ATTI

DEL IV CONGRESSO INTERNAZIONALE

DEI

MATEMATICI

(Roma, 6-11 Aprile 1908)

PUBBLICATI

PER CURA DEL SEGRETARIO GENERALE

G. CASTELNUOVO

PROF. ALL'UNIVERSITÀ DI ROMA

VOL. III.

COMUNICAZIONI DELLE SEZIONI III-A, III-B e IV.

ROMA

TIPOGRAFIA DELLA R. ACCADEMIA DEI LINCEI

PROPRIETÀ DEL CAV. V. SALVIUCCI

—

1909

PARTE III

COMUNICAZIONI

Sezione III-a

MECCANICA, FISICA MATEMATICA, GEODESIA

G. H. DARWIN

THE RIGIDITY OF THE EARTH

Recent investigations prove without any room for doubt that, quite apart from earthquakes, the solid earth is never at rest, but is heaving up and down almost as though it were breathing, and I wish explain the chain of argument by which we have become convinced of the truth of the existence of this rhythmic motion. The lines of reasoning by which this conclusion is established are of various kinds, but they all lead to results closely concordant with one another.

The first suggestion on the subject, which carried much weight, was by that great physicist Lord KELVIN. His recent death, at a ripe old age, has been deplored by men of science of every civilised country in the world. In Rome, where he was an honoured member of the Accademia dei Lincei, his loss is felt no less than elsewhere.

Lord KELVIN attacked the difficult problem of determining the deformation of an elastic sphere, with the object of considering the earth as placed under strain by the attraction of the moon. LAMÉ had solved the problem previously, although I do not think Lord KELVIN was aware of the fact; but LAMÉ's solution has comparatively little interest in connection with our present subject, because he drew no conclusions as to the rigidity of the earth.

Lord KELVIN found that if the earth were throughout its mass only as stiff as glass, it would rise and fall under the tidal forces due to the moon's attraction more than half as much as if it were liquid throughout. Even if it were made of steel the tidal movements would be one third as great.

Now we are only able to scratch the surface of the earth, and thus we know but little about the inside; yet it is difficult to suppose that the earth is constructed of a material possessing a degree of stiffness incomparably greater than that of any of the materials with which we are acquainted. Accordingly Lord KELVIN concluded that the solid earth must be rising and falling with the tide, like the waters of the ocean, but of course to a less extent.

It then remained to consider the means whereby we ought to be able to perceive this tidal motion of the solid earth, and he concluded that it would be by its effect on the movements of the waters of the ocean. If the solid earth rose and fell exactly as much as if it were liquid, it is clear that the waters of the sea would not move at all relatively to the land, for the whole would move up and down together. Thus the existence of oceanic tides shows that the solid earth moves to a less extent than if it were liquid. This line of argument may be carried further, and we may conclude that if the solid earth moves by half as much as if it were liquid, the oceanic tides will be reduced to half as much as if the earth were liquid. Or again, since a globe of steel of the size of the earth would pulsate tidally one third as much as one of water, Lord KELVIN concluded that the oceanic tides would be two thirds as great as if the solid earth were at rest.

He then stated conjecturally that our tides are certainly more than half as high as they would be on an unyielding earth, although perhaps not more than two-thirds as great. Hence he pronounced the earth to be stiffer than glass but perhaps not so stiff as steel. This conclusion is, as we now know, very nearly correct, but it must be considered more as an intuition than as a proof, although nearly 40 years ago his conclusion seemed justifiable.

If the earth were to rotate very slowly on its axis whilst the moon moved in the heavens with corresponding slowness, the waters of the ocean would have time to assume a definite position of rest at each moment of time. This position of rest or of equilibrium can be calculated with all the accuracy desired, and it enables us to determine what would be the height of tide according to this hypothesis, which is called the Equilibrium Theory.

In his celebrated investigation of the tides, LAPLACE, following NEWTON, showed that the equilibrium theory was useless as a means of tidal prediction and that the actual motion must be incomparably more complex. He proved in fact that it is impossible to predict the height of the tides of oceans broken by continents, as on the earth. And since the time when Lord KELVIN wrote, the researches of Mr. HOUGH have shown that the semidiurnal oscillations of the sea, on a planet completely covered with water, are of even greater complexity than was supposed by LAPLACE. Indeed Mr. HOUGH has proved that the semidiurnal oceanic tides may in some places have an amplitude ten times as great as that deduced from the equilibrium theory. In such places a reduction of the tide to even a half of its amplitude on a rigid earth might easily remain unnoticed.

Within a few years after Lord KELVIN had written, our knowledge of the tides had begun to increase very rapidly. This was largely due to the inauguration of the harmonic analysis of tidal observations, which by the way was also due to Lord KELVIN. Amongst the tidal oscillations which were then actually measured for the first time were those oscillations which were called oscillations of the first species by LAPLACE and are now more commonly described as tides of long period. These oscillations consist of a slow rise and fall of the mean level of the sea, continually disturbed as it is by the ordinary semidiurnal tide. The most important of these oscillations has a period of fourteen days, and another has a period of a month. They are called in English the fortnightly and monthly tides. These tidal oscillations are so minute that they escaped detection in all the older tidal observations, but they have now been measured with some degree of accuracy at a large number of places.

LAPLACE adduced considerations which seemed to prove that these tides of long period would, in consequence of fluid friction, obey the equilibrium law pretty closely — that is to say the ocean would, as regards this group of forces, have time enough to assume the position of equilibrium. Thus he held that it was possible to calculate the amplitudes of oscillation of these tides on the hypothesis that the solid earth was absolutely unyielding.

About 1881 I had the honour of helping Lord KELVIN to pass through the press the second edition of THOMSON and TAIT's Natural Philosophy, and it occurred to me that it might be possible to supplement Lord KELVIN's interesting conjecture by a numerical evaluation from the data which were at that time available. Accordingly I took the observed results for 33 years of the fortnightly and monthly tides at various places, and compared them with the results as calculated by the equilibrium theory. I concluded that these tides had on the average an amplitude of two thirds as much as they would have had if the earth had been quite unyielding. The result exactly confirmed Lord KELVIN's suggestion, and it seemed safe to assert that the earth was about as stiff as steel.

However within a year or two it occurred to me to doubt the justice of LAPLACE's reasoning by which he believed that he had proved that the tides of long period should nearly obey the equilibrium law. On investigating the dynamical problem offered by these tides of long-period on an ocean-covered planet I found that they might differ in height considerably from their equilibrium value. This then seemed to throw doubt on the exactness of the conclusion that the earth was as stiff as steel, although it confirmed the view that the degree of rigidity of the earth's mass must be very great.

The matter rested in this state until 1903 when Lord RAYLEIGH (1) pointed out that the existence of the land barriers formed by our continents would have the effect of annulling those modes of motion in the ocean which are responsible for making these tidal oscillations on an ocean-covered planet so different from what they would be according to the equilibrium theory. He thus went far to reinstate LAPLACE's conclusion, as to the rigidity of the earth.

Since that time an immense amount of tidal data has been accumulating, and in 1907 Dr. WILHELM SCHWEYDAR of Potsdam reduced the observations of the tides of long period for 195 years at a number of ports all over the world (2). The result attained by him from this extremely laborious reduction is that these tides have a height between .62 and .60 of their equilibrium amount, my old result being .67. The weight to be attached to Dr. SCHWEYDAR's result, which points to a rigidity a little less than that of steel, is of course immensely greater than that which my conclusion possessed, based as it was on far more limited data. From this line of research then we conclude that the earth is a little less stiff, on the average, than steel, and we must now turn to another line of investigation.

If the earth were to yield like a perfect fluid and were to be a figure of equilibrium at every moment the moon's tide generating force would seem to vanish to

(1) Phil. Mag., vol. 5 (1903), p. 136.

(2) Beiträge zur Geophysik, vol. 9 (1907), p. 41.

an observer capable of measuring it, who supposed the earth to be absolutely unyielding. The horizontal force due to the moon's attraction only amounts at greatest to one eleven-millionth part of gravity, and a pendulum will oscillate to and fro through an angle which is only 1/55th of a second of arc. It obviously then requires observations of extraordinary delicacy to measure so small a deflection of the plumb-line; indeed the measurement is quite impossible without some apparatus by which the deflections may be multiplied enormously. My brother and I madé the attempt some 25 years ago, but found ourselves altogether defeated by those minute movements of the soil which form the subject of research of seismologists. Since our time however von REBEUR PASCHWITZ invented, or rather revived and perfected, an instrument of great delicacy, the horizontal pendulum. It must suffice to say here that it can be given almost any degree of sensitiveness to minute horizontal forces which disturb the apparent direction of the vertical. PASCHWITZ himself, and after his death EHLERT and KORTAZZI all undertook the measurement of the moon's horizontal force, and concluded that its apparent amount was from one half to two thirds of the amount on a rigid earth. Dr. SCHWEYDAR has also combined the observations of PASCHWITZ, EHLERT and KORTAZZI, and finds them to give a factor of oceanic tide of two thirds.

And now at length in the skilful hands of Dr. HECKER at Potsdam the problem has received a far more complete solution, the substantial correctness of which is not open to doubt (1). He erected in a recess in the side of a well at 25 m. below the surface at Potsdam two horizontal pendulums arranged in azimuths at right angles to one another, so that it is possible to measure the deflections of the vertical in the two directions N. E. and N. W. These two pendulums are arranged so as to furnish continuous automatic records, and have been under observation almost continuously from December 1902 to April 1905. The series still continues, but Dr. HECKER has published a first account of his researches.

The situation of these pendulums is incomparably superior to those used by any previous observer, and Dr. HECKER has known how to take full advantage of the superiority of his installation. The reduction of his observations shows that the oscillations of the pendulum are almost exactly two-thirds of the amount they would have on a rigid earth. The result derived from tidal observations is thus in substantial agreement with that from the horizontal pendulum. This mutual confirmation is important, and it goes far to remove the uncertainty which is inherent in the tidal method, in consequence of the doubt as to whether the oceanic tides of long period conform exactly to the equilibrium theory. It will perhaps not be generally recognised how remarkable is the accuracy of Dr. HECKER's observations, and I therefore propose to point out some of the most striking details. They appear to me moreover to be of the greatest interest in themselves, and to open the way to other researches as to the constitution of the earth.

The great difficulty which besets measurements of this kind resides in the fact that it is impossible to avoid the disturbances due to the sun's radiation. Whatever

(1) *Beobachtungen an Horizontalpendeln.* k. Preus. Geodätischen Institutes. Neue Folge, N. 32 (1907).

effect the sun's heat can have must be periodic in a solar day, whilst the magnitude of that periodic inequality must undergo a variability in the course of a year. The most important of the lunar effects, which it is sought to measure, has a period of a lunar day, and 29 lunar days are equal to 30 solar days. Hence we see that any inequality depending on solar time will be obliterated on the average, if we group the observations according to lunar time.

The horizontal pendulums are found to move with oscillations of a fairly regular character under the influence of the sun's heat, and these oscillations undergo a variability of amplitude with a yearly period. But even at a depth of 25 m. below the earth's surface the amplitude of the solar thermal daily oscillation is often twenty times as great as that of the lunar oscillation to be measured. My brother and I in our attempt made at the earth's surface found the diurnal solar effect so large that we concluded, erroneously as we now see, that it would completely mask the lunar effect. Now Dr. HECKER's observations are so accurate that even this enormous perturbation disappears in the average, and we find the lunar effect standing out quite clearly by itself.

Besides the thermal perturbation the sun of course exercises a tidal influence, which is about four-elevenths of that of the moon. The thermal effect of the sun has a diurnal period, the amplitude being variable in the course of the year as the seasons change, but the tidal effect of the sun has a semidiurnal period. Dr. HECKER therefore grouped together the observations for separate months, and in this way he is even able to evaluate the solar tide. As far as concerns one of the two pendulums the result is the same as for the moon, namely a reduction of amplitude of two-thirds. The second pendulum was much more affected by temperature than the first, and here the result is not so satisfactory, since the observed oscillation is somewhat greater instead of being less than the computed oscillation on a rigid earth. It is amazing that the large thermal diurnal oscillation of the pendulum should disappear sufficiently to render it possible to detect the tidal semidiurnal one. There can however be little room for doubt that this is the case, although we may suspect that the close concordance of the result from one of the two pendulums is to some extent a matter of chance.

Dr. HECKER has kindly sent me two diagrams of the greatest interest, which he is so good as to allow me to use. He has not himself had time fully to discuss the meaning of these curves, but they are so interesting that I shall explain the result of my own examination. It is proper to say that I do not in any way represent Dr. HECKER in the remarks I shall make, and it is quite possible that when he shall have discussed the whole completed series of observations, he may be led to conclusions which will differ from mine.

In these diagrams then Dr. HECKER has grouped together all the days on which the moon's declination was greater than 12° N., with a mean of 16° 15′ N; and also all the days with the moon's declination greater than 12° S., with a mean of 16° 20′ S. For each group he has plotted the path of the pendulum during 24 hours. That path when the moon's declination is northerly, is shown in the somewhat irregular curve in fig. 1; the horizontal and vertical scales are marked in thousandths of a second of arc, so that the scale is of the extremest refinement. The numbers of the successive hours from 0 to 23 are written along the curve of observation and along the red curve deduced from theory, as will be expained hereafter. I do not reproduce the figure corresponding to southern declination, but it shows a very similar result.

It will be remembered that Dr. HECKER finds a mean reduction of deflections to two-thirds of the amount on a rigid earth. I have therefore drawn a red line over Dr. HECKER's curves, which exhibits the theoretical deflections on a rigid earth reduced in magnitude to two-thirds of the full scale. It will be seen that there is a general concordance between the two curves, for we have the larger loop and the smaller one; but there are also some very remarkable discrepancies.

In the first place it is obvious that the observed curve is considerably flatter than the computed curve in the N.-S. direction and longer in the E.-W. direction.

I have accordingly tried what would be the result if we might suppose that the N.-S. computed deflections are reduced by a different factor from the E.-W. deflections. I find that for northerly declination of the moon the N.-S. deflections should be reduced by a factor .336. and the E.-W. deflections by a factor .836. I have not made the similar reduction for southerly declination. The result is exhibited in Figure 2, and it will be seen that the concordance has become so good that it is difficult not to admit, at least provisionally, that this result represents an actual fact. I am unable to suggest any physical hypothesis which would, as regards the whole earth, justify the supposition that the north and south deflections are about one-third of those computed, whilst the east and west deflections are only reduced by eleven twelfths. But it does not seem impossible that the configuration of the continent of Europe alongside the Atlantic Ocean might cause this remarkable inequality in the two azimuths.

Then there is another remarkable abnormality in the observed curve, and this holds good both for northern and for southern declination of the moon. It is that the larger loop of the curve is displaced westward and the smaller one to the eastward. Dr. HECKER himself has suggested to me that this may be due to inequalities in the elasticity in the two directions. If, as is likely, this suggestion is correct, it again looks as if it was due to the position of the place of observation not very far from the western edge of the great European-Asiatic continent.

I may finally remark that the small loop of the observed curve is smaller than in the computed curve. Some calculations I have made seem to show that this would be represented by supposing the diurnal inequality to be reduced by the factor two-thirds, whilst the semidiurnal inequality is reduced by the factor three-quarters. However a different method of reduction, which I believe Dr. HECKER will adopt in his final discussion, will probably bring this point into clearer relief.

Whatever may be thought of this discussion it will be generally admitted that the results are astonishingly consistent amongst themselves, and that we have before us a new and interesting method of discussing the elasticity of the earth. I should hope that the method may throw some light on the inequalities in the elasticity of the earth in various directions. This will show whether or not the superficial inequalities represented by the continents, have their corresponding deep-seated inequalities

Fig. 2.

Scale of $\frac{1}{1000}$ths of seconds of arc.

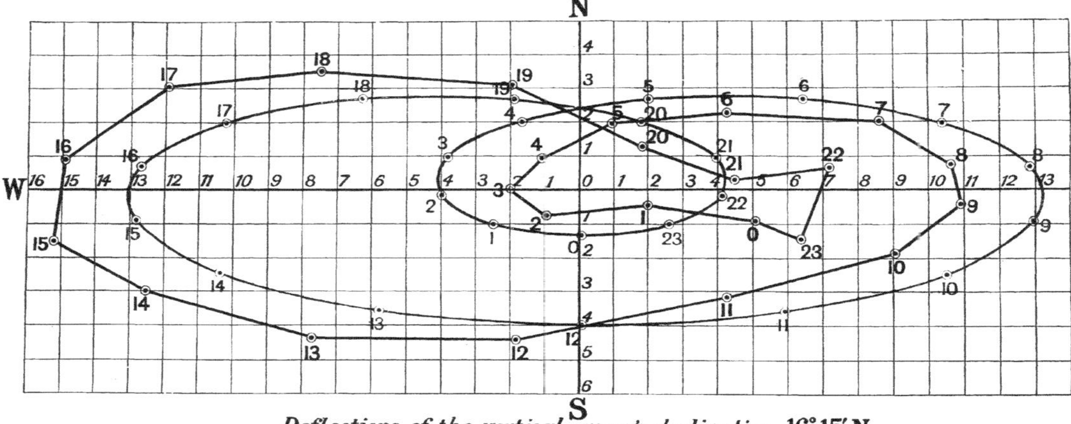

***Deflections of the vertical, moon's declination* 16° 15′ N.**

Theoretical deflections reduced N. *and* S. *by* ·336, *and* E. *and* W. *by* ·836.

Fig. 1.

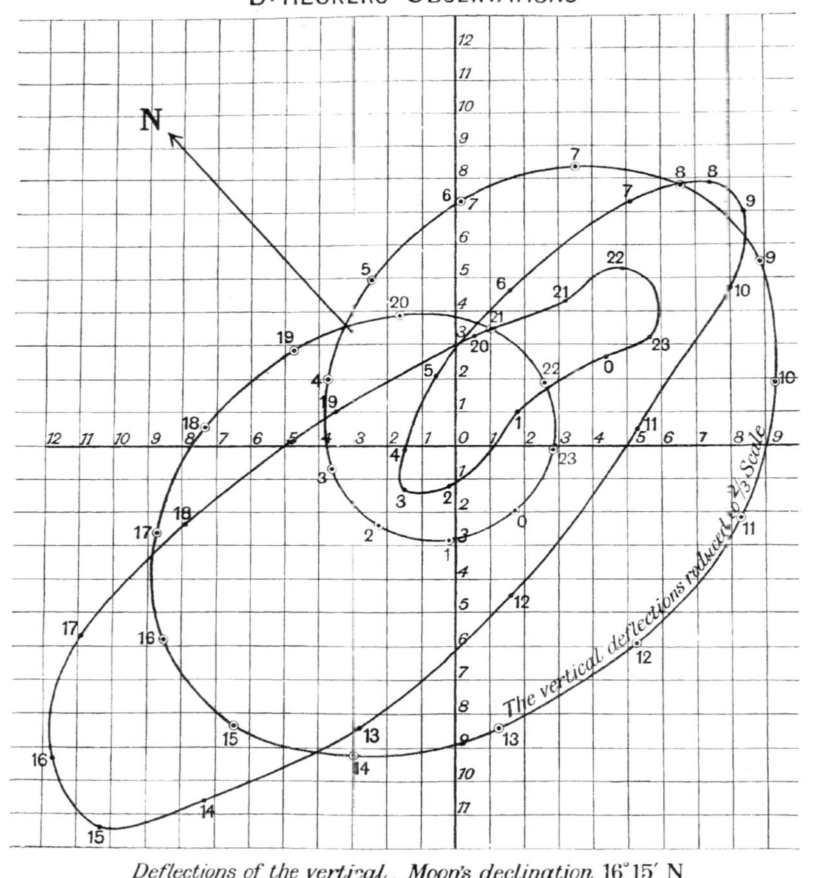

Deflections of the vertical, Moon's declination 16° 15′ N.
Scale of $\frac{1}{1000}$ ths. of seconds of arc.

of elasticity. It is hoped that the Russians will, at the suggestion of the International Seismological Association, undertake a similar series of observations. A series of researches ought also to be instituted in the middle of the United States. Such observations will be of special interest, since the results will be free from doubts occasioned by the neighbourhood to the ocean; for certain calculations which I made a good many years ago, seemed to show that the varying weight imposed on the solid earth as the tide rises and falls might produce sensible flexure of the solid earth even at a great distance from the sea-coast (1).

Then again barometric inequalities must produce similar flexures, and it would be of great interest if Dr. HECKER would discuss his observations with respect to the distributions of high and low pressure with reference to Berlin. I believe that some measurable influence would be detected, and it is not impossible that the result would throw light on the inequalities of elasticity in various directions.

I will now endeavour to examine the amount by which we must suppose the solid earth to rise and fall with the combined lunar and solar tides. It is impossible to attain accuracy, but we may obtain an approximate estimate. At the equator the principal lunar semidiurnal tide has according to the equilibrium theory an amplitude of 23 cm.; but if all the conditions as to the position of the moon are favorable it may rise 35 cm., or if unfavorable it may fall to 12 cm. Let us consider only the greatest possible amplitude of 35 cm.; the corresponding solar tide is 16 cm. For a globe of steel the rise and fall will be one third as great, say 12 cm. for the lunar tide and 5 cm. for the solar tide. Hence it is probable that at spring-tide and at the equator we should be alternately, at intervals of 6 hours, 17 cm. nearer and 17 cm. further from the centre of the earth. Some calculations which I made seemed to show that the earth's surface may be lower by as much as 9 cm. under a high barometer than under low barometer. I think then that the change of the surface might amount to twice 17 cm. + 9 cm., or say 45 cm. The estimate is of course very rough, but it shows that we must be moving up and down by an amount which would be easily perceptible without the aid of instruments, if we had any fixed point by which to estimate the change.

I shall not attempt to discuss another wholly independent method of estimating the rigidity of the earth, namely that arising from the variation of latitude. It must suffice to say that the prolongation of the Eulerian Nutation of the earth from 305 to 430 days, shows according to the researches of NEWCOMB and after him of HOUGH, that the earth is yielding about as much as if it were made of steel. Thus the tides, the direct measurement of the lunar attraction and the variation of latitude agree in giving the same estimate of the elastic yielding of the solid earth. On the other hand the seismological researches of MILNE, OMORI, WIECHERT, ODDONE and of many others indicate that at a few hundred miles below the earth's surface matter possesses a rigidity far greater than that of steel. Thus seismology gives a discordant estimate, and it is not, as yet, easy to suggest the source of the discrepancy.

(1) Report to the British Assoc. 1882, pp. 95-119; or G. H. DARWIN, *Scientific Papers*, vol. I (1907) p. 430.

H. LAMB

ON THE FLEXURE OF A NARROW BEAM

1. For the sake of mathematical simplicity I take the case of a beam of rectangular section, whose breadth is small compared with the (vertical) depth, so that the problem is virtually one of plane stress. The beam is in the first instance supposed to be infinitely long, and to be subject to a periodic distribution of load, but inferences are afterward drawn relating to beams of finite length.

Investigations on a somewhat similar plan have been instituted by previous writers, and results have been deduced by processes of approximation (1); but the *degree* of approximation is not easily estimated, and in the treatment of terminal conditions and allied questions appeal is made simply to DE SAINT-VENANT's principle of « equipollent loads ».

I find that some light is thrown on these points, and in particular on the range of validity of DE SAINT-VENANT's principle, if we apply CAUCHY's theory of « residues » to the transformation of the FOURIER series which are in the first instance obtained.

As regards the particular distribution of force which is to be assumed for study, a great variety of suppositions is open to us; and in this way we might construct a whole series of exact solutions of the equations of internal equilibrium under various conditions of concentrated or continuous load. The main intererest of such calculations lies of course in the comparison with the ordinary EULER-BERNOULLI theory of flexure, and with the more or less tentative additions and corrections by which this theory is often supplemented. I have thought it sufficient to work out a few typical cases which are of interest from this point of view; their number might easily be greatly extended.

2. In the case first to be considered we have an infinitely long horizontal beam acted on by equal and opposite forces alternately, at equal intervals a. This distri-

(1) L. N. G. FILON, *On an Approximate Solution for the Bending of a Beam of Rectangular Cross-Section....* (*Phil. Trans.*, 201, p. 63, 1902).

The more difficult case of a cylinder of circular section was discussed by L. POCHHAMMER, *Beitrag zur Theorie der Biegung des Kreiscylinders* (J. f. Math. 81, p. 33, 1875).

bution of isolated loads may be regarded as the limit of a continuous load of the type

$$(1)\quad \varphi(x) = \ldots + \chi(x-2a) - \chi(x-a) + \chi(x) - \chi(x+a) + \chi(x+2a) - \ldots,$$

where $\chi(x)$ ir an even function of x. This may be expressed by a FOURIER's series, viz (¹)

$$(2)\qquad \varphi(x) = A_1 \cos\frac{\pi x}{a} + A_3 \cos\frac{3\pi x}{a} + A_5 \cos\frac{5\pi x}{a} + \ldots,$$

where

$$(3)\qquad \begin{cases} A_s = \dfrac{2}{a}\displaystyle\int_0^a \varphi(x)\cos\frac{s\pi x}{a}\,dx = \frac{2}{a}\int_{-\infty}^{\infty}\chi(x)\cos\frac{s\pi x}{a}\,dx \\ [s = 1, 3, 5, \ldots]. \end{cases}$$

For the present purpose we put

$$(4)\qquad \chi(x) = \frac{\alpha}{\pi}\cdot\frac{1}{x^2+\alpha^2};$$

this makes

$$(5)\qquad A_s = \frac{4\alpha}{\pi a}\int_0^{\infty}\cos\frac{s\pi x}{a}\,\frac{dx}{x^2+\alpha^2} = \frac{2}{a}\,e^{-\frac{s\pi\alpha}{a}}.$$

In the applications of this paper α is ultimately supposed to be infinitesimal.

It will appear that the elastic problem involves the summation of FOURIER series of the type

$$(6)\qquad \sum_s \frac{F(\zeta_s)}{\zeta_s(\sinh 2\zeta_s - 2\zeta_s)}\cos\frac{\zeta_s x}{h},$$

where $\zeta_s = s\pi h/a$, the integers s being odd, and $F(\zeta_s)$ is a certain integral even function of ζ. We shall find

$$(7)\qquad \frac{F(\zeta)}{\zeta(\sinh 2\zeta - 2\zeta)} = \frac{A}{\zeta^4} + \frac{B}{\zeta^2} + f(\zeta),$$

(¹) Sir W. THOMSON, *Math. and Phys. Papers*, 2, p. 56.

where A , B are certain constants (which may vanish), and $f(\zeta)$ is finite for $\zeta = 0$. The finite singularities of the expression

(8) $$f(\zeta)\,\frac{\sin\left(\tfrac{1}{2}a - x\right)\dfrac{\zeta}{h}}{\cos\tfrac{1}{2}\dfrac{a\zeta}{h}},$$

considered as a function of the complex variable $\zeta = \xi + i\eta$, will therefore consist of simple poles, viz, the roots (other than zero) of the equation

(9) $$\sinh 2\zeta - 2\zeta = 0,$$

and the points

(10) $$\zeta = \pm\frac{s\pi h}{a}, \quad [s = 1, 3, 5, \dots].$$

The finite roots of (9) occur in sets of four, of the type

(11) $$\zeta = \pm\,\xi_n \pm i\eta_n.$$

The values of ξ_n, η_n may be found graphicallv. as the intersections of the curves

(12) $$\cos 2\eta = \frac{2\xi}{\sinh 2\xi}, \quad \cosh 2\xi = \frac{2\eta}{\sin 2\eta},$$

the asymptotic forms being

(13) $$\xi_n = \tfrac{1}{2}\log(2n + \tfrac{1}{2})\pi, \quad \eta_n = (n + \tfrac{1}{4})\pi,$$

where n is a positive integer; see Fig. 1. The formulae (12) also lend themselves to a well-known process of successive approximation. If we assume a rough value of η_n, the second equation gives an approximate value of ξ_n; this substituted in the first equation gives an improved value of η_n; and so on. I find

(14) $$\left\{\begin{array}{ll} \xi_1 = 1.384, & \eta_1 = 4.773 \times \tfrac{1}{2}\pi, \\ \xi_2 = 1.676, & \eta_2 = 8.849 \times \tfrac{1}{2}\pi, \\ \xi_3 = 1.856, & \eta_3 = 12.884 \times \tfrac{1}{2}\pi. \end{array}\right.$$

Now consider the rectangle bounded by the lines

(15) $$\xi = \pm(s + 1)\,\frac{\pi h}{a}, \quad \eta = \pm(n + \tfrac{3}{4})\pi,$$

where n and s are positive integers, s being odd. Having regard to the special forms of $F(\zeta)$ with which we have to deal, it will appear that the value of the integral

$$(16) \qquad \int f(\zeta) \frac{\sin(\frac{1}{2} a - x)\frac{\zeta}{h}}{\cos \frac{1}{2} \frac{a\zeta}{h}} d\zeta ,$$

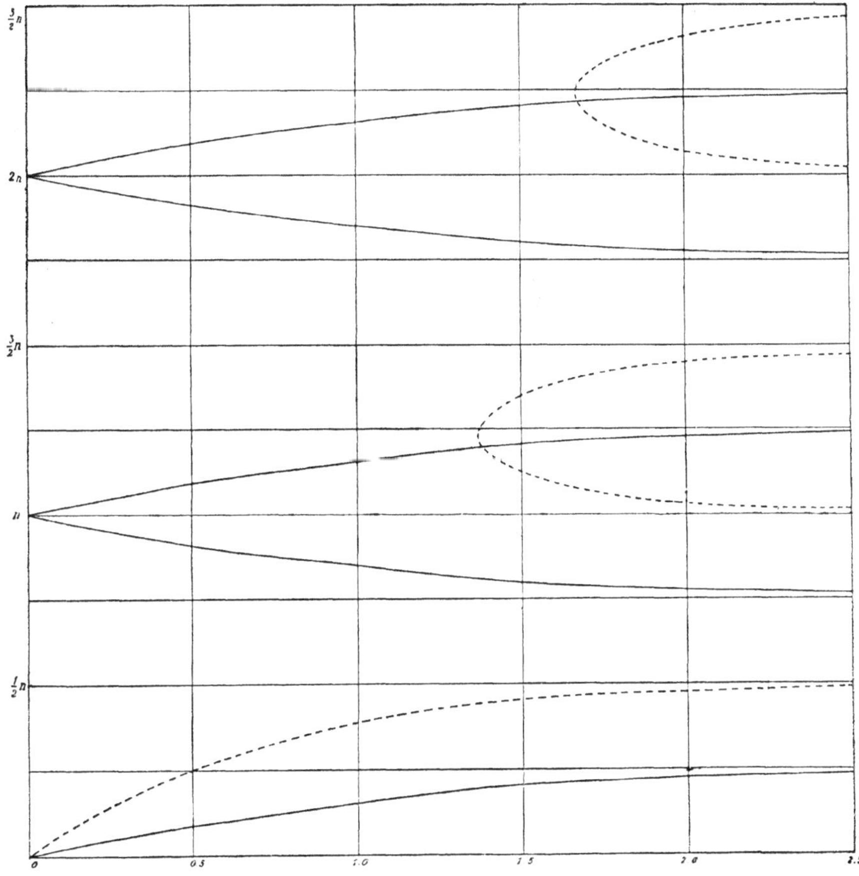

Fig. 1.

taken round the contour of this rectangle, tends, when n and s are indefinitely increased, to the limit zero, provided $|\frac{1}{2} a - x| < \frac{1}{2} a$, that is, provided x lies between the limits 0 and a. Hence the sum of the « residues » of the function (8) will be zero, provided the poles be properly grouped. Now the sum of the residues with respect to the four poles forming a set of the type (11) is

$$\text{(17)} \qquad Re\left[\frac{F(\zeta_n)}{\zeta_n \sinh^2 \zeta_n} \cdot \frac{\sin(\tfrac{1}{2}a - x)\dfrac{\zeta_n}{h}}{\cos\tfrac{1}{2}\dfrac{a\zeta_n}{h}}\right],$$

where $\zeta_n = \xi_n + i\eta_n$, and the symbol Re is used to denote that the real part of the expression which follows is to be taken. Again, the sum of the residues with respect to a pair of poles of the type (10) is

$$\text{(18)} \qquad -4\frac{h}{a}f'\left(\frac{s\pi h}{a}\right)\cos\frac{s\pi x}{a}.$$

Hence the sum of the series (6) is

$$\text{(19)} \quad \frac{Aa^4}{\pi^4 h^4}\sum_s \frac{1}{s^4}\cos\frac{s\pi x}{a} + \frac{Ba^2}{\pi^2 h^2}\sum_s \frac{1}{s^2}\cos\frac{s\pi x}{a} + \tfrac{1}{4}\frac{a}{h}\sum_n \mathrm{Re}\left[C_n \frac{\sin(\tfrac{1}{2}a - x)\dfrac{\zeta_n}{h}}{\cos\tfrac{1}{2}\dfrac{a\zeta_n}{h}}\right],$$

where the summation Σ_n related to those roots (other than zero) of the equation (9) which lie in the first quadrant of the ζ-plane, and

$$\text{(20)} \qquad C_n = \frac{F(\zeta_n)}{\zeta_n \sinh^2 \zeta_n}.$$

For values of x ranging from 0 to a we have

$$\text{(21)} \qquad \left\{\begin{aligned} &\sum_s \frac{1}{s^2}\cos\frac{s\pi x}{a} = \frac{\pi^2}{8}\left(1 - 2\frac{x}{a}\right), \\ &\sum_s \frac{1}{s^4}\cos\frac{s\pi x}{a} = \frac{\pi^4}{96}\left(1 - 6\frac{x^2}{a^2} + 4\frac{x^3}{a^3}\right), \\ &\qquad [s = 1, 3, 5, \ldots]. \end{aligned}\right.$$

Hence finally, we have, under certain restrictions as to the form of $F(\zeta)$ which are always fulfilled in the applications which follow,

$$\text{(22)} \quad \left\{\begin{aligned} &\sum_s \frac{F\left(\dfrac{s\pi h}{a}\right)}{\dfrac{s\pi h}{a}\left(\sinh\dfrac{2s\pi h}{a} - \dfrac{2s\pi h}{a}\right)}\cos\frac{s\pi x}{a} = \frac{A}{96}\frac{a^4}{h^4}\left(1 - 6\frac{x^2}{a^2} + \frac{4x^3}{a^3}\right) \\ &\qquad + \frac{B}{8}\frac{a^2}{h^2}\left(1 - 2\frac{x}{a}\right) + \frac{1}{4}\frac{a}{h}\sum_n \mathrm{Re}\left[C_n \frac{\sin(\tfrac{1}{2}a - x)\dfrac{\zeta_n}{h}}{\cos\tfrac{1}{2}\dfrac{a\zeta_n}{h}}\right]. \end{aligned}\right.$$

By differentation with respect to x we infer that

$$(23)\quad \begin{cases} \displaystyle\sum_s \frac{F\left(\frac{s\pi h}{a}\right)}{\sinh\frac{2s\pi h}{a}-\frac{2s\pi h}{a}}\sin\frac{s\pi x}{a} \\ \displaystyle\quad =\frac{A}{8}\frac{a^3}{h^3}\frac{x}{a}\left(1-\frac{x}{a}\right)+\frac{B}{4}\frac{a}{h}+\frac{1}{4}\frac{a}{h}\sum_n \mathrm{Re}\left[\zeta_n C_n\frac{\cos(\frac{1}{2}a-x)\frac{\zeta_n}{h}}{\cos\frac{1}{2}\frac{a\zeta_n}{h}}\right]. \end{cases}$$

3. In some further problems we have to deal with periodic functions of the type

$$(24)\quad \varphi(x)=\ldots+\chi(x-2a)+\chi(x-a)+\chi(x)+\chi(x+a)+(x+2a)+\ldots,$$

where, as before, $\chi(x)$ is an even function. We find

$$(25)\quad \varphi(x)=A_0+A_2\cos\frac{2\pi x}{a}+A_4\cos\frac{4\pi x}{a}+\ldots,$$

where

$$(26)\quad \begin{cases} \displaystyle A_0=\frac{1}{a}\int_0^u\varphi(x)dx=\frac{1}{a}\int_{-\infty}^{\infty}\chi(x)dx\,, \\ \displaystyle A_r=\frac{2}{a}\int_0^a\varphi(x)\cos\frac{r\pi x}{a}\,dx=\frac{2}{a}\int_{-\infty}^{\infty}\chi(x)\cos\frac{r\pi x}{a}\,dx\,, \\ \qquad [r=2,4,6,\ldots]. \end{cases}$$

With the value (4) of $\chi(x)$ we have

$$(27)\quad A_0=\frac{1}{a}\quad,\quad A_r=\frac{2}{a}e^{-\frac{r\pi\alpha}{a}}.$$

In some applications a constant term is added to $\varphi(x)$ which has the effect of annulling A_0.

In the same connection we meet with Fourier series of the type

$$(28)\quad \sum_r\frac{F(\zeta_r)}{\zeta_r(\sinh 2\zeta_r-2\zeta_r)}\cos\frac{\zeta_r x}{h}\,,$$

where $\zeta_r=r\pi h/a$, the integers r being even, and $F(\zeta)$ is an even function of ζ having the same general properties as before. With the same notation as in (7) we have to consider the residues of the function

$$f(\zeta)\,\frac{\cos(\frac{1}{2}a-x)\dfrac{\zeta}{h}}{\sin\frac{1}{2}\dfrac{a\zeta}{h}}\,. \tag{29}$$

The residue with respect to $\zeta=0$ (which is a simple pole) is

$$2\,\frac{h}{a}\,f(0)\,; \tag{30}$$

and the sum of the residues with respect to $\zeta=\pm r\pi h/a$ is

$$4\,\frac{h}{a}\,f\left(\frac{r\pi h}{a}\right)\cos\frac{r\pi x}{a}\,. \tag{31}$$

The sum of the residues with respect to a set of four poles of the type (11) is

$$Re\left[\frac{F(\zeta_n)}{\zeta_n\sinh^2\zeta_n}\cdot\frac{\cos(\frac{1}{2}a-x)\dfrac{\zeta_n}{h}}{\sin\frac{1}{2}\dfrac{a\zeta_n}{h}}\right]. \tag{32}$$

The sum of the series (28) is therefore

$$\left\{\begin{aligned}&\frac{Aa^4}{\pi^4h^4}\sum_r\frac{1}{r^4}\cos\frac{r\pi x}{a}+\frac{Ba^2}{\pi^2h^2}\sum_r\frac{1}{r^2}\cos\frac{r\pi x}{a}-\tfrac{1}{2}f(0)\\&\qquad\qquad+\frac{1}{4}\frac{a}{h}\sum_n Re\left[C_n\frac{\cos(\frac{1}{2}a-x)\dfrac{\zeta_n}{h}}{\sin\frac{1}{2}\dfrac{a\zeta_n}{h}}\right],\end{aligned}\right. \tag{33}$$

where C_n has the value given in (20). For values of x ranging from 0 to a we have

$$\left\{\begin{aligned}&\sum_r\frac{1}{r^4}\cos\frac{r\pi x}{a}=\frac{\pi^2}{24}\left(1-6\frac{x}{a}+6\frac{x^2}{a^2}\right),\\&\sum_r\frac{1}{r^4}\cos\frac{r\pi x}{a}=\frac{\pi^4}{1440}\left(1-30\frac{x^2}{a^2}+60\frac{x^3}{a^3}-30\frac{x^4}{a^4}\right),\\&\qquad[r=2,4,6,\ldots].\end{aligned}\right. \tag{34}$$

Hence, with the same implications as before,

$$(35)\qquad \sum_r \frac{F\left(\dfrac{r\pi h}{a}\right)}{\dfrac{r\pi h}{a}\left(\sinh\dfrac{2r\pi h}{a}-\dfrac{2r\pi h}{a}\right)}\cos\frac{r\pi x}{a}$$

$$=\frac{A}{1440}\frac{a^4}{h^4}\left(1-30\frac{x^2}{a^2}+60\frac{x^3}{a^3}-30\frac{x^4}{a^4}\right)$$

$$+\frac{B}{24}\frac{a^2}{h^2}\left(1-6\frac{x}{a}+6\frac{x^2}{a^2}\right)-\tfrac{1}{2}f(0)$$

$$+\frac{1}{4}\frac{a}{h}\sum_n \mathrm{Re}\left[C_n\frac{\cos(\frac{1}{2}a-x)\dfrac{\zeta_n}{h}}{\sin\frac{1}{2}\dfrac{a\zeta_n}{h}}\right].$$

4. The way is now clear for the discussion of the special problems of this paper. If the axis of x be taken along the middle line of the beam, the equations of the upper and lower faces being $y=\pm h$, the component displacements u, v due to a vertical body-force whose amount, per unit area of the middle surface ($y=0$), is $H\cos mx$ are

$$(36)\quad u=-\frac{H}{2\mu m}\left\{\cosh mh\sinh my-\frac{\sinh mh}{mh}\left(my\cosh my+\frac{\lambda'+2\mu}{\lambda'+\mu}\sinh my\right)\right\}\sin mx$$
$$\div(\sinh 2mh-2mh),$$

$$(37)\quad v=\frac{H}{2\mu m^2 h}\cos mx$$
$$+\frac{H}{2\mu m}\left\{\cosh mh\cosh my-\frac{\sinh mh}{mh}\left(my\sinh my-\frac{\mu}{\lambda'+\mu}\cos my\right)\right\}\cos mx$$
$$\div(\sinh 2mh-2mh),$$

where

$$(38)\qquad \lambda'=\frac{2\lambda\mu}{\lambda+2\mu},$$

the notation of the elastic constants being that of Lamé. The formulae were obtained in the first instance [1] for the case of a *plate* unlimited in the direction of the breadth, but Mr. Filon has shown that in order to pass to the case of a narrow beam it is only necessary to replace the original λ by λ' [2].

(1) H. Lamb, *On the Flexure of an Elastic Plate* (Proc. Lond. Math. Soc., 21, p. 86, 1889).
(2) See A. E. H. Love, *Elasticity* (Cambridge, 1906, p. 135).

The corresponding formulae for the stresses are

$$(39)\quad p_{xx} = \mathrm{H}\left\{\frac{\sinh mh}{mh}(my\cosh my + 2\sinh my) - \cosh mh \sinh my\right\}\cos mx$$
$$\div(\sinh 2mh - 2mh),$$

$$(40)\quad p_{xy} = -\frac{\mathrm{H}}{2mh}\sin mx$$
$$+\mathrm{H}\left\{\frac{\sinh mh}{mh}(my\sinh my + \cosh my) - \cosh mh\cosh my\right\}\sin mx$$
$$\div(\sinh 2mh - 2mh),$$

$$(41)\quad p_{yy} = \mathrm{H}\left\{\cosh mh\sinh my - \frac{\sinh mh}{mh}my\cosh my\right\}\cos mx$$
$$\div(\sinh 2mh - 2mh).$$

It is easily verified that these formulae satisfy the equations of internal equilibrium, viz.

$$(42)\qquad \frac{\partial p_{xx}}{\partial x} + \frac{\partial p_{xy}}{\partial y} = 0\ , \quad \frac{\partial p_{xy}}{\partial x} + \frac{\partial p_{yy}}{\partial y} + \mathrm{H}\cos mx = 0\ ,$$

and make

$$p_{xy} = 0\ , \quad p_{yy} = 0 \quad \text{for } y = \pm h\ .$$

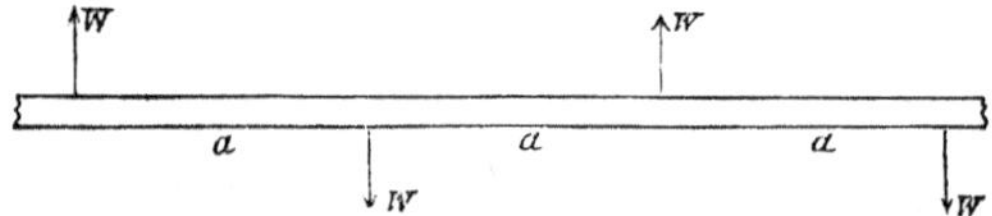

Fig. 2.

To calculate the effect of the system of forces indicated in Fig. 2, when these consist of body-forces concentrated uniformly in the sections $x = 0, x = \pm a, x = \pm 2a, \ldots$, it appears, on reference to (1) and (5), that we must write

$$(43)\qquad \mathrm{H} = \frac{2\mathrm{W}}{ba}\ , \quad m = \frac{s\pi}{a}\ ,$$

where b denotes the breadth of the beam, and sum for odd values of s. Thus we have, for the form of tho middle line $(y=0)$,

$$(44)\qquad v_0=\frac{\mathrm{W}a}{\pi^2\mu bh}\sum_s\frac{1}{s^2}\cos\frac{s\pi x}{a}$$

$$+\frac{\mathrm{W}h}{\mu ba}\sum_s\frac{\cosh\frac{s\pi h}{a}+\frac{\mu}{\lambda'+\mu}\frac{\sinh\frac{s\pi h}{a}}{\frac{s\pi h}{a}}}{\frac{s\pi h}{a}\left(\sinh\frac{2s\pi h}{a}-\frac{2s\pi h}{a}\right)}\cos\frac{s\pi x}{a}$$

The sum in the second term comes under the form (6); viz. we have

$$(45)\qquad \mathrm{F}(\zeta)=\cosh\zeta+\frac{\mu}{\lambda'+\mu}\frac{\sinh\zeta}{\zeta},$$

and the constants A , B of the formula (7) have accordingly the values

$$(46)\qquad \mathrm{A}=\frac{3(\lambda'+2\mu)}{4(\lambda'+\mu)}\;,\quad \mathrm{B}=\frac{9\lambda'+8\mu}{\lambda'+\mu}\,.$$

Hence, by (22) and (21),

$$(47)\qquad v_0=\frac{\lambda'+2\mu}{128(\lambda'+\mu)\mu}\frac{\mathrm{W}a^3}{bh^3}\left(1-6\frac{x^2}{a^2}+4\frac{x^3}{a^3}\right)$$

$$+\frac{49\lambda'+48\mu}{320(\lambda'+\mu)\mu}\frac{\mathrm{W}a}{bh}\left(1-2\frac{x}{a}\right)$$

$$+\frac{\mathrm{W}}{4\mu b}\sum_n Re\left[\mathrm{C}_n\frac{\sin(\frac{1}{2}a-x)\frac{\zeta_n}{h}}{\cos\frac{1}{2}\frac{a\zeta_n}{h}}\right].$$

The first part of this expression is identical with the deflection as given by the ordinary Euler-Bernoulli theory, viz.

$$(48)\qquad v_0=\frac{\mathrm{W}a^3}{48\mathrm{EI}}\left(1-6\frac{x^2}{a^2}+4\frac{x^3}{a^3}\right),$$

where E is Young's modulus, and I is the moment of inertia of the cross-section with respect to a transverse axis through its centre; for we have

$$(49)\qquad \frac{\mu(3\lambda+2\mu)}{\lambda+\mu}=\frac{4\mu(\lambda'+\mu)}{\lambda'+2\mu},\quad \mathrm{I}=\tfrac{2}{3}\,bh^3.$$

This part of the deflection is shewn in fig. 3.

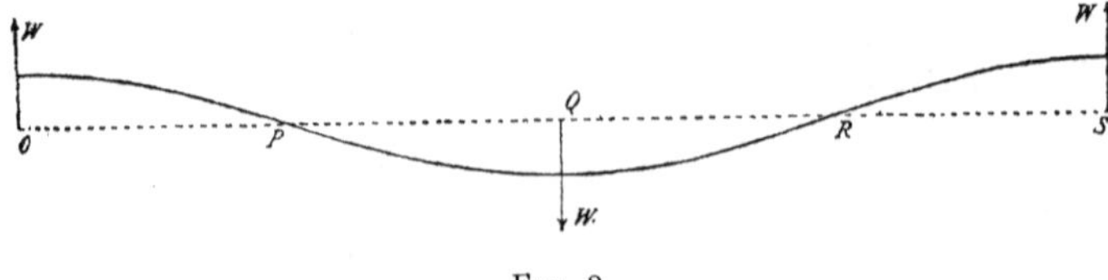

Fig. 3.

The additional deflection indicated by the second line in (47) is of the order h^2/a^2 as compared with the former; it is represented by a zig-zag line whose successive straight portions make very obtuse angles with one another at the load-points. If the ratio a/h be moderately large the remaining terms in (47) are negligible except in the immediate neighbourhood of the loads. For if we write $\zeta_n = \xi_n + i\eta_n$, it appears from (14) that the ratio $\eta_n a/h$ will be considerable even for $n = 1$; hence, taking account only of the most important terms in the numerators and denominators, we obtain

(50) $$\frac{W}{4\mu b} \sum_n \operatorname{Re}\left[iC_n e^{-\frac{\eta_n x}{h}} \cdot e^{\frac{i\xi_n x}{h}} \right].$$

When x is comparable with h this is quite insensible; but for very small values of x the second and third lines in (47) are of equal importance. This has the effect of rounding off the angles of the zig-zag.

The formulae for the stresses can be treated in a similar manner. Thus in the evaluation of p_{xx} we write (see equation (39))

(51) $$F(\zeta) = \sinh\zeta\left(\frac{\zeta y}{h}\cosh\frac{\zeta y}{h} + 2\sinh\frac{\zeta y}{h}\right) - \zeta\cosh\frac{\zeta y}{h}\sinh\frac{\zeta y}{h},$$

and therefore, in the notation of (7),

(52) $$A = 0 \quad , \quad B = \tfrac{3}{2}.$$

The final results, obtained by means of the formulae (22) and (23), are

(53) $$p_{xx} = \frac{3}{8}\frac{Wa}{bh^2}\left(1 - 2\frac{x}{a}\right)\frac{y}{h} + \text{etc.},$$

(54) $$p_{xy} = -\frac{3}{8}\frac{Wa}{bh}\left(1 - \frac{y^2}{h^2}\right) + \text{etc.},$$

(55) $$p_{yy} = 0 + \text{etc.},$$

the terms which when h/a is small are insensible except in the immediate neighbourhood of the loads being omitted for brevity. The terms retained agree with the expressions to which we should be led by the usual process of correction to the EULER-BERNOULLI theory (1).

It may be worth while, without entering into the details of the work, to give the values of the displacements u, v to the same degree of approximation. I find

$$u = \frac{3(\lambda' + 2\mu)}{32(\lambda' + \mu)\mu} \frac{Wa^2}{bh^2} \frac{x}{a}\left(1 - \frac{x}{a}\right)\frac{y}{h} - \frac{11\lambda' + 12\mu}{160(\lambda' + \mu)\mu} \frac{W}{b} \frac{y}{h} + \frac{3\lambda' + \mu}{32(\lambda' + \mu)\mu} \frac{W}{b} \frac{y^3}{h^3} + \text{etc.} \tag{56}$$

$$v = v_0 - \frac{3\lambda'}{64(\lambda' + \mu)\mu} \frac{Wa}{bh}\left(1 - 2\frac{x}{a}\right)\frac{y^2}{h^2} + \text{etc.} \tag{57}$$

From these, again, we may deduce the preceding expressions for the stresses.

5. We next make the more practical supposition that the forces in Fig. 2 consist of a series of isolated loads W on the upper face of the beam together with

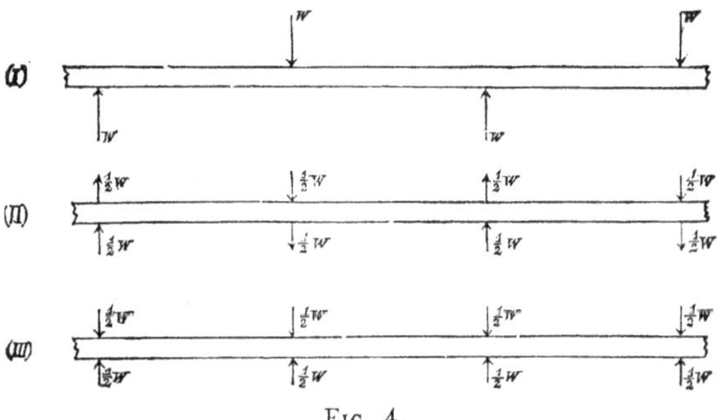

FIG. 4.

a series of equal and opposite supporting pressures on the lower face, half way between the loads. This distribution of force, which is indicated in Fig. 4 (I), may be

(1) The process is briefly as follows. Assuming that the horizontal elongation at a distance y from the middle line is proportional to y and to the curvature of this line, we have

$$p_{xx} = -\text{E}y\frac{\partial^2 v_0}{\partial x^2}. \tag{a}$$

Hence

$$\frac{\partial p_{xy}}{\partial y} = -\frac{\partial p_{xx}}{\partial x} = \text{E}y\frac{\partial^3 v_0}{\partial x^3},$$

and therefore

$$p_{xy} = -\tfrac{1}{2}\text{E}h^2\left(1 - \frac{y^2}{h^2}\right)\frac{\partial^3 v_0}{\partial x^3}, \tag{b}$$

the additive constant being chosen so as to make p_{xy} vanish for $y = \pm h$. Again

$$\frac{\partial p_{yy}}{\partial y} = -\frac{\partial p_{xy}}{\partial x} = \tfrac{1}{2}\text{E}h^2\left(1 - \frac{y^2}{h^2}\right)\frac{\partial^4 v_0}{\partial x^4},$$

and therefore

$$p_{yy} = -\frac{1}{6}\text{E}h^3\left(2 - 3\frac{y}{h} + \frac{y^3}{h^3}\right)\frac{\partial^4 v_0}{\partial x^4}. \tag{c}$$

If we substitute the values of v_0 and E from (48) and (49), the results agree with the values given in the text.

resolved into the sum of the two distributions (II) and (III), which are most conveniently treated separately. The distribution (III) will evidently not affect the form of the middle line.

The effect of the surface-tractions

$$(58) \qquad p_{yy} = \pm \tfrac{1}{2} \mathrm{H} \cos mx \ , \ p_{xy} = 0$$

on the faces $y = \pm h$, respectively, is given by the formulae [1]

$$(59) \quad u = \frac{\mathrm{H}}{2\mu m} \left\{ \cosh mh \left(my \cosh my + \frac{\mu}{\lambda' + \mu} \sinh my \right) - mh \sinh mh \sinh my \right\} \sin mx$$
$$\div (\sinh 2mh - 2mh),$$

$$(60) \quad v = \frac{\mathrm{H}}{2\mu m} \left\{ \cosh mh \left(\frac{\lambda' + 2\mu}{\lambda' + \mu} \cosh my - my \sinh my \right) + mh \sinh mh \cosh my \right\} \cos mx$$
$$\div (\sinh 2mh - 2mh).$$

The corresponding stresses are

$$(61) \quad p_{xx} = \mathrm{H} \left\{ \cosh mh (\sinh my + my \cosh my) - mh \sinh mh \sinh my \right\} \cos mx$$
$$\div (\sinh 2mh - 2mh),$$

$$(62) \quad p_{xy} = \mathrm{H} \left\{ \cosh mh \, . \, my \sinh my - mh \sinh mh \cosh my \right\} \sin mx$$
$$\div (\sinh 2mh - 2mh),$$

$$(63) \quad p_{yy} = \mathrm{H} \left\{ \cosh mh (\sinh my - my \cosh my) + mh \sinh mh \sinh my \right\} \cos mx$$
$$\div (\sinh 2mh - 2mh).$$

The form assumed by the middle line under the distribution (I) or (II) of Fig. 4 is therefore

$$(64) \qquad v_0 = \frac{\mathrm{W}h}{\mu b a} \sum_s \frac{\dfrac{\lambda' + 2\mu}{\lambda' + \mu} \cosh \dfrac{s\pi h}{a} + \dfrac{s\pi h}{a} \sinh \dfrac{s\pi h}{a}}{\dfrac{s\pi h}{a} \left(\sinh \dfrac{2s\pi h}{a} - \dfrac{2s\pi h}{a} \right)} \cos \frac{s\pi x}{a}$$

where $s = 1, 3, 5, \ldots$ The discussion of this formula follows the same course as that of (44). We have now

$$(65) \qquad \mathrm{F}(\zeta) = \frac{\lambda' + 2\mu}{\lambda' + \mu} \cosh \zeta + \zeta \sinh \zeta \, ,$$

$$(66) \qquad \mathrm{A} = \frac{3(\lambda' + 2\mu)}{4(\lambda' + \mu)} \ , \ \mathrm{B} = \frac{39\lambda' + 48\mu}{40(\lambda' + \mu)} \, ,$$

$$(67) \qquad \mathrm{C}_n = \frac{\dfrac{\lambda' + 2\mu}{\lambda' + \mu} \cosh \zeta_n + \zeta_n \sinh \zeta_n}{\zeta_n \sinh^2 \zeta_n} = \frac{\lambda' + 2\mu}{\lambda' + \mu} \frac{1}{\sinh^3 \zeta_n} + \frac{1}{\sinh \zeta_n} \, .$$

(1) H. Lamb, loc. cit.

We obtain, finally, for values of x ranging from 0 to a,

$$(68)\quad v_0 = \frac{\lambda' + 2\mu}{128(\lambda' + \mu)\mu}\frac{Wa^3}{bh^3}\left(1 - 6\frac{x^2}{a^2} + 4\frac{x^3}{a^3}\right) + \frac{39\lambda' + 48}{320(\lambda' + \mu)\mu}\frac{Wa}{bh}\left(1 - 2\frac{x}{a}\right)$$

$$+ \frac{W}{4\mu b}\sum_n Re\left[C_n \frac{\sin(\frac{1}{2}a - x)\frac{\zeta_n}{h}}{\cos\frac{1}{2}a\frac{\zeta_n}{h}}\right].$$

The first term is the same as in (47), as was to be expected. The change in the mode of application of the extraneous forces has, however, an effect on the coefficient of the second term, and the gradient of the « zig-zag » correction is accordingly somewhat diminished. The expression in the third line is affected by the altered value of C_n, but it is as before quite insensible except in the immediate neighbourhood of the points of application of the forces.

The general values of the displacements (in the distribution (II)) are found to be

$$(69)\quad u = \frac{3(\lambda' + 2\mu)}{32(\lambda' + \mu)\mu}\frac{Wa^2 x}{bh^2 a}\left(1 - \frac{x}{a}\right)\frac{y}{h} - \frac{21\lambda' + 12\mu}{160(\lambda' + \mu)\mu}\frac{W}{b}\frac{y}{h}$$

$$+ \frac{3\lambda' + 4\mu}{32(\lambda' + \mu)\mu}\frac{W}{b}\frac{y^3}{h^3} + \text{etc.},$$

$$(70)\quad v = v_0 - \frac{3\lambda'}{64(\lambda' + \mu)\mu}\frac{Wa}{bh}\left(1 - 2\frac{x}{a}\right)\frac{y^2}{h^2} + \text{etc.}$$

These correspond to (56) and (57). The approximate values of the stresses are exactly as in (53), (54), (55).

In the case of the distribution (III) of Fig. 4 we have to deal with a periodic function of the type represented by (24) and (25). The surface-traction

$$(71)\quad p_{yy} = \tfrac{1}{2}H\cos mx \;,\; p_{xy} = 0$$

on the faces $y = \pm h$ would produce the internal stresses

$$(72)\quad p_{xx} = H\{\sinh mh(\cosh my + my\sinh my) - mh\cosh mh\cosh my\}\cos mx \div (\sinh 2mh + 2mh),$$

$$(73)\quad p_{xy} = H\{- mh\cosh mh\sinh my + \sinh mh\,.\,my\cosh my\}\sin mx \div (\sinh 2mh + 2mh),$$

$$(74)\quad p_{yy} = H\{\sinh mh(\cosh my - my\sinh my) + mh\cosh mh\cosh my\}\cos mx \div (\sinh 2mh + 2mh).$$

In these, as in the corresponding formulae for the displacements, we must put $m = r\pi/a$, and $H = W/ba$ or $H = 2W/ba$, according as $r = 0$ or > 0, and sum

4

for $r = 0, 2, 4, 6, \ldots$ It is unnecessary to go through the work in detail, as it is easily seen from the analytical character of the functions involved that the resulting values of the stresses will be quite insensible (when h/a is small) except in the immediate neighbourhood of the points of application of the forces. There will, however be an elongation of the middle line, of integral amount

$$\frac{\lambda' + 2\mu}{4(\lambda' + \mu)\mu} \frac{W}{b}, \tag{75}$$

in the neighbourhood of each of these points.

6. We are now is a position to draw some conclusions as to the validity of the Euler-Bernoulli theory of flexure of finite beams, and of the usual somewhat empirical adjuncts to it. Considering the portion represented by OS in Fig. 3, we have a beam of length $2a$ clamped horizontally at the ends and carrying a load W at the centre. The difference between the two solutions contained in §§ 4 and 5 is due to variations in the mode of clamping, and in the mode of appplication of the central load.

Again, considering the portion PR we have a beam of length a supported by vertical shearing stresses of integral amount $\frac{1}{2}$W on the two terminal sections, and carrying a load W at the centre. The ratio $2h/a$ being assumed to be small, say not greater than 0.1, the distribution of stress over the two ends will practically be exactly the same in the two solutions, viz

$$p_{xx} = 0, \quad p_{xy} = -\frac{3}{8}\frac{W}{bh}\left(1 - \frac{y^2}{h^2}\right), \tag{76}$$

the only essential difference being in the mode of application of the central load. In the one case this is supposed applied uniformly over the central section; in the other the load rests on the upper surface of the beam. The first parts of the expressions (47) and (68) for the form of the middle line (1) are as given by the ordinary theory. The correction represented by the second terms is, however, somewhat different (2). If, for example, we put $\lambda = \mu$, $\lambda' = \frac{2}{3}\mu$, as on Poisson's view of the relation between the elastic constants, we find that the maximum additional deflection given by this correction is respectively

$$3.025\left(\frac{2h}{a}\right)^2 \quad \text{and} \quad 2.775\left(\frac{2h}{a}\right)^2$$

of the deflection given by the Euler-Bernoulli formula. The distribution of stresses throughout the beam is given (for small values of $2h/a$) with abundant accuracy by the formulae (53), (54), (55).

(1) The origin of x may be transferred to the middle point Q by merely changing the signe of W.
(2) This corresponds to the « additional deflection due to shearing » of technical writers.

Again by considering the portion OP of the beam we are able to illustrate the case of a cantilever carrying a terminal load. The variation in the form of the middle line is here due to a difference in the manner of clamping at the fixed end O.

The state of strain in the immediate neighbourhood of the points of application of the force is a matter for separate examination. This is not attempted here (¹), but it may be remarked that the horizontal extent of the regions which are excluded from the scope of the above statements diminishes very rapidly with diminution of the ratio $2h/a$.

7. We proceed to consider some cases of continuous load. Suppose, in the first place, that we have an infinitely long beam bent by its own weight, and supported by a body-force concentrated uniformly in the sections $x = 0, \pm a, \pm 2a, \ldots$ The total distribution of body-force is evidently of the type (25), with $A_0 = 0$. In the formulae of § 4 we must write

$$(77) \qquad H = \frac{2\varpi a}{b}, \quad m = \frac{r\pi}{a},$$

where ϖ is the weight per unit length, and sum for $r = 2, 4, 6, \ldots$ Thus we find for the equation of the middle line

$$(78) \quad v_0 = \frac{\varpi a^2}{\pi^2 \mu b h} \sum_r \frac{1}{r^2} \cos\frac{r\pi x}{a} + \frac{\varpi h}{\mu b} \sum_r \frac{\cosh\dfrac{r\pi h}{a} + \dfrac{\mu}{\lambda' + \mu}\dfrac{\sinh\dfrac{r\pi h}{a}}{\dfrac{r\pi h}{a}}}{\dfrac{r\pi h}{a}\left(\sinh\dfrac{2r\pi h}{a} - \dfrac{2r\pi h}{a}\right)} \cos\frac{r\pi x}{a}.$$

To sum the latter series we make use of the formula (35), writing, as in (45),

$$(79) \qquad F(\zeta) = \cosh\zeta + \frac{\mu}{\lambda' + \mu}\frac{\sinh\zeta}{\zeta},$$

and therefore

$$(80) \qquad A = \frac{3(\lambda' + 2\mu)}{4(\lambda' + \mu)}, \quad B = \frac{9\lambda' + 8\mu}{40(\lambda' + \mu)}.$$

Omitting constant terms, we have for values of x ranging from 0 to a

$$(81) \quad v_0 = -\frac{\lambda' + 2\mu}{64(\lambda' + \mu)\mu}\frac{\varpi a^4}{bh^3}\frac{x^2}{a^2}\left(1 - \frac{x}{a}\right)^2 - \frac{49\lambda' + 48\mu}{160(\lambda' + \mu)\mu}\frac{\varpi a^2}{bh}\frac{x}{a}\left(1 - \frac{x}{a}\right)$$
$$+ \frac{\varpi a}{4\mu b}\sum_n\left[C_n \frac{\cos(\tfrac{1}{2}a - x)\dfrac{\zeta_n}{h}}{\sin\tfrac{1}{2}\dfrac{a\zeta_n}{h}}\right],$$

(¹) For a discussion of such points reference may be made to Mr. Filon's paper, already cited.

where C_n is defined by (20). When the ratio h/a is small the last term will be quite insensible except near the points of support.

The approximate formulae for the stresses are found to be

$$(82)\qquad p_{xx} = \frac{1}{8}\frac{\varpi a^2}{bh^2}\left(1 - 6\frac{x}{h} + 6\frac{x^2}{h^2}\right)\frac{y}{h} + \frac{3}{10}\frac{\varpi}{b}\frac{y}{h} + \tfrac{1}{2}\frac{\varpi}{b}\frac{y^3}{h^3} + \text{etc.},$$

$$(83)\qquad p_{xy} = -\frac{3}{8}\frac{\varpi a}{bh}\left(1 - 2\frac{x}{a}\right)\left(1 - \frac{y^2}{h^2}\right) + \text{etc.},$$

$$(84)\qquad p_{yy} = -\frac{1}{4}\frac{\varpi}{b}\frac{y}{h}\left(1 - \frac{y^2}{h^2}\right) + \text{etc.}$$

It is to be noticed that the second and third terms in the value of p_{xx} contribute (together) nothing to the bending movement, viz.

$$(85)\qquad b\int_{-h}^{h} p_{xx} y\, dy = \frac{1}{12}\varpi a^2\left(1 - 6\frac{x}{a} + 6\frac{x^2}{a^2}\right).$$

The displacements u, v are a little more troublesome to work out, owing to the terms corresponding to $f(0)$ in (35). I find

$$(86)\qquad u = \frac{\lambda' + 2\mu}{32(\lambda' + \mu)\mu}\frac{\varpi a^3}{bh^2}\frac{x}{a}\left(1 - \frac{x}{a}\right)\left(1 - \frac{2x}{a}\right)\frac{y}{h}$$
$$- \frac{11\lambda' + 12\mu}{160(\lambda' + \mu)\mu}\frac{\varpi a}{b}\left(1 - 2\frac{x}{a}\right)\frac{y}{h} + \frac{3\lambda' + 4\mu}{32(\lambda' + \mu)\mu}\frac{\varpi a}{b}\left(1 - 2\frac{x}{a}\right)\frac{y^3}{h^3} + \text{etc.},$$

$$(87)\qquad v = v_0 - \frac{\lambda'}{64(\lambda' + \mu)\mu}\frac{\varpi a^2}{bh}\left(1 - 6\frac{x}{a} + 6\frac{x^2}{h^2}\right)\frac{y}{h} - \frac{11\lambda' + 10\mu}{160(\lambda' + \mu)\mu}\frac{\varpi h}{b}\frac{y^2}{h^2}$$
$$+ \frac{3\lambda' + 2\mu}{84(\lambda' + \mu)\mu}\frac{\varpi h}{b}\frac{y^4}{h^4} + \text{etc.}$$

It is easily verified that these lead to the preceding values of the stresses, which were obtained independently.

8. As a variation on this problem we may imagine the load to consist of a uniform distribution of surface-stress

$$(88)\qquad p_{yy} = \mp\tfrac{1}{2}\frac{\varpi}{b}, \quad p_{xy} = 0$$

on the two faces $y = \pm\frac{1}{2}h$, respectively, and that the support is effected by means of concentrated upward forces $\frac{1}{2}\varpi a/b$ applied to these faces at the points $x = 0, \pm a, \pm 2a, \ldots$ Using the formulae of § 5 we find

$$(89)\qquad v_0 = \frac{\varpi h}{\mu b}\sum_r \frac{\dfrac{\lambda' + 2\mu}{\lambda' + \mu}\cosh\dfrac{r\pi h}{a} + \dfrac{r\pi h}{a}\sinh\dfrac{r\pi h}{a}}{\left|\dfrac{r\pi h}{a}\left(\sinh\dfrac{2r\pi h}{a} - \dfrac{2r\pi h}{a}\right)\right.}\cos\frac{r\pi x}{a},$$

where $r = 2, 4, 6, \ldots$ The reduction is as before, except that the formulae (80) are replaced by

$$\text{(90)} \qquad A = \frac{3(\lambda' + 2\mu)}{4(\lambda' + \mu)}, \quad B = \frac{39\lambda' + 48\mu}{40(\lambda' + \mu)},$$

as in (66). The result is

$$\text{(91)} \quad v_0 = -\frac{\lambda' + 2\mu}{64(\lambda' + \mu)\mu} \frac{\varpi a^3}{bh^3} \frac{x^2}{a^2}\left(1 - \frac{x}{a}\right)^2 - \frac{39\lambda' + 48\mu}{160(\lambda' + \mu)\mu} \frac{\varpi a^2}{bh} \frac{x}{a}\left(1 - \frac{x}{a}\right)$$

$$+ \frac{\varpi a}{4\mu b} \sum_n \mathrm{Re}\left[C_n \frac{\cos(\frac{1}{2}a - x)\frac{\zeta_n}{h}}{\sin \frac{1}{2}\frac{a\zeta_n}{h}} \right],$$

where C_n has now the value (67).

For the stresses I find

$$\text{(92)} \qquad p_{xx} = \frac{\varpi a^2}{8bh^2}\left(1 - 2\frac{x}{a} + 6\frac{x^2}{a^2}\right)\frac{y}{h} + \frac{3}{10}\frac{\varpi}{b}\frac{y}{h} - \frac{1}{2}\frac{\varpi}{b}\frac{y^3}{h^3} + \text{etc}.$$

$$\text{(93)} \qquad p_{xy} = -\frac{3}{8}\frac{\varpi a}{bh}\left(1 - 2\frac{x}{a}\right)\left(1 - \frac{y^2}{h^2}\right) + \text{etc.},$$

$$\text{(94)} \qquad p_{yy} = -\frac{\varpi}{4b}\left(3\frac{y}{h} + \frac{y^3}{h^3}\right) + \text{etc.},$$

The distribution of applied force in this problem is indicated in Fig. 5 (I), the short arrows representing the uniform part of the load. If we superpose the distri-

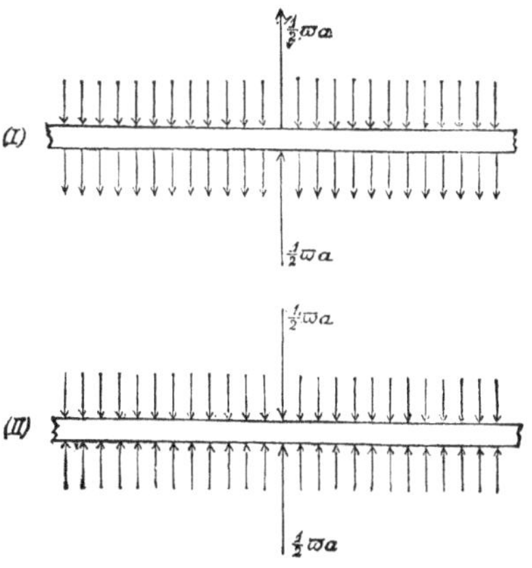

Fig. 5.

bution (II) we get the case of a beam loaded uniformly along the upper face and supported by concentrated pressures at equal intervals along the lower face. It is evident without detailed calculation that the effect of the distribution (II) will be merely to produce a horizontal extension of the beam which is sensibly uniform except in the immediate neighbourhood of the supports.

9. The investigations of §§ 7, 8 may be used to illustrate the case of a uniformly loaded beam of finite length a clamped horizontally at the ends. In § 7 the load consists of the beam's own weight; in § 8 it is divided equally between the upper and lower faces, but except for the horizontal extension just referred to the result is practically the same as if the load were applied to the upper face alone.

The first term in the expression (81) or (91) is identical with the result given by the ordinary theory, viz.

$$(95) \qquad v_0 = -\frac{1}{24}\frac{\varpi}{\mathrm{EI}}x^2(a-x)^2,$$

where the origin of x is at one end, and the values of E, I are as in (49). The second terms give a parabolic correction which is of the order h^2/a^2 as compared with (95); the slight difference in the value of the coefficient is to be attributed to the variation in the modes of clamping and of application of the load.

To illustrate the case of a beam loaded uniformly, and « supported » at the ends, it is convenient to change the origin of x, writing $x+\frac{1}{2}a$ for a, and to put $a^2=3l^2$. In this way (81) becomes

$$(96) \quad v_0 = -\frac{\lambda'+2\mu}{64(\lambda'+\mu)\mu}\frac{\varpi l^4}{bh^3}\left(5-6\frac{x^2}{l^2}+\frac{x^4}{l^4}\right)-\frac{49\lambda'+48\mu}{160(\lambda'+\mu)\mu}\frac{\varpi l^2}{bh}\left(1-\frac{x^2}{l^2}\right)+\text{etc.},$$

where constants have been added so as to make the expression vanish for $x=\pm l$. The formulae (82), (83), (84) for the stresses become

$$(97) \qquad p_{xx} = -\frac{3}{4}\frac{\varpi l^2}{bh^2}\left(1-\frac{x^2}{l^2}\right)\frac{y}{h}+\frac{3}{10}\frac{\varpi}{b}\frac{y}{h}-\frac{1}{2}\frac{\varpi}{b}\frac{y^3}{h^3}+\text{etc.},$$

$$(98) \qquad p_{xy} = \frac{3}{4}\frac{\varpi}{bh}x\left(1-\frac{y^2}{h^2}\right)+\text{etc.},$$

$$(99) \qquad p_{yy} = -\frac{1}{4}\frac{\varpi}{b}\frac{y}{h}\left(1-\frac{y^2}{h^2}\right)+\text{etc.},$$

These formulae refer to the case of a beam of length $2l$ supported at the ends $x=\pm l$ (where the bending moment as given by (85) vanishes) and bent by its own weight. The formulae for the case of a uniform surface-load differ only in the value of the coefficient in the second term of v_0, and in the form (94) of p_{yy}. If we put $\lambda'=\frac{2}{3}\mu$ the maximum value of the parabolic correction to the form of the middle line is found to be

$$2.42\left(\frac{h}{l}\right)^2 \quad \text{or} \quad 2.22\left(\frac{h}{l}\right)^2$$

of the deflection at the centre as given by the Eulerian theory, according to the manner in which the uniform load is applied. The supporting stresses on the ends are (practically) exactly the same (when h/l is small) in the two cases, viz.

$$(100) \qquad p_{xx} = \frac{3}{10}\frac{\varpi}{b}\frac{y}{h} - \frac{1}{2}\frac{\varpi}{b}\frac{y^3}{h^3}\,, \quad p_{xy} = \frac{3}{4}\frac{\varpi l}{bh}\left(1 = \frac{y^2}{h^2}\right).$$

The distribution of stress on either end is equivalent to a vertical force ϖl. If it were replaced by any other statically equivalent distribution, this would again involve a slight change in the parabolic correction to the form of the middle line, but would not affect the internal stresses except within a distance from the ends which is of the order h.

The stresses given in (82), (83), (84) differ slightly from those to which we should be led by the « empirical » methods [1], viz.

$$(101) \qquad p_{xx} = \frac{3}{4}\frac{\varpi l^2}{bh^2}\left(1 - \frac{x^2}{l^2}\right)\frac{y}{h}\,,$$

$$(102) \qquad p_{xy} = \frac{3}{4}\frac{\varpi}{bh}\left(1 - \frac{y^2}{h^2}\right),$$

$$(103) \qquad p_{yy} = -\frac{1}{4}\frac{\varpi}{b}\frac{y}{h}\left(1 - \frac{y^2}{h^2}\right).$$

The difference is in the value of p_{xy}, but the proportional error is of the order h^2/a^2.

Writers who have discussed the validity of the EULER-BERNOULLI theory from the point of view of the exact equations of elasticity have naturally been led to dwell, perhaps unduly, on the defects of the theory. No one, of course, would expect it to lead to good results when the dimensions of the cross-section are not small compared with the horizontal distances between points of loading and of support,

[1] In the case of a body force the determination of in the foot-note on p. 23 requires modification. We now have

$$\frac{\partial p_{yy}}{\partial y} = -\frac{\partial p_{xy}}{\partial x} + \frac{\varpi}{2bh} = \tfrac{1}{2}\,Eh^3\left(1 - \frac{y^2}{h^2}\right)\frac{\partial^4 v_0}{\partial x^4} + \frac{\varpi}{2bh}\,.$$

On the EULER-BERNOULLI theory

$$EI\frac{\partial^4 v_0}{\partial x^4} = -\varpi,$$

and therefore

$$\frac{\partial p_{yy}}{\partial y} = -\frac{1}{4}\frac{\varpi}{bh}\left(1 - 3\frac{y^2}{h^2}\right).$$

This leads on integration to the formula (103) in the text. The formulae (101), (102) are obtained by substituting

$$v_0 = -\frac{1}{24}\frac{\varpi l^4}{EI}\left(5 - 6\frac{x^2}{l^2} + \frac{x^4}{l^4}\right),$$

which is the equivalent of the first term of (96), in the equations (a) and (b) of the footnote referred to.

or (more generally) between points of discontinuity of the applied forces. But, apart from this qualification, it would appear that in the case of a narrow beam the theory in question is entitled to considerable respect. In the case of isolated loads it leads to a distribution of internal stress which is practically exact, except at distances from the loads which are comparable with the depth. The form of the middle line given by the theory is subject to a correction which may be sensible, but the magnitude of this correction is in practical cases somewhat uncertain, owing to its variability with the mode of application of the extraneous forces. This uncertainty is present in an especial degree in the case of a clamped beam. In cases of continuous load the stresses indicated by the approximate theory are no longer exact; the requisite correction is determinate, but is under practical conditions usually small.

The methods of this paper might be employed without much trouble to examine the effect of other variations in the mode of application of the forces. For example, we might consider the effect of concentrated forces applied at points of the middle line. This would correspond to the case of a beam loaded and supported by means of horizontal stanchions passing through it at points of the middle line.

G. LAURICELLA

SULL'EQUAZIONE $\Delta^{2i}V = 0$ E SU ALCUNE ESTENSIONI DELLE EQUAZIONI DELL'EQUILIBRIO DEI CORPI ELASTICI ISOTROPI

Alla dimostrazione diretta, da me data, sull'esistenza dell'integrale dell'equazione $\Delta^4 V = 0$ in un campo piano, per dati valori al contorno di V e della sua derivata normale ([1]), ne aggiunsi recentemente una nuova ([2]), che vale per un numero qualsiasi di dimensioni, e che si fonda sopra un teorema, il quale riconduce la ricerca dell'integrale suddetto, alla integrazione delle equazioni dell'equilibrio dei corpi elastici isotropi per un valore *speciale* della costante di isotropia ([3]).

Ora mi propongo di estendere questo nuovo metodo al problema dell'integrazione dell'equazione $\Delta^{2i}V = 0$, per dati valori al contorno della funzione V e delle sue derivate normali dei primi $i-1$ ordini, e ad altri problemi analoghi ancora più generali. Tale estensione conduce alla considerazione di un certo sistema di equazioni alle derivate parziali del 2° ordine, che è una facile estensione del sistema di equazioni dell'equilibrio dei corpi elastici isotropi. La sua integrazione comprende, come casi particolari, l'integrazione dell'equazione $\Delta^{2i}V = 0$ e di varii altri sistemi, pure di ordine superiore, più generali; e si può eseguire applicando i noti risultati di Fredholm sulle equazioni integrali, indipendentemente da qualsiasi altro problema al contorno più semplice.

Per ragione di semplicità, nella presente comunicazione mi limiterò al caso di $i = 3$ e delle *tre* dimensioni, e mi limiterò ancora a quelle estensioni, che sono necessarie per dimostrare l'esistenza in generale degli integrali delle equazioni che dovrò considerare. Gli elementi, che così verranno introdotti, sono sufficienti a fare comprendere come bisogna procedere nel caso di i qualsiasi e di un numero qualsiasi di dimensioni; ed ancora ad indicare la via che bisogna percorrere nell'eseguire le varie generalizzazioni che si presentano spontanee.

([1]) *Sur l'intégration de l'équation relative à l'équilibre des plaques...* Acta mathematica, t. 32.

([2]) *Sull'integrazione dell'equazione* $\Delta^4 V = 0$ (Rendiconti della R. Acc. dei Lincei, vol. XVI, 2° semestre).

([3]) Per il caso delle due dimensioni questo teorema era stato notato già dal prof. Boggio nella sua Nota *Sull'equilibrio delle membrane elastiche piane*, § 8 (Atti della R. Acc. delle Sc. di Torino, vol. XXXV).

Preliminari.

1. Indichiamo con σ una superficie chiusa, con S lo spazio finito da essa limitato, con n la normale nei punti di σ; e fissiamo la direzione positiva di n in modo che sia rivolta verso il campo S. Supponiamo poi che la superficie σ soddisfaccia alle seguenti condizioni:

1°. Ammetta un piano tangente determinato in ogni suo punto, variabile con continuità al variare con continuità del punto di contatto;

2°. Esista un numero fisso positivo α tale che, indicando con $\widehat{nn'}$ l'angolo formato dalle direzioni positive delle normali n, n' in due punti qualsiasi p, p' di σ e con r' il vettore $\overline{pp'}$, si abbia:

$$\widehat{nn'} < \alpha r'.$$

Riferiamo i punti dello spazio ad una terna di assi cartesiani ortogonali; e indichiamo con r il vettore che congiunge due punti qualsiasi dello spazio, le cui coordinate siano rispettivamente x, y, z ; ξ, η, ζ. Finalmente si ponga:

$$\Delta^2 = \frac{\partial^2}{\partial\xi^2} + \frac{\partial^2}{\partial\eta^2} + \frac{\partial^2}{\partial\zeta^2}\,, \quad \Delta^{2i} = \Delta^2(\Delta^{2(i-1)}) \; ; \quad \Delta = \left(\frac{\partial}{\partial\xi}\right)^2 + \left(\frac{\partial}{\partial\eta}\right)^2 + \left(\frac{\partial}{\partial\zeta}\right)^2 ;$$

$$\frac{d}{dn} = \frac{\partial}{\partial x}\cos\widehat{nx} + \frac{\partial}{\partial y}\cos\widehat{ny} + \frac{\partial}{\partial z}\cos\widehat{nz}\,, \quad \frac{d^i}{dn^i} = \frac{d}{dn}\left(\frac{d^{i-1}}{dn^{i-1}}\right),$$

supponendo nelle due ultime formole (*derivata normale prima*, *derivata normale* i^{esima}) che il punto (x, y, z) sia su σ e che n sia la normale in questo punto.

Teoremi di equivalenza.

2. Quando di una funzione V sono dati nei punti di σ i suoi valori e quelli delle sue derivate normali prima e seconda, si possono subito ottenere i valori di $\frac{\partial V}{\partial x}, \frac{\partial V}{\partial y}, \frac{\partial V}{\partial z}, \frac{d}{dn}\frac{\partial V}{\partial x}, \frac{d}{dn}\frac{\partial V}{\partial y}, \frac{d}{dn}\frac{\partial V}{\partial z}$ negli stessi punti di σ, supposto che queste derivate esistano.

Viceversa, se di una funzione V sono dati nei punti di σ i valori di $\frac{\partial V}{\partial x}, \frac{\partial V}{\partial y}$, $\frac{\partial V}{\partial z}, \frac{d}{dn}\frac{\partial V}{\partial x}, \frac{d}{dn}\frac{\partial V}{\partial y}, \frac{d}{dn}\frac{\partial V}{\partial z}$, si possono subito determinare negli stessi punti di σ i valori di $\frac{d^2V}{dn^2}, \frac{dV}{dn}$ e, a meno di una costante, quelli di V.

Di qui segue che *al problema di determinare una funzione* V *dei punti del campo* S, *la quale soddisfaccia alle equazioni*:

$$(1)\quad\begin{cases}(\text{nei punti di S})\quad \Delta^6 V=0,\\ (\text{nei punti di }\sigma)\quad V=f_1(\alpha,\beta)\ ,\ \dfrac{dV}{dn}=f_2(\alpha,\beta)\ ,\ \dfrac{d^2V}{dn^2}=f_3(\alpha,\beta),\end{cases}$$

dove α,β *sono i parametri relativi ad un sistema ortogonale su* σ, *e dove* $f_1(\alpha,\beta)$, $f_2(\alpha,\beta)$, $f_3(\alpha,\beta)$ *sono funzioni finite e continue arbitrariamente date, delle quali le prime due abbiano le derivate prime finite e continue, si può sostituire l'altro di determinare una funzione* V_1 *dei punti del campo* S, *la quale soddisfaccia alle equazioni*:

$$(1)_1\quad\begin{cases}(\text{nei punti di S})\quad \Delta^6 V_1=0,\\ (\text{nei punti di }\sigma)\ \begin{cases}\dfrac{\partial V_1}{\partial x}=u_\sigma\ ,\ \dfrac{\partial V_1}{\partial y}=v_\sigma\ ,\ \dfrac{\partial V_1}{\partial z}=w_\sigma\ ,\\ \dfrac{d}{dn}\dfrac{\partial V_1}{\partial x}=u'_\sigma\ ,\ \dfrac{d}{dn}\dfrac{\partial V_1}{\partial y}=v'_\sigma\ ,\ \dfrac{d}{dn}\dfrac{\partial V_1}{\partial z}=w'_\sigma\ ,\end{cases}\end{cases}$$

dove si è posto

$$u_\sigma=\frac{\partial V}{\partial x}\ ,\ v_\sigma=\frac{\partial V}{\partial y}\ ,\ w_\sigma=\frac{\partial V}{\partial z}\ ,\ u'_\sigma=\frac{d}{dn}\frac{\partial V}{\partial x}\ ,\ v'_\sigma=\frac{d}{dn}\frac{\partial V}{\partial y}\ ,\ w'_\sigma=\frac{d}{dn}\frac{\partial V}{\partial z}\,.$$

Infatti, determinato in un modo qualsiasi un integrale V_1 delle equazioni $(1)_1$, questo differirà da un integrale V delle equazioni (1) per una costante additiva, la quale si potrà determinare, tenendo conto del valore di $f_1(\alpha,\beta)$ in un punto qualsiasi di σ.

3. Se V_1 è integrale delle equazioni $(1)_1$, posto:

$$u=\frac{\partial V_1}{\partial \xi}\ ,\ v=\frac{\partial V_1}{\partial \eta}\ ,\ w=\frac{\partial V_1}{\partial \zeta}\quad ,\quad \theta=\frac{\partial u}{\partial \xi}+\frac{\partial v}{\partial \eta}+\frac{\partial w}{\partial \zeta}=\Delta^2 V_1,$$

risulterà:

$$(1)_2\quad\begin{cases}(\text{nei punti di S})\ \begin{cases}\Delta^2\Big(\Delta^2 u-\dfrac{\partial\theta}{\partial\xi}\Big)=0\ ,\ \Delta^2\Big(\Delta^2 v-\dfrac{\partial\theta}{\partial\eta}\Big)=0,\\ \Delta^2\Big(\Delta^2 w-\dfrac{\partial\theta}{\partial\zeta}\Big)=0,\\ \Delta^4\theta=0,\end{cases}\\ (\text{nei punti di }\sigma)\quad u=u_\sigma\ ,\ v=v_\sigma\ ,\ w=w_\sigma\ ,\ \dfrac{du}{dn}=u'_\sigma\ ,\ \dfrac{dv}{dn}=v'_\sigma\ ,\ \dfrac{dw}{dn}=w'_\sigma\ ,\end{cases}$$

nelle quali u_σ, v_σ, w_σ sono rispettivamente i valori nei punti di σ delle derivate parziali del 1° ordine rapporto a ξ, η, ζ di una medesima funzione, ed u'_σ, v'_σ, w'_σ sono rispettivamente i valori nei punti di σ delle derivate normali di queste tre derivate parziali.

Viceversa supponiamo che le funzioni u, v, w formino un sistema di integrali delle equazioni $(1)_2$, nelle quali u_σ, v_σ, w_σ siano rispettivamente i valori nei punti di σ delle derivate parziali del 1° ordine rapporto a ξ, η, ζ di una medesima funzione $V_2(\xi, \eta, \zeta)$, ed u'_σ, v'_σ, w'_σ siano rispettivamente i valori nei punti di σ delle derivate normali prime di $\frac{\partial V_2}{\partial \xi}, \frac{\partial V_2}{\partial \eta}, \frac{\partial V_2}{\partial \zeta}$. Posto:

$$\tau_1 = \frac{\partial w}{\partial \eta} - \frac{\partial v}{\partial \zeta}, \quad \tau_2 = \frac{\partial u}{\partial \zeta} - \frac{\partial w}{\partial \xi}, \quad \tau_3 = \frac{\partial v}{\partial \xi} - \frac{\partial u}{\partial \eta}, \tag{2}$$

le prime tre delle $(1)_2$ diverranno:

$$\Delta^2\left(\frac{\partial \tau_2}{\partial \zeta} - \frac{\partial \tau_3}{\partial \eta}\right) = 0, \quad \Delta^2\left(\frac{\partial \tau_3}{\partial \xi} - \frac{\partial \tau_1}{\partial \zeta}\right) = 0, \quad \Delta^2\left(\frac{\partial \tau_1}{\partial \eta} - \frac{\partial \tau_2}{\partial \xi}\right) = 0,$$

ossia:

$$\frac{\partial \Delta^2 \tau_2}{\partial \zeta} - \frac{\partial \Delta^2 \tau_3}{\partial \eta} = 0, \quad \frac{\partial \Delta^2 \tau_3}{\partial \xi} - \frac{\partial \Delta^2 \tau_1}{\partial \zeta} = 0, \quad \frac{\partial \Delta^2 \tau_1}{\partial \eta} - \frac{\partial \Delta^2 \tau_2}{\partial \xi} = 0; \tag{3}$$

e quindi esisterà una funzione $U(\xi, \eta, \zeta)$ tale che:

$$\Delta^2 \tau_1 = \frac{\partial U}{\partial \xi}, \quad \Delta^2 \tau_2 = \frac{\partial U}{\partial \eta}, \quad \Delta^2 \tau_3 = \frac{\partial U}{\partial \zeta}. \tag{4}$$

Dalle (3) si ha ancora integrando per parti,

$$\left\{\begin{aligned} 0 = & -\int_S \Big\{ u\left(\frac{\partial \Delta^2 \tau_2}{\partial \zeta} - \frac{\partial \Delta^2 \tau_3}{\partial \eta}\right) + v\left(\frac{\partial \Delta^2 \tau_3}{\partial \xi} - \frac{\partial \Delta^2 \tau_1}{\partial \zeta}\right) + \\ & \qquad + w\left(\frac{\partial \Delta^2 \tau_1}{\partial \eta} - \frac{\partial \Delta^2 \tau_2}{\partial \xi}\right)\Big\} dS = \\ = & \int_S (\tau_1 \Delta^2 \tau_1 + \tau_2 \Delta^2 \tau_2 + \tau_3 \Delta^2 \tau_3)\, dS + \int_\sigma \Big\{ \Delta^2 \tau_1 (w \cos \widehat{ny} - v \cos \widehat{nz}) + \\ & \qquad + \Delta^2 \tau_2 (u \cos \widehat{nz} - w \cos \widehat{nx}) + \Delta^2 \tau_3 (v \cos \widehat{nx} - u \cos \widehat{ny}) \Big\} d\sigma = \\ = & -\int_S (\Delta \tau_1 + \Delta \tau_2 + \Delta \tau_3)\, dS - \int_\sigma \left(\tau_1 \frac{d\tau_1}{dn} + \tau_2 \frac{d\tau_2}{dn} + \tau_3 \frac{d\tau_3}{dn}\right) d\sigma + \\ & \qquad + \int_\sigma \Big\{ \Delta^2 \tau_1 (w \cos \widehat{ny} - v \cos \widehat{nz}) + \dots \Big\} d\sigma; \end{aligned}\right. \tag{5}$$

e dalle (4), pure integrando per parti,

$$
(6)\quad \begin{cases}
\int_\sigma \left\{ \Delta^2\tau_1 (w \cos\widehat{ny} - v \cos\widehat{nz}) + \Delta^2\tau_2(u \cos\widehat{nz} - w \cos\widehat{nx}) + \dots \right\} d\sigma = \\
= \int_\sigma \left\{ \frac{\partial U}{\partial x}\left(\frac{\partial V_2}{\partial z}\cos\widehat{ny} - \frac{\partial V_2}{\partial y}\cos\widehat{nz}\right) + \right. \\
\qquad \left. + \frac{\partial U}{\partial y}\left(\frac{\partial V_2}{\partial x}\cos\widehat{nz} - \frac{\partial V_2}{\partial z}\cos\widehat{nx}\right) + \cdots \right\} d\sigma = \\
= -\int_S \left\{ \frac{\partial}{\partial \eta}\left(\frac{\partial U}{\partial \xi}\frac{\partial V_2}{\partial \zeta}\right) - \frac{\partial}{\partial \zeta}\left(\frac{\partial U}{\partial \xi}\frac{\partial V_2}{\partial \eta}\right) + \frac{\partial}{\partial \zeta}\left(\frac{\partial U}{\partial \eta}\frac{\partial V_2}{\partial \xi}\right) - \frac{\partial}{\partial \xi}\left(\frac{\partial U}{\partial \eta}\frac{\partial V_2}{\partial \zeta}\right) + \right. \\
\qquad \left. + \frac{\partial}{\partial \xi}\left(\frac{\partial U}{\partial \zeta}\frac{\partial V_2}{\partial \eta}\right) - \frac{\partial}{\partial \eta}\left(\frac{\partial U}{\partial \zeta}\frac{\partial V_2}{\partial \xi}\right) \right\} dS = 0 .
\end{cases}
$$

Le ultime *sei* delle $(1)_2$ ci dànno nei punti di σ:

$$
\frac{\partial u_\sigma}{\partial \alpha} = \frac{\partial u}{\partial x}\cos\widehat{\alpha x} + \frac{\partial u}{\partial y}\cos\widehat{\alpha y} + \frac{\partial u}{\partial z}\cos\widehat{\alpha z} = \frac{\partial}{\partial \alpha}\left(\frac{\partial V_2}{\partial x}\right) =
$$

$$
= \frac{\partial^2 V_2}{\partial x^2}\cos\widehat{\alpha x} + \frac{\partial^2 V_2}{\partial x\,\partial y}\cos\widehat{\alpha y} + \frac{\partial^2 V_2}{\partial x\,\partial z}\cos\widehat{\alpha z} ,
$$

$$
\frac{\partial u_\sigma}{\partial \beta} = \frac{\partial u}{\partial x}\cos\widehat{\beta x} + \quad \cdot \quad \cdot \quad \cdot \quad = \frac{\partial}{\partial \beta}\left(\frac{\partial V_2}{\partial x}\right) = \frac{\partial^2 V_2}{\partial x^2}\cos\widehat{\beta x} + \cdots ,
$$

$$
\frac{du}{dn} = \frac{\partial u}{\partial x}\cos\widehat{nx} + \quad \cdot \quad \cdot \quad \cdot \quad = \frac{d}{dn}\left(\frac{\partial V_2}{\partial \xi}\right) = \frac{\partial^2 V_2}{\partial x^2}\cos\widehat{nx} + \cdots ;
$$

allora si avrà nei punti di σ:

$$
\frac{\partial u}{\partial x} = \frac{\partial^2 V_2}{\partial x^2} \quad , \quad \frac{\partial u}{\partial y} = \frac{\partial^2 V_2}{\partial x\,\partial y} \quad , \quad \frac{\partial u}{\partial z} = \frac{\partial^2 V_2}{\partial x\,\partial z} ,
$$

e similmente:

$$
\frac{\partial v}{\partial x} = \frac{\partial^2 V_2}{\partial y\,\partial z} \quad , \quad \frac{\partial v}{\partial y} = \frac{\partial^2 V_2}{\partial y^2} \quad , \quad \frac{\partial v}{\partial z} = \frac{\partial^2 V_2}{\partial y\,\partial z} \quad , \quad \frac{\partial w}{\partial x} = \frac{\partial^2 V_2}{\partial z\,\partial x} , \dots ;
$$

quindi, ammettendo per la funzione V_2 la proprietà dell'inversione dell'ordine di derivazione sulle derivate seconde, sarà:

$$
(7)\quad \text{(nei punti di } \sigma) \quad \tau_1 = \frac{\partial w}{\partial y} - \frac{\partial v}{\partial z} = \frac{\partial^2 V_2}{\partial z\,\partial y} - \frac{\partial^2 V_2}{\partial y\,\partial z} = 0 \ , \ \tau_2 = 0 \ , \ \tau_3 = 0.
$$

Queste, insieme alle formule (5), (6), ci dànno immediatamente:

$$
\int_S (\Delta\tau_1 + \Delta\tau_2 + \Delta\tau_3)\, dS = 0 ;
$$

donde:

$$\text{(nei punti di S)} \qquad \frac{\partial\tau_1}{\partial\xi} = \frac{\partial\tau_1}{\partial\eta} = \frac{\partial\tau_1}{\partial\zeta} = \frac{\partial\tau_2}{\partial\xi} = \cdots = \frac{\partial\tau_3}{\partial\xi} = \cdots = 0\,;$$

e quindi, in virtù delle (7),

$$\text{(nei punti di S)} \qquad \tau_1 = \tau_2 = \tau_3 = 0\,,$$

ossia:

$$\text{(nei punti di S)} \qquad \frac{\partial w}{\partial\eta} = \frac{\partial v}{\partial\zeta}\,, \quad \frac{\partial u}{\partial\zeta} = \frac{\partial w}{\partial\xi}\,, \quad \frac{\partial v}{\partial\xi} = \frac{\partial u}{\partial\eta}\,.$$

Di qui segue l'esistenza di una funzione $V_1(\xi, \eta, \zeta)$ tale che:

$$u = \frac{\partial V_1}{\partial\xi}\,, \quad v = \frac{\partial V_1}{\partial\eta}\,, \quad w = \frac{\partial V_1}{\partial\eta}\,;$$

e così otteniamo per la $V_1(\xi, \eta, \zeta)$, in virtù delle $(1)_2$,

$$\text{(nei punti di S)} \qquad \Delta^6 V_1 = 0\,,$$

$$\text{(nei punti di } \sigma) \qquad \frac{\partial V_1}{\partial x} = u_\sigma\,, \quad \frac{\partial V_1}{\partial y} = u_\sigma\,, \ldots, \quad \frac{d}{dn}\frac{\partial V_1}{\partial x} = u'_\sigma\,, \quad \frac{d}{dn}\frac{\partial V_1}{\partial y} = v'_\sigma\,, \ldots$$

Riepilogando, si ha che *l'integrazione delle equazioni* $(1)_1$ *equivale all'integrazione delle equazioni* $(1)_2$.

4. Ciò premesso, si considerino le equazioni:

$$(8) \quad \begin{cases} \text{(nei punti di S)} \begin{cases} \Delta^2\left(\Delta^2 u + k\dfrac{\partial\theta}{\partial\xi}\right) = 0\,, \quad \Delta^2\left(\Delta^2 u + k\dfrac{\partial\theta}{\partial\eta}\right) = 0\,, \\ \Delta^2\left(\Delta^2 w + k\dfrac{\partial\theta}{\partial\zeta}\right) = 0\,, \quad \Delta^4\theta = 0\,; \end{cases} \\ \text{(nei punti di } \sigma) \quad u = u_\sigma\,,\ v = v_\sigma\,,\ w = w_\sigma\,,\ \dfrac{du}{dn} = u'_\sigma\,, \ldots, \end{cases}$$

che sono una estensione delle equazioni dell'equilibrio dei corpi elastici isotropi. Le prime *tre* per $k \neq -1$ dànno, come conseguenza, la quarta $\Delta^4\theta = 0$, la quale per $k = -1$ non è conseguenza delle prime *tre*.

Le equazioni (8), *nel caso particolare in cui le funzioni finite e continue* $u_\sigma, v_\sigma, w_\sigma$ *sono rispettivamente i valori nei punti di* σ *delle derivate parziali del primo ordine rapporto a* ξ, η, ζ *di una medesima funzione* $V_2(\xi, \eta, \zeta)$, *e le altre* $u'_\sigma, v'_\sigma, w'_\sigma$ *sono rispettivamente i valori nei punti di* σ *delle derivate normali di* $\dfrac{\partial V_2}{\partial\xi}, \dfrac{\partial V_2}{\partial\eta}, \dfrac{\partial V_2}{\partial\zeta}$, *coincidono per* $k = -1$ *con le* $(1)_2$.

2bis. Quando di una funzione u sono dati nei punti di σ i suoi valori e quelli della sua derivata normale, si possono subito ottenere i valori di $\frac{\partial u}{\partial x}$, $\frac{\partial u}{\partial y}$, $\frac{\partial u}{\partial z}$ negli stessi punti di σ, supposto che queste derivate esistano.

Viceversa, se di una funzione u sono dati su σ i valori di $\frac{\partial u}{\partial x}$, $\frac{\partial u}{\partial y}$, $\frac{\partial u}{\partial z}$, si possono subito determinare negli stessi punti di σ i valori di $\frac{du}{dn}$ e, a meno di una costante additiva, quelli di u.

Di qui segue che *al problema di determinare tre funzioni* u, v, w *dei punti del campo* S, *le quali soddisfacciano alle equazioni* (8), *con* $u_\sigma(\alpha, \beta)$, $v_\sigma(\alpha, \beta)$, $w_\sigma(\alpha, \beta)$, $u'_\sigma(\alpha, \beta)$, $v'_\sigma(\alpha, \beta)$, $w'_\sigma(\alpha, \beta)$ *funzioni finite e continue arbitrariamente date, delle quali le prime tre abbiano le derivate del primo ordine finite e continue, si può sostituire l'altro problema di determinare tre funzioni* u_1, v_1, w_1 *dei punti del campo* S, *le quali soddisfacciano alle equazioni*:

$$(8)_1 \begin{cases} \text{(nei punti di S)} \begin{cases} \Delta^2\left(\Delta^2 u_1 + k\frac{\partial \theta_1}{\partial \xi}\right) = 0, & \Delta^2\left(\Delta^2 v_1 + k\frac{\partial \theta_1}{\partial \eta}\right) = 0, \\ \Delta^2\left(\Delta^2 w_1 + k\frac{\partial \theta_1}{\partial \zeta}\right) = 0, & \Delta^4 \theta_1 = 0, \end{cases} \\ \text{(nei punti di } \sigma) \quad \frac{\partial u_1}{\partial x} = u_\sigma^{(1)}, \quad \frac{\partial u_1}{\partial y} = u_\sigma^{(2)}, \quad \frac{\partial u_1}{\partial z} = u_\sigma^{(3)}, \quad \frac{\partial v_1}{\partial x} = v_\sigma^{(1)}, \dots, \\ \qquad\qquad \frac{\partial w_1}{\partial x} = w_\sigma^{(1)}, \dots, \end{cases}$$

dove si è posto

$$u_\sigma^{(1)} = \frac{\partial u}{\partial x}, \quad u_\sigma^{(2)} = \frac{\partial u}{\partial y}, \quad u_\sigma^{(3)} = \frac{\partial u}{\partial z}, \quad v_\sigma^{(1)} = \frac{\partial v}{\partial x}, \dots, \quad w_\sigma^{(1)} = \frac{\partial w}{\partial x}, \dots.$$

Infatti, determinato in un modo qualsiasi un sistema integrale u_1, v_1, w_1 di queste equazioni, le u_1, v_1, w_1 differiranno da un sistema integrale u, v, w delle equazioni (8) rispettivamente per *tre* costanti additive, le quali si potranno determinare tenendo conto rispettivamente dei valori di $u_\sigma(\alpha, \beta)$, $v_\sigma(\alpha, \beta)$, $w_\sigma(\alpha, \beta)$ in un punto qualsiasi di σ.

3bis. Se le funzioni $u_1(\xi, \eta, \zeta)$, $v_1(\xi, \eta, \zeta)$, $w_1(\xi, \eta, \zeta)$ sono integrali delle equazioni $(8)_1$, posto

$$u^{(1)} = \frac{\partial u_1}{\partial \xi}, \quad u^{(2)} = \frac{\partial u_1}{\partial \eta}, \quad u^{(3)} = \frac{\partial u_1}{\partial \zeta}, \quad v^{(1)} = \frac{\partial v_1}{\partial \xi}, \dots, \quad w^{(1)} = \frac{\partial w_1}{\partial \xi}, \dots;$$

$$\theta_u = \frac{\partial u^{(1)}}{\partial \xi} + \frac{\partial u^{(2)}}{\partial \eta} + \frac{\partial u^{(3)}}{\partial \zeta}, \quad \theta_v = \frac{\partial v^{(1)}}{\partial \xi} + \frac{\partial v^{(2)}}{\partial \eta} + \cdots, \quad \theta_w = \frac{\partial w^{(1)}}{\partial \xi} + \cdots;$$

$$\theta^{(1)} = \frac{\partial u^{(1)}}{\partial \xi} + \frac{\partial v^{(1)}}{\partial \eta} + \frac{\partial w^{(1)}}{\partial \zeta}, \quad \theta^{(2)} = \frac{\partial u^{(2)}}{\partial \xi} + \frac{\partial v^{(2)}}{\partial \eta} + \cdots, \quad \theta^{(3)} = \frac{\partial u^{(3)}}{\partial \xi} + \cdots;$$

$$\theta' = \frac{\partial \theta_u}{\partial \xi} + \frac{\partial \theta_v}{\partial \eta} + \frac{\partial \theta_w}{\partial \zeta} = \frac{\partial \theta^{(1)}}{\partial \xi} + \frac{\partial \theta^{(2)}}{\partial \eta} + \frac{\partial \theta^{(3)}}{\partial \zeta},$$

risulterà

$$\theta_u = \Delta^2 u_1 \ , \ \theta_v = \Delta^2 v_1 \ , \ \theta_w = \Delta^2 w_1 \ ,$$

$$\Delta^2\theta_1 = \Delta^2\left(\frac{\partial u_1}{\partial\xi} + \frac{\partial v_1}{\partial\eta} + \frac{\partial w_1}{\partial\zeta}\right) = \frac{\partial\Delta^2 u_1}{\partial\xi} + \frac{\partial\Delta^2 v_1}{\partial\eta} + \frac{\partial\Delta^2 w_1}{\partial\zeta} =$$

$$= \frac{\partial\theta_u}{\partial\xi} + \frac{\partial\theta_v}{\partial\eta} + \frac{\partial\theta_w}{\partial\zeta} = \theta' ;$$

e per conseguenza:

$$(8)_2 \left\{\begin{array}{ll} \text{(nei punti di S)} & \begin{array}{l} (a) \left\{\begin{array}{l} \Delta^2 u^{(1)} - \dfrac{\partial\theta_u}{\partial\xi} = 0 \ , \quad \Delta^2 v^{(1)} - \dfrac{\partial\theta_v}{\partial\xi} = 0 \ , \quad \Delta^2 w^{(1)} - \dfrac{\partial\theta_w}{\partial\xi} = 0 \ , \\ \Delta^2 u^{(2)} - \dfrac{\partial\theta_u}{\partial\eta} = 0 \ , \quad \Delta^2 v^{(2)} - \dfrac{\partial\theta_v}{\partial\eta} = 0 \ , \ \ldots\ldots\ldots \ , \\ \Delta^2 u^{(3)} - \dfrac{\partial\theta_u}{\partial\zeta} = 0 \ , \ \ldots\ldots\ldots\ldots\ldots \ , \ \ldots\ldots\ldots \ , \end{array}\right. \\ (b) \left\{\begin{array}{l} \Delta^2\theta_u + k\dfrac{\partial\theta'}{\partial\xi} = 0 \ , \quad \Delta^2\theta' = 0 \ ; \\ \Delta^2\theta_v + k\dfrac{\partial\theta'}{\partial\eta} = 0 \ , \\ \Delta^2\theta_w + k\dfrac{\partial\theta'}{\partial\zeta} = 0 \ , \end{array}\right. \end{array} \\ \text{(nei punti di } \sigma) & u^{(1)} = u_\sigma^{(1)}, u^{(2)} = u_\sigma^{(2)}, u^{(3)} = u_\sigma^{(3)}, v^{(1)} = v_\sigma^{(1)}, \ldots, w^{(1)} = w_\sigma^{(1)}, \ldots \end{array}\right.$$

nelle quali $u_\sigma^{(1)}$, $u_\sigma^{(2)}$, $u_\sigma^{(3)}$ sono rispettivamente i valori nei punti di σ delle derivate prime rapporto a ξ, η, ζ di una medesima funzione, $v_\sigma^{(1)}$, $v_\sigma^{(2)}$, $v_\sigma^{(3)}$ sono rispettivamente i valori nei punti di σ delle derivate prime rapporto a ξ, η, ζ di una medesima seconda funzione, $w_\sigma^{(1)}$, $w_\sigma^{(2)}$, $w_\sigma^{(3)}$ sono ... di una medesima terza funzione.

Viceversa supponiamo che le funzioni $u^{(1)}$, $u^{(2)}$, $u^{(3)}$, $v^{(1)}$, ..., $w^{(1)}$, ... dei punti di S formino un sistema di integrali delle equazioni $(8)_2$, nelle quali $u_\sigma^{(1)}$, $u_\sigma^{(2)}$, $u_\sigma^{(3)}$ siano rispettivamente i valori nei punti di σ delle derivate prime rispetto a ξ, η, ζ di una medesima funzione $u_2(\xi, \eta, \zeta)$; $v_\sigma^{(1)}$, $v_\sigma^{(2)}$, $v_\sigma^{(3)}$ siano rispettivamente ... di una medesima funzione $v_2(\xi, \eta, \zeta)$; $w_\sigma^{(1)}$, $w_\sigma^{(2)}$, $w_\sigma^{(3)}$ siano ....

Posto:

$$(9) \qquad \tau_{1u} = \frac{\partial u^{(3)}}{\partial \eta} - \frac{\partial u^{(2)}}{\partial \zeta}, \quad \tau_{2u} = \frac{\partial u^{(1)}}{\partial \zeta} - \frac{\partial u^{(3)}}{\partial \xi}, \quad \tau_{3u} = \frac{\partial u^{(2)}}{\partial \xi} - \frac{\partial u^{(1)}}{\partial \eta},$$

$$\tau_{1v} = \frac{\partial v^{(3)}}{\partial \eta} - \frac{\partial v^{(2)}}{\partial \zeta}, \ldots, \tau_{1w} = \frac{\partial w^{(3)}}{\partial \eta} - \frac{\partial w^{(2)}}{\partial \zeta}, \ldots,$$

le equazioni (a) delle $(8)_2$ diverranno:

$$(10) \qquad \left\{ \begin{array}{l} \dfrac{\partial \tau_{2u}}{\partial \zeta} - \dfrac{\partial \tau_{3u}}{\partial \eta} = 0, \quad \dfrac{\partial \tau_{3u}}{\partial \xi} - \dfrac{\partial \tau_{1u}}{\partial \zeta} = 0, \quad \dfrac{\partial \tau_{1u}}{\partial \eta} - \dfrac{\partial \tau_{2u}}{\partial \xi} = 0, \\ \dfrac{\partial \tau_{2v}}{\partial \zeta} - \dfrac{\partial \tau_{3v}}{\partial \eta} = 0, \ldots, \dfrac{\partial \tau_{2w}}{\partial \zeta} - \dfrac{\partial \tau_{3w}}{\partial \eta} = 0, \ldots; \end{array} \right.$$

e quindi risulterà [1] che esistono *tre* funzioni $u_1(\xi, \eta, \zeta)$, $v_1(\xi, \eta, \zeta)$, $w_1(\xi, \eta, \zeta)$ dei punti del campo S, tali che

$$u^{(1)} = \frac{\partial u_1}{\partial \xi}, \quad u^{(2)} = \frac{\partial u_1}{\partial \eta}, \quad u^{(3)} = \frac{\partial u_1}{\partial \zeta}, \quad v^{(1)} = \frac{\partial v_1}{\partial \xi}, \quad v^{(2)} = \frac{\partial v_1}{\partial \eta}, \quad v^{(3)} = \frac{\partial v_1}{\partial \zeta},$$

$$w^{(1)} = \frac{\partial w_1}{\partial \xi}, \quad w^{(2)} = \frac{\partial w_1}{\partial \eta}, \quad w^{(3)} = \frac{\partial w_1}{\partial \zeta}.$$

Avremo allora:

$$\theta_u = \Delta^2 u_1, \quad \theta_v = \Delta^2 v_1, \quad \theta_w = \Delta^2 w_1, \quad \theta' = \frac{\partial \theta_u}{\partial \xi} + \frac{\partial \theta_v}{\partial \eta} + \frac{\partial \theta_w}{\partial \zeta} =$$

$$= \Delta^2 \left(\frac{\partial u_1}{\partial \xi} + \frac{\partial v_1}{\partial \eta} + \frac{\partial w_1}{\partial \zeta} \right);$$

e per conseguenza, posto:

$$\theta_1 = \frac{\partial u_1}{\partial \xi} + \frac{\partial v_1}{\partial \eta} + \frac{\partial w_1}{\partial \zeta},$$

in virtù delle (b) e delle rimanenti delle $(8)_2$, si avrà ancora che le funzioni $u_1(\xi, \eta, \zeta)$, $v_1(\xi, \eta, \zeta)$, $w_1(\xi, \eta, \zeta)$ sono integrali delle equazioni $(8)_1$.

Riepilogando si ha che *l'integrazione delle equazioni* $(8)_1$ *equivale all'integrazione delle equazioni* $(8)_2$.

[1] Ripetendo i ragionamenti a p. 377 della mia citata Nota dei Lincei.

4bis. Ciò premesso, si considerino le equazioni:

$$
(11)\left\{\begin{array}{l}
\text{(nei punti di S)}\left\{\begin{array}{ll}
(a)_1 & \left\{\begin{array}{l}
\Delta^2 u^{(1)} + \lambda \dfrac{\partial \theta_u}{\partial \xi} + (1+\lambda) k \dfrac{\partial \theta^{(1)}}{\partial \xi} = 0 , \\
\Delta^2 v^{(1)} + \lambda \dfrac{\partial \theta_v}{\partial \xi} + (1+\lambda) k \dfrac{\partial \theta^{(1)}}{\partial \eta} = 0 , \\
\Delta^2 w^{(1)} + \lambda \dfrac{\partial \theta_w}{\partial \xi} + (1+\lambda) k \dfrac{\partial \theta^{(1)}}{\partial \zeta} = 0 , \\
\\
\Delta^2 u^{(2)} + \lambda \dfrac{\partial \theta_u}{\partial \eta} + (1+\lambda) k \dfrac{\partial \theta^{(2)}}{\partial \xi} = 0 , \\
\Delta^2 v^{(2)} + \lambda \dfrac{\partial \theta_v}{\partial \eta} + (1+\lambda) k \dfrac{\partial \theta^{(2)}}{\partial \eta} = 0 , \\
\ldots\ldots\ldots\ldots\ldots , \\
\\
\Delta^2 u^{(3)} + \lambda \dfrac{\partial \theta_u}{\partial \zeta} + (1+\lambda) k \dfrac{\partial \theta^{(3)}}{\partial \xi} = 0 , \\
\ldots\ldots\ldots\ldots\ldots , \\
\ldots\ldots\ldots\ldots\ldots ,
\end{array}\right. \\
\\
(b)_1 & \Delta^2 \theta_u + k \dfrac{\partial \theta'}{\partial \xi} = 0 , \ \Delta^2 \theta_v + k \dfrac{\partial \theta'}{\partial \eta} = 0 , \ \Delta^2 \theta_w + k \dfrac{\partial \theta'}{\partial \zeta} = 0 , \ \Delta^2 \theta' = 0 ;
\end{array}\right. \\
\\
\text{(nei punti di } \sigma) \quad u^{(1)} = u_\sigma^{(1)} , \ u^{(2)} = u_\sigma^{(2)} , \ u^{(3)} = u_\sigma^{(3)} , \ v^{(1)} = v_\sigma^{(1)} , \ldots , w^{(1)} = w_\sigma^{(1)} , \ldots ,
\end{array}\right.
$$

che sono una nuova estensione delle equazioni dell'equilibrio dei corpi elastici isotropi. Le $(a)_1$ per $\lambda \neq -1$ dànno come conseguenza le prime tre delle $(b)_1$, e queste per $k \neq -1$, e quindi ancora le $(a)_1$ per $\lambda \neq -1$, $k \neq -1$, dànno come conseguenza la quarta delle $(b)_1$. Le prime tre delle $(b)_1$ non sono conseguenza delle $(a)_1$ per $\lambda = -1$, così come la quarta delle $(b)_1$ non è conseguenza delle prime tre delle $(b)_1$ per $k = -1$.

Le equazioni (11), *nel caso particolare in cui le funzioni finite e continue* $u_\sigma^{(1)}$, $u_\sigma^{(2)}$, $u_\sigma^{(3)}$ *sono rispettivamente i valori nei punti di* σ *delle derivate parziali del primo ordine rispetto a* ξ, η, ζ *di una medesima funzione* $u_2(\xi, \eta, \zeta)$, $v_\sigma^{(1)}$, $v_\sigma^{(2)}$, $v_\sigma^{(3)}$ *sono rispettivamente i valori nei punti di* σ *delle derivate parziali del primo ordine rispetto a* ξ, η, ζ *di una medesima funzione* $v_2(\xi, \eta, \zeta)$, $w_\sigma^{(1)}$, $w_\sigma^{(2)}$, $w_\sigma^{(3)}$ *sono rispettivamente ...... di una medesima funzione* $w_2(\xi, \eta, \zeta)$, *coincidono per* $\lambda = -1$ *con le* $(8)_2$.

2ter. Quando di una funzione V sono dati nei punti di σ i suoi valori e quelli delle sue derivate normali prime e seconde, si possono subito ottenere i valori di $\dfrac{\partial^2 V}{\partial x^2}$, $\dfrac{\partial^2 V}{\partial y^2}$, $\dfrac{\partial^2 V}{\partial z^2}$, $\dfrac{\partial^2 V}{\partial x \partial y}$, $\dfrac{\partial^2 V}{\partial y \partial z}$, $\dfrac{\partial^2 V}{\partial z \partial x}$ negli stessi punti di σ, supposto che queste derivate esistano. Viceversa, se di nna funzione V sono dati nei punti di σ

i valori di $\frac{\partial^2 V}{\partial x^2}, \ldots, \frac{\partial^2 V}{\partial x \, \partial y}, \ldots$, si possono subito determinare negli stessi punti di σ i valori di $\frac{d^2 V}{dn^2}$, quelli di $\frac{dV}{dn}$ a meno di una costante, e quelli di V a meno di una funzione lineare di α e di β.

Di qui segue che *al problema di determinare una funzione* V *dei punti del campo* S, *la quale soddisfaccia alle equazioni* (1), *nell'ipotesi che la funzione* $f_1(\alpha, \beta)$ *abbia le derivate dei due primi ordini finite e continue e che la funzione* $f_2(\alpha, \beta)$ *abbia le derivate del primo ordine pure finite e continue, si può sostituire l'altro di determinare una funzione* V_2 *dei punti del campo* S, *la quale soddisfaccia alle equazioni:*

$$(12) \begin{cases} \text{(nei punti di S)} \quad \Delta^6 V_2 = 0\,, \\ \text{(nei punti di } \sigma) \begin{cases} \frac{\partial^2 V_2}{\partial x^2} = u_\sigma^{(1)}\,, \quad \frac{\partial^2 V_2}{\partial y^2} = v_\sigma^{(2)}\,, \quad \frac{\partial^2 V_2}{\partial z^2} = w_\sigma^{(3)}\,, \quad \frac{\partial^2 V_2}{\partial x \, \partial y} = u_\sigma^{(2)} = v_\sigma^{(1)}\,, \\ \frac{\partial^2 V_2}{\partial y \, \partial z} = v_\sigma^{(3)} = w_\sigma^{(2)}\,, \quad \frac{\partial^2 V_2}{\partial z \, \partial x} = w_\sigma^{(1)} = u_\sigma^{(3)}\,, \end{cases} \end{cases}$$

dove si è posto:

$$u_\sigma^{(1)} = \frac{\partial^2 V}{\partial x^2}\,, \quad v_\sigma^{(2)} = \frac{\partial^2 V}{\partial y^2}\,, \quad w_\sigma^{(3)} = \frac{\partial^2 V}{\partial z^2}\,, \quad u_\sigma^{(2)} = v_\sigma^{(1)} = \frac{\partial^2 V}{\partial x \, \partial y}\,,$$

$$v_\sigma^{(3)} = w_\sigma^{(2)} = \frac{\partial^2 V}{\partial y \, \partial z}\,, \quad w_\sigma^{(1)} = u_\sigma^{(3)} = \frac{\partial^2 V}{\partial z \, \partial x}\,.$$

Infatti, determinato in un modo qualsiasi un integrale V_2 delle equazioni (12), questo differirà da un integrale V delle equazioni (1) per una funzione additiva lineare nelle ξ, η, ζ, la quale si potrà determinare, tenendo conto dei valori di $\frac{\partial V}{\partial x}, \frac{\partial V}{\partial y}, \frac{\partial V}{\partial z}$, V in un punto qualsiasi di σ.

5. Dai risultati che precedono segue ovviamente che *l'integrazione delle equazioni* (12) *equivale all'integrazione delle equazioni* $(8)_2$ *per* $k = -1$, *nelle quali:*

$$(13) \begin{cases} u_\sigma^{(1)} = \frac{\partial^2 V_3}{\partial x^2}\,, \quad v_\sigma^{(2)} = \frac{\partial^2 V_3}{\partial y^2}\,, \quad w_\sigma^{(3)} = \frac{\partial^2 V_3}{\partial z^2}\,, \\ u_\sigma^{(2)} = v_\sigma^{(1)} = \frac{\partial^2 V_3}{\partial x \, \partial y}\,, \quad v_\sigma^{(3)} = w_\sigma^{(2)} = \frac{\partial^2 V_3}{\partial y \, \partial z}\,, \quad w_\sigma^{(1)} = u_\sigma^{(3)} = \frac{\partial^2 V_3}{\partial z \, \partial x}\,, \end{cases}$$

con $V_3(\xi, \eta, \zeta)$ *funzione data ad arbitrio.*

Indipendentemente dai risultati dei paragrafi precedenti, questo teorema può ancora stabilirsi nel seguente modo.

3ter. Se la funzione $V_2(\xi, \eta, \zeta)$ è integrale delle equazioni (12), posto:

$$u^{(1)} = \frac{\partial^2 V_2}{\partial \xi^2}, \quad v^{(2)} = \frac{\partial^2 V_2}{\partial \eta^2}, \quad w^{(3)} = \frac{\partial^2 V_2}{\partial \zeta^2},$$

$$u^{(2)} = v^{(1)} = \frac{\partial^2 V_2}{\partial \xi \, \partial \eta}, \quad v^{(3)} = w^{(2)} = \frac{\partial^2 V_2}{\partial \eta \, \partial \zeta}, \quad w^{(1)} = u^{(3)} = \frac{\partial^2 V_2}{\partial \zeta \, \partial \xi},$$

risulterà:

$$\theta_u = \frac{\partial \Delta^2 V_2}{\partial \xi}, \quad \theta_v = \frac{\partial \Delta^2 V_2}{\partial \eta}, \quad \theta_w = \frac{\partial \Delta^2 V_2}{\partial \zeta}, \quad \theta' = \Delta^4 V_2;$$

e per conseguenza:

$$(11)_1 \left\{ \begin{array}{l} \text{(nei punti di S)} \left\{ \begin{array}{ll} (a) & \left\{ \begin{array}{l} \Delta^2 u^{(1)} - \dfrac{\partial \theta_u}{\partial \xi} = 0, \quad \Delta^2 v^{(1)} - \dfrac{\partial \theta_v}{\partial \xi} = 0, \quad \Delta^2 w^{(1)} - \dfrac{\partial \theta_w}{\partial \xi} = 0, \\ \Delta^2 u^{(2)} - \dfrac{\partial \theta_u}{\partial \eta} = 0, \quad \Delta^2 v^{(2)} - \dfrac{\partial \theta_v}{\partial \eta} = 0, \quad \Delta^2 w^{(2)} - \dfrac{\partial \theta_w}{\partial \eta} = 0, \\ \Delta^2 u^{(3)} - \dfrac{\partial \theta_u}{\partial \zeta} = 0, \quad \Delta^2 v^{(3)} - \dfrac{\partial \theta_v}{\partial \zeta} = 0, \quad \Delta^2 w^{(3)} - \dfrac{\partial \theta_w}{\partial \zeta} = 0, \end{array} \right. \\ (b) & \Delta^2 \theta_u - \dfrac{\partial \theta'}{\partial \xi} = 0, \quad \Delta^2 \theta_v - \dfrac{\partial \theta'}{\partial \eta} = 0, \quad \Delta^2 \theta_w - \dfrac{\partial \theta'}{\partial \zeta} = 0, \quad \Delta^2 \theta' = 0; \end{array} \right. \\ \text{(nei punti di } \sigma) \quad u^{(1)} = u_\sigma^{(1)}, \quad u^{(2)} = u_\sigma^{(2)}, \quad u^{(3)} = u_\sigma^{(3)}, \quad \ldots. \end{array} \right.$$

Viceversa supponiamo che le funzioni $u^{(1)}, u^{(2)}, u^{(3)}, v^{(1)}, \ldots, w^{(1)}, \ldots$ dei punti di S formino un sistema di integrali delle equazioni $(11)_1$, nelle quali $u_\sigma^{(1)}, u_\sigma^{(2)}, \ldots$ abbiano la forma (13) con $V_3(\xi, \eta, \zeta)$ funzione qualsiasi.

Come al § 3bis risulta intanto l'esistenza di tre funzioni $u_1(\xi, \eta, \zeta)$, $v_1(\xi, \eta, \zeta)$, $w_1(\xi, \eta, \zeta)$ dei punti del campo S, tali che:

$$(14) \qquad \left\{ \begin{array}{l} u^{(1)} = \dfrac{\partial u_1}{\partial \xi}, \quad u^{(2)} = \dfrac{\partial u_1}{\partial \eta}, \quad u^{(3)} = \dfrac{\partial u_1}{\partial \zeta}, \\ v^{(1)} = \dfrac{\partial v_1}{\partial \xi}, \quad v^{(2)} = \dfrac{\partial v_1}{\partial \eta}, \quad v^{(3)} = \dfrac{\partial v_1}{\partial \zeta}, \\ w^{(1)} = \dfrac{\partial w_1}{\partial \xi}, \quad w^{(2)} = \dfrac{\partial w_1}{\partial \eta}, \quad w^{(3)} = \dfrac{\partial w_1}{\partial \zeta}, \end{array} \right.$$

ed ancora:

$$(15) \qquad \text{(nei punti di S)} \left\{ \begin{array}{l} \Delta^2\left(\Delta^2 u_1 - \dfrac{\partial \theta_1}{\partial \xi}\right) = 0, \quad \Delta^2\left(\Delta^2 v_1 - \dfrac{\partial \theta_1}{\partial \eta}\right) = 0, \\ \Delta^2\left(\Delta^2 w_1 - \dfrac{\partial \theta_1}{\partial \zeta}\right) = 0, \quad \Delta^4 \theta_1 = 0. \end{array} \right.$$

Posto, come al § 3,

$$(16)\qquad \tau_1 = \frac{\partial w_1}{\partial \eta} - \frac{\partial v_1}{\partial \zeta}\ ,\quad \tau_2 = \frac{\partial u_1}{\partial \zeta} - \frac{\partial w_1}{\partial \xi}\ ,\quad \tau_3 = \frac{\partial v_1}{\partial \xi} - \frac{\partial u_1}{\partial \eta}\ ,$$

risulterà, come in quel paragrafo, dalle prime tre delle (15), che esiste una funzione $U(\xi, \eta, \zeta)$ tale che:

$$(4)_1\qquad \Delta^2\tau_1 = \frac{\partial U}{\partial \xi}\ ,\quad \Delta^2\tau_2 = \frac{\partial U}{\partial \eta}\ ,\quad \Delta^2\tau_3 = \frac{\partial U}{\partial \zeta}\ ,$$

e si avrà inoltre una formola perfettamente analoga alla (5).

Dall'ipotesi che le $u_\sigma^{(1)}, u_\sigma^{(2)}, u_\sigma^{(3)}, \ldots$ delle equazioni $(11)_1$ hanno la forma (13), risulta, in virtù delle (14),

$$(17)\quad \text{(nei punti di } \sigma) \left\{ \begin{array}{l} \tau_1 = \dfrac{\partial w_1}{\partial y} - \dfrac{\partial v_1}{\partial z} = w_\sigma^{(2)} - v_\sigma^{(3)} = 0\ ,\ \tau_2 = u_\sigma^{(3)} - w_\sigma^{(1)} = 0\ , \\ \tau_3 = v_\sigma^{(1)} - u_\sigma^{(2)} = 0\ , \end{array} \right.$$

$$\text{(nei punti di } \sigma)\quad u_1 = \frac{\partial V_3}{\partial x} + a\ ,\quad v_1 = \frac{\partial V_3}{\partial y} + b\ ,\quad w_1 = \frac{\partial V_3}{\partial z} + c$$

con a, b, c quantità costanti; sicchè, posto $V_3'(\xi, \eta, \zeta) = V_3(\xi, \eta, \zeta) + a\xi + b\eta + c\zeta$, si avrà:

$$(18)\qquad \text{(nei punti di } \sigma)\quad u_1 = \frac{\partial V_3'}{\partial x}\ ,\quad v_1 = \frac{\partial V_3'}{\partial y}\ ,\quad w_1 = \frac{\partial V_3'}{\partial z}.$$

Da queste formole, dalle equazioni (15) e dalle $(4)_1$ risulta, come al § 3, una formola perfettamente analoga alla (6) di quel paragrafo; e quindi si avrà, ragionando ancora come al § 3, che esiste una funzione $V_2(\xi, \eta, \zeta)$ tale che:

$$u_1(\xi, \eta, \zeta) = \frac{\partial V_2}{\partial \xi}\ ,\quad v_1(\xi, \eta, \zeta) = \frac{\partial V_2}{\partial \eta}\ ,\quad w_1(\xi, \eta, \zeta) = \frac{\partial V_2}{\partial \zeta}.$$

In virtù delle (14) sarà allora:

$$u^{(1)}(\xi, \eta, \zeta) = \frac{\partial^2 V_2}{\partial \xi^2}\ ,\quad v^{(2)}(\xi, \eta, \zeta) = \frac{\partial^2 V_2}{\partial \eta^2}\ ,\quad w^{(3)}(\xi, \eta, \zeta) = \frac{\partial^2 V_2}{\partial \zeta^2}\ ,$$

$$u^{(2)}(\xi, \eta, \zeta) = v^{(1)}(\xi, \eta, \zeta) = \frac{\partial^2 V_2}{\partial \xi\, \partial \eta}\ ,\quad v^{(3)}(\xi, \eta, \zeta) = w^{(2)}(\xi, \eta, \zeta) = \frac{\partial^2 V_2}{\partial \eta\, \partial \zeta}\ ,$$

$$w^{(1)}(\xi, \eta, \zeta) = u^{(3)}(\xi, \eta, \zeta) = \frac{\partial^2 V_2}{\partial \zeta\, \partial \xi}\ ;$$

e quindi risulterà, dall'ultima delle (15) e dalle condizioni nei punti di σ che compariscono nelle $(11)_1$,

$$\text{(nei punti di S)} \quad \Delta^6 V_2 = 0,$$

$$\text{(nei punti di } \sigma) \quad \frac{\partial^2 V_2}{\partial x^2} = u_\sigma^{(1)}, \frac{\partial^2 V_2}{\partial y^2} = v_\sigma^{(2)}, \frac{\partial^2 V_2}{\partial z^2} = w_\sigma^{(3)}, \frac{\partial^2 V_2}{\partial\xi\partial\eta} = u_\sigma^{(2)} = v_\sigma^{(1)}, \ldots.$$

Riepilogando, si ha il teorema del § 5, ossia risulta che *l'integrazione delle equazioni* (12) *equivale all'integrazione delle equazioni* $(11)_1$, *nelle quali le funzioni* $u_\sigma^{(1)}, u_\sigma^{(2)}, u_\sigma^{(3)}, \ldots.$ *hanno la forma* (13).

4ter. Introducendo anche qui le equazioni (11) del § 4bis, si ha che *le equazioni* (11) *nel caso particolare in cui le funzioni finite e continue* $u_\sigma^{(1)}, u_\sigma^{(2)}, u_\sigma^{(3)}, v_\sigma^{(1)}, \ldots$ *hanno la forma* (13) *con* $V_3(\xi,\eta,\zeta)$ *funzione qualsiasi, coincidono per* $\lambda = k = -1$ *con le* $(11)_1$.

Teoremi di unicità.

6. Facendo uso delle posizioni (2) al § 3, le prime tre equazioni indefinite delle (8) si possono scrivere:

$$(8)' \quad \left\{ \begin{aligned} &\Delta^2 \left\{ (1+k)\,\Delta^2 u + k\left(\frac{\partial\tau_3}{\partial\eta} - \frac{\partial\tau_2}{\partial\zeta}\right) \right\} = 0, \\ &\Delta^2 \left\{ (1+k)\,\Delta^2 v + k\left(\frac{\partial\tau_1}{\partial\zeta} - \frac{\partial\tau_3}{\partial\xi}\right) \right\} = 0, \\ &\Delta^2 \left\{ (1+k)\,\Delta^2 w + k\left(\frac{\partial\tau_2}{\partial\xi} - \frac{\partial\tau_1}{\partial\eta}\right) \right\} = 0. \end{aligned} \right.$$

Integrando per parti, dalle prime tre delle (8) si ha:

$$(19) \quad \left\{ \begin{aligned} 0 = &\int_S \left\{ u.\Delta^2\left(\Delta^2 u + k\frac{\partial\theta}{\partial\xi}\right) + v.\Delta^2\left(\Delta^2 v + k\frac{\partial\theta}{\partial\eta}\right) + w.\Delta^2\left(\Delta^2 w + k\frac{\partial\theta}{\partial\zeta}\right) \right\} dS = \\ &= \int_S \left\{ (\Delta^2 u)^2 + (\Delta^2 v)^2 + (\Delta^2 w)^2 + k\Delta\theta \right\} dS + \\ &+ \int_\sigma \left\{ \Delta^2 u\frac{du}{dn} + \Delta^2 v\frac{dv}{dn} + \Delta^2 w\frac{dw}{dn} + k\theta\frac{d\theta}{dn} - u\left(\frac{d\Delta^2 u}{dn} + k\Delta^2\theta.\cos\widehat{nx}\right) - \right. \\ &\left. - v\left(\frac{d\Delta^2 v}{dn} + k\Delta^2\theta.\cos\widehat{ny}\right) - w\left(\frac{d\Delta^2 w}{dn} + k\Delta^2\theta.\cos\widehat{nz}\right) \right\} d\sigma, \end{aligned} \right.$$

dalle (8)' si ha ancora:

$$(19)'\left\{\begin{aligned}0=&\int_S\Big[u\Delta^2\Big\{(1+k)\Delta^2u+k\Big(\frac{\partial\tau_3}{\partial\eta}-\frac{\partial\tau_2}{\partial\zeta}\Big)\Big\}+\\&+v\Delta^2\Big\{(1+k)\Delta^2v+k\Big(\frac{\partial\tau_1}{\partial\zeta}-\frac{\partial\tau_3}{\partial\xi}\Big)\Big\}+\cdots\Big]dS=\\=&\int_S\Big[(1+k)\Big\{(\Delta^2u)^2+(\Delta^2v)^2+(\Delta^2w)^2\Big\}-k(\Delta\tau_1+\Delta\tau_2+\Delta\tau_3)\Big]dS+\\&+\int_\sigma\Big[(1+k)\Big\{\Big(\Delta^2u\frac{du}{dn}-u\frac{d\Delta^2u}{dn}\Big)+\Big(\Delta^2v\frac{dv}{dn}-v\frac{d\Delta^2v}{dn}\Big)+\cdots\Big\}-\\&-k\Big(\tau_1\frac{d\tau_1}{dn}+\tau_2\frac{d\tau_2}{dn}+\cdots\Big)+k\Delta^2\tau_1(w\cos\widehat{ny}-v\cos\widehat{nz})+\\&+k\Delta^2\tau_2(u\cos\widehat{nz}-w\cos\widehat{nx})+\cdots\Big]d\sigma.\end{aligned}\right.$$

7. Siano $u(\xi,\eta,\zeta)$, $v(\xi,\eta,\zeta)$, $w(\xi,\eta,\zeta)$ integrali delle equazioni (8) e si abbia:

$$u_\sigma=v_\sigma=w_\sigma=u'_\sigma=v'_\sigma=w'_\sigma=0.$$

Si avrà intanto nei punti di σ:

$$\frac{\partial u}{\partial x}=\frac{\partial u}{\partial y}=\frac{\partial u}{\partial z}=\frac{\partial v}{\partial x}=\frac{\partial v}{\partial y}=\cdots=\frac{\partial w}{\partial x}=\cdots=0;$$

e quindi:

$$(\text{nei punti di } \sigma)\quad \theta=\tau_1=\tau_2=\tau_3=0.$$

Ciò premesso, risulterà dalla (19) per $k\geq 0$:

$$(\text{nei punti di S})\quad \Delta^2u=\Delta^2v=\Delta^2w=0;$$

e quindi ancora per $k\geq 0$.

$$(\text{nei punti di S})\quad u=v=w=0.$$

Risulterà similmente dalla (19)' per $0>k>-1$:

$$(\text{nei punti di S})\quad u=v=w=0.$$

Per $1+k=0$ la (19)' ci dà in tutto il campo S:

$$\tau_1=\tau_2=\tau_3=0,$$

donde segue l'esistenza di una funzione $V(\xi,\eta,\zeta)$ tale che:

$$u=\frac{\partial V}{\partial\xi}\ ,\ v=\frac{\partial V}{\partial\eta}\ ,\ w=\frac{\partial V}{\partial\zeta};$$

sicchè, in virtù della quarta e delle rimanenti delle (8), risulterà:

$$(\text{nei punti di S})\quad \Delta^6V=0,$$

$$(\text{nei punti di } \sigma)\quad \frac{\partial V}{\partial x}=\frac{\partial V}{\partial y}=\frac{\partial V}{\partial z}=\frac{d}{dn}\frac{\partial V}{\partial x}=\frac{d}{dn}\frac{\partial V}{\partial y}=\cdots=0.$$

Da queste equazioni risulta, come è notorio,

$$\text{(nei punti di S)}\quad V = \text{cost.};$$

e quindi ancora, come si voleva dimostrare, per $k = -1$:

$$\text{(nei punti di S)}\quad u = v = w = 0.$$

I risultati precedenti ci dimostrano che *per* $k \geq -1$ *i valori degli integrali* u, v, w *delle equazioni* (8) *sono pienamente determinati in tutti i punti del campo* S.

8. Facendo uso delle notazioni (9) e ponendo ancora:

$$\tau_1^{(i)} = \frac{\partial w^{(i)}}{\partial \eta} - \frac{\partial v^{(i)}}{\partial \zeta}, \quad \tau_2^{(i)} = \frac{\partial u^{(i)}}{\partial \zeta} - \frac{\partial w^{(i)}}{\partial \xi}, \quad \tau_3^{(i)} = \frac{\partial v^{(i)}}{\partial \xi} - \frac{\partial u^{(i)}}{\partial \eta},$$

le equazioni $(a)_1$ delle (11) possono scriversi nelle seguenti diverse maniere:

$$(a)_1' \left\{ \begin{array}{l} (1+\lambda)\,\Delta^2 u^{(1)} + \lambda\left(\frac{\partial \tau_{3u}}{\partial \eta} - \frac{\partial \tau_{2u}}{\partial \zeta}\right) + (1+\lambda)\,k\,\frac{\partial \theta^{(1)}}{\partial \xi} = 0, \\ (1+\lambda)\,\Delta^2 u^{(2)} + \lambda\left(\frac{\partial \tau_{1u}}{\partial \zeta} - \frac{\partial \tau_{3u}}{\partial \xi}\right) + (1+\lambda)\,k\,\frac{\partial \theta^{(2)}}{\partial \xi} = 0, \\ \cdots\cdots \qquad , \\ (1+\lambda)\,\Delta^2 v^{(1)} + \lambda\left(\frac{\partial \tau_{3v}}{\partial \eta} - \frac{\partial \tau_{2v}}{\partial \zeta}\right) + (1+\lambda)\,k\,\frac{\partial \theta^{(1)}}{\partial \eta} = 0, \\ \cdots\cdots \qquad , \\ \cdots\cdots \qquad ; \end{array} \right.$$

$$(a)_1'' \left\{ \begin{array}{l} (1+k+\lambda k)\,\Delta^2 u^{(1)} + \lambda\,\frac{\partial \theta_u}{\partial \xi} + (1+\lambda)\,k\left(\frac{\partial \tau_3^{(1)}}{\partial \eta} - \frac{\partial \tau_2^{(1)}}{\partial \zeta}\right) = 0, \\ (1+k+\lambda k)\,\Delta^2 u^{(2)} + \lambda\,\frac{\partial \theta_u}{\partial \eta} + (1+\lambda)\,k\left(\frac{\partial \tau_3^{(2)}}{\partial \eta} - \frac{\partial \tau_2^{(2)}}{\partial \zeta}\right) = 0, \\ \cdots\cdots \qquad , \\ (1+k+\lambda k)\,\Delta^2 v^{(1)} + \lambda\,\frac{\partial \theta_v}{\partial \xi} + (1+\lambda)\,k\left(\frac{\partial \tau_1^{(1)}}{\partial \zeta} - \frac{\partial \tau_3^{(1)}}{\partial \xi}\right) = 0, \\ \cdots\cdots \qquad , \\ \cdots\cdots \qquad ; \end{array} \right.$$

$$(a)_1''' \left\{ \begin{array}{l} (1+\lambda)(1+k)\,\Delta^2 u^{(1)} + \lambda\left(\frac{\partial \tau_{3u}}{\partial \eta} - \frac{\partial \tau_{2u}}{\partial \zeta}\right) + (1+\lambda)\,k\left(\frac{\partial \tau_3^{(1)}}{\partial \eta} - \frac{\partial \tau_2^{(1)}}{\partial \zeta}\right) = 0, \\ (1+\lambda)(1+k)\,\Delta^2 u^{(2)} + \lambda\left(\frac{\partial \tau_{1u}}{\partial \zeta} - \frac{\partial \tau_{3u}}{\partial \xi}\right) + (1+\lambda)\,k\left(\frac{\partial \tau_3^{(2)}}{\partial \eta} - \frac{\partial \tau_2^{(2)}}{\partial \zeta}\right) = 0, \\ \cdots\cdots \qquad , \\ (1+\lambda)(1+k)\,\Delta^2 v^{(1)} + \lambda\left(\frac{\partial \tau_{3v}}{\partial \eta} - \frac{\partial \tau_{2v}}{\partial \zeta}\right) + (1+\lambda)\,k\left(\frac{\partial \tau_1^{(1)}}{\partial \zeta} - \frac{\partial \tau_3^{(1)}}{\partial \xi}\right) = 0, \\ \cdots\cdots \qquad , \\ \cdots\cdots \qquad . \end{array} \right.$$

Integrando per parti, si ha dalle $(a)_1$ delle (11):

$$(20)\quad \begin{cases} 0 = \int_S \Big[u^{(1)} \Big\{ \Delta^2 u^{(1)} + \lambda \frac{\partial \theta_u}{\partial \xi} + (1+\lambda) k \frac{\partial \theta^{(1)}}{\partial \xi} \Big\} + \\ \qquad + u^{(2)} \Big\{ \cdots \Big\} + u^{(3)} \Big\{ \cdots \Big\} + v^{(1)} \Big\{ \cdots \Big\} + \cdots \Big] dS = \\ = - \int_S \Big[\Delta u^{(1)} + \Delta u^{(2)} + \Delta u^{(3)} + \Delta v^{(1)} + \cdots + \lambda (\theta_u^2 + \theta_v^2 + \theta_w^2) + \\ \qquad + (1+\lambda) k \Big\{ (\theta^{(1)})^2 + (\theta^{(2)})^2 + (\theta^{(3)})^2 \Big\} \Big] dS - \\ - \int_\sigma \Big[u^{(1)} \Big\{ \frac{du^{(1)}}{dn} + \lambda \theta_u \cos \widehat{nx} + (1+\lambda) k \theta^{(1)} \cos \widehat{nx} \Big\} + \\ \qquad + u^{(2)} \Big\{ \cdots \Big\} + u^{(3)} \Big\{ \cdots \Big\} + v^{(1)} \Big\{ \cdots \Big\} + \cdots \Big] d\sigma, \end{cases}$$

dalle $(a)'_1$:

$$(20)'\quad \begin{cases} 0 = \int_S \Big[u^{(1)} \Big\{ (1+\lambda) \Delta^2 u^{(1)} + \lambda \Big(\frac{\partial \tau_{3u}}{\partial \eta} - \frac{\partial \tau_{2u}}{\partial \zeta} \Big) + (1+\lambda) k \frac{\partial \theta^{(1)}}{\partial \xi} \Big\} + \\ \qquad + u^{(2)} \Big\{ \cdots \Big\} + u^{(3)} \Big\{ \cdots \Big\} + v^{(1)} \Big\{ \cdots \Big\} + \cdots \Big] dS = \\ = - \int_S \Big[(1+\lambda) (\Delta u^{(1)} + \Delta u^{(2)} + \Delta u^{(3)} + \Delta v^{(1)} + \cdots) - \\ - \lambda (\tau_{1u}^2 + \tau_{2u}^2 + \tau_{3u}^2 + \tau_{1v}^2 + \cdots) + (1+\lambda) k \Big\{ (\theta^{(1)})^2 + (\theta^{(2)})^2 + (\theta^{(3)})^2 \Big\} \Big] dS - \\ - \int_\sigma \Big[u^{(1)} \Big\{ (1+\lambda) \frac{du^{(1)}}{dn} + \lambda (\tau_{3u} \cos \widehat{ny} - \tau_{2u} \cos \widehat{nz}) + \\ + (1+\lambda) k \theta^{(1)} \cos \widehat{nx} \Big\} + u^{(2)} \Big\{ \cdots \Big\} + u^{(3)} \Big\{ \cdots \Big\} + v^{(1)} \Big\{ \cdots \Big\} + \cdots \Big] d\sigma, \end{cases}$$

dalle $(a)''_1$:

$$(20)''\quad \begin{cases} 0 = \int_S \Big[u^{(1)} \Big\{ (1+k+\lambda k) \Delta^2 u^{(1)} + \lambda \frac{\partial \theta_u}{\partial \xi} + (1+\lambda) k \Big(\frac{\partial \tau_3^{(1)}}{\partial \eta} - \frac{\partial \tau_2^{(1)}}{\partial \zeta} \Big) \Big\} + \\ \qquad + u^{(2)} \Big\{ \cdots \Big\} + u^{(3)} \Big\{ \cdots \Big\} + v^{(1)} \Big\{ \cdots \Big\} + \cdots \Big] dS = \\ = - \int_S \Big[(1+k+\lambda k) (\Delta u^{(1)} + \Delta u^{(2)} + \Delta u^{(3)} + \Delta v^{(1)} + \cdots) + \\ + \lambda (\theta_u^2 + \theta_v^2 + \theta_w^2) - (1+\lambda) k \Big\{ (\tau_1^{(1)})^2 + (\tau_2^{(1)})^2 + (\tau_3^{(1)})^2 + (\tau_1^{(2)})^2 + \cdots \Big\} \Big] dS - \\ - \int_\sigma \Big[u^{(1)} \Big\{ (1+k+\lambda k) \frac{du^{(1)}}{dn} + \lambda \theta_u \cos \widehat{nx} + \\ \qquad + (1+\lambda) k (\tau_3^{(1)} \cos \widehat{ny} - \tau_2^{(1)} \cos \widehat{nz}) \Big\} + u^{(2)} \Big\{ \cdots \Big\} + \cdots \Big] d\sigma, \end{cases}$$

dalle $(a)_1'''$:

$$
(20)''' \left\{
\begin{aligned}
0 &= \int_S \Big[u^{(1)} \Big\{ (1+\lambda)(1+k)\,\Delta^2 u^{(1)} + \lambda \Big(\frac{\partial \tau_{3u}}{\partial \eta} - \frac{\partial \tau_{2u}}{\partial \zeta} \Big) + \\
&\qquad + (1+\lambda)\,k \Big(\frac{\partial \tau_3^{(1)}}{\partial \eta} - \frac{\partial \tau_2^{(1)}}{\partial \zeta} \Big) \Big\} + u^{(2)} \Big\{ \cdots \Big\} + \cdots \Big] dS = \\
&= - \int_S \Big[(1+\lambda)(1+k)(\Delta u^{(1)} + \Delta u^{(2)} + \cdots + \Delta v^{(1)} + \cdots) - \\
&\quad - \lambda(\tau_{1u}^2 + \tau_{2u}^2 + \tau_{3u}^2 + \tau_{1v}^2 + \cdots) - (1+\lambda)k \Big\{ (\tau_1^{(1)})^2 + (\tau_2^{(1)})^2 + \cdots + (\tau_1^{(2)})^2 + \cdots \Big\} \Big] dS - \\
&\quad - \int_\sigma \Big[u^{(1)} \Big\{ (1+\lambda)(1+k) \frac{du^{(1)}}{dn} + \lambda(\tau_{3u} \cos \widehat{ny} - \tau_{2u} \cos \widehat{nz}) + \\
&\qquad + (1+\lambda)\,k(\tau_3^{(1)} \cos \widehat{ny} - \tau_2^{(1)} \cos \widehat{nz}) \Big\} + u^{(2)} \Big\{ \cdots \Big\} + \cdots \Big] d\sigma .
\end{aligned}
\right.
$$

9. Siano $u^{(1)}, u^{(2)}, u^{(3)}, v^{(1)}, \ldots$ integrali delle equazioni (11), e si abbia:

$$u_\sigma^{(1)} = u_\sigma^{(2)} = u_\sigma^{(3)} = v_\sigma^{(1)} = \cdots = 0.$$

Dalla (20) si ha per $\lambda \geq 0$, $k \geq 0$:

$$\text{(nei punti di S)} \quad \Delta u^{(1)} = \Delta u^{(2)} = \Delta u^{(3)} = \Delta v^{(1)} = \cdots = 0 ;$$

e quindi per $\lambda \geq 0$, $k \geq 0$:

$$\text{(nei punti di S)} \quad u^{(1)} = u^{(2)} = u^{(3)} = v^{(1)} = \cdots = 0 .$$

Dalla (20)' si ha similmente per $0 \geq \lambda > -1$, $k \geq 0$:

$$\text{(nei punti di S)} \quad u^{(1)} = u^{(2)} = u^{(3)} = v^{(1)} = \cdots = 0 .$$

Dalla medesima (20)' si ha ancora per $1 + \lambda = 0$ e k quantità finita qualsiasi:

$$\text{(nei punti di S)} \quad \tau_{1u} = \tau_{2u} = \tau_{3u} = \tau_{1v} = \cdots = 0 ;$$

donde risulta l'esistenza di tre funzioni $u(\xi, \eta, \zeta)$, $v(\xi, \eta, \zeta)$, $w(\xi, \eta, \zeta)$ tali che:

$$(21) \quad u^{(1)}(\xi,\eta,\zeta) = \frac{\partial u}{\partial \xi}, \; u^{(2)}(\xi,\eta,\zeta) = \frac{\partial u}{\partial \eta}, \; u^{(3)}(\xi,\eta,\zeta) = \frac{\partial u}{\partial \zeta}, \; v^{(1)}(\xi,\eta,\zeta) = \frac{\partial v}{\partial \xi}, \ldots ;$$

e quindi ancora:

$$\theta_u = \Delta^2 u \;,\; \theta_v = \Delta^2 v \;,\; \theta_w = \Delta^2 w \;,\; \theta' = \Delta^2 \Big(\frac{\partial u}{\partial \xi} + \frac{\partial v}{\partial \eta} + \frac{\partial w}{\partial \zeta} \Big) = \Delta^2 \theta .$$

Queste ci dànno, in virtù delle equazioni $(b)_1$ e delle rimanenti delle (11),

$$\text{(nei punti di S)} \quad \Delta^2\Big(\Delta^2 u + k \frac{\partial \theta}{\partial \xi}\Big) = 0 \,,\; \Delta^2\Big(\Delta^2 v + k \frac{\partial \theta}{\partial \eta}\Big) = 0 \,,\; \Delta^2\Big(\Delta^2 w + k \frac{\partial \theta}{\partial \zeta}\Big) = 0 ,$$

$$\text{(nei punti di } \sigma) \quad \frac{\partial u}{\partial x} = \frac{\partial u}{\partial y} = \frac{\partial u}{\partial z} = \frac{\partial v}{\partial x} = \cdots = 0 ;$$

sicchè avremo, applicando il risultato stabilito al § 7, che le funzioni u, v, w per $k \geqq -1$ sono costanti in tutto il campo S; e, in forza delle (21), si avrà per $1+\lambda=0$, $k \geqq -1$:

$$\text{(nei punti di S)} \quad u^{(1)}=u^{(2)}=u^{(3)}=v^{(1)}=\cdots=0 .$$

Dalla (20)'' si ha ovviamente per $\lambda \geqq 0$, $k<0$, $1+k+\lambda k>0$, ossia per $\lambda \geqq 0$, $0>k>\frac{-1}{1+\lambda}$:

$$\text{(nei punti di S)} \quad u^{(1)}=u^{(2)}=u^{(3)}=v^{(1)}=\cdots=0 .$$

Dalla (20)''' si ha similmente per $\lambda \leqq 0$, $k \leqq 0$, $1+\lambda>0$, $1+k>0$, ossia per $0 \geqq \lambda > 1$, $0 \geqq k > -1$:

$$\text{(nei punti di S)} \quad u^{(1)}=u^{(2)}=u^{(3)}=v^{(1)}=\cdots=0 .$$

Dalla (20)''' si ha poi per $\lambda<0$, $1+\lambda \geqq 0$, $1+k=0$:

$$\text{(nei punti di S)} \quad \tau_{1u}=\tau_{2u}=\tau_{3u}=\tau_{1v}=\cdots=0 ;$$

e quindi, ragionando come sopra, si avrà per $0>\lambda \geqq -1$, $k=-1$:

$$\text{(nei punti di S)} \quad u^{(1)}=u^{(2)}=u^{(3)}=v^{(1)}=\cdots=0 .$$

Se si riferiscono i valori reali di λ e di k a due assi cartesiani ortogonali, e se si considera sul piano l'area indefinita A, che contiene il punto $(\lambda=0, k=0)$, e che è limitata dalla semiretta avente per estremi i punti $(\lambda=-1, k=\infty)$, $(\lambda=-1, k=-1)$, dal segmento avente per estremi i punti $(\lambda=-1, k=-1)$, $(\lambda=0, k=-1)$ e dal ramo di iperbole equilatera, avente per assintoti l'asse delle λ e la retta $\lambda=-1$, con gli estremi nei punti $(\lambda=0, k=-1)$, $(\lambda=\infty, k=0)$, i precedenti risultati si possono riassumere nel seguente teorema: *per tutti i valori reali di λ e di k, corrispondenti a punti dell'area* A, *esclusi al più i punti della porzione di contorno formata dal ramo di iperbole, i valori degli integrali $u^{(1)}, u^{(2)}, u^{(3)}, v^{(1)}, \ldots$ delle equazioni* (11) *sono pienamente determinati in tutti i punti del campo* S.

Formole fondamentali per l'integrazione delle equazioni (11).

10. Posto $\mu=(1+\lambda)k$, le equazioni $(a)_1$ delle (11) divengono:

$$(22) \quad \begin{cases} \Delta^2 u^{(1)}+\lambda \dfrac{\partial \theta_u}{\partial \xi}+\mu \dfrac{\partial \theta^{(1)}}{\partial \xi}=0, \quad \Delta^2 v^{(1)}+\lambda \dfrac{\partial \theta_v}{\partial \xi}+\mu \dfrac{\partial \theta^{(1)}}{\partial \eta}=0, \ldots, \\ \Delta^2 u^{(2)}+\lambda \dfrac{\partial \theta_u}{\partial \eta}+\mu \dfrac{\partial \theta^{(2)}}{\partial \xi}=0, \ldots \qquad\qquad , \ldots, \\ \ldots \qquad\qquad , \ldots \qquad\qquad , \ldots . \end{cases}$$

Chiameremo *componenti delle tensioni generali* nei punti di σ le seguenti espressioni:

$$
(23)\quad \left\{
\begin{array}{l}
\dfrac{du^{(1)}}{dn}+\lambda\theta_u\cos\widehat{nx}+\mu\theta^{(1)}\cos\widehat{nx}+\\
\quad +h_1\left(\dfrac{\partial u^{(1)}}{\partial x}\cos\widehat{nx}+\dfrac{\partial v^{(1)}}{\partial x}\cos\widehat{ny}+\dfrac{\partial w^{(1)}}{\partial x}\cos\widehat{nz}-\theta^{(1)}\cos\widehat{nx}\right)+\\
\quad +h_2\left(\dfrac{\partial u^{(1)}}{\partial x}\cos\widehat{nx}+\dfrac{\partial u^{(2)}}{\partial x}\cos\widehat{ny}+\dfrac{\partial u^{(3)}}{\partial x}\cos\widehat{nz}-\theta_u\cos\widehat{nx}\right)+\\
\quad +h_3\left(\dfrac{\partial u^{(1)}}{\partial x}\cos\widehat{nx}+\dfrac{\partial v^{(1)}}{\partial x}\cos\widehat{ny}+\dfrac{\partial w^{(1)}}{\partial x}\cos\widehat{nz}-\theta^{(1)}\cos\widehat{nx}\right)+\\
\quad +h_4\left(\dfrac{\partial u^{(1)}}{\partial x}\cos\widehat{nx}+\dfrac{\partial u^{(2)}}{\partial x}\cos\widehat{ny}+\dfrac{\partial u^{(3)}}{\partial x}\cos\widehat{nz}-\theta_u\cos\widehat{nx}\right),\\
\dfrac{du^{(2)}}{dn}+\lambda\theta_u\cos\widehat{ny}+\mu\theta^{(2)}\cos\widehat{nx}+\\
\quad +h_1\left(\dfrac{\partial u^{(2)}}{\partial x}\cos\widehat{nx}+\dfrac{\partial v^{(2)}}{\partial x}\cos\widehat{ny}+\dfrac{\partial w^{(2)}}{\partial x}\cos\widehat{nz}-\theta^{(2)}\cos\widehat{nx}\right)+\\
\quad +h_2\left(\dfrac{\partial v^{(1)}}{\partial x}\cos\widehat{nx}+\dfrac{\partial v^{(2)}}{\partial x}\cos\widehat{ny}+\dfrac{\partial v^{(3)}}{\partial x}\cos\widehat{nz}-\theta_v\cos\widehat{nx}\right)+\\
\quad +h_3\left(\dfrac{\partial u^{(1)}}{\partial y}\cos\widehat{nx}+\dfrac{\partial v^{(1)}}{\partial y}\cos\widehat{ny}+\dfrac{\partial w^{(1)}}{\partial y}\cos\widehat{nz}-\theta^{(1)}\cos\widehat{ny}\right)+\\
\quad +h_4\left(\dfrac{\partial u^{(1)}}{\partial y}\cos\widehat{nx}+\dfrac{\partial u^{(2)}}{\partial y}\cos\widehat{ny}+\dfrac{\partial u^{(3)}}{\partial y}\cos\widehat{nz}-\theta_u\cos\widehat{ny}\right),\\
\dfrac{du^{(3)}}{dn}+\lambda\theta_u\cos\widehat{nz}+\mu\theta^{(3)}\cos\widehat{nx}+\\
\quad +h_1\left(\dfrac{\partial u^{(3)}}{\partial x}\cos\widehat{nx}+\dfrac{\partial v^{(3)}}{\partial x}\cos\widehat{ny}+\dfrac{\partial w^{(3)}}{\partial x}\cos\widehat{nz}-\theta^{(3)}\cos\widehat{nx}\right)+\\
\quad +h_2\left(\dfrac{\partial w^{(1)}}{\partial x}\cos\widehat{nx}+\dfrac{\partial w^{(2)}}{\partial x}\cos\widehat{ny}+\dfrac{\partial w^{(3)}}{\partial x}\cos\widehat{nz}-\theta_w\cos\widehat{nx}\right)+\\
\quad +h_3\left(\dfrac{\partial u^{(1)}}{\partial z}\cos\widehat{nx}+\dfrac{\partial v^{(1)}}{\partial z}\cos\widehat{ny}+\dfrac{\partial w^{(1)}}{\partial z}\cos\widehat{nz}-\theta^{(1)}\cos\widehat{nz}\right)+\\
\quad +h_4\left(\dfrac{\partial u^{(1)}}{\partial z}\cos\widehat{nx}+\dfrac{\partial u^{(2)}}{\partial z}\cos\widehat{ny}+\dfrac{\partial u^{(3)}}{\partial z}\cos\widehat{nz}-\theta_u\cos\widehat{nz}\right),\\
\dfrac{dv^{(1)}}{dn}+\lambda\theta_v\cos\widehat{nx}+\mu\theta^{(1)}\cos\widehat{ny}+\\
\quad +h_1\left(\dfrac{\partial u^{(1)}}{\partial y}\cos\widehat{nx}+\dfrac{\partial v^{(1)}}{\partial y}\cos\widehat{ny}+\dfrac{\partial w^{(1)}}{\partial y}\cos\widehat{nz}-\theta^{(1)}\cos\widehat{ny}\right)+\\
\quad +h_2\left(\dfrac{\partial u^{(1)}}{\partial y}\cos\widehat{nx}+\dfrac{\partial u^{(2)}}{\partial y}\cos\widehat{ny}+\dfrac{\partial u^{(3)}}{\partial y}\cos\widehat{nz}-\theta_u\cos\widehat{ny}\right)+\\
\quad +h_3\left(\dfrac{\partial u^{(2)}}{\partial x}\cos\widehat{nx}+\dfrac{\partial v^{(2)}}{\partial x}\cos\widehat{ny}+\dfrac{\partial w^{(2)}}{\partial x}\cos\widehat{nz}-\theta^{(2)}\cos\widehat{nx}\right)+\\
\quad +h_4\left(\dfrac{\partial v^{(1)}}{\partial x}\cos\widehat{nx}+\dfrac{\partial v^{(2)}}{\partial x}\cos\widehat{ny}+\dfrac{\partial v^{(3)}}{\partial x}\cos\widehat{nz}-\theta_v\cos\widehat{nx}\right),\\
\quad \cdot\ \cdot\ \cdot\ \cdot\ \cdot\ \cdot\ \cdot\ \cdot\ \cdot\ \cdot\ \cdot\ \cdot\\
\quad \cdot\ \cdot\ \cdot\ \cdot\ \cdot\ \cdot\ \cdot\ \cdot\ \cdot\ \cdot\ \cdot\ \cdot\ \cdot\ ,
\end{array}\right.
$$

nelle quali h_1, h_2, h_3, h_4 sono parametri arbitrarî ed indipendenti fra di loro.

Chiameremo *componenti delle pseudo-tensioni* nei punti di σ, ciò che divengono le (23) nel caso particolare in cui h_1, h_2, h_3, h_4 sono le radici delle equazioni simultanee:

$$
(24)\left\{
\begin{aligned}
&\frac{2+\mu}{1+\mu} h_1 + \frac{2+\lambda}{1+\lambda} h_2 = \frac{\mu}{1+\mu}\,, \quad \frac{2+\mu}{1+\mu} h_3 + \frac{2+\lambda}{1+\lambda} h_4 = \frac{\lambda}{1+\lambda}\,, \\
&\lambda\mu(2+\lambda+\mu)(h_1+h_2) + \lambda(4+4\lambda+2\mu+\lambda\mu+\mu^2)\, h_3 + \\
&\qquad + \mu(4+2\lambda+4\mu+\lambda\mu+\lambda^2)\, h_4 = \lambda\mu(2-\lambda+3\mu)\,, \\
&\lambda\mu(2+\lambda+\mu)(h_3+h_4) + \lambda(4+4\lambda+2\mu+\lambda\mu+\mu^2)\, h_1 + \\
&\qquad + \mu(4+2\lambda+4\mu+\lambda\mu+\lambda^2)\, h_2 = \lambda\mu(2-\mu+3\lambda)\,.
\end{aligned}
\right.
$$

11. Ricordando di avere posto al § 1:

$$
r = \sqrt{(x-\xi)^2 + (y-\eta)^2 + (z-\zeta)^2}\,,
$$

si verifica facilmente che sono integrali delle equazioni (22) i seguenti *nove* sistemi di funzioni di ξ, η, ζ:

$$
(\mathrm{I})\left\{
\begin{aligned}
u_1^{(1)} &= \frac{1}{r} - \frac{\lambda}{2!(1+\lambda)} \cdot \frac{\partial^2 r}{\partial x^2} - \frac{\mu}{2!(1+\mu)} \cdot \frac{\partial^2 r}{\partial x^2} + \\
&\qquad + \frac{\lambda\mu(2+\lambda+\mu)}{4!(1+\lambda)(1+\mu)(1+\lambda+\mu)} \cdot \frac{\partial^4 r^3}{\partial x^4}\,, \\
u_1^{(2)} &= -\frac{\lambda}{2!(1+\lambda)} \cdot \frac{\partial^2 r}{\partial x\,\partial y} + \frac{\lambda\mu(2+\lambda+\mu)}{4!(1+\lambda)(1+\mu)(1+\lambda+\mu)} \cdot \frac{\partial^4 r^3}{\partial x^3\,\partial y}\,, \\
u_1^{(3)} &= -\frac{\lambda}{2!(1+\lambda)} \cdot \frac{\partial^2 r}{\partial x\,\partial z} + \frac{\lambda\mu(2+\lambda+\mu)}{4!(1+\lambda)(1+\mu)(1+\lambda+\mu)} \cdot \frac{\partial^4 r^3}{\partial x^3\,\partial z}\,, \\
v_1^{(1)} &= -\frac{\mu}{2!(1+\mu)} \cdot \frac{\partial^2 r}{\partial x\,\partial y} + \frac{\lambda\mu(2+\lambda+\mu)}{4!(1+\lambda)(1+\mu)(1+\lambda+\mu)} \cdot \frac{\partial^4 r^3}{\partial x^3\,\partial y}\,, \\
v_1^{(2)} &= \frac{\lambda\mu(2+\lambda+\mu)}{4!(1+\lambda)(1+\mu)(1+\lambda+\mu)} \cdot \frac{\partial^4 r^3}{\partial x^2\,\partial y^2}\,, \\
v_1^{(3)} &= \frac{\lambda\mu(2+\lambda+\mu)}{4!(1+\lambda)(1+\mu)(1+\lambda+\mu)} \cdot \frac{\partial^4 r^3}{\partial x^2\,\partial y\,\partial z}\,, \\
w_1^{(1)} &= -\frac{\mu}{2!(1+\mu)} \cdot \frac{\partial^2 r}{\partial x\,\partial z} + \frac{\lambda\mu(2+\lambda+\mu)}{4!(1+\lambda)(1+\mu)(1+\lambda+\mu)} \cdot \frac{\partial^4 r^3}{\partial x^3\,\partial z}\,, \\
w_1^{(2)} &= \frac{\lambda\mu(2+\lambda+\mu)}{4!(1+\lambda)(1+\mu)(1+\lambda+\mu)} \cdot \frac{\partial^4 r^3}{\partial x^2\,\partial y\,\partial z}\,, \\
w_1^{(3)} &= \frac{\lambda\mu(2+\lambda+\mu)}{4!(1+\lambda)(1+\mu)(1+\lambda+\mu)} \cdot \frac{\partial^4 r^3}{\partial x^2\,\partial z^2}\,;
\end{aligned}
\right.
$$

$$
(\mathrm{II})\left\{
\begin{aligned}
u_2^{(1)} &= -\frac{\lambda}{2!(1+\lambda)}\cdot\frac{\partial^2 r}{\partial x\,\partial y}+\frac{\lambda\mu(2+\lambda+\mu)}{4!(1+\lambda)(1+\mu)(1+\lambda+\mu)}\cdot\frac{\partial^4 r^3}{\partial x^3\,\partial y},\\
u_2^{(2)} &= \frac{1}{r}-\frac{\lambda}{2!(1+\lambda)}\cdot\frac{\partial^2 r}{\partial y^2}-\frac{\mu}{2!(1+\mu)}\cdot\frac{\partial^2 r}{\partial x^2}+\\
&\qquad+\frac{\lambda\mu(2+\lambda+\mu)}{4!(1+\lambda)(1+\mu)(1+\lambda+\mu)}\cdot\frac{\partial^4 r^3}{\partial x^2\,\partial y^2},\\
u_2^{(3)} &= -\frac{\lambda}{2!(1+\lambda)}\cdot\frac{\partial^2 r}{\partial y\,\partial z}+\frac{\lambda\mu(2+\lambda+\mu)}{4!(1+\lambda)(1+\mu)(1+\lambda+\mu)}\cdot\frac{\partial^4 r^3}{\partial x^2\,\partial y\,\partial z},\\
v_2^{(1)} &= \frac{\lambda\mu(2+\lambda+\mu)}{4!(1+\lambda)(1+\mu)(1+\lambda+\mu)}\cdot\frac{\partial^4 r^3}{\partial x^2\,\partial y^2},\\
v_2^{(2)} &= -\frac{\mu}{2!(1+\mu)}\cdot\frac{\partial^2 r}{\partial x\,\partial y}+\frac{\lambda\mu(2+\lambda+\mu)}{4!(1+\lambda)(1+\mu)(1+\lambda+\mu)}\cdot\frac{\partial^4 r^3}{\partial x\,\partial y^3},\\
v_2^{(3)} &= \frac{\lambda\mu(2+\lambda+\mu)}{4!(1+\lambda)(1+\mu)(1+\lambda+\mu)}\cdot\frac{\partial^4 r^3}{\partial x\,\partial y^2\,\partial z},\\
w_2^{(1)} &= \frac{\lambda\mu(2+\lambda+\mu)}{4!(1+\lambda)(1+\mu)(1+\lambda+\mu)}\cdot\frac{\partial^4 r^3}{\partial x^2\,\partial y\,\partial z},\\
w_2^{(2)} &= -\frac{\mu}{2!(1+\mu)}\cdot\frac{\partial^2 r}{\partial x\,\partial z}+\frac{\lambda\mu(2+\lambda+\mu)}{4!(1+\lambda)(1+\mu)(1+\lambda+\mu)}\cdot\frac{\partial^4 r^3}{\partial x\,\partial y^2\,\partial z},\\
w_2^{(3)} &= \frac{\lambda\mu(2+\lambda+\mu)}{4!(1+\lambda)(1+\mu)(1+\lambda+\mu)}\cdot\frac{\partial^4 r^3}{\partial x\,\partial y\,\partial z^2};
\end{aligned}\right.
$$

. . . .

. . . .

Posto:

$$
\theta_{iu}=\frac{\partial u_i^{(1)}}{\partial\xi}+\frac{\partial u_i^{(2)}}{\partial\eta}+\frac{\partial u_i^{(3)}}{\partial\zeta},\ \theta_{iv}=\frac{\partial v_i^{(1)}}{\partial\xi}+\frac{\partial v_i^{(2)}}{\partial\eta}+\frac{\partial v_i^{(3)}}{\partial\zeta},\ \theta_{iw}=\frac{\partial w_i^{(1)}}{\partial\xi}+\frac{\partial w_i^{(2)}}{\partial\eta}+\frac{\partial w_i^{(3)}}{\partial\zeta},
$$

$$
\theta_i^{(1)}=\frac{\partial u_i^{(1)}}{\partial\xi}+\frac{\partial v_i^{(1)}}{\partial\eta}+\frac{\partial w_i^{(1)}}{\partial\zeta},\ \ldots,\qquad\qquad \ldots,
$$

si ha, corrispondentemente ai soprascritti sistemi di integrali,

$$
(\mathrm{I})'\left\{
\begin{aligned}
\theta_{1u} &= \frac{1}{1+\lambda}\cdot\frac{\partial}{\partial\xi}\left(\frac{1}{r}-\frac{\mu}{2(1+\lambda+\mu)}\,\frac{\partial^2 r}{\partial\xi^2}\right),\\
\theta_{1v} &= \frac{1}{1+\lambda}\cdot\frac{\partial}{\partial\xi}\left(-\frac{\mu}{2(1+\lambda+\mu)}\,\frac{\partial^2 r}{\partial\xi\,\partial\eta}\right),\\
\theta_{1w} &= \frac{1}{1+\lambda}\cdot\frac{\partial}{\partial\xi}\left(-\frac{\mu}{2(1+\lambda+\mu)}\,\frac{\partial^2 r}{\partial\xi\,\partial\zeta}\right),\\
\theta_1^{(1)} &= \frac{1}{1+\mu}\cdot\frac{\partial}{\partial\xi}\left(\frac{1}{r}-\frac{\lambda}{2(1+\lambda+\mu)}\,\frac{\partial^2 r}{\partial\xi^2}\right),\\
\theta_1^{(2)} &= \frac{1}{1+\mu}\cdot\frac{\partial}{\partial\xi}\left(-\frac{\lambda}{2(1+\lambda+\mu)}\,\frac{\partial^2 r}{\partial\xi\,\partial\eta}\right),\\
\theta_1^{(3)} &= \frac{1}{1+\mu}\cdot\frac{\partial}{\partial\xi}\left(-\frac{\lambda}{2(1+\lambda+\mu)}\,\frac{\partial^2 r}{\partial\xi\,\partial\zeta}\right);
\end{aligned}\right.
$$

$$
(\mathrm{II})' \quad \left\{
\begin{aligned}
\theta_{2u} &= \frac{1}{1+\lambda}\cdot\frac{\partial}{\partial\eta}\left(\frac{1}{r} - \frac{\mu}{2\,(1+\lambda+\mu)}\,\frac{\partial^2 r}{\partial\xi^2}\right),\\
\theta_{2v} &= \frac{1}{1+\lambda}\cdot\frac{\partial}{\partial\eta}\left(-\frac{\mu}{2\,(1+\lambda+\mu)}\,\frac{\partial^2 r}{\partial\xi\,\partial\eta}\right),\\
\theta_{2w} &= \frac{1}{1+\lambda}\cdot\frac{\partial}{\partial\eta}\left(-\frac{\mu}{2\,(1+\lambda+\mu)}\,\frac{\partial^2 r}{\partial\xi\,\partial\zeta}\right),\\
\theta_2^{(1)} &= \frac{1}{1+\mu}\cdot\frac{\partial}{\partial\xi}\left(-\frac{\lambda}{2\,(1+\lambda+\mu)}\,\frac{\partial^2 r}{\partial\xi\,\partial\eta}\right),\\
\theta_2^{(2)} &= \frac{1}{1+\mu}\cdot\frac{\partial}{\partial\xi}\left(\frac{1}{r} - \frac{\lambda}{2\,(1+\lambda+\mu)}\,\frac{\partial^2 r}{\partial\eta^2}\right),\\
\theta_2^{(3)} &= \frac{1}{1+\mu}\cdot\frac{\partial}{\partial\xi}\left(-\frac{\lambda}{2\,(1+\lambda+\mu)}\,\frac{\partial^2 r}{\partial\eta\,\partial\zeta}\right);
\end{aligned}
\right.
$$

. . . .

. . . .

12. Le espressioni delle componenti delle pseudo-tensioni, corrispondenti ai *nove* sistemi di integrali (I), (II), ..., sono formate ciascuna del prodotto di una funzione, che si mantiene sempre finita qualunque sia la posizione dei punti (x, y, z), (ξ, η, ζ) nello spazio, per la funzione $\dfrac{d\frac{1}{r}}{dn}$. Esse sono rispettivamente:

$$
(\mathrm{I})'' \quad \left\{
\begin{aligned}
\mathrm{U}_1^{(1)} &= \Bigg[1 - (h_1 + h_2 + h_3 + h_4)\left\{1 - 3\left(\frac{\partial r}{\partial x}\right)^2\right\} +\\
&\qquad + \frac{3\lambda\mu(2+\lambda+\mu)}{2^3(1+\lambda)(1+\mu)(1+\lambda+\mu)}(1 + h_1 + h_2 + h_3 + h_4)\times\\
&\qquad\qquad \times\left\{1 - 6\left(\frac{\partial r}{\partial x}\right)^2 + 5\left(\frac{\partial r}{\partial x}\right)^4\right\}\Bigg]\frac{d\frac{1}{r}}{dn},\\
\mathrm{U}_1^{(2)} &= \Bigg[3(h_3 + h_4)\frac{\partial r}{\partial x}\frac{\partial r}{\partial y} + \frac{3\lambda\mu(2+\lambda+\mu)}{2^3(1+\lambda)(1+\mu)(1+\lambda+\mu)}(1+h_1+h_2+h_3+h_4)\times\\
&\qquad\qquad \times\left\{-3\frac{\partial r}{\partial x}\frac{\partial r}{\partial y} + 5\left(\frac{\partial r}{\partial x}\right)^3\frac{\partial r}{\partial y}\right\}\Bigg]\frac{d\frac{1}{r}}{dn},\\
\mathrm{U}_1^{(3)} &= \Bigg[3(h_3 + h_4)\frac{\partial r}{\partial x}\frac{\partial r}{\partial z} + \frac{3\lambda\mu(2+\lambda+\mu)}{2^3(1+\lambda)(1+\mu)(1+\lambda+\mu)}(1+h_1+h_2+h_3+h_4)\times\\
&\qquad\qquad \times\left\{-3\frac{\partial r}{\partial x}\frac{\partial r}{\partial z} + 5\left(\frac{\partial r}{\partial x}\right)^3\frac{\partial r}{\partial z}\right\}\Bigg]\frac{d\frac{1}{r}}{dn},
\end{aligned}
\right.
$$

$$
(\mathrm{I})''\left\{\begin{aligned}
\mathrm{V}_1^{(1)} &= \Big[3(h_1+h_2)\frac{\partial r}{\partial x}\frac{\partial r}{\partial y} + \frac{3\lambda\mu(2+\lambda+\mu)}{2^3(1+\lambda)(1+\mu)(1+\lambda+\mu)}(1+h_1+h_2+h_3+h_4)\times \\
&\qquad \times\Big\{-3\frac{\partial r}{\partial x}\frac{\partial r}{\partial y}+5\Big(\frac{\partial r}{\partial x}\Big)^3\frac{\partial r}{\partial y}\Big\}\Big]\frac{d\frac{1}{r}}{dn}, \\
\mathrm{V}_1^{(2)} &= \Big[\frac{3\lambda\mu(2+\lambda+\mu)}{2^3(1+\lambda)(1+\mu)(1+\lambda+\mu)}(1+h_1+h_2+h_3+h_4)\times \\
&\qquad \times\Big\{\frac{1}{3}-\Big(\frac{\partial r}{\partial x}\Big)^2-\Big(\frac{\partial r}{\partial y}\Big)^2+5\Big(\frac{\partial r}{\partial x}\Big)^2\Big(\frac{\partial r}{\partial y}\Big)^2\Big\}\Big]\frac{d\frac{1}{r}}{dn}, \\
\mathrm{V}_1^{(3)} &= \Big[\frac{3}{2}\Big\{\frac{\lambda}{1+\lambda}(h_1+h_3)+\frac{\mu}{1+\mu}(h_2+h_4)\Big\}\frac{\partial r}{\partial y}\frac{\partial r}{\partial z}+ \\
&\qquad +\frac{3\lambda\mu(2+\lambda+\mu)}{2^3(1+\lambda)(1+\mu)(1+\lambda+\mu)}(1+h_1+h_2+h_3+h_4)\times \\
&\qquad \times\Big\{-3\frac{\partial r}{\partial y}\frac{\partial r}{\partial z}+5\Big(\frac{\partial r}{\partial x}\Big)^2\frac{\partial r}{\partial y}\frac{\partial r}{\partial z}\Big\}\Big]\frac{d\frac{1}{r}}{dn}, \\
\mathrm{W}_1^{(1)} &= \Big[3(h_1+h_2)\frac{\partial r}{\partial x}\frac{\partial r}{\partial z} + \frac{3\lambda\mu(2+\lambda+\mu)}{2^3(1+\lambda)(1+\mu)(1+\lambda+\mu)}(1+h_1+h_2+h_3+h_4)\times \\
&\qquad \times\Big\{-3\frac{\partial r}{\partial x}\frac{\partial r}{\partial z}+5\Big(\frac{\partial r}{\partial x}\Big)^3\frac{\partial r}{\partial z}\Big\}\Big]\frac{d\frac{1}{r}}{dn}, \\
\mathrm{W}_1^{(2)} &= \Big[\frac{3}{2}\Big\{\frac{\lambda}{1+\lambda}(h_1+h_3)+\frac{\mu}{1+\mu}(h_2+h_4)\Big\}\frac{\partial r}{\partial y}\frac{\partial r}{\partial z}+ \\
&\qquad +\frac{3\lambda\mu(2+\lambda+\mu)}{2^3(1+\lambda)(1+\mu)(1+\lambda+\mu)}(1+h_1+h_2+h_3+h_4)\times \\
&\qquad \times\Big\{-3\frac{\partial r}{\partial y}\frac{\partial r}{\partial z}+5\Big(\frac{\partial r}{\partial x}\Big)^2\frac{\partial r}{\partial y}\frac{\partial r}{\partial z}\Big\}\Big]\frac{d\frac{1}{r}}{dn}, \\
\mathrm{W}_1^{(3)} &= \Big[\frac{3\lambda\mu(2+\lambda+\mu)}{2^3(1+\lambda)(1+\mu)(1+\lambda+\mu)}(1+h_1+h_2+h_3+h_4)\times \\
&\qquad \times\Big\{\frac{1}{3}-\Big(\frac{\partial r}{\partial x}\Big)^2-\Big(\frac{\partial r}{\partial z}\Big)^2+5\Big(\frac{\partial r}{\partial x}\Big)^2\Big(\frac{\partial r}{\partial z}\Big)^2\Big\}\Big]\frac{d\frac{1}{r}}{dn};
\end{aligned}\right.
$$

. . . .

. . . .

13. Supposto il punto (ξ, η, ζ) nell'interno del campo S si ha, come è noto,

$$\int_\sigma \frac{d\frac{1}{r}}{dn}d\sigma = 4\pi\,, \qquad \int_\sigma \Big(\frac{\partial r}{\partial x}\Big)^2\frac{d\frac{1}{r}}{dn}d\sigma = \frac{4}{3}\pi\,, \qquad \int_\sigma \frac{\partial r}{\partial x}\frac{\partial r}{\partial y}\frac{d\frac{1}{r}}{dn}d\sigma = 0\,,$$

$$\int_\sigma \Big(\frac{\partial r}{\partial x}\Big)^4\frac{d\frac{1}{r}}{dn}d\sigma = \frac{4}{5}\pi\,, \int_\sigma \Big(\frac{\partial r}{\partial x}\Big)^3\frac{\partial r}{\partial y}\frac{d\frac{1}{r}}{dn}d\sigma = 0\,, \quad \int_\sigma \Big(\frac{\partial r}{\partial x}\Big)^2\Big(\frac{\partial r}{\partial y}\Big)^2\frac{d\frac{1}{r}}{\partial n}d\sigma = \frac{4}{3.5}\pi\,,$$

$$\int_\sigma \Big(\frac{\partial r}{\partial x}\Big)^2\frac{\partial r}{\partial y}\frac{\partial r}{\partial z}\frac{d\frac{1}{r}}{dn}d\sigma = 0\,.$$

Da queste formole e dalle analoghe, che non si sono scritte, risulta, sempre nell'ipotesi che il punto (ξ, η, ζ) sia nell'interno del campo S,

$$\int_\sigma U_1^{(1)} d\sigma = 4\pi , \int_\sigma U_1^{(2)} d\sigma = \int_\sigma U_1^{(3)} d\sigma = \int_\sigma V_1^{(1)} d\sigma = \int_\sigma V_1^{(2)} d\sigma = \int_\sigma V_1^{(3)} d\sigma =$$
$$= \int_\sigma W_1^{(1)} d\sigma = \int_\sigma W_1^{(2)} d\sigma = \int_\sigma W_1^{(3)} d\sigma = 0 .$$

Se il punto (ξ, η, ζ) poi è nell'interno del campo infinito S' limitato da σ, si ha similmente:

$$\int_\sigma U_1^{(1)} d\sigma = \int_\sigma U_1^{(2)} d\sigma = \int_\sigma U_1^{(3)} d\sigma = \int_\sigma V_1^{(1)} d\sigma = \int_\sigma V_1^{(2)} d\sigma = \int_\sigma V_1^{(3)} d\sigma =$$
$$= \int_\sigma W_1^{(1)} d\sigma = \int_\sigma W_1^{(2)} d\sigma = \int_\sigma W_1^{(3)} d\sigma = 0 ;$$

mentre se il punto (ξ, η, ζ) è su σ, si ha:

$$\int_\sigma \frac{d\frac{1}{r}}{dn} d\sigma = 2\pi \quad , \quad \int_\sigma \left(\frac{\partial r}{\partial x}\right)^2 \frac{d\frac{1}{r}}{dn} d\sigma = \frac{2}{3}\pi , \ldots ,$$

e quindi ancora:

$$\int_\sigma U_1^{(1)} d\sigma = 2\pi \quad , \quad \int_\sigma U_1^{(2)} d\sigma = \int_\sigma U_1^{(3)} d\sigma = \cdots = 0.$$

Formole perfettamente analoghe alle precedenti si hanno ovviamente per le espressioni (II)'', (III)''', ... che non si sono scritte.

14. Ciò premesso, siano $\varphi_1(\alpha, \beta), \varphi_2(\alpha, \beta), \varphi_3(\alpha, \beta), \psi_1(\alpha, \beta), \psi_2(\alpha, \beta), \psi_3(\alpha, \beta), \chi_1(\alpha, \beta), \chi_2(\alpha, \beta), \chi_3(\alpha, \beta)$ *nove* funzioni finite e continue dei punti (α, β) di σ, e si ponga:

$$(25) \left\{ \begin{aligned} \Phi_1(\xi, \eta, \zeta) &= \frac{1}{2\pi} \int_\sigma \Big(U_1^{(1)} \varphi_1 + U_2^{(1)} \varphi_2 + U_3^{(1)} \varphi_3 + U_4^{(1)} \psi_1 + U_5^{(1)} \psi_2 + \\ &\qquad + U_6^{(1)} \psi_3 + U_7^{(1)} \chi_1 + U_8^{(1)} \chi_2 + U_9^{(1)} \chi_3 \Big) d\sigma , \\ \Phi_2(\xi, \eta, \zeta) &= \frac{1}{2\pi} \int_\sigma \Big(U_1^{(2)} \varphi_1 + U_2^{(2)} \varphi_2 + U_3^{(2)} \varphi_3 + U_4^{(2)} \psi_1 + U_5^{(2)} \psi_2 + \\ &\qquad + U_6^{(2)} \psi_3 + U_7^{(2)} \chi_1 + U_8^{(2)} \chi_2 + U_9^{(2)} \chi_3 \Big) d\sigma , \\ &\cdots\cdots\cdots , \\ \Psi_1(\xi, \eta, \zeta) &= \frac{1}{2\pi} \int_\sigma \Big(V_1^{(1)} \varphi_1 + V_2^{(1)} \varphi_2 + V_3^{(1)} \varphi_3 + V_4^{(1)} \psi_1 + \cdots \Big) d\sigma , \\ &\cdots\cdots\cdots \\ &\cdots\cdots\cdots \end{aligned} \right.$$

Chiameremo le funzioni $\Phi_1(\xi, \eta, \zeta)$, $\Phi_2(\xi, \eta, \zeta)$, ..., $\Psi_1(\xi, \eta, \zeta)$, ... *pseudo-doppi strati*. Esse godono di proprietà perfettamente analoghe ai doppi strati della teoria del potenziale newtoniano. In particolare, se si indicano rispettivamente con

$\Phi_1(\alpha', \beta')$, $\Phi_2(\alpha', \beta')$, ..., $\Psi_1(\alpha', \beta')$, ... i valori che le espressioni (25) prendono nel punto $P' \equiv (\alpha', \beta')$, preso ad arbitrio su σ, si hanno le seguenti formole di discontinuità: *se il punto* $P \equiv (\xi, \eta, \zeta)$ *si avvicina indefinitamente al punto* $P' \equiv (\alpha', \beta')$ *di* σ, *mantenendosi sempre nell'interno del campo finito* S, *sarà*:

$$(26) \quad \begin{cases} \lim\limits_{P=P'} \Phi_1(\xi, \eta, \zeta) = \varphi_1(\alpha', \beta') + \Phi_1(\alpha', \beta'), \\ \lim\limits_{P=P'} \Phi_2(\xi, \eta, \zeta) = \varphi_2(\alpha', \beta') + \Phi_2(\alpha', \beta'), \ldots; \end{cases}$$

se il punto $P \equiv (\xi, \eta, \zeta)$ *si avvicina indefinitamente al punto* $P' \equiv (\alpha', \beta')$ *di* σ, *mantenendosi sempre nell'interno del campo infinito* S', *sarà*:

$$(27) \quad \begin{cases} \lim\limits_{P=P'} \Phi_1(\xi, \eta, \zeta) = -\varphi_1(\alpha', \beta') + \Phi_1(\alpha', \beta'), \\ \lim\limits_{P=P'} \Phi_2(\xi, \eta, \zeta) = -\varphi_2(\alpha', \beta') + \Phi_2(\alpha', \beta'), \ldots . \end{cases}$$

15. Si possono pure scrivere delle formole analoghe a quelle di discontinuità degli strati semplici, ad altre formole ancora analoghe a quella di reciprocità del BETTI, a quelle del SOMIGLIANA, ecc. Similmente si possono introdurre delle funzioni analoghe a quelle di GREEN, che in alcuni casi particolari porterebbero alla integrazione delle equazioni (22) per dati valori di $u^{(1)}, u^{(2)}, u^{(3)}, v^{(1)}, \ldots$ nei punti di σ.

Un edifizio simile a quello precedentemente costruito per le equazioni (22), e simile ancora a quello ben noto relativo all'equazione doppia di LAPLACE, può costruirsi per le equazioni (8) del § 4.

16. Siano $u_\sigma^{(1)}(\alpha, \beta)$, $u_\sigma^{(2)}(\alpha, \beta)$, $u_\sigma^{(3)}(\alpha, \beta)$, $v_\sigma^{(1)}(\alpha, \beta)$, ... funzioni finite e continue dei punti (α, β) di σ, date ad arbitrio. Indichiamo rispettivamente con $U_1^{(1)}(\alpha, \beta; \alpha', \beta'; \lambda, \mu)$, $U_1^{(2)}(\alpha, \beta; \alpha', \beta'; \lambda, \mu)$, ... ciò che divengono le espressioni (I)'', quando i punti (x, y, z), (ξ, η, ζ) coincidono rispettivamente con i punti (α, β), $P' \equiv (\alpha', \beta')$ di σ; con $U_2^{(1)}(\alpha, \beta; \alpha', \beta'; \lambda, \mu)$, ... ciò che divengono le espressioni (II)'', ecc.; e consideriamo il seguente sistema di equazioni integrali:

$$(28) \quad \begin{cases} \varphi_1(\alpha', \beta'; \lambda, \mu) + \dfrac{1}{2\pi} \displaystyle\int_\sigma \Big\{ U_1^{(1)}(\alpha, \beta; \alpha', \beta'; \lambda, \mu)\, \varphi_1(\alpha, \beta; \lambda, \mu) + \\ \qquad + U_2^{(1)}(\ldots)\, \varphi_2(\alpha, \beta; \lambda, \mu) + U_3^{(1)}(\ldots)\, \varphi_3(\alpha, \beta; \lambda, \mu) + \\ \qquad + U_4^{(1)}(\ldots)\, \psi_1(\alpha, \beta; \lambda, \mu) + \cdots + U_7^{(1)}(\ldots)\, \chi_1(\alpha, \beta; \lambda, \mu) + \cdots \Big\} d\sigma = u_\sigma^{(1)}(\alpha', \beta') \\ \varphi_2(\alpha', \beta'; \lambda, \mu) + \dfrac{1}{2\pi} \displaystyle\int_\sigma \Big\{ U_1^{(2)}(\alpha, \beta; \alpha', \beta'; \lambda, \mu)\, \varphi_1(\alpha, \beta; \lambda, \mu) + \cdots \Big\} d\sigma = u_\sigma^{(2)}(\alpha', \beta') \\ \cdots\cdots\cdots \\ \psi_1(\alpha', \beta'; \lambda, \mu) + \dfrac{1}{2\pi} \displaystyle\int_\sigma \Big\{ V_1^{(1)}(\alpha, \beta; \alpha', \beta'; \lambda, \mu)\, \varphi_1(\alpha, \beta; \lambda, \mu) + \cdots \Big\} d\sigma = v_\sigma^{(1)}(\alpha', \beta') \\ \cdots\cdots\cdots \\ \cdots\cdots\cdots \end{cases}$$

con $\varphi_1, \varphi_2, \varphi_3, \psi_1, \psi_2, \psi_3, \chi_1, \chi_2, \chi_3$ funzioni incognite.

La natura delle funzioni $U_1^{(1)}(\alpha, \beta; \alpha', \beta'; \lambda, \mu), \ldots$ è tale (cfr. il § 12) che alle precedenti equazioni integrali si possono applicare i noti risultati di FREDHOLM [1]; ed allora, posto $\mu = (1 + \lambda)k$ e ragionando come ai §§ 6, 7, 8, 9 della mia citata Nota dei Lincei, si dimostra il seguente teorema: *Esiste un sistema di funzioni meromorfe di λ e di k:*

$$u^{(1)}(\xi, \eta, \zeta; \lambda, k) \ , \ u^{(2)}(\xi, \eta, \zeta; \lambda, k) \ , \ u^{(3)}(\xi, \eta, \zeta; \lambda, k) \ , \ v^{(1)}(\xi, \eta, \zeta; \lambda, k), \ldots,$$

le quali, per tutti i valori non singolari di λ e di k, sono finite e continue in tutto il campo S *(i punti di σ inclusi), hanno le derivate rispetto a ξ, η, ζ finite e continue in qualunque campo interno al campo* S, *e soddisfano alle equazioni* (11). *Nessun valore singolare di λ e di k può appartenere all'area* A, *i punti del contorno iperbolico al più esclusi.*

Questo teorema, nel caso particolare in cui le $u_\sigma^{(1)}, u_\sigma^{(2)}, u_\sigma^{(3)}$, sono rispettivamente i valori nei punti di σ delle derivate parziali del primo ordine rispetto a ξ, η, ζ di una medesima funzione, le $v_\sigma^{(1)}, v_\sigma^{(2)}, v_\sigma^{(3)}$ sono rispettivamente i valori nei punti di σ delle derivate parziali del primo ordine rispetto a ξ, η, ζ di una medesima seconda funzione, le $w_\sigma^{(1)}, w_\sigma^{(2)}, w_\sigma^{(3)}$ sono rispettivamente .... di una medesima terza funzione, ci dimostra per $\lambda = -1$ l'esistenza degli integrali regolari delle equazioni $(8)_2$; nel caso particolare in cui le $u_\sigma^{(1)}, u_\sigma^{(2)}, u_\sigma^{(3)}, v_\sigma^{(1)}, \ldots$ hanno la forma (13), ci dimostra per $\lambda = k = -1$ l'esistenza degli integrali regolari delle equazioni $(11)_1$. In questo modo *risulta dimostrata l'esistenza del sistema di integrali regolari delle equazioni* (8) *per tutti i valori non singolari di k od in particolare per i valori di k appartenenti al campo* $-1, \infty$; ed ancora *risulta dimostrata l'esistenza dell'integrale regolare delle equazioni* (1).

OSSERVAZIONE. — Le condizioni poste in principio sulla natura della superficie σ si sono introdotte per potere dimostrare il precedente teorema di esistenza relativo alle equazioni (11). Qualunque sia la superficie σ, *tutte le volte che, in un modo qualsiasi, si conoscono le formole che dànno gli integrali delle equazioni* (11), *il procedimento generale, indicato nei* §§ 2bis, 3bis, *ci dà il mezzo di risolvere il problema dell'integrazione delle equazioni* (8) *con sole quadrature, ed il procedimento generale, indicato nei* §§ 2ter, 3ter, *ci dà il mezzo di risolvere il problema dell'integrazione delle equazioni* (1) *pure con sole quadrature.*

(1) LAURICELLA, *Alcune applicazioni della teoria delle equazioni funzionali alla fisica-matematica,* Cap. III, §§ 1, 2, 3 (Nuovo Cimento, 1907).

C. SOMIGLIANA

SULLE DEFORMAZIONI ELASTICHE NON REGOLARI

I.

La teoria classica della elasticità, dopo un rigoglioso sviluppo quasi secolare, presentava ancora, fino a qualche tempo fa, una singolare lacuna. Alcuni fenomeni, che pur sono oggetto della esperienza più comune e diretta, erano sfuggiti completamente agli elasticisti teorici e sperimentali, sebbene fra questi si debbano annoverare quasi tutti i più illustri cultori della fisica-matematica del passato secolo.

I fondatori della teoria avevano avuto di mira le deformazioni prodotte nei corpi elastici da forze esterne. Spetta al prof. WEINGARTEN (1) il merito di aver richiamato l'attenzione su quegli stati di tensione in cui può trovarsi un corpo elastico senza che esso sia sottoposto all'azione di alcuna forza esterna, e che possono considerarsi come dovuti alla infiltrazione, o alla soppressione, di sottili strati di materia nell'interno del corpo stesso.

In seguito alle osservazioni del WEINGARTEN, il prof. VOLTERRA ha svolto una vasta ed elegante teoria (2), che può considerarsi come una delle più complete che ora possediamo nella statica elastica, anche pel fatto che le previsioni teoriche hanno potuto trovare delle conferme sperimentali semplici e convincenti quanto si poteva desiderare.

Tuttavia non si può dire ancora che i fatti d'osservazione abbiano con ciò trovato una rappresentazione completa. La teoria delle cosidette *distorsioni* svolta dal prof. VOLTERRA contempla le tensioni che si sviluppano in un corpo non semplicemente connesso, quando, praticato in esso un taglio che non ne interrompa la connessione, i lembi del taglio stesso subiscono spostamenti relativi rigidi, dopo i quali la continuità materiale del corpo viene ristabilita con opportuna immissione o sottrazione di materia.

Ma è ovvio pensare che, oltre questi casi, altri ne esistono, offertici dall'osservazione. Noi possiamo immaginare che i lembi del taglio, oltre che spostati rigidamente fra loro subiscano delle leggere deformazioni, come quando in un taglio prodotto

(1) WEINGARTEN, Rendiconti della R. Acc. dei Lincei, 1901, 1° Sem.
(2) VOLTERRA, Rendiconti della R. Acc. dei Lincei, 1905.

in un corpo anulare incastriamo una sottile lente a faccie curve. Ed inoltre noi possiamo immaginare incastrati, od estratti, in corpi semplicemente connessi, come una sfera od un ellissoide, dei sottili corpi lentiformi ed avere così in essi delle tensioni elastiche prodotte parimenti in assenza di forze esterne.

Ora è lecito domandare: questi fatti di così ovvia osservazione, già considerati anche dal WEINGARTEN, non sono suscettibili di uno studio che abbia qualche analogia con quello delle distorsioni del VOLTERRA? oppure la teoria della elasticità nella sua forma attuale non è ancora in grado di attaccare questi problemi?

Per rispondere a tali domande è necessario prendere in esame e discutere i punti di partenza della teoria.

L'ipotesi fondamentale che sta a base delle considerazioni del WEINGARTEN, è che le sei componenti delle tensioni interne variino con continuità da punto a punto, dopo ristabilita nel corpo la continuità materiale, così che esso possa considerarsi nelle stesse condizioni statiche di un corpo compatto. Da ciò segue che anche le sei caratteristiche della deformazione (che sono funzioni lineari indipendenti delle tensioni) debbono godere delle stesse proprietà di continuità. Le ipotesi del VOLTERRA sono più restrittive. Egli ammette:

1° la continuità delle caratteristiche della deformazione (da cui segue la continuità delle tensioni);

2° la continuità delle loro derivate prime e seconde.

Ora, per l'estensione che noi abbiamo di mira, nulla vieta di lasciare da parte questa seconda ipotesi, per la quale non è evidente una assoluta necessità meccanica. Ritorneremo così alle ipotesi del WEINGARTEN, e potremo proporci di cercare se esistono deformazioni che soddisfacciano a queste ipotesi e non a quelle del VOLTERRA. Per semplicità e chiarezza di linguaggio chiamerò *distorsioni di* VOLTERRA le deformazioni che soddisfanno alle precedenti condizioni 1ª e 2ª; *distorsioni di* WEINGARTEN quelle che soddisfanno solamente alla 1ª. Non mi propongo qui di risolvere in modo generale la quistione enunciata, ma mostrerò con un esempio, che è però di una notevole generalità, che *esistono distorsioni di* WEINGARTEN *che non sono distorsioni di* VOLTERRA.

Consideriamo un mezzo elastico isotropo indefinito, nel quale immaginiamo praticato un taglio piano σ, limitato da un contorno s. Immaginiamo poi che le due faccie del taglio vengano spostate facendo percorrere ad ogni punto un piccolo tratto lungo la normale al piano del taglio. Presi nello spazio tre assi ortogonali ξ, η, ζ, possiamo supporre che la superficie σ cada sul piano $\eta\,\zeta$; indicheremo con $U = U(\eta, \zeta)$ la distanza fra due punti corrispondenti sulla stessa normale dopo la deformazione. Possiamo allora proporci di determinare la deformazione del mezzo prodotta dalla discontinuità sopra indicata, quando si supponga che lungo il taglio, nè in alcuna altra parte del mezzo agiscano forze e quindi che le due faccie del taglio si trovino in equilibrio come due parti di uno stesso corpo che sono a contatto fra loro. Analiticamente ciò equivale a supporre che le pressioni elastiche relative agli elementi superficiali di σ variino con continuità quando passiamo da una parte all'altra di questa superficie. Un tal problema è staticamente determinato, quando si supponga che all'infinito la deformazione si annulli colle condizioni solite dei mezzi indefinitamente estesi, e che la funzione $U(\eta, \zeta)$ sia finita e continua insieme alle sue derivate prime e seconde.

Per trovare effettivamente una tale deformazione indichiamo con $\varphi = \varphi(x, y, z)$ la funzione potenziale newtoniana della superficie σ, quando sopra di essa si suppone uno strato di densità U; cioè poniamo

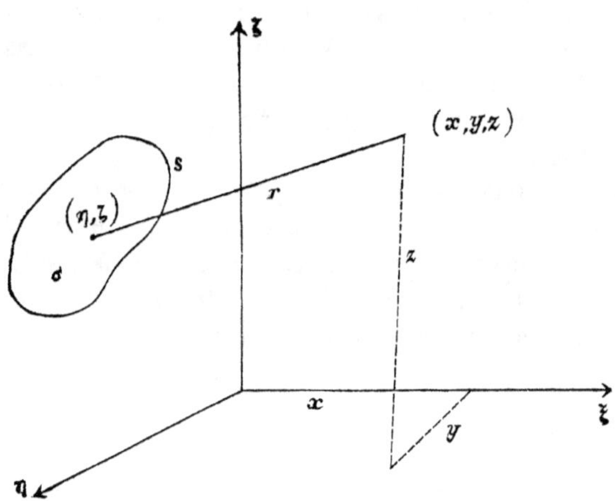

$$\varphi(x, y, z) = \int_\sigma U(\eta, \zeta) \frac{d\sigma}{r} \quad , \quad r = \sqrt{x^2 + (\eta - y)^2 + (\zeta - z)^2}. \tag{1}$$

Consideriamo poi la deformazione le cui componenti di spostamento u, v, w sono date dalle formole

$$u = \alpha x \frac{\partial^2 \varphi}{\partial x^2} + \beta \frac{\partial \varphi}{\partial x} \quad , \quad v = \alpha x \frac{\partial^2 \varphi}{\partial x \, \partial y} + \gamma \frac{\partial \varphi}{\partial y} \quad , \quad w = \alpha x \frac{\partial^2 \varphi}{\partial x \, \partial z} + \gamma \frac{\partial \varphi}{\partial z}. \tag{2}$$

Le equazioni di equilibrio

$$(\lambda + \mu) \frac{\partial \theta}{\partial (x, y, z)} + \mu \Delta_2(u, v, w) = 0$$

sono soddisfatte se fra le costanti α, β, γ sussiste la relazione

$$(\lambda + \mu)(\alpha + \beta - \gamma) + 2\mu \alpha = 0. \tag{3}$$

Indichiamo con $u'_\sigma, v'_\sigma, w'_\sigma$, e $u''_\sigma, v''_\sigma, w''_\sigma$ rispettivamente i valori delle u, v, w sulla faccia positiva e negativa di σ. Per le note proprietà delle derivate delle funzioni potenziali di superficie avremo, posto $\beta = -\frac{1}{4\pi}$,

$$(4) \qquad u'_\sigma - u''_\sigma = \mathrm{U} \quad , \quad v'_\sigma - v''_\sigma = 0 \quad , \quad w'_\sigma - w''_\sigma = 0$$

per tutti i punti di σ, escluso al più il contorno.

Le caratteristiche della deformazione (2) sono colle notazioni di KIRCHHOFF:

$$(5) \qquad \begin{aligned} x_x &= (\alpha + \beta) \frac{\partial^2\varphi}{\partial x^2} + \alpha x \frac{\partial^3\varphi}{\partial x^3} \quad , \quad y_z = 2\gamma \frac{\partial^2\varphi}{\partial y\, \partial z} + 2\alpha x \frac{\partial^3\varphi}{\partial x\, \partial y\, \partial z} \\ y_y &= \gamma \frac{\partial^2\varphi}{\partial y^2} + \alpha x \frac{\partial^3\varphi}{\partial x\, \partial y^2} \quad , \quad z_x = (\alpha + \beta + \gamma) \frac{\partial^2\varphi}{\partial x\, \partial z} + 2\alpha x \frac{\partial x^2 \partial z}{\partial^3\varphi} \frac{\partial^3\varphi}{\partial x^2 \partial z} \\ z_z &= \gamma \frac{\partial^2\varphi}{\partial z^2} + \alpha x \frac{\partial^3\varphi}{\partial x\, \partial z^2} \quad , \quad x_y = (\alpha + \beta + \gamma) \frac{\partial^3\varphi}{\partial x^2 \partial y} + 2\alpha x \frac{\partial^3\varphi}{\partial x^2 \partial y} \end{aligned}$$

e per le componenti delle tensioni relative ad elemento normale all'asse ξ, abbiamo

$$(6) \qquad \begin{aligned} \mathrm{X}_x &= \lambda\theta + 2\mu x_x = [(\lambda + 2\mu)(\alpha + \beta) - \lambda\gamma] \frac{\partial^2\varphi}{\partial x^2} + 2\mu\alpha x \frac{\partial^3\varphi}{\partial x^3} \\ \mathrm{Y}_x &= \mu y_x = \mu(\alpha + \beta + \gamma) \frac{\partial^2\varphi}{\partial x\, \partial y} + 2\mu\alpha x \frac{\partial^3\varphi}{\partial x^2 \partial y} \\ \mathrm{Z}_x &= \mu z_x = \mu(\alpha + \beta + \gamma) \frac{\partial^2\varphi}{\partial x\, \partial z} + 2\mu\alpha x \frac{\partial^3\varphi}{\partial x^2 \partial z} . \end{aligned}$$

Queste tre espressioni devono essere continue attraverso il pezzo di superficie σ. Ma per poter stabilire le condizioni di tale continuità, determineremo prima, col metodo NEUMANN-BELTRAMI, le discontinuità delle derivate della funzione potenziale φ sulla superficie attraente σ.

Indicando con ν la normale interna al contorno s di σ, si ha

$$(7) \qquad \begin{aligned} \frac{\partial\varphi}{\partial y} &= \int_s \mathrm{U} \frac{\partial\eta}{\partial\nu} \frac{ds}{r} + \int_\sigma \frac{\partial \mathrm{U}}{\partial\eta} \frac{\partial\sigma}{r} \\ \frac{\partial\varphi}{\partial z} &= \int_s \mathrm{U} \frac{\partial\zeta}{\partial\nu} \frac{ds}{r} + \int_\sigma \frac{\partial \mathrm{U}}{\partial\zeta} \frac{\partial\sigma}{r} \end{aligned}$$

da cui appare la continuità delle derivate tangenziali, escluso al più il contorno. Inoltre analogamente si trova

$$(8) \qquad \begin{aligned} \frac{\partial^2\varphi}{\partial y^2} &= \int_s \mathrm{U} \frac{\partial \frac{1}{r}}{\partial y} \frac{\partial y}{\partial\nu} ds + \int_s \frac{\partial \mathrm{U}}{\partial y} \frac{d\eta}{\partial\nu} \frac{ds}{r} + \int_\sigma \frac{\partial^2 \mathrm{U}}{\partial\eta^2} \frac{d\sigma}{r} \\ \frac{\partial^2\varphi}{\partial y\, \partial z} &= \int_s \mathrm{U} \frac{\partial \frac{1}{r}}{\partial z} \frac{\partial\eta}{\partial\nu} ds + \int_s \frac{\partial \mathrm{U}}{\partial\eta} \frac{\partial\zeta}{\partial\nu} \frac{ds}{r} + \int_\sigma \frac{\partial^2 \mathrm{U}}{\partial\eta\, \partial\zeta} \frac{d\sigma}{r} \\ \frac{\partial^2\varphi}{\partial z^2} &= \int_s \mathrm{U} \frac{\partial \frac{1}{r}}{\partial z} \frac{\partial\zeta}{\partial\nu} ds + \int_s \frac{\partial \mathrm{U}}{\partial\xi} \frac{\partial\xi}{\partial\nu} \frac{ds}{r} + \int_\sigma \frac{\partial^2 \mathrm{U}}{\partial\zeta^2} \frac{d\sigma}{r} \end{aligned}$$

da cui appare la continuità di queste tre derivate seconde e quindi anche della $\frac{\partial^2\varphi}{\partial x^2}$ a cagione della relazione

$$\frac{\partial^2\varphi}{\partial x^2}=-\frac{\partial^2\varphi}{\partial y^2}-\frac{\partial^2\varphi}{\partial z^2} \tag{9}$$

mentre dalle (7) risulta la discontinuità delle $\frac{\partial^2\varphi}{\partial x\,\partial y}$, $\frac{\partial^2\varphi}{\partial x\,\partial z}$, per le quali sopra σ avremo

$$\begin{aligned}\left(\frac{\partial^2\varphi}{\partial x\,\partial y}\right)'_\sigma-\left(\frac{\partial^2\varphi}{\partial x\,\partial z}\right)''_\sigma&=-4\pi\frac{\partial U}{\partial y}\\ \left(\frac{\partial^2\varphi}{\partial x\,\partial z}\right)'_\sigma-\left(\frac{\partial^2\varphi}{\partial x\,\partial z}\right)''_\sigma&=-4\pi\frac{\partial U}{\partial z}.\end{aligned} \tag{10}$$

Procedendo in tal modo per determinare le discontinuità delle derivate di qualsiasi ordine, si vede facilmente che il risultato finale è il seguente: *Le derivate che contengono un numero pari di derivazioni rispetto ad x, ossia rispetto alla normale alla superficie attraente σ, sono continue, quelle che ne contengono un numero dispari sono discontinue.*

Così dalle formole (8) si ricava

$$\begin{aligned}\left(\frac{\partial^3\varphi}{\partial y^2\partial x}\right)'_\sigma-\left(\frac{\partial^3\varphi}{\partial y^2\partial x}\right)''_\sigma&=-4\pi\frac{\partial^2 U}{\partial y^2}\\ \left(\frac{\partial^2\varphi}{\partial x\,\partial y\,\partial z}\right)'_\sigma-\left(\frac{\partial^3\varphi}{\partial x\,\partial y\,\partial z}\right)''_\sigma&=-4\pi\frac{\partial^2 U}{\partial y\,\partial z}\\ \left(\frac{\partial^3\varphi}{\partial z^2\partial x}\right)'_\sigma-\left(\frac{\partial^3\varphi}{\partial z^2\partial x}\right)''_\sigma&=-4\pi\frac{\partial^2 U}{\partial z^2}\end{aligned} \tag{11}$$

e dalla (9)

$$\left(\frac{\partial^3\varphi}{\partial x^3}\right)'_\sigma-\left(\frac{\partial^3\varphi}{\partial x^3}\right)''_\sigma=4\pi\left(\frac{\partial^2 U}{\partial y^2}+\frac{\partial^2 U}{\partial z^2}\right).$$

Da questi risultati deriva che per la continuità delle X_x, Y_x, Z_x date dalle (6) è necessario e sufficiente che sia

$$\alpha+\beta+\gamma=0. \tag{3''}$$

Le tre costanti α,β,γ che entrano nelle (1) sono così completamente determinate dalle (3) (3′) (3″) e si ha

$$\alpha=\frac{1}{4\pi}\,\frac{\lambda+\mu}{\lambda+2\mu}\quad,\quad\beta=-\frac{1}{4\pi}\quad,\quad\gamma=\frac{1}{4\pi}\,\frac{\mu}{\lambda+2\mu}.$$

Con ciò il problema proposto è risoluto.

Ma la soluzione trovata soddisfa certe condizioni che non sono implicite nei dati del problema. Difatti la condizione (3″) $\alpha+\beta+\gamma=0$ è sufficiente anche per stabilire *la continuità attraverso* σ *di tutte le sei caratteristiche della deformazione*, come risulta dalle (5) e dalle proprietà trovate circa la discontinuità delle derivate seconde dalla φ. Sono perciò continue anche le sei componenti delle tensioni, e quindi possiamo concludere che:

La deformazione considerata è una distorsione di WEINGARTEN.

Le proprietà trovate per le derivate terze della φ ci permettono di assegnare il modo di comportarsi delle derivate delle $x_x, y_y, \ldots x_y$. Si trova così che le x_z, x_y hanno le loro tre derivate continue; e che le altre quattro caratteristiche x_x, y_y, z_z, y_z hanno continue le derivate rispetto ad y e z, cioè le derivate tangenziali, ma discontinue quelle rispetto ad x, cioè le normali. Proprietà analoghe si hanno per le sei componenti di pressione. A cagione di queste discontinuità possiamo concludere che la deformazione considerata *non è una distorsione di* VOLTERRA.

È facile vedere quali siano le conseguenze di questi risultati dal punto di vista della teoria delle deformazioni prodotte in assenza di forze esterne. Se noi consideriamo un corpo non semplicemente connesso, ed in esso praticati dei tagli piani che non ne interrompano la connessione, noi potremo deformare e allontanare i lembi del taglio con spostamenti arbitrari lungo la normale al piano del taglio, poi ristabilire la continuità materiale con opportune aggiunte o soppressioni di materia, ed ottenere così un corpo in istato di tensione senza che su di esso agiscano forze, come quelli considerati dal WEINGARTEN. Inoltre lo studio della distribuzione delle tensioni e degli spostamenti necessari a ricondurlo allo stato naturale, si potrà fare in modo analogo a quello indicato dal VOLTERRA pel caso delle sue distorsioni.

Difatti se in un corpo di forma identica a quello considerato, fissata in modo qualsiasi la sezione piana σ, si immagina la deformazione rappresentata dalle formole (1), questa darà luogo a tensioni superficiali finite e continue. Quindi sovrapponendo a tale deformazione quella *regolare*, a cui corrispondano tensioni superficiali uguali e contrarie alle precedenti, si otterrà una deformazione compatibile colle condizioni di equilibrio per forze esterne tutte nulle. Il problema delle distorsioni della specie considerata in corpi di dimensioni finite e non semplicemente connessi è così ricondotto, come nei casi di VOLTERRA, ad un problema della statica ordinaria.

Ma importa ora di notare che tali distorsioni sono possibili anche *in corpi semplicemente connessi*. Infatti il teorema di VOLTERRA, secondo il quale non sono possibili deformazioni a spostamenti discontinui in corpi semplicemente connessi, cessa di essere valido a cagione delle discontinuità che si verificano nelle derivate prime delle caratteristiche della deformazione sopra la σ. Nulla quindi impedisce di considerare queste distorsioni prodotte in corpi semplicemente connessi con tagli che non ne interrompano la connessione.

Una sola difficoltà si presenta in questi casi. A differenza di quanto avviene nei corpi a connessione multipla, in questi casi il contorno dei tagli è sempre, almeno in parte, contenuto nell'interno del corpo. Ora le derivate della funzione φ, che compaiono nelle nostre formole, possono sul contorno s di φ presentare degli infiniti, come risulta dalle formole (7), (8), ecc. Però da queste stesse formole appare che supponendo nulla sul contorno s la funzione U, e le sue derivate, vengono a scomparire quegli integrali di contorno, a cui appunto sono dovuti gli infiniti.

Segue da ciò che per evitare la comparsa degli infiniti, basta aggiungere la condizione che la funzione U, che rappresenta la discontinuità normale dello spostamento, sia nulla sul contorno del taglio (od almeno su quella parte del contorno che è interna al corpo) insieme alle derivate di alcuni dei primi ordini. Quando la discontinuità sia prodotta dalla introduzione di un sottile corpo esterno, questa condizione ha un'interpretazione assai semplice: *questo corpo esterno dovrà essere a bordo tagliente, come un filo di rasoio*. Ogni sua sezione normale al contorno dovrà presentare una specie di cuspide. Dal punto di vista analitico basterà supporre che la funzione U sia della forma

$$U = [f(\eta, \zeta)]^n \, U_1(\eta\zeta)$$

se $f(\eta, \zeta) = 0$ rappresenta la linea di contorno che è interna al corpo, ed n un numero abbastanza grande.

Passiamo ora ad un'altra quistione. Si è visto come siano possibili distorsioni di Weingarten dovute a spostamenti *normali* al piano del taglio. Cerchiamo ora se sono possibili distorsioni della stessa specie prodotte da spostamenti *tangenziali*.

Supponiamo che gli spostamenti avvengano nella direzione delle η, il che non è una restrinzione. Indichiamo con $V = V(\eta, \zeta)$ la discontinuità di spostamento. Dovranno sussistere in questo caso sulla superficie σ le relazioni

$$(12) \qquad u'_\sigma - u''_\sigma = 0 \ , \quad v'_\sigma - v''_\sigma = V \ , \quad w'_\sigma - w''_\sigma = 0 .$$

Noi possiamo risolvere in questo caso il problema analogo a quello precedentemente considerato, ponendo

$$(13) \qquad u = \alpha x \frac{\partial^2 \psi}{\partial x \, \partial y} + \beta \frac{\partial \psi}{\partial y} \ , \quad v = \alpha x \frac{\partial^2 \psi}{\partial y^2} + \gamma \frac{\partial \psi}{\partial x} \ , \quad w = \alpha x \frac{\partial^2 \psi}{\partial y \, \partial z}$$

ove

$$\psi = \int_\sigma V \frac{d\sigma}{r} .$$

Le equazioni di equilibrio sono soddisfatte se

$$(14) \qquad (\alpha + \beta + \gamma)(\lambda + \mu) + 2\alpha\mu = 0$$

e le (12) sono pure verificate se

$$(14') \qquad \gamma = -\frac{1}{4\pi} .$$

Per le caratteristiche della deformazione troviamo

$$(15) \qquad \begin{aligned} x_x &= (\alpha + \beta) \frac{\partial^2 \psi}{\partial x \, \partial y} + \alpha x \frac{\partial^3 \psi}{\partial x^2 \partial y} \ , & y_z &= \gamma \frac{\partial^2 \psi}{\partial x \, \partial z} + 2\alpha x \frac{\partial^3 \psi}{\partial y^2 \partial z} \\ y_y &= \gamma \frac{\partial^2 \psi}{\partial x \, \partial y} + \alpha x \frac{\partial^3 \psi}{\partial y^3} \ , & z_x &= (\alpha + \beta) \frac{\partial^2 \psi}{\partial y \, \partial z} + 2\alpha x \frac{\partial^3 \psi}{\partial x \, \partial y \, \partial z} \\ z_z &= \alpha x \frac{\partial^2 \psi}{\partial y \, \partial z^2} \ , & x_y &= (\alpha + \beta) \frac{\partial^2 \psi}{\partial y^2} + \gamma \frac{\partial^2 \psi}{\partial x^2} + 2\alpha x \frac{\partial^3 \psi}{\partial x \partial y^2} \end{aligned}$$

e per le componenti della tensione sopra un elemento normale a ξ

$$X_x = [(\lambda + 2\mu)(\alpha + \beta) + \lambda\gamma] \frac{\partial^2 \psi}{\partial x \, \partial y} + 2\mu\alpha x \frac{\partial^3 \psi}{\partial x^2 \, \partial y}$$

$$Y_x = \mu(\alpha + \beta) \frac{\partial^2 \psi}{\partial y^2} + \mu\gamma \frac{\partial^2 \psi}{\partial x^2} + 2\mu\alpha x \frac{\partial^3 \psi}{\partial x \, \partial y^2}$$

$$Z_x = \mu(\alpha + \beta) \frac{\partial^2 \psi}{\partial y \, \partial z} + 2\alpha\mu x \frac{\partial^3 \psi}{\partial x \, \partial y \, \partial z}.$$

Sulle due faccie della superficie σ risulta da queste formole che Y_x, Z_x hanno valori uguali, e perchè risulti continua anche X_x, dovremo porre

$$(14'') \qquad (\lambda + 2\mu)(\alpha + \beta) + \lambda\gamma = 0.$$

Queste relazioni (14) (14') (14'') determinano le costanti α, β, γ e ci dànno

$$\alpha = \frac{1}{4\pi} \frac{\lambda + \mu}{\lambda + 2\mu}, \quad \beta = -\frac{1}{4\pi} \frac{\mu}{\lambda + 2\mu}, \quad \gamma = -\frac{1}{4\pi}.$$

Con ciò il problema proposto è risoluto. Ma in questo caso la deformazione non è più in generale, come nel caso precedente, una *distorsione di* Weinngarten, poichè le x_x, y_y, z_z risultano discontinue attraversando la superficie σ. Queste discontinuità sono dovute alle discontinuità delle derivate $\frac{\partial^2 \psi}{\partial x \, \partial y}, \frac{\partial^2 \psi}{\partial x \, \partial z}$, discontinuità le quali si annullano solo quando V è una costante, come risulta dalle (10). Ma in questo caso la deformazione diviene una *distorsione di* VOLTERRA, poichè gli spostamenti tangenziali relativi sopra σ sono rigidi. Siamo quindi in un caso noto.

Considerazioni perfettamente analoghe si possono fare per spostamenti tangenziali paralleli all'asse ζ. Ora se osserviamo che uno spostamento qualsiasi può sempre decomporsi in uno spostamento normale ed in uno tangenziale, e che perciò qualunque distorsione di WEINGARTEN relativa ad un taglio piano deve essere compresa fra le deformazioni che si ottengono sovrapponendo le due categorie speciali di deformazioni che abbiamo considerato, possiamo concludere che:

Le distorsioni di WEINGARTEN *relative ad un taglio piano non sono altro che le deformazioni prodotte, in assenza di forze esterne, da spostamenti normali arbitrari variabili da punto a punto lungo i lembi del taglio; alle quali naturalmente si può sempre aggiungere una qualsiasi distorsione di* VOLTERRA.

Con ciò si può considerare come esaurita la quistione delle distorsioni relative a tagli piani.

II.

Dal punto di vista analitico la teoria delle distorsioni può considerarsi come la teoria delle deformazioni elastiche, nelle quali le componenti u, v, w dello spostamento non sono funzioni regolari nell'interno del corpo, ma presentano delle discontinuità, le quali portano alla possibilità di uno stato di tensione elastica in assenza di forze esterne. Ma, oltre le discontinuità, esistono altre singolarità per le u, v, w o per le loro derivate, le quali parimenti possono produrre stati di tensione compatibili coll'assenza di qualsiasi forza esterna.

Il prof. MORERA in una Nota pubblicata lo scorso anno negli Atti della R. Accademia delle Scienze di Torino [1] ha richiamato l'attenzione su quelle distribuzioni di tensioni elastiche, le quali in un punto isolato del corpo (o anche lungo una linea) diventano infinitamente grandi, mentre secondo il concetto di STOKES e THOMSON di forza agente in un punto, esse non dànno luogo ad alcuna forza o ad alcun momento risultante. Vi è anche la possibilità di una interpretazione fisica di questi stati di tensione. Le cosidette *lagrime di Batavia* si trovano in uno stato di tensione che non è dovuto ad alcuna forza esterna (quando si faccia astrazione dalla pressione atmosferica) e che può essere spiegato coll'esistenza di uno o più centri di pressione, i quali fanno sì che il ritorno del corpo allo stato naturale non sia possibile che colla completa disgregazione di esso. La violenta esplosione delle lagrime allorchè si produce la rottura della cosidetta *coda* è una appariscente conferma di questo stato di tensione.

Ora è possibile costruire un esempio teorico di un corpo, il quale si trova in uno stato di tensione della natura indicata.

Consideriamo la deformazione rappresentata dalle formole

$$(1)\qquad u = -\frac{\partial \frac{1}{r}}{\partial x}\,,\quad v = -\frac{\partial \frac{1}{r}}{\partial y}\,,\quad w = -\frac{\partial \frac{1}{r}}{\partial z}$$

ove r rappresenta la distanza da un punto, che possiamo supporre sia l'origine delle coordinate. Questa deformazione ha un punto isolato di singolarità in $r = 0$, ma all'infuori di questo punto, essa è compatibile colle equazioni generali dell'equilibrio in mancanza di forze di massa. Le tensioni a cui essa dà luogo sono

$$(2)\qquad \begin{aligned} X_x &= -2\mu \frac{\partial^2 \frac{1}{r}}{\partial x^2}\,, & Y_z &= -2\mu \frac{\partial^2 \frac{1}{r}}{\partial y\,\partial z} \\ Y_y &= -2\mu \frac{\partial^2 \frac{1}{r}}{\partial y^2}\,, & Z_x &= -2\mu \frac{\partial^2 \frac{1}{r}}{\partial z\,\partial x} \\ Z_z &= -2\mu \frac{\partial^2 \frac{1}{r}}{\partial z^2}\,, & X_y &= -2\mu \frac{\partial^2 \frac{1}{r}}{\partial x\,\partial y}\,. \end{aligned}$$

Di qui risulta che un elemento superficiale di normale n è soggetto ad una tensione le cui componenti sono

$$(3)\qquad X_n = -2\mu \frac{\partial}{\partial n}\frac{\partial \frac{1}{r}}{\partial x}\,,\quad Y_n = -2\mu \frac{\partial}{\partial n}\frac{\partial \frac{1}{r}}{\partial y}\,,\quad Z_n = -2\mu \frac{\partial}{\partial n}\frac{\partial \frac{1}{r}}{\partial z}\,.$$

[1] MORERA, *Intorno all'equilibrio dei corpi elastici isotropi* (1907, §§ 5-6).

Se supponiamo che l'elemento appartenga ad una sfera col centro in $r=0$, e con un raggio r, sarà

$$(4)\qquad X_r = -\frac{4\mu}{r^3}\cos(rx)\ ,\ Y_r = -\frac{4\mu}{r^3}\cos(ry)\ ,\ Z_r = -\frac{4\mu}{r^3}\cos(rz)\,.$$

Di qui appare che considerando una sfera piccolissima σ col centro nel centro di pressione, si ha

$$\int_\sigma X_r\,d\sigma = \int_\sigma Y_r\,d\sigma = \int_\sigma Z_r\,d\sigma = 0$$

$$\int_\sigma (Y_r z - Z_r y)\,d\sigma = \int_\sigma (Z_r x - X_r z)\,d\sigma = \int_\sigma (X_r y - Y_r x)\,d\sigma = 0$$

cioè, sebbene queste pressioni divengano infinitamente grandi avvicinandosi al centro di pressione, esse non producono alcuna azione o momento risultante [1].

Se ora immaginiamo un corpo qualsiasi di dimensioni finite nel quale avvenga la deformazione (1), essendo interno ad esso il centro di pressione, le tensioni elastiche corrispondenti saranno finite e continue sulla superficie s del corpo. Noi potremo quindi stabilire l'equilibrio sia applicando alla superficie delle forze che neutralizzino queste tensioni, sia sottoponendo il corpo ad una seconda deformazione *regolare* che produca in superficie tensioni uguali e contrarie. Questo secondo procedimento è analogo a quello considerato nel caso delle distorsioni ed usato da VOLTERRA. Esso ci mostra che colla sovrapposizione di queste due deformazioni è possibile ottenere quello stato di tensione in assenza di forze esterne e dovuto alla presenza di un centro di dilatazione o di pressione, al quale abbiamo accennato da principio.

È quasi superfluo indicare che queste considerazioni valgono qualunque sia la forma del corpo e che si possono estendere al caso di un numero qualunque di centri di pressione. Importa invece vedere un caso in cui si può molto facilmente avere una rappresentazione completa di una tale distribuzione di tensioni.

Supponiamo che il corpo sia una sfera di raggio R e che il centro di dilatazione sia nel centro della sfera. In questo caso le (4) ci mostrano che ogni elemento posto sulla superficie della sfera è soggetto ad una tensione le cui componenti sono

$$(5)\qquad X_r = -\frac{4\mu}{R^3}\cos(rx)\ ,\ Y_r = -\frac{4\mu}{R^3}\cos(ry)\ ,\ Z_r = -\frac{4\mu}{R^3}\cos(rz)\,.$$

Se ora supponiamo la sfera sottoposta ad una dilatazione uniforme

$$(6)\qquad u = \alpha x\ ,\ v = \alpha y\ ,\ x = \alpha z$$

[1] Anche il Sig. LOVE nella Memoria: *The propagation of wav-motion in isotropic elastic solid medium,* considerando il moto vibratorio di forma analoga alla deformazione (1), osserva che le pressioni in vicinanza del centro di dilatazione *have no statical resultant or moment.*

ove α è una costante, ogni elemento di normale n sarà soggetto ad una tensione di componenti

$$X_n = (3\lambda + 2\mu)\, \alpha \cos(nx)$$
$$Y_n = (3\lambda + 2\mu)\, \alpha \cos(ny)$$
$$Z_n = (3\lambda + 2\mu)\, \alpha \cos(nz)\,.$$

Perciò, se determiniamo α in modo che sia

$$(7) \qquad -\frac{4\mu}{R^3} + (3\lambda + 3\mu)\, \alpha = 0$$

gli elementi superficiali della sfera si troveranno soggetti a tensioni nulle, ed avremo l'esempio cercato di un corpo avente nel suo interno un centro di pressione e che si trova in equilibrio senza che ad esso siano applicate forze esterne.

Giova studiare con qualche precisione le particolarità della deformazione ottenuta. Sommando le deformazioni (1) (6) e mettendo per α il valore determinato dalla (7), si trova che tale deformazione è una *dilatazione*, in cui ogni punto subisce spostamenti radiali. Questi sono dati dalla formola

$$(8) \qquad s_r = \frac{1}{r^2} + \frac{4\mu}{3\lambda + 2\mu}\, \frac{r}{R^3}\,.$$

Il coefficiente di dilatazione cubica è costante ed uguale a $\dfrac{12\mu}{3\lambda + 2\mu}$.

Le componenti della tensione corrispondente ad un elemento di normale n

$$X_n = -\, 2\mu \frac{\partial}{\partial n} \frac{\partial \frac{1}{r}}{\partial x} + \frac{4\mu}{R^3} \cos(nx)\,, \ldots$$

si possono porre sotto la forma:

$$(9) \qquad \begin{aligned} X_n &= 2\mu \left(\frac{1}{r^3} + \frac{2}{R^3}\right) \cos(nx) - \frac{6\mu}{r^3} \cos(rx) \cos(rn) \\ Y_n &= 2\mu \left(\frac{1}{r^3} + \frac{2}{R^3}\right) \cos(ny) - \frac{6\mu}{r^3} \cos(ry) \cos(rn) \\ Z_n &= 2\mu \left(\frac{1}{r^3} + \frac{2}{R^3}\right) \cos(nz) - \frac{6\mu}{r^3} \cos(rz) \cos(rn)\,. \end{aligned}$$

Se consideriamo un elemento superficiale normale al raggio, si ha $\cos(rn) = 1$, quindi

$$X_r = -\, 4\mu \left(\frac{1}{r^3} - \frac{1}{R^3}\right) \cos(rx)$$
$$Y_r = -\, 4\mu \left(\frac{1}{r^3} - \frac{1}{R^3}\right) \cos(ry)$$
$$Z_r = -\, 4\mu \left(\frac{1}{r^3} - \frac{1}{R^3}\right) \cos(rz)\,.$$

Considerando invece un elemento passante pel raggio, si ha $\cos(rn) = 0$, e se s è la normale

$$X_s = -2\mu\left(\frac{1}{r^3} + \frac{2}{R^3}\right)\cos(sx)$$

$$Y_s = -2\mu\left(\frac{1}{r^3} + \frac{2}{R^3}\right)\cos(sy)$$

$$Z_s = -2\mu\left(\frac{1}{r^3} + \frac{2}{R^3}\right)\cos(sz).$$

Per cui, sia in un caso che nell'altro, l'elemento è soggetto ad una tensione normale, che nel primo caso è negativa e data da

$$T_r = -4\mu\left(\frac{1}{r^3} - \frac{1}{R^3}\right),$$

nel secondo positiva

$$T_s = 2\mu\left(\frac{1}{r^3} + \frac{1}{R^3}\right).$$

Sulla superficie della sfera abbiamo

$$T_r = 0 \quad , \quad T_s = \frac{6\mu}{R^3}$$

cioè: *la superficie esterna è uniformemente tesa come una membrana.*

Dalle (9) risulta che ogni elemento può considerarsi come soggetto a due tensioni, di cui l'una T'_r diretta secondo il raggio è data da

$$T'_r = -\frac{6\mu}{r^3}\cos(nr)$$

l'altra, diretta secondo la normale, è data da

$$T'_n = 2\mu\left(\frac{1}{r^3} + \frac{2}{R^3}\right).$$

La relazione

$$T'_n + T'_r\cos(nr) = 0$$

ci determina le normali n di elementi soggetti a pressione normale nulla, cioè tesi soltanto tangenzialmente. Questa relazione ci dà

$$\operatorname{tang}(rn) = \sqrt{\frac{2(R^3 - r^3)}{R^3 + 2r^3}}$$

Quindi in ogni punto della sfera gli elementi soggetti a sola tensione tangenziale inviluppano un cono la cui apertura θ_r rispetto al raggio è determinata dalla formola

$$\operatorname{tang}\theta_r = \sqrt{\frac{R^3 + 2r^3}{2(R^3 - r^3)}}$$

Al centro

$$\operatorname{tang}\theta_0 = \frac{1}{\sqrt{2}}\ , \quad \theta_0 = 35^\circ.15' .$$

Il coefficiente $\frac{4\mu}{3\lambda + 2\mu}$ che compare nella espressione (8) degli spostamenti dipende unicamente dal coefficiente di Poisson e si ha, indicando con σ questo coefficiente,

$$\frac{4\mu}{3\lambda + 2\mu} = \frac{2}{1 + \sigma} .$$

Pel vetro σ è compreso fra 0,245 e 0,258 (Love, *Lehrbuch der Elasticität*, pag. 125).

M. ABRAHAM

ZUR THEORIE DER WIRBELSTROMBREMSEN

Auch in den Kreisen der Elektrotechniker beginnt man jetzt, die Vorzüge der MAXWELL'schen Theorie zu würdigen. Die einheitliche Darstellung des Gesamtfeldes erweist sich meist als zweckmässiger, als die künstlichen Zerlegungen, welche man früher vorzunehmen pflegte. Besonders wichtig für die Elektrotechnik sind die Probleme, die sich auf die durch Bewegung erzeugten Wirbelströme in Metallen beziehen. Bei der Behandlung dieser Probleme kann man sich auf den Boden der HERTZ'schen Elektrodynamik bewegter Körper stellen; denn in den Metallen kommt der Verschiebungsstrom nicht in Betracht, und damit fallen die Unterschiede hinsichtlich des Verschiebungsstromes in bewegten Körpern fort, welche die HERTZ'sche Theorie von der LORENTZ'schen trennen.

Ein in diesem Gebiete liegendes Problem ist das der *massiven Wirbelstrombremse*:

Unterhalb eines Systemes von Magnetpolen, die im Abstand τ auf einander folgen, bewegt sich der Bremskörper (s. Figur): dieser erstreckt sich im Sinne der

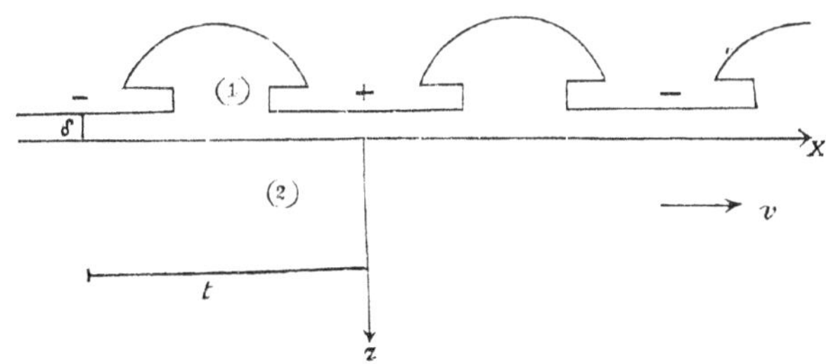

positiven z-Achse so weit, dass der Einfluss der dortigen Begrenzung nicht in Betracht kommt. Dieses Problem befindet sich unter denen, die R. RUEDENBERG in seiner lehrreichen Schrift: *Energie der Wirbelströme in elektrischen Bremsen und Dynamomaschinen* (Stuttgart, F. Enke, 1906) behandelt.

Die von RUEDENBERG angewandte Methode bedeutet gerade im Sinne der Annäherung an die MAXWELL'sche Theorie einen Fortschritt; dennoch kann man, wie mir scheint, gerade in dieser Richtung noch wesentlich weiter gehen, und durch consequente Verwendung der Differentialgleichungen und der Grenzbedingungen der MAXWELL-HERTZ'schen Theorie eine Vereinfachung und Verallgemeinerung der Problemstellung erzielen.

Als gegeben denke ich mir die zur Oberfläche des Bremskörpers parallele magnetische Feldkomponente an der gegenüberliegenden Begrenzungsebene des Luftspaltes ($z = -\delta$)

(1) $$\{\mathfrak{G}_{1x}\}_{z=-\delta} = \sum_{1=1}^{\infty} -i\, A_n\, e^{in\alpha x} \; ; \; \alpha = \frac{\pi}{\tau} \, .$$

Aus der ersten Hauptgleichung folgt, an der Grenzebene ($z = 0$) des Bremskörpers selbst, für die magnetischen Komponenten eine Beziehung, die man, wenn $\delta\alpha$ klein ist, schreiben kann

(2) $$\{\mathfrak{G}_{1x}\}_{z=0} - \delta \left\{ \frac{\partial \mathfrak{G}_{1z}}{\partial x} \right\}_{z=0} = \{\mathfrak{G}_{1x}\}_{z=-\delta} \, .$$

Die Oberfläche des Bremskörpers spielt die Rolle einer Gleitfläche: da sie von magnetischem Induktionsfluss durchsetzt wird, so besitzen, gemäss der HERTZ'schen Elektrodynamik bewegter Körper, die tangentiellen elektrischen Feldkomponenten dort eine Unstetigkeit:

(3) $$\mathfrak{f}_{1y} - \mathfrak{f}_{2y} = v\, \mathfrak{L}_z \, .$$

Im Innern des Bremskörpers, also für $z > 0$, gelten die Differentialgleichungen (σ Leitfähigkeit in abs. elm. Maass)

(I) $$\operatorname{curl} \mathfrak{G} = 4\pi \mathfrak{i} = 4\pi\sigma \mathfrak{f} \, ,$$

(II) $$\operatorname{curl} \mathfrak{f} = -\frac{\partial \mathfrak{L}}{\partial t} - \operatorname{curl} [\mathfrak{L}\, \mathfrak{v}] \, ,$$

(III) $$\operatorname{div} \mathfrak{L} = \operatorname{div} \mu \mathfrak{G} = 0 \, .$$

Ist, wie wir annehmen wollen, der Vektor $\mathfrak{L}$ der (x, z)-Ebene parallel, so wird (III) gelöst durch

(4) $$\mathfrak{L}_x = \mu \mathfrak{G}_x = -\frac{\partial \psi}{\partial z} \, , \qquad \mathfrak{L}_z = \mu \mathfrak{G}_z = \frac{\partial \psi}{\partial x} \, .$$

Da $\mathfrak{v}$ der x-Achse parallel ist, so ist das äussere Produkt von $\mathfrak{L}$ und $\mathfrak{v}$ der

y-Achse parallel, und es wird (II) für den stationären Zustand $\left(\frac{\partial}{\partial t}=0\right)$ gelöst durch:

(5) $$\mathfrak{f}_y = -[\mathfrak{L}\mathfrak{v}]_y = -v\,\mathrm{L}_z\ ,\ \mathfrak{f}_x = \mathfrak{f}_z = 0\,.$$

Demnach folgt, für die Stromfunktion ψ, aus I die partielle Differentialgleichung:

(6) $$\frac{\partial^2\psi}{\partial z^2}+\frac{\partial^2\psi}{\partial x^2}-\eta\frac{\partial\psi}{\partial x}=0\ ,\ \eta=4\pi v\sigma\mu.$$

Durch (5) wird auch die Grenzbedingung (3) erfüllt, ohne dass man in Luftspalt ein elektrisches Feld anzunehmen hat:

$$\mathfrak{f}_1 = 0\,.$$

Dadurch vereinfacht sich hier die Behandlung wesentlich; die Grenzbedingungen des magnetischen Feldes ergeben jetzt:

(7) $$\{\mathfrak{G}_{1x}\}_{z=0} = -\frac{1}{\mu}\left\{\frac{\partial\psi}{\partial z}\right\}_{z=0}\quad ;\quad \{\mathfrak{G}_{1z}\}_{z=0} = \frac{1}{\mu}\left\{\frac{\partial\psi}{\partial x}\right\}_{z=0}$$

Somit folgt aus (2) und (1) für ψ die Grenzbedingung:

(8) $$\frac{1}{\mu}\left\{\frac{\partial\psi}{\partial z}\right\}_{z=0}+\delta\left\{\frac{\partial^2\psi}{\partial x^2}\right\}_{z=0} = -\{\mathfrak{G}_{1x}\}_{z=0} = \sum_{n=1}^{\infty} i\mathrm{A}_n\, e^{inax}\,.$$

Durch den complexen Ansatz

(9) $$\psi=\sum_{n=1}^{\infty}\frac{\mathrm{B}_n}{i\alpha n}\,e^{i\alpha nx}\,.\,e^{-r_n\alpha nz}$$

können wir (6) und (8) genügen.

Für die complexe Grösse $r_n = k_n + i\lambda_n$ folgt aus (6)

(10) $$r_n^2 = k_n^2-\lambda_n^2+2ik_n\lambda_n = 1+i\zeta_n\,,$$
$$\zeta_n=\frac{\eta}{\alpha n}=\frac{4\pi v\sigma\mu}{\alpha n}\,,$$

so dass für k_n, λ_n die positiven Wurzeln der complexen Ausdrücke zu setzen sind:

(10 a) $$k_n^2=\tfrac{1}{2}\left\{1+\sqrt{1+\zeta_n^2}\right\},$$

(10 b) $$\lambda_n^2=\tfrac{1}{2}\left\{-1+\sqrt{1+\zeta_n^2}\right\}.$$

Die Grenzbedingung (8) ergibt sodann

$$\text{(11)} \qquad B_n = A_n \cdot \frac{\mu}{k_n + \delta \alpha \mu n + i \lambda_n} .$$

Die complexen Coeffizienten B_n sind massgebend für die Reihenentwicklung des Ausdrucks der zur Oberfläche des Bremskörpers senkrechten Komponente der magnetischen Induktion; denn aus (4) und (9) folgt:

$$\text{(12)} \qquad \left\{ \mathfrak{L}_z \right\}_{z=0} = \sum_{n=1}^{\infty} B_n \cdot e^{i\alpha n x} .$$

Die Gleichung (11) lehrt den Zusammenhang kennen, in dem diese Coeffizienten mit den durch (1) ursprünglich eingeführten reellen Coeffizienten stehen.

Die Hauptaufgabe einer Theorie der Wirbelstrombremse ist es, die Abhängigkeit der *Bremskraft* von der Geschwindigkeit v zu ermitteln. Um diese Aufgabe zu lösen, muss man irgend welche Grössen als von der Geschwindigkeit unabhängig einführen. Von der Geschwindigkeit unabhängig ist der Strom in den Bewickelungen der Elektromagnete. Dagegen ist das magnetische Feld dieses Stromes von dem Verlaufe der Feldlinien im Bremskörper, und damit von dessen Geschwindigkeit abhängig. Theoretisch diese Abhängigkeit für irgend eine Gestalt der Feldmagnete zu ermitteln, dürfte sehr schwierig sein. Doch kann man wohl ohne weiteres annahmen, dass die Coeffizienten A_n langsamer mit v variieren, als irgend welche auf das Feld in Gebiete $z > -\delta$ bezügliche Grössen. Beschränkt man sich insbesondere bei der weiteren Verfolgung des Ansatzes auf die Grundwelle, so hat man die Amplitude A_1, weil sie durch die erste Hauptgleichung unmittelbar mit dem Strome, welcher die Elektromagnete erregt, verknüpft ist, als von der Geschwindigkeit des Bremskörpers unabhängig anzusehen. Es mag für diesen Fall die weitere Ausführung der Theorie angedeutet werden.

Die elektromagnetische Kraft, die am Bremskörper angreift ist pro Volumeinheit, nach (5),

$$\text{(13)} \qquad [i\,\mathfrak{L}]_x = i_y\,\mathfrak{L}_z = \sigma\,\mathfrak{f}_y\,\mathfrak{L}_z = -\,v\sigma\mathfrak{L}_z^2 ;$$

dabei soll, unter Beschränkung auf die Grundwelle, gesetzt werden

$$\mathfrak{L}_z = R \left\{ B_1\, e^{-k_1 \alpha z} \cdot {}^{i\alpha(x - \lambda_1 z)} \right\} .$$

Die mittlere Bremskraft, berechnet für einen Cylinder von 1 cm² Querschnitt, findet sich jetzt gleich

$$\text{(14)} \qquad -R_x = \frac{v\sigma}{2\tau} \int_0^{2\tau} dx \int_0^{\infty} dz\, \mathfrak{L}_z^2 = \frac{v\sigma}{4\alpha k_1} |B_1|^2 .$$

Dabei ist, nach (11), zu setzen:

$$|B_1|^2 = A_1^2 \cdot \frac{\mu^2}{(k_1 + \delta\alpha\mu)^2 + \lambda_1^2}, \tag{15}$$

und es bestimmen sich k_1 und λ_1 aus $(10\,a, b)$, wobei die Geschwindigkeit v eingeht vermittelst der Grösse

$$\zeta_1 = \frac{4\pi v \sigma \mu}{\alpha} = 4 v \sigma \mu \tau. \tag{16}$$

Man kann somit den Ausdruck (14) der Bremskraft auch schreiben:

$$-R_x = \frac{\mu A_1^2}{16\pi} \cdot Z(\zeta_1), \tag{17}$$

wobei

$$Z(\zeta_1) = \frac{\zeta_1}{k_1} \cdot \frac{1}{(k_1 + \vartheta)^2 + \lambda_1^2}, \quad \vartheta = \delta\alpha\mu \tag{17a}$$

die Abhängigkeit von ζ_1, und damit von der Geschwindigkeit v bestimmt.

Setzen wir etwa $\delta = 0{,}1$ cm., $\tau = 10\pi$ cm., so wird $\delta\alpha = 0{,}01$: es wird somit für Kupfer, wo $\mu = 1$, $\vartheta = 0{,}01$ gegen $k_1 > 1$ zu vernachlässigen sein, dagegen für Eisen ($\mu = 1000$ circa) keineswegs. Demgemäss sind die beiden Fälle gesondert zu discutieren.

Für Kupfer wird

$$Z = \frac{\zeta_1}{k_1} \cdot \frac{1}{k_1^2 + \lambda_1^2} = \sqrt{\frac{\zeta_1^2}{1 + \zeta_1^2} \cdot \frac{2}{1 + \sqrt{1 + \zeta_1^2}}}. \tag{18}$$

Für kleine ζ_1 nimmt demnach die Bremskraft proportional zu v zu, um für grosse ζ_1 umgekehrt prop. zu $\sqrt{v}$ abzunehmen. Das *Maximum der Bremskraft* liegt bei

$$\zeta_1 = \sqrt{3}, \quad v = \frac{\sqrt{3}}{4\sigma\mu\tau},$$

und beträgt

$$\{-R_x\}_m = \frac{A_1^2}{16\pi\sqrt{2}}. \tag{18a}$$

Es ist also von der Breite des Luftspaltes unabhängig.

Bei Eisen ist $\sigma\mu$ etwa 100-mal so gross, wie bei Kupfer, es hat also ζ_1, caeteris paribus, einen 100 mal so grossen Wert. Man kann hier in allen praktischen Fällen mit den Näherungswerten rechnen:

$$k_1 = \lambda_1 = \sqrt{\frac{\zeta_1}{2}},$$

darf aber ϑ in $(17a)$ nicht streichen.

Es wird demnach:

(19)
$$Z = \frac{\sqrt{2\zeta_1}}{\vartheta^2 + \vartheta\sqrt{2\zeta_1} + \zeta_1}.$$

Hier steigt die Bremskraft zuerst prop. zu $\sqrt{v}$ an, um schliesslich wie $1/\sqrt{v}$ zu sinken, was mit Rüdenbergs Ergebnissen übereinstimmt. Die *maximale Bremskraft* liegt bei

$$\zeta_1 = \vartheta^2 \quad , \quad v = \frac{\vartheta^2}{4\sigma\mu\tau} = \frac{\delta^2\pi^2\mu}{4\sigma\tau^3}$$

und beträgt

(19 *a*)
$$\left\{-R_x\right\}_m = \frac{A_1^2}{16\pi} \cdot \frac{1}{\delta\alpha\left(1+\sqrt{2}\right)}.$$

Bei einem eisernen Bremskörper ist also der maximale Wert der Bremskraft wesentlich von dem Quotienten: Breite des Luftspaltes durch Polabstand, abhängig. Bei den oben angenommenen Daten ist dieser Wert etwa 60 mal so gross, als bei einem kupfernen Bremskörper.

J. ANDRADE

SUR UNE NOUVELLE MÉTHODE DE MESURE DES FROTTEMENTS

Entre deux supports en bêton, une roue lestée et fermée oscille sur une arête de couteau placée en son axe. Les supports soutiennent le couteau par l'intermédiaire de deux chapes sphériques en acier trempé qui permettent au couteau de chercher une assiette d'égale usure, les chapes sont ensuite immobilisées.

C'est à M. Fénon que je dois le secours de ces chapes.

Le frottement systématique est exercé par un levier dont un bras, en fourchette, appuie de part et d'autre des faces de la roue pendule sur les deux moitiés d'un *épaulement* cylindrique concentrique à la roue (de 10^{cm} de rayon); mais un épaulement de rayon double pourra aussi être pressé par le même levier dont l'axe d'oscillation peut être à cet effet surélevé.

Dans *les deux expériences* le levier fourchette *horizontal* exerce une même pression (30 à 50 Kilogr. environ) sur chacun des deux épaulements, mais le frottement produit par cette pression s'exercera, dans les deux expériences, avec deux *moments* différents sur la roue oscillante. On observe dans chaque expérience les petites oscillations de la roue pendule.

Sur la roue fermée la résistance balistique de l'air n'existe pas, la viscosité est négligeable; et si les oscillations sont assez réduites les demi-amplitudes de même orientation décroissent en progression arithmétique; on mesure dans une expérience deux écarts extrêmes de MÊME PARITÉ et on divise la différence obtenue par le nombre des oscillations.

Le quotient obtenu q équivaut à une quantité proportionnelle à la somme du moment de frottement systématique et du moment de roulement.

Cette expérience a été faite en pressant sur l'épaulement de rayon ϱ, en faisant la seconde expérience en pressant sur l'épaulement de rayon ϱ' on trouve un second quotient analogue à q : soit q'.

Le noveau quotient $\frac{q'-q}{\varrho'-\varrho}$ a éliminé le roulement, il est proportionnel à la pression systématique P et au coefficient du frottement produit sur les deux épaulements, que pour simplifier ici, nous supposons formés de même matière. Il est d'ailleurs loisible de ne faire varier la matière à *essayer* que sur l'un des épaulements.

La roue, de 2^m de diamètre, que je viens de faire construire est en fonte, elle pèse $\frac{1}{2}$ tonne environ et elle est disposée pour faire l'expérience sous de petites oscillations. Une autre méthode opératoire, beaucoup moins facilement calculable, mais offrant d'autres avantages, pourrait utiliser l'extinction rapide d'une grande oscillation. En m'en tenant à la première méthode, celle des petites oscillations à extinctions d'une lenteur modérée, je compte obtenir aisément l'approximation du millième et j'espère atteindre le dix millième.

A. KORN

UEBER DIE THEORIE DER UNIVERSELLEN SCHWINGUNGEN MIT ANWENDUNGEN AUF DIE THEORIE DER GRAVITATION UND DER INTRAMOLEKULAREN KRAEFTE

Obwohl die MAXWELL'sche Theorie und noch besser die Theorien von LORENTZ und COHN mit ihren formalen Hypothesen eine grosse Zahl der elektro-magnetischen Erscheinungen darstellen, ist doch der Wunsch noch in vielen lebendig, die Hypothesen der genannten formalen Theorien auf eine intuitive, mechanische Grundlage zu stellen. Im besonderen würde es erwünscht sein, dem Elektron und dem vom ihm hervorgebrachten Felde einen mechanisch definierbaren Begriff zu substituieren; wenn dies gelingt, werden uns die Hypothesen MAXWELL's und seiner Nachfolger nicht blos mehr befriedigen, sondern es wird auch zweifellos aus solchen mechanischen Deutungen weitere Anregung zu neuen Forschungen entstehen.

Es ist bekannt, dass man dem gravitierenden Teilchen mit Hilfe des BJERKNES'schen Modells der in einer Flüssigkeit pulsierenden Kugel eine mechanische Bedeutung beilegen kann. Lässt man in einer inkompressiblen Flüssigkeit zwei Kugeln mit gleicher Schwingungsdauer und gleicher Phase pulsieren (d. h. periodisch ihr Volumen verändern, so dass beide Kugeln stets zu gleicher Zeit das Maximum ihres Volumens erreichen), so wirken die beiden Kugeln auf einander mit einer scheinbaren Anziehungskraft, welche dem Quadrate ihrer Centraldistanzen umgekehrt proportional ist, wenn wir gegen diese die Radien der Kugeln klein annehmen. Während so die mechanische Deutung der gravitierenden Teilchen in der Weise möglich ist, dass man dieselben als mit gleicher Phase pulsierende Teilchen in einem Medium voraussetzt, das wenigstens gegen sehr schnelle Schwingungen sich wie eine inkompressible Flüssigkeit verhält, ergiebt eine mechanische Deutung der Elektronen in einem ähnlichen Sinne die folgende Schwierigkeit: Wenn wir pulsierende Teilchen von gleicher Phase als gleichartige Elektronen, pulsierende Teilchen von entgegengesetzter Phase als ungleichartige Elektronen ansehen, so erhalten wir zwischen gleichartigen Elektronen Anziehung und zwischen ungleichartigen Elektronen Abstossung. BJERKNES hat daher die Erscheinungen zwischen pulsierenden Teilchen als invers elektrische bezeichnet. Wenn man Elektronen als pulsierende Teilchen erklären will, muss man offenbar nach einem mechanischen Unterschiede zwischen solchen pulsierenden Teilchen suchen, die als gravitierende Teilchen zu bezeichnen sind, und solchen pulsierenden Teilchen, welche als Elektronen aufgefasst werden können. Im besonderen wird für die Wechselwirkung der Elektronen noch die Umkehrung des Vorzeichens auf mechanischer Grundlage zu begründen sein. Die kurze Untersuchung, welche ich hier vortragen will, soll eine Antwort auf diese Fragen zu geben versuchen, also über den mechanischen Unterschied zwischen gravitierenden Teilchen und Elektronen handeln, wenn beide als pulsierende Teilchen in einer empirisch inkompressiblen Flüssigkeit aufgefasst werden.

Wir wollen uns zunächst die gravitierenden Teilchen als pulsierende Teilchen zurechtlegen, wie ich es in meiner Theorie der universellen Schwingungen der Materie gethan habe. Die einzige Schwierigkeit bei der Erklärung der Gravitation war die Frage: Warum sollen alle materiellen Teilchen, die wir uns in einem für sehr rasche Schwingungen nahe inkompressiblen Aether eingebettet denken, mit derselben Schwingungsdauer und Phase pulsieren? Die erste, etwas bequeme Annahme, etwa das Sonnensystem unter einem periodischen Druck stehend anzunehmen, der, als von aussen kommend, nicht weiter zu erklären wäre und bei der Inkompressibilität des Zwischenmediums von den Pulsationen der eingebetteten, schwach kompressiblen materiellen Teilchen mit derselben Phase und derselben Schwingungsdauer Rechenschaft ablegen würde, habe ich später verändert, und ich habe die weit befriedigendere Annahme durchführen können, dass die Schwingungen, welche die Gravitation hervorrufen, Eigenschwingungen der Materie sind, so dass keine äussere Ursache hinzugenommen werden braucht. In der That ist der inkompressible Aether mit den eingebetteten, schwach kompressiblen Teilchen, als welche wir die materiellen Teilchen ansehen wollen, ein mechanisches System, welches einer unendlich grossen Zahl von Eigenschwingungen fähig ist; das mathematische Problem ist das folgende:

Es ist eine einfache Schwingung:

$$u \sin \frac{t}{T} 2\pi ,$$

$$v \sin \frac{t}{T} 2\pi ,$$

$$w \sin \frac{t}{T} 2\pi ,$$

so zu finden, dass die Funktionen u, v, w der Stelle $(x\, y\, z)$ in den materiellen Teilchen den Differentialgleichungen für schwach kompressible Medien, im Aussenraume den hydrodynamischen Gleichungen genügen, und dass diese Funktionen an der Grenze, wie im Innen- und Aussenraume überall eindeutig und stetig sind. Es ergiebt sich nun das Resultat, die Funktionen $u\, v\, w$ müssen die Ableitungen einer Funktion

$$\Phi (x , y , z)$$

sein, die im Innen- und Aussenraume und auch bei dem Durchgange durch die Grenze mit ihren ersten Ableitungen eindeutig und stetig ist und im Unendlichen, wie ein

Potential, unendlich klein wird; diese Funktion muss im Aussenraume der LAPLACE'schen Differentialgleichung:

$$\Delta \Phi = 0$$

und im Innenraume der materiellen Teilchen der Differentialgleichung:

$$\Delta \Phi + k^2 \Phi = 0$$

genügen, wo:

$$k^2 = 4\pi^2 \frac{a^2}{T^2}$$

und a^2 eine der Kompressibilität des Mediums zugehörige Konstante ist.

Hier haben wir nun ein ganz bestimmtes mathematische Problem vor uns. und die mathematische Analyse ergiebt, dass das Problem eine unendlich grosse Zahl von Lösungen zulässt

$$\Phi_0, \Phi_1, \Phi_2 \ldots,$$

mit zugehörigen Zahlen:

$$k_0^2 < k_1^2 < k_2^2 < \ldots,$$

also mit zugehörigen Schwingungsdauern

$$T_0 > T_1 > T_2 > \ldots.$$

Die Lösung mit grösster Schwingungsdauer T_0 werden wir als die der Grundschwingung zugehörige Lösung zu bezeichnen haben, die anderen Lösungen wird man als die den Obertönen zugehörigen Lösungen ansehen können. Alle diese Schwingungen wollen wir als die universellen Schwingungen der Materie bezeichnen.

Es ist eine ganz bestimmte, mathematische Aufgabe, die Formen dieser Schwingungen zu bestimmen, und im besonderen ist die Bestimmung der Grundschwingung ziemlich einfach, wenn wir alle materiellen Teilchen in erster Annäherung als kugelförmig annehmen, und zwar als Kugeln, deren Centraldistanzen gegen ihre Radien sehr gross sind. Es ergiebt sich als Form der Grundschwingung eine Pulsation aller materieller Teilchen mit gleicher Phase, also grade die Form der Schwingung, welche wir zur Erklärung der Gravitationswirkungen brauchen. Die Erklärung der gravitierenden Teilchen als pulsierender Teilchen ergiebt sich also mechanisch am ungezwungensten, wenn man die Pulsationsschwingungen der gravitierenden Teilchen als die universelle Grundschwingung der Materie ansieht, unter der Voraussetzung, dass die materiellen Teilchen als schwach kompressible Medien in einem für sehr rasche Schwingungen empirisch inkompressiblen Zwichenmedium aufzufassen sind.

Um nun zu versuchen, auch für die Elektronen eine Auffassung in ähnlicher Weise vorzubereiten und zugleich den Unterschied zu untersuchen, welcher zwischen gravitierenden Teilchen und Elektronen vorhanden sein muss, wenn wir beide Arten von Teilchen als pulsierende Teilchen in einem inkompressiblen Zwischenmedium auffassen, will ich von dem Princip der lebendigen Kraft ausgehen. Das Problem, das ich soeben kurz angedeutet hatte, das Problem, die universelle Grundschwingung zweier materieller Teilchen zu bestimmen, ist mechanisch vollständig und eindeutig bestimmt, wenn uns noch die lebendige Kraft der Schwingungsbewegung im Ganzen oder auch nur die lebendige Kraft der Schwingungsbewegung der intermediären Flüssigkeit

$$\frac{\mu}{2}\int_a\left[\left(\frac{\partial\Phi_0}{\partial x}\right)^2+\left(\frac{\partial\Phi_0}{\partial y}\right)^2+\left(\frac{\partial\Phi_0}{\partial z}\right)^2\right]d\tau\,\sin^2\frac{t}{T_0}\,2\pi \quad (\mu \text{ Dichtigkeit der Flüssigkeit})$$

bzw. ihr Mittelwert im Verlaufe einer Schwingungsdauer T_0 bekannt ist:

$$\text{(1)} \qquad T_a=\frac{\mu}{4}\int_a\left[\left(\frac{\partial\Phi_0}{\partial x}\right)^2+\left(\frac{\partial\Phi_0}{\partial y}\right)^2+\left(\frac{\partial\Phi_0}{\partial z}\right)^2\right]d\tau\,.$$

Wenn T_a gegeben ist, ist die Funktion Φ_0 im ganzen Raume eindeutig bestimmt.

Setzt man:

$$\text{(2)} \qquad e=\sqrt{\frac{\mu}{8\pi}}\int\limits_{\omega_1}\frac{\partial\Phi_0}{\partial n}\,d\omega=\sqrt{\frac{\mu}{8\pi}}\int\limits_{\omega_2}\frac{\partial\Phi_0}{\partial n}\,d\omega$$

(ω_1, ω_2 die Oberflächen der Teilchen, n die in die Flüssigkeit hineingehende Normale) so ergiebt sich durch nicht besonders schwierige Rechnungen, die ich hier nicht ausführlich geben möchte:

$$\text{(3)} \qquad T_a=\frac{e^2}{R}+\frac{e^2}{\varrho}\,,$$

wo ϱ die Centraldistanz der beiden Kugeln und R ihren mittleren Radius bezeichnet und wir Grössen vernachlässigen, welche gegen $\frac{e^2}{\varrho}$ von der Ordnung $\frac{R}{\varrho}$ klein sind. Wir wollen nun das Centrum des einen Teilchens als fest annehmen, während das Centrum des zweiten Teilchens in der Richtung ϱ $(1\rightarrow 2)$ die sichtbare Geschwindigkeit ϱ' haben möge.

Die gesammte lebendige Kraft des Systems (Mittelwert während einer Schwingungsdauer T_0) setzt sich dann aus folgenden Teilen zusammen:

Aus der lebendigen, translatorischen Kraft des beweglichen Teilchens

$\frac{1}{2}M\varrho'^2$, (M Gesammtmasse des beweglichen Teilchens)

den beiden Pulsationsenergieen der Teilchen

$$2\,T_i$$

und der lebendigen Kraft der intermediären Flüssigkeit

$$T_a = e^2\left(\frac{1}{R} + \frac{1}{\varrho}\right)$$

Das Princip der lebendigen Kraft ergiebt:

$$\frac{d}{dt}\left\{\frac{1}{2}M\varrho'^2 + 2T_i + e^2\left(\frac{1}{R} + \frac{1}{\varrho}\right)\right\} = 0$$

oder:

$$M\varrho'\varrho'' + 2\frac{dT_i}{dt} + \left(\frac{1}{R} + \frac{1}{\varrho}\right)\frac{de^2}{dt} - \frac{e^2}{\varrho^2}\varrho' = 0$$

oder:

(4) $$M\varrho'' = \frac{e^2}{\varrho^2} - \frac{1}{\varrho'}\left\{2\frac{dT_i}{dt} + \left(\frac{1}{R} + \frac{1}{\varrho}\right)\frac{de^2}{dt}\right\}$$

d. h. wir erhielten das Coulomb'sche Gesetz zwischen den beiden Teilchen, mit dem richtigen Vorzeichen:

(5) $$M\varrho'' = \frac{e^2}{\varrho^2},$$

wenn

$$T_i \text{ und } e^2$$

oder, da T_i auch nur von e abhängt, wenn e, also die Pulsationsgeschwindigkeit, von der Zeit unabhängig ist. Da sich nun aber bei der strengen Durchführung des rechnerischen Problems der universellen Grundschwingung ergiebt, dass die auf das zweite Teilchen ausgeübte Kraft nicht

$$+\frac{e^2}{\varrho^2},$$

sondern

$$-\frac{e^2}{\varrho^2}$$

ist, so kann bei dem Problem der universellen Grundschwingung e nicht unveränderlich sein, sondern, wenn die Teilchen einmal den Abstand ϱ_1, das andere Mal den Abstand ϱ_2 haben, sind die mittleren Pulsationsgeschwindigkeiten der Teilchen verschieden, das ursprüngliche e ist in e' übergegangen. Allerdings unterscheiden sich e und e' nur um ausserordentlich kleine Grössen, die von der Ordnung $\frac{R}{\varrho}$ klein sind. Es ergiebt namlich die Rechnung, es ist bei einer kleinen Verschiebung:

$$(6) \qquad e' = e\left(1 + \alpha \frac{R}{\varrho} + \text{kleine Grössen von der Ordnung } \frac{R^2}{\varrho^2}\right),$$

wo α einen Zahlenfaktor vorstellt; aber dieser kleine Unterschied genügt, wie leicht aus der Formel (4) hervorgeht, dass von der äusseren lebendigen Kraft

$$\text{die Grösse } \frac{e^2}{\varrho}$$

in jede der Kugeln gewissermassen hineinkriecht und dass so das Vorzeichen der Wechselwirkung

$$\frac{e^2}{\varrho^2}$$

grade in das entgegengesetzte umgekehrt wird.

Bei der universellen Grundschwingung sind also die Pulsationsgeschwindigkeiten der pulsierenden Teilchen, gewissermassen die Massen der gravitierenden Teilchen, nicht rigorös konstant, und aus diesem Grunde ergiebt sich die Anziehung gravitierender Teilchen; würde dagegen dem System eine Bedingung auferlegt, welche die strenge Konstanz der mittleren Pulsationsgeschwindigkeiten, also die strenge Konstanz von e, zur Folge haben würde, so würde sich zwischen den Teilchen Abstossung ergeben, wie es zwischen gleichnamig elektrischen Teilchen der Fall sein muss. Damit sind wir nun tatsächlich zu dem mechanischen Unterschied gelangt, der zwischen pulsierenden Teilchen, welche Gravitationselemente darstellen, und pulsierenden Teilchen, welche Elektronen darstellen, vorhanden sein muss: Die Pulsationsgeschwindigkeiten der Gravitationselemente sind nicht absolut konstant, sondern wechseln mit der Konfiguration der Teilchen gegen einander; die Unterschiede sind natürlich äusserst klein, von der Ordnung der Radien der Teilchen, dividiert durch ihre Abstände, so dass sie experimentell gar nicht verfolgt werden können. Die Pulsationsgeschwindigkeiten der pulsierenden Teilchen, welche als Elektronen aufzufassen sind, sind rigorös konstant; dieser Unterschied bedingt die Umkehrung des Vorzeichens der Wechselwirkung.

Um Wechselwirkung zwischen Teilchen der einen Art (Gravitationselemente) einerseits und Teilchen der anderen Art (Elektronen) andererseits auszuschliessen, kann angenommen werden, dass die Schwingungsdauern der Pulsationen für die beiden Arten von Teilchen verschieden sind; es deuten aber andere Momente darauf hin, dass die Schwingungsdauern für beide Arten dieselben sind, und dann bleibt nur die Annahme übrig, das sich die Phasen der Teilchen der einen und der anderen Art um $\frac{\pi}{2}$ unterscheiden. Wir würden, nach einer bestimmten Festsetzung des Anfangspunktes der Zeit, von gravitierenden Teilchen herrührend Schwingungen der äusseren Flüssigkeit von der Form

$$u' \sin \frac{t}{T} 2\pi ,$$

$$v' \sin \frac{t}{T} 2\pi ,$$

$$w' \sin \frac{t}{T} 2\pi ,$$

von Elektronen herrührend Schwingungen von der Form:

$$u \cos \frac{t}{T} 2\pi ,$$

$$v \cos \frac{t}{T} 2\pi ,$$

$$w \cos \frac{t}{T} 2\pi ,$$

haben, die Sinusschwingung wäre die universelle Grundschwingung des gesammten Himmelssystems, welche durch die Konfiguration der materiellen Teilchen vollständig bestimmt ist, und da sich einer Veränderung der durch die Konfiguration bedingten Pulsation ganz ausserordentlich grosse Kräfte entgegenstellen würden, kann sich die Pulsationsschwingung der in der Phase un $\frac{\pi}{2}$ verschiedenen Elektronenpulsationen mit der Zeit nicht ändern; darum grade ergeben sich, wie wir gesehen haben, die Wechselwirkungen von Gravitationselementen unter einander und von Elektronen unter einander mit verschiedenem Vorzeichen.

Es war lediglich die Absicht dieser kurzen Mitteilung, den Unterschied zwischen Gravitationselementen und Elektronen mechanisch zu begründen, ich kann hier nicht auf die sich anschliessenden Fragen näher eingehen, auf welche Weise bei der Bewegung non Elektronen in der umgebenden Flüssigkeit Drehungsbewegungen auftreten, ohne welche die elektrischen Erscheinungen nicht erklärt werden können, ich schliesse nur mit der kurzen Andeutung über das mechanische Bild der hydrodynamischen Theorie, dass die Geschwindigkeiten in einem elektromagnetischen Felde ganz allgemein von der Form

$$u_0 + u_1 \cos \frac{t}{T} 2\pi + u_2 \sin \frac{t}{T} 2\pi ,$$

$$v_0 + v_1 \cos \frac{t}{T} 2\pi + v_2 \sin \frac{t}{T} 2\pi ,$$

$$w_0 + w_1 \cos \frac{t}{T} 2\pi + w_2 \sin \frac{t}{T} 2\pi$$

gedacht werden müssen, die $u_0\, v_0\, w_0$ sind gewissermassen die sichtbaren Geschwindigkeiten, $u_1\, v_1\, w_1$ sind den Grössen X Y Z, $u_2\, v_2\, w_2$ den Grössen L M N in den verschiedenen Theorien von Maxwell, Cohn, Lorentz proportional zu setzen; welche Theorie man hier auch annehmen mag, immer wird diese Auffassung ein klares mechanisches Bild liefern; man kann so jede der genannten Theorien in eine mechanische Theorie umsetzen, wenn auch noch vieles zu erledigen bleibt.

T. LEVI-CIVITA

SULLA ESPRESSIONE ASINTOTICA DEI POTENZIALI RITARDATI

1. — *Richiamo della equazione di* DÖPPLER.

Sia P un punto mobile con data legge, rispetto ad un certo sistema di riferimento; O un punto fisso.

Dette

$$(1)\qquad \begin{cases} x = x(t), \\ y = y(t), \\ z = z(t), \end{cases}$$

le coordinate di P in un generico istante t; x_0, y_0, z_0 le coordinate di O, si designi al solito la distanza $\overline{OP}$ con

$$(2)\qquad r = \sqrt{(x-x_0)^2 + (y-y_0)^2 + (z-z_0)^2}\,.$$

Si supponga che da P emanino azioni di tipo newtoniano, propagantisi per onde sferiche con velocità costante c.

Si fissi un istante t, e sia in questo istante la posizione di P distinta da O, cioè $r > 0$.

Ammesso che la velocità v di P sia stata, prima dell'istante considerato, co-

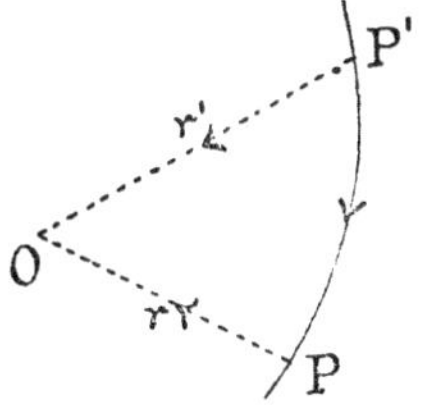

stantemente inferiore ad un limite fisso $< c$, esiste sulla traiettoria una ed una sola posizione *di utile emissione*; voglio dire una ed una sola posizione anteriore P', tale che, partendone un'azione nell'istante t', in cui vi transita il mobile, l'arrivo in O segue proprio all'istante t.

Tale univoca esistenza si dimostra subito dando forma analitica alla definizione dell'istante t' e della corrispondente posizione P'.

La proprietà caratteristica è che l'intervallo di tempo $t - t'$ risulti eguale a quello che si richiede per la propagazione con velocità c da P' fino in O.

Sarà pertanto

$$t' = t - \frac{r'}{c} \tag{3}$$

designando r' la distanza $\overline{OP'}$.

D'altra parte la stessa r' non è altro che il valore per $t = t'$ della funzione $r(t)$, definita dalla (2).

Si ha così, per determinare r', la equazione implicita ben nota

$$r' = r\left(t - \frac{r'}{c}\right), \tag{D}$$

che si può a buon diritto chiamare *equazione di* DÖPPLER.

Trovato r', la (3) dà il corrispondente istante t'.

Indichiamo con $\mathbf{v}$ (vettore) la velocità di P nell'istante t, con $\mathbf{v}'$ l'analoga velocità nell'istante t'.

Le componenti di $\mathbf{v}$ sono manifestamente $\dot{x}, \dot{y}, \dot{z}$, il punto sovrapposto significando derivazione rapporto a t.

Dalla (2) si ha

$$\dot{r} = \frac{x - x_0}{r}\dot{x} + \frac{y - y_0}{r}\dot{y} + \frac{z - z_0}{r}\dot{z},$$

in cui il secondo membro può essere interpretato come la componente di $\mathbf{v}$ secondo la direzione O → P. Adottando come direzione positiva del segmento r quella che corrisponde al senso di propagazione, cioè la P → O, potremo scrivere

$$\dot{r} = -v_r. \tag{4}$$

Ciò posto, consideriamo la differenza

$$r' - r\left(t - \frac{r'}{c}\right)$$

come funzione dell'argomento (positivo) r'.

Derivando rapporto a r', e badando alla (4) $\left(\text{riferita all'istante anteriore}\right.$ $\left. t' = t - \frac{r'}{c}\right)$, si ha

$$1 - \frac{v'_r}{c}.$$

Comunque vari r' (per valori positivi), questa espressione ha un limite inferiore > 0, in base all'ipotesi che la velocità v (e a fortiori una sua componente v_r) si mantenga, in ogni istante anteriore a t, al disotto di una quantità costante $< c$. Segue da ciò che la differenza in questione va crescendo costantemente al crescere di r'.

Per $r' = 0$, essa ha il valore negativo $-r(t)$; si incontrerà dunque, facendo crescere r', uno ed un sol valore positivo, che la rende nulla.

Dacchè la (D) equivale all'annullarsi della differenza

$$r' - r\left(t - \frac{r'}{c}\right),$$

rimane provata l'univoca esistenza di una sua radice positiva r' (funzione del parametro t).

2. — *Definizione* (cinetica) *di potenziale ritardato*

Un potenziale newtoniano ordinario si presenta sotto la forma

$$\frac{k}{r},$$

essendo k (per un dato punto potenziante) funzione determinata di t.

Supponiamo per un momento che il punto potenziante sia in quiete ed esprimiamo che la propagazione non è istantanea, ma si compie con velocità c.

All'uopo, basta manifestamente riportare la funzione k all'istante dell'emissione, che precede t di $\frac{r}{c}$. Ciò dà

$$\frac{k\left(t - \frac{r}{c}\right)}{r},$$

che può ben dirsi la forma statica di un potenziale ritardato. Essa si presenta nel modo il più diretto e spontaneo, quando si ha riguardo ad una posizione di emissione fissa.

Se il punto potenziante P si muove, interviene una duplice modificazione [1], rilevata dai sigg. Liénard e Wiechert. Anzitutto bisogna riferirsi alla posizione di utile emissione P'; inoltre va introdotto il fattore

$$\frac{dt'}{dt} = \frac{1}{1 - \frac{v'_r}{c}} .$$

Si ha così in generale (cioè comunque [2] si muova il punto potenziante P), per un potenziale ritardato f, la forma analitica seguente:

$$f = \frac{k\left(t - \frac{r'}{c}\right)}{r'\left(1 - \frac{v'_r}{c}\right)} . \tag{5}$$

Come si vede, la f dipende dalla posizione e dalla velocità del punto P, non nell'istante attuale t, ma in un certo istante anteriore t', a caratterizzare il quale interviene [a norma della (D)] la storia del mobile, cioè la natura delle funzioni $x(t)$, $y(t)$, $z(t)$ in un intervallo *finito* di tempo, precedente t.

3. — *Casi limiti e relativi intorni — Condizioni cinematiche caratteristiche — Relazione del secondo caso limite colla quasi-stazionarietà di* Abraham.

Vi sono due casi limiti, in cui il carattere funzionale della dipendenza di f dallo stato di moto del punto P, viene a sparire:

1° quando si ritorni all'ipotesi classica di una propagazione istantanea $\left(\frac{1}{c} = 0\right)$; r' e t' coincidono allora naturalmente con r e t;

2° quando, pur essendo qualunque la velocità di propagazione, la posizione attuale del mobile tenda a confondersi con quella del punto potenziato O ($\lim r = 0$). È chiaro infatti che, ove sia nullo il cammino da percorrere, le cose vanno come se la propagazione fosse istantanea.

Per rendersene conto analiticamente, basta osservare la (D): il valore limite della radice r', al convergere di $r(t)$ a zero, è manifestamente $r' = 0$.

Particolarmente importante è il comportamento dei potenziali ritardati in prossimità di questi due casi limiti: cioè rispettivamente per c molto grande, o per r molto piccolo.

[1] Cfr. per es. la nota *Sul campo elettromagnetico generato*, ecc. (Nuovo Cimento, Ser. V, T. VI, 1903, pagg. 153-162); oppure Abraham, *Elektromagnetische Theorie der Strahlung* (Leipzig, Teubner, 1905, pp. 82-84).

[2] Rispettando, beninteso, la restrizione qualitativa $v < c$.

Interessa prima di tutto farsi un'idea del significato concreto delle qualifiche « grande » e « piccolo », in relazione ad altri elementi omogenei del fenomeno di cui si tratta.

Si è prossimi al primo caso limite $\left(\frac{1}{c} = 0\right)$, quando la velocità v del mobile (in tutto l'intervallo di tempo, che occorre considerare) è molto piccola di fronte alla velocità di propagazione c.

Si è invece prossimi al secondo caso limite, quando è piccolo il rapporto numerico

$$\frac{r\,a}{c^2},$$

designando a l'accelerazione del mobile, anzi il limite superiore delle accelerazioni, che esso assume, durante l'intervallo di tempo considerato.

Si osservi che $\frac{r}{c}$ non è altro che il tempo di propagazione da P, fino in O, e che di conseguenza $a\frac{r}{c}$ porge un limite superiore per la differenza di velocità del mobile fra l'istante dell'emissione e quello dell'arrivo in O.

La piccolezza del rapporto $\frac{r\,a}{c^2}$ è così suscettibile della interpretazione seguente:

la velocità v del mobile (anche senza essere di per sè piccola di fronte a c) subisce durante il tempo di propagazione (fino al punto potenziato O), variazioni, le quali restano sempre piccole di fronte a c.

Lo sviluppo dei potenziali ritardati, nell'intorno di $\frac{1}{c} = 0$ (1), e le espressioni approssimate, che ne conseguono, allorchè ci si limita a termini di dato ordine in $\frac{v}{c}$ sono, si può dire, d'uso corrente. Nè io mi permetterò di spendervi parola, desiderando piuttosto di richiamare l'attenzione sull'altro caso limite e sui corrispondenti sviluppi, che dirò asintotici, visto che un potenziale f tende a crescere indefinitamente, quando r, e con esso r', converge a zero.

Prima però di esporre il lato matematico della questione, debbo far presente come essa si colleghi indirettamente colle ricerche del sig. ABRAHAM (2).

È ben noto che, anteriormente a tali ricerche, l'unico criterio di riduzione (inteso a sostituire alle espressioni funzionali delle espressioni differenziali approssimate) fu di operare nell'intorno di $\frac{1}{c} = 0$, sfruttando la piccolezza del rapporto $\frac{v}{c}$.

Il sig. ABRAHAM seppe rinunciare a tale ipotesi restrittiva e riescì a trovare (non proprio per i potenziali, ma per gli elementi fisici, che ne dipendono) un nuovo cri-

(1) Si vegga per lo sviluppo completo la bella Nota del sig. HERGLOTZ, *Ueber die Berechnung retardierter Potentiale* (Göttinger Nachrichten, 1904, pp. 549-556).

(2) Cfr. in particolare i §§ 16-23 della citata sua opera.

terio di riduzione, basato sopra una felice intuizione di analogia meccanica: quella dei fenomeni quasi-stazionari.

Dal punto di vista matematico, l'origine e la giustificazione di un tale procedimento risiede negli sviluppi asintotici. Renderò conto di ciò in un prossimo lavoro, dove farò vedere, illustrandone le conseguenze, come si precisino e si completino alcuni risultati di meccanica elettromagnetica.

Dovrò qui limitarmi a brevi considerazioni di natura analitica.

4. — *Risoluzione asintotica della equazione di Döppler.*

Si tratta sostanzialmente di esplicitare la funzione $r'(t)$ definita dalla

$$r' = r\left(t - \frac{r'}{c}\right) \tag{D}$$

in un intorno di $r(t) = 0$. Più precisamente si richiede di trovare uno sviluppo dell'incognita r', il quale metta in evidenza i termini di vario ordine rispetto ad $r(t)$, nell'ipotesi che, pur restando regolare il moto di P, la traiettoria tenda a passare per O. La regolarità del moto va intesa nel consueto significato cinematico: le funzioni $x(t)$, $y(t)$, $z(t)$, sono cioè a ritenersi finite, continue e derivabili quanto occorre.

La difficoltà della questione — se pur ve n'è una — risiede nel fatto che, quando la traiettoria tende a passare per O, la funzione (data) $r(t)$, la quale compare nel secondo membro della (D), non si comporta regolarmente, come fanno le coordinate cartesiane, ma ha già una derivata seconda, che non resta finita.

Per girare la difficoltà, conviene quadrare i due membri della (D) e studiare l'equazione

$$r'^2 - q\left(t - \frac{r'}{c}\right) = 0\,, \tag{D'}$$

dove

$$q(t) = r^2 = (x - x_0)^2 + (y - y_0)^2 + (z - z_0)^2 \tag{6}$$

è funzione perfettamente regolare di t, assieme ad $x(t)$, $y(t)$, $z(t)$, e resta tale anche quando (facendo per es. variare dei parametri, che per lo scopo attuale non importa specificare) $x(t)$, $y(t)$, $z(t)$ tendono rispettivamente ad assumere (per un qualche valore di t) i valori x_0, y_0, z_0.

La (D') possiede naturalmente, al pari della (D), una ed una sola radice positiva. Per riconoscerne il comportamento nel senso dichiarato, porremo

$$r' = \lambda r\,, \tag{7}$$

e applicheremo alla funzione $q\left(t - \frac{\lambda r}{c}\right)$ lo sviluppo (abbreviato) di Taylor fino al terz'ordine (inclusivo).

La (D') diviene con ciò

$$\lambda^2 r^2 - q + \frac{\lambda}{c} \dot{q} r - \frac{\lambda^2}{2c^2} \ddot{q} r^2 + \frac{\lambda^3}{6c^3} \dddot{q} r^3 + Q r^4 = 0,$$

dove $q, \dot{q}, \ddot{q}, \dddot{q}$ si riferiscono al valore t dell'argomento, e il coefficiente Q è a ritenersi finito e continuo anche per r convergente a zero.

Si noti che la derivazione della (6) porge

$$\dot{q} = 2\Sigma(x - x_0)\dot{x} = -2rv_r, \tag{8}$$

il simbolo $\sum$ designando la somma del termine scritto e di quelli che si ottengono da esso, cambiando successivamente x in y ed in z.

Per ulteriore derivazione si ha poi

$$\left\{\begin{aligned} \frac{1}{2}\ddot{q} &= \Sigma \dot{x}^2 + \Sigma(x - x_0)\ddot{x} = v^2 - ra_r, \\ \frac{1}{6}\dddot{q} &= \Sigma \dot{x}\ddot{x} + \frac{1}{3}\Sigma(x - x_0)\dddot{x} = va_v - \frac{1}{3} r\dot{a}_r, \end{aligned}\right. \tag{9}$$

dove a_v rappresenta la componente dell'accelerazione $\mathbf{a}$ di P nel senso del moto, e $\dot{\mathbf{a}}$ il vettore derivato di $\mathbf{a}$, rapporto a t.

Se ora si divide per r^2 la equazione in λ, ricavata dalla (D'), e si ha riguardo alle (6), (8) e (9), ove si ponga per brevità

$$\frac{1}{c}\mathbf{v} = \boldsymbol{\beta}, \tag{10}$$

e di conseguenza

$$\frac{1}{c} v = \beta \quad , \quad \frac{1}{c} v_r = \beta_r;$$

nonchè

$$(1 - \beta^2)\lambda^2 - 2\beta_r \lambda - 1 = \omega_0, \tag{11}$$

$$\frac{1}{c^2}(a_r \lambda^2 + \beta a_v \lambda^3) = \omega_1, \tag{12}$$

$$-\frac{1}{3}\frac{\lambda^3}{c^3}\dot{a}_r + Q = \Omega, \tag{13}$$

con che Ω resta finita, anche per r convergente a zero, risulta

$$\frac{r'^2 - q\left(t - \frac{r'}{c}\right)}{r^2} = \omega = \omega_0 + \omega_1 r + \Omega r^2 = 0. \tag{D''}$$

Prendendo sotto questa forma la equazione di definizione di λ, si è raggiunto lo scopo di esplicitare i termini di ordine zero e quelli di ordine 1 rispetto a r. È chiaro del resto che, protraendo abbastanza lo sviluppo di $q\left(t-\frac{\lambda r}{c}\right)$, si potrebbero analogamente esplicitare i termini successivi del primo membro ω, fino ad un ordine comunque elevato.

Eguagliando a zero il termine ω_0, d'ordine zero, si ha

$$(1-\beta^2)\lambda^2-2\beta_r\lambda-1=0,$$

equazione di secondo grado in λ, la quale, per essere $\beta=\frac{v}{c}<1$, ammette due radici di segno opposto

$$(14)\qquad \begin{cases} \lambda_1=\dfrac{\beta_r+s}{1-\beta^2}, \\ \lambda_2=\dfrac{\beta_r-s}{1-\beta^2}, \end{cases}$$

dove

$$(15)\qquad s=\sqrt{1-\beta^2+\beta_r^2},$$

intendendosi attribuito al radicale il suo valore aritmetico. λ_1 rappresenta così la radice positiva, e si ha identicamente

$$(11')\qquad \omega_0=(1-\beta^2)(\lambda-\lambda_1)(\lambda-\lambda_2).$$

Ciò premesso, trattiamo l'r, *in quanto compare esplicitamente in* ω (in quanto cioè segna l'ordine dei vari termini), come un parametro, in funzione del quale debba definirsi λ dalla (D''). Per l'equivalenza colla originaria (D), siamo a priori sicuri (in base alla posizione $r'=\lambda r$) che la (D'') ammette una ed una sola radice positiva.

Dacchè, per $r=0$, essa è soddisfatta da $\lambda=\lambda_1$, e la derivata del primo membro

$$\left(\frac{\partial\omega}{\partial\lambda}\right)_{\substack{\lambda=\lambda_1\\ r=0}}=(1-\beta^2)(\lambda_1-\lambda_2)=2s$$

non si annulla, si può trarne λ come funzione di r, per r abbastanza piccolo. È questa la soluzione, che a noi interessa. A meno di termini in r, si avrà manifestamente $\lambda=\lambda_1$.

Formando la

$$\frac{d\lambda}{dr}=-\frac{\dfrac{\partial\omega}{\partial r}}{\dfrac{\partial\omega}{\partial\lambda}}$$

e ponendovi $r=0$, si otterrà il coefficiente del termine in r.

In generale, se nella (D″) si trovano esplicitati i termini fino ad un certo ordine n, si potrà, per derivazione successiva, trarne i corrispondenti termini della radice λ.

5. — *Espressione asintotica di un potenziale ritardato.*

Determinato per λ (e quindi per $r' = \lambda r$) uno sviluppo valido nell'intorno di $r = 0$, è subito risoluta l'analoga questione per un potenziale ritardato.

Ecco del resto come conviene procedere per abbreviare il calcolo.

Data l'espressione (6) di q, si ha

$$\frac{1}{2}\frac{\partial}{\partial r'} q\left(t - \frac{r'}{c}\right) = r'\left(1 - \frac{v'_r}{c}\right),$$

quindi anche

$$\frac{1}{2}\frac{\partial}{\partial r'}\left\{r'^2 - q\left(t - \frac{r'}{c}\right)\right\} = r'\left(1 - \frac{v'_r}{c}\right).$$

Sostituendo nel primo membro λr al posto di r', e badando alla posizione

$$\frac{r'^2 - q\left(t - \frac{r'}{c}\right)}{r^2} = \omega,$$

potremo scrivere

$$\frac{1}{2} r \frac{\partial \omega}{\partial \lambda} = r'\left(1 - \frac{v'_r}{c}\right),$$

donde, ponendo ancora

$$\mu = 2\,\frac{k\left(t - \frac{\lambda r}{c}\right)}{\frac{\partial \omega}{\partial \lambda}}, \tag{16}$$

e confrontando colla (5),

$$f = \frac{\mu}{r}. \tag{5'}$$

Si intende che in μ va sostituito per λ il suo valore definito dalla (D″), cioè quella tale radice di $\omega = 0$, che si riduce a λ_1 per $r = 0$.

Al pari di λ, la funzione μ è suscettibile di uno sviluppo procedente per termini d'ordine sempre più elevato rispetto a r. Per quello d'ordine zero, si avrà in particolare dalla (16), ponendovi $r = 0$ e quindi $\lambda = \lambda_1$,

$$\mu_0 = (\mu)_{r=0} = 2 \frac{k(t)}{\left(\frac{\partial \omega_0}{\partial \lambda}\right)_{\lambda=\lambda_1}} = \frac{k}{s}. \tag{17}$$

Di qua risulta subito *l'espressione asintotica* di f:

$$\frac{\mu_0}{r} = \frac{k}{r} \cdot \frac{1}{s} = \frac{k(t)}{r} \frac{1}{\sqrt{1 - \beta^2 + \beta_r^2}}; \tag{I}$$

È il caso di parlare di espressione asintotica perchè, mentre, al convergere di r a zero, tanto $\frac{\mu}{r}$, quanto $\frac{\mu_0}{r}$ crescono indefinitamente, siamo sicuri che la differenza $\frac{\mu - \mu_0}{r}$ resta finita.

Più generalmente, si potrà chiamare asintotico anche lo sviluppo di f, che si ottiene esplicitando l'ordine dei vari termini rispetto ad r.

6. — *Calcolo del secondo termine — Considerazioni riassuntive.*

Valutiamo anche il termine in r, $\mu_1 r$, nello sviluppo di μ.

Essendo, a meno di termini in r^2,

$$k\left(t - \frac{\lambda r}{c}\right) = k - \dot{k} \frac{\lambda}{c} r$$

(dove k e $\dot{k}$ si riferiscono all'istante attuale t), nonchè

$$\frac{\partial \omega}{\partial \lambda} = \frac{\partial \omega_0}{\partial \lambda} + \frac{\partial \omega_1}{\partial \lambda} r,$$

avremo colla stessa approssimazione

$$\mu = 2 \frac{k\left(t - \frac{\lambda r}{c}\right)}{\frac{\partial \omega}{\partial \lambda}} = \frac{2k}{\frac{\partial \omega_0}{\partial \lambda}} - 2 \left\{ \frac{k \frac{\partial \omega_1}{\partial \lambda}}{\left(\frac{\partial \omega_0}{\partial \lambda}\right)^2} + \frac{\dot{k} \frac{\lambda}{c}}{\frac{\partial \omega_0}{\partial \lambda}} \right\} r.$$

Nel secondo addendo si può porre senz'altro $\lambda = \lambda_1$. Non così nel primo, dacchè vogliamo trascurare soltanto i termini in r^2.

Osserveremo perciò che dalla (D″) segue

$$\left(\frac{d\lambda}{dr}\right)_{r=0} = -\frac{\omega_1}{\frac{\partial\omega_0}{\partial\lambda}},$$

e quindi $\left(\frac{\partial\omega_0}{\partial\lambda}\right.$ dipendendo da r — in quanto parametro dell'ordine — solo pel tramite di $\left.\lambda\right)$

$$\frac{1}{\frac{\partial\omega_0}{\partial\lambda}} = \frac{1}{\left(\frac{\partial\omega_0}{\partial\lambda}\right)_{\lambda=\lambda_1}} + \left\{\frac{\frac{\partial^2\omega_0}{\partial\lambda^2}\,\omega_1}{\left(\frac{\partial\omega_0}{\partial\lambda}\right)^3}\right\}_{\lambda=\lambda_1} r\,.$$

Il coefficiente di r nella espressione di μ è dunque

$$\mu_1 = \frac{2k}{\left(\frac{\partial\omega_0}{\partial\lambda}\right)^3}\left\{\frac{\partial^2\omega_0}{\partial\lambda^2}\,\omega_1 - \frac{\partial\omega_0}{\partial\lambda}\frac{\partial\omega_1}{\partial\lambda}\right\} - \frac{2\dot{k}}{\frac{\partial\omega_0}{\partial\lambda}}\frac{\lambda}{c},$$

nella quale λ va dappertutto posto eguale a λ_1, e ω_0, ω_1 hanno i valori (11), (12).

Eseguendo materialmente il calcolo, si trova

$$(18)\qquad \mu_1 = -\frac{k}{2c^2s^3}\left\{a_r + \beta a_v\,\beta_r\,\frac{3(1-\beta^2)+2\beta_r^2}{(1-\beta^2)^2}\right\} - \\ - k\,\frac{\beta a_v}{c^2(1-\beta^2)^2} - \frac{\dot{k}}{c(1-\beta^2)}\left(1+\frac{\beta_r}{s}\right),$$

dove, a norma della (15), s sta per il radicale

$$\sqrt{1-\beta^2+\beta_r^2}\,.$$

Usufruendo dello sviluppo $\mu_0 + \mu_1 r + \ldots$ di μ, si ha dalla (5′)

$$(\text{II})\qquad f = \frac{\mu_0}{r} + \mu_1 + \ldots,$$

in cui μ_0 *e* μ_1 *hanno i valori* (17) *e* (18), *e i termini omessi convergono a zero con* r.

Si potrebbe naturalmente procedere nel calcolo dei termini successivi, d'ordine $1, 2, \ldots$, rispetto ad r. Il loro carattere comune è di dipendere esclusivamente dallo stato di moto del punto nell'istante attuale t. Però, mentre in $\frac{\mu_0}{r}$ intervengono soltanto posizione e velocità, in μ_1 si presenta anche l'accelerazione; e, in generale, da un termine al successivo, il massimo ordine delle derivate, che vi compariscono, aumenta di una unità.

Di ciò è ben facile rendersi conto. Debbo però confessare che non sono riescito a trovare, per la struttura dei vari termini, o, ciò che è lo stesso, per lo sviluppo asintotico di f, una forma compendiosa ed espressiva, sul tipo di quella che la serie di LAGRANGE (1) fornisce per l'altro sviluppo (nell'intorno della propagazione istantanea).

Dal punto di vista delle applicazioni, interessano, si può dire, esclusivamente i due termini che abbiamo già esplicitato.

Infatti, per r abbastanza piccolo, essi preponderano sugli altri in modo che l'influenza di questi ultimi riesce quasi trascurabile. A dire il vero, lo stesso può affermarsi, quanto all'ordine di grandezza, per $\frac{\mu_0}{r}$ in confronto di μ_1, e parrebbe che si potesse addirittura limitarsi al termine asintotico.

Ciò sta indiscutibilmente per f, e anche per le sue derivate, finchè si considera un valore locale; ma per lo più, occorre piuttosto aver riguardo a certi valori medi, relativi a sistemi continui di punti.

Può allora accadere (e accade infatti) che intervengano dei compensi, per cui il contributo del primo termine $\frac{\mu_0}{r}$ risulti identicamente nullo.

Ecco perchè, di fronte alle applicazioni elettromagnetiche, viene ad acquistare speciale importanza anche il termine μ_1.

(1) Cfr. HERGLOTZ, loc. cit.

A. GARBASSO

SU LO SPETTRO NORMALE DI UNA VIBRAZIONE SMORZATA

§ 1.

Secondo una teoria classica di Lord Kelvin, la corrente di scarica in un circuito, fornito di autoinduzione, di resistenza e di capacità, è sinussoidale e smorzata ([1]).

Questo risultato trovò più tardi, per opera del Bjerknes, una verifica sperimentale ([2]).

Ludwig Zehnder dimostrò a sua volta che un oscillatore di Hertz fornisce per diffrazione uno spettro continuo ([3]); e la stessa cosa fu riconosciuta, nel caso della rifrazione prismatica, da Aschkinass e da me ([4]).

Cercai di rendermi conto di codesti fenomeni, rappresentando la funzione

$$e^{-at} \sin bt$$

con un integrale di Fourier, secondo la formola ([5])

$$(1) \qquad e^{-at} \sin bt = \frac{1}{\pi} \int_0^\infty \sin \alpha t \, . \, d\alpha \left[\frac{a}{(\alpha - b)^2 + a^2} - \frac{a}{(\alpha + b)^2 + a^2} \right] .$$

La (1) deriva immediatamènte, sebbene a suo tempo io l'avessi dedotta per altra via, dall'espressione consueta del teorema di Fourier, vale a dire dalla

$$f(t) = \frac{1}{\pi} \int_0^\infty d\alpha \int_{-\infty}^{+\infty} f(\lambda) \, . \, \cos \alpha (\lambda - t) \, . \, d\lambda \, .$$

([1]) W. Thomson, *On transient electric currents* (Math. and physical Papers, I, 534, 1882).

([2]) V. Bjerknes, *Ueber die Dämpfung schneller elektrischer Schwingungen* (Wied. Ann., XLIV, 74, 1891).

([3]) L. Zehnder, *Messungen mit Strahlen elektrischer Kraft* (Wied. Ann., LIII, 162, 1894).

([4]) A. Garbasso und E. Aschkinass, *Ueber Brechung und Dispersion der Strahle elektrischer Kraft* (Wied. Ann., LIII, 534, 1894).

([5]) A. Garbasso, *Sulla luce bianca* (Atti R. Acc. d. Sc. di Torino, XXX, 186, 1894).

Se la rappresentazione si limita ai valori *positivi* della t, e si pone, *come è perfettamente lecito*,

$$f(-t) = -f(t),$$

risulta infatti

$$f(t) = \frac{2}{\pi} \int_0^\infty \sin \alpha t \, . \, d\alpha \int_0^\infty f(\lambda) \sin \alpha\lambda \, . \, d\lambda \, ;$$

e nel caso nostro, sostituendo per $f(t)$ il suo valore, si ottiene appunto la (1).

Codesta equazione fa vedere chiaramente che una vibrazione smorzata risulta in fondo dalla sopraposizione di infinite vibrazioni semplici, i cui periodi variano con continuità; e cioè possiede uno spettro continuo nel comune significato ottico della parola.

Cercai del resto più tardi, insieme a mio fratello Alberto, di dimostrare la stessa cosa per altra via ([1]).

§ 2.

Le nostre conclusioni furono contestate dal sig. E. CARVALLO, in una sua Nota, vecchia già di parecchi anni, della quale conobbi però l'esistenza, casualmente, solo in questi ultimi tempi. Il CARVALLO scrive ([2]):

« ..... Je refuterai d'abord le travail de MM. GARBASSO. Il repose sur une « faute materielle, ... La faute est que les auteurs admettent pour formule de « FOURIER

$$f(t) = \int_0^\infty dx \, . \, \varphi(x) \, . \sin \frac{2\pi t}{x}$$

« oubliant ainsi la phase, fonction de la variable x, comme l'amplitude $\varphi(x)$, et « qui doit figurer sous le signe sinus. Cette faute est le fondement de la méthode ».

All'egregio A. è manifestamente sfuggito che la vibrazione smorzata ha un senso fisico solo a partire da un istante determinato. La vibrazione *comincia* a un certo tempo, con una certa ampiezza; e il prolungarla fino a $t = -\infty$ può essere comodo per il calcolo, ma fisicamente non significa nulla o anzi è un errore. Bisogna limitarsi invece ai valori positivi della variabile e allora la (1) è legittima, come ho fatto osservare.

Questa svista del sig. CARVALLO diventa subito appresso « le fondement de sa méthode ». Egli prende infatti la funzione

$$e^{-at} \sin bt \, ,$$

([1]) A. et A. GARBASSO, *Sur la forme de la perturbation dans un rayon de lumière solaire* (Arch. des sc. phys. et nat., (4), IV, 105, 1897).

([2]) E. CARVALLO, *Sur la nature de la lumière blanche* (Journal de physique, (3), IX, 138, 1900).

senza curarsi del campo in cui rappresenta il fenomeno fisico, e dimostra che essa deve attraversare il reticolo appunto come un'oscillazione semplice, dando dunque uno spettro normale di righe chiare ed oscure.

§ 3.

Io non sono riuscito per mia parte a trattare il problema in modo rigoroso, ma mi lusingo di proporne una soluzione più approssimata di quella del CARVALLO.

Se si rappresenta graficamente la

$$e^{-at} \sin bt$$

si trova un andamento ben noto, e l'area compresa fra la curva e l'asse delle t ha per valore assoluto [1]

$$A = \cdots + \int_{-2\frac{\pi}{b}}^{-\frac{\pi}{b}} e^{-at} \sin bt \,.\, dt - \int_{-\frac{\pi}{b}}^{0} + \int_{0}^{+\frac{\pi}{b}} - \int_{+\frac{\pi}{b}}^{+2\frac{\pi}{b}} + \cdots$$

Ma l'integrale indefinito è

$$\int e^{-at} \sin bt \,.\, dt = - \frac{e^{-at}}{a^2 + b^2} (a \sin bt + b \cos bt) \,,$$

e dunque

$$A = \frac{1}{a^2 + b^2} \Big\{ \cdots - \Big[e^{-at}(a \sin bt + b \cos bt) \Big]_{-2\frac{\pi}{b}}^{-\frac{\pi}{b}} +$$

$$+ \Big[\;\Big]_{-\frac{\pi}{b}}^{0} - \Big[\;\Big]_{0}^{+\frac{\pi}{b}} + \Big[\;\Big]_{+\frac{\pi}{b}}^{+2\frac{\pi}{b}} - \cdots \Big\} ,$$

$$= \frac{b}{a^2 + b^2} \Big[\Big(\cdots e^{+2\frac{\pi}{b}a} + 2e^{+\frac{\pi}{b}a} + 1 \Big) + \Big(1 + 2e^{-\frac{\pi}{b}a} + e^{-2\frac{\pi}{b}a} + \cdots \Big) \Big] .$$

La prima parentesi corrisponde alle aree che stanno a sinistra del punto $t = 0$, la seconda alle aree che stanno a destra dello stesso punto.

Ma la seconda soltanto entra in giuoco, ed entra in giuoco tutta intera, se vogliamo calcolare il fenomeno fisico.

Ora io vedo due modi di condurre il calcolo. Il primo, ed è quello del sig. CARVALLO, consiste nel tener conto delle due parentesi, il secondo, ed è quello che in-

[1] Se $e^{-at} \sin bt$ è un'intensità di corrente, la **A** è la quantità complessiva di elettricità che passa, nei due sensi, attraverso alla sezione del conduttore.

tendo indicare qui, consiste nel limitare la seconda somma ad un numero finito di termini.

È facile vedere a quali errori si vada incontro nell'uno e nell'altro caso.

Poniamo all'uopo

$$A = A_1 + A_2,$$

$$A_1 = \frac{b}{a^2+b^2}\left(\ldots e^{+2\frac{\pi}{b}a} + 2e^{+\frac{\pi}{b}a} + 1\right),$$

$$A_2 = \frac{b}{a^2+b^2}\left(1 + 2e^{-\frac{\pi}{b}a} + e^{-2\frac{\pi}{b}a} + \cdots\right).$$

Sommando verrà, come è facile verificare

$$A_1 = \infty,$$

$$A_2 = \frac{b}{a^2+b^2}\cdot\frac{1+e^{-\frac{\pi}{b}a}}{1-e^{-\frac{\pi}{b}a}}\cdot\lim_{k=\infty}\left(1-e^{-2k\frac{\pi}{b}a}\right),$$

(2) $$= \frac{b}{a^2+b^2}\cdot\frac{1+e^{-\frac{\pi}{b}a}}{1-e^{-\frac{\pi}{b}a}}.$$

Se ci limitiamo nella seconda somma ad un numero finito k di vibrazioni complete, risulta invece

$$A_2' = \frac{b}{a^2-b^2}\cdot\frac{1+e^{-\frac{\pi}{b}a}}{1-e^{-\frac{\pi}{b}a}}\cdot\left(1-e^{-2k\frac{\pi}{b}a}\right),$$

e per la (2)

$$\frac{A_2'}{A_2} = 1 - e^{-2k\frac{\pi}{b}a}.$$

Ma in un caso pratico è facile verificare che l'esponenziale $e^{-2k\frac{\pi}{b}a}$ diviene assai presto (p. e. per $k = 50$ o 100) dell'ordine di 10^{-6} [1].

[1] Se si ricorda che Bjerknes ha trovato in una misura diretta 0,77 come rapporto fra le ampiezze della seconda e della prima onda, per un oscillatore di Hertz, e si pone, arrotondando, $e^{-2k\frac{\pi}{b}a} = 0{,}8$, risulta

k	$e^{-2k\frac{\pi}{b}a}$
1	0,8
20	0,01152921
40	0,00013292
60	0,00000153
80	0,00000002

E dunque si conclude che col processo del CARVALLO noi portiamo di nostro arbitrio nel calcolo un termine (A_1), che è infinito rispetto a quello (A_2), che entra in giuoco realmente nel fenomeno; dove considerando A_2' in luogo di A_2, e facendo k un po' grande, si trascura invece un termine trascurabile.

Ciò posto, nell'intervallo da zero a $2k\frac{\pi}{b}$, la funzione $e^{-at}\sin bt$ si potrà svolgere in una serie di soli seni, e apparirà dunque come la sopraposizione di un numero infinito di treni *limitati* di onde.

Di ciascuno di questi sarà facile dimostrare, col procedimento del SCHUSTER (¹), che gli corrisponde uno spettro continuo, e la stessa cosa risulterà dunque vera per la vibrazione smorzata.

(¹) A. SCHUSTER, *On interference phenomena* (Phil. Mag., (5), XXXVII, 509, 1894).

G. GREENHILL

GEOMETRY OF THE MOTION OF A SPINNING TOP

I have the honour to bring before this Congress a method of drawing, with ease and accuracy, a family of curves described by a point on the axis of a spinning top; and the family can be varied indefinitely.

Considering that there are three constants disposible in the motion, there is a triply infinite assemblage (∞^3) in number; and the selection of an illustrative numerical example is at first sight an embarrassing one in its variety.

But if we avail ourself of Darboux's theorem of the representation of the gyroscopic motion of the axis by a deformable hyperboloid (such as those designed by Wiener, procurable now from Teubner) the constants of the motion are given by geometrical magnitudes, and calculation is replaced by measurement on a drawing.

Darboux's theorem asserts that if one generating line of the hyperboloid is held fixed in a vertical position, and the opposite parallel generator is moved so as to describe with its lower end a certain Poinsot herpolhode on the horizontal table; then the generating lines crossing the fixed vertical generator describe each a cone about its fixed point of intersection, and the cone is a gyroscopic cone of the axis of a top, with respect to space revolving about the vertical with an appropriate constant angular velocity.

Or reducing the space to rest, the Poinsot herpolhode must receive a rotation reversed, the effect of which is equivalent to Sylvester's extension of Poinsot's theorem, which asserts that ellipsoids confocal with Poinsot's momental ellipsoid will roll on parallel planes, provided with an appropriate constant angular velocity.

Having selected then a deformable hyperboloid for illustration, the focal ellipse, which is seen when the hyperboloid is flattened in its plane, will give the modulus k of the elliptic function of the motion by the ratio of its axes, and the excentricity will be the comodulus k', required for the elliptic function of the imaginary period in the parameter of the Third Elliptic Integral which arises in the motion.

This parameter is determined by the choice of the generating line which is to be held vertical, a tangent PQ of the focal ellipse, touching it at P, OQ being the perpendicular on it from the centre O.

The semi-axes OA and OB being denoted by a and $b = ka$, the angle AOQ or ω is put equal to am fK$'$, where fK$'$ is a fraction f of the co-period K$'$, and either ω or fK$'$ is called the parameter of the Third Elliptic Integral required.

To realise the deformation of the hyperboloid, the tangent generator PQ is moved so as to describe the herpolhode, while the parallel generator $P_0 Q_0$ is held fixed and vertical; but for the geometrical argument it is simpler to suppose that the parallel line through the centre O is the fixed generator of a deformable hyperboloid of half the size, and that PQ is moved to describe the herpolhode, reduced one half.

Having selected a point H on PQ to describe the appropriate herpolhode, OH will be taken to represent the vector of angular momentum of the associated motion of the top, and the axis of the top to be the generating line through O parallel to HP$'$, the other tangent to the focal ellipse from H, not only at the start from the plane of the focal ellipse, but during all the subsequent motion, until the hyperboloid is flattened in the plane of the focal hyperbola.

The point H is guided in its herpolhode (ϱ, ϖ) in a plane perpendicular to PQ, and the hodograph of the motion will give a curve the projection of a point C fixed in the axis of the top.

The axis OI of resultant angular velocity will join O with I, a point fixed in the generator through H, and so I will describe a spherical curve.

These theorems were brought before the Mathematical Congress at Heidelberg; and I shall avail myself again of the privilege of addressing an instructed audience, and confine myself to a statement of some further results, as you will prefer to invent your own demonstration.

Recalling the notation given there, and EULER's angles θ, ψ, φ, I find it more convenient to measure θ from the downward vertical; so that, putting $\cos\theta = z$,

(1) $$nt = \int \frac{dz}{\sqrt{(2Z)}}$$

(2) $$Z = (z - F)(1 - z^2) - \frac{G^2 - 2GG'z + G'^2}{2A^2 n^2}$$

$$= (z - E)(1 - z^2) - \tfrac{1}{2}\left(\frac{Gz - G'}{An}\right)^2$$

$$= (z - D)(1 - z^2) - \tfrac{1}{2}\left(\frac{G - G'z}{An}\right)^2$$

$$= (z_3 - z)(z - z_2)(z - z_1),$$

(3) $$1 > z_3 > z > z_2 > -1 > z_1$$

(4) $$z_1 + z_2 + z_3 = F = E - \frac{G^2}{2A^2 n^2} = D - \frac{G'^2}{2A^2 n^2}.$$

Normalising (1) by the factor

(5) $$\sqrt{\frac{z_3 - z_1}{2}} = \frac{\mathrm{OA}}{\mathrm{OD}}, \text{ and putting } n\sqrt{\frac{z_3 - z_1}{2}} = m,$$

(6) $$mt = \int_z^{z_3} \frac{\sqrt{(z_3 - z_1)}\, dz}{\sqrt{(4 . z_3 - z . z - z_2 . z - z_1)}}$$

$$= \mathrm{sn}^{-1}\sqrt{\frac{z_3 - z}{z_3 - z_2}} = \mathrm{cn}^{-1}\sqrt{\frac{z - z_2}{z_3 - z_2}} = \mathrm{dn}^{-1}\sqrt{\frac{z - z_1}{z_3 - z_1}},$$

(7) $$z = z_2 \,\mathrm{sn}^2\, mt + z_3 \,\mathrm{cn}^2\, mt, \quad k^2 = \frac{z_3 - z_2}{z_3 - z_1}.$$

The vectorial angle ϖ in the herpolhode described by H is connected with ψ by the relation

(8) $$\psi - \varpi = \tan^{-1} \frac{\sqrt{(2\mathrm{Z})}}{\frac{\mathrm{G}z - \mathrm{G}'}{\mathrm{A}n}}$$

and

(9) $$\varpi = \int_z^{z_3} \frac{\frac{\mathrm{G}z - \mathrm{G}'}{2\mathrm{A}n}}{z - \mathrm{E}} \frac{dz}{\sqrt{(2\mathrm{Z})}}$$

(10) $$\psi = \int \frac{\frac{\mathrm{G} - \mathrm{G}'z}{\mathrm{A}n}}{1 - z^2} \frac{dz}{\sqrt{(2\mathrm{Z})}}$$

so that (8) gives the result of the addition of the two Third Elliptic Integrals in (10) into the single one in (9).

Then

(11) $$\int_{\mathrm{E}}^{z_3} \frac{\sqrt{(z_3 - z_1)}\, dz}{\sqrt{(4\mathrm{Z})}} = \int_{z_2}^{z_3} + \int_{\mathrm{E}}^{z_2} = \mathrm{K} + f\mathrm{K}'i$$

(12) $$f\mathrm{K}' = \int_{\mathrm{E}}^{z_2} \frac{\sqrt{(z_3 - z_1)}\, dz}{\sqrt{(-4\mathrm{Z})}}$$

(13) $$\mathrm{K} = \int_{z_2}^{z_3} \frac{\sqrt{(z_3 - z_1)}\, dz}{\sqrt{(4\mathrm{Z})}} = \int_{-\infty}^{z_1} \frac{\sqrt{(z_3 - z_1)}\, dz}{\sqrt{(4\mathrm{Z})}}$$

(14) $$\mathrm{K}' = \int_{z_1}^{z_2} \frac{\sqrt{(z_3 - z_1)}\, dz}{\sqrt{(-4\mathrm{Z})}} = \int_{z_3}^{\infty} \frac{\sqrt{(z_2 - z_1)}\, dz}{\sqrt{(-4\mathrm{Z})}}.$$

For the complete determination of the motion of any point of the Top, EULER's third angle φ is required, and the Third Elliptic Integral with pole at

$$z = D\ ,\ -1\ ,\ +1\ , \tag{15}$$

and parameter $f'K'$, f_1K', f_2K', defined as above by

$$\int_{D,-1}^{z_3} \frac{\sqrt{(z_3 - z_1)}\,dz}{\sqrt{(4Z)}} = \int_{z_2}^{z_3} + \int_{D,-1}^{z_2} = K + (f', f_1)K', \tag{16}$$

$$(f', f_1)K' = \int_{D,-1}^{z_2} \frac{\sqrt{(z_3 - z_1)}\,dz}{\sqrt{(-4Z)}}, \tag{17}$$

$$f_2K'i = \int_{z_3}^{1} \frac{\sqrt{(z_3 - z_1)}\,dz}{\sqrt{(4Z)}}\ ,\quad f_2K' = \int_{z_3}^{'} \frac{\sqrt{(z_3 - z_1)}\,dz}{\sqrt{(-4Z)}} \tag{18}$$

and then

$$f = f_1 - f_2\ ,\quad f' = f_1 + f_2; \tag{19}$$

and keeping f constant, the value of f_1, f_2, f' is given in the columns, showing their gradual change.

When f' as well as f is a rational fraction, so that f_1 and f_2 are rational, the Multiplicative Elliptic functions employed by KLEIN become pseudo-elliptic, and may be replaced by algebraical function qualified by an exponential function of the time as a secular term.

Of all the positions of H on the line PQ, we select a certain L as the starting point, determined by making QL to LP the ratio of $\text{zn}\, fK'$ to $\text{zn}(1-f)K'$, and so requiring the use of LEGENDRE's Table; because we find that when H is placed at L, the apsidal angle of ϖ and ψ, which we denote by Π and Ψ, becomes $\frac{1}{2}\pi f$.

Moving H to a position above L,

$$\Pi = \Psi = \tfrac{1}{2}\pi f + \frac{LH}{OA}K, \tag{20}$$

or in degrees

$$\Pi^\circ = \Psi^\circ = \left(f + \frac{LK}{OA}\frac{K}{\frac{1}{2}\pi}\right)90^\circ, \tag{21}$$

but if H is placed below L, the apsidal angle is reduced by a corresponding amount, proportional to the distance from L; so that having calculated the length LH which makes

$$\frac{LH}{OA}\frac{K}{\frac{1}{2}\pi} = 1, \tag{22}$$

any fraction h of this length will displace H to a point where the apsidal angle is increased or diminished by this fraction h of 90°.

We may notice here that, as interpreted geometrically on the focal ellipse

(23) $$\operatorname{zn} f\mathrm{K}' = \frac{\mathrm{LQ}}{\mathrm{OA}} \quad , \quad -\operatorname{zd} f\mathrm{K}' = \frac{\mathrm{LP}}{\mathrm{OA}},$$

$$\operatorname{zs} f\mathrm{K}' = \frac{\mathrm{LV}}{\mathrm{OA}} \quad , \quad -\operatorname{zc} f\mathrm{K}' = \frac{\mathrm{LT}}{\mathrm{OA}},$$

employing GLAISHER's notation for the Zeta functions zn, zd, zs, zc.

And putting $z_3 = \cos\theta_3$, $z_2 = \cos\theta_2$, $z_1 = -\operatorname{ch}\theta_1$, θ_3 is the angle between the tangents HP and HP′, θ_2 is the angle between S′H and HS, and

(24) $$\operatorname{ch}\theta_1 = \frac{\mathrm{SH}^2 + \mathrm{S'H}^2}{2\mathrm{SH}.\mathrm{S'H}} \quad , \quad e^{\theta_1} = \frac{\mathrm{S'H}}{\mathrm{SH}}.$$

The perpendicular SQ_2 on OQ will cut off the length OQ_2 to which OQ diminishes as θ increases from θ_3 to θ_2.

The angle θ_2 and θ_3 is read off in the figure from

(25) $$\mathrm{SHI'} = \frac{\theta_2 - \theta_3}{2} \quad , \quad \mathrm{S'HI} = \frac{\theta_2 + \theta_3}{2}.$$

Also

(26) $$z_3 = \cos\theta_3 = \frac{\mathrm{AB}^2 - \mathrm{OH}^2}{\mathrm{HS}.\mathrm{HS'}},$$

(27) $$z_2 = \cos\theta_2 = \frac{\mathrm{OS}^2 - \mathrm{OH}^2}{\mathrm{HS}.\mathrm{HS'}},$$

(28) $$\frac{z_3 - z_2}{2} = \frac{\mathrm{OB}^2}{\mathrm{HS}.\mathrm{HS'}},$$

and this appears to determine HS . HS′ or OD^2 in the easiest way.

We have put HS . HS′ $= c^2$, so that

(29) $$c = \frac{\mathrm{OB}}{\sqrt{\dfrac{z_3 - z_2}{2}}}$$

and denoting HQ, HQ′ by δ, δ'

(30) $$\frac{\mathrm{G}, \mathrm{G'}}{2\mathrm{A}n} = \frac{\delta, \delta'}{c}$$

which enables these dynamical constants to be read from the diagram, with proper attention to the sign.

We are now in a position to determine the apsidal angle, and the limiting inclination θ_3 and θ_2 of the axis of the top for a family of such cases, where the modulus k and the fraction fK′ of the coperiod K′ have been decided by the focal ellipse of a deformable hyperboloid, and by a tangent line PQ, such that

$$\text{(31)} \qquad AOQ = \omega = \operatorname{am} f K' \quad , \quad f K' = F(\omega, k').$$

When f is a rational fraction, such as $\frac{1}{2}, \frac{2}{3}, \frac{1}{3}, \frac{1}{5}, \ldots$ the theory of ABEL's *Pseudo-Elliptic Integral* may be utilised for the reduction of the transcendental expressions to an algebrical result, capable of exact numerical calculation; and so I had made a start in fig. 1 with $f = \frac{1}{2}$, and choosing $k = \frac{4}{5}$, somewhat larger than before, so as to give more character to the algebraical herpolode and associated top-motion, shown in the central figure; these have been calculated by a number of points and so we may be certain of the general features.

The other figures are obtained by moving H to a position above or below L; Π and Ψ, θ_3, θ_3, z_3, z_2, z_1, ... are measured on Table I from the ellipse; the curve is then drawn in freehand, and the general appearance can be inferred; the red colour shews the path above the equator, and the blue below.

The same in a Table and Fig. 2, where $f = \frac{2}{3}$, so as to give a central trefoil figure, and then the subsequent variations, which can be multiplied indefinitely.

In a Table and Figure 3 and 4, a small value of k and f had been selected: $k = \sin 15°$, $f = \frac{1}{3}$, and $k = \sin 10°$, $f = \frac{1}{5}$; corresponding to a stereoscopic figure exhibited; with the object of showing the true shape in a penultimate form of the pseudo-regular Precession, described in KLEIN-SOMMERFELD's *Kreisel-Theorie*, p. 326 obtained when H in placed between b and P, or T and b'.

In filling in the Table, a start is made at L, with the value of the apsidal angle Π and Ψ, also of θ_3 and θ_2, and z_3, z_2, z_1.

Next the value of θ_3 and θ_2 is entered at certain cardinal points where it can be inferred with certainty, after which it is easy to interpolate any intermediate value; and it will be noticed that a rule of sign must be observed carefully, to preserve the continuity. The value of Π and Ψ can then be filled in, and an aliquot value chosen when it is desired to construct a figure which closes on itself.

If a start is made with H at I, at an infinite distance above L, it will be noticed that θ_3 and θ_2 are both $+180°$ and $\frac{G \cdot G'}{2An}$ unity; but since

$$\text{(32)} \qquad nT = \frac{c}{a} K$$

the motion of the axis is very sluggish, T denoting the time in seconds of a beat of the axis.

As H is moved down gradually past L to I′ an infinite distance below, the angle θ_3 diminishes from 180° to 0°, when H is at P, after which θ_3 is taken as negative and diminishing ultimately to $-180°$, when $\frac{G , G'}{2An} = -1$.

But θ_2 diminishes from 180° till H reaches b, where PQ crosses the tangent at B, and now there are cusps at θ_2; as H proceeds downward, θ_2 increases again up to 180°, when H is at T, and afterwards increases beyond 180° to a maximum at b', where PQ crosses the tangent at B', and here again there are cusps; below this, θ_2 diminishes again to 180° when H reaches L'.

If PQ crosses the tangents at A and A' in a and a', the auxiliary circle in α and α', and the orthoptic circle in β and β', we find

$$\theta_2 \text{ (at } a') = \theta_2 \text{ (at } a) \tag{33}$$

$$\theta_3 \text{ (at } a') = 90° + \theta_3 \text{ (at } b) = 180° + \theta_3 \text{ (at } a') = 270° + \theta_3 \text{ (at } b')$$

$$\theta_3 \text{ (at V)} = 180° - 2\omega \quad , \quad \theta_3 \text{ (at P)} = 0 \quad , \quad \theta_2 \text{ (at P)} = \theta_2 \text{ (at V)} = 2\text{QO}\alpha ,$$

$$\theta_3 \text{ (at T)} = -2\omega \quad , \quad \theta_2 \text{ (at T)} = 180° ,$$

$$\theta_3 (\beta) = \theta_3 (\beta') = 90°$$

values which are filled in at once on the Table.

So also $\frac{G}{2An}$ starts at $+1$ when H is at I, diminishes to zero with H at Q, and beyond is a taker negative till it reaches -1 with H at 1'; and $\frac{G'}{2An}$ starts in the same manner, changing sign by passing through zero where PQ crosses the pedal of the ellipse and the Spherical Pendulum condition is realised, finishing also at the value -1 when H reaches I'.

A few remarks may be added about the system of quadric surfaces, homothetic with confocals and contrafocals, which generate by their rolling the herpolhode curve of angular momentum described by H, in its various position on PQ.

Writing the equation of a rolling surface

$$Ax^2 + By^2 + Cz^2 = D\delta^2 , \tag{34}$$

we find

$$\frac{A}{D} = \frac{HQ}{HV} \ , \ \frac{B}{D} = \frac{HQ}{HT} \ , \ \frac{C}{D} = \frac{HQ}{HP} , \tag{35}$$

with proper attention to sign, the surface being coaxial with the deformable hyperboloid.

We are not restricted now to momental ellipsoids of real positive matter, in which A, B, C are positive, and can make up the sides of a triangle; the rolling surface may be an ellipsoid of any shape, or a hyperboloid of one or two sheets, so that points of inflexion may come into existence, as discussed by De Sparre and Hess; a point of inflexion on H corresponding to a stationery value of Ψ.

The same curve of H may be supposed generated by the rolling on the plane of a line of curvature, the intersection of the ellipsoid and hyperboloid of two sheets confocal with the deformable hyperboloid, and passing through H.

With H at V, T, or P, then A, B, or C is infinite, and the rolling surface is a plate, an elliptic plate at V and T, but hyperbolic at P.

When H is at Q, the rolling surface must be supposed a cone; and the point Q separates the rolling surfaces into two families, each confocal among themselves, but contrafocal with the rest.

Moving H upward from I makes the apsidal angle Π and Ψ increase, and opens out the herpolhode curve of H in a fan like manner.

But a movement of H downward causes the herpolhode to close up; and as H passes through b, when there are cusps on the gyroscopic curve at P_2, the herpolhode becomes crumpled into inflexions, which imply a stationary value of Ψ, and loops of C.

This goes on till H reaches P, when there are cusps at H_3, and the axis passes through the downward vertical and $\theta_3 = 0$.

We must take θ_3 negative when H is below P, and Ψ must be taken as $\Pi - 180°$, until H passes T when Ψ is again the same as Π. Thus at a certain point between P and T, Π changes sign by passing through zero, and there $\Psi = -180°$.

With H at T, $\theta_2 = 180°$, the axis passes through the highest vertical (a Rosette curve in Klein's name) and there are cusps at H_2.

From T to b', there are inflexions on H, and loops on C, shrinking into cusps when H reaches b'; and beyond b' the curves become featureless.

Loops in the curve of H correspond to undulations produced by the rolling of the associated surface

$$A' x^2 + B' y^2 + C' z^2 = D' \delta'^2 \tag{36}$$

required in the complete discussion in Jacobi's manner of the third Euler's angle φ; and conversely; so that loops and undulations in H should receive consideration as reciprocal properties, in a complete discussion of the theorems of Hess and de Sparre on this question.

The various symmetrical relations given by Darboux (in Despeyrous, *Mécanique*) between

$$A, B, C, D \text{ and } A', B', C', D',$$

or their reciprocal in his notation,

$$a, b, c, h, \text{ and } a', b', c', h',$$

can be interpreted by geometrical relations on the diagram.

To give an instance,

$$\frac{B - C}{A} + \frac{B' - C'}{A'} = 0 \tag{37}$$

is the equivalent of

$$\frac{HV \cdot PT}{HT \cdot HP} = \frac{HV' \cdot PT'}{HT' \cdot HP'}; \tag{38}$$

and

(39) $$\left(1-\frac{A}{B}\right)\left(1-\frac{A}{C}\right)=\left(1-\frac{A'}{B'}\right)\left(1-\frac{B'}{C'}\right)$$

of

(40) $$\frac{TV\,.\,PV}{HV^2}=\frac{T'V'\,.\,P'V'}{HV'^2}=\frac{OX}{OR};$$

and so on.

It will be an interesting enquiry to pursue these interpretations throughout the deformation of the hyperboloid, out of the focal ellipse, and up to the focal hyperbola.

In the state of Steady Motion the modulus k is undistinguishable from zero, and the focal ellipse is seen as a straight line, and its pedal with respect to O becomes two circles.

The deformable ellipsoid is now practically a rigid lattice of rods radiating from S and S′, and in the motion it revolves round one rod held vertical.

The period K′ is infinite, so that $f=0$, but $\operatorname{zn} fK'=\sin\omega$; so that L coincides with S; and for the apsidal angle Ψ,

(41) $$\frac{\Psi}{\frac{1}{2}\pi}=\frac{HS}{OS},$$

(42) $$\frac{nT}{\pi}=\frac{OS}{\sqrt{(HS\,.\,HS')}}.$$

For a spherical pendulum H must be placed at a point where SQ crosses the circle on the diameter OS′.

A geometrical interpretation can then be given to Bravais's result for the apsidal angle of a spherical pendulum moving in the neighbourhood of the downward vertical, when SQ, SO are nearly coincident.

In the general case putting $z=\mp 1$ in (2),

(43) $$\frac{\delta-\delta'}{c}=2\operatorname{ch}\tfrac{1}{2}\theta_1\sin\tfrac{1}{2}\theta_2\sin\tfrac{1}{2}\theta_3,$$

(44) $$\frac{\delta+\delta'}{c}=2\operatorname{sh}\tfrac{1}{2}\theta_1\cos\tfrac{1}{2}\theta_2\cos\tfrac{1}{2}\theta_3;$$

so that in the spherical pendulum, with $\delta'=0$,

(45) $$\tan\tfrac{1}{2}\theta_2\tan\tfrac{1}{2}\theta_3=\operatorname{th}\tfrac{1}{2}\theta_1,$$

and with θ_2 and θ_3 small c may be replaced by OS, and

(46) $$\frac{\delta}{c}=\frac{HQ}{OS}=2\operatorname{ch}\tfrac{1}{2}\theta_1\sin\tfrac{1}{2}\theta_2\sin\tfrac{1}{2}\theta_3.$$

Make $Sq = SO$; then

(47) $$\operatorname{lt}\frac{Vq}{VQ} = \tfrac{1}{2}\ ,\ \operatorname{lt}\frac{VQ}{HQ} = \tfrac{1}{2}\ ,\ \operatorname{lt}\frac{Vq}{HQ} = \tfrac{1}{4}\ ,\ \operatorname{lt}\frac{Hq}{HQ} = \tfrac{3}{4},$$

$$\operatorname{lt}\frac{Hq}{OS} = \operatorname{lt}\frac{Hq}{HQ}\operatorname{lt}\frac{HQ}{OS} = \tfrac{3}{2}\sin\tfrac{1}{2}\theta_2 \sin\tfrac{1}{2}\theta_3\ ,\ \text{with ch}\,\tfrac{1}{2}\theta_1 = 1;$$

and for the apsidal angle in (41)

(48) $$\frac{\Psi}{\frac{1}{2}\pi} = \frac{HS}{OS} = 1 + \frac{Hq}{OS} = 1 + \tfrac{3}{2}\sin\tfrac{1}{2}\theta_2\ \sin\tfrac{1}{2}\theta_3 = 1 + \frac{3}{8}\frac{ab}{l^2},$$

Bravais's result correcting that given by Lagrange.

The result may be generalised for the motion of a smooth particle in the neighbourhood of the lowest part of any surface of revolution

(49) $$r^2 = 2lz + \lambda z^2 + \mu z^3 + \cdots;$$

We find now that

(50) $$\frac{\Psi}{\frac{1}{2}\pi} = 1 + \frac{ab}{8l^2}(4 + \lambda),$$

(51) $$\frac{nT}{\pi} = 1 + \frac{a^2 + b^2}{16\, l^2}(4 + 3\lambda),$$

agreeing with Bravais's result, when $\lambda = -1$, $\mu = 0, \ldots,$ on the sphere.

To recapitulate, this method of drawing gyroscopic curves consists in the selection of an ellipse, and a fixed tangent; and thence of reading off the limiting inclinations θ_2 and θ_3 of the axis, and Ψ the apsidal angle, which can be made an aliquot part of the circumference when it is desired to have a closed figure.

A simple formula can be calculated for the curvature of the projection P, to give greater accuracy to the drawing.

In this way a series of diagrams can be supplied for use in a formal treatise, such as Kreisel-Sommerfeld, *Kreisel-Theorie*, and they can be compared with experimental results, as given in Webster's, *Dynamics*.

The use of the two colours, red and blue, is I think essential, to distinguish the upper and under part of the curve; bnt the direction of motion may be reversed, dynamically by a reversal of the angular velocity, or in appearance according as the diagram is looked at as a star chart, fixed to the cieling, or a sea-chart on the floor.

I had intended to exibit to the Congress the apparatus described above, and the diagram to which reference has been made; but diagrams and apparatus went astray in the transit, and did not arrive in time.

A. SOMMERFELD

EIN BEITRAG ZUR HYDRODYNAMISCHEN ERKLAERUNG DER TURBULENTEN FLUESSIGKEITSBEWEGUNGEN

§ 1.

Uebersicht über die Litteratur des Gegenstandes.

Die Kluft zwischen der technischen Hydraulik einerseits und der theoretischen Hydrodynamik andererseits, zwischen den Versuchen grossen Massstabes einerseits und den Laboratoriumsversuchen an Capillaren andererseits ist oft betont und beklagt worden.

Bekanntlich hat Osborne Reynolds diese Kluft überbrückt und den physikalischen Sachverhalt geklärt durch den Begriff der « Turbulenz » oder der Instabilität von Flüssigkeitsbewegungen. Reynolds [1] wies nämlich das Vorhandensein einer kritischen Grenze für die Stabilität experimentell nach, deren qualitatives Gesetz er durch eine Dimensionsbetrachtung bestimmte. Bedeutet ϱ die Dichte, μ die Viscositätskonstante der Flüssigkeit, U die Geschwindigkeit der linearen Strömung, die auf ihre Stabilität untersucht werden soll (genauer gesagt, bei Reynolds die mittlere Geschwindigkeit im Querschnitt) und h den Durchmesser der Röhre, so ist

$$R = \frac{\varrho U h}{\mu} \tag{1}$$

eine reine Zahl, die wir die *Reynolds'sche Zahl* nennen wollen. Je nachdem diese einen gewissen kritischen Wert, etwa 2000, überschreitet oder nicht, wird die Strömung U instabil oder stabil. Vergrösserung der Viskosität wirkt also auf Stabilität, Vergrösserung der Trägheit auf Instabilität hin.

Die sehr instruktiven theoretischen Betrachtungen von Reynolds gründen sich auf ein Energiekriterium und auf die Bildung von Mittelwerten, führen aber nicht

[1] Phil. Trans. London R. Soc. Vol. 174 (1883) p. 935 und Vol. 186 (1895) p. 123.

zu einer genauen Berechnung des kritischen Wertes von R. Sie sind von H. A. Lorentz [1] wesentlich vereinfacht und erweitert worden.

Lorentz erkannte, dass der von Couette [2] experimentell behandelte Fall einer Strömung zwischen zwei parallelen Cylinderwandungen, von denen die eine ruht, die andere umgedreht wird — ähnlich der Strömung des Schmiermittels in einer Dampfmaschine zwischen Zapfen und Lagerschale — einfacher ist als der Fall der Strömung in einer Röhre. Ferner vereinfachte Lorentz den Couette'schen Fall noch dahin, dass er von der Krümmung der Cylinderflächen absah und das folgende ebene Problem untersuchte, das auch schon in einer Arbeit von Lord Kelvin [3] formulirt wird:

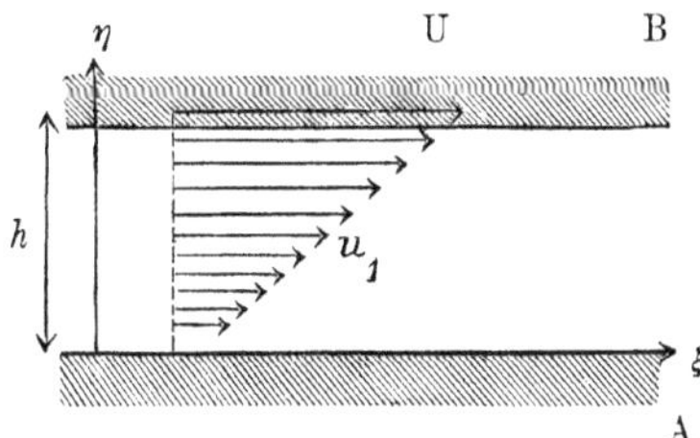

Von den beiden Platten A und B im Abstande h von einander, an denen die Flüssigkeit haftet, wird B mit der Geschwindigkeit U im Sinne des Pfeiles der Figur bewegt, A ruht. Zwischen beiden bildet sich ein lineares Geschwindigkeitsgefälle aus. Unter welchen Umständen ist diese Strömung stabil?

Eben dieses Problem werden wir nach einer von der Lorentz'schen gänzlich verschiedenen, nämlich nach der klassischen *Methode der kleinen Schwingungen* behandeln. Die allgemeine Lösung desselben kann leicht durch Integrale mit Bessel'schen Funktionen gefunden werden. Die Instabilitätsbedingung erscheint dann in der Form einer transcendenten Gleichung.

Die gegenwärtige Mitteilung führt nur bis zur Aufstellung jener Gleichung; ihre vollständige Diskussion, die mir den eingentlichen Inhalt des Problems der Turbulenz zu bilden scheint, habe ich noch nicht beendigt; ich bemerke nur, dass unsere allgemeine Methode in dem einfachsten Spezialfalle verschwindend kleiner Geschwindigkeit der Hauptbewegung zu Ergebnissen führt, welche bereits Lord Rayleigh [4] gefunden hat.

Unsere Methode kann nur dazu dienen, die Stabilitätsgrenze, d. h. den *Eintritt* der turbulenten Bewegung festzustellen, nicht der Charakter der turbulenten Bewegung, die sich nach *Ueberschreiten* der Stabilitätsgrenze ausbildet. Letztere zu finden,

(1) *Abhandlungen über theoretische Physik*. Nr. 3. *Ueber turbulente Flüssigkeitsbewegungen.*

(2) Annales de chim. et phys. Vol. 21 (1890) p. 433.

(3) Phil. Mag. (5) 24 August 1887.

(4) Scientific Papers, vol. III, Nr. 194 p. 575. *On the Question of the Stability of the Flow of Fluids.* Vgl. auch die kritischen Bemerkungen von p. 582 über die eben citirte Arbeit von Kelvin, denen ich mich anschliesse.

ist ein viel schwierigeres Problem, welches wohl nur mit den RIEMANN'schen Methoden für Schwingungen endlicher Amplitude erfolgreich in Angriff genommen werden könnte. Die Schwierigkeit liegt dabei in dem nicht linearen Charakter der hydrodynamischen Gleichungen, von dem die Methode der kleinen Schwingungen bis zu einem gewissen Grade abzusehen gestattet.

§ 2.

Die allgemeine Lösung der Differentialgleichungen.

Im Anschluss an die Figur sehen wir unser Problem als eben an, betrachten also nur die zwei Geschwindigkeitskomponenten u und v.

Die hydrodynamischen Gleichungen einer kräftefreien incompressibeln zweidimensionalen Strömung lauten:

$$\varrho\left(\frac{\partial u}{\partial t}+u\frac{\partial u}{\partial x}+v\frac{\partial u}{\partial y}\right)=\mu\Delta u-\frac{\partial p}{\partial x},$$

$$\varrho\left(\frac{\partial v}{\partial t}+u\frac{\partial v}{\partial x}+v\frac{\partial v}{\partial y}\right)=\mu\Delta v-\frac{\partial p}{\partial y},$$

$$\frac{\partial u}{\partial x}+\frac{\partial v}{\partial y}=0.$$

Der dritten Gleichung genügen wir durch Einführung eines Potentials (genauer gesagt, eines senkrecht zur xy — Ebene gerichteten Vektorpotentials), indem wir setzen:

$$u=\frac{\partial \Pi}{\partial y},\; v=-\frac{\partial \Pi}{\partial x}.$$

Wenn wir aus den beiden ersten Gleichungen p eliminieren, ergiebt sich die Differentialgleichung für Π:

$$\frac{\varrho}{\mu}\left(\frac{\partial}{\partial t}\Delta\Pi+\frac{\partial \Pi}{\partial y}\frac{\partial}{\partial x}\Delta\Pi-\frac{\partial \Pi}{\partial x}\frac{\partial}{\partial y}\Delta\Pi\right)=\Delta\Delta\Pi. \tag{2}$$

Wir setzen

$$u=u_1+u_2\,,\quad v=v_1+v_2\,,\quad \Pi=\Pi_1+\Pi_2,$$

und nennen u_1, v_1 die *Hauptbewegung*, Π_1 ihr Potential, u_2, v_2 die *Störung*, Π_2 das Störungspotential.

Nach der Figur gilt für die Hauptbewegung

$$u_1 = \mathrm{U}\frac{y}{h} = \frac{\partial \Pi_1}{\partial y}\,, \quad v_1 = 0 = -\frac{\partial \Pi_1}{\partial x}\,. \tag{3}$$

Die Störung u_2, v_2 und daher auch das Störungspotential Π_2 wird als klein vorausgesetzt, so dass Grössen zweiter Ordnung in den Differentialquotienten von Π_2 zu streichen sind. Aus (2) ergibt sich daraufhin mit Rücksicht auf (3):

$$\Delta\Delta\Pi_2 = \frac{\varrho}{\mu}\left(\frac{\partial}{\partial t}\Delta\Pi_2 + \mathrm{U}\frac{y}{h}\frac{\partial}{\partial x}\Delta\Pi_2\right). \tag{4}$$

Die Grösse $-\Delta\Pi_2 = \frac{\partial v_2}{\partial x} - \frac{\partial u_2}{\partial y}$ bedeutet die « Rotation » der Störung; dass nur diese in unserer Gleichung auftritt, letztere sich also in zwei Differentialgleichungen zweiter Ordnung auflöst, ist die besondere Vereinfachung, die der Couette'sche Fall mit sich bringt. Bei dem Problem der Strömung in einer Röhre würde die Differentialgleichung unzerlegbar von der vierten Ordnung sein.

Wir wählen h zur Längeneinheit und führen dementsprechend die unbenannten Coordinaten ein:

$$\xi = \frac{x}{h}\,, \quad \eta = \frac{y}{h}\,. \tag{5}$$

Um auch t durch eine unbenannte Coordinate zu ersetzen, können wir schreiben

$$\tau = \frac{\mathrm{U}}{h}t \tag{6}$$

Eine Lösung von (4) erhalten wir in der Form:

$$\begin{cases} \Delta\Pi_2 = e^{i(\beta\tau - \alpha\xi)}\varphi(\eta)\,, \\ \Pi_2 = e^{i(\beta\tau - \alpha\xi)}f(\eta)\,, \end{cases} \tag{7}$$

falls φ und f den folgenden Differentialgleichungen unterworfen werden:

$$\begin{cases} \dfrac{d^2\varphi}{d\eta^2} - \alpha^2\varphi = i\mathrm{R}(\beta - \alpha\eta)\varphi\,, \\[2ex] \dfrac{d^2 f}{d\eta^2} - \alpha^2 f = \varphi\,; \end{cases} \tag{8}$$

R bedeutet die durch (1) eingeführte Reynolds'sche Zahl.

Die erste Gleichung (8) ist eine RICCATI'sche. Um sie auf ihre einfachste Form zu bringen, kann man die folgende lineare Funktion von η als unabhängige Variable einführen:

$$z = \frac{\alpha^2 + i\mathrm{R}(\beta - \alpha\eta)}{(\alpha\mathrm{R})^{2/3}}\,; \tag{9}$$

dann wird einfach:

$$\frac{d^2\varphi}{dz^2} + z\varphi = 0. \tag{10}$$

Die allgemeine Lösung dieser Gleichung setzt sich aus den beiden partikulären Integralen zusammen:

$$\left\{\begin{aligned} \varphi_1 &= 1 - \frac{1}{3!}z^3 + \frac{1\,.\,4}{6!}z^6 - \frac{1\,.\,4\,.\,7}{9!}z^9 + \ldots \\ \varphi_2 &= z - \frac{2}{4!}z^4 + \frac{2\,.\,5}{7!}z^7 - \frac{2\,.\,5\,.\,8}{10!}z^{10} + \ldots \end{aligned}\right. \tag{11}$$

die sich unmittelbar nach der Methode der unbestimmten Coefficienten berechnen ([1]). Dieselben lassen sich auch durch die BESSEL'schen Funktionen mit dem Index $+\,{}^1/_3$ und $-\,{}^1/_3$ ausdrücken:

$$\left\{\begin{aligned} \varphi_1 &= \left(\frac{1}{3}\right)^{-1/3} \Gamma\left(\frac{2}{3}\right) z^{1/2} J_{-1/3}\left(\frac{2}{3}z^{3/2}\right), \\ \varphi_2 &= \left(\frac{2}{3}\right)^{-1/3} \Gamma\left(\frac{4}{3}\right) z^{1/2} J_{+1/3}\left(\frac{2}{3}z^{3/2}\right), \end{aligned}\right. \tag{12}$$

wie man entweder aus der Form der Reihen oder daraus schliesst, dass die RICCATI'sche Gleichung (10) durch eine geeignete Substitution für φ und z in die BESSEL'sche Gleichung übergeht.

Nachdem die erste Gleichung (8) allgemein integriert ist, lässt sich die Integration der zweiten Gleichnung (8) nach der Methode der Variation der Constanten auf Quadraturen zurückführen. In der Variabeln z geschrieben, lautet dieselbe:

$$\frac{d^2f}{dz^2} + k^2 f = -\frac{k^2}{\alpha^2}\varphi\,, \tag{13}$$

mit der Abkürzung

$$k^3 = \frac{\alpha^2}{\mathrm{R}}\,. \tag{14}$$

Setzen wir hier $\varphi = \mathrm{A}\varphi_1 + \mathrm{B}\varphi_2$, wo A und B die bei der Integration von (10)

([1]) Diese Reihen treten bereits bei Lord KELVIN l. c. auf.

auftretenden willkürlichen Constanten sind, so findet man ein partikuläres Integral von (13) in der Form

$$A f_1(z) + B f_2(z),$$

wo f_1, f_2 die folgenden mit φ_1 und φ_2 gebildeten Integralausdrücke sind, in denen die unteren Grenzen willkürlich gewählt werden können:

$$(15)\quad \begin{cases} f_1(z) = \dfrac{k}{\alpha^2}\displaystyle\int^z \varphi_1(z') \sin k(z' - z) dz', \\ f_2(z) = \dfrac{k}{\alpha^2}\displaystyle\int^z \varphi_2(z') \sin k(z' - z) dz'. \end{cases}$$

Das allgemeine Integral von (13) lautet nunmehr bei Benützung zweier weiterer Integrationskonstanten C und D:

$$(16)\quad f = A f_1(z) + B f_2(z) + C e^{ikz} + D e^{-ikz}.$$

Wenn auch nach dem Vorangehenden deutlich ist, dass wir in (16) die allgemeinste Form unserer Funktion f gefunden haben, so könnte doch in Zweifel gezogen werden, dass wir auf diesem Wege zugleich auch einen hinreichend allgemeinen Ansatz für das Störungspotential Π_2 gewinnen. Um die Stabilität der Hauptbewegung nachzuweisen, müssten wir diese nämlich mit einer ganz willkürlichen Anfangsstörung überlagern, welche an keine als die Incompressibilitätsbedingung gebunden ist, und müssten die zeitliche Entwickelung dieser Störung verfolgen. Einer solchen willkürlichen Anfangsstörung würde es entsprechen, dass wir das Störungspotential Π_2 für $t = 0$ gleich einer willkürlichen Funktion von ξ und η machen. Unser Ansatz (7) ist aber sowohl in seiner Abhängigkeit von ξ wie von η speziell gewählt. Indessen übersieht man leicht, dass man, was die Abhängigkeit von ξ betrifft, durch Ueberlagerung solcher spezieller Störungspotentiale (7) mit continuirlich variabelem α nach den Vorschriften der Fourier'schen Integraldarstellung in der Tat zu einer willkürlichen Abhängigkeit von ξ zwischen $\xi = -\infty$ und $\xi = +\infty$ übergehen kann. Wir dürfen uns daher begnügen, unter α irgend eine reelle Zahl verstehend, die Stabilität der Bewegung in Hinsicht auf die spezielle Störung (7) zu untersuchen. Dieselbe ist dann auch in Hinsicht auf eine nach der ξ-Richtung willkürliche Störung gesichert.

Nicht so einfach liegen die Verhältnisse, was die η-Richtung angeht. Auch hier müssten wir zeigen, dass wir eine willkürliche Funktion von η zwischen $\eta = 0$ und $\eta = 1$ durch Ueberlagerung von Störungen des speziellen Typus (7) erzeugen können. Dies wird in dem besonderen Falle einer kleinen Geschwindigkeit tatsächlich leicht bestätigt. Die transcendente Gleichung, zu der man hier gelangt, hat nämlich in Uebereinstimmung mit den oben zitierten Ergebnissen von Lord Rayleigh unendlich viele Wurzeln, deren jede einer bestimmten Unterteilung des Gebietes zwischen $\eta = 0$ und $\eta = 1$ in Partialwirbel entspricht, oder, wie wir sagen können, einer bestimmten Anzahl von Oscillationen der betr. Funktion $f(z)$. Gerade so, wie man nun bei den Fourier'schen Reihen eine willkürliche Funktion innerhalb eines endlichen Gebietes durch Ueberlagerung einer Reihe immer häufiger oscillierender Funktionen darstellt, ist eine solche Darstellung auch hier im Falle kleiner Geschwindigkeit und nach Analogie wohl auch im allgemeinen Falle möglich. Wir dürfen uns daher auch in Rücksicht auf η damit begnügen, eine Störung von dem speziellen Typus (7) zu betrachten und die Stabilität der Hauptbewegung unter dem Einfluss derselben zu untersuchen.

§ 3.

Grenzbedingungen und Aufstellung der transcendenten Gleichung.

An der ruhenden und bewegten Wand A und B (vergl. die Fig.) muss die Flüssigkeit haften und darf nicht in dieselbe eindringen. Für unsere Störungsbewegung folgt hieraus, dass für $\eta = 0$ und $\eta = 1$ gilt:

$$u_2 = v_2 = 0$$

oder

$$\frac{\partial \Pi_2}{\partial x} = \frac{\partial \Pi_2}{\partial y} = 0$$

oder

$$f = \frac{df}{d\eta} = 0.$$

In der Variabeln z mögen den Werten $\eta = 0$ und $\eta = 1$ die Werte $z = z_0$ und $z = z_1$ entsprechen, wobei nach (9) und (14)

$$(17) \qquad \left\{ \begin{aligned} z_0 &= \frac{\alpha^2 + i\mathrm{R}\beta}{(\alpha\mathrm{R})^{2/3}} = k^2 + \frac{i\beta}{k}, \\ z_1 &= \frac{\alpha^2 + i\mathrm{R}(\beta - \alpha)}{(\alpha\mathrm{R})^{2/3}} = k^2 + \frac{i(\beta - \alpha)}{k}. \end{aligned} \right.$$

Wir haben dann auch zu verlangen, dass für z_0 und z_1 gelte:

$$(18) \qquad f = \frac{df}{dz} = 0.$$

Es bestehen also vier Grenzbedingungen. Andrerseits haben wir noch vier willkürliche Konstanten zu unserer Verfügung, nämlich die Verhältnisse der Integrationsconstanten A : B : C : D in (16) und die in z implicite vorkommende Grösse β, welche nach (7) den zeitlichen Ablauf der Störung regelt. Dagegen sind die Grössen R und α gegeben, erstere durch die Geschwindigkeit der Hauptbewegung, letztere durch die Wellenlänge $^{2\pi h}/_{\alpha}$ der ihr überlagerten Störung. Zugleich mit R und α ist wegen (14) auch die Grösse k gegeben.

Unsere Grenzbedingungen (18) lauten:

$$(19)\quad \left\{\begin{array}{l} Af_1(z_0) + Bf_2(z_0) + Ce^{ikz_0} + De^{-ikz_0} = 0\,, \\ Af_1'(z_0) + Bf_2'(z_0) + ikCe^{ikz_0} - ikDe^{-ikz_0} = 0\,, \\ Af_1(z_1) + Bf_2(z_1) + Ce^{ikz_1} + De^{-ikz_1} = 0\,, \\ Af_1'(z_1) + Cf_2'(z_1) + ikCe^{ikz_1} - ikDe^{-ikz_1} = 0\,. \end{array}\right.$$

Sie lassen sich durch passende Normirung der partikulären Lösungen f_1, f_2 sehr vereinfachen. Wählen wir nämlich die untere Grenze der Integrale (15) gleich z_0, so wird nicht nur

$$f_1(z_0) = f_2(z_0) = 0$$

sondern auch

$$f_1'(z_0) = f_2'(z_0) = 0\,.$$

Die beiden ersten Gleichungen (19) verlangen daher notwendiger Weise

$$C = D = 0\,.$$

Die beiden letzten geben nach Elimination von A : B die Bedingung:

$$\left|\begin{array}{l} f_1(z_1)\,,\ f_2(z_1) \\ f_1'(z_1)\,,\ f_2'(z_1) \end{array}\right| = 0$$

oder

$$(20)\qquad \frac{f_1'(z_1)}{f_1(z_1)} = \frac{f_2'(z_1)}{f_2(z_1)}\,.$$

Wir sind also zu einer ganz bestimmten transcendenten Gleichung für die in z_0 und z_1 vorkommende Zeitkonstante β gekommen, welche im Allgemeinen einen complexen Wert von β liefern wird. Dabei sind zwei Fälle zu unterscheiden:

1) Der, oder genauer gesagt, einer der aus (20) zu berechnenden Werte von β ist *complex mit positiv imaginärem Teil.* Dann verhält sich die Hauptbewegung (R) gegenüber der betrachteten Störung (α) *stabil*, indem letztere mit der Zeit abnimmt. Zeigt sich überdies, dass alle aus (20) zu berechnenden Werte von β für alle möglichen Werte von α complex mit positiv imaginärem Teil werden, so verhält sich die Hauptbewegung *absolut stabil.*

2) Einer der aus (20) zu berechnenden Werte von β ist für gewisse Werte von α *complex mit negativ imaginärem Teil.* Dann gibt es Störungen (α), welche mit der Zeit anwachsen und die Hauptbewegung (R) verhält sich *instabil.*

Die Grenze zwischen 1) und 2) bildet der Fall, wo zwar der betrachtete « Zweig » von β für keinen Wert von α einen negativen, aber für einen derselben einen verschwindenden imaginären Teil hat. Die Hauptbewegung befindet sich dann gegenüber dieser Störung auf der Grenze von Stabilität und Labilität; bei einer geringen Abänderung (Erhöhung) von R werden wirklich instabile Bewegungen auftreten. Zu jedem besonderen Zweige von β wird man je einen besonderen Wert von R finden können, bei welchem jene Grenze erreicht wird. Unter allen so erhaltenen (unendlich vielen) R-Werten muss es einen kleinsten geben. Dies ist der *kritische Wert von* R.

Hiernach hätten wir für alle möglichen Combinationen der Werte α und R, d. h. für die verschiedenen Gebiete einer « α, R-Ebene » die zugehörigen Werte von β zu bestimmen, wobei man die Grenzfälle αR klein und αR gross voranzustellen haben wird. Der kritische Wert von R ergiebt sich dann, indem man diejenigen Grenzkurven construirt, welche die « stabilen » und « instabilen Gebiete » der α, R-Ebene (mit negativem oder positivem reellem Teil von β) von einander trennen, von jeder dieser Grenzcurven die kleinste Ordinate aufsucht und unter den letzteren die absolut kleinste bestimmt.

T. BOGGIO

SOPRA ALCUNI TEOREMI DI FISICA-MATEMATICA

Nella maggior parte dei problemi di fisica-matematica, le funzioni incognite soddisfano a sistemi d'equazioni, ove figurano dei parametri costanti, dipendenti dalla natura del corpo considerato.

Tali funzioni incognite dipendono perciò anche da questi parametri; orbene qui dimostrerò che, supponendo che esse, per rispetto ad uno dei parametri, abbiano dei poli, questi poli debbono necessariamente essere *semplici*.

Tale proprietà si può dimostrare in modo molto elementare, operando opportunamente sulle equazioni differenziali del problema. Qui esporrò la dimostrazione per i problemi dell'equilibrio elastico, quando, in superficie, si conoscono gli spostamenti, o le tensioni, o parte degli spostamenti e delle tensioni; la proprietà in questione vale anche per alcuni corpi non isotropi, e per le equazioni da cui dipende il problema del moto dei solidi elastici isotropi.

Tratto poi anche le equazioni del problema delle temperature stazionarie e dell'induzione magnetica.

1. Denotando con $X_x, \ldots, Y_z$ le sei componenti delle tensioni interne di un corpo elastico in equilibrio, e con X, Y, Z le componenti delle forze di massa, per unità di volume, sussistono le equazioni indefinite:

$$(1) \quad \begin{cases} \dfrac{dX_x}{dx} + \dfrac{dX_y}{dy} + \dfrac{dX_z}{dz} = X \\ \ldots\ldots\ldots\ldots \\ \ldots\ldots\ldots\ldots \end{cases}$$

$$X_y = Y_x \,, \; X_z = Z_x \,, \; Y_z = Z_y \,.$$

Inoltre, se L, M, N indicano le componenti delle tensioni superficiali, per unità di area, si ha:

$$(2) \quad \begin{cases} X_x \dfrac{dx}{dn} + X_y \dfrac{dy}{dn} + X_z \dfrac{dz}{dn} = L \\ \ldots\ldots\ldots\ldots \\ \ldots\ldots\ldots\ldots , \end{cases}$$

ove n indica la normale alla superficie σ del solido S considerato, diretta verso l'interno.

Indicando con u, v, w le componenti dello spostamento di un punto qualsiasi di S, con $x_x, \ldots, y_z$ le sei componenti di deformazione, cioè:

$$x_x = \frac{du}{dx}, \ldots, y_z = \frac{dv}{dz} + \frac{dw}{dy}, \tag{3}$$

e con Π il potenziale di elasticità, avremo allora:

$$2\Pi = c_{11} x_x^2 + c_{22} y_y^2 + \cdots + c_{66} x_y^2 + 2c_{12} x_x y_y + \cdots, \tag{4}$$

ove le c sono le costanti isotermiche di elasticità.

Si ha poi:

$$X_x = -\frac{d\Pi}{dx_x}, \ldots, Y_z = -\frac{d\Pi}{dy_z}. \tag{5}$$

Le funzioni u, v, w sono determinate dalla condizione di dover soddisfare, nei punti di S, alle (1), e nei punti della superficie σ ad uno qualunque dei sistemi:

$$\left\{\begin{array}{l} u = \varphi_1 \\ v = \varphi_2 \\ w = \varphi_3 \end{array}\right. \quad \left\{\begin{array}{l} L = \varphi_1 \\ M = \varphi_2 \\ N = \varphi_3 \end{array}\right. \quad \left\{\begin{array}{l} u = \varphi_1 \\ v = \varphi_2 \\ N = \varphi_3 \end{array}\right. \quad \left\{\begin{array}{l} u = \varphi_1 \\ M = \varphi_2 \\ N = \varphi_3, \end{array}\right. \tag{6}$$

ove $\varphi_1, \varphi_2, \varphi_3$ sono funzioni date nei punti di σ. Queste varie condizioni ai limiti corrispondono ai casi in cui sul contorno si conoscono gli spostamenti, ovvero le tensioni, ovvero parte degli spostamenti e delle tensioni.

2. Le funzioni u, v, w dipendono dai parametri $c_{11}, c_{22}, \ldots$; supponendo che questi parametri siano funzioni lineari di uno stesso parametro k, anche u, v, w saranno funzioni di k, e mostreremo ora, nel caso dei corpi isotropi, e di qualche corpo non isotropo, che se u, v, w riguardate come funzioni del parametro k, hanno dei poli, essi dovranno essere necessariamente *semplici e reali*.

Per dimostrare questa proprietà, stabiliamo alcune formole, valide nel caso generale dei corpi non isotropi.

Supponiamo che le funzioni u, v, w ammettano per $k = k_0$ un polo d'ordine m $(m > 1)$. Potremo allora porre:

$$\left\{\begin{array}{l} u = \dfrac{u'}{(k-k_0)^m} + \dfrac{u''}{(k-k_0)^{m-1}} + \cdots \\[2ex] v = \dfrac{v'}{(k-k_0)^m} + \dfrac{v''}{(k-k_0)^{m-1}} + \cdots \\[2ex] w = \dfrac{w'}{(k-k_0)^m} + \dfrac{w''}{(k-k_0)^{m-1}} + \cdots, \end{array}\right. \tag{7}$$

ove i residui u', v', w' non possono essere tutti identicamente nulli.

Ne segue, dalle (3), che anche le sei componenti di deformazione avranno, per $k = k_0$, un polo d'ordine m, e lo stesso avverrà delle sei componenti delle tensioni, in guisa che potremo scrivere:

$$
(8) \quad \left\{
\begin{array}{l}
X_x = \dfrac{X'_x}{(k-k_0)^m} + \dfrac{X''_x}{(k-k_0)^{m-1}} + \cdots \\
\cdot\ \cdot\ \cdot\ \cdot\ \cdot\ \cdot\ \cdot\ \cdot\ \cdot\ \cdot\ \cdot\ \cdot\ \cdot\ \cdot \\
\cdot\ \cdot\ \cdot\ \cdot\ \cdot\ \cdot\ \cdot\ \cdot\ \cdot\ \cdot\ \cdot\ \cdot\ \cdot\ \cdot \\
\cdot\ \cdot\ \cdot\ \cdot\ \cdot\ \cdot\ \cdot\ \cdot\ \cdot\ \cdot\ \cdot\ \cdot\ \cdot\ \cdot\ ,
\end{array}
\right.
$$

e a causa delle (4), (5) le funzioni $X'_x, \ldots, Y'_z$ contengono linearmente le costanti c, e quindi anche la k.

Sostituendo nelle (1) si ha:

$$
(9) \quad \left\{
\begin{array}{l}
\dfrac{dX'_x}{dx} + \dfrac{dX'_y}{dy} + \dfrac{dX'_z}{dz} + (k-k_0)\left(\dfrac{dX''_x}{dx} + \dfrac{dX''_y}{dy} + \dfrac{dX''_z}{dz}\right) + \cdots = (k-k_0)^m X \\
\cdot\ \cdot \\
\cdot\ ;
\end{array}
\right.
$$

ponendo $k = k_0$ si deduce:

$$
(10) \quad \left\{
\begin{array}{l}
\dfrac{dX'_x}{dx} + \dfrac{dX'_y}{dy} + \dfrac{dX'_z}{dz} = 0 \\
\cdot\ \cdot\ \cdot\ \cdot\ \cdot\ \cdot\ \cdot\ \cdot\ \cdot\ \cdot \\
\cdot\ \cdot\ \cdot\ \cdot\ \cdot\ \cdot\ \cdot\ \cdot\ \cdot\ \cdot\ ;
\end{array}
\right.
$$

derivando invece le (9) rispetto a k e ponendo poi $k = k_0$, si ha:

$$
(11) \quad \left\{
\begin{array}{l}
\dfrac{dX''_x}{dx} + \dfrac{dX''_y}{dy} + \dfrac{dX''_z}{dz} = -\dfrac{d}{dk}\left(\dfrac{dX'_x}{dx} + \dfrac{dX'_y}{dy} + \dfrac{dX'_z}{dz}\right) = X'' \\
\cdot\ \cdot\ \cdot\ \cdot\ \cdot\ \cdot\ \cdot\ \cdot\ \cdot\ \cdot\ \cdot\ \cdot\ \cdot\ \cdot\ \cdot\ \cdot\ \cdot\ \cdot\ \cdot \\
\cdot\ \cdot\ \cdot\ \cdot\ \cdot\ \cdot\ \cdot\ \cdot\ \cdot\ \cdot\ \cdot\ \cdot\ \cdot\ \cdot\ \cdot\ \cdot\ \cdot\ \cdot\ \cdot\ .
\end{array}
\right.
$$

Sostituendo i valori (7) (8) nelle (6) si ottiene, collo stesso procedimento:

$$
(12) \quad \left\{
\begin{array}{l}
u' = 0 \\
v' = 0 \\
w' = 0
\end{array}
\right.
\quad
\left\{
\begin{array}{l}
L' = 0 \\
M' = 0 \\
N' = 0
\end{array}
\right.
\quad
\left\{
\begin{array}{l}
u' = 0 \\
v' = 0 \\
N' = 0
\end{array}
\right.
\quad
\left\{
\begin{array}{l}
u' = 0 \\
M' = 0 \\
N' = 0
\end{array}
\right.
$$

$$
(13) \quad \left\{
\begin{array}{l}
u'' = 0 \\[2ex]
v'' = 0 \\[2ex]
w'' = 0
\end{array}
\right.
\quad
\left\{
\begin{array}{l}
L'' = -\dfrac{dL'}{dk} \\
M'' = -\dfrac{dM'}{dk} \\
N'' = -\dfrac{dN'}{dk}
\end{array}
\right.
\quad
\left\{
\begin{array}{l}
u'' = 0 \\[2ex]
v'' = 0 \\[2ex]
N'' = -\dfrac{dN'}{dk}
\end{array}
\right.
\quad
\left\{
\begin{array}{l}
u'' = 0 \\[2ex]
M'' = -\dfrac{dM'}{dk} \\
N'' = -\dfrac{dN'}{dk}\ .
\end{array}
\right.
$$

È evidente che per ciascuna delle condizioni precedenti è soddisfatta l'equazione:

$$\int_\sigma (u'' L' + v'' M' + w'' N')\, d\sigma = 0 ,$$

da cui si trae, mediante il teorema di reciprocità del Betti:

$$\int_S (u' X'' + v' Y'' + w' Z'')\, dS + \int_\sigma (u' L'' + v' M'' + w' N'')\, d\sigma = 0 .$$

Sostituendo i valori (11), (13) ed integrando per parti, l'equazione precedente si riduce a:

(14) $$\int_S \frac{d}{dk}(x'_x X'_x + \cdots + y'_z Y'_z)\, dS = 0 ,$$

cioè:

(14') $$\int_S \frac{d\Pi'}{dk}\, dS = 0 ,$$

ove Π' indica il potenziale di elasticità formato colle $x'_x, \ldots, y'_z$.

Inoltre, dalle equazioni (10), (12) si trae, com'è noto:

(15) $$\int_S \Pi'\, dS = 0 .$$

3. Supponiamo ora che il corpo S sia *isotropo*; allora si ha [1]:

$$2\Pi = c_{11}(x_x + y_y + z_z)^2 + c_{44}(x_y^2 + x_z^2 + y_z^2 - 4x_x y_y - 4x_x z_z - 4y_y z_z) ,$$

e riguardando come parametro k la costante c_{11}, la (14') porge:

$$\int_S (x'_x + y'_y + z'_z)^2\, dS = 0 ,$$

onde, in tutto S:

(16) $$x'_x + y'_y + z'_z = 0 .$$

Siccome poi è facile verificare che la precedente espressione di 2Π può pure scriversi:

$$2\Pi = \left(c_{11} - \frac{4}{3}c_{44}\right)(x_x + y_y + z_z)^2 +$$
$$+ c_{44}\left\{x_y^2 + x_z^2 + y_z^2 + \frac{2}{3}[(x_x - y_y)^2 + (x_x - z_z)^2 + (y_y - z_z)^2]\right\} ,$$

(1) Cfr. ad es. Marcolongo, *Teoria matematica dell'equilibrio dei corpi elastici*, pag. 192 (Milano, a. 1904).

si trae, dalle (15), (16):

$$x'_x = y'_y = z'_z = x'_y = x'_z = y'_z = 0\,,$$

in ogni punto di S.

Le sei componenti di deformazione relative allo spostamento (u', v', w') sono dunque identicamente nulle in S, quindi, prescindendo da spostamenti rigidi del corpo S, risultano pure identicamente nulle in S le funzioni u', v', w'.

Questo risultato è in contraddizione con quanto è espresso dalle (7), a meno che non sia $m = 1$, perciò si conclude che se u, v, w, riguardate come funzioni del parametro c_{11}, ammettono dei poli, essi sono necessariamente *semplici*.

Se il corpo S, anzichè isotropo, è cristallino, ma del *sistema monometrico*, allora si ha ([1]):

$$2\Pi = c_{11}(x_x^2 + y_y^2 + z_z^2) + 2c_{12}(x_x y_y + x_x z_z + y_y z_z) + c_{44}(x_y^2 + x_z^2 + y_z^2)\,,$$

e riguardando come parametro k la costante c_{11}, si trae dalla (14'):

$$\int_S (x_x'^2 + y_y'^2 + z_z'^2)\, dS = 0\,,$$

perciò, in tutto S:

$$x'_x = y'_y = z'_z = 0\,.$$

Da queste eguaglianze e dalla (15) risulta:

$$x'_y = x'_z = y'_z = 0\,.$$

Per conseguenza, anche in questo caso, le sei componenti di deformazione relative allo spostamento (u', v', w') sono identicamente nulle in S, quindi la stessa proprietà compete alle funzioni u', v', w'.

Essendo questo risultato in contraddizione con ciò che è espresso dalle (7), si conclude che se u, v, w riguardate come funzioni del parametro c_{11} hanno dei poli, essi saranno *semplici*.

Per altri sistemi cristallini si può, con qualche ulteriore ipotesi, stabilire proprietà analoghe; così ad es. per i cristalli del *sistema dimetrico* si ha ([2]):

$$2\Pi = c_{11}(x_x^2 + y_y^2) + c_{33} z_z^2 + 2c_{23}(y_y z_z + x_x z_z) + 2c_{12} x_x y_y + c_{44}(y_z^2 + x_z^2) + c_{66} x_y^2\,,$$

([1]) Cfr. Op. cit., pag. 186.
([2]) Cfr. Op. cit., pag. 185.

quindi, riguardando come parametro k la costante c_{11}, dalla (14′) si conclude:

$$\int_S (x'^2_x + y'^2_y)\, dS = 0 ,$$

ossia, in tutto S:

$$x'_x = y'_y = 0 ;$$

da esse e dalla (15) si deduce:

$$\int_S [c_{33}\, z'^2_z + c_{44}\,(y'^2_z + x'^2_z) + c_{66}\, x'^2_y]\, dS = 0 ,$$

perciò, se le costanti c_{33}, c_{44}, c_{66} hanno lo stesso segno ([1]), dovrà essere in tutto S:

$$z'_z = y'_z = x'_z = x'_y = 0 ;$$

le sei componenti di deformazione sono dunque nulle in S, e si conclude perciò che se riguardando u, v, w come funzioni del parametro c_{11}, tali funzioni hanno dei poli, questi saranno certamente *semplici*.

4. Per stabilire, nei varî casi considerati, che i poli sono *reali*, conviene premettere un'altra formola generale.

Siano k', k'' due poli *differenti* delle funzioni u, v, w, e diciamo u', v', w' ed u'', v'', w'' i corrispondenti residui. Formando le componenti di deformazione $x'_x, \ldots y'_z$, $x''_x, \ldots y''_z$ e di tensione $X'_x, \ldots Y'_z$, $X''_x, \ldots Y''_z$ corrispondenti a tali residui, è chiaro che tali componenti di tensione verificheranno le equazioni indefinite (10), e le equazioni ai limiti (12).

Indicando con $X^0_x, \ldots Y^0_z$ i valori assunti da $X''_x, \ldots Y''_z$ ove vi si ponga k' al posto di k'', le equazioni relative alle funzioni $X''_x, \ldots Y''_z$ potranno scriversi:

$$\left\{\begin{array}{l} \dfrac{dX^0_x}{dx} + \dfrac{dX^0_y}{dy} + \dfrac{dX^0_z}{dz} = (k' - k'')\, \dfrac{d}{dk'}\left(\dfrac{dX^0_x}{dx} + \dfrac{dX^0_y}{dy} + \dfrac{dX^0_z}{dz}\right) \\ \ldots\ldots\ldots\ldots\ldots\ldots\ldots\ldots \\ \ldots\ldots\ldots\ldots\ldots\ldots\ldots\ldots \end{array}\right.$$

Indicando con L′, M′, N′ ed L″, M″, N″ le componenti delle tensioni superficiali relative agli spostamenti (u', v', w'), (u'', v'', w''), saranno soddisfatte nei punti della superficie σ di S le equazioni (12). Chiamando poi L^0, M^0, N^0 i valori assunti da L″, M″, N″ quando vi si pone k' al posto di k'', le equazioni ai limiti relative alle funzioni L″, M″, N″ e ad es. al caso in cui sono date le tensioni superficiali, possono scriversi:

$$L^0 = (k' - k'')\, \frac{dL^0}{dk'} , \ldots , \ldots$$

([1]) Questa restrizione diventa inutile, se si suppone che, nella precedente espressione di Π, le costanti c (esclusa c_{11}) abbiano valori fisicamente possibili.

In ogni caso però è verificata l'equazione:

$$\int_\sigma (u'' \mathrm{L}' + v'' \mathrm{M}' + w'' \mathrm{N}')\, d\sigma = 0,$$

di qui, applicando il teorema di Betti e le equazioni precedenti, e poi procedendo come nel n. 2, si ottiene:

$$(17) \qquad (k' - k'') \int_\mathrm{S} \frac{d}{dk'} (x'_x \mathrm{X}^0_x + \cdots + y'_z \mathrm{Y}^0_z)\, d\mathrm{S} = 0,$$

che è analoga alla (14); poichè k' è differente da k'', dovrà esser nullo l'integrale.

La funzione entro parentesi non è altro che la forma *polare* del potenziale Π'. Supponendo ora che il corpo S sia isotropo e considerando (come nel n. 3) come parametro k la costante c_{11}, si deduce, dalla corrispondente espressione del potenziale e dalla (17):

$$\int_\mathrm{S} (x'_x + y'_y + z'_z)(x''_x + y''_y + z''_z)\, d\mathrm{S} = 0.$$

Se il corpo cristallino è del sistema monometrico, si ottiene analogamente:

$$\int_\mathrm{S} (x'_x x''_x + y'_y y''_y + z'_z z''_z)\, d\mathrm{S} = 0.$$

Se invece il corpo appartiene al sistema dimetrico, si conclude, allo stesso modo:

$$\int_\mathrm{S} (x'_x x''_x + y'_y y''_y)\, d\mathrm{S} = 0.$$

Da queste relazioni di ortogonalità si deduce subito, con un noto ragionamento, che i poli debbono essere *reali*.

5. Assumendo le equazioni indefinite a cui soddisfano gli spostamenti, sotto la forma:

$$\Delta_2 u + k \frac{d\theta}{dx} = 0, \ldots,$$

ove θ indica la dilatazione cubica, segue dalle proprietà precedenti, che se u, v, w riguardate come funzioni del parametro k, hanno dei poli, essi sono necessariamente semplici e reali.

Si può, in modo completamente analogo, stabilire la stessa proprietà per le equazioni dalle quali dipende il problema del moto dei solidi elastici isotropi. Tali equazioni sono:

$$(18) \qquad \Delta_2 u + h \frac{d\theta}{dx} + ku = 0, \ldots,$$

inoltre, sulla superficie del corpo, valgono ancora le (6) nei casi in cui in superficie si conoscono gli spostamenti, le tensioni, o parte degli spostamenti e delle tensioni.

Considerando u, v, w come funzioni del parametro k, e supponendo che tali funzioni abbiano dei poli, essi saranno dunque semplici e reali (anzi, come è facile riconoscere, negativi). Perciò se $k = k_0$ è un polo, si potrà porre:

$$u = \frac{u'}{k - k_0} + u'', \ldots,$$

e i residui u', v', w' verificheranno le (18) ove $k = k_0$, e le (6) ove i secondi membri siano sostituiti con zero.

Le funzioni u'', v'', w'' sono finite per $k = k_0$ e soddisfano alle equazioni indefinite

$$\Delta_2 u'' + k \frac{d\theta''}{dx} + k_0 u'' = -u', \ldots, \tag{19}$$

e ad equazioni ai limiti del tipo (6).

Quando si sappia che le sole singolarità delle funzioni u, v, w sono dei poli (necessariamente semplici, per quanto si è or ora dimostrato), è chiaro che per dimostrare l'esistenza effettiva di infiniti poli, basta dimostrare l'esistenza di un primo polo k_0, perchè poi dalle (19), che sono riducibili al tipo (18), si dedurrà nell'identico modo l'esistenza di un nuovo polo k_1 che sarà certo maggiore (in valore assoluto) di k_0, perchè le funzioni u'', v'', w'' sono finite per $k \leq k_0$. E così procedendo si proverà l'esistenza di altri poli successivi $k_2, k_3, \ldots$ in numero infinito ([1]).

6. Consideriamo una funzione u che verifichi le equazioni:

$$\left\{ \begin{array}{ll} \Delta_2 u + \lambda c u = f & \text{(in S)} \\ b \dfrac{du}{dn} - a u = \varphi & \text{(su } \sigma), \end{array} \right. \tag{20}$$

ove a, b, c, f, φ sono funzioni date, inoltre c ha un segno *costante* in S, e λ è una costante ed n è la normale interna.

La u può riguardarsi come funzione del parametro λ, e allora si può dimostrare che se essa ammette dei poli, essi dovranno essere *semplici e reali.*

Infatti, nel caso contrario, se λ_0 è un polo d'ordine m $(m > 1)$ per la funzione u, si può porre:

$$u = \frac{u'}{(\lambda - \lambda_0)^m} + \frac{u''}{(\lambda - \lambda_0)^{m-1}} + \cdots$$

([1]) Circa il modo di provare l'esistenza del primo polo, cfr. LAURICELLA, *Sulle equazioni del moto dei corpi elastici* (Memorie della R. Accademia delle Scienze di Torino, serie II, t. XLV, a. 1896).

Sostituendo nelle (20) e procedendo come nel n. 2, si trovano per le funzioni u', u'' le equazioni:

$$(21)\qquad \begin{cases} \Delta_2 u' + \lambda_0 c u' = 0 & \text{(in S)} \\ b\dfrac{du'}{dn} - a u' = 0 & \text{(su } \sigma) \end{cases}$$

$$(21')\qquad \begin{cases} \Delta_2 u'' + \lambda_0 c u'' = -\,c u' & \text{(in S)} \\ b\dfrac{du''}{dn} - a u'' = 0 & \text{(su } \sigma). \end{cases}$$

Ora, dalla identità:

$$(22)\qquad \int_S [v(\Delta_2 u + \lambda c u) - u(\Delta_2 v + \lambda c v)]\, dS + \int_\sigma \left(v\frac{du}{dn} - u\frac{dv}{dn}\right) d\sigma = 0,$$

applicata alle funzioni u', u'' che verificano le (21), (21'), si deduce:

$$\int_S c\, u'^2\, dS = 0,$$

onde dovrebbe essere identicamente $u' = 0$, contro l'ipotesi.

Pertanto dovrà essere $m = 1$, quindi il polo λ_0 sarà semplice e il residuo u' verificherà le (21). La funzione u sarà perciò della forma:

$$u = \frac{u'}{\lambda - \lambda_0} + u'',$$

ove u'' è una funzione finita per $\lambda = \lambda_0$.

Sostituendo nelle (20) si riconosce subito che u'' dovrà verificare le equazioni:

$$(23)\qquad \begin{cases} \Delta_2 u'' + \lambda_0 c u'' = f - c u' & \text{(in S)} \\ b\dfrac{du''}{dn} - a u'' = \varphi & \text{(su } \sigma). \end{cases}$$

Consideriamo ora due poli λ', λ'_1 *differenti* tra loro, e siano u', u'_1 i corrispondenti residui; dalla (22) si trae tosto:

$$\int_S c\, u' u'_1\, dS = 0,$$

di qui risulta subito che i poli debbono essere reali.

7. Dall'identità:

$$\int_S u(\Delta_2 u + \lambda c u)\, dS = -\int_\sigma u\frac{du}{dn}\, d\sigma - \int_S (\Delta u - \lambda c u^2)\, dS,$$

applicata alla funzione u' che soddisfa alle (21), si deduce:

$$\int_S (\Delta u' - \lambda_0 c u'^2)\, dS + \int_\sigma \frac{a}{b} u'^2\, d\sigma = 0,$$

perciò se la funzione c è positiva in S, e le funzioni a, b hanno lo stesso segno (che possiamo benissimo supporre positivo), i poli debbono essere *positivi* ($\lambda_0 > 0$).

Questo risultato vale anche se $b = 0$ ($a \neq 0$), come si riconosce facilmente. Se invece $a = 0$ ($b \neq 0$) l'eguaglianza precedente può essere soddisfatta da:

$$\lambda_0 = 0 \quad , \quad u' = \text{costante}.$$

È facile trovare il valore di questa costante: la funzione u sarà ora della forma:

$$u = \frac{u'}{\lambda} + u'',$$

ove u'' è una funzione finita per $\lambda = 0$, la quale verifica le (23) ove $a = 0$. Ponendo in esse $\lambda_0 = 0$ e notando l'identità:

$$\int_S \Delta_2 v dS + \int_\sigma \frac{dv}{dn} d\sigma = 0,$$

si trova:

$$\int_S (f - cu') dS + \int_\sigma \frac{\varphi}{b} d\sigma = 0,$$

la quale determina la costante u'.

Quando si sappia che le sole singolarità della funzione u che soddisfa alle (20), sono dei poli, è chiaro che per dimostrare l'esistenza effettiva di infiniti poli, basta dimostrare l'esistenza di un primo polo λ_0, perchè poi dalle (23), che sono identiche alle (20), salvo che la funzione f è sostituita da $f - cu'$, si dedurrà nell'identico modo l'esistenza di un nuovo polo λ_1, che dovrà certo essere maggiore di λ_0, perchè la funzione u'' è finita per $\lambda \leq \lambda_0$. Così procedendo si proverà l'esistenza di altri poli successivi $\lambda_2, \lambda_3, \ldots$ in numero infinito.

Nel caso particolare $b = c = 1$ ed a = costante reale non negativa, le proprietà precedenti sono state ottenute con metodo del tutto diverso (ricorrendo alle equazioni integrali) dal prof. LAURICELLA [1].

8. Considerando invece del sistema (20) il seguente:

$$(20') \qquad \begin{cases} \Delta_2 u + \lambda c u = f & \text{(in S)} \\ kb \dfrac{du}{dn} - hau = \varphi & (\text{su } \sigma), \end{cases}$$

ove h, k sono costanti, è chiaro che la funzione u che soddisfa alle (20'), può pure riguardarsi come funzione del parametro h. Si può allora dimostrare, con procedimento del tutto simile a quello adoperato dianzi, che se $\lambda c \leq 0$, i poli della funzione u sono tutti *semplici e reali*; inoltre se le funzioni a, kb hanno lo stesso segno, i poli debbono essere *negativi*.

Analogamente se si riguarda la u come funzione del parametro k.

(1) LAURICELLA, *Applicazione della teoria di Fredholm al problema del raffreddamento dei corpi* (Annali di Matematica, serie III, t. XIV, a. 1907).

Consideriamo ancora la funzione u che soddisfa all'equazione:

$$\Delta_{2m} u + \lambda c u = f \qquad \text{(in S)},$$

ove λ è un parametro, c una funzione che ha segno costante nel campo S, ed f una funzione data; supponiamo inoltre che la funzione u e le sue derivate normali successive dei primi $m-1$ ordini, prendano sulla superficie di S dei valori assegnati. Allora si può stabilire, col metodo adoperato precedentemente, che se la u considerata come funzione di λ, ha dei poli, questi debbono essere semplici e reali. Se poi ad es. m è dispari e c è positiva in S, allora i poli sono *positivi*.

L'esistenza di tali poli si può mostrare poi con procedimento simile a quello adoperato dal PICARD [1] nel caso di $m = 1$.

9. Consideriamo infine il problema dell'induzione magnetica, dal punto di vista della teoria di POISSON.

La questione si riduce a cercare una funzione u continua e armonica in tutto lo spazio, che si comporti all'infinito come una funzione potenziale, e le cui derivate normali, interna ed esterna $\frac{du}{dn_i}$, $\frac{du}{dn_e}$ verifichino, nei punti della superficie σ del corpo S, l'equazione:

$$k \frac{du}{dn_e} + \frac{du}{dn_i} = \varphi, \tag{24}$$

ove k è una costante, e φ una funzione data nei punti di σ.

Si può dimostrare che se la u, riguardata come funzione di k, ha dei poli, essi debbono essere *semplici e reali*.

Infatti, nel caso contrario, se k_0 è un polo d'ordine m $(m > 1)$ per la funzione u, si può porre:

$$u = \frac{u'}{(k-k_0)^m} + \frac{u''}{(k-k_0)^{m-1}} + \cdots,$$

ed è chiaro che u', u'' saranno, al pari di u, funzioni armoniche e continue in tutto lo spazio, e si comporteranno all'infinito come funzioni potenziali.

Sostituendo nella (24) e procedendo nel modo solito, si trova che nei punti di σ debbono essere verificate le equazioni:

$$\text{(25)} \qquad \begin{aligned} k_0 \frac{du'}{dn_e} + \frac{du'}{dn_i} &= 0 \\ k_0 \frac{du''}{dn_e} + \frac{du''}{dn_i} &= -\frac{du'}{dn_e}. \end{aligned}$$

(1) PICARD, *Sur quelques applications de l'équation fonctionnelle de M. Fredholm* (Rendiconti del Circolo Matematico di Palermo, tomo XXII, a. 1906).

Ora, se S' indica lo spazio esterno a σ, dal lemma di GREEN si ricava l'identità:

$$\int_S (v\Delta_2 u - u\Delta_2 v)\, dS + k_0 \int_{S'} (v\Delta_2 u - u\Delta_2 v)\, dS' +$$
$$+ \int_\sigma \left[v\left(k_0 \frac{du}{dn_e} + \frac{du}{dn_i}\right) - u\left(k_0 \frac{dv}{dn_e} + \frac{dv}{dn_i}\right)\right] d\sigma = 0,$$

che, applicata alle funzioni u', u'' porge:

$$\int_\sigma u' \frac{du'}{dn_e} d\sigma = 0,$$

ovvero:

$$\int_{S'} \Delta u' dS' = 0 ;$$

la funzione u' dovrebbe dunque essere costante in S', ma essendo nulla all'infinito, sarà nulla in S', quindi pure su σ, e perciò anche in S; tale funzione sarebbe dunque identicamente nulla in tutto lo spazio, ciò che è contrario all'ipotesi.

Dovrà dunque essere $m = 1$, quindi il polo k_0 sarà semplice, e il corrispondente residuo u' verificherà la (25).

Considerando poi due poli k', k'_1 differenti fra loro, e i corrispondenti residui u', u'_1, dall'identità precedente si trae tosto:

$$(k' - k'_1) \int_\sigma u' \frac{du'_1}{dn_e} d\sigma = 0,$$

ossia:

$$\int_{S'} \Delta(u', u'_1)\, dS' = 0,$$

dalla quale è facile dedurre che i poli debbono essere reali.

Inoltre i poli sono *negativi*. Infatti, dalla (25) si ha:

$$\int_\sigma u' \left(k_0 \frac{du'}{dn_e} + \frac{du'}{dn_i}\right) d\sigma = 0,$$

da cui:

$$k_0 \int_{S'} \Delta u' dS' + \int_S \Delta u' dS = 0,$$

di qui si deduce $k_0 \leq 0$. Si ha precisamente $k_0 = 0$ solo se $u' =$ costante in S.

Si può considerare la funzione u, che è armonica e continua in tutto lo spazio, come la funzione potenziale di uno strato semplice, di densità ϱ, disteso sulla superficie σ; allora sussistono le note formole:

$$\begin{cases} \dfrac{du}{dn_i} + \dfrac{du}{dn_e} = -4\pi\varrho \\ \dfrac{du}{dn_i} - \dfrac{du}{dn_e} = 2\displaystyle\int_\sigma \varrho \frac{\cos\psi}{r^2} d\sigma, \end{cases}$$

ove r è la distanza di un punto variabile di σ, dal punto potenziato, pure situato su σ, e ψ è l'angolo che la normale interna a σ nel punto potenziato fa col raggio vettore r.

Ricavando da esse $\frac{du}{dn_i}$, $\frac{du}{dn_e}$ e sostituendo nella (24) si ha l'equazione integrale per la densità ϱ:

$$\varrho + \lambda \int_\sigma \varrho \frac{\cos\psi}{2\pi r^2} d\sigma = \varphi_1 ,$$

ove:

$$\lambda = 1 - \frac{2}{k+1} \quad , \quad \varphi_1 = -\frac{1}{2\pi(k+1)}\varphi .$$

Dalle proprietà stabilite poc'anzi per la funzione u, si trae che *i poli* λ *di questa equazione integrale sono tutti semplici, reali, ed almeno eguali ad* 1 *in valore assoluto.*

Ritroviamo così, con procedimento molto elementare, un teorema del Plemelj ([1]), il quale lo stabilì con metodo completamente diverso e meno semplice.

([1]) Plemelj, *Ueber lineare Randwertaufgaben der Potentialtheorie*, § 15 (Monatshefte für Mathematik und Physik, XVI, a. 1904).

J. BOCCARDI [1]

SUR UNE NOUVELLE ÉQUATION DANS LES OBSERVATIONS DES PASSAGES

Nous ne sommes plus au temps où l'astronome MASKELYNE se croyait en devoir de déclarer à l'un de ses assistants qu'il n'était pas fait pour la carrière astronomique, par la seule raison qu'il n'observait pas les passages des étoiles au méridien de la même manière que son directeur. L'équation personnelle est un fait bien connu aujourd'hui, et à mesure que les méthodes d'observation se perfectionnent, on découvre de nouvelles formes de cette équation. Dans ces dernières années on a reconnu l'équation décimale et l'équation de grandeur, ou, pour mieux dire, l'équation d'éclat, dont sont affectés les passages d'étoiles de grandeurs différentes.

A l'occasion d'un travail de réobservation de 500 étoiles du catalogue d'ALBANY (de l'Association Allemande), que j'ai faite dernièrement à Turin, je me suis proposé d'examiner si les ascensions droites observées et réduites à un même équinoxe moyen, étaient affectées par les variations des conditions atmosphériques. D'autres avant moi avaient essayé de faire des recherches dans cette direction, sans constater aucune variation systématique. C'est que le nombre des observations relatif à chaque étoile n'était pas grand pour ces observateurs. D'après mon plan, je devais observer pendant plusieurs années de suite les étoiles que j'avais choisies du catalogue d'ALBANY, en commençant plusieurs heures après minuit et en terminant au crépuscule du soir.

J'ai observé avec un instrument des passages de 108 mm. d'ouverture et de 160 cm. de distance focale, en employant toujours un grossissement de 129. Cet instrument n'avait pas alors de micromètre dit impersonnel. A l'exception de l'inclinaison de l'axe horizontal qui était mesurée directement avec un excellent niveau à bulle d'air, les constantes instrumentales étaient déterminées au moyen d'observations de fondamentales, alternées avec celles des petites étoiles au cours de chaque soirée. Le nombre des fondamentales était considérable, c'est-à-dire de 10, 15 jusqu'à 21. Ceci était nécessaire pour pouvoir appliquer la méthode des moindres carrés pour déduire les valeurs des inconnues suivantes: azimut, collimation, correction de

[1] Je donne ici un résumé de la communication que j'ai faite au Congrès de Rome. On trouvera de plus amples details dans un Mémoire qui va paraître bientôt.

l'horloge pour un instant donné et sa marche pendant les observations [1]. Autant qu'il a été possible, j'ai choisi des fondamentales entre les grandeurs $4^m,0$ et $5^m,0$. Pour les étoiles d'ALBANY sur lesquelles ont porté mes observations, je me suis aussi borné aux étoiles de $7^m,0$ à $8^m,2$.

Sans doute, les observations des petites étoiles réduites avec les constantes déterminées au moyen des étoiles d'un éclat plus grand seront affectées par l'équation de grandeur; mais si cette dernière reste constante pendant toute la série des observations, les ascensions droites de chaque étoile réduites à l'équinoxe moyen doivent s'accorder dans les limites des erreurs d'observation. Je dis en passant que l'erreur probable d'une de mes observations a été au commencement de $\pm 0^s,029$ et ensuite elle est descendue à $\pm 0^s,024$. Mais si les variations des conditions atmosphériques, pendant les mois embrassés par les observations de chaque étoile, ont produit un changement dans l'observation des pasages, les ascensions droites seront assujetties à des fluctuations, ou, si l'on veut, l'équation de grandeur doit varier.

Mes observations de passages au méridien ont commencé le 2 juillet 1904 et elles ont fini le 29 novembre 1906. Leur nombre a atteint 12000. Dès la première année, puisque j'ai fait marcher de front les calculs de réduction — que j'ai fait moi-même, aussi bien que toutes les observations — j'ai remarqué que pour les 600 étoiles d'ALBANY, en commençant par 20^h, les ascensions droites réduites à l'équinoxe moyen de 1904,0 étaient un peu plus faibles pour les observations de juillet, plus fortes pour celles de septembre et des mois suivants. La différence était plus sensible pour les étoiles de $7^m,7$ à $8^m,2$. J'ai soupçonné d'abord une équation qu'on aurait pu appeler de saison, ou bien horaire, puisque elle était en rapport avec les heures des observations; mais en poursuivant celles-ci je me suis aperçu que la différence de clarté de l'atmosphère jouait un rôle prépondérant dans cette variation des ascensions droites.

Le climat de Turin, surtout à cause de la proximité du Po, est assujetti à des variations subites dans l'état du ciel. Il arrive souvent que l'on commence les observations avec un ciel superbe, et ensuite tout-à-coup le brouillard se lève et quelquefois on est obligé d'interrompre les observations. D'autres fois il arrive le contraire; on commence les observations avec un ciel brumeux et au bout d'une heure le ciel se découvre et il devient très clair. Ce climat était donc tout indiqué pour des recherches sur l'influence des conditions atmosphériques sur les observations des passages. Or, en examinant avec soin l'allure des ascensions droites de chaque étoile pour de différents degrés de clarté du ciel, j'ai constaté la loi suivante pour mes observations: « lorsque « le ciel est très clair, les passages sont observés avec avance, lorsque le ciel est « brumeux les passages sont pris en retard. Les observations avec du vent sont aussi « en avance, celles marquées difficiles sont en retard ». A cause de la variabilité du ciel de Turin, j'ai pu bien souvent constater ces lois pendant la même soirée. Et voilà comment. J'ai jugé à propos d'appliquer à mes observations la méthode général de correction proposée par M. SCHIAPARELLI dans l'introduction au catalogue de Brera (Milan), et qui consiste à perfectionner les observations, en les débarassant d'une

[1] Voyez l'Annuario Astronomico del R. Osservatorio di Torino, pour 1906.

erreur systématique que l'on découvre en comparant pour chacune des étoiles observées dans une soirée l'observation de tel jour à la position très exacte que l'on forme en faisant la moyenne de toutes les observations pour chaque étoile. Cette moyenne, lorsque le nombre des observations est très grand, peut être regardée comme très près de la vérité, par conséquent pour chaque étoile l'écart entre la position d'une soirée et la moyenne donne l'erreur de l'observation. Or, si l'on fait cette comparaison pour toutes les étoiles d'une soirée, on découvre une allure systématique dans ces écarts, que l'on peut représenter avec un diagramme. Dès lors, chaque coordonnée observée est affectée par deux erreurs, l'une qui est due au système dont j'ai parlé tout à l'heure, l'autre qui est tout à fait accidentelle. D'après les principes de la théorie des erreurs, on est autorisé à délivrer chaque observation de l'erreur systématique, et alors il ne restera sur l'observation ainsi modifiée que l'erreur accidentelle.

Contre cette manière de perfectionner, pour ainsi dire, les observations, je pense qu'il n'y à rien à objecter. Du moment que l'erreur systématique existe, et qu'elle se révèle d'une manière évidente, on est autorisé, on est même obligé de la faire disparaître, de même que l'on corrige les passages des erreurs d'azimut, de collimation, etc.

En appliquant cette méthode aux dates auxquelles l'état du ciel avait changé pendant la série des observations, j'ai reconnu d'une manière évidente sur le diagramme que les ascensions droites des étoiles observées par un ciel très clair étaient au-dessous de la moyenne, tandis que pour les étoiles observées avec du brouillard les ascensions droites étaient plus fortes. Par là l'augmentation des ascensions droites de juillet à septembre s'explique parfaitement. A Turin, contrairement à ce qui a lieu ailleurs, l'automne ordinairement n'est pas favorable aux observations. Ceci est arrivé surtout en 1904. Le ciel a été pendant cet automne presque constamment brumeux. Au contraire en juillet 1904 l'atmosphère, surtout après minuit, a été d'une transparence remarquable. Voilà pourquoi mes ascensions droites de juillet sont plus faibles, comme vous pouvez le remarquer sur les feuilles que j'ai l'honneur de vous présenter.

J'ajoute qu'à Turin le mois janvier est incontestablement le meilleur de tous pour les observations. Le ciel, surtout pendant les deux ou trois premières semaines, est alors d'une transparence merveilleuse. Il s'ensuit que, pour les mêmes étoiles, les ascensions droites observées en janvier sont un peu plus faibles que celles observées en septembre, quoique les observations de septembre — pour ces étoiles — se fassent après minuit, lorsque l'air est plus calme, la poussière atmosphérique s'est deposée et, pour tout dire, la radiation de l'éclairage de la ville est moindre, tandis que les observations de janvier se font aux premières heures du soir.

Après avoir bien constaté sur mes observations la loi que j'ai énoncée plus haut, j'ai pu dresser un tableau donnant les modifications que subissent les ascensions droites observées par moi suivant les variations de l'état du ciel. Ce tableau se trouve sur les feuilles que je vous ai déjà présentées.

Mais après avoir reconnu cette loi sur mes observations, j'ai essayé de rechercher s'il s'agit là d'une équation personnelle dans le sens le plus étroit de ce mot, c'est-à-dire si je suis le seul à l'avoir, ou bien si elle est commune à d'autres. Cette recherche n'était pas facile, d'abord parce que si l'on a fait de longues séries d'observations de déclinaisons, surtout à l'occasion des recherches sur la variations des latitudes, il n'existe pas de longues séries d'observations d'ascensions droites; et ensuite parce que, ordinairement, les renseignements sur le conditions atmosphériques ne sont pas donnés avec tous les détails. Toutefois j'ai utilisé la belle série d'observations faites à Arcetri (Florence) par M. B. Viaro. Lui aussi a employé un grand nombre de fondamentales pour la détermination des constantes instrumentales, et il a assez clairement indiqué les conditions du ciel pour chaque soirée et même les variations survenues pendant la même soirée. Pour chaque étoile il n'a fait que 4 à 6 observations, de sorte que la valeur moyenne d'une coordonnée reposant sur un petit nombre d'observations, n'est pas, à la rigueur très près de la vérité. Mais, faute de mieux, je l'ai adoptée comme une valeur plus près de la vérité que n'importe quelle observation isolée. Je n'ai pas osé former un tableau des variations des ascensions droites de M. Viaro, analogue, au mien, puisque le nombre de ses observations n'est pas grand. Toutefois j'ai fait les différences entre les α correspondant à des états différents de transparence de l'atmosphère, ces états allant de I à IV dans le sens croissant de la transparence. J'ai donc trouvé que pour M. Viaro aussi les α diminuent avec le vent et avec une grande clarté du ciel et augmentent avec la brume et le brouillard. Le tableau de ces comparaisons est à côté de celui basé sur mes observations. Σ est la somme des différences entre les α se rapportant aux indications: I, II, III, etc.; n est le nombre des étoiles; m est la moyenne arithmétique de la différence.

Enfin il est tellement certain que le manque de clarté de l'athmosphére retarde mes observations de passages, que bien souvent j'ai pu le constater pendant le passage d'une même étoile, c'est-à-dire que lorsque l'observation à quelque fil du micromètre a été faite à travers le brouillard, etc.... l'α correspondante est résultée plus forte.

J'appelle donc l'attention des astronomes sur cette nouvelle forme d'équation dans les observations des passages. Si ce fait est confirmé par d'autres observations, il résulterait la nécessité d'avoir égard aux conditions atmosphériques par lesquelles les observations sont faites. Quant à mon modeste catalogue de 600 étoiles d'Albany, puisque le nombre des observations pour chaque étoile est très grand, et elles ont été faites dans toutes les conditions du ciel, mes positions basées sur la moyenne de toutes les observations relatives à chaque étoile correspondent à un état moyen de transparence. Mais pour les autres catalogues d'ascensions droites qui ne reposent pas sur un grand nombre d'observations, l'influence de cette nouvelle équation doit être sensible. Ceci pourrait expliquer, du moins en partie, les différences systématiques que l'on remarque entre les α données pour les mêmes étoiles par différents catalogues, même lorsqu'ils ont adopté le même système de fondamentales.

Si l'on admet que par le micromètre auto-régistreur l'équation de grandeur est supprimée, on pourrait observer les passages des étoiles par tous les états de l'atmosphère, et comparer chaque observation à celles qui auraient été faites avec le micromètre sus-dit. Par ce moyen on déterminerait les variations de l'équation de grandeur suivant la clarté du ciel, et le tableau de l'équation de transparence, que l'on formerait ainsi, serait certainement plus exact que le mien.

J. ANDRADE

SYNCHRONISATION PAR LE FER DOUX

I.

C'est en 1847 que Foucault a prévu, avec une grande généralité, le phénomène de la synchronisation des horloges; mais, à ma connaissance du moins, aucune théorie systématique adéquate à la généralité du phénomène n'a encore été donnée.

En 1894, cependant, dans un célèbre Mémoire présenté au Congrès des électriciens à Paris, Cornu a étudié et *illustré expérimentalement* le cas pour ainsi dire *type*, le cas de *première approximation* des phénomènes de synchronisation: ce phénomène se produit en effet lorsqu'une force, fonction périodique du temps, vient à troubler un mouvement pendulaire uniformément amorti; en d'autres termes le cas *type* et *simple* du phénomène de synchronisation se ramène à ce théorème très simple: P *et* Q *désignant deux coefficients positifs, l'intégrale de l'equation différentielle*:

$$(1)\qquad \frac{d^2x}{dt^2} = -Px - Q\frac{dx}{dt} + F(t),$$

dans laquelle on suppose: 1° $Q < 2\sqrt{P}$; 2° $F(t)$, *fonction périodique du temps* t *à période* T′, *cette intégrale, disons nous, ou bien sera rigoureusement périodique ou bien tend asymptotiquement pour* $t = nT' + \theta$, ($\theta > 0$ *et* $n = \infty$) *vers une intégrale périodique de période* T′.

La fonction $F(t)$ représente en ce cas *la force synchronisante* qui finit *pratiquement* par imposer sa période T′ au mouvement (1); si la force synchronisante était supprimée le mouvement serait uniformément amorti mais isochrone et de période $T = \dfrac{2\pi}{\sqrt{P - \frac{Q^2}{4}}}$.

II.

Pratiquement la force synchronisante est réalisée par un barreau circulaire aimanté lié au pendule de l'horloge synchronisée et dont un pôle est mobile dans une bobine actionnée périodiquement par l'horloge synchronisante dont les battements ont pour période T'. Il est recommandé que le régime de synchronisation comporte une attraction du barreau plutôt qu'une répulsion.

Tel est le procédé de la synchronisation par un aimant *permanent* influencé par un courant périodique.

Ce procédé emprunté à la prévision de FOUCAULT a été d'abord réalisé par JONES.

Dans la théorie et dans les illustrations expérimentales qu'il a faites du mouvement (1), CORNU a beacouup insisté sur le rôle *joué par l'amortissement* c'est à dire par le coëfficient Q de la résistance visqueuse, et même il a augmenté systématiquement ce coëfficient Q par l'addition d'une résistance d' induction.

À quoi sert la synchronisation en dehors du service des observatoires?

CORNU m'a donné, dans une lettre, son opinion sur l'opportunité de la synchronisation des horloges; il estimait qu'il ne fallait synchroniser que des horloges médiocres, celles qu'il appelait des *sabots*; selon lui la synchronisation peut en faire de bonnes horloges, sauf à augmenter l'amortissement naturel de l'horloge synchronisée, à *le régulariser* pour ainsi dire par une résistance complémentaire d'induction; celle ci était produite dans le procédé CORNU par un déplacement du barreau aimanté à travers une masse isolée de cuivre rouge. Dans son Mémoire de 1894 CORNU insiste fortement sur cet amortissemment additionnel qui, dit-il, distingue complètement sa méthode de celle de JONES.

En somme CORNU, n'a jamais considéré que la synchronisation par un aimant permanent.

La règle de FOUCAULT est d'ailleurs peu explicite à cet égard, mais l'artiste VÉRITÉ, de Beauvais, tout en s'inspirant de la règle de FOUCAULT a réalisé des synchronisation soit par l'acier aimanté, soit par le fer doux.

Il est assez curieux, d'une part, que CORNU ne se soit pas préoccupé de l'emploi du fer doux, et que, d'autre part, ayant parfaitement senti qu'un amortissement complémentaire pouvait perfectionner une horloge médiocre soumise à la synchronisation, il n'ait pas eu l'idée d'étudier le rôle de l'échappement dans le phénomène de la synchronisation.

III.

En me limitant d'abord à la synchronisation par un aimant permanent j'ai, par la méthode de la variation des constantes, complété la théorie de CORNU en tenant compte du rôle de l'échappement; en considérant la partie principale E de *l'effet* de l'échappement, qui est sensiblement indépendante de l'amplitude en cours, j'ai (Comptes Rendus de l'Académie de Paris, Juillet 1903) obtenu le résultat suivant:

Si l'on appelle λ le coëfficient d'amortissement relatif au régime de synchronisation, μ une quantité proportionnelle au retard relatif des deux horloges, u_0 l'amplitude de régime, la synchronisation pourra être réalisée si

$$\frac{E}{u_0} + \sqrt{(1-\lambda)^2 + \mu^2} < 1 \qquad (2)$$

d'où l'on voit que si λ et μ sont de petites quantités de même ordre, la condition de sécurité pour la synchronisation sera :

$$(3) \qquad \lambda > \frac{E}{u_0};$$

en comparant cette condition à la relation qui, dans l'horloge synchronisée fonctionnant isolément, lie son amortissement naturel λ_0 à l'effet E_0 de l'echappement, relation qui est :

$$\lambda_0 = \frac{E_0}{u_0},$$

on aura deux moyens principaux d'assurer la condition (3).

Soit $E = E_0$, $\lambda > \lambda_0$; soit $\lambda = \lambda_0$, $E < E_0$; l'amplitude de régime restant d'ailleurs u_0; ce qui nous donne soit la règle de CORNU : aider la synchronisation par un amortissement complémentaire, soit la règle de FOUCAULT : aider la synchronisation par *l'atténuation* de l'échappement.

IV.

Dans les résultats qui sont ici fournis par l'application de la méthode de variation des constantes, il y a des circonstances mathématiques intéressantes à signaler.

La méthode d'intégration des équations différentielles par séries de quadratures que l'on doit à M. PICARD nous permet de nous servir ici de la méthode de la variation des constantes avec une entière rigueur et d'aboutir aux résultats intéressants que voici :

THÉORÈME I. — *Pour des résistances fonctions de la vitesse qui suivent une loi peu différente de la loi de résistance proportionnelle à la vitesse, on peut toujours modifier la partie sinusoïdale du premier ordre de la force synchronisante de manière à rendre le mouvement de l'horloge influencée rigoureusement périodique, avec une période égale à celle de la force synchronisante ; pour des conditions initiales déterminées.*

THÉORÈME II. — *Les choses étant ainsi disposées, si l'on modifie suffisamment peu les conditions initiales, le mouvement du pendule influencé par la force synchronisante et soumis d'ailleurs à son échappement propre va tendre effectivement vers un régime limite périodique de période* T'.

V.

Dans les théorèmes qui précèdent, la force modificatrice du mouvement naturel de l'horloge était rigoureusement périodique.

Or, voici un cas extrêmement intéressant où, touyours par la même méthode d'approximations de M. PICARD, on peut *étendre* les conclusions précédentes.

Supposons qu'au lieu de faire agir une force synchronisante fonction périodique du temps, on fasse agir une force dont la valeur soit le produit d'une telle fonction $F(t)$ par une force, fonction de la position du pendule caracterisée par sa déviation actuelle x ; soit $F(t) \times \varphi(x)$ une pareille force. Mais supposons que dans le voisinage de $x = x_1$, la fonction $\varphi(x)$ soit à peu près constante et présente à l'égard de la variable x soit un maximum soit un minimum.

Dans ces conditions les théorèmes précédents, avec une légère modification du second, sont encore applicables, comme on peut d'ailleurs le pressentir intuitivement et le démontrer rigoureusement par la méthode de M. Picard.

En tous cas, on peut encore régler la fonction F(t) *de manière, à assurer la synchronisation.*

VI.

Voici, maintenant l'intérêt pratique de la remarque qui précède.

Dans la synchronisation par le fer doux, la bobine excitée périodiquement par l'horloge-mère exerce une induction magnétique sur une plaque de fer doux entrainée par le pendule de l'horloge synchronisée et cette induction est fonction de la position relative de la bobine et du pendule, c'est à dire de l'angle d'écart x, l'action magnétique est d'ailleurs proportionnelle à l'intensité du courant qui parcourt la bobine, la force synchronisante a donc bien ici la forme $F(t) . \varphi(x)$ signalée plus haut; si, pour fixer les idées, la bobine synchronisante est verticale, au point mort du pendule synchronisé, la fonction $\varphi(x)$ aura un maximum ou un minimum pour $x = x_1$, et pour $x = -x_1$ et nous sommes alors dans les conditions où on peut appliquer les remarques précédentes.

VII.

En résumé j'ai, grâce aux méthodes d'approximations successives, *élargi* le cas type mais *isolé*, considéré d'abord par Cornu pour envisager une infinité de cas voisins; en d'autres termes j'ai démontré la *stabilité* du phénomène de synchronisation qui devient ainsi étendu aux mouvements *à peu-près* pendulaires, amortis par une résistance *à peu-près* proportionnelle à la vitesse et soumis à une action synchronisante agissant soit sur l'acier aimanté soit sur le fer doux.

Pour être tout à fait précis je dois ajouter que mon instrument de calcul a été une combinaison de la méthode d'approximations de M. Picard avec la théorie des substitutions répétées dont l'emploi m'a été suggéré par le théorème de M. Koenigs sur les substitutions répétées à une variable.

R. W. GENESE

APPLICATION OF THE METHOD OF RECIPROCAL POLARS TO FORCES IN SPACE

In 1886 I communicated to the London Mathematical Society a method of reciprocating forces in a plane: the object of the present paper is to extend the theory to forces in space, and to show how simply the whole is evolved by GRASSMANN's methods (for a practical acquaintance with which I am greatly indebted to the works of Prof. PEANO).

1°.

In Plano.

If P and p be pole and polar with respect to a circle, centre O, radius unity, I define $|f$ the reciprocal of a *force* f acting along p as a *weight* at P whose measure is the moment of f about O, i. e. $\pm\left(f \times \frac{1}{\mathrm{OP}}\right)$; and if x be any scalar $|xf = x|f$.

Similarly I define $|x\mathrm{P}$, the reciprocal of a *weight* x at P as a *force* along p measured by the moment of x about O, i. e. $x \times \mathrm{OP}$. (The moment of this force about $\mathrm{O} = x \,.\, \mathrm{OP} \times \frac{1}{\mathrm{OP}}$; so that $||x\mathrm{P} = x\mathrm{P}$). Then the bar sign $|$ as an operator is distributive; thus from an equation of weights (MÖBIUS'masses)

(1) $$(m + n)\,\mathrm{R} = m\mathrm{P} + n\mathrm{Q}$$

there follows

(2) $$(m + n)\,|\,\mathrm{R} = m\,|\,\mathrm{P} + n\,|\,\mathrm{Q}\,.$$

For, the points P, Q, R being collinear, their polars meet in a point, T say (fig. 1).

By LEIBNIZ' theorem, we derive from (1) the equation of *forces*

$$(a) \qquad (m+n) \,.\, \mathrm{OR} = m\mathrm{OP} + n\mathrm{OQ} \,.$$

If now we suppose these forces translated to T and turned through a right angle, we obtain equation (2).

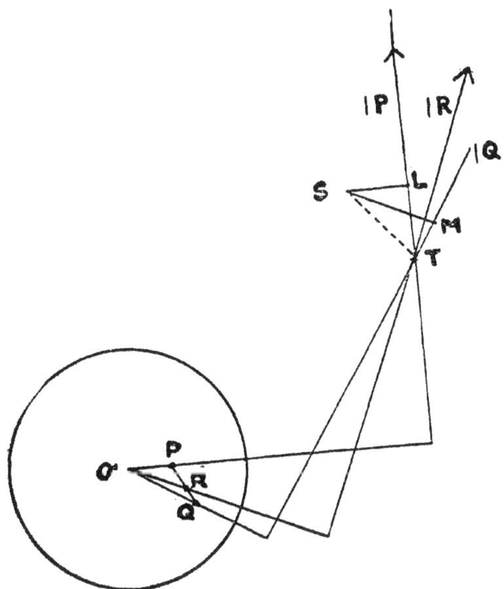

FIG. 1.

The case of the couple ($n = -m$) is of special interest.

Here the weight R is at infinity along PQ or any parallel to it; therefore its reciprocal (of definite intensity, viz, the moment of the couple) passes through O and therefore acts along OT, which is perpendicular to QP.

It is convenient to consider the weights as acting at right angles to the plane of the paper, and then we may say that all couples in parallel planes of the same moment reciprocate into the same force at O.

Again if we take a couple formed by parallel forces f, g *in the plane*, their poles P, Q are along the same perpendicular from O; the moments about O of the reciprocal weights, $f/\mathrm{OP} \times \mathrm{OP}$, $g/\mathrm{OQ} \times \mathrm{OQ}$ being equal and opposite, the resultant weight acts at O, and its measure is the algebraic sum of the moments of f and g, i. e. the moment of the couple f, g.

Or, again, any equation of forces may be thrown into the form (a), and (1) may be inferred.

The reciprocity of (1) and (2) may be extended in the usual manner to any number of weights and forces.

The following illustration may be useful. If successive elements of arc of a closed curve represent forces, the system is equivalent to a couple measured by the area of the curve. Reciprocating we obtain an infinite number of weights acting at the points of the reciprocal curve each weight being measured by the moment of the corresponding element of the first curve about the centre chosen O, and the resultant weight acts at O. Hence, making the necessary changes to pass from the elements of one curve to those of the other, we learn that a wire of any form may be so weighted that its centroid may be any assigned point O, viz. by giving each element ds the weight $\frac{ds}{p^2 \varrho}$ where p is the perpendicular from O on ds (i. e. a tangent) and ϱ is the radius of curvature.

The analytical condition $\int \frac{ds}{p^2 \varrho} x = 0$ round any curve whose reciprocal is closed (for *any* axis x) is a fruitful source of definite integrals.

If we use Leibniz' theorem, multiplying each elementary weight by r we obtain a theorem in Attractions, viz. if each element ds attract a particle at O according to the law $\frac{d}{dr}\left(-\frac{1}{p}\right) ds$, the particle is in equilibrium. As an example, if the perimeter of an infinite parabola attract according to the law $r^{-\frac{3}{2}}$, a particle at the focus is in equilibrium.

Returning to the theory, we have next the equation of moments,

(3) $$P \mid Q = Q \mid P.$$

The left hand side = distance of P from the polar of $Q \times OQ$, and the right hand side = distance of Q from the polar $P \times OP$. These are equal by Salmon's theorem (*Conics*, Art 101).

It may be observed, en passant, that $P|P = \left(\frac{1}{\overline{OP}} - \overline{OP}\right) OP = 1 - OP^2$ is variable. Grassmann's $P|P = 1$ would require the reciprocation to be with respect to « the absolute » (in *areal coordinates* not the same curve as in trilinear coordinates).

In Regressive Multiplication we may define [1] the product of two lines as *their intersection* with intensity equal to the product of the measures of the lines and the sine of the included angle.

Then (fig. 1)

(4)
$$\begin{aligned} |P . |Q &= T \text{ with weight } \overline{OP} . \overline{PQ} \sin (\widehat{|P, |Q}) \\ &= T \quad " \quad " \quad " \quad " \ \widehat{POQ} \text{ in same sense.} \\ &= T \quad " \quad " \quad 2\Delta OPQ \text{ (carrying sign)} \\ &= |PQ \end{aligned}$$

[1] This mode of presenting the subject frees it from the necessity of considering units of reference and from the condition $e|e = 1$.

Further, if S be any point in the plane.

(5) $$S|PQ = S|Q.|P - S|P.|Q.$$

For, drawing SL, SM perpendicular to $|P$, $|Q$, by LAMI's theorem, a force sinMTL along TS can be resolved into sinMTS along TL and sinSTL along TM. Multiplying by ST and reversing forces,

$$\text{ST sinMTL along ST} = \text{SM along LT and SL along MT}.$$

Multiplying by the measures of $|P$, $|Q$ we obtain equation (5).

Adding three such equation

(6) $$P|QR + Q|RP + R|PQ = 0$$

i. e. if P', Q', R' be the poles of the sides of a triangle PQR certain forces along PP', QQ', RR' balance. (If O be the centroid of PQR, the measures of $|QR$ etc. are equal and the forces are represented by PP', QQ', RR'). Since also

$$P'|Q'R' + Q'|R'P' + R'|P'Q' = 0,$$

and the ratios of the measures of the forces are definite, we must have

$$\frac{\Delta OQ'R'}{\Delta OQR} = \frac{\Delta OP'Q'}{\Delta ORP} = \frac{\Delta OP'Q'}{\Delta OPQ}.$$

(Cf. Question by Prof. NEUBERG in Educational Times, March 1908). Reciprocally

(7) $$QR|P + RP|Q + PQ|R = 0$$

or certain weights at the intersections of QR, $Q'R'$, etc. balance, and these points are in directum.

2°.

In Spatio.

DEF. — If π be the polar plane of P with respect to unit sphere, centre O, the reciprocal $|xP$ of a weight x at P is a twist (Blatt, not Feld) in the plane π of intensity xOP so that its moment about O is $xOP \times \frac{1}{OP} = x$; further, if x be positive, the twist viewed from O shall have a positive i. e. counter-clock-wise aspect, and shall appear clock-wise if x be negative. This, too, supplies the definition of the reciprocal $|\pi$ of a given twist.

The reciprocal, $|PQ$, of a force PQ is another force along the polar of PQ whose intensity is measured by $\overline{OPQ}$ (i. e. the moment of PQ about O treated as a scalar) and *whose sense is such that a rotation* OPQ *forms with it a left-handed screw.*

Theorem. — From a relation of weights

$$(m+n)\,R = mP + nQ$$

we may infer one of twists

$$(m+n)\,|R = m\,|P + n\,|Q\,.$$

In fig. 2 we suppose OPQ to be the plane of the paper meeting the sphere in the circle C and $|P, |Q$ in the lines LT, TM. The planes $|P, |Q$ meet in a line perpendicular to the paper along which unit vector u is taken towards the reader.

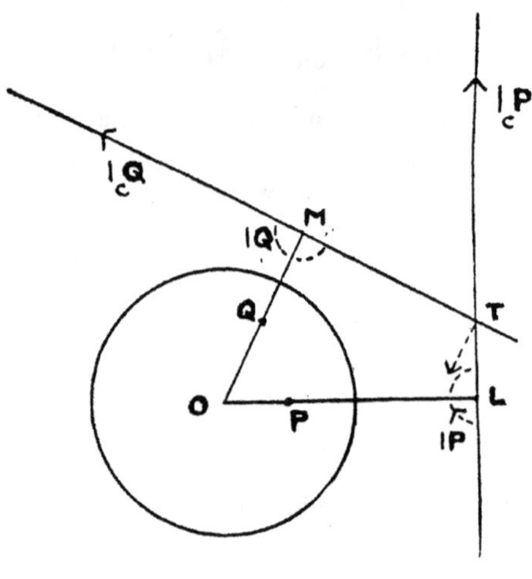

Fig. 2.

Let $|_c$ denote the reciprocal of a point with respect to the circle.

$$\text{Then } |P = u\,|_c P\,,\ |Q = u\,|_c Q\,.$$
$$\text{But } (m+n)\,|_c R = m\,|_c P + n\,|_c Q\,.$$

Multiplying by u the theorem follows.

The reciprocal of a couple $P - Q$ may be shown to be a twist through O of intensity QP in a plane perpendicular to $P - Q$ and in the proper sense.

Salmon's theorem again gives

$$P\,|Q = Q\,|P\,.$$

Coming to Regressive Multiplication I define the product of two twists as a force along their line of intersection, in the proper sense (See page 444 of the Book of the Heidelberg Congress), whose intensity is the product of the measures of the twists and the sine of the angle between their planes in the order of factors (thus $\alpha\beta = -\beta\alpha$).

Here, $|P.|Q =$ a forces along u reversed whose intensity is

$\overline{OP}.\overline{OQ}$ sinPOQ i. e. moment of PQ about O

$= |PQ$ by above definition.

It will be found by considering various positions of P, Q inside and outside sphere that the signs agree.

$$\text{Clearly } |Q.|P = |QP = -|PQ = -|P.|Q.$$

Theorem. — From an equation of forces in equilibrium.

$$\Sigma P_r Q_r = 0$$

the reciprocal

$$\Sigma |P_r Q_r = 0$$

may be inferred.

For, let ABCD be a tetrahedron of reference

$$\begin{aligned} P_r &= a_r A + b_r B + c_r C + d_r D \\ Q_r &= f_r A + g_r B + h_r c + k_r D \\ \text{then } P_r Q_r &= (a_r g_r - f_r b_r) AB + \text{ etc.} \\ \text{Also } \quad |P_r &= a_r |A + b_r |B + \text{ etc.} \end{aligned}$$

(where $|A$ has the meaning of this paper and is not equal to BCD).

$$\begin{aligned} |Q_r &= f_r |A + g_r |B + \text{ etc.} \\ \therefore \; |P_r Q_r &= |P_r.|Q_r = (a_r g_r - f_r b_r)|AB + \text{ etc.} \end{aligned}$$

Now $\Sigma P_r Q_r = 0$ requires the coefficients of AB, AC etc. to vanish separately, because no forces along the edges of a tetrahedron can balance, therefore also

$$\Sigma |P_r Q_r = 0.$$

The theorem admits of independent proof.

Let AB be one of a system of balancing forces and let it be replaced by an equal and parallel force OP together with a couple OAB.

We have then

$$\begin{aligned} &\text{in forces } \; \Sigma OP = 0. \\ &\text{in couples } \; \Sigma OAB = 0. \end{aligned}$$

Now let ONR be perpendicular to AB and $|AB$, then

$$\text{moment of couple } O|AB = \overline{OAB}\,.\,\overline{OR}$$
$$= \overline{AB}\,.\,\overline{ON}\,.\,\overline{OR}$$
$$= \overline{AB}$$

Hence OP may be taken as the axis of this couple, and the first of the above conditions then shows that $\Sigma\, O|AB = 0$.

Again $|AB$ translated to O may be taken as the axis of tfie couple OAB; the second condition then shows that forces $\Sigma|AB$ translated to O would balance.

The two results show that

$$\Sigma|AB = 0\,.$$

As a simple case it may be noticed that to every theorem concerning forces in one plane π there is a reciprocal about forces meeting in a point P the pole of π; and if the first set be equivalent to a couple, the second set will reduce to a force perpendicular to π.

Also to any theorem concerning forces acting along tangents to a sphere will correspond a theorem concerning forces respectively equal to them but turned through a right angle in the tangent planes containing them.

The equation in space corresponding to (6) in plano is

$$P|QRS - Q|PRS + R|PQS - S|PQR = 0$$

or, if P', Q', R', S' be the poles, $\alpha, \beta, \gamma, \delta$ the tetrahedral co-ordinates of the centre O with respect to the tetrahedron PQRS.

$$\alpha PP' + \beta QQ' + \gamma RR' + \delta SS' = 0\,.$$

Mutatis mutandis, we have reciprocally

$$\alpha' P'P + \beta' Q'Q + \gamma' R'R + \delta' S'S = 0$$
$$\therefore\ \frac{\alpha}{\alpha^1} = \frac{\beta}{\beta^1} = \text{etc. (Neuberg's problem)}$$

or, if we understand by α the ratio of OQRS to PQRS, etc., then $\alpha = \alpha'$ etc.

But we may derive another interpretation.

By Leibnitz' theorem, O being the centroid of weights $\alpha, \beta, \gamma, \delta$ at P, Q, R, S.

$$\alpha PO + \beta QO + \gamma RO + \delta SO = 0$$
$$\text{Hence}\quad \alpha P(P' - O) + \beta Q(Q' - O) + \text{etc.} = 0\,.$$

$P(P' - O)$ is a force through P parallel and equal to OP′, the magnitude being equal to $1 \div$ the distance of O from the plane QRS, etc.

We return thus to the old theorem that forces through P, Q, R, S perpendicular and proportional to the opposite faces are in equilibrium.

A. MACFARLANE

ON THE SQUARE OF HAMILTON'S DELTA

In JOLY's Manual, the most recent treatise on the quaternion analysis, it is assumed, but nowhere proved, that ∇^2 is a scalar operator. In this paper I propose to show that what has hitherto been taken for the square of ∇ is only the scalar part of the complete square.

This investigation was suggested by the more simple and logically prior one « What is the complete square of a sum of vectors? » Let, as is now usual, a, b, c denote three simple vectors; that is, vectors of the vector-analysts, not the right quaternions of HAMILTON (¹). Their sum is denoted by

$$a + b + c;$$

their order in this sum may indicate a real order, in which case commutation is not indifferent. Let the square be denoted by

$$(a + b + c)^2.$$

In works on vector-analysis it is assumed that this square is formed by writing one trinomial after the other, and then taking the several partial products, always preserving in the partial product the order in which the symbols appear in the trinomial factors. That is

$$(a + b + c)(a + b + c)$$
$$= a^2 + b^2 + c^2 + ab + ba + ac + ca + bc + cb.$$

But

$$ab = \mathrm{S}ab + \sqrt{-1}\,\mathrm{V}ab$$
$$ba = \mathrm{S}ab - \sqrt{-1}\,\mathrm{V}ab.$$

Hence according to the above process of forming the square

$$(a + b + c)^2 = a^2 + b^2 + c^2 + 2\,\}\,\mathrm{S}ab + \mathrm{S}ac + \mathrm{S}bc\,\{\,.$$

(¹) To indicate clearly that a, b, c are vectors, some authors print them in fat Italic type.

The three vector terms Vab, Vac, Vbc do not appear: they have been eliminated by the manner of effecting the multiplication. But the mode of multiplying is incorrect, for it destroys the natural order of the terms in the trinomial; for instance a is prior to b, but in one partial product a is placed after b.

But the square can be formed so as to preserve the natural order, as follows:

$$\begin{aligned}(a+b+c)^2 &= a^2+b^2+c^2+2(ab+ac+bc)\\ &= a^2+b^2+c^2+2(Sab+Sac+Sbc)\\ &\quad +2\sqrt{-1}\,(Vab+Vac+Vbc)\,.\end{aligned}$$

That this is the correct square is proved by the fact that with it the exponential theorem remains true; whereas with the other form of square it does not. The exponentials $e^{\sqrt{-1}\,a}$, $e^{\sqrt{-1}\,b}$, $e^{\sqrt{-1}\,c}$ denote angles in space; and

$$e^{\sqrt{-1}\,a}\,e^{\sqrt{-1}\,b}\,e^{\sqrt{-1}\,c} = e^{\sqrt{-1}\,a+\sqrt{-1}\,b+\sqrt{-1}\,c}$$

is true, provided the square and other powers are formed on the above principle, and not otherwise.

The common way of forming the square of the sum of three vectors gives merely the scalar part of the complete square. Does a similar distinction hold in forming the square of Hamilton's operator ∇, which is well known to be a kind of symbolic vector?

In the case of rectangular co-ordinates,

$$\nabla = \frac{\partial(\,)}{\partial x}\frac{1}{i}+\frac{\partial(\,)}{\partial y}\frac{1}{j}+\frac{\partial(\,)}{\partial z}\frac{1}{k}$$

where ( ) denotes the place for the function; and ∇^2 is taken to be

$$\frac{\partial^2(\,)}{\partial x^2}\frac{1}{i^2}+\frac{\partial^2(\,)}{\partial y^2}\frac{1}{j^2}+\frac{\partial^2(\,)}{\partial z^2}\frac{1}{k^2}$$

which reduces to

$$\frac{\partial^2}{\partial x^2}+\frac{\partial^2}{\partial y^2}+\frac{\partial^2}{\partial z^2}\,.$$

But the vector part has been cancelled by an artificial order of the factors, just as in the trinomial of vectors. When it is restored, the complete square has the additional term

$$2\left\{\frac{\partial^2(\,)}{\partial x\,\partial y}\frac{1}{ij}+\frac{\partial^2(\,)}{\partial x\,\partial z}\frac{1}{ik}+\frac{\partial^2(\,)}{\partial y\,\partial z}\frac{1}{jk}\right\}.$$

In the case of polar co-ordinates, the square of ∇ is considered to be

$$\frac{\partial^2}{\partial r^2}+\frac{\partial^2}{(r\partial\theta)^2}+\frac{\partial^2}{(r\sin\theta\,\partial\varphi)^2}+\frac{2}{r}\frac{\partial}{\partial r}+\cot\theta\frac{\partial}{\partial\theta}\,.$$

Looking at this expression from the point of view of symmetry, we ask, « What has become of the term in $\frac{\partial}{\partial\varphi}$; and are there no cross terms? ».

In this case the radius-vector $R = r\varrho_1$ where

$$\varrho_1 = \cos\theta \,.\, i + \sin\theta\,(\cos\varphi\,.\,j + \sin\varphi\,.\,k)$$

$$\frac{\partial\varrho_1}{\partial\theta} = \varrho_2 = -\sin\theta\,.\,i + \cos\theta\,(\cos\varphi\,.\,j + \sin\varphi\,.\,k)$$

and

$$\frac{1}{\sin\theta}\frac{\partial\varrho_1}{\partial\varphi} = \varrho_3 = -\sin\varphi\,.\,j + \cos\varphi\,.\,k\,;$$

and these three unit-vectors $\varrho_1, \varrho_2, \varrho_3$ form an orthogonal system.

And then

$$\nabla = \frac{\partial()}{\partial r}\frac{1}{\varrho_1} + \frac{\partial()}{\partial\theta}\frac{1}{r\varrho_2} + \frac{\partial()}{\partial\varphi}\frac{1}{r\sin\theta\varrho_3}\,.$$

If we write one operator after the other

$$\left(\frac{\partial()}{\partial r}\frac{1}{\varrho_1} + \frac{\partial()}{\partial\theta}\frac{1}{r\varrho_2} + \frac{\partial()}{\partial\varphi}\frac{1}{r\sin\theta\varrho_3}\right)\left(\frac{\partial()}{\partial r}\frac{1}{\varrho_1} + \frac{\partial()}{\partial\theta}\frac{1}{r\varrho_2} + \frac{\partial()}{\partial\varphi}\frac{1}{r\sin\theta\varrho_3}\right)$$

and form the nine partial products after the usual mode we obtain,

$$\frac{\partial^2()}{\partial r^2}\frac{1}{\varrho_1^2} + \frac{\partial}{\partial\theta}\left(\frac{\partial()}{\partial\theta}\frac{1}{r\varrho_2}\right)\frac{1}{r\varrho_2} + \frac{\partial}{\partial\varphi}\left(\frac{\partial()}{\partial\varphi}\frac{1}{r\sin\theta\varrho_3}\right)\frac{1}{r\sin\theta\varrho_3}$$

$$+\frac{\partial}{\partial r}\left(\frac{\partial()}{\partial\theta}\frac{1}{r\varrho_2}\right)\frac{1}{\varrho_1} + \frac{\partial}{\partial\theta}\left(\frac{\partial()}{\partial r}\frac{1}{\varrho_1}\right)\frac{1}{r\varrho_2}$$

$$+\frac{\partial}{\partial r}\left(\frac{\partial()}{\partial\varphi}\frac{1}{r\sin\theta\varrho_3}\right)\frac{1}{\varrho_1} + \frac{\partial}{\partial\varphi}\left(\frac{\partial()}{\partial r}\frac{1}{\varrho_1}\right)\frac{1}{r\sin\theta\varrho_3}$$

$$+\frac{\partial}{\partial\theta}\left(\frac{\partial()}{\partial\varphi}\frac{1}{r\sin\theta\varrho_3}\right)\frac{1}{r\varrho_2} + \frac{\partial}{\partial\varphi}\left(\frac{\partial()}{\partial\theta}\frac{1}{r\varrho_2}\right)\frac{1}{r\sin\theta\varrho_3}\,.$$

The latter eight terms are expanded by differentiation by parts in which the order of the vectors must be preserved. There is also need of the additional principle that the differential coefficient of $\frac{1}{\varrho}$ is $\frac{1}{\varrho^2}$, not $-\frac{1}{\varrho^2}$. What is remarkable is having no minus. When these differentiations are performed, we obtain

$$\frac{\partial^2(\,)}{\partial r^2}\frac{1}{\varrho^2}+\frac{\partial^2(\,)}{\partial\theta^2}\frac{1}{(r\varrho_2)^2}+\frac{\partial(\,)}{\partial\theta}\frac{1}{\varrho_2^2}\frac{\partial\varrho_2}{\partial\theta}\frac{1}{\varrho_2 r^2}$$
$$+\frac{\partial^2(\,)}{\partial\varphi^2}\frac{1}{(r\sin\theta\varrho_3)^2}+\frac{\partial(\,)}{\partial\varphi}\frac{1}{\varrho_3^2}\frac{\partial\varrho_3}{\partial\varphi}\frac{1}{\varrho_3}\frac{1}{(r\sin\theta)^2}$$
$$+\frac{\partial^2(\,)}{\partial r\,\partial\theta}\frac{1}{r\varrho_2\varrho_1}-\frac{\partial(\,)}{\partial\theta}\frac{1}{r^2\varrho_2\varrho_1}$$
$$+\frac{\partial^2(\,)}{\partial\theta\,\partial r}\frac{1}{r\varrho_2\varrho_1}+\frac{\partial(\,)}{\partial r}\frac{1}{\varrho_1^2}\varrho_2\frac{1}{r\varrho_2}$$
$$+\frac{\partial^2(\,)}{\partial r\,\partial\varphi}\frac{1}{r\sin\theta\,\varrho_3\varrho_1}-\frac{\partial(\,)}{\partial\varphi}\frac{1}{r^2\sin\theta\,\varrho_3\varrho_1}$$
$$+\frac{\partial^2}{\partial\varphi\,\partial r}\frac{1}{r\sin\theta\,\varrho_1\varrho_3}+\frac{\partial(\,)}{\partial r}\frac{1}{\varrho_1^2}\sin\theta\varrho_3\frac{1}{r\sin\theta\varrho_3}$$
$$+\frac{\partial^2}{\partial\theta\,\partial\varphi}\frac{1}{r^2\sin\theta\,\varrho_3\varrho_1}-\frac{\partial(\,)}{\partial\varphi}\frac{1}{r^2\sin^2\theta}\cos\theta\frac{1}{\varrho_3\varrho_2}$$
$$+\frac{\partial^2(\,)}{\partial\varphi\,\partial\theta}\frac{1}{r^2\sin\theta\,\varrho_2\varrho_3}+\frac{\partial(\,)}{\partial\theta}\frac{1}{\varrho_2^2}\cos\theta\,\varrho_3\frac{1}{r^2\sin\theta\,\varrho_3}.$$

Introduce the absolute principle of reduction, namely, $\varrho\frac{1}{\varrho}=1$, as a result we obtain the three square terms

$$\frac{\partial^2(\,)}{\partial r^2}\frac{1}{\varrho_1^2}+\frac{\partial^2(\,)}{\partial\theta^2}\frac{1}{(r\varrho_2)^2}+\frac{\partial^2(\,)}{\partial\varphi^2}\frac{1}{(r\sin\theta\,\varrho_3)^2}.$$

Also three pairs of cross terms of the form

$$\frac{\partial^2(\,)}{\partial r\,\partial\theta}\left\{\frac{1}{r\varrho_1\varrho_2}+\frac{1}{r\varrho_2\varrho_1}\right\}$$

which vanish in pairs, because the unit-vectors $\varrho_1, \varrho_2, \varrho_3$ are mutually perpendicular.

And finally we have the terms

$$\frac{\partial(\,)}{\partial r}\frac{2}{r}\frac{1}{\varrho_1^2}$$
$$\frac{\partial(\,)}{\partial\theta}\left\{-\varrho_2\frac{1}{\varrho_1}-\varrho_1\frac{1}{\varrho_2}+\cot\theta\right\}\frac{1}{(r\varrho_2)^2}$$
$$\frac{\partial(\,)}{\partial\varphi}\left\{-\sin\theta\varrho_3\frac{1}{\varrho_1}-\cos\theta\varrho_3\frac{1}{\varrho_2}+\frac{\partial\varrho_3}{\partial\varphi}\frac{1}{\varrho_3}\right\}\frac{1}{(r\sin\theta\,\varrho_3)^2}.$$

It will be observed that throughout these equations the important principle of equality of dimensions remains good for the vectors. According to the above mode of formation of the square the first and second terms of $\frac{\partial}{\partial\theta}$ cancel one another; and in the case of $\frac{\partial}{\partial\varphi}$ the sum of the first and second cancels the third. As a consequence, the result is a scalar expression. But if we suppose this cancelling of the vector terms due to the artificial order of the factors, we obtain for a pair of cross terms the form $2\frac{\partial^2(\,)}{\partial r\,\partial\theta}\frac{1}{r\varrho_1\varrho_2}$ which is vector and imaginary. The co-efficient of $\frac{\partial}{\partial\theta}$ then becomes $\}\cot\theta + 2\sqrt{-1}\,\varrho_3\{\frac{1}{r^2}$ and the coefficient of $\frac{\partial}{\partial\varphi}$ becomes

$$2\sqrt{-1}\,i\,\frac{1}{(r\sin\theta)^2}\,.$$

The complete square of ∇ becomes

$$\frac{\partial^2(\,)}{\partial r^2}+\frac{\partial^2(\,)}{\partial\theta^2}\frac{1}{r^2}+\frac{\partial^2(\,)}{\partial\varphi^2}\frac{1}{(r\sin\theta)^2}$$

$$+2\sqrt{-1}\left\{\frac{\partial^2(\,)}{\partial r\,\partial\theta}\frac{\varrho_3}{r}+\frac{\partial^2(\,)}{\partial r\,\partial\varphi}\frac{\varrho_2}{r\sin\theta}+\frac{\partial^2(\,)}{\partial\theta\,\partial\varphi}\frac{\varrho_1}{r^2\sin\theta}\right\}$$

$$+\frac{\partial(\,)}{\partial r}\frac{2}{r}+\frac{\partial(\,)}{\partial\theta}\frac{1}{r^2}\}\cot\theta+2\sqrt{-1}\,\varrho_3\{+\frac{\partial(\,)}{\partial\varphi}2i\frac{1}{(r\sin\theta)^2}\,.$$

The scalar part of this expression gives the square of ∇ as usually formed; the additional part is all vector and imaginary, but nevertheless geometrically real. From the point of view of symmetry, it is the latter expression evidently which is the complete square of ∇.

O. TEDONE

SUL PROBLEMA DI LAMÉ

1. Il problema di determinare i sistemi di coordinate curvilinee (q_1, q_2, q_3) per i quali l'equazione di Laplace ammette infinite soluzioni (soluzioni elementari) della forma $P f_1(q_1) f_2(q_2) f_3(q_3)$ dove P è una funzione determinata, la stessa per tutte le infinite soluzioni, può portare convenientemente il nome di *problema di Lamé*. Ad esso sono legati definitivamente i nomi di Darboux e di Klein le di cui ricerche si trovano raccolte rispettivamente nel libro di Darboux stesso: *Leçons sur les systèmes orthogonaux...* (1) ed in quello del Bôcher, *Ueber die Reihenentwickelungen der Potentialtheorie* (2). Molte e fondamentali sono però ancora le lacune che restano da colmare affinchè si possa dire di avere una soluzione completa e soddisfacente di questo problema; spero quindi di interessare la *Sezione* mostrando come alcune di queste lacune possano essere colmate nel caso particolarmente importante in cui il sistema delle superficie $q_1 = \text{cost.}$, $q_2 = \text{cost.}$, $q_3 = \text{cost.}$ forma un sistema triplo ortogonale di rotazione o che ad un sistema triplo di questa natura si possa ridurre con una trasformazione per raggi vettori reciproci. Questo caso speciale del problema di Lamé pare indipendente dal problema generale nel senso che il metodo atto a risolvere il problema generale non indica che tutte le soluzioni del problema particolare sieno necessariamente comprese fra le soluzioni del problema generale. I primi e più fondamentali risultati sulla quistione di cui noi vogliamo occuparci sono dovuti al prof. Wangerin (3). Di essa si è poi occupato l'Haentzschel (4),

(1) Paris, Gauthier Villars, 1898.

(2) Leipzig, Teubner, 1894.

(3) *Reduction der Potentialgleichung für gewisse Rotationskörper auf eine gewöhnliche Differentialgleichung* (Preisschriften der Fürstlich Jablonowski'schen Gesellschaft der Wissenschaften, n. 18, Leipzig, 1875). — *Ueber die Reduction der Gleichung* $\frac{\partial^2 V}{\partial x^2} + \frac{\partial^2 V}{\partial y^2} + \frac{\partial^2 V}{\partial z^2} = 0$ *auf gewöhnliche Differentialgl* (Monatsberichte der kgl. Akademie der Wissenschaften zu Berlin, 21 Febr., 1878).

(4) *Studien über die Reduktion der Potentialgl. auf gewöhnliche Differentialgl.* (Georg Reimer, Berlin, 1893). — *Rotationszykliden und Lamesche Produkte* (Archiv der Math. und Physik, III Reihe, Bd. 4, S. 57-65, 1902). — *Ueber ein orthogonales System von bizirkularen Kurven vierter Ordnung* (Wissenschaftliche Beilage zum Jahresbericht des Köllnischen Gymnasiums zu Berlin, Ostern, 1908, Programm Nr. 70).

scolaro del WANGERIN, i risultati del quale sono stati in parte contestati dal SOFFORD [1]. Sono ben lontano dal voler entrare terzo nella disputa; e solo avrò per iscopo di enunciare e di dimostrare chiaramente alcune proposizioni fondamentali.

2. Assumiamo come asse di rotazione l'asse x e sia r la distanza di un punto qualunque dello spazio da questo asse. Se, in un piano qualunque passante per l'asse x, poniamo

$$(1) \qquad x+ir=f(\alpha+i\beta)\ , \ \text{ovvero}\ \ (1')\ x-ir=f(\alpha+i\beta)\,,\ i=\sqrt{-1}\ ,$$

dove f è il simbolo di una funzione qualunque di variabile complessa, le linee $\alpha=\text{cost.}$, $\beta=\text{cost.}$ formano, in quel piano, un sistema di linee ortogonali, isotermo, il quale, rotando intorno all'asse x, genera, insieme ai piani passanti per l'asse x, un sistema triplo ortogonale di rotazione. È noto d'altra parte che tutti i sistemi tripli di rotazione che possono essere soluzioni del nostro problema possono essere generati a questo modo. Indicando con ω l'angolo che un piano meridiano qualunque fa con un piano meridiano fisso, il quadrato dell'elemento lineare dello spazio sarà dato, in ciascuno dei due casi, dalla formola

$$(2) \qquad ds^2=h^2(d\alpha^2+d\beta^2)+r^2d\omega^2\ \ ,\ \ h^2=f'(\alpha+i\beta)f'_0(\alpha-i\beta)\,,$$

f_0 essendo la funzione coniugata di f, e l'equazione di LAPLACE, trasformata nelle coordinate curvilinee $\alpha\,,\beta\,,\omega$, si scriverà

$$(3) \qquad \frac{\partial}{\partial\alpha}\left(r\frac{\partial V}{\partial\alpha}\right)+\frac{\partial}{\partial\beta}\left(r\frac{\partial V}{\partial\beta}\right)+\frac{h^2}{r}\frac{\partial^2 V}{\partial\omega^2}=0.$$

Inoltre sarà, nel caso (1),

$$(4) \qquad r=\frac{1}{2i}\Big[f(\alpha+i\beta)-f_0(\alpha-i\beta)\Big],$$

e nel caso (1'),

$$(4') \qquad r=-\frac{1}{2i}\Big[f(\alpha+i\beta)-f_0(\alpha-i\beta)\Big].$$

[1] *Systems of revolution and their relation to conical systems in the theory of Lamé's products* (American Journal of Math., vol. 21, pp. 1-23, 1899). *Surfaces of revolutions in the theory of Lamé's products.* (Bulletin of the American Math. Society, 2. serie, V. 5, pp. 431-437, 1899). — *Rotation Cyclids and Lamé's products* (Arch. der Math. und Physik, III Reihe, Bd. 10, S. 234-237, 1906).

Quando feci la mia comunicazione non mi erano noti i lavori dell'HAENTZSCHEL e del SAFFORD sicchè una quantità di risultati che credevo di aver trovati per primo erano contenuti nei lavori citati che io non conoscevo, soprattutto le relazioni fra le ovali di CARTESIO, le curve Cartesiane e la funzione $\wp$ di WEIERSTRASS che sono dovute all'HAENTZSCHEL. Il prof. WANGERIN che presiedeva la Sezione durante la mia comunicazione, mi dette notizia gentilmente dei lavori dell'HAENTZSCHEL ed allora ho, nel manoscritto di questa comunicazione, soppresso quanto nei precedenti lavori era detto espressamente e chiaramente, come pure ho approfittato di essi per migliorare in qualche punto la redazione del mio.

Ciò posto cerchiamo di soddisfare alla (3) con un prodotto della forma

$$V = P \, . \, A \, . \, B \, . \, \Omega \tag{5}$$

dove P è una funzione determinata ed A , B , Ω dipendono rispettivamente da α , β , ω soltanto e soddisfano ad equazioni differenziali, ordinarie del second'ordine. Si trova senza difficoltà che il modo più generale di risolvere la nostra quistione, incorporando, se occorre, i fattori di α , β , ω che possono far parte di P, rispettivamente in A , B , Ω, consiste nel prendere

$$P = \frac{1}{\sqrt{r}} \tag{6}$$

e nel determinare A , B , Ω come soluzioni delle equazioni:

$$\frac{d^2A}{d\alpha^2} + \varphi(\alpha)A = 0 \ , \ \frac{d^2B}{d\beta^2} + \varphi_1(\beta)B = 0 \ , \ \frac{d^2\Omega}{d\omega^2} + n^2\Omega = 0 \tag{7}$$

$\varphi(\alpha)$ e $\varphi_1(\beta)$ essendo due opportune funzioni ed n^2 una costante qualunque positiva, o negativa.

3. Ponendo nella (3) $V = \frac{U}{\sqrt{r}}$ si ha la trasformata in U

$$\frac{\partial^2 U}{\partial\alpha^2} + \frac{\partial^2 U}{\partial\beta^2} + \frac{h^2}{r^2}\left(\frac{\partial^2 U}{\partial\omega^2} + \frac{1}{4}U\right) = 0 \tag{3'}$$

e questa trasformata mostra subito che le soluzioni della nostra quistione corrispondono a quei valori di f per i quali $\frac{h^2}{r^2}$ si può porre sotto la forma della somma di una funzione di α e di una funzione di β. Dev'essere quindi

$$\frac{\partial^2}{\partial\alpha\,\partial\beta}\frac{h^2}{r^2} = 0 \ , \ \text{ossia} \ \frac{\partial^2}{\partial\xi^2}\frac{h^2}{r^2} = \frac{\partial^2}{\partial\eta^2}\frac{h^2}{r^2} \ , \ \xi = \alpha + i\beta \ , \ \eta = \alpha - i\beta \, . \tag{8}$$

Seguendo il Darboux (¹) poniamo:

$$X = f'^2(\alpha + i\beta) \quad , \quad Y = f_0'^2(\alpha - i\beta)$$

e supponiamo anche che X , Y sieno espresse, con l'aiuto della (1), ovvero (1'), rispettivamente per mezzo di f e di f_0. Nel caso (1) avremo:

$$r = \frac{1}{2i}(f - f_0) \quad , \quad h^2 = \sqrt{XY}$$

(¹) *Théorie des surfaces*, 2e partie, p. 208.

e l'equazione (8), divisa per $\sqrt{XY}$, si potrà scrivere

$$(9) \qquad \frac{\partial}{\partial f}\left[\sqrt{X}\frac{\partial}{\partial f}\frac{\sqrt{X}}{(f-f_0)^2}\right]=\frac{\partial}{\partial f_0}\left[\sqrt{Y}\frac{\partial}{\partial f_0}\frac{\sqrt{Y}}{(f-f_0)^2}\right];$$

così nel caso (1') avremo:

$$r=-\frac{1}{2i}(f-f_0) \quad , \quad h^2=\sqrt{XY}$$

e l'equazione (8), divisa ancora per $\sqrt{XY}$, acquista la stessa forma (9).

Eseguendo nella (9) le operazioni di derivazione indicate si ha

$$(10) \qquad 12(X-Y)-6(f-f_0)(X'+Y')+(f-f_0)^2(X''-Y'')=0,$$

dove gli accenti sono sempre simboli di derivazione. E da questa equazione, derivando successivamente due volte rispetto a f e due volte rispetto ad f_0, si ottiene

$$(11) \qquad X^{IV}=Y^{IV}.$$

Ne viene

$$(12) \qquad \left(\frac{df}{d\xi}\right)^2=X=a_0f^4+a_1f^3+a_2f^2+a_3f+a_4$$

e le costanti a_0, a_1, a_2, a_3, a_4, come le costanti coniugate di esse che entrano nell'espressione di Y, sono soggette alle sole condizioni di rendere identicamente soddisfatta la (10). Se indichiamo con a_i^0 la costante coniugata di a_i, facendo nella (10) $f=f_0$, si trova

$$(a_0-a_0^0)f^4+(a_1-a_1^0)f^3+(a_1-a_2^0)f^2+(a_3-a_3^0)f+a_4-a_4^0=0,$$

per cui le costanti a_0, a_1,... a_4 devono essere tutte reali. Si trova pure facilmente che, sotto questa condizione, la (10), effettivamente, è soddisfatta identicamente. Per rendere più agevole questa verifica, notiamo che, ponendo $\boldsymbol{\Xi}=t^4X$, $\boldsymbol{H}=t^4Y$ e mutando f ed f_0 rispettivamente in $\frac{f}{t}$, $\frac{f_0}{t}$, la (10) assume la forma

$$(13) \qquad f_0^2\boldsymbol{\Xi}''_{f,f}-f^2\boldsymbol{H}''_{f_0,f_0}+2t(f_0\boldsymbol{\Xi}''_{f,t}-f\boldsymbol{H}''_{f_0,t})+t^2(\boldsymbol{\Xi}''_{t,t}-\boldsymbol{H}''_{t,t})=0.$$

Possiamo dunque enunciare il risultato: *Tutte le soluzioni possibili del nostro problema si ottengono prendendo*

$$\left.\begin{array}{l} 1^\circ.\quad x+ir=f(\alpha+i\beta)=f(\xi) \\ 2^\circ.\quad x-ir=f(\alpha+i\beta)=f(\xi) \end{array}\right\} \text{con } \left(\frac{df}{d\xi}\right)^2=a_0f^4+a_1f^3+a_2f^2+a_3f+a_4,$$

le costanti a_0, a_1, ..., a_4 *essendo reali e completamente arbitrarie.*

4. Un sistema isotermo determinato da una relazione qualunque $x \pm ir = f(\alpha + i\beta)$ è anche un sistema di linee confocali, nel senso che le linee del sistema hanno in comune tutti i fochi reali, giacchè questi fochi si ottengono ponendo

$$f'(\alpha + i\beta) = 0.$$

Possiamo enunciare quindi il risultato precedente sotto questa forma: *Affinchè un sistema isotermo sia soluzione del nostro problema è necessario e basta che esso abbia al più quattro fochi reali e che questi fochi sieno situati sull'asse di rotazione ovvero, simmetricamente rispetto a quest'asse.*

5. Alle due soluzioni del nostro problema $x + ir = f(\alpha + i\beta)$, $x - ir = f(\alpha + i\beta)$ corrisponde lo stesso valore di $\frac{h^2}{r^2}$ cioè

$$-\frac{4f'(\alpha + i\beta)\, f'_0(\alpha - i\beta)}{[f(\alpha + i\beta) - f_0(\alpha - i\beta)]^2}.$$

Così tutte le funzioni $F(\alpha + i\beta)$, legate ad $f(\alpha + i\beta)$ da una relazione lineare fratta a coefficienti reali

$$F = \frac{af + b}{cf + d}, \tag{14}$$

conducono pure allo stesso valore di $\frac{h^2}{r^2}$, ossia $\frac{h^2}{r^2}$ è un invariante rispetto alle sostituzioni della forma (14). Un calcolo semplicissimo dimostra questo fatto. Tenendo conto dell'interpretazione geometrica della trasformazione (14), possiamo dire che dal sistema isotermo corrispondente alla funzione f si passa al sistema isotermo corrispondente alla funzione F, se non teniamo conto di traslazioni lungo l'asse di rotazione, con una inversione per raggi vettori reciproci rispetto ad una circonferenza che ha il centro in un punto dell'asse di rotazione stesso accompagnata da una simmetria rispetto a questo asse, con una omotetia avente il centro nello stesso punto dell'asse di rotazione, e con una simmetria rispetto a questo punto, al più. Dunque: *se un sistema isotermo è una soluzione del nostro problema, anche i sistemi isotermi che si ottengono dal primo con una inversione per raggi vettori reciproci rispetto ad una circonferenza che ha il centro in un punto qualunque dell'asse di rotazione, con una simmetria rispetto all'asse di rotazione, o con una simmetria rispetto ad un punto qualunque dell'asse di rotazione, sono soluzioni del nostro problema.*

Volendo fare una classificazione di tutti i casi possibili è naturale di raggruppare in una unica categoria tutti quelli che corrispondono allo stesso valore di $\frac{h^2}{r^2}$.

6. Prenderemo come punto di partenza, per eseguire questa classificazione, l'equazione

$$\left(\frac{df}{d\xi}\right)^2 = X = a_0 f^4 + a_1 f^3 + a_2 f^2 + a_3 f + a_4 \tag{12}$$

con $a_0, a_1, \ldots, a_4$ costanti reali arbitrarie. E ricordiamo che una trasformazione lineare fratta arbitraria trasforma la (12) in una equazione dello stesso tipo e conserva l'ordine di multiplicità delle radici del polinomio del quarto grado che compare al secondo membro; che, inoltre, se la trasformazione lineare fratta è a coefficienti reali, l'equazione trasformata della (12) è pure, come la (12), a coefficienti reali, ed a radici reali, ovvero a coppie di radici coniugate, immaginarie, del secondo membro di (12), corrispondono rispettivamente radici reali, ovvero coppie di radici immaginarie coniugate del secondo membro della equazione trasformata. Viceversa due equazioni

$$\left(\frac{df}{d\xi}\right)^2 = \mathrm{X} \ , \ \left(\frac{d\bar{f}}{d\bar{\xi}}\right)^2 = \bar{\mathrm{X}}$$

dove X e $\bar{\mathrm{X}}$ sono due polinomii di quarto grado in f e in $\bar{f}$ rispettivamente, tutti e due a coefficienti reali ed aventi lo stesso numero di radici immaginarie e ciascuna radice avente lo stesso grado di multiplicità, mutando, in una di esse, se occorre, ξ in ξ moltiplicato per un'opportuna costante τ, il che non porta che a mutare i valori degli argomenti α e β, sono trasformabili l'una nell'altra con una trasformazione lineare fratta a coefficienti reali, purchè, se X e $\bar{\mathrm{X}}$ hanno soltanto radici semplici, il rapporto anarmonico delle radici di X sia eguale al rapporto anarmonico delle radici corrispondenti di $\bar{\mathrm{X}}$. Si hanno quindi i seguenti casi distinti:

I) X ha una radice quadrupla, naturalmente, reale;
II) X ha una radice tripla ed una semplice tutte e due, natnralmente, reali;
III^a) X ha una coppia di radici doppie reali;
III^b) X ha una coppia di radici doppie coniugate, immaginarie;
IV^a) X ha una radice doppia reale e due radici semplici reali;
IV^b) X ha una radice doppia reale e due radici coniugate, immaginarie;
V^a) X ha quattro radici semplici e reali;
V^b) X ha due radici semplici e reali e due coniugate immaginarie;
V^c) X ha due coppie di radici semplici, immaginarie, coniugate.

Bisogna tener conto poi che ciascuno dei casi V^a, V^b, V^c si scinde a sua volta in infiniti casi speciali caratterizzati ciascuno dal valore del rapporto anarmonico delle quattro radici di X. Però dal punto di vista analitico tutti gli infiniti casi appartenenti a ciascuna delle categorie V^a, V^b, V^c comportano le stesse considerazioni.

Con una trasformazione del solito tipo, cioè lineare fratta a coefficienti reali, possiamo ridurre la (12) ed f, per ciascun caso, a forma tipica determinata:

I. $$\frac{df}{d\xi} = 1 \ , \ f = \xi \ ; \ \frac{h^2}{r^2} = \frac{1}{\beta^2} \, .$$

Le equazioni a cui soddisfano A e B sono:

$$\frac{d^2\mathrm{A}}{d\alpha^2} = m\mathrm{A} \ , \ \frac{d^2\mathrm{B}}{d\beta^2} + \left[m - \left(n^2 - \frac{1}{4}\right)\frac{1}{\beta^2}\right]\mathrm{B} = 0$$

dove m, come n, è una costante arbitraria. Ed i sistemi isotermi che corrispondono a questo caso sono quello formato dalle rette parallele all'asse di rotazione e dalle rette a queste perpendicolari e quello più generale formato dal fascio dei cerchi tangenti in uno stesso punto all'asse di rotazione e dal fascio di cerchi analogo ortogonale al primo.

II. $$\left(\frac{df}{d\xi}\right)^2 - 4f = 0 \ , \ f = \xi^2 \ , \ \frac{h^2}{r^2} = \frac{1}{\alpha^2} + \frac{1}{\beta^2} .$$

Le equazioni a cui soddisfano A e B sono:

$$\frac{d^2\mathrm{A}}{d\alpha^2} - \left[m + \left(n^2 - \frac{1}{4}\right)\frac{1}{\alpha^2}\right]\mathrm{A} = 0 \ , \ \frac{d^2\mathrm{B}}{d\beta^2} + \left[m - \left(n^2 - \frac{1}{4}\right)\frac{1}{\beta^2}\right]\mathrm{B} = 0$$

dove m ed n sono costanti arbitrarie. Ed i sistemi isotermi, soluzioni del nostro problema, in questo caso, sono: 1° la rete di parabole confocali aventi il foco comune in un punto dell'asse di rotazione e per asse comune l'asse stesso di rotazione; 2°, più in generale, il sistema di quartiche bicircolari, confocali aventi tutte una cuspide in uno stesso punto dell'asse di rotazione e l'asse di rotazione stesso per tangente cuspidale.

III^a. $$\frac{df}{d\xi} + f^2 - 1 = 0 \ , \ f = \frac{e^{\xi} + e^{-\xi}}{e^{\xi} - e^{-\xi}} \ , \ \frac{h^2}{r^2} = \frac{4}{\mathrm{sen}^2(2\beta)} .$$

Le equazioni a cui soddisfano A e B sono:

$$\frac{d^2\mathrm{A}}{d(2\alpha)^2} - m\mathrm{A} = 0 \ , \ \frac{d^2\mathrm{B}}{d(2\beta)^2} + \left[m - \left(n^2 - \frac{1}{4}\right)\frac{1}{\mathrm{sen}^2(2\beta)}\right]\mathrm{B} = 0 .$$

Ed i sistemi isotermi soluzioni del nostro problema sono: 1° il fascio di cerchi che taglia l'asse di rotazione nei due punti reali $z = \pm 1$ ed il fascio dei cerchi ortogonali; 2° il caso particolare del precedente formato da un fascio di cerchi concentrici col centro in un punto dell'asse di rotazione e dalle rette uscenti dal centro comune.

III^b. $$\frac{df}{d\xi} + f^2 + 1 = 0 \ , \ f = \cot g\, \xi \ , \ \frac{h^2}{r^2} = -\frac{4}{\mathrm{sen}^2(2i\beta)}$$

Le equazioni a cui soddisfano A e B sono:

$$\frac{d^2\mathrm{A}}{d(2\alpha)^2} - m\mathrm{A} = 0 \ , \ \frac{d^2\mathrm{B}}{d(2\beta)^2} + \left[m + \left(n^2 + \frac{1}{4}\right)\frac{1}{\mathrm{sen}^2(2i\beta)}\right]\mathrm{B} = 0 ,$$

e l'unico sistema isotermo che risolve il nostro problema in questo caso è formato da un fascio di cerchi che si tagliano in due punti simmetrici rispetto all'asse di rotazione e dal fascio di cerchi ortogonali.

IV^a. $$\left(\frac{df}{d\xi}\right)^2 + f^2 - 1 = 0 \ , \ f = \cos\xi \ , \ \frac{h^2}{r^2} = \frac{1}{\mathrm{sen}^2\alpha} - \frac{1}{\mathrm{sen}^2(i\beta)} .$$

Le equazioni a cui soddisfano A e B sono:

$$\frac{d^2A}{d\alpha^2} - \left[m - \left(n^2 - \frac{1}{4}\right)\frac{1}{\operatorname{sen}^2\alpha}\right]A = 0 \ , \ \frac{d^2B}{d\beta^2} + \left[m - \left(n^2 - \frac{1}{4}\right)\frac{1}{\operatorname{sen}^2(i\beta)}\right]B = 0;$$

ed i sistemi isotermi appartenenti a questo caso sono: 1° la schiera delle coniche confocali aventi i fochi reali comuni sull'asse di rotazione; 2° più in generale, ogni schiera di quartiche bicircolari aventi un punto doppio sull'asse di rotazione e su quest'asse i due fochi reali.

IV^b. $$\left(\frac{df}{d\xi}\right)^2 + f^2 + 1 = 0 \ , \ f = \frac{1}{2}(e^{\xi} + e^{-\xi}) \ , \ \frac{h^2}{r^2} = \frac{1}{\operatorname{sen}^2(i\alpha)} - \frac{1}{\operatorname{sen}^2\beta}$$

Le equazioni a cui soddisfano A e B sono

$$\frac{d^2A}{d\alpha^2} - \left[m - \left(n^2 - \frac{1}{4}\right)\frac{1}{\operatorname{sen}^2(i\alpha)}\right]A = 0 \ , \ \frac{d^2B}{d\beta^2} + \left[m - \left(n^2 - \frac{1}{4}\right)\frac{1}{\operatorname{sen}^2(i\beta)}\right]B = 0;$$

ed i sistemi isotermi corrispondenti a questo caso sono: 1° la schiera delle coniche confocali aventi i fochi reali comuni in due punti simmetrici rispetto all'asse di rotazione; 2° più in generale, ogni schiera di quartiche bicircolari aventi un punto doppio sull'asse di rotazione e i due fochi reali in punti simmetrici rispetto a quest' asse.

V^a. $$\left(\frac{df}{d\xi}\right)^2 - 4f^3 + g_2 f + g_3 = 0 \ , \ g_2^3 - 27g_3^2 > 0 \ , \ f = p\xi \ ,$$

la p essendo la funzione ellittica fondamentale di Weierstrass.

$$\frac{h^2}{r^2} = -4\frac{p'(\alpha + i\beta)p'(\alpha - \beta)}{[p(\alpha + i\beta) - p(\alpha - i\beta)]^2} = 4[p(2\alpha) - p(2i\beta)]$$

e le equazioni a cui soddisfano A e B sono:

$$\frac{d^2A}{d(2\alpha)^2} + \left[m - \left(n^2 - \frac{1}{4}\right)p(2\alpha)\right]A = 0 \ , \ \frac{d^2B}{d(2i\beta)^2} + \left[m - \left(n^2 - \frac{1}{4}\right)p(2i\beta)\right]B = 0.$$

Quando si voglia risolvere il problema di Diriclhet per un corpo intero di rotazione, n è un numero intero e le equazioni precedenti sono equazioni di Lamé corrispondenti ad un valore dell'indice eguale alla metà di un numero intero, equazioni studiate dal Brioschi.

Il sistema isotermo corrispondente alla funzione $p\xi$, in questo caso è formato da ovali di Cartesio. Se, come al solito, si indicano con e_1, e_2, e_3 le tre radici dell'equazione $4f^3 - g_2 f - g_3 = 0$, i fochi di queste ovali sono disposti sull'asse di rotazione ed hanno per ascisse i valori $x = e_1, e_2, e_3$. L'equazione delle curve $\alpha =$ cost. si può porre sotto una qualunque delle forme seguenti:

$$(15)\begin{cases} \{[x - p(2\alpha)]^2 + r^2 - \frac{1}{2}p''(2\alpha)\}^2 - p'^2(2\alpha)[2x + p(2\alpha)] = 0, \\ \sum_1^3 i \frac{(x^2 + r^2 - 2e_i x - e_i^2 - e_{i+1}e_{i+2})^2}{(e_i - e_{i+1})(e_i - e_{i+2})[p(2\alpha) - e_i]} = 0 \end{cases}$$

e cambiando α in $i\beta$ si ottengono le equazioni delle curve $\beta =$ cost. Queste curve hanno, oltre l'asse di rotazione per asse di simmetria, tre cerchi di simmetria nei cerchi

$$(16) \qquad C_i \equiv x^2 + r^2 - 2e_i x - e_i^2 - e_{i+1}e_{i-2} = 0$$

di cui C_1 e C_2 sono reali e C_3 immaginario. Inoltre il punto dell'asse di rotazione che ha per ascissa $x = p(2\alpha)$, ovvero $x = p(2i\beta)$, è il foco straordinario delle curve $\alpha =$ cost., ovvero $\beta =$ cost.

A questa soluzione bisogna aggiungere, nel caso che ora consideriamo, tutti i sistemi isotermi che si ottengono dal precedente con una simmetria rispetto ad un punto dell'asse di rotazione, ovvero con una inversione per raggi vettori reciproci rispetto ad un punto dello stesso asse di rotazione. Con quest'ultima operazione si ottengono sistemi di quartiche bicircolari aventi quattro fochi sull'asse di rotazione.

$$\text{V}^b. \qquad \left(\frac{df}{d\xi}\right)^2 - 4f^3 + g_2 f + g_3 = 0 \ , \ g_2^3 - 27g_3^2 < 0 \ , \ f = p\xi .$$

A e B, in questo caso, soddisfano alle stesse equazioni che nel caso V^a. Però il sistema isotermo corrispondente alla funzione $p\xi$ è formato dalle così dette *curve Cartesiane*. Le equazioni di queste curve sono ancora le (15) e valgono tutte le considerazioni precedenti con queste differenze che dei tre fochi uno è sull'asse di rotazione ed ha per ascissa $x = e_2$ e gli altri due $x + ir = e_1, e_3$ sono disposti simmetricamente rispetto all'asse di rotazione stesso e, dei tre cerchi di simmetria C_i, C_2 è reale, mentre C_1 e C_3 sono immaginarii.

V^c. Si ha quest'ultimo caso quando il secondo membro della (12) ha quattro radici a due, a due, immaginarie, coniugate. Allora la (12) non può ridursi alla forma normale di Weierstrass altro che con una sostituzione lineare, fratta a coefficienti complessi. Se indichiamo con f_1, f_2, f_3, f_4 le radici del secondo membro della (12), in questo caso, se è f_2 coniugata di f_1 ed f_4 coniugata di f_3 ed indichiamo pure con e_1, e_2, e_3 le tre radici dell'equazione $4f^3 - g_2 f - g_3 = 0$, dove può supporsi, per fissare le idee, $g_2^3 - 27g_3^2 > 0$, si potrà porre questa sostituzione sotto la forma

$$(17) \qquad \frac{f - f_1}{f - f_2} \cdot \frac{f_3 - f_2}{f_3 - f_1} = \frac{p\xi - e_1}{p\xi - e_2} \cdot \frac{e_3 - e_2}{e_3 - e_1}$$

con la condizione

$$(18) \qquad \frac{f_4 - f_1}{f_4 - f_2} \cdot \frac{f_3 - f_2}{f_3 - f_1} = \frac{e_3 - e_2}{e_3 - e_1} ,$$

la p essendo la funzione di WEIERSTRASS costruita con gli invarianti g_2 e g_3, e nell'ipotesi che ad f_1, f_2, f_3, f_4 corrispondano, rispettivamente, i valori e_1, e_2, e_3, ∞. Se indichiamo con K l'espressione $\frac{f_4 - f_1}{f_4 - f_2}$ e con K_0 l'espressione coniugata $\frac{f_3 - f_2}{f_3 - f_1}$; se indichiamo ancora con F la funzione $K \frac{p\xi - e_1}{p\xi - e_2}$ e con F_0, f_0 le funzioni coniugate di F ed f, potremo porre la (17) sotto una delle forme

$$(17') \qquad \frac{f - f_1}{f - f_2} = F \ , \ f = \frac{f_1 - f_2 F}{1 - F}.$$

Avremo quindi

$$\frac{h^2}{r^2} = 4 \frac{F'F'_0}{(FF_0 - 1)^2} = 4 \frac{KK_0(e_1 - e_2)^2 p'(\xi)p'\eta}{[KK_0(p\xi - e_1)(p\eta - e_1) - (p\xi - e_2)(p\eta - e_2)]^2}$$
$$= 4 \frac{(e_3 - e_1)(e_3 - e_2) p'\xi p'\eta}{[p\xi p\eta - e_3(p\xi + p\eta) - e_3^2 - e_1 e_2]^2}.$$

Si trova ora subito

$$p\xi p\eta - e_3(p\xi + p\eta) - e_3^2 - e_1 e_2 =$$
$$= \frac{[p^2\alpha - 2e_3 p\alpha - e_3^2 - e_1 e_2][p^2(i\beta) - 2e_3 p(i\beta) - e_3^2 - e_1 e_2]}{[p\alpha - p(i\beta)]^2} \ (^1)$$

e, d'altra parte, è pure

$$[p^2\alpha - 2e_3 p\alpha - e_3^2 - e_1 e_2]^2 = (p^2\alpha + \tfrac{1}{4} g_2)^2 + 2g_3 p\alpha - e_3 p'^2\alpha = p'^2\alpha[p(2\alpha) - e_3]$$

. . . .

$$p'\xi p'\xi = -[p\xi - p\eta]^2 [p(2\alpha) - p(2i\beta)] = \frac{p'^2\alpha\, p'^2(i\beta)}{[p\alpha - p(i\beta)]^4} [p(2\alpha) - p(2i\beta)]$$

per cui si trova, finalmente

$$(19) \qquad \frac{h^2}{r^2} = 4 \frac{(e_3 - e_1)(e_3 - e_2)[p(2\alpha) - p(2i\beta)]}{[p(2\alpha) - e_3][p(2i\beta) - e_3]}$$
$$= 4 \frac{(e_3 - e_1)(e_3 - e_2)}{p(2\alpha) - e_3} - 4 \frac{(e_3 - e_1)(e_3 - e_1)}{p(2i\beta) - e_3}.$$

Da questo risultato discende che le equazioni differenziali a cui soddisfano A e B, in questo caso, sono:

$$\frac{d^2 A}{d(2\alpha)^2} - \left[m + (n - \tfrac{1}{4}) \frac{(e_3 - e_1)(e_3 - e_2)}{p(2\alpha) - e_3}\right] A = 0 \ ,$$
$$\frac{d^2 B}{d(2i\beta)^2} - \left[m + (n^2 - \tfrac{1}{4}) \frac{(e_3 - e_1)(e_3 - e_2)}{p(2i\beta) - e_3}\right] B = 0.$$

(1) Si consulti: WEIERSTRASS-SCHWARZ, *Förmeln und Lehrsätze*....... S. 14.

I sistemi isotermi che si ottengono così sono i sistemi di quartiche bicircolari aventi quattro fochi a due, a due disposti simmetricamente rispetto all'asse di rotazione.

Dalla (17') e dall'espressione di F risulta

$$f(\xi) - f_0(\eta) = \frac{(f_1 - f_2)(1 - \mathrm{F}\mathrm{F}_0)}{(1 - \mathrm{F})(1 - \mathrm{F}_0)},$$

$$1 - \mathrm{F}\mathrm{F}_0 = \frac{e_1 - e_2}{(e_3 - e_1)(p\xi - e_2)(p\eta - e_2)}[p\xi\, p\eta - e_3(p\xi + p\eta) - e_3^2 - e_1 e_2]$$

quindi al cerchio C_3 di simmetria per le curve $x + ir = p\xi$ corrisponde l'asse x come asse di simmetria per le curve $x + ir = f(\xi)$. Ne viene che con la rotazione anche queste curve generano superficie del quarto ordine.

J. H. POYNTING

THE MOMENTUM OF A BEAM OF LIGHT

The existence of Light Pressure, and therefore the existence of Momentum, in a beam of light follows directly from NEWTON's Corpuscular Theory; but that a pressure also exists when light is regarded as undulatory was first deduced by MAXWELL from his Electromagnetic Theory of light.

It can be shown however that the pressure must follow as a consequence of any wave motion, without making assumptions as to the nature of the type of wave which constitutes light, provided only that the medium is such that a reflecting solid can move through it without disturbing the medium except by reflecting the waves which it meets. This important generalization was first indicated by BARTOLI, and afterwords more fully worked out by LARMOR. The proof given by the latter may be put in a simple form as follows:

Consider a train of waves incident normally on a perfectly reflecting wall which is moving towards the beam with velocity v, and let V be the wave velocity. Then evidently a length $V+v$ of the incident beam which is just beginning to meet the reflector at any instant will after an interval of one second be transformed into a length $V-v$ of the reflected beam.

These two lengths must contain the same number of waves; hence if λ is the wave length of the incident beam, the reflected beam must have the shorter wave length $\lambda' = \frac{V-v}{V+v} \cdot \lambda$ which is in accordance with DOPPLER's principle.

The perfect reflection requires that the resultant disturbance at the surface shall always be zero, and the incident and reflected trains must therefore have equal amplitudes. We must now assume that for a given amplitude the average energy density is inversely as the square of the wave length. This is evidently true for elastic waves, and it holds also for Electromagnetic waves when the amplitude is that of the Vector Potential.

The effect of the change in wave length will therefore be to increase the energy density from E, the value in the incident beam, to E', the value for the reflected beam, where

$$E' = \left(\frac{V+v}{V-v}\right)^2 . E .$$

Regarding then a beam of unit cross section, the total energy before reflection is $(V+v)E$, and after reflection it is $(V-v)E'$, so that in one second the energy of wave motion in the medium is increased by an amount

$$(V-v)E'-(V+v)E$$
$$=\frac{V+v}{V-v}\,.\,2v\,.\,E\,.$$

This gain in energy is to be accounted for by supposing that the reflecting surface is pressed back by the waves, so that work has to be done in moving it forward. If then p is the pressure on the reflector when moving with velocity v, the work done per second on each square unit of surface will be pv, and we obtain at once:

$$p=\frac{V+v}{V-v}\,.\,2E$$

When the reflector is at rest $v=0$, and hence

$$p_0=2E$$

or, since the incident and reflected beams are now equal and therefore $E'=E$, we have the simple result that the pressure is equal to the total energy density in front of the reflector. This relation, it should be noticed, does not hold in the case of motion, for the total energy density is then

$$E+E'=E+\left(\frac{V+v}{V-v}\right)^2.\,E$$
$$=\frac{V^2+v^2}{(V-v)^2}\,.\,2\,E$$

and hence

$$p=\frac{V^2-v^2}{V^2+v^2}\,.\,(E+E')$$
$$=\left(1-\frac{2v^2}{V^2}\right)(E+E')\quad\text{approximately.}$$

This shows that the pressure is only equal to the energy density if the second power of $\frac{v}{V}$ can be neglected.

If the incident beam is not reflected but totally absorbed by a surface at rest it produces half the pressure, and we still have the pressure equal to the energy density.

The wave train can therefore be regarded as carrying with it a stream of momentum, and since the absorption of this momentum gives rise to a pressure on the absorbing surface equal in amount to the energy density E of the waves, we may consider that the stream of momentum has a density $\frac{E}{V}$ and is moving with the velocity of light V.

The idea of momentum in the wave train enables us to see at once what is the nature of the action of a beam of light on a surface at which it is reflected, refracted, absorbed, or emitted, without making any further appeal to the theory of the wave motion. Several important cases will now be considered from this point of view.

If the surface upon which a beam falls is a perfect absorber, and is at rest, the pressure p_0 on it must equal the momentum received per second per unit area, or

$$p_0 = \left(\frac{E}{V}\right) . V = E .$$

Now suppose that the absorber is moving towards the beam with velocity v, in one second it will sweep up the momentum in a lenght $V + v$ of the incident beam and the pressure is therefore increased to

$$p = (V + v) . \frac{E}{V}$$
$$= \left(1 + \frac{v}{V}\right) E.$$

Consider now a surface at rest which is emitting a parallel beam of light normally; there will be a back pressure on it which is again equal to the energy density of the beam. This follows from the fact that the momentum stream sent out comes from the surface and therefore the latter must experience the corresponding reaction. Or we may deduce the pressure from the case of perfect reflection already discused by regarding the reflected light as *emitted* by the surface.

When the source is moving with velocity v in the direction in which it is radiating, let E' be the energy density of the beam emitted. Since the momentum density is $\frac{E'}{V}$, and a length $V - v$ is emitted in each second, the pressure must be given by

$$p = \frac{V - v}{V} \cdot E'$$

We have as yet made no assumption as to the value of E'. Suppose that the source when at rest emits waves having energy density E_0, and assume that when in motion the emitting surface always converts its internal energy into radient energy at the same rate E_0V as when at rest, but that the work pv done per second against the pressure is also transformed into radiant energy. We have then

$$E_0V + pv = E'(V - v)$$

and hence from last equation

$$p = \frac{V}{V - v} \cdot E_0$$

or

$$p = \frac{V}{V - v} p_0 .$$

The pressure is therefore increased by the forward motion.

The existence of the pressure when a beam of light falls normally upon a surface has been fully proved by the experiments of LEBEDEW and of NICHOLS and HULL.

In the experiments which we shall now describe, illustrating the momentum in a beam of light, we shall for convenience consider the energy E_1 per unit length of the beam, and the total pressure force, so avoiding any necessity for taking into account the cross section of the beam. The beam of light then carries a quantity of momentum $\frac{E_1}{V}$ in unit length, and exerts a force equal to E_1 on any totally absorbing surface at rest, and this force is always in the direction of the beam.

Thus for oblique incidence on an absorbing surface at an angle θ with the normal, the force on the surface has components

$$E_1 \cos\theta \text{ normally}$$

$$E_1 \sin\theta \text{ tangentially.}$$

In the more general case when the surface has reflection coefficient r, it is easily seen that the components are $(1 + r) E_1 \cos\theta$ and $(1 - r) E_1 \sin\theta$ respectively

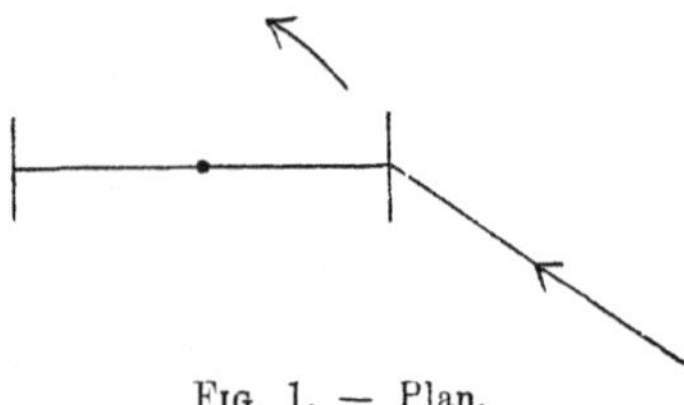

FIG. 1. — Plan.

The tangential stress is of especial interest as it may be detected more easily than the normal effect. For generally the disturbing action of the surrounding gas gives a resultant force along the normal to the surface, and it is always difficult to separate this from the normal light pressure. On the other hand it is merely necessary to arrange that the absorbing surface is free to move only in its own plane in order to eliminate the gas action and exhibit the tangential component of the light pressure.

In the first experiment to show this effect, two circular glass disks, 2 cm. diameter, were fixed to the ends of a horizontal glass rod, length 5.3 cm., the disks being perpendicular to the rod (Fig. 1. plan). One of the disks was coated with camphor black, and the other brightly silvered. The whole system was then suspended by a fine quartz fibre within an exhausted chamber. A parallel beam of light from a Nernst Lamp was directed horizontally on either disk at an angle of 45° as shown by the arrow in Fig. 1. When the beam fell on the black disk the system was pushed round by the tangential force, but when it fell on the silvered disk the push round was very small. The deflections of the system were observed by the usual telescope and mirror method. The energy of the beam was determined, after the manner of NICHOLS and HULL, by allowing it to be absorbed by a blackened silver disk of known thermal capacity and measuring the rise in temperature by means of a thermoelectric junction. Some irregular disturbances due to gas action were never entirely eliminated, but these were found to be at a *minimum*, as in the experiments of NICHOLS and HULL, for gas pressures near 1 cm. of mercury. The calculated and observed deflections were in good agreement.

Another, and much more successful, form of the experiment has been recently

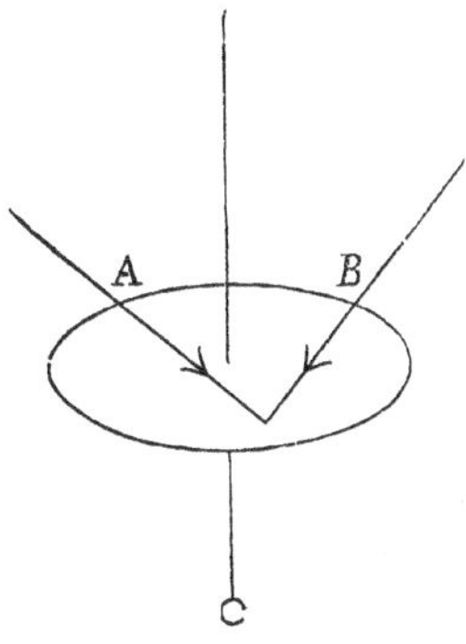

FIG. 2.

carried out. A single circular disk of camphor blacked mica, 3.5 cm. diameter, was suspended with its plane horizontal by a quartz fibre from its centre (Fig. 2). Two equal beams of light, A and B, were thrown down at an angle of 45° on exacthy the same part of the disk: these beams were in the same vertical plane, and therefore mutually at right angles, and hence the two tangential stresses on the disk were equal and tended to rotate it in opposite directions. The amount of rotation was determined (*a*) for A alone (*b*) for B alone and (*c*) for A and B together. The algebraical difference between the deflections (*a*) and (*b*) gives twice the tangential effect, for the heating of the mica disc, and therefore any uneliminated gas action, may be assumed to be the same in both cases. On the other hand the deflection (*c*) will give merely twice the gas action. Observations made with widely varying gas pressures in both air and hydrogen (in which gas the disturbing action is much less than in air) demonstrated beyond all doubt the existence of a tangential stress of the magnitude, always within 15 per cent, required by theory.

If by means of any system of reflecting or refracting surfaces a beam of light be displaced parallel to its original direction, we see at once from the momentum idea that the system must be acted upon by a couple. Two such cases have been examined experimentally.

A rectangular block of glass (Fig. 3. Plan) 3 cm. × 1 cm. × 1 cm., was suspended by a quartz fibre so that the long axis of the block was horizontal. A parallel beam

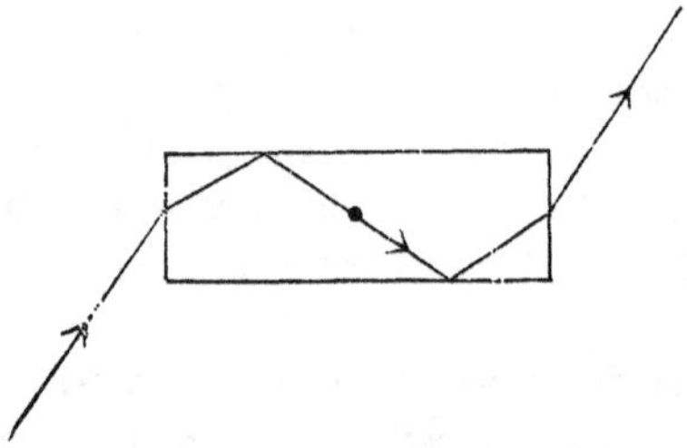

Fig. 3. — Plan.

of light was directed horizontally on to one end of the block and at an angle of incidence of 55°. After two internal total reflections it emerged from the other end in a direction parallel to the incident beam, as indicated by the arrows in Fig. 3.

The couple on the block produced by this lateral shift of the beam of light was found to be in close agreement with the value calculated from measurements of the energy of the beam.

In the other experiment two glass prisms (Fig. 4. Plan) each having a refracting angle of 34° and with refracting edge 1.6 cm. long. were fixed at the ends of a

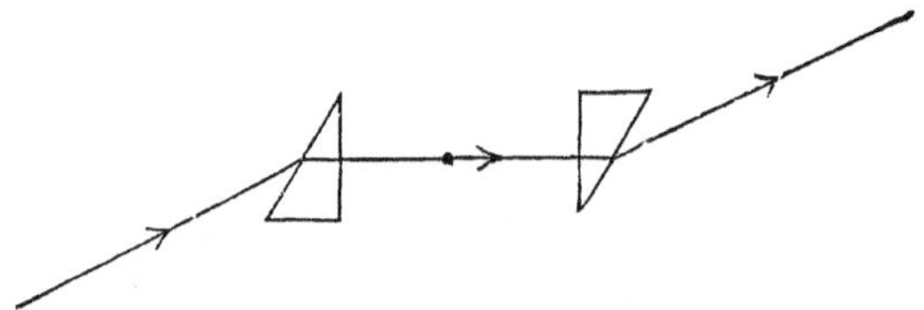

Fig. 4. — Plan.

thin brass torsion arm suspended at its middle point from a quartz fibre. The two inner faces of the prisms were perpendicular to the torsion arm and 3 cm. apart. When a parallel beam of light was sent symmetrically throngh the system, as shown by the arrows in the diagram, the lateral diplacement of the beam, 1.64 cms. in this experiment, produced an easily measurable couple in the direction and within a few per cent of the magnitude indicated by theory. This experiment was also successfully repeated with another and smaller pair of prisms.

These experiments were performed with reduced air pressure, but the absence of serious gas action was probably due to the fact that in such a system of reflections and refractions at glass surfaces only a very small fraction of the energy of the light is absorbed by the system.

The experiments were made in collaboration with my colleague Dr. Guy Barlow.

C. STÖRMER

SUR LES TRAJECTOIRES DES CORPUSCULES ÉLECTRISÉS DANS LE CHAMP D'UN AIMANT ÉLÉMENTAIRE AVEC APPLICATION AUX AURORES BORÉALES

J'aurai le grand honneur de vous entretenir ce soir d'une série de recherches faites par moi au cours de ces dernières années relativement à une théorie mathématique du phénomène des aurores boréales et des perturbations magnétiques.

L'origine de mes recherches a été une série d'expériences remarquables sur les rayons cathodiques dans un champ magnétique faites par mon collègue le professeur Birkeland pendant les dernières années du siècle précédent. Pour l'enchaînement naturel des idées, il sera nécessaire de parler d'abord un peu de ces expériences.

Ce fut en 1896, que M. Birkeland découvrit le phénomène si intéressant qu'il a appelé la succion des rayons cathodiques vers un pôle magnétique. Voici (fig. 1) une photographie de son expérience.

On voit comment un aimant très-fort, placé sous une ampoule de Crookes et dont l'action peut être assimilée à celle d'un pôle magnétique unique, aura la propriété de faire converger les rayons cathodiques comme une leutille fait converger les rayons lumineux vers un foyer. Ce phénomène peut être expliqué complètement par la théorie, comme l'a fait voir M. Poincaré, en utilisant un résultat analytique obtenu par M. Darboux relativement à l'intégration des équations de mouvement des corpuscules cathodiques en question.

Guidé par ce beau phénomène, M. Birkeland a ensuite été conduit à une théorie féconde sur l'origine des aurores boréales; en effet, dans un Mémoire paru en 1896 dans les Archives de Genève, il dit après avoir cité l'hypothèse du météorologiste danois Paulsen, selon laquelle l'aurore boréale provient d'une phosphorescence de l'air dûe à des rayons cathodiques venant des plus hautes couches de l'atmosphère :

« D'après ce qui précède, on peut admettre que les rayons proviennent de l'espace cosmique et sont surtout absorbés au pôle magnétique terrestre et qu'il faut les attribuer d'une manière ou de l'autre au soleil ».

Depuis lors Birkeland a organisé et dirigé à trois reprises des expéditions dans les régions polaires pour étudier les aurores boréales et les perturbations magnétiques. La dernière fois, en 1902-1903, il avait 4 stations simultanées dans le Firmarken, en Islande, au Spitzberg et à la Nouvelle-Zemble: les résultats de cette expédition seront bientôt publiés (1).

Dans des Mémoires subséquents, M. Birkeland est revenu à diverses reprises à cette hypothèse, et il a tâché de la vérifier par une série d'expériences très-remarquables. Dans ces expériences il a soumis un faisceau de rayons cathodiques à l'action d'un petit globe magnétique représentant la terre. Il a donc vu, dans certaines conditions, des phénomènes qui rendent son hypothèse très-vraisemblable.

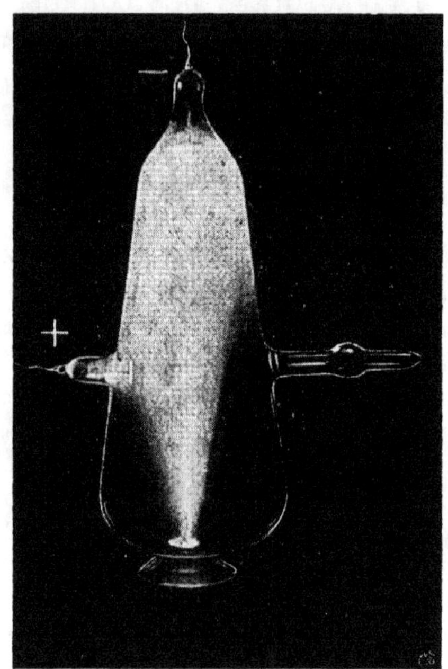

Fig. 1

Ainsi, sur la fig. 2, on voit le tube de décharge avec la petite terre magnétique suspendue à l'intérieur. Le globe est recouvert d'une couche de cyanure double de platine et de baryum, pour rendre visibles les endroits frappés par les rayons cathodiques. Le pôle magnétique sud, qui est tourné vers le haut, est marqué par une croix. On voit ici se former un anneau lumineux autour de la sphère.

Sur la fig. 3, on voit une sphère semblable dont le magnétisme est plus fort et qui a un diamètre plus petit que celle de la fig. 2; elle est aussi munie d'un écran phosphorescent. Les photographies sont prises dans des directions faisant des angles

(1) Le volume I ayant le titre: *The norvegian aurora polaris expedition 1902-1903. On the cause of magnetic storms and the origin of terrestial magnetism, first section,* vient d'être publié (chez M. C. Klincksieck, Paris).

(Note de l'auteur pendant la correction des epreuves).

de 120° et 240° avec la ligne qui va de la cathode au centre du globe, ces angles étant comptés dans le plan horizontal de l'ouest à l'est, en passant par le sud. On voit ici comment les rayons cathodiques frappent le globe sur deux bandes phospho-

Fig. 2.

rescentes entourant les pôles magnétiques et rappelant les ceintures de fréquence

Fig. 3.

maximum des aurores boréales. Il est à remarquer que, pour obtenir des bandes étroites, il faut diminuer les dimensions du globe en le rendant en même temps aussi magnétique que possible.

Il m'a paru extrêmement intéressant de tâcher de retrouver par l'analyse mathématique les détails de tous ces remarquables phénomènes, en partant des lois connues pour le mouvement d'une particule cathodique dans un champ magnétique. Pendant les 4 dernières années j'ai été occupé de ces recherches, dont on trouve un résumé dans un Mémoire paru l'année dernière dans les Archives de Genève ([1]). J'ai ainsi réussi non seulement à expliquer par l'analyse les traits principaux des phénomènes observés par M. Birkeland, mais aussi à retrouver théoriquement une série de propriétés caractéristiques des phénomènes d'aurore boréale et des perturbations magnétiques.

Nous allons donner un court résumé des résultats obtenus; pour les détails je renvoie à mon Mémoire cité plus haut.

Disons d'abord quelques mots sur la mise en équation du problème.

Si l'on admet que l'aurore boréale et les perturbations magnétiques sont dûes à des corpuscules électrisés venant de l'espace cosmique, on est tout de suite conduit au problème consistant à trouver les trajectoires de ces corpuscules sous l'action du magnétisme terrestre. On est d'abord forcé de faire une série l'hypothèses pour simplifier le calcul; le problème simplifié une fois résolu il faut ensuite essayer de résoudre le problème primitif. Comme hypothèses simplifiantes nous avons choisi les suivantes:

1°. Nous négligeons les mouvements propres de la terre et du soleil pour ne considérer que leurs positions relatives; en effet, à cause de vitesses énormes des corpuscules en questions cette position relative ne change pas sensiblement pendant qu'un corpuscule chemine du soleil à la terre.

2°. Nous supposons que les corpuscules ne sont pas soumis à d'autres forces que le magnétisme terrestre et qu'ils se meuvent d'après les lois qu'on a observées pour les rayons cathodiques dans un champ magnétique.

3°. Enfin nous supposons que le magnétisme terrestre est dû à les masses magnétiques situées à l'*intérieur* de la terre, de sorte qu'on a pour le potentiel magnétique dans l'espace extérieur la représentation connue en série convergente suivant les puissances de $\frac{R}{r}$, R étant le rayon de la terre et r le rayon vecteur, avec des coefficients qui sont des fonctions de Laplace.

De cette dernière hypothèse résulte le fait connu, qu'à des distances très-grandes de la terre, p. ex. excédant 1 million de km., le champ du magnétisme terrestre peut être assimilé, avec beaucoup d'approximation, au champ d'un aimant élémentaire, d'un moment égal à environ $8{,}52.10^{25}$ unités magnétiques, aimant placé au centre de la terre, et dont l'axe coïncide avec l'axe magnétique du globe.

De là résulte une simplification considérable du problème; en effet, il suffit alors, comme première approximation de *trouver les trajectoires des corpuscules électrisés sous l'action d'un aimant élémentaire*, problème analogue à celui où le champ est dû à un seul pôle, mais beaucoup plus difficile à résoudre.

([1]) *Sur les trajectoires des corpuscules électrisés dans l'espace sous l'action du magnétisme terrestre, avec application aux aurores boréales* (Juillet-Octobre 1907).

Considérons les équations différentielles des trajectoires d'un corpuscule électrisé dans un pareil champ. Prenons pour unité de longueur une longueur de C centimètres, C étant défini par l'équation

$$C = \sqrt{\frac{M}{H_0 \varrho_0}}$$

où M est le moment de l'aimant élémentaire et où $H_0 \varrho_0$ est une constante caractéristique pour les corpuscules en question; ainsi, pour les corpuscules formant les rayons cathodique, $H_0 \varrho_0$ varie entre 100 et 600, pour ceux des rayons β de radium entre 1500 et 5000 et pour ceux des rayons α de radium entre 200000 et 400000.

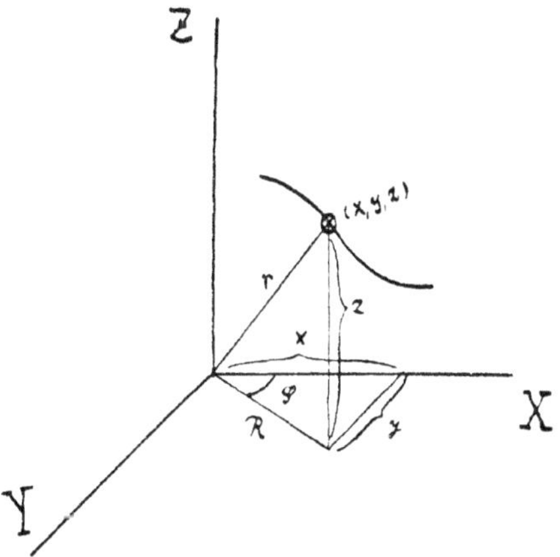

Fig. 4.

Plaçons ensuite un système de coordonnées cartésiennes de manière que l'aimant élémentaire soit à l'origine, son axe coincidant avec l'axe des z et le pôle sud tourné vers les z positifs (Voir fig. 4).

Cela posé, si (x, y, z) est un point de la trajectoire et que l'arc s de celle-ci soit choisi comme variable indépendante, les équations différentielles de la trajectoire seront [1], pour un corpuscule chargé d'électricité négative

$$(1) \quad \begin{cases} \dfrac{d^2x}{ds^2} = \dfrac{3yz}{r^5}\dfrac{dz}{ds} - \dfrac{3z^2 - r^2}{r^5}\dfrac{dy}{ds} \\ \dfrac{d^2y}{ds^2} = \dfrac{3z^2 - r^2}{r^5}\dfrac{dx}{ds} - \dfrac{3xz}{r^5}\dfrac{dz}{ds} \\ \dfrac{d^2z}{ds^2} = \dfrac{3xz}{r^5}\dfrac{dy}{ds} - \dfrac{3yz}{r^5}\dfrac{dx}{ds} \end{cases}$$

où $r^2 = x^2 + y^2 + z^2$.

[1] Voir mon Mémoire cité, p. 21.

Si la charge électrique est positive, il faut changer le signe des seconds membres, d'où on conclut que pour la même valeur de C, les trajectoires des corpuscules positifs sont symétriques à celles des corpuscules négatifs par rapport à un plan passant par l'axe de l'aimant; il suffit donc d'étudier ces dernières.

On obtient tout de suite une intégrale première en introduisant des coordonnées semi-polaires R et φ définies par les équations $x = \mathrm{R}\cos\varphi$, $y = \mathrm{R}\sin\varphi$.

En effet, on trouve

$$\frac{d}{ds}\left(\mathrm{R}^2\frac{d\varphi}{ds}\right) = -\frac{3\mathrm{R}^2 z}{r^5}\frac{dz}{ds} - \frac{r^2 - 3z^2}{r^5}\mathrm{R}\frac{d\mathrm{R}}{ds}$$

et le second membre est ici la dérivée de $\frac{\mathrm{R}^2}{r^3}$, de manière qu'on obtient en intégrant

$$\mathrm{R}^2\frac{d\varphi}{ds} = 2\gamma + \frac{\mathrm{R}^2}{r^3} \tag{2}$$

γ étant une constante d'intégration.

En éliminant ensuite φ à l'aide de cette relation, on arrive au système

$$\left\{\begin{aligned} &\frac{d^2\mathrm{R}}{ds^2} = \frac{1}{2}\frac{\partial \mathrm{Q}}{\partial \mathrm{R}}, \quad \frac{d^2 z}{ds^2} = \frac{1}{2}\frac{\partial \mathrm{Q}}{\partial z} \\ &\left(\frac{d\mathrm{R}}{ds}\right)^2 + \left(\frac{dz}{ds}\right)^2 = \mathrm{Q} \end{aligned}\right. \tag{3}$$

où nous avons posé

$$\mathrm{Q} = 1 - \left[\frac{2\gamma}{\mathrm{R}} + \frac{\mathrm{R}}{r^3}\right]^2.$$

Dans mon Mémoire, j'ai fait voir quelles conséquences utiles on peut tirer des équations (2) et (3) relativement aux propriétés des trajectoires. Il en résulte p. ex. une condition qui doit être vérifiée tout le long de la trajectoire, à savoir que

$$-1 \leqq \frac{2\gamma}{\mathrm{R}} + \frac{\mathrm{R}}{r^3} \leqq 1$$

ce qui définit une certaine partie de l'espace, que nous appellerons Q_γ d'où les trajectoires ne peuvent sortir. Toutes les trajectoires possibles se trouvent donc classées en une série infinie de familles, chaque famille étant caractérisée par une valeur particulière de γ et les trajectoires de cette famille ne sortant jamais de l'espace Q_γ correspondant.

Sur les figures (fig. 5 et fig. 6), on peut voir une série de formes caractéristiques de ces espaces; l'aimant est placé au centre de chaque figure. Comme on le voit, à chaque figure de la série inférieure en correspond une autre de la série supérieure représentant la section des espaces en question par un plan passant par l'axe magnétique. Les parties blanches sont celles qui par leur révolution autour de cet axe engendrent nos espaces Q_γ.

Nous allons tout de suite en faire une application aux aurores. Pour le cas du magnétisme terrestre, notre unité de longueur C est d'environ 13 fois la distance de la terre à la lune pour les rayons cathodiques ordinaires, 4 fois la même distance pour les rayons β de radium et enfin la moitié de la même distance pour les rayons α de radium. Les dimensions des espaces Q_γ sont donc énormes par rapport à la terre, ce qu'on peut voir sur la figure 7 qui représente les sections des espaces Q_γ aux

Fig. 7.

environs de l'aimant élémentaire; les dimensions relatives de la terre y sont indiquées par des cercles pointillés.

On comprend alors que la terre sera frappée par des corpuscules solaires en des régions situées dans les zônes arctiques et antarctiques ce qui est conforme à la fréquence ordinaire des aurores.

Cependant, pour étudier en détail les trajectoires possibles, il était nécessaire d'intégrer au moins approximativement les équations différentielles. Pour cela, nous nous sommes servis des méthodes d'intégration graphique et numérique permettant de suivre les trajectoires pas à pas du soleil jusqu'à la terre. Nous n'entrerons pas dans les détails de ces utiles méthodes: il suffit de renvoyer à mon Mémoire cité plus haut et à une note qui vient de paraître en anglais [1]. À l'aide de ces mé-

[1] Voir: *On graphic solution of dynamical problems.* Videnskabs Selskabets Skrifter Christiania, 1908.

thodes nous avons, mes assistants et moi-même, pendant les 3 dernières années, calculé une multitude de trajectoires différentes, dont on peut voir quelques-unes sur les figures suivantes. C'est là un travail immense de calcul qui a exigé en tout plus que 5000 heures de travail.

Nous allons voir d'abord un modèle (Voir fig. 8 et 9) représentant un faisceau de rayons cathodiques sous l'action d'un aimant élémentaire et correspondant à l'expérience de M. Birkeland reproduite fig. 2. On voit ici l'anneau correspondant à l'anneau lumineux de l'expérience, son rayon est égal à notre unité de longueur C.

Cependant la majeure partie des rayons n'arrive pas à l'aimant élémentaire, mais s'en approche seulement à une certaine distance, pour continuer ensuite vers

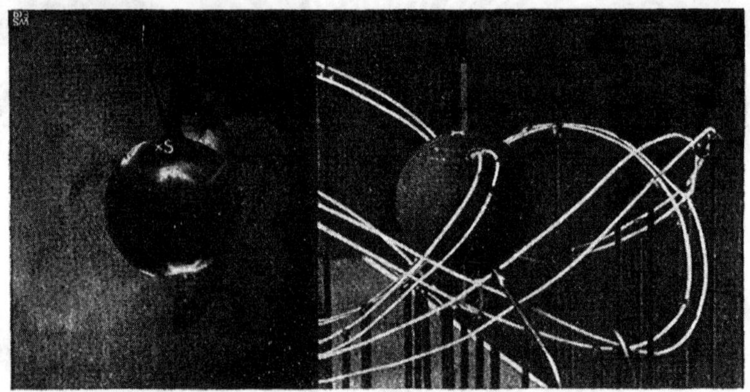

Fig. 11.

l'infini; c'est là une loi générale qui résulte d'ailleurs de la théorie. En effet, si l'on considère tous les corpuscules correspondants à la même valeur de $H_\sigma \varrho_0$ et émanant d'un point situé à grande distance de l'aimant, il n'y a que ceux jetés dans *certaines directions distinctes* qui arrivent à l'aimant, tandis qu'aucun des autres n'y arrive; nous appelerons ces directions *directions distinguées*. Sur la figure 10 on peut voir de pareilles trajectoires correspondant aux directions distinguées émanant de deux points différents.

On voit comment les corpuscules frappent le petit globe en des endroits différents situés dans des ceintures entourant l'axe magnétique.

En comparant cela avec l'expérience de M. Birkeland on est frappé par la coïncidence qui existe entre la théorie et l'expérience (voir fig. 11).

Faisons l'application de ce qui précède aux aurores boréales:

Considérons tous les corpuscules émanant p. ex. d'une tache solaire et se mouvant vers la terre. À cause de la petitesse de la terre par rapport à notre unité de longueur C, il n'y a que les corpuscules jetés dans des directions différant très peu des directions distinguées qui puissent arriver à la terre pour y donner lieu à l'aurore. Or le soleil ne peut avoir toutes les situations possibles par rapport à l'axe magnétique de la terre; en effet, il ne peut pas monter ou descendre de plus de 35° environ au dessus ou au dessous du plan magnétique équatorial; il en résulte que les trajectoires correspondantes à des situations impossibles devront être rejetées, ce qui limite les zônes théoriques d'aurore à *des ceintures entourant les points d'inter-*

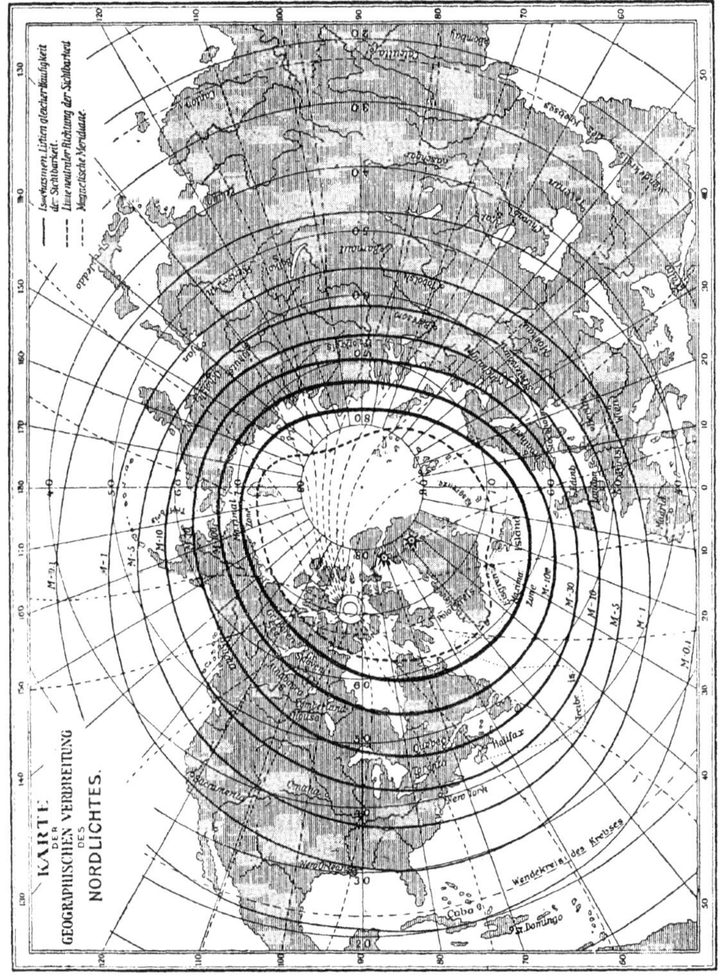

Fig 12.

section de l'axe magnétique de la terre avec sa surface. Ceci s'accorde bien avec la zône de fréquence maximum, ainsi qu'on peut le voir par la carte ci-jointe:

Sur cette carte, le point d'intersection de l'axe magnétique et de la surface de la terre est indiqué par des étoiles: celui situé le plus à l'ouest correspond à l'année 1900, l'autre à l'année 1700.

Par les théories anciennes, il était fort difficile d'expliquer le fait que les au-

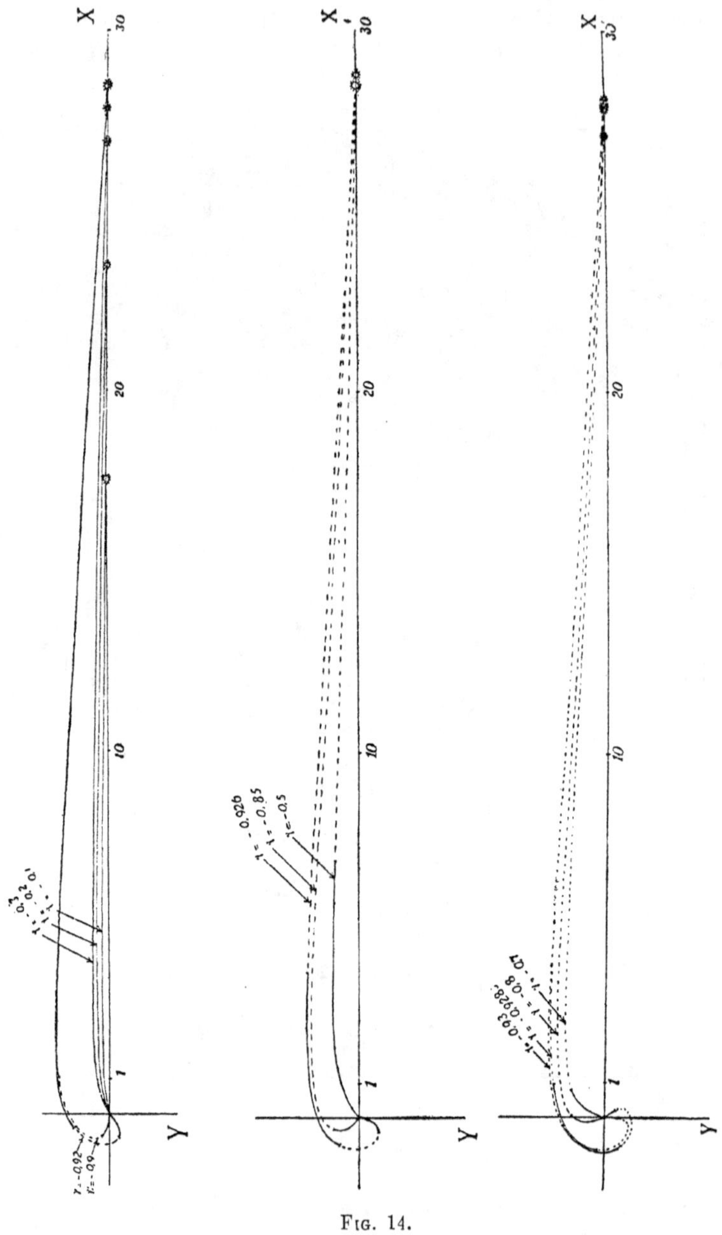

Fig. 14.

rores peuvent apparaître pendant la nuit; ce fait est une conséquence immédiate de la forme des trajectoires comme on peut le voir sur les figures 13 et 14.

Considérons maintenant un faisceau de rayons très-étroit émanant d'un même point et situés si près d'une des directions distinguées qu'ils arrivent jusqu'à l'atmosphère de la terre. La théorie fait alors voir qu'ils formeront à l'entrée de l'atmosphère des hélices autour d'une ligne de force magnétique (Voir fig. 15), d'où il résultera ce qu'on appelle un rayon auroral typique. La largeur de ce rayon auroral variera beaucoup pour les diverses sortes de rayons: depuis quelques mètres pour les rayons cathodiques jusqu'à plusieurs kilomètres pour les rayons α de radium.

Si l'on déplace un peu le point d'émanation des rayons, il en résulte un déplacement correspondant du rayon auroral dans l'atmosphère et par les calculs numériques que nous avons faits, il est possible de calculer ce dernier déplacement en fonction du premier.

Il en résulte qu'il sera possible de trouver par le calcul toute la partie de l'atmosphère frappée par des corpuscules venant de tous les points d'une surface d'émanation située sur le soleil et cela donne une explication toute naturelle des phénomènes remarquables qu'on appelle des *draperies d'aurores*. En effet, il arrive pour certaines situations de la surface d'émanation par rapport à l'axe magnétique qu'un faisceau ayant d'abord une section circulaire se déforme en s'approchant de la terre de telle sorte qu'il sera allongé énormément dans la direction de l'ouest-est magnétique; à leur entrée dans l'atmosphère, les rayons du faisceau seront alors distribués en forme de draperie aurorale très-longue et très-étroite.

Sur les tableaux ci-joints on peut voir les dimensions théoriques d'une pareille draperie correspondant à un cas particulier traité dans mon Mémoire. Ici E désigne l'étendue angulaire de la surface d'émanation sur le soleil, dans une direction parallèle à l'axe magnétique de la terre:

Dimensions de la région frappée par le faisceau, sur une sphère concentrique à la terre et ayant 500000 km. de rayon:

E	LARGEUR	LONGUEUR
1″	3,2 km.	1950 km.
10″	10,2 »	6160 »
1′	25 »	15090 »
3′	43,2 »	26145 »

Dimensions théoriques de la draperie dans l'atmosphère:

E	ÉPAISSEUR	LONGUEUR
1″	15 mètres	20 km.
10″	26 »	65 »
1′	46 »	160 »
3′	72 »	275 »

Il est même possible d'expliquer par la théorie le phénomène si remarquable de plusieurs draperies situées l'une derrière l'autre. Les situations favorables à la formation des draperies seront vite passées en raison du mouvement de l'axe magnétique de la terre autour de l'axe de rotation; en général les directions distinguées, leur groupement et leur nombre varient extrêmement avec le temps, ce qui s'accorde bien avec les changements si brusques des phénomènes d'aurore correspondants.

Nous allons pour finir exposer quelques formes typiques de ces draperies aurorales (Voir fig. 16).

Je vous prie de m'excuser si cette conférence est devenue un peu longue; cela tient à la richesse de la matière; il reste cependant encore des points obscurs à éclairer et pour cela les recherches sur les perturbations magnétiques, dont mon collègue le prof. BIRKELAND s'occupe pour le moment, seront sans doute d'une importance capitale pour le développement ultérieur de la théorie.

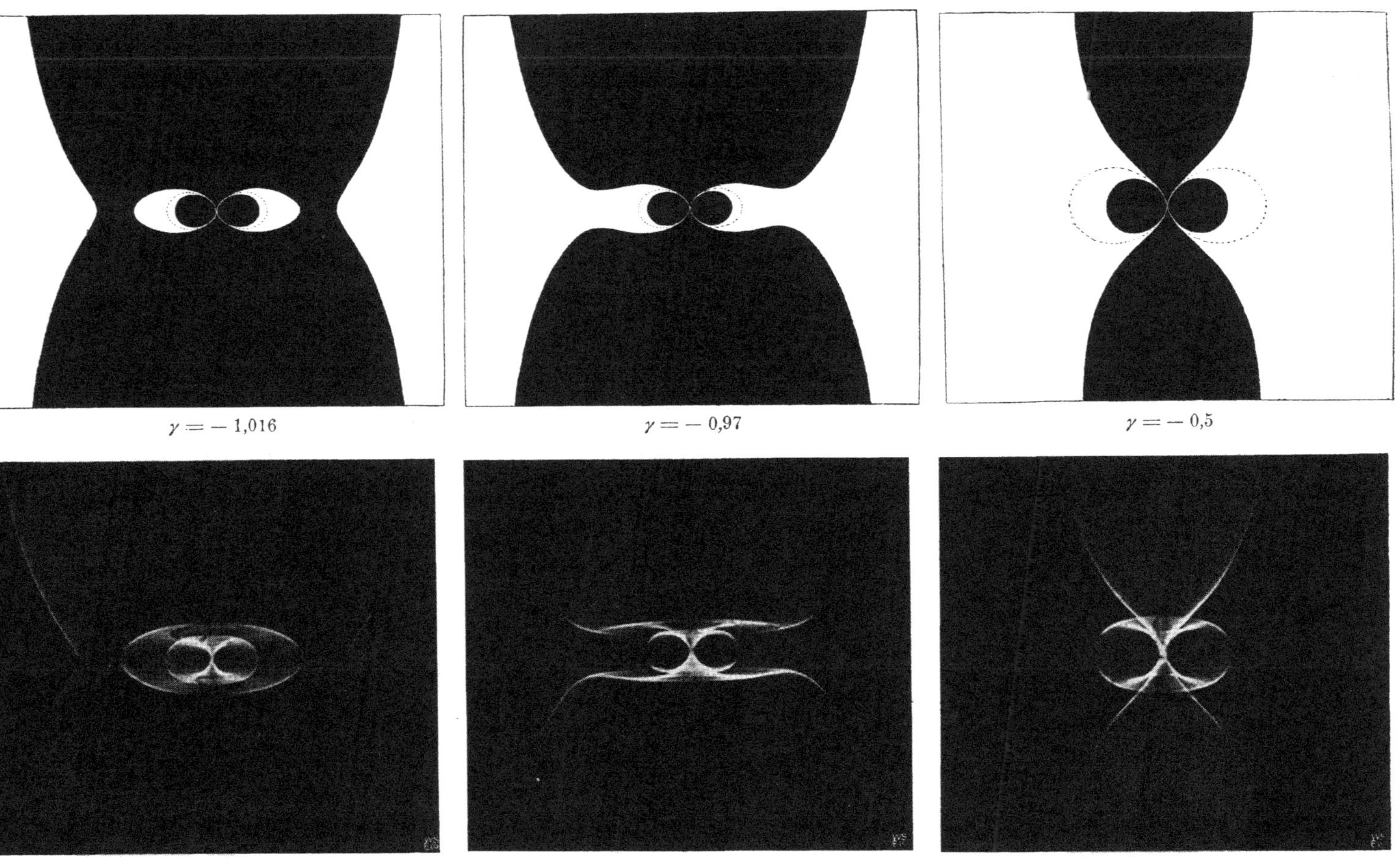

Fig. 5.

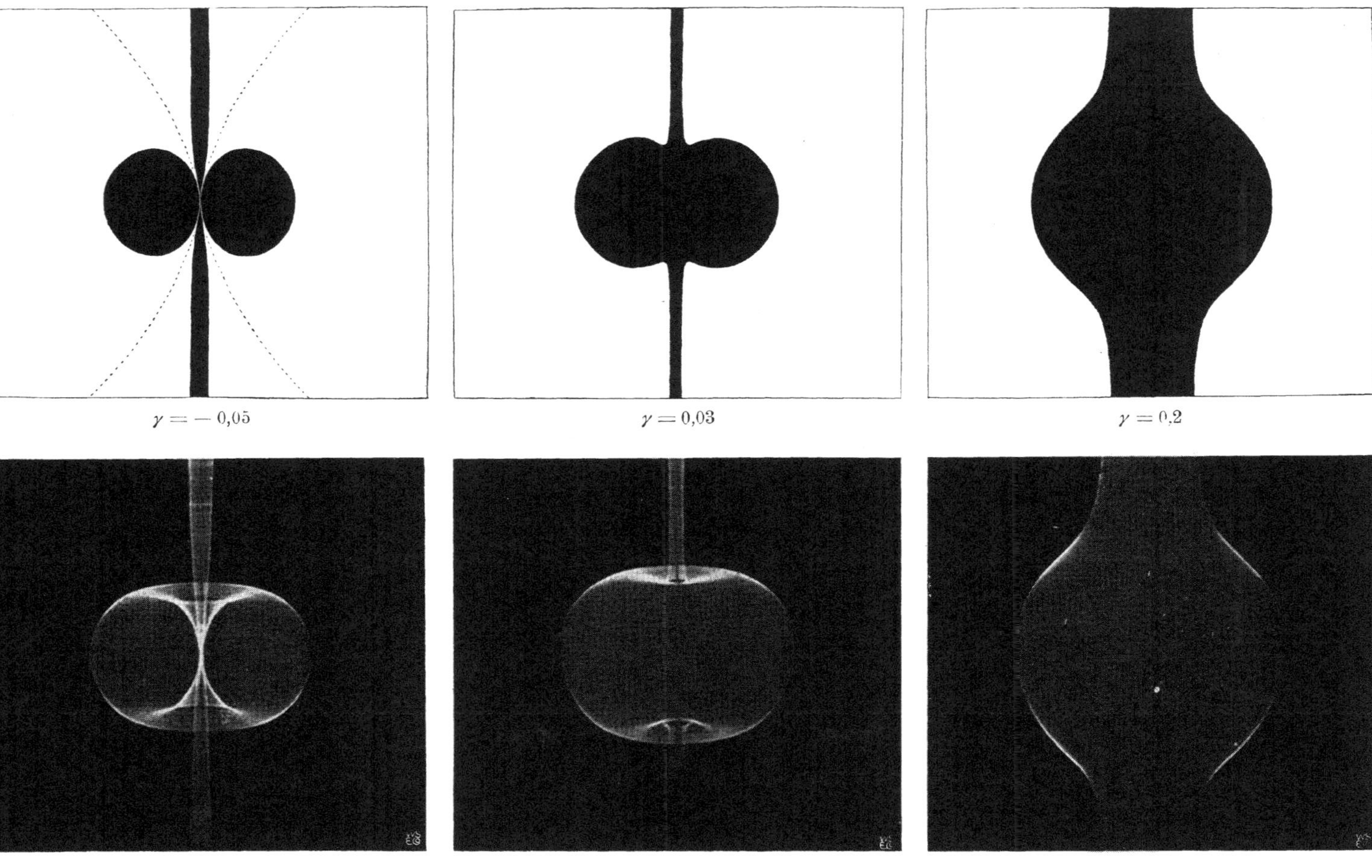

Fig. 6.

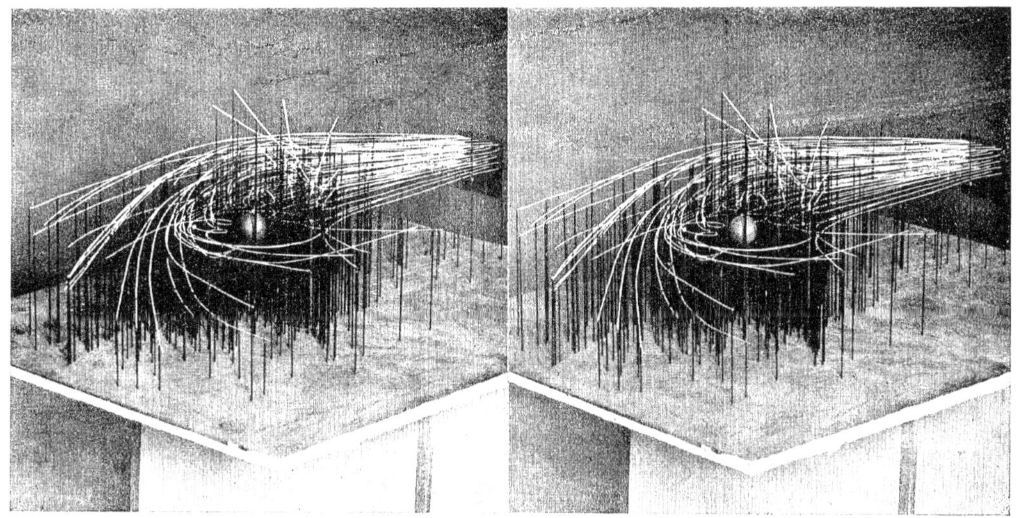

Fig. 8.

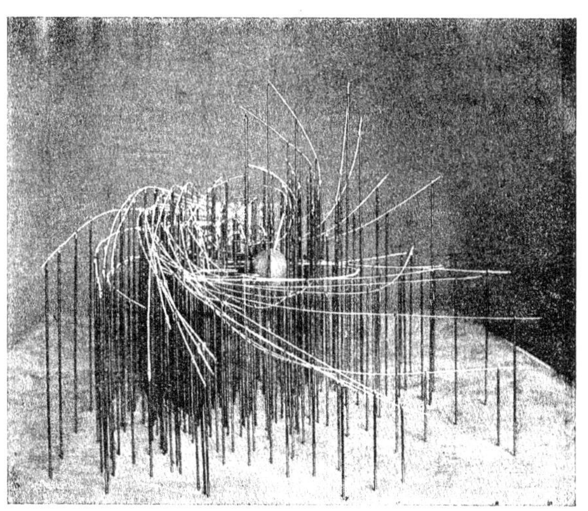

Fig. 9.

Fig. 10.

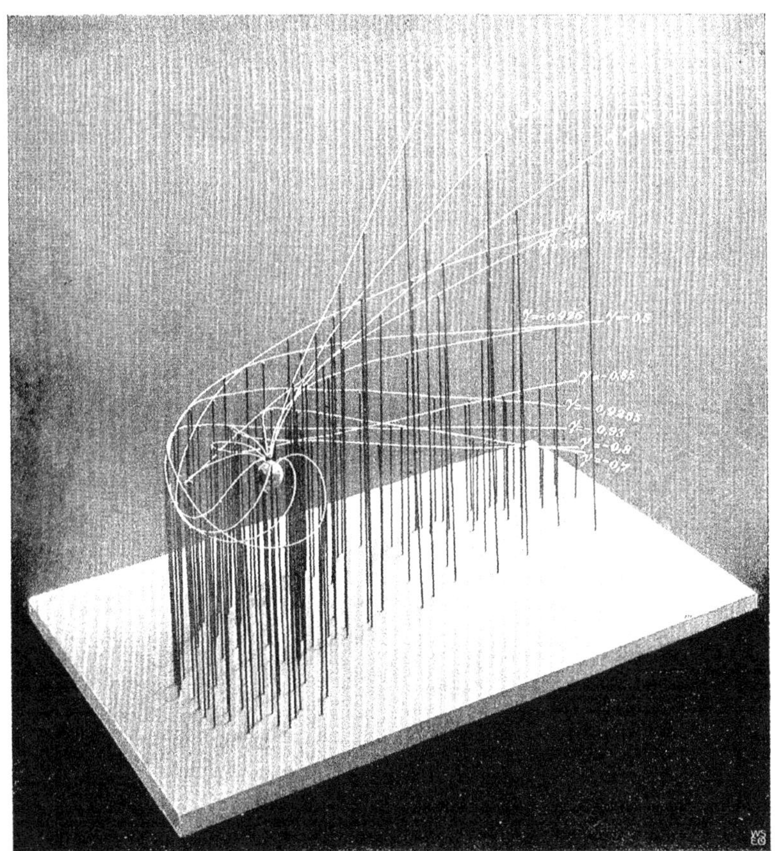

Fig. 13.

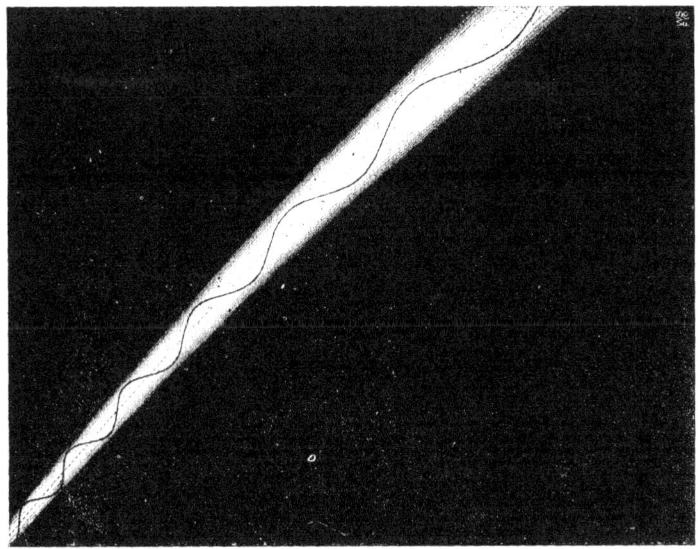

Fig. 15.

Fig. 16.

G. KOLOSSOFF

SUR LE PROBLÈME PLAN DANS LA THÉORIE D'ÉLASTICITÉ

Dans une note aux Comptes rendus 1908, nº. 10, nous avons donné un nouveau moyen pour obtenir diverses solutions du problème plan de la théorie d'élasticité. Soient N_1 et N_2 les efforts normaux sur les éléments perpendiculaires à 2 axes rectangulaires Ox, Oy et T les efforts tangentiels.

D'après le théorème de M. Maurice Levy (Comptes rendus, t. CXXVI, nº. 18) pour l'équilibre d'élasticité dans les problèmes à 2 dimensions, on a à satisfaire aux 3 équations:

$$(1) \qquad \frac{\partial N_1}{\partial x} + \frac{\partial T}{\partial y} = 0 \,, \frac{\partial N_2}{\partial y} + \frac{\partial T}{\partial x} = 0 \,, \qquad \Delta_2(N_1 + N_2) = 0$$

et en outre aux conditions à la frontière. Ces équations peuvent être écrites

$$(2) \qquad \left\{ \begin{array}{l} \dfrac{\partial 2T}{\partial y} + \dfrac{\partial (N_1 - N_2)}{\partial x} = - \dfrac{\partial (N_1 + N_2)}{\partial x} \,, \\ \dfrac{\partial 2T}{\partial x} - \dfrac{\partial (N_1 - N_2)}{\partial y} = - \dfrac{\partial (N_1 + N_2)}{\partial y} \,, \\ \Delta_2(N_1 + N_2) = 0 \,. \end{array} \right.$$

Pour satisfaire à (2) il faut et il suffit

$$(3) \qquad \left\{ \begin{array}{l} 2T = \alpha \dfrac{\partial (N_1 + N_2)}{\partial y} - \beta \dfrac{\partial (N_1 + N_2)}{\partial x} + \varphi \,, \\ N_1 - N_2 = \beta \dfrac{\partial (N_1 + N_2)}{\partial y} + \alpha \dfrac{\partial (N_1 + N_2)}{\partial x} + \psi \end{array} \right.$$

où α et β satisfont aux équations auxiliaires:

$$(4) \qquad \frac{\partial \alpha}{\partial x} - \frac{\partial \beta}{\partial y} = -1 \,, \; \frac{\partial \alpha}{\partial y} + \frac{\partial \beta}{\partial x} = 0 \quad \text{et} \quad \varphi + i\psi = F(z)$$

est une fonction de la variable complexe $x + iy = z$. Pour α et β on n'a besoin que d'une solution particulière de (4); nous pouvons poser par exemple

$$(5) \qquad \ldots \alpha = -x \, , \beta = 0$$

ou

$$(6) \qquad \ldots \alpha = 0 \; \beta = y \, ,$$

ou

$$(7) \qquad \ldots \alpha = -\frac{x}{2} \, , \beta = \frac{y}{2} \, .$$

Les équations (3) peuvent être écrites

$$(8) \qquad \ldots 2T + i(N_1 - N_2) = i(\alpha + i\beta) \frac{d\varphi_0(z)}{dz} + F(z) \, ,$$

en introduisant la fonction de la variable complexe $\varphi_0(z)$, dont la partie réelle est $N_1 + N_2$. Au moyen de (3) et de (8) on peut recevoir une infinité de solutions du problème plan en coordonnées x, y.

Exemples. — 1°) Posons:

$$N_1 + N_2 = \Sigma(A_m e^{my} + A_{-m} e^{-my}) \cos mx \, ,$$
$$\varphi = \Sigma(B_m e^{my} + B_{-m} e^{-my}) \sin mx \, ,$$
$$\psi = \Sigma(B_m e^{my} - B_{-m} e^{-my}) \cos mx \, ,$$

en prenant pour α et β (5) nous trouverons la solutions de M. Ribière [Comptes rendus, t. CXXVI, n.° 5; $A_m = 4ma_2$, $A_{-m} = -4mb_2$, $B_m = 2(a_2 - 2a_1) m$, $B_{-m} = 2(b_2 - 2b_1) m$].

2°) Posons:

$$N_1 + N_2 = A_m \Phi_m + A_{1m} \Phi_{1m} \, ,$$
$$\varphi = B_m \Phi_m + B_{1m} \Phi_{1m} \, ,$$
$$\psi = B_m \Phi_{1m} - B_{1m} \Phi_m \, ,$$

où Φ_m et Φ_{1m} sont 2 polynomes harmoniques de degré m, tels que

$$\Phi_m + i\Phi_{1m} = (x + iy)^m \, ,$$

nous trouverons la solution de M. Mesnager (Comptes rendus, t. CXXXII, n. 24). La théorie s'étend aux coordonnées curvilignes et la formule (8) offre un moyen très simple de recevoir des solutions en coordonnées curvilignes. Soient par exemple ξ, η les coordonnées curvilignes isothermes, ainsi que $\zeta = \xi + i\eta = f(z)$ et $z = f_{-1}(\zeta)$ où $z = x + iy$, R et Φ les efforts normaux sur les éléments perpendiculaires aux axes ξ, η, U les efforts tangentiels, θ l'angle, que l'axe Ox fait avec l'axe ξ. Nous avons les formules de transformation des efforts:

$$2T = 2U \cos 2\theta + (R - \Phi) \sin 2\theta ,$$
$$N_1 - N_2 = (R - \Phi) \cos 2\theta - 2U \sin 2\theta ,$$
$$2T + i(N_1 - N_2) = \{ 2U + i(R - \Phi) \} e^{-2i\theta} .$$

En remarquant que $-\lg h + i\theta$ (1) est une fonction de la variable complexe z (ou ζ) (LAMÉ, *Leçons sur les coordonnées curvilignes*, § CVII) ainsi que $-\lg h + i\theta = \lg f'_{-1}(\zeta)$ nous obtiendrons au moyen de (8):

$$\frac{1}{h^2}[2U + i(R - \Phi)] = i f'^2_{-1}(\zeta)(\alpha + i\beta) \frac{d\varphi_0(z)}{dz} + f'^2_{-1}(\zeta) F(z) .$$

En prenant pour α et β (7), nous aurons:

$$\frac{1}{h^2}[2U + i(R - \Phi)] = -\frac{i}{2} f'_{-1}(\zeta) f_{-1}(\zeta_1) \frac{d\varphi_{01}(\zeta)}{d\zeta} + \Omega(\zeta) ,$$

où

$$\varphi_{01}(\zeta) = \varphi_0(z) , \zeta_1 = \xi - i\eta ,$$

$$f'_{-1}(\zeta) = \frac{df_{-1}(\zeta)}{d\zeta} = \frac{dz}{d\zeta} , \Omega(\zeta) = f'^2_{-1}(\zeta) F(z) .$$

Exemples. — 1°):

$$z = e^\zeta = f_{-1}(\zeta) , \zeta = \xi + i\eta = \lg(x + iy) = \lg r + i\varphi ;$$
$$\xi = lgr , \theta = \varphi , \eta = \varphi , h = \frac{1}{r} \quad f'_{-1}(\zeta) f_{-1}(\zeta_1) = e^\zeta e^{\zeta_1} = e^{2\zeta}$$

nous aurons pour les coordonnées polaires r, φ la formule:

$$r^2 [2U + i(R - \Phi)] = -i \frac{r^2}{2} \frac{d\varphi_{01}(\zeta)}{d\zeta} + \Omega(\zeta) ,$$

où

$$\varphi_{01}(\zeta) = R + \Phi + i\omega(r, \varphi)$$

et

$$2Ur^2 = -\frac{r^2}{2} \frac{\partial(R + \Phi)}{\partial\varphi} + \varphi_{2T}$$

$$(R - \Phi) r^2 = -\frac{r^2}{2} \frac{\partial(R + \Phi)}{\partial lgr} + \varphi_{R-\Phi} ,$$

(1) h est le paramètre différentiel $= \sqrt{\left(\frac{\partial\xi}{\partial x}\right)^2 + \left(\frac{\partial\xi}{\partial y}\right)^2} = \sqrt{\left(\frac{\partial\eta}{\partial x}\right)^2 + \left(\frac{\partial\eta}{\partial y}\right)^2}$.

où

$$\varphi_{2T} + i\varphi_{R-\Phi} = \Omega(\zeta) .$$

En posant

$$R + \Phi = N_1 + N_2 = \Sigma(A_m r^m + A_{-m} r^{-m}) \cos m\varphi$$

$$\varphi_{2T} = \Sigma(B_m r^m + B_{-m} r^{-m}) \sin m\varphi$$

$$\varphi_{R-\Phi} = \Sigma(- B_m r^m + B_{-m} r^{-m}) \cos m\varphi$$

nous trouverons la solution de M. Ribière [1] et en ajoutant à $R + \Phi$ les membres $C_1 \lg r + C_2$ la solution de M. Belzecki (Comptes rendus, t. CXL, n.° 15).

Le cas particulier de la solution de M. Ribière $m = 1$ a été decouvert par le professeur russe M. Golowine (Annales de l'Institut technologique de S. Pétersbourg, 1881).

2°):

$$x + yi = f_{-1}(\zeta) = \cos h(\xi + i\eta) , \quad h = \frac{1}{\sqrt{\cos h^2 \xi - \cos^2 \eta}} ,$$

$$f'_{-1}(\zeta)\, f_{-1}(\zeta_1) = \cos h(\xi - i\eta) \sin h(\xi + i\eta) = \tfrac{1}{2} (\sin h2\xi + i \sin 2\eta)$$

$$\frac{1}{h^2} [2U + i(R - \Phi)] = - \frac{i}{4} (\sin h2\xi + i \sin 2\eta) \frac{d\varphi_{01}(\zeta)}{d\zeta} + \Omega(\zeta) .$$

En posant:

$$R + \Phi = \Sigma A_m e^{m\xi} \cos m\eta ,$$

nous aurons:

$$\frac{2T}{h^2} = \Sigma \frac{m}{4} A_m e^{m\xi} (\cos m\eta \sin 2\eta + \sin m\eta \sin 2h\xi) + \varphi_{2T} ,$$

$$\frac{R - \Phi}{h^2} = \Sigma \frac{m}{4} A_m e^{m\xi} (\sin m\eta \sin 2\eta - \cos m\eta \sin 2h\xi) + \varphi_{R-\Phi}$$

qu'on peut déduire des formules pour ce cas de M. Belzecki (Annales de l'assemblée des ingenieurs russes, 1905).

La méthode exposée donne: 1°) le moyen d'appliquer au problème plan la théorie des représentations conformes comme on l'applique dans l'hydrodynamique (méthode Helmholtz-Kirchhoff); 2°) une infinité de moyens de *transformer* les solutions et d'une solution en tirer d'autres. La transformation de M. Michell (Proceedings of the London mathematical Society t. XXXIV) *l'inversion* est un cas particulier de ces transformations. Beaucoup d'exemples et la théorie détaillée de notre méthode et de ces transformations paraîtront dans notre Mémoire russe vers la fin de 1909.

[1] Comptes rendus, t. CVIII, n°. 11 et t. CXXXII, n°. 6.

R. MARCOLONGO

PER L'UNIFICAZIONE DELLE NOTAZIONI VETTORIALI

(Proposte di E. BURALI-FORTI e R. MARCOLONGO)

In una serie di articoli pubblicati nei Rendiconti del Circolo Matematico di Palermo, dall'aprile dell'anno scorso, il collega BURALI ed io abbiamo richiamato l'attenzione dei matematici e dei fisici sulla necessità, spesso anzi invocata, di una comune intesa al fine di unificare le notazioni vettoriali.

Attualmente si adottano notazioni diverse non soltanto da paese a paese; ma in uno stesso paese ogni autore, a capriccio, segue le notazioni che più gli talentano. Tale anarchia non agevola certamente i progressi dei metodi semplici ed eleganti del calcolo vettoriale, e non ne facilita le applicazioni.

Abbiamo creduto far cosa utile sottoporre ad un esame lungo, paziente, e non sempre facile, i vari enti vettoriali; abbiamo raccolto, confrontato, vagliato e criticato le varie notazioni proposte e seguìte da tutti coloro che, da BELLAVITIS, GRASSMANN, MÖBIUS, HAMILTON in poi sino al PEANO, si sono occupati di calcolo vettoriale, non escluse naturalmente quelle di cui in lavori precedenti ci siamo serviti il BURALI ed io. Questo esame e queste critiche ci hanno condotto a fare delle proposte concrete e semplicissime, che crediamo necessario far conoscere al Congresso.

*
* *

Noi ci siamo occupati del cosidetto *sistema minimo* di calcolo vettoriale; cioè di quel sistema fondato sulla considerazione di *numero* (reale), *punto* e *vettore* e le cui operazioni producono numeri, punti, vettori. È ben vero che non tutte le questioni geometriche, meccaniche e fisico-matematiche possono essere trattate col sistema minimo; il quale, quindi, presenta delle deficienze; ma ciò nondimeno il campo di applicabilità di un tal sistema è immenso ed è da questo sistema che assolutamente e recisamente conviene cominciare, prima di passare allo studio di altri sistemi ben più ampi; come, p. es., quello dei baricentri di MÖBIUS, dei quaternioni di HAMILTON e delle forme geometriche di GRASSMANN. L'uno studio dovendo completare l'altro, è troppo naturale fissare uno dei principî fondamentali a cui tutte le notazioni debbono uniformarsi; cioè:

Le notazioni fondamentali del sistema minimo vettoriale non devono essere in contradizione con quelle dei più ampi sistemi di Möbius, Hamilton, Grassmann.

Si deve poi osservare che sebbene l'algoritmo del sistema minimo sia assai limitato e si riduca: *alla somma di un punto con un vettore, alla somma dei vettori, prodotto di un vettore per un numero, prodotto scalare e prodotto vettoriale di due vettori, derivata di un punto e di un vettore, gradiente di un numero, divergenza e rotazione di un vettore,* non è assolutamente conveniente allontanarsi, possibilmente, dall'identità coll'algebra per la somma, prodotto per un numero, ecc. Quindi il secondo principio:

Le operazioni devono essere soggette, quanto più è possibile, a leggi formali simili a quelle universalmeute note dell'analisi.

Nessuno, crediamo, potrà revocare in dubbio la giustezza e la convenienza di questi due principî riguardanti rispettivamente le notazioni e le operazioni.

Ciò posto ecco le nostre proposte.

I.

Seguendo Grassmann, Hamilton, Bellavitis, Möbius *proponiamo di indicare il vettore da* A *a* B *con* B — A *(differenza di due punti). Nel caso poi che sia conveniente, come spesso accade in fisica-matematica, fissare un criterio speciale, proponiamo indicare un vettore con una sola lettera, e seguendo* Heaviside, *di servirsi dei tipi di* Clarendon: *lettere grassette* **a**, **b**, *ecc.*

La notazione proposta, seguìta già da moltissimi autori, soddisfa ai due principî fondamentali; mentre non avviene così delle altre come AB, $\overline{AB}$, ecc.

È inoltre semplicissima.

II.

La grandezza o modulo del vettore B — A *o* **a** *proponiamo si accenni con* mod **a**, *come è indicata da* Argand *e* Cauchy.

Il mod è simbolo di funzione che, conforme alle leggi ordinarie, si scrive da una parte della lettera cui si applica. Se in analisi pura può essere anche comodo adoperare il simbolo di Weierstrass, |**a**|, le due aste producono confusione nel calcolo di Grassmann, dove | preposto ad un vettore o a un bivettore, produce un bivettore o un vettore.

III.

La somma di un punto con un vettore, la somma o differenza di due vettori, il prodotto di un numero (reale) con un vettore sia indicata, con Grassmann *e* Hamilton, *rispettivamente*

$$\mathrm{A} + \mathbf{a} \;,\; \mathbf{a} \pm \mathbf{b} \;,\; m\mathbf{a} .$$

Su questa è unanime il consenso di tutti coloro che hanno scritto sul calcolo vettoriale.

***

Fin qui, come si vede, non soltanto non proponiamo nulla di nuovo, ma seguiamo notazioni di autori classici. L'accordo sarebbe dunque assai facile ad ottenersi; nè i vari autori dovrebbero essere troppo restii di seguire le orme dei grandi.

Le divergenze diventano un po' più profonde per i due prodotti scalare e vettoriale, che così frequentemente occorre considerare in geometria, meccanica, ecc. Le notazioni più semplici e più precise, in riguardo al sistema minimo, sono state iniziate, ci sia concessa la frase, da Gibbs. Il prodotto scalare e vettoriale sono da lui rispettivamente indicati con **a** . **b** e **a** × **b**; e ciò, ripetiamo, ha senza dubbio costituito un immenso progresso sulle notazioni scorrette dell'Heaviside e sulle altre, così seguite in Germania, di $(a\,.\,b)$ e $[a\,,\,b]$ che non sono soggette allo stesso algoritmo algebrico così semplice, dei prodotti scalare e vettoriale, e in cui la sola forma delle parentesi, che in algebra è puramente accidentale, deve far distinguere tra di loro i due prodotti scalare e vettoriale. Basta del resto averle, anche per poco, adoperate in un corso di lezioni, per sapere quanto siano incomode. Il Gibbs ha dunque iniziato un grandissimo progresso. Ma occorre avvertire che in algebra il punto . viene adoperato, con grandissimo profitto della chiarezza, come separatore di termini di una stessa formula, e non serve a indicare la moltiplicazione di due grandezze. La prima modificazione, necessaria, da arrecare alla notazione di Gibbs, parrebbe dunque dover esser questa: di sopprimere il *punto* tra **a** e **b** nell'indicazione del prodotto scalare, che quindi dovrebbe scriversi **ab**. Ma nel calcolo di Grassmann con **ab** si intende un nuovo ente, il *bivettore*, inutile nel sistema minimo, che segue le ordinarie leggi algebriche. Accettando questa modificazione non rispetteremmo adunque il primo e più importante dei principî fondamentali.

A noi, dopo ciò, è parso utile fare una modificazione alla notazione di Gibbs e accettare, tornando all'antico, pel prodotto scalare la notazione **a** × **b** già proposta da Grassmann. Veniva quindi a mancare un segno conveniente per esprimere il prodotto vettoriale e non volendo in verun modo abbandonare la semplicità delle notazioni di Gibbs, ci siamo permessi, per la prima ed unica volta, di costruire e di proporre un simbolo nuovo che da un lato stia a ricordare l'ente prodotto vettoriale e sia nel tempo stesso tra gli attuali simboli delle casse tipografiche. Quanto poi ai nomi di prodotto scalare e vettoriale essi sono oramai già vecchi e seguìti quasi universalmente. Queste poche considerazioni dànno dunque ragione della nostra seguente proposta.

IV.

Seguendo Grassmann, Somoff, Resal proponiamo di indicare con **a** × **b** *il prodotto interno o scalare di* **a** *per* **b**.

Pel prodotto esterno o vettoriale proponiamo la notazione nuova **a** ∧ **b**.

Notiamo subito che l'algoritmo del prodotto scalare e vettoriale, con queste notazioni, è dei più semplici e facili e segue leggi completamente simili a quelle degli ordinari prodotti. Ci permettiamo soltanto di far osservare e rilevare due teoremi che sono implicitamente dati da GRASSMANN e poi dal GIBBS e di cui noi abbiamo fatto uso costante in tutti i nostri articoli e che hanno applicazioni svariatissime e cioè: il teorema sul duplice prodotto vettoriale e il teorema sulla inversione dei simboli $\wedge$ e $\times$.

Ed osservamio ancora che la notazione precisa di GASSMANN, |**ab**, esige la introduzione di bivettore, che, come dicemmo è estranea al sistema minimo. In Italia fu seguìta dal PEANO, e poi dal BURALI e da me.

Qualche osservazione è ancora assolutamdnte indispensabile per riguardo alle notazioni seguite dal TAIT e poscia da HEAVISIDE e quindi assai comuni in Inghilterra, e desunte dal calcolo dei quaternioni.

E cominciamo col segnalare il fatto, che ben si rileva dal libro del GIBBS e da tutti i nostri articoli, cioè che tutte le questioni che si possono risolvere col calcolo dei quaternioni, eccettuata la composizione diretta delle rotazioni finite intorno ad assi non paralleli, si possono risolvere col sistema minimo. In questo anzi figurano enti, notazioni più semplici, leggi simili alle algebriche e si può anche (come in parte già dimostrammo) prescindere da qualunque sistema di riferimento. Per tale ragione non abbiamo compreso i quaternioni nel *sistema minimo di calcolo vettoriale autonomo.*

D'altra parte è assai facile dedurre dal sistema minimo non solamente i quaternioni, ma anche il *Calcolo geometrico di GRASSMANN* che di tutti i sistemi noti è il più ampio e che con le trasformazioni lineari, contiene non soltanto i quaternioni, ma altre funzioni importantissime, comprese tutte le *proiettività*, *omografie*, *correlazioni* ecc., di continuo uso in geometria; e tutto sotto la forma mirabilmente chiara e semplice data dal PEANO, cui noi siamo grandemente debitori.

Le formazioni di 1ª, 2ª, 3ª specie hanno le forme simboliche

$$\Sigma x_i \mathrm{A}_i \;,\; \Sigma x_i \mathrm{A}_i \mathrm{B}_i \;,\; \Sigma x_i \mathrm{A}_i \mathrm{B}_i \mathrm{C}_i$$

deve le x sono *numeri reali* e A , B , C *punti*. Esse restano definite per astrazione mediante le condizioni di uguaglianza

$$\Sigma x_i \mathrm{A}_i = \Sigma y_i \mathrm{B}_i$$

soltanto quando

$$\Sigma x_i (\mathrm{A}_i - 0) = \Sigma y_i (\mathrm{B}_i - 0);$$

$$\Sigma x_i \mathrm{A}_i \mathrm{B}_i = \Sigma y_i \mathrm{P}_i \mathrm{Q}_i$$

soltanto quando

$$\Sigma x_i (\mathrm{A}_i - 0) \wedge (\mathrm{B}_i - 0) = \Sigma y_i (\mathrm{P}_i - 0) \wedge (\mathrm{Q}_i - 0);$$

$$\Sigma x_i \mathrm{A}_i \mathrm{B}_i \mathrm{C}_i = \Sigma y_i \mathrm{P}_i \mathrm{Q}_i \mathrm{R}_i$$

soltanto quando

$$\Sigma x_i (\mathrm{A}_i - 0) \times (\mathrm{B}_i - 0 \wedge (\mathrm{C}_i - 0) = \Sigma y_i (\mathrm{P}_i - 0) \times (\mathrm{Q}_i - 0) \wedge (\mathrm{R}_i - 0),$$

comunque si fissi il punto O.

Basta poi convenire che

$$\mathrm{ABCD} = \frac{1}{6} (\mathrm{B} - \mathrm{A}) \times (\mathrm{C} - \mathrm{A}) \wedge (\mathrm{D} - \mathrm{A})$$

per ottenere il calcolo geometrico di GRASSMANN sotto la forma semplice e concreta data da PEANO.

Passiamo piuttosto a qualche cenno sui quaternioni, in vista appunto delle notazioni proposte.

Se s è un numere reale, **u** un vettore, con

$$q = s + \mathbf{u} \wedge$$

s'intende il *simbolo di funzione*, operatore, applicabile ai vettori **x** normali ad **u**, tale che

$$q\mathbf{x} = s\mathbf{x} + \mathbf{u} \wedge \mathbf{x}.$$

La forma q, definita univocamente insieme al suo campo di variabilità, che è quello dei vettori normali ad uno dato, dicesi *quaternione* di cui s è lo scalare, Sq, e **u** il vettore, o asse, Vq. Se $s = 0$ abbiamo un quaternione retto

$$q\mathbf{x} = \mathbf{u} \wedge \mathbf{x}.$$

Di qui si deduce

$$q^2\mathbf{x} = q(q\mathbf{x}) = \mathbf{u} \wedge (\mathbf{u} \wedge \mathbf{x}) = \mathbf{u} \times \mathbf{x} . \mathbf{u} - \mathbf{u}^2\mathbf{x} = -\mathbf{u}^2\mathbf{x},$$

cioè

$$q^2 = -\mathbf{u}^2,$$

e quindi, in conformità di quanto dice HAMILTON, il quaternione retto è tale che il suo quadrato produce il quadrato del suo modulo con il segno negativo.

Si noti poi che $\wedge$ è simbolo di funzione, operatore a destra come !, che applicato ad un qualunque vettore produce il quaternione retto che lo ha come vettore. Si può quindi porre

$$\mathbf{u} \wedge = q \ , \ \mathbf{u} = q \wedge^{-1},$$

le quali corrispondono rispettivamente alle

$$\mathrm{I}^{-1}\mathbf{u} = q \ , \ \mathbf{u} = \mathrm{I}q$$

di HAMILTON; il quale, in sul primo, ben distingue tra vettore e quaternione retto.

Se ora α è un quaternione qualunque, con la notazione completa

$$\alpha(\mathrm{I}^{-1}\mathbf{u})$$

si indica il prodotto di α per il quaternione retto $\mathrm{I}^{-1}\mathbf{u}$; con la notazione $\alpha\mathbf{u}$ invece si deve intendere il vettore ottenuto da **u** con l'operazione α (quaternione) quante volte l'asse di α sia normale ad **u**. Ora HAMILTON deve aver notato che la prima notazione è complicata e non si presenta nelle applicazioni nel primitivo significato e però ha abbreviato la prima in $\alpha\mathbf{u}$; cioè a cominciare dal III libro della sua opera, egli sopprime i simboli di operazione I ed I^{-1} ed identifica il quaternione retto $\mathrm{I}^{-1}\mathbf{u}$, al suo vettore; il vettore Iq al suo quaternione retto q. E quindi dal III libro in poi il vettore per HAMILTON è propriamente una *funzione vettoriale*. Ciò non fu tenuto presente dai volgarizzatori dell'opera di HAMILTON e sopratutto dal TAIT in cui regna sovrana la confusione tra vettore e quaternione retto.

Ciò ricordato osserviamo che per prodotto quaternionale di due vettori **u** e **v** si deve intendere il prodotto dei due quaternioni retti $\mathrm{I}^{-1}\mathbf{u}$, $\mathrm{I}^{-1}\mathbf{v}$; ora è facile mostrare che essendo **x** normale a **v** si ha

$$(\mathbf{u}\wedge)(\mathbf{v}\wedge)\mathbf{x} = \}-\mathbf{u}\times\mathbf{v}+(\mathbf{u}\wedge\mathbf{v})\wedge\{\,\mathbf{x}\,;$$

cioè coi simboli di HAMILTON

$$(\mathrm{I}^{-1}\mathbf{u})(\mathrm{I}^{-1}\mathbf{v}) = -\mathbf{u}\times\mathbf{v}+\mathrm{I}^{-1}(\mathbf{u}\wedge\mathbf{v})\,;$$

abbiamo cioè un quaternione il cui scalare è $-\mathbf{u}\times\mathbf{v}$, e il cui vettore è $\mathbf{u}\wedge\mathbf{v}$. Questa è appunto l'origine delle notazioni abbreviate

$$-\mathrm{S}(\mathbf{uv}),\ \text{e}\ \mathrm{V}(\mathbf{uv})$$

per indicare il prodotto scalare e vettoriale di **u** per **v**. Le notazioni complete sarebbero invece

$$-\mathrm{S}\,\}(\mathrm{I}^{-1}\mathbf{u})(\mathrm{I}^{-1}\mathbf{v})\{\ ,\ \mathrm{V}\,\}(\mathrm{I}^{-1}\mathbf{u})(\mathrm{I}^{-1}\mathbf{v})\{.$$

Non v'ha dubbio che esse siano regolari e complete quando si siano introdotti i quaternioni; ma non facendo uso di questi (e nel sistema minimo, torniamo a ripeterlo, non ce n'è bisogno) le due notazioni suddette debbono indicare funzioni delle due variabili **u** e **v** e dànno luogo ad un algoritmo diverso e notevolmente più complicato delle altre $\mathbf{u}\times\mathbf{v}$ e $\mathbf{u}\wedge\mathbf{v}$.

***

Le altre nostre proposte si riferiscono alle tre funzioni vettoriali *gradiente*, *divergenza* e *rotazione* che così frequentemente occorre considerare in meccanica e la cui definizione può essere data, conforme all'indole del sistema minimo autonomo, pure in modo autonomo e diretto. Si riassumono nelle seguenti:

V.

Seguendo MAXWELL, RIEMANN-WEBER, CLIFFORD, LORENTZ, FERRARIS, proponiamo di indicare il gradiente di un numero u, la rotazione e la divergenza di un vettore **u** *con le notazioni*:

$$\mathit{grad}\,u\ ,\ \mathit{rot}\,\mathbf{u}\ ,\ \mathit{div}\,\mathbf{u}\,.$$

La prima è ora quasi universalmente seguìta. La notazione di HAMILTON è, come è noto, ∇u (e sotto forma completa $\mathrm{I}\nabla u$); il simbolo ∇ (nabla) è simbolo di funzione lineare o distributiva che applicato ad un quaternione funzione del punto P produce pure un quaternione funzione di P. È dunque notazione precisa ed appropriata nel calcolo dei quaternioni e quindi, in tale significato, non applicabile nel sistema minimo.

Le notazioni hamiltoniane per la divergenza e la rotazione si deducono osservando che

$$\nabla I^{-1}\mathbf{u} = S(\nabla I^{-1}\mathbf{u}) + I^{-1}V(\nabla I^{-1}\mathbf{u}).$$

Ora, secondo Hamilton,

$$\begin{aligned} \operatorname{div}\mathbf{u} &= -S\nabla I^{-1}\mathbf{u} = -S\nabla\mathbf{u}, \\ \operatorname{rot}\mathbf{u} &= V\nabla I^{-1}\mathbf{u} = V\nabla\mathbf{u}; \end{aligned}$$

e per questo si ripetono le stesse osservazioni di prima per non accoglierle nel sistema minimo.

Nelle notazioni di Gibbs il ∇ funziona invece come vettore simbolico ed è ben diverso dall'operatore di Hamilton; cioè: $\nabla \times$ e $\nabla \wedge$ (o secondo Gibbs $\nabla.$, $\nabla\times$) sono due nuovi operatori, il primo dei quali applicato ad un vettore dà un numero, che hanno forma tachigrafica cartesiana e non godono delle proprietà dei vettori rispetto, p. es., alla operazione $\times$.

L'algoritmo molto limitato delle funzioni grad, div, rot si può stabilire semplicemente ed in modo autonomo; le formule relative alla div e alla rot presentano una specie di legge di reciprocità per rispetto alle operazioni $\times$ e $\wedge$; ma al tempo stesso esso presenta notevoli deficienze. Non permette p. es. di esprimere alcuni dei prodotti div grad u, grad div $\mathbf{u}$, rot rot $\mathbf{u}$; ma è tuttavia sufficiente per gli scopi delle applicazioni più notevoli.

***

Riepilogando adunque le notazioni razionali che noi proponiamo soddisfano in tutto ai due principî posti a base del nostro lavoro; abbiamo scelto il buono dovunque lo abbiamo riscontrato e quindi, meno in un sol punto relativamente al prodotto vettoriale, le notazioni proposte, senza appartenere ad un solo autore, sono però conformi a quelle usate dai grandi matematici che fondarono il calcolo vettoriale e lo applicarono alla meccanica, alla fisica-matematica, ecc. Queste notazioni sono semplicissime; tutti in poco tempo possono rendersene padroni ed uno di noi ebbe già a sperimentarle con pieno successo nel proprio insegnamento.

Della eleganza e della semplicità di questi metodi non è il caso di parlare; esse sono ben note a tutti. Coloro che hanno letto una delle nostre ultime note avranno potuto vedere quanto si guadagni in chiarezza ed in brevità, coi soli elementi del calcolo vettoriale a sistema minimo ed autonomo, nella esposizione oramai classica di note teorie.

Non dubitiamo che il Congresso vorrà prendere in considerazione queste nostre proposte e confidiamo che, dopo matura discussione, vorrà approvarle (1).

(1) Il Congresso, in una delle sue ultime sedute plenarie, su proposta del sig. J. Hadamard, che riassunse la discussione fatta in seguito alla precedente lettura, approvò la nomina di una Commissione internazionale, coll'incarico di risolvere la questione dell'unificazione delle notazioni vettoriali.

P. PIZZETTI

SULLA RIDUZIONE DELLE LATITUDINI E LONGITUDINI AL LIVELLO DEL MARE

Il Prof. Pizzetti discorre delle formole e dei metodi sperimentali recentemente proposti ed usati dal barone prof. Eötvös per determinare le curvature principali del Geoide in un punto, la inflessione delle verticali, e le variazioni locali della Gravità. Ricorda anche un proprio lavoro pubblicato nel 1895 e reclama la priorità per quanto riguarda l'idea di dedurre la inflessione della verticale dalle misurazioni della Gravità.

J. BELJANKIN

EXEMPLE D'UNE FORCE CENTRALE TELLE QU'UN POINT MATÉRIEL PEUT DECRIRE UNE COURBE DU 2ème ORDRE

Soit

$$P = \frac{\sqrt{x^2 + y^2}}{\{L + My + a\sqrt{L + 2My + Ny^2}\}^3}$$

une force centrale, dirigée vers l'origine. Les équations du mouvement sont :

$$\left.\begin{aligned} x'' &= \frac{\mu x}{r} P \\ y'' &= \frac{\mu y}{r} P \end{aligned}\right\} \quad (r = \sqrt{x^2 + y^2})$$

et l'intégrale des aires est

$$xy' - x'y = h .$$

Introduisons trois variables nouvelles par les formules :

$$X = \frac{x}{y} \ , \ Y = \frac{1}{y} \ , \ dT = \frac{dt}{y^2} .$$

Alors on trouve, que :

$$\frac{dX}{dT} = \left(\frac{x}{y}\right)' \frac{dt}{dT} = x'y - xy' = -h ,$$

$$\frac{dY}{dT} = \left(\frac{1}{y}\right)' \frac{dt}{dT} = -y' ,$$

$$\frac{d^2Y}{dT^2} = -y''y^2 = -P\mu \frac{y^3}{r} ,$$

$$\frac{d^2Y}{dT^2} = \frac{d^2Y}{dX^2} \cdot h^2 ;$$

on peut écrire l'équation :

$$\frac{d^2Y}{dX^2} = -\frac{\mu}{h^2} \cdot \frac{1}{\left\{ LY + M + a\sqrt{LY^2 + 2MY + N} \right\}^3},$$

d'où l'on tire :

$$\frac{d^2Y}{dX^2} = \frac{\mu}{2h^2(LN - M^2)} \frac{d}{dY} \left\{ \frac{1}{\left[a + \frac{LY + M}{\sqrt{LY^2 + 2MY + N}} \right]^2} \right\}.$$

En intégrant, on trouve :

$$\left(\frac{dY}{dX}\right)^2 = \frac{\mu}{h^2(LN - M^2)} \cdot \frac{1}{\left[a + \frac{LY + M}{\sqrt{LY^2 + 2MY + N}} \right]^2} + H$$

Si l'on a

$$H = 0,$$

on déduit facilement :

$$aY + \sqrt{LY^2 + 2MY + N} = \frac{1}{h}\sqrt{\frac{\mu}{LN - M^2}}\, X + K;$$

on finit par écrire :

$$L + 2My + Ny^2 = \left\{ \frac{1}{h}\sqrt{\frac{\mu}{LN - M^2}}\, x + Ky - a \right\}^2.$$

G. CASAZZA

NUOVE DEDUZIONI DALLA TEORIA DELLA COMPOSIZIONE DEI MOTI

Dovendo esprimere dei giudizi di critica intorno a teorie le quali da tempo ebbero la sanzione piena e definitiva della scienza, non posso avere, nè ho, la pretesa di convincere, ma solo la speranza di riuscire a richiamare sopra di essi l'attenzione dei competenti, nella lusinga che dopo ponderato esame si riconosca che non del tutto inutile fu questa mia Comunicazione.

Dovendo condensare in poche righe un argomento per sè vasto, cercherò di esprimermi con uno stile telegrafico, persuaso che sarò compreso anche in quei punti sui quali sorvolo.

Il principio del parallelogr. delle forze statiche mi pare non possa avere il suo corrispondente (come è creduto) nella composizione delle forze dinamiche, ossia dei moti; tanto meno poi il parallelogr. delle forze statiche può avere il suo corrispondente nel parallelogr. del lavoro.

Si vuole che il *lavoro della risultante sia eguale alla somma dei lavori delle componenti.* Questo criterio, unito a quell'altro che il lavoro consumato è sempre eguale al lavoro prodotto, conduce al principio che qualunque sia il modo con cui si compongono due moti o due forze dinamiche, non vi è mai nè vantaggio nè svantaggio. Il che è contrario allo spirito stesso della scienza dei moti, come è contrario all'evidenza dei fatti.

Sia P (fig. 1) un piano contro cui va a scomporsi la forza F, e sieno f' ed f le sue due scomponenti. La somma dei segmenti f' ed f è maggiore di FA.

Ebbene, ciò può essere vero come principio statico, ma non lo può essere come principio dinamico. Staticamente una forza può far equilibrio a due altre la di cui somma sia maggiore della forza stessa, ma dinamicamente no, se trattasi di moto equabile.

La ragione di ciò sta nel fatto che nella statica la forza F, ad esempio, si oppone, non propriamente alle due forze f' ed f, *ma alla loro risultante*; vale a dire queste forze, prima di opporsi alla F, si distruggono parzialmente e vicendevolmente, così che esse potrebbero essere anche infinite (purchè fossero eguali e contrarie); ma tutto ciò non ha il suo riscontro nel caso nostro in cui le f' ed f sono *generate* dalla F.

Che dinamicamente e graficamente la somma $f' + f$ non possa essere superiore ad F lo dimostra anche il fatto che se noi prendiamo le due f' ed f così ottenute e le componiamo per es. parallelamente e nello stesso senso, otteniamo una risultante eguale alla loro somma e quindi maggiore di F, il che è assurdo.

Ma che cosa ci risponde qui la fisica? che se le F, f' ed f invece di considerarle come *quantità di moto* le consideriamo come *forze vive*, allora il conto torna, perchè $F^2 = f'^2 + f^2$. Il conto torna infatti, ma non torna, a me pare, la logica, perchè se per far più presto noi facciamo $f' = f$ e la massa su cui devono agire chiamiamo m, siccome f' ed f sono anche due spazî s, così il lavoro di f' sarà $= ms$ e quello di f pure $= ms$. Se questi due moti invece di farli comporre normalmente li facciamo comporre parallelamente, in virtù del principio che le velocità parallele nello stesso senso si sommano, la risultante *sarà necessariamente rappresentata da un segmento che riuscirà maggiore del segmento* FA, e precisamente $= 2s$, e se la massa su cui agiscono le forze è m, il lavoro sarà $m \times 2s = 2ms$ che è maggiore di mFA. Le forze f' ed f non possono dare nè più nè meno di quel che sono, per essere *finite*. Insomma, in nessuna maniera la risultante di f' ed f parallele può essere eguale ad FA, come sarebbe richiesto dalla teoria della composizione dei moti, in confronto alla conservazione dell'energia.

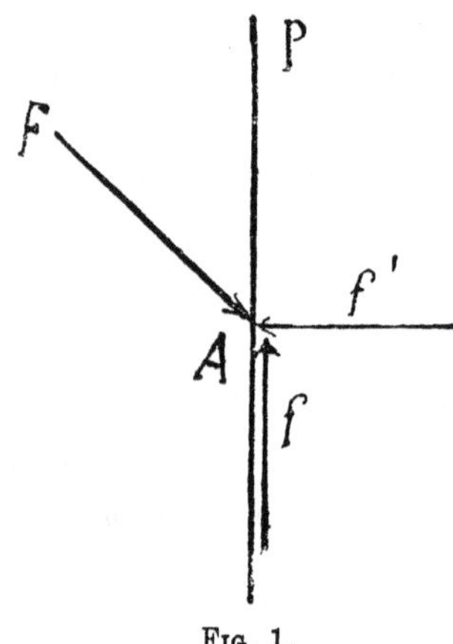

Fig. 1.

Ma vediamo un poco i singoli casi di composizione se corrispondono al principio che il lavoro della risultante è eguale alla somma dei lavori delle componenti.

I caso. — Sieno AB ed AC (fig. 2) due forze istantanee che superano per attrito le resistenze AB, AC, evidentemente il lavoro della risultante R sarà rappresentato da AR, che non è la somma di AB e di AC.

II caso. — AB ed AC sieno ancora due forze istantanee che agiscano sopra una massa libera, la risultante sarà ancora rappresentata da AR e non dalla somma dei lavori secondo le proiezioni di AR su AB ed AC, poichè allora evidentemente si avrebbe *creazione di energia*.

III CASO. — Le forze A B ed A C sono costanti, di moto reso uniforme per attrito, con v trascurabile; la risultante sarà ancora A R, poichè il lavoro è sempre *la medesima resistenza* moltiplicata per lo spazio superato. Questo criterio d'altronde risulta chiarito anche nel caso che segue. Avremo quindi $AR < AB + AC$ come lavoro.

IV CASO. — A B ed A C sieno due forze costanti che agiscono sopra una massa libera; la risultante in lavoro dico che sarà ancora A R. Non così però la pensa la fisica, poichè vi trova una contraddizione con la teoria della *forza viva*. Siccome è qui dove si riscontra il maggior equivoco, dobbiamo fermare un momento la nostra attenzione. Rammentiamo la definizione del lavoro: *Una resistenza moltiplicata per lo spazio superato*. Ebbene, stando a questa definizione ed ammettendo, quanto la fisica ammette, che il lavoro di una forza costante agente sopra una massa libera, è come gli spazi, evidentemente il lavoro della nostra risultante R sarà $=$ A R.

Ma la fisica, veduto qui che il conto non tornava, che cosa fece? invece di moltiplicare la resistenza per lo spazio superato, moltiplicò le forze, o la somma delle forze risolute secondo AR; ma ciò è arbitrario e *contro la definizione del lavoro* (1).

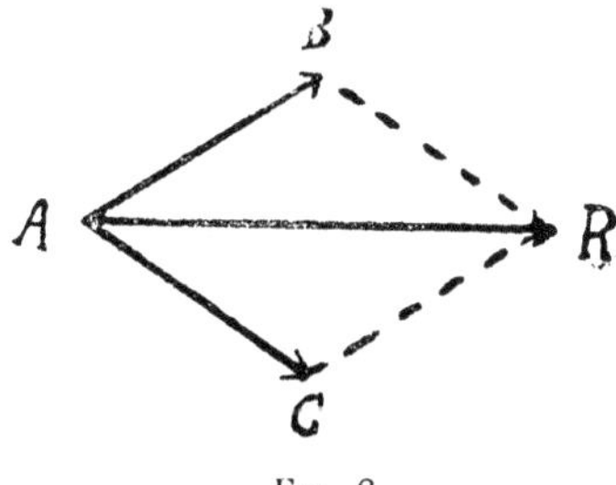

FIG. 2.

Per meglio rendere chiare le idee su questo principio fondamentale, supponiamo che le forze A B ed A C agiscano parallelamente nella stessa direzione e che sieno eguali. Se agisce una sola di esse il lavoro l che fa si dice che è fs; se agiscono tutte e due per il medesimo tempo, quale lavoro fanno? si risponde: $4l$. E come si ricava questo $4l$? facendo $2f \times 2s = 4fs = 4l$. Ma ciò è logico? evidentemente no, poichè è vero che doppia f fa doppia s, ma la resistenza che vince è la medesima, per cui stando alla definizione vera del lavoro nel caso che una f agisca da sola, si ha $l = rs$ (ove r è la resistenza) e nel caso agiscano tutte e due insieme, si ha $l = r \times 2s = 2rs = 2l$. Ma siccome si ha doppia velocità, la quale secondo la fisica darebbe luogo a quadruplo lavoro, il conto non torna. Visto ciò, si moltiplicò $2f$ per $2s$, ammettendo implicitamente l'errore che doppia f nel mentre fa doppio s vince anche doppia resistenza; ciò che è non vero, perchè è saputo ed ammesso che doppia f che incontri doppia resistenza fa il medesimo s. La formola del lavoro che doveva essere rs si trasformò arbitrariamente in fs, credendo di togliere con ciò una contraddizione, mentre in effetto si copriva un errore.

(1) Non dovrebbe essere necessario rammentare che la risultante come lavoro si fa $= \overline{AR}^2$, uguale sforzo AR moltiplicato per spazio AR, mentre dovrebbe essere $m \times AR$. Se $m = 1$ la risultante è $= AR$.

Ma c'è un'altra cosa da rilevare. Qui si ammette che le forze agiscono secondo gli spazî, mentre è *cosa evidente* che le forze naturali agiscono secondo i tempi.

Nella stessa storica controversia del XVIII secolo, intorno alla misura della energia di moto, i contendenti convenivano tutti in un'idea: che le forze naturali non possono agire che secondo i tempi. Mentre in qual modo si dà ragione del prodotto $4l = 4fs$? nel modo seguente.

Facciamo $R = f + f'$, questa somma può rappresentare anche la velocità risultante v che esprime un lavoro $= v^2$. Ma $(f + f')^2 = f^2 + f'^2 + ff' = Rf + Rf'$; ma siccome R è anche s, si ricava il lavoro l facendo $l = fs + f's$. Vale a dire si moltiplica ciascuna f per tutto lo spazio che percorre il suo punto di applicazione. Orbene, qui si fa entrare nella fisica un principio il quale, quando non fosse condannato dall'evidenza e dagli stessi fisici, quali Newton, Cartesio, Leibnitz, Bernoulli, ecc., dovrebbe per lo meno essere discusso e dimostrato. Si confonde il lavoro prodotto col lavoro consumato, perchè la fisica ammette che il primo è sempre eguale al secondo. Solo nel caso che s sia resistente, il lavoro prodotto è rs, ma allora il lavoro consumato è sempre maggiore del lavoro prodotto. In altri termini: mentre il primo (qui e sempre) è come i tempi, il secondo risulta secondo gli spazî; ma se lo spazio non è resistente, cioè se la forza agisce sopra una massa libera, allora tanto il lavoro consumato, quanto il lavoro prodotto, risultano secondo i tempi. La stessa gravità presenta il più bell'esempio di forza che agisce secondo i tempi. Infatti, in ogni unità di tempo successiva viene sempre aggiunto al moto lo stesso spazio e la stessa velocità; ma la fisica ha il torto di credere che la forza costante agisca anche per quegli spazî che il mobile percorrerebbe egualmente da se stesso senza l'azione di alcuna forza. Così avviene che la più piccola forza può *in un secondo* produrre tanta energia da fermare il corso ad un astro, e basta a tal fine che sia unita ad un'altra di sufficiente grandezza: ma ciò non è un assurdo? L'effetto di una forza aumenterebbe coll'aumentare della forza a cui si unisce; se la prima la si considera un moto equabile, si ha anche una *creazione* di energia, e quindi la possibilità del moto perpetuo [1].

Dopo questi schiarimenti, si capisce come anche nel IV caso non si possa ritenere che il lavoro della risultante sia eguale alla somma dei lavori delle componenti. Vi sarebbe però un quinto caso da considerare: quello cioè presentato da una forza costante che vince un'altra forza costante, quale potrebbe essere quello presentato dal *piano inclinato*. Ma che anche la teoria del piano inclinato sia errata, mi pare non difficile a dimostrarlo.

Abbiamo già detto, e, spero anche dimostrato, che il parallelogramma delle forze non può avere il suo corrispondente nella composizione dei moti, e ciò anche indipendentemente dall'idea che il lavoro della risultante sia eguale al lavoro delle componenti, valutato secondo la proiezione della risultante stessa sulla direzione delle compo-

[1] Questo aspetto della questione è ampiamente illustrato nell'ultimo mio libro: *Il più grande errore scientifico del secolo XIX* (*La supposta indistruttibilità della forza*). Milano, editore Paolo Carrara.

nenti medesime; ma non possiamo toccare un simile argomento senza guardare alla teoria del piano inclinato che ne è l'essenza.

Sia A B (fig. 3) un piano inclinato, G la gravità, e sia A F = F la stessa gravità relativa risoluta secondo A B. Allo scopo di rendere più breve la dimostrazione, supponiamo che sia A G = G B: in tal modo la forza F risoluta secondo A B sarà eguale a quella risoluta normalmente al piano A B; vale a dire la forza G viene scomposta in due parti eguali.

Noi non sappiamo ora come si chiameranno, come si valuteranno, ecc., queste forze, poichè anzi ciò è quanto vogliamo controllare; basti a noi l'esser certi di questo: *che la G è divisa in due parti eguali.* C'è quindi lecito valutare separatamente l'azione di queste forze scomponenti. Ebbene, la fisica dice che le forze che agiscono separatamente sopra la stessa massa, stanno fra loro come le velocità: ossia come gli spazî percorsi nell'unità di tempo.

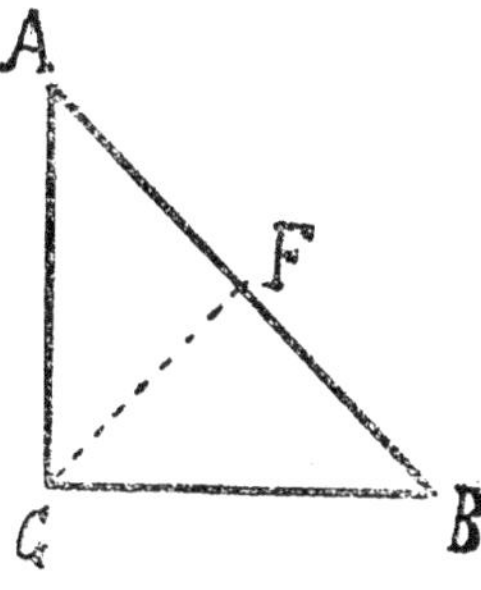

FIG. 3.

Ora, la forza risoluta secondo A B si può rappresentare con quel segmento o con quel diavolo che si vuole, ma per questo non cessa di essere la metà di G, e siccome questa nell'unità di tempo si suppone che percorra A G, la sua metà, scomposta secondo A B, deve percorrere, ossia far percorrere al suo punto di applicazione, uno spazio $= \frac{1}{2}$ A G; mentre la fisica gli fa percorrere $\frac{1}{2}$ A B.

Inoltre l'erroneità della teoria del piano inclinato risulta evidente anche dal fatto che secondo essa sarebbe possibile il moto perpetuo, poichè stabilisce il parvente errore che per comunicare ad una massa una determinata velocità occorrerebbe sempre la spesa della stessa energia, *qualunque sia l'angolo che la direzione del moto fa con l'orizzonte*, e quindi anche se tale direzione è orizzontale; mentre ognuno può vedere che se p è il peso del corpo e se f è la forza necessaria per spingerlo orizzontalmente, per spingerlo verticalmente con la stessa velocità occorrerà una forza $= p + f$.

La teoria della composizione dei moti non considera il peso. Così occorrerebbe sempre il medesimo impulso alla massa m per fare ad essa superare la salita B A; mentre l'energia richiesta sarà $= mv + p'$ $\left(\text{e non } \frac{mv^2}{2}\right)$; ma quando cadesse verticalmente ci renderebbe una energia $= mv + p$; *ove però p' è sempre una frazione di p.*

Non si capisce come abbia potuto la fisica generalizzare la formola del lavoro $\frac{mv^2}{2}$, mentre essendo essa ricavata, come è noto, dalle formole della gravità $\frac{v^2}{2g}$; $l = P\frac{v^2}{2g}$; $P = mg$, e quindi $l = \frac{mv^2}{2}$, anche quando quest'ultima fosse giusta (ciò che non può essere, perchè cessa di essere anche una funzione variabile di g) evidentemente, data l'origine sua, l dovrebbe variare col variare di g; quando l debba rappresentare non solo il lavoro prodotto, ma anche il lavoro consumato. In altri termini: nella formola $\frac{mv^2}{2}$ si pretende che il lavoro della forza motrice non solo debba vincere l'inerzia della massa m, ma anche il suo peso g; ma nel caso che m venga spinta, per es., orizzontalmente, il peso dov'è? vi è solo l'enerzia della massa da vincere. Ed è per questo che il marinaio con lo sforzo di una mano mette in moto un grosso barcone carico, mentre per innalzarlo non basterebbero cento cavalli.

Da qui risulta subito errata anche la teoria della parabola dei proiettili. Infatti, la velocità iniziale comunicata al proiettile dall'esplosione deve essere quella reale sotto l'influenza della gravità, e non quella che si otterrebbe se l'esplosivo agisse sul proiettile, nell'ipotesi che esso fosse sottratto alla gravità. Ciò dicasi anche nel caso della spinta verticale in alto dello stesso proiettile. Secondo la teoria della composizione dei moti, in questo caso si spenderebbe un lavoro cha risulta proporzionale alla velocità ed all'inerzia della massa; mentre questa poi cadendo ci fornirebbe evidentemente un lavoro proporzionale alla *stessa* massa, alla *stessa* velocità *ed al peso*; ossia all'azione statica della gravità; per cui si renderebbe possibile il moto perpetuo.

La teoria del piano inclinato stabilisce quest'altro errore evidente. Per far salire un grave da B ad A si spenderebbe sempre la stessa energia qualunque sia l'angolo che la direzione della forza forma col piano AB. Ma chi non sa che ciò non è vero! Ammette la fisica che per far equilibrio al grave occorre uno sforzo maggiore nel caso che la direzione dello sforzo sia per es. parallela alla base del piano anzichè al piano stesso; ma dunque uno sforzo maggiore moltiplicato per uno stesso spazio deve dare un prodotto maggiore. La fisica valutando qui per spazio la proiezione orizzontale del piano confonde, come sempre, il lavoro prodotto col lavoro consumato; il lavoro *prodotto* è sempre il medesimo, ma il lavoro *consumato* varia col variare dell'angolo che la direzione della forza fa col piano. La forza risoluta normalmente alla direzione del piano *si distrugge*. L'errore nacque quindi dal fatto che si crede che lo sforzo statico non consumi la propria causa. Un tale criterio errato ha l'origine comune a non pochi altri, cioè ha per origine il supposto modo invisibile di agire della gravità; modo di agire supposto che non si riscontra in nessuna forza conosciuta e controllabile.

Infatti, secondo la fisica, la gravità sarebbe una forza la quale può comunicare ad una massa una qualsiasi energia senza consumare se stessa menomamente; orbene, niuna forza conosciuta si comporta in tal modo. La gravità sarebbe pure una forza la quale sopra una *massa libera* agisce in modo costante; ma dov'è in natura un'altra forza che possa in tal modo agire? Di più, la gravità (come l'elasticità) sarebbe una forza la quale nel produrre lo sforzo statico non consuma se stessa; ma niuna forza nota e controllabile si comporta in tal modo. Eppure fu dalla gravità che si trassero i principî fondamentali della dinamica: ma se una tale forza si rendesse *visibile*, noi vedremmo che non si comporta in modo diverso dalle altre, ed allora i principî fondamentali della dinamica li vedremmo cadere per se stessi. Allora, per es., vedremmo quanto sia assurdo il principio dedotto immediatamente dalla teoria del piano inclinato, che due buoi per un medesimo solco consumano la medesima energia, qualunque sia il modo con cui sono aggiogati rispetto alla direzione del solco: cioè tanto se agiscono parallelamente quanto se agiscono obliquamente al solco stesso; criterio tale che farebbe tener il ventre dal ridere ad ogni buon contadino che l'udisse. Per la stessa ragione vedremmo quanto sia assurdo il volere che la formola del lavoro $\left(\frac{mv^2}{2}\right)$ sia generale; cioè che non si debba tener calcolo della direzione di m destinata a muoversi sotto l'influenza costante di una forza (gravità) che per avere una direzione invariabile ha un *effetto statico* (peso) variabile. O forse tutte queste mie idee non costituiscono che una fenomenale illusione della mia mente? È quanto spero di sapere presto dalla critica illuminata che, mi lusingo, i competenti non vorranno negarmi.

PARTE III

COMUNICAZIONI

SEZIONE III-B

APPLICAZIONI VARIE DELLA MATEMATICA

G. TOJA

ALCUNE CONSIDERAZIONI SUI RAPPORTI TRA LA MATEMATICA E LA SCIENZA ATTUARIALE

Chiamato, soltanto da ragioni di anzianità professionale, a coprire la carica di « Introduttore » per la Sezione Attuariale di questo Congresso, rivolgo il mio omaggio affettuoso e devoto agli Egregi Colleghi che vollero accogliere tanto favorevolmente l'invito di partecipare ai lavori di questa nuova Sezione e formulo l'augurio vivissimo che l'attuale Congresso segni una data memorabile per la Scienza Attuariale che alla matematica deve la sua origine, il suo sviluppo, il suo progresso.

L'opera scientifica dell'attuario si svolge nel campo statistico, finanziario e matematico, e trova applicazione nell'ordinamento tecnico delle istituzioni di Previdenza, sian queste Compagnie di Assicurazione, Società di Mutuo Soccorso o Casse Pensioni. L'interesse della collettività previdente è salvaguardato dal rigore dell'indagine scientifica, la quale ha lo scopo eminentemente pratico di ricercare ed imporre le condizioni dell'equilibrio finanziario in aziende a cui sono affidati interessi rilevantissimi. All'infuori di tutti gli elementi di carattere industriale, che pure hanno una parte notevole nella pratica professionale, la scienza dell'attuario indica i metodi per determinare gl'impegni finanziarii che scaturiscono da un razionale ordinamento delle istituzioni di previdenza, per vigilare affinchè le valutazioni corrispondano bene alla realtà dei fatti, per analizzare gli scarti che l'esperienza presenta di fronte alle previsioni. Essa studia inoltre le cause degli scarti stessi, ne propone i rimedi, quando l'origine dei medesimi non sia puramente accidentale ma dovuta a cause sistematiche ad eliminare le quali occorre riformare totalmente o parzialmente l'edificio statistico sul quale le previsioni erano fondate.

Dall'annualità vitalizia e dall'assicurazione sulla vita che rappresentano i problemi più semplici dell'ordinamento tecnico della previdenza, al calcolo aprioristico di pensioni da corrispondersi, dopo la morte di un iscritto a cassa pensioni, alla famiglia superstite, esiste una serie numerosa di questioni le cui soluzioni, se semplici, peccano spesso di rigore, se esatte nel senso matematico, riescono il più delle volte inapplicabili per mancanza di dati statistici o per la grande quantità di calcoli numerici richiesti.

Considerati i fenomeni demografici elementari come resultati dell'esperienza, definite e calcolate le probabilità ad essi corrispondenti, corrette le imperfezioni dovute al caso, al sistema, al numero limitato di osservazioni, la teoria formale delle probabilità, mediante l'applicazione di noti teoremi, permette di valutare le probabilità del fenomeno che forma oggetto delle operazioni finanziarie da studiare, e permette altresì con la scorta delle funzioni del saggio d'interesse, valutato secondo i principî della teoria della finanza, di calcolare i valori probabili o le speranze matematiche che risolvono il quesito attuariale.

L'applicazione del calcolo formale e della teoria della finanza fatta generalmente con metodi aritmetici è semplice, ma riesce di scarso interesse al matematico il quale potrebbe invece tentare l'uso del metodo continuo e l'introduzione di speciali funzioni che permettessero di sostituire alle valutazioni aritmetiche il calcolo d'integrali definiti. In tal senso i tentativi fatti non hanno dato finora buoni resultati, giacchè, spesso, se la quadratura è semplice, la funzione integrale non rappresenta bene il fenomeno demografico, e se altrimenti la funzione interpreta con un certo rigore il fenonomeno osservato, la quadratura corrispondente non si ottiene senza ricorrere ad uno sviluppo in serie che riesce in ultima analisi più laborioso dei calcoli aritmetici adottati nella pratica. Il metodo aritmetico, fondato sui simboli di commutazione, conta ormai più di un secolo di vita.

Affinchè l'attuario possa procedere a valutazioni razionali è necessario ammettere che ciascuno dei fenomeni demografici sottoposti al suo studio sia governato da una legge definita. Fatta l'ipotesi della esistenza di questa legge, la prima ricerca sarà rivolta alla sua determinazione eseguita con i metodi più accurati.

La natura stessa dei fenomeni demografici esige che tale determinazione sia ricavata dall'esperienza; si presenta così un problema comune a tutte le scienze di osservazione che consiste sostanzialmente nello stabilire una distribuzione di casi o, il che è lo stesso, la probabilità che un dato fenomeno si presenti in un determinato intervallo finito od infinitesimo di tempo.

La via da seguire per la soluzione di questo problema è additata, com'è noto, dal calcolo delle probabilità, e più specialmente dalla legge dei grandi numeri.

Usando della consueta rappresentazione geometrica, possiamo dire che una prima classe di osservazioni relative al fenomeno conduce alla costruzione di un diagramma che già fornisce un'idea grossolana della legge cercata, una classe più numerosa di osservazioni ugualmente accurate dà al diagramma una forma meno incerta, e, così procedendo, ove col crescere del numero delle osservazioni si noti nel diagramma la tendenza a disporsi secondo un andamento sempre più definito, è naturale e intuitivo ammettere che esiste una linea verso la quale il diagramma tende col crescere all'infinito del numero delle osservazioni, e che questa linea rappresenta effettivamente la legge che governa il fenomeno. I precedenti scostamenti fuori del limite si attribuiscono alla imperfezione e limitazione del materiale statistico.

Può darsi invece che la tendenza ad accostarsi ad una forma limite non si verifichi, ma in questo caso dobbiamo concludere che le osservazioni compiute non furono buone o che non fu rispettata qualcuna di quelle cautele che debbono guidare ogni corretta elaborazione dei materiali statistici.

Come opportunamente pone in rilevo THIELE nel suo geniale lavoro sulla Teoria delle osservazioni, quando studia le leggi degli errori, vi ha in questa questione della analogia con le note considerazioni sulle serie convergenti e indeterminate.

In sostanza il metodo adottato procede dall'ipotesi che anche per fenomeni complessi, come quelli che formano oggetto dei nostri studî, si possa parlare di probabilità, che questo elemento debba determinarsi a posteriori e che sia legittima l'applicazione dei noti principî su cui si basano determinazioni di questa natura.

Ordinato il materiale statistico ed ottenuta così una serie di valori grezzi relativa al fenomeno considerato, occorre introdurre la continuità ed eliminare l'influenza degli errori accidentali di osservazione: sorge allora lo studio delle leggi degli errori e il problema della perequazione.

Come è noto sono vari i metodi grafici, meccanici, analitici. Limitandoci alla considerazione di questi ultimi che hanno maggiore interesse dal punto di vista scientifico il problema può porsi sotto questa forma: Presupposto che una determinata funzione analitica sia atta a rappresentare la legge di variazione di un fenomeno, determinare, in base ad osservazioni compiute, i valori più convenienti delle costanti sicchè ne segua la legge più probabile che governa il fenomeno.

I postulati su i quali si fonda il classico metodo dei minimi quadrati, mentre possono essere concessi in molti fenomeni studiati dalle scienze sperimentali, in alcuni fenomeni demografici molto complessi non possono logicamente giustificarsi: la conferma ci è infatti fornita dal resultato che qualche volta è tale da escludere assolutamente l'opportunità di tale applicazione.

Un metodo che assai frequentemente dà resultati soddisfacenti è quello dei momenti del PEARSON: altri metodi suggeriti da varî autori mentre rispondono in alcuni casi fallano affatto in altri.

Un metodo che potrebbe considerarsi come una estensione di quello di PEARSON è il seguente:

Detta $f(x)$ la funzione analitica scelta per rappresentare la legge in istudio e $\varphi_1, \varphi_2, \dots \varphi_n$, n funzioni arbitrarie, da scegliersi poi convenientemente, si pongano le equazioni:

$$\int_{-\infty}^{+\infty} f(x)\,\varphi_1(x)\,dx = A_1$$

$$\dots\dots\dots\dots$$

$$\int_{-\infty}^{+\infty} f(x)\,\varphi_n(x)\,dx = A_n$$

dove $A_1, A_2, \dots A_n$, sono i valori corrispondenti degli stessi integrali ricavati dall'esperienza. Le equazioni saranno destinate a determinare le costanti della $f(x)$. La questione che si presenta consiste allora nello scegliere opportunamente le funzioni $\varphi_1, \varphi_2, \dots \varphi_n$, e converrebbe stabilire qualche principio che valesse a suggerirle.

Per altro, riassumendo, i metodi di cui possiamo disporre sono d'incerta applicazione e mancano altresì criterii rigorosi atti a giudicare della bontà di una effettuata perequazione.

Assai più complesso apparisce il problema quando la funzione perequatrice dipende da due variabili indipendenti: alla curva viene sostituita una superficie e la soluzione può essere cercata con successive perequazioni effettuate secondo le intersezioni di quella superficie con piani paralleli ai piani coordinati, oppure immaginando un qualche metodo che usufruisca simultaneamente di tutte le osservazioni.

Altra questione a parer nostro di grande interesse per i problemi attuariali è quella della scelta di una adatta funzione analitica per rappresentare l'andamento di un fenomeno demografico.

Sino ad ora si procedè od in base a criterii di indole metafisica, del resto confermati dalla prova sperimentale, od in base a criterî di opportunità inspirati all'uso della funzione e alle formule nelle quali doveva poi comparire. L'uno e l'altro metodo hanno un fondo di vero e non intendiamo disconoscere il buon successo che determinarono in matematica attuariale: basti citare la nota legge di sopravvivenza di Gompertz-Makeham pel primo caso, e per il secondo le belle ricerche del Sig. Quiquet su leggi di sopravvivenza soddisfacenti a determinate ed opportune condizioni.

Considerata la cosa in generale e indipendentemente dalla natura specifica del fenomeno in quistione, converrebbe ricercare se è possibile stabilire dei principî atti, se non a determinare univocamente la funzione da adottarsi, a suggerirne una che rappresenti il fenomeno considerato in modo soddisfacente.

È certo che il problema posto sotto questa forma apparisce indeterminato, benchè il significato ne sia intuitivo; ma la maggiore difficoltà consiste appunto nel trovare una forma adatta per rendere il problema matematicamente trattabile. Forse sarebbe necessario sottoporre la funzione ad opportune condizioni, di semplicità ad esempio, e quindi dovrebbe stabilirsi cosa debba intendersi per semplicità in questo caso, o cosa per rappresentazione analitica soddisfacente di un fenomeno osservato.

La questione, anche dal lato matematico, presenta molto interesse, e riteniamo, come altri ha già osservato, non sia azzardato pensare ch'essa possa collegarsi con la teoria generale delle funzioni.

Frattanto, riassumendo quanto abbiamo esposto fin qui, riconosciamo che già lo studio di questi tre problemi offre largo campo di ricerche all'indagine matematica. La legittimità del concetto di probabilità e della sua determinazione a posteriori, la legittimità dell'applicazione dei noti principî del calcolo formale fondati su ipotesi che non trovano la loro piena corrispondenza nel carattere dei fenomeni demografici, i varî problemi di perequazione, e infine la scelta di una funzione atta a rappresentare analiticamente in modo soddisfacente un fenomeno osservato sono tutte questioni nelle quali sino ad oggi permangono inevitabili incertezze e che solo una sapiente ed efficace analisi matematica potrebbe eliminare.

Rilevati così alcuni degli argomenti di scienza attuariale che appariscono connessi con le teorie della matematica, riteniamo opportuno di accennare ad alcuni problemi che avemmo occasione di risolvere nella nostra pratica professionale e che mentre presentano qualche interesse anche dal lato matematico, mostrano il carattere di alcuni artifizi attuariali.

Abbiamo tratto tre esempi, che potremmo dire tipici, da un nostro studio sulle Casse Pensioni.

Il primo di essi è essenzialmente basato sull'uso delle linee di frequenza e presenta i caratteri normali del fenomeno demografico: il secondo invece è di natura più complessa ed è soltanto mediante qualche ulteriore ipotesi, che dobbiamo supporre soddisfatta, che si può giustificare l'uso delle linee di frequenza: il terzo infine rappresenta uno di quei casi che trattati con procedimenti ordinari conducono a formule troppo complesse, o a risultati di scarso valore per la limitazione del materiale statistico, ma che in virtù di un conveniente artifizio possono essere risoluti con semplicità ed in modo soddisfacente dal punto di vista applicativo.

1° Problema. — Determinare il valore di una Rendita vedovile da corrispondersi dopo la morte di un socio di una Istituzione di Previdenza alla vedova superstite fino alla data della morte o del passaggio a seconde nozze. Si conosce l'età del Socio e nulla si sa del suo stato di famiglia: il calcolo delle probabilità indica la via da seguirsi: il procedimento è normale.

I dati necessari alla soluzione del quesito sono i seguenti:

a) Funzione di sopravvivenza dei Soci inscritti alla istituzione di previdenza.

b) Funzione di sopravvivenza vedovile.

c) Probabilità che alla morte il socio lasci la vedova.

d) Linea di distribuzione delle vedove per età.

La funzione l_x di sopravvivenza dei soci non presenta nessuna particolarità e si determina con i metodi ordinari di ordinamento statistico e di perequazione.

La funzione di sopravvivenza vedovile rappresenta un fenomeno affetto da una particolare selezione dovuta al passaggio a seconde nozze e deve rigorosamente dipendere da due variabili indipendenti: età della vedova e durata del periodo vedovile. Indicheremo il valore dell'annualità su testa di vedova da corrispondersi all'età y con a_y.

La probabilità Θ^c_x che alla morte il socio lasci la vedova riguarda la frequenza alle diverse età dei soci coniugati vedovi e celibi. Il rapporto tra il numero dei soci coniugati ad una determinata età al numero totale dei soci osservati, indicherà il valore più probabile della probabilità che all'età considerata il socio sia coniugato. I valori più probabili così determinati rappresentano elementi grezzi che naturalmente vanno sottoposti all'ordinaria perequazione.

La linea di frequenza della vedova si ottiene raccogliendo tutte le osservazioni relative alle successive età del socio e distribuendo le osservazioni stesse per età della moglie.

Detta y l'età della moglie, x quella del marito alla morte, ad ogni valore di x corrisponde una speciale distribuzione di y: tra x ed y sussiste ciò che ordinariamente si dice correlazione.

La probabilità che avvenendo la morte del marito all'età x, l'età della moglie sia y sarà data da:

$$\varphi(x, y)\, dy\,.$$

Ciò posto, usando dei simboli ora introdotti e di quelli ordinariamente adottati nelle questioni attuariali ed applicando i consueti principî del calcolo delle probabilità si ha che il valore dell'impegno della Cassa verso la moglie quando il marito ha raggiunto l'età x è espressa da:

$$\frac{1}{l_x}\int_0^\infty l_{x+t}\,.\,\mu_{x+t}\,.\,v^t\,.\,\Theta^c{}_{x+t}\,.\,dt\int_a^b \varphi(x+t\,,y)\,\bar{a}_y\,.\,dy\,.$$

La funzione φ come si scorge dalla distribuzione grezza ha la forma delle curve asimmetriche degli errori.

2° **Problema.** — Gruppi d'Orfani. Annualità composte $a[\bar{0}_r]$.

La teoria delle annualità composte insegna il modo di ricavare il valore di un'annualità sul gruppo $[\bar{0}_r]$ mediante combinazioni lineari delle annualità a_{x_r}, $a_{x_r x_s}$, al 1° caso di morte su 1, 2 o più teste note le età $x_1, x_2, \ldots x_n$ degli orfani componenti il gruppo $[\bar{0}_r]$.

Le annualità semplici nel caso di gruppi di orfani s'intendono sempre temporenee da corrispondersi cioè al massimo fino al compimento di una determinata età dell'orfano minore. In pratica per la determinazione di tale impegno, non potendo seguire mediante estese tavole di annualità tutte le possibili combinazioni di età, dobbiamo ricorrere a sistemi di calcolo abbreviati basati su speciali medie e tali da far dipendere il valore dell'annualità composta da una sola variabile: ad esempio dall'età dell'orfano minore. S'immagini che i gruppi d'orfani a favore dei quali vengono corrisposte le pensioni siano distribuiti uniformemente, in altri termini, supponiamo un ambiente in condizioni stazionarie nel quale le distribuzioni dei gruppi siano soggette a leggi statistiche costanti. Riferendoci allora ai gruppi d'orfani, anzichè ad un singolo individuo, dobbiamo determinare il valore dell'annualità corrispondente ad un gruppo di orfani qualunque, tenendo conto soltanto dell'età dell'orfano minore. Il numero r di orfani può essere qualunque. Non cerchiamo così la soluzione del quesito dell'ammontare dell'annualità composta relativa ad un determinato gruppo, quesito che si risolverebbe, note le età degli orfani, con procedimenti ordinari, ma determiniamo invece il valore medio che possiamo attribuire all'annualità per un gruppo di orfani appartenente ad una collettività in condizioni stazionarie.

Detta x l'età dell'orfano minore, $[0]_x$ il gruppo corrispondente, indicheremo con ξ_x la probabilità che il gruppo $[0]_x$ sia composto da due 2 o più orfani. Indicheremo inoltre con $\eta_\Delta\ d\Delta$ la probabilità che la differenza di età tra l'orfano minore ed il successivo sia Δ. (Evidentemente la funzione η_Δ vale al disopra di un certo valore h).

Detto $a_{[0]_x}$ il valore dell'annualità da determinare e p_x, q_x, le probabilità di vita e di morte nell'anno $x, \ldots.. x+1$, è facile convincersi della seguente formula ricorrente:

$$a_{[0]_x} = vp_x(1 + a_{[0]_{x+1}}) + \xi_{x+1}\,.\,q_x\,.\,v\,.\left(1 + \int_h^{n-x-1} \eta_\Delta\,.\,a[0]_{x+\Delta+1}\,.\,d\Delta\right)$$

estensione di una nota formula di Scienza Attuariale.

ξ e η in una Cassa Pensione a movimento uniforme hanno carattere di stabilità tale da poter far pensare a linee di frequenza: determinati così questi elementi, si procede al calcolo delle annualità applicando successivamente la precedente formula. L'elemento tipico da considerare in questo secondo problema è il concetto di linea di frequenza esteso anche ai fenomeni di probabilità ξ e η.

3° Problema. — Annualità di Famiglia.

Per una determinata età x alla morte dell'inscritto all'Istituzione di Previdenza definiamo annualità di famiglia il valore capitale probabile della pensione da corrispondersi in base ad un determinato regolamento alla famiglia superstite, pensione che varia col variare della composizione della famiglia stessa. Indicheremo tale annualità con a_{F_x}.

Per l'età x alla morte del socio, consideriamo $L_{x,0}$ famiglie la cui composizione potrà essere di tre specie:

Famiglia con la sola vedova $[v]$

Famiglia con soli orfani $[o]$

Famiglia con vedove ed orfani $[v\,o]$

Se tra L_{x_0} famiglie considerate ne abbiamo l_{x_0} con sole vedove, le rimanenti $L_{x_0} - l_{x_0}$ rappresentano le famiglie contenenti soltanto orfani.

Un ordinamento statistico opportuno ci permette di ricavare la legge di eliminazione delle famiglie dopo $1, 2, \ldots t$ anni dalla morte del socio, cioè:

$$L_{x_0}, L_{x_1}, L_{x_2}, \ldots L_{x_t} \ldots$$

La pensione π_{x_0} da corrispondersi alle famiglie superstiti in base ad un determinato regolamento, sarà funzione della composizione della famiglia stessa, e per potere studiare la legge di variazione di queste pensioni dopo la morte del socio, dovremo immaginare un mezzo per rendere omogeneo il materiale statistico: l'artifizio al quale abbiamo ricorso consiste nel riferire il valore di π all'unità di pensione alla quale avrebbe avuto diritto la vedova nell'ipotesi di mancanza di orfani.

Indicando allora con $\pi_{x_0}, \pi_{x_1}, \ldots \pi_{x_t}$ la legge di variazione delle pensioni così valutate, il valore grezzo della pensione di famiglia sarà dato dall'espressione:

$$a_{F_x} = \frac{1}{L_{x_0}} \sum L_{x_t} \cdot \pi_{x_t} v^t .$$

A questo punto dobbiamo notare che la Pensione vedovile si potè precedentemente determinare con procedimento più rigoroso. ond'è che per valutare l'influenza che producono gli orfani sul valore della pensione, in più od in meno rispetto a quella che sarebbe stata liquidata alla sola vedova, abbiamo ricorso al seguente artifizio.

Con una semplice trasformazione l'annnualità di famiglia può scriversi:

$$a_{F_x} = \frac{1}{L_{x,t}} \sum (L_{x,t} \, . \, \pi_{x,t} - l_{x,t}) \, v_t + \frac{l_{x,0}}{L_{x,0}} \, a_{|v|_x}$$

per cui avendo determinato il valore di $a_{F\,x}$ della pensione vedovile potremo mediante un'opportuna perequazione dei valori $\sum (L_{x_t} \, \pi_{x_t} - l_{x_t}) \, v^t$ riconoscere dalla precedente relazione l'influenza prodotta nella pensione integrale di famiglia, dagli orfani.

È in tal modo che per via indiretta è stato valutato un elemento che sarebbe stato impossibile ricavare con procedimenti ordinari per la scarsità degli elementi statistici che avevamo a disposizione.

A. QUIQUET

SUR UNE NOUVELLE APPLICATION DES JACOBIENS AUX PROBABILITÉS VIAGÈRES

I.

Applications antérieures. Exposé succinct.

1. Dans deux circonstances, j'ai déjà eu l'occasion d'appliquer aux probabilités viagères les déterminants fonctionnels de JACOBI, et grâce à eux j'ai résolu deux problèmes que je vais rappeler succinctement.

Une formule célèbre, donnée d'abord par GOMPERTZ, puis étendue par MAKEHAM, a été maintes fois utilisée, depuis ces deux éminents actuaires anglais, pour la représentation analytique des Tables de survie et de mortalité.

La « loi de survie » de GOMPERTZ et de MAKEHAM jouit d'une propriété, fort précieuse dans les assurances sur la vie, que je formulerai de la façon suivante:

« Pour un nombre déterminé de naissances, lorsque le nombre des survivants à un âge quelconque est figuré par une loi de GOMPERTZ ou par une loi de MAKEHAM, la probabilité, pour un groupe quelconque d'individus obéissant à cette loi, d'exister encore tout entier au bout du temps t, peut s'exprimer à l'aide de t et d'*une seule variable* indépendante de t: la variable en question ne dépend que des âges de ces individus à un même moment ».

2. C'est cette propriété que j'ai cherché à généraliser, d'abord en 1892 dans le premier chapitre de la Thèse qui m'a valu le titre de membre agrégé de l'*Institut des Actuaires français*, puis en 1903 dans une communication que j'ai lue à New-York devant le IVe Congrès international d'Actuaires.

Le problème de ma Thèse rentre dans celui que j'ai traité à New-York, où je ne me suis plus astreint à ne considérer que des individus obéissant, comme dans ma Thèse, à *une seule loi* de survie, mais où j'ai supposé qu'ils obéissaient à des lois de survie *distinctes ou non*. Je me borne donc à l'énoncé le plus général du problème que je m'étais posé:

« Soient $a, b, \ldots, k$ les âges de N individus, qui suivent des lois de survie distinctes ou non, et supposons que, pour un nombre donné de naissances, le nombre des vivants à l'âge x soit figuré par

$$l_1(x), l_2(x), \ldots, l_N(x),$$

suivant qu'il s'agit du premier, du second,..., du N^e individu. Soient, d'autre part, n fonctions de $a, b, \ldots, k$, que j'appelle $\alpha, \beta, \ldots, \theta$, indépendantes entre elles et indépendantes de t. Quelle doit être la forme respective de $l_1(x), l_2(x), \ldots$ $l_N(x)$, pour que l'on ait, quel que soit t, et n étant inférieur à N,

$$\text{(1)} \qquad \frac{l_1(a+t)}{l_1(a)} \cdot \frac{l_2(b+t)}{l_2(b)} \cdots \frac{l_N(k+t)}{l_N(k)} = G(\alpha, \beta, \ldots, \theta, t)\text{ ? »}$$

3. J'ai établi à New-York que si l'on représente par $l_g(x)$ une quelconque des fonctions

$$l_1(x), l_2(x), \ldots, l_N(x),$$

et par $\mu_g(x)$, conformément aux notations anglaises, la dérivée logarithmique changée de signe de $l_g(x)$, c'est-à-dire

$$\mu_g(x) = -\frac{l'_g(x)}{l_g(x)},$$

l'une quelconque de ces fonctions satisfait à l'équation différentielle

$$\text{(2)} \qquad A_0\mu'_g(x) + A_1\mu''_g(x) + \ldots + A_n\mu_g^{(n+1)}(x) = 0,$$

où les $A_0, A_1, \ldots, A_n$ sont indépendants de x et de g, c'est-à-dire constants.

J'ai donné l'expression générale des fonctions $l_g(x)$, fort simple à déduire de ce résultat.

$$\text{(3)} \qquad l_g(x) = e^{A+Bx+\Sigma e^{r_i x} f_i(x)}$$

Dans cette formule, r_i est une quelconque des racines de l'équation *caractéristique*:

$$\text{(4)} \qquad A_0 + A_1 r + \cdots + A_n r^n = 0;$$

et si λ_i est son ordre de multiplicité, $f_i(x)$ est un polynôme de degré $\lambda_i - 1$ quand r_i n'est pas nulle, de degré $\lambda_i + 1$ quand r_i est nulle. Le signe Σ s'étend d'ailleurs à toutes les racines distinctes de l'équation caractéristique.

Je conserverai ces notations pour la nouvelle étude que je vais exposer. Je conserverai aussi une convention sur le polynôme $f_i(x)$ quand r_i est nulle: je supposerai dans ce cas que le terme constant de ce polynôme et son terme en x se fondent avec le binôme $A + Bx$.

De la sorte, le logarithme népérien de $l_g(x)$,

$$Ll_g(x) = A + Bx + \Sigma e^{r_i x} f_i(x),$$

sera toujours une fonction linéaire de A, de B, et de n paramètres introduits par les polynômes $f_i(x)$: ces $n + 2$ paramètres servent à différencier entre elles les N fonctions $l_g(x)$.

Enfin, pour rappeler le point de contact de ces fonctions par le degré n de leur commune caractéristique, je les ai appelées *fonctions de survie d'ordre n.*

En particulier, les lois de GOMPERTZ et de MAKEHAM sont des fonctions de survie d'ordre 1.

II.

Complément du problème résolu à New-York. Intervention de n fonctions identiques.

4. En possession de ces anciens résultats, je me propose aujourd'hui de donner un complément au problème que j'ai résolu à New-York.

Ce complément, relatif au second membre de l'équation (1),

$$G(\alpha, \beta, \ldots, \theta, t),$$

m'a été inspiré par la forme spéciale que j'ai choisie pour cette fonction dans le troisième chapitre de ma Thèse. Comme celle-ci n'a trait qu'à N fonctions de survie *identiques*, il convient d'y introduire les modifications qui la rendront applicable au cas de N fonctions *distinctes ou non.*

Cette forme spéciale de $G(\alpha, \beta, \ldots, \theta, t)$ a son intérêt, car elle s'adapte fort bien aux besoins courants des Compagnies d'assurances, notamment en ce qui concerne leurs opérations sur plusieurs têtes telles que les annuités viagères.

5. Pour bien préciser la marche que j'ai suivie dans le troisième chapitre de ma Thèse, je vais en reproduire le passage principal. Je n'y introduirai que les légères modifications nécessitées par l'intervention de N fonctions non identiques $l_g(x)$, au lieu d'une seule, $l(x)$.

Aucune relation jusqu'ici n'a été imposée entre $a, b, \ldots, k$, et $\alpha, \beta, \ldots, \theta$; lorsque les fonctions de survie d'ordre n envisagées sont N des fonctions $l_g(x)$ définies par (3), si l'on établit arbitrairement n relations indépendantes entre $a, b, \ldots, k$, et $\alpha, \beta, \ldots, \theta$, la fonction

$$G(\alpha, \beta, \ldots, \theta, t)$$

se trouvera entièrement connue en vertu de l'équation (1).

Les deux membres de cette équation ne sont en effet qu'une double manière d'écrire la même chose, et ils doivent être identiques, quel que soit t, dès que l'on y remplace $\alpha, \beta, \ldots, \theta$, par leurs valeurs en $a, b, \ldots, k$, ou réciproquement.

Ces n relations dépendant exclusivement du choix du calculateur, il lui est permis de se demander quelles sont celles qui lui rendront le plus de services. Sous cet aspect, c'est surtout la forme de $G(\alpha, \beta, \ldots, \theta, t)$ qu'il envisagera d'abord.

Le problème est ainsi renversé, car le calculateur choisira arbitrairement cette forme, et il en déduira les n relations cherchées au lieu de prendre celles-ci comme point de départ.

Voyons maintenant par quel procédé ces considérations de ma Thèse vont s'étendre au présent problème.

6. Je vais d'abord considérer $\alpha, \beta, \ldots, \theta$ comme les âges au même moment de n individus.

Je pourrais supposer que chacun d'eux obéisse à une loi particulière de survie, qui serait d'ailleurs réelle ou *fictive*: l'intervention de lois fictives n'est pas pour nous arrêter, puisqu'il ne s'agit présentement que des commodités du calcul. J'aurais ainsi affaire à n lois distinctes ou non.

Quoique ces n lois, envisagées simultanément, puissent ne pas être inutiles dans certaines applications, je ne m'y arrêterai pas ici pour ne pas développer outre mesure cette communication. Je passe de suite à un cas plus limité, celui où les n individus obéissent par hypothèse à *une seule* loi de survie, réelle ou fictive. La démonstration que je vais donner suffira du reste pour montrer qu'elle ne serait pas à changer bien essentiellement dans le cas de n lois non identiques entre elles.

7. Soit donc $H(x)$ cette loi unique cherchée.

Pour le groupe d'individus d'âges $\alpha, \beta, \ldots, \theta$, la probabilité d'exister encore tout entier au bout du temps t s'exprimera alors par

$$\frac{H(\alpha+t)}{H(\alpha)} \cdot \frac{H(\beta+t)}{H(\beta)} \cdots \frac{H(\theta+t)}{H(\theta)}.$$

C'est par cette probabilité que je remplace $G(\alpha, \beta, \ldots, \theta, t)$.

$$G(\alpha, \beta, \ldots, \theta, t) = \frac{H(\alpha+t)}{H(\alpha)} \cdot \frac{H(\beta+t)}{H(\beta)} \cdots \frac{H(\theta+t)}{H(\theta)};$$

et je vais maintenant chercher à déterminer la fonction $\mathrm{H}(x)$ de manière à avoir identiquement, quel que soit t,

$$(5)\qquad \frac{l_1(a+t)}{l_1(a)}\cdot\frac{l_2(b+t)}{l_2(b)}\cdots\frac{l_N(k+t)}{l_N(k)}=\frac{\mathrm{H}(\alpha+t)}{\mathrm{H}(\alpha)}\cdot\frac{\mathrm{H}(\beta+t)}{\mathrm{H}(\beta)}\cdots\frac{\mathrm{H}(\theta+t)}{\mathrm{H}(\theta)}.$$

8. Comme dans ma Thèse, je pose

$$\frac{\mathrm{H}'(x)}{\mathrm{H}(x)}=-\mathrm{J}(x).$$

Après avoir pris par rapport à t la dérivée logarithmique des deux membres de (5), je dérive encore n fois par rapport à t cette dérivée logarithmique.

En faisant ensuite $t=0$ dans tous les résultats, j'arrive au système:

$$\left\{\begin{array}{l}\mu_1(a)+\mu_2(b)+\cdots+\mu_N(k)=\mathrm{J}(\alpha)+\mathrm{J}(\beta)+\cdots+\mathrm{J}(\theta)\\ \mu_1'(a)+\mu_2'(b)+\cdots+\mu_N'(k)=\mathrm{J}'(\alpha)+\mathrm{J}'(\beta)+\cdots+\mathrm{J}'(\theta)\\ \cdots\cdots\cdots\cdots\cdots\cdots\cdots\cdots\\ \mu_1^{(n)}(a)+\mu_2^{(n)}(b)+\cdots+\mu_N^{(n)}(k)=\mathrm{J}^{(n)}(\alpha)+\mathrm{J}^{(n)}(\beta)+\cdots+\mathrm{J}^{(n)}(\theta)\end{array}\right.$$

C'est à ce système que je pourrais étendre la méthode qui m'a déjà servi dans ma Thèse et à New-York, et qui est l'application directe du fameux mémoire de Jacobi, *De determinantibus functionalibus.*

9. Je modifie cependant un peu ce système, pour arriver plus immédiatement à la connaissance de $\mathrm{J}(x)$: je fais passer dans le premier membre toutes les fonctions d'une des variables, par exemple α, du second membre; en même temps, je fais passer dans le second membre toutes les fonctions d'une des variables, par exemple k, du premier membre. J'obtiens ainsi un nouveau système:

$$(6)\quad\left\{\begin{array}{l}\mu_1(a)+\mu_2(b)+\cdots-\mathrm{J}(\alpha)=-\mu_N(k)+\mathrm{J}(\beta)+\cdots+\mathrm{J}(\theta)\\ \mu_1'(a)+\mu_2'(b)+\cdots-\mathrm{J}'(\alpha)=-\mu_N'(k)+\mathrm{J}'(\beta)+\cdots+\mathrm{J}'(\theta)\\ \cdots\cdots\cdots\cdots\cdots\cdots\cdots\cdots\\ \mu_1^{(n)}(a)+\mu_2^{(n)}(b)+\cdots-\mathrm{J}^{(n)}(\alpha)=-\mu_N^{(n)}(k)+\mathrm{J}^{(n)}(\beta)+\cdots+\mathrm{J}^{(n)}(\theta)\end{array}\right.$$

Les nouvelles variables des seconds membres, $k,\beta,\ldots,\theta$, peuvent être prises comme n variables indépendantes. Ces seconds membres sont au nombre de $n+1$, et par hypothèse ces $n+1$ fonctions ne dépendent que de n variables indépendantes. Il y a donc une relation entre les premiers membres du système (6).

10. Ces premiers membres constituent $n+1$ fonctions de N variables indépendantes, qui sont $a, b, \ldots, \alpha$. En vertu du mémoire de JACOBI, la condition nécessaire et suffisante est bien connue pour qu'il y ait entre les premiers membres une relation indépendante de ces variables: il faut et il suffit que les déterminants fonctionnels de ces $n+1$ fonctions par rapport à $n+1$ quelconques des variables soient tous égaux à zéro.

Il suffit d'examiner l'un de ces déterminants à annuler, par exemple le déterminant

$$\begin{vmatrix} \mu_1'(a) & \ldots & J'(\alpha) \\ \mu_1''(a) & \ldots & J''(\alpha) \\ \ldots & \ldots & \ldots \\ \mu_1^{(n+1)}(a) & \ldots & J^{(n+1)}(\alpha) \end{vmatrix}$$

11. Pour que ce déterminant soit identiquement nul, il faut et il suffit qu'il y ait une même relation linéaire et homogène entre tous les éléments de chacune de ses lignes ou de chacune de ses colonnes. Or nous connaissons la relation de ce genre qui unit tous les éléments de chacune des n premières colonnes. Par exemple, pour la première, cette relation est, en vertu de (2):

$$A_0\mu_1'(a) + A_1\mu_1''(a) + \cdots + A_n\mu_1^{(n+1)}(a) = 0.$$

On a donc:

$$A_0J'(\alpha) + A_1J''(\alpha) + \cdots + A_nJ^{(n+1)}(\alpha) = 0;$$

autrement dit, α étant quelconque:

$$A_0J'(x) + A_1J''(x) + \cdots + A_nJ^{(n+1)}(x) = 0,$$

les $A_0, A_1, \cdots, A_n$ étant les *mêmes* que dans la caractéristique (4) commune aux fonctions $l_g(x)$.

12. De cet important résultat on déduit sans peine que

$$H(x) = e^{A' + B'x + \Sigma e^{r_i x} F_i(x)},$$

où les r_i sont les mêmes que dans les fonctions $l_g(x)$, et où les polynômes $F_i(x)$ jouent le même rôle que les polynômes $f_i(x)$, mais avec des paramètres différents.

Ainsi le problème est résolu, et dans l'expression de $H(x)$ interviennent encore $n+2$ paramètres, à savoir A', B', et les n paramètres des polynômes $F_i(x)$: ils serviront à poursuivre les identifications.

13. Je n'ai pas à insister, dans ce Congrès, sur les conséquences que la pratique actuarielle peut tirer de l'existence des fonctions $H(x)$. Pour n'en citer qu'une, on voit de suite la réduction des calculs d'annuités viagères sur N têtes, obéissant à N lois de survie distinctes, $l_g(x)$, du même ordre n: non seulement ces annuités se ramèneront à des annuités sur un nombre n de têtes, moindre que N; mais encore ces dernières têtes obéiront toutes, par des artifices appropriés, à une *unique* loi de survie, $H(x)$.

III.

De certaines lois "gompertziennes".

14. Avant de terminer, je ne crois pas oiseux de m'arrêter à une particularité de certaines fonctions $l_g(x)$. Cette particularité permet d'abréger considérablement la recherche de la fonction $H(x)$, en ce sens que la fonction $H(x)$, une fois trouvée pour un groupe de N fonctions $l_g(x)$, reste *la même* pour toute autre valeur de N.

La loi de GOMPERTZ est le premier exemple historique de cette particularité. Aussi ai-je cru pouvoir appeler jadis *gompertziennes* toutes les lois $l_g(x)$ qui présentent cette particularité, et *makehamiennes* toutes celles qui ne la présentent pas: ce second cas en effet est celui de la loi de MAKEHAM.

Je me bornerai ici à rechercher le caractère gompertzien des fonctions $l_g(x)$ dont la caractéristique (4) n'a pas de racines nulles: cette communication est déjà longue, et je ne veux pas l'étendre par le cas des racines nulles.

15. Enonçons d'abord un *lemme.*

Soient α et α' deux valeurs distinctes de α; calculons les quotients

$$\frac{H(\alpha'+t)}{H(\alpha')} \quad \text{et} \quad \frac{H(\alpha+t)}{H(\alpha)},$$

puis faisons le rapport de ces deux quotients.

Comme il est aisé de s'en convaincre, ce rapport est indépendant de B'.

16. Supposons maintenant que l'on ait déjà trouvé une fonction $H(x)$ telle que, pour une valeur déterminée de N, on ait:

$$(7) \qquad \frac{l_1(a+t)}{l_1(a)} \cdot \frac{l_2(b+t)}{l_2(b)} \cdots \frac{l_N(k+t)}{l_N(k)} = \frac{H(\alpha+t)}{H(\alpha)} \cdot \frac{H(\beta+t)}{H(\beta)} \cdots \frac{H(\theta+t)}{H(\theta)}.$$

Supposons que nous puissions continuer à employer *la même loi* $H(x)$ lorsque le premier membre contiendra une tête de plus, d'âge a', qui obéisse à une $(N+1)^e$

loi, $l_{N+1}(x)$, ayant la même caractéristique que les N premières lois. Dans ce cas-là, $l_{N+1}(x)$ aura le caractère gompertzien, c'est-à-dire que toutes les lois $l_g(x)$ intervenues auront ce caractère, si on convient de prendre d'une façon quelconque dans le premier membre de (7) les $N+1$ fonctions dont on s'occupe.

17. Sous le bénéfice de ces diverses restrictions, appellons α', β', ..., θ', ce que deviennent $\alpha, \beta, \ldots, \theta$ quand s'introduit la $(N+1)^e$ tête d'âge a'.

Par hypothèse on doit avoir :

$$(8) \quad \frac{l_1(a+t)}{l_1(a)} \cdot \frac{l_2(b+t)}{l_2(b)} \cdots \frac{l_N(k+t)}{l_N(k)} \cdot \frac{l_{N+1}(a'+t)}{l_{N+1}(a')} = \frac{H(\alpha'+t)}{H(\alpha')} \cdot \frac{H(\beta'+t)}{H(\beta')} \cdots \frac{H(\theta'+t)}{H(\theta')}$$

Divisons membre à membre l'équation (8) par l'équation (7).

Il restera dans le premier membre seulement

$$\frac{l_{N+1}(a'+t)}{l_{N+1}(a')} .$$

Dans le second membre il restera un produit de n rapports tels que celui de

$$\frac{H(\alpha'+t)}{H(\alpha')} \quad \text{à} \quad \frac{H(\alpha+t)}{H(\alpha)} .$$

Or, d'après le lemme, ces rapports sont indépendants de B'. Leur produit l'est aussi; en d'autres termes

$$\frac{l_{N+1}(a'+t)}{l_{N+1}(a')}$$

est indépendant de B'.

On en déduit, en faisant $a'=0$ et $t=x$, que $l_{N+1}(x)$ ne contient pas le terme en B qui figure dans l'expression générale (3) des $l_g(x)$, et qu'elle se borne à

$$l_{N+1}(x) = e^{A+\Sigma e^{r_i x} f_i(x)} .$$

18. Comme, du cas de $N+1$ fonctions, ou passerait de même au cas de $N+2$ fonctions, de $N+3$ fonctions, et ainsi de suite, on voit à quelle condition, dans les limites faites au cours de la démonstration, $H(x)$ reste la même quelle que soit N.

IV.

Conclusion.

19. Pour conclure, qu'on me permette de soumettre une réflexion à ceux de mes confrères du Congrès que ce modeste travail intéressera.

S'ils sont actuaires, ils observeront avec moi qu'il n'est pas indispensable, pour les fonctions $l_g(x)$, de représenter des nombres de vivants à l'âge x: elles peuvent représenter d'autres fonctions de cet âge, le taux de mortalité par exemple, etc., ou même à la fois diverses de ces fonctions.

S'ils se livrent à l'étude des mathématiques dans un but moins professionnel, ils se diront sans doute qu'il n'est pas non plus indispensable, pour la variable x, de représenter un âge: elle peut être quelconque, et les fonctions $l_g(x)$ ne sont pas restreintes à celles dont usent les assurances sur la vie.

Je m'estimerais alors très heureux que les uns et les autres trouvent ici la solution toute préparée d'une question susceptible de se présenter dans leurs recherches, à savoir: dans quelles circonstances un produit de N fonctions d'une variable (ou la somme de N fonctions, si l'on veut bien passer aux logarithmes des précédentes) peut être remplacé par le produit (ou la somme) d'un nombre n, inférieur à N, de fonctions convenablement choisies et identiques entre elles. Ces fonctions de remplacement offrent d'ailleurs des ressources étendues pour les simplifications de calculs, surtout si l'on rencontre le caractère que j'ai appelé « gompertzien ».

R. POUSSIN

SUR L'APPLICATION DU GRAPHICISME AUX CALCULS D'ASSURANCES

J'ai traité par ailleurs, en 1904, dans une thèse d'agrégation à l'Institut des Actuaires Français, « de l'application des procédés graphiques aux calculs d'assurance sur la vie » ([1]).

Le sujet m'avait été inspirée par la lecture d'une brochure do M. Quiquet, intitulée: *Sur 3 modes de réduction des assurances mixtes aux assurances en cas de décès.*

Une préference pour les solutions géométriques; le sentiment que j'ai eu, après quelques recherches, que la Géométrie apporterait à la science actuarielle, des procédés de calculs universels, je veux dire par là, applicables à toute loi de mortalité; la preuve que ces procédés comportaient une approximations suffisante quand ils étaient maniés avec quelque art du dessin. Tels sont les motifs d'origine de ma thèse et les raisons qui m'ont attaché au sujet qui est aujourd'hui soumis au présent Congrès.

J'ai notamment montré que la plupart des calculs de prix de revient de contrat et de réserves mathématiques, sont justiciables de solutions graphiques, quel que soit le sujet assuré (tête ou groupe de têtes).

On trouvera réunies dans un album spécialement composé pour le Congrès, les épures contenues dans ma thèse ainsi que les planches de la brochure de M. Quiquet ([2]).

J'ai classé les graphiques d'après les méthodes que j'ai employées: abaques et coordonnées parallèles de droites, statique graphique, intégration graphique, statique géométrique.

On remarque entre autres choses, l'usage qu'a été fait de la statique graphique pour la réduction des annuités sur plusieurs têtes à des annuités sur une seule ou sur un moindre nombre de têtes, pour la réduction des capitaux de survie à des capitaux simplement assurés en cas de décès, etc:

([1]) Éditeur Dulac, 8 Rue Lamartine, Paris.

([2]) Cet album fut présenté à Mrs les Congressistes.

C'est ce qui m'a toujours paru la partie la plus intéréssante de mon travail. Cette réduction d'ordre géométrique doit être rapprochée de la réduction d'ordre analytique fondée sur les lois particulières de Makeham. C'est une solution qui semble bien conforme à notre esprit français.

Je ne sais dans quelle mesure ces études ont déjà été utiles et quelles applications on en a faites.

J'ai recherché pour le présent Congrès quel problème aurait été laissé en dehors des exemples traités en 1904. On trouvera peut être quelque intérêt à l'application que je vais indiquer ci après, de la statique graphique aux assurances dotales avec contre-assurance des primes versées.

On sait que ce contrat comporte pour l'assureur l'engagement de payer à l'échéance un capital fixé, si la tête assurée est vivante, ou de rembourser les primes versées si cette tête décède avant l'expiration du contrat. C'est une assurance dotale parce que la tête assurée est une tête d'enfant, que la duréee est choisie de telle façon que le capital assuré ait le caractère d'une dot et que le contrat est généralement souscrit par un père de famille qui paie les primes.

Soit x l'âge du père, y l'âge de l'enfant, au début du contrat, n la durée du contrat et m le capital assuré.

Soit Π le prix de revient pur du contrat — la prime unique — et α la prime annuelle commerciale payable pendant la durée commune des deux têtes X et Y, et au plus pendant n années.

Pour mettre le problème en équation, j'appliquerai ce que j'ai appelé la méthode directe (v. *Traité élémentaire des assurances sur la vie.* Paris 1906, Dulac éditeur, 8 Rue Lamartine). Je considère à cet effet une société élémentaire de $v_x . v_y$ contractants. Je groupe par échéances communes les recettes et les dépenses qu'elle apporte à l'assurance, et je prends les valeurs à une même époque, des unes et des autres par le moyen des commutations. En conduisant ensuite convenablement les calculs, on pourra mettre le résultat sous une forme simple susceptible d'une solution graphique.

$$|v_x v_y \Pi| = |\alpha\, d_y v_x| + |2\alpha\, d_{y+1} . v_{y+1} + \alpha\, d_{y+1} . dx| + \cdots$$
$$\cdots + |n\alpha\, d_{y+n-1} . v_{x+n-1} + (n-1)\,\alpha\, d_{y+n-1} . v_{x+n-2} + \cdots| + |m . v_{y+n} . v_x| .$$

Soit, en prenant les commutations par rapport à Y

$$(1) \quad v_x . D_y . \Pi = \left| \begin{array}{l} C_y . v_x \\ 2\, C_{y+1} . v_{x+1} + C_{y+1} . d_x \\ \cdot\ \cdot\ \cdot\ \cdot\ \cdot\ \cdot\ \cdot\ \cdot\ \cdot \\ nC_{y+n-1} . v_{x+n-1} + (n-1)\, C_{y+n-1} . v_{x+n-2} + \cdots + C_{y+n-1} . d_x \end{array} \right| + m . D_{y+n} . v_x$$

D'autre part, en désignant par f le chargement, et par p la fraction de prime utile, frais d'encaissement déduit, on peut écrire

$$(2) \qquad \Pi + f = p . \alpha (1 + a_{xy}^{(n-1)}) .$$

En éliminant Π entre les équations (1) et (2) on tirera α.

On peut transformer comme suit:

$$v_x . D_y . \Pi = \alpha \begin{vmatrix} C_y . v_x \\ C_{y+1} . v_x + C_{y+1} . v_{x+1} \\ . \quad . \quad . \quad . \quad . \quad . \quad . \quad . \quad . \quad . \\ C_{y+n-1} . v_x + C_{y+n-1} . v_{x+1} + \cdots + C_{y+n-1} . v_{x+n-1} \end{vmatrix} + m D_{y+n} . v_x$$

$$= \alpha [(M_y - M_{y+n}) . v_x + (M_{y+1} - M_{y+n-1}) . v_{x+1} + \cdots + (M_{y+n-1} - M_{y+n}) v_{x+n-1}] + m D_{y+n} . v_x$$

$$= \alpha [M_y v_x + M_{y+1} v_{x+1} + \cdots + M_{y+n-1} v_{x+n-1} - M_{y+n} (v_x + \cdots + v_{x+n-1})] . + m D_{y+n} . v_x$$

Sous cette forme, il est aisé de voir que la statique graphique permet de déterminer une quantité K_y^n telle que

$$M_y v_x + M_{y+1} v_{x+1} + \cdots + M_{y+n-1} v_{x+n-1} = K_y^n (v_x + v_{x+1} + \cdots + v_{x+n-1}) .$$

La relation prend alors la forme suivante:

$$\Pi = \alpha . \frac{K_y^n - M_{y+n}}{D_y} \cdot \frac{v_x + v_{x+1} + \cdots + v_{x+n-1}}{v_x} + m \cdot \frac{D_{y+n}}{D_y}$$

ce qu'on peut encore écrire

$$\Pi = \frac{D_{y+n}}{D_y} \left[\alpha . \frac{K_y^n - M_{y+n}}{D_{y+n}} \cdot \left(\frac{1}{2} + m_x^{(n)} \right) + m \right]$$

$m_x^{(m)}$ est la vie moyenne temporaire, le calcul en est facile.

En dressant d'ailleurs une table de population donnant des nombres L_x tels que $L_x = v_x + v_{x+1} + \cdots + v_\omega$, si ω est l'âge limite de la table, on a

$$\frac{1}{2} + m_x^{(n)} = \frac{L_x - L_{x+n}}{v_x} .$$

La statique graphiue donnera le rapport

$$\frac{K_y^n - M_{y+n}}{D_{y+n}} .$$

On disposera la figure ainsi qu'il est indiqué d'autre part.

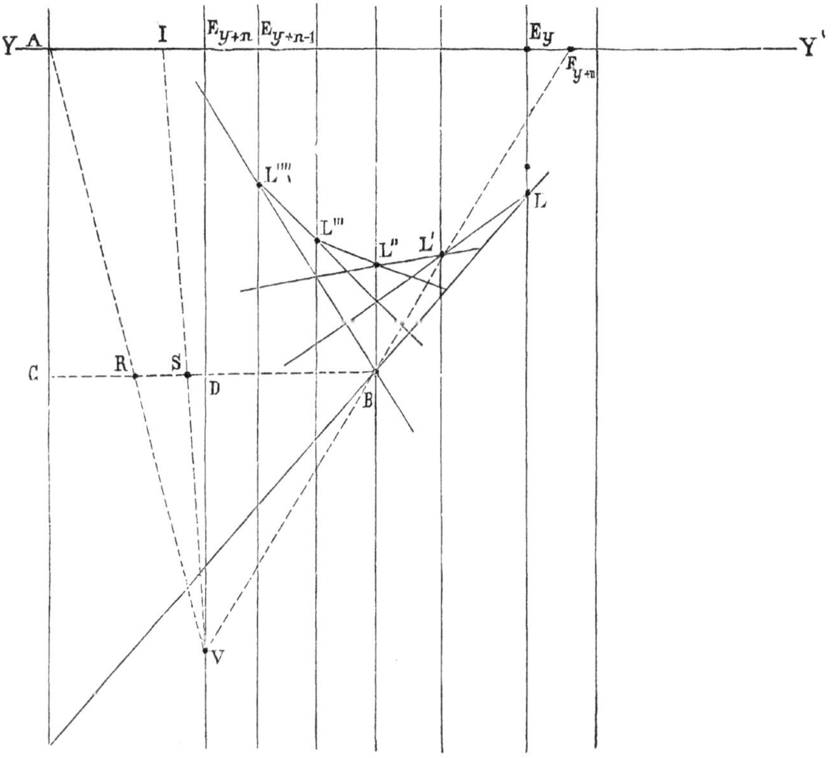

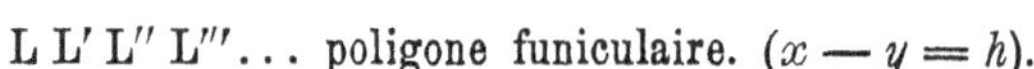
L L' L'' L'''... poligone funiculaire. ($x - y = h$).

$AE_{y+n} = M_{y+n}$ $\qquad E_{y+n}\, F_{y+n} = D_{y+n}$

$BD = K_y^n - M_{y+n}$ $\qquad AI = 1$

$$RS = \frac{K_y^n - M_{y+n}}{D_{y+n}}$$

V point d'intérsection de $F_{y+n}B$ et de la verticale E_{y+n}

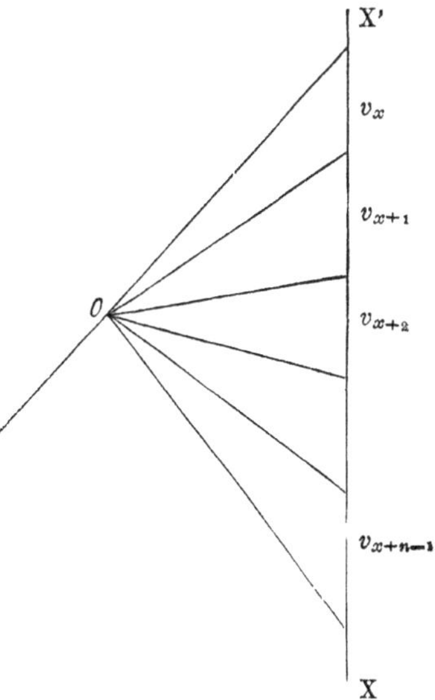

Sur un axe vertical XX′, on portera à une échelle convenable, à la suite les unes des autres, des longueurs $v_\omega\ v_{\omega-1} \ldots v_x \ldots$ en restant dans les limites des âges qu'on rencontre en pratique. On tracera le dynamique en choisissant un pôle O de façon que les rayons soient convenablement disposés.

Sur un axe horizontal YY′, on portera, à partir d'une même origine A, des longueurs représentant

$$M_y\ M_{y+1} \ldots M_{y+n} \ldots \quad \text{telles que} \quad AE_{y+n} = M_{y+n}.$$

On tracera par chacun des points E ainsi obtenus sur l'axe YY′, des parallèles à XX′. Choisissant alors une différence d'âges $x - y$ (35 ans, par exemple), on tracera le polygone funiculaire correspondant.

Pour cette différence d'âges. $x - y$, le même polygone servira quel que soit l'âge initial y et quelle que soit la durée n du contrat. On tracera d'autres polygones pour d'autres différences d'âges, 25 et 45 : quand la différence d'âges ne coincidera pas avec celle du tracé, on solutionnera le problème pour la différence la plus proche, ou pour deux valeurs situées de part et d'autre, l'une par défaut, l'autre par excès, et on intérpolera les résultats.

Pour chaque groupe de valeurs y et n, on trouvera le point B à l'intérsection des côtés du polygone funiculaire numérotés y et $y + n$. C'est le sommet de fermeture du polygone convenant à ces valeurs extrèmes, pour une différence $x - y$ donnée

$$K_y^n = BC\,, \quad \text{lu sur une parallèle à YY}'$$

$$K_y^n - M_{y+n} = BD.$$

Pour obtenir facilement $\dfrac{K_y^n - M_{y+n}}{D_{y+n}}$, on portera sur YY′, en une graduation convenable, des points F_{y+n} tels que $E_{y+n}\,F_{y+n} = D_{y+n}$. Dans ces conditions, si AI représente l'unitè, en tirant

$$F_{y+n}\,BV \quad , \quad VA \text{ et } VI$$

RS mesurera, à l'échelle AI, le rapport $\dfrac{K_y^n - M_{y+n}}{D_{y+n}}$.

On lira RS, en déplaçant convenablement, une échelle graduée, tenue parallelement à YY′, sans qu'on ait besoin de tracer BC.

Ce tracé ne comporte que des droites. Il est donc d'une construction commode En outre les âges x et y restent en pratique inclus dans des limites assez resserrées.

Les polygones n'ont, de ce fait, qu'un petit nombre de côtés. On peut, par suite, agrandir les échelles et obtenir une grande précision.

Enfin, les rétultats varient peu avec la différeuce $x - y$ et il suffira de tracer 2 ou 3 polygones pour résoudre tous les cas possibles.

Il m'a semblé qu'il y avait là un ensemble de circonstances de nature à justifier cette nouvelle applications des méthodes graphiques.

W. PALIN ELDERTON

A COMPARISON OF SOME CURVES USED FOR GRADUATING CHANCE-DISTRIBUTIONS

I.

Introductory.

The object by any system of frequency curves is to explain the facts that have been collected about a variety of subjects connected with chance. The system is useless if it does not give approximately the distributions that actually occur. The binomial series is justified from this point of view as a description of the number of times events happen because we have found from experience that the numbers given by it are realised approximately by trial. When one considers the matter one is almost compelled to admit that the real justification of any theory of probability is that events happen in the way such a theory leads one to expect, and it seems to the present writer that if one wishes to compare the systems of frequency curves that have been suggested in recent years it should be done not only by examining the ways in which they have been derived but also by seeing what classes of distributions they represent and by noticing carefully the cases of failure and the difficulties of application. One is hardly justified in describing a curve as « empirical » because it has not been derived from the binomial series, or because some assumption having the sanction of history (such as the independence of elementary cause groups) has been discarded.

Since, however, we know from experience that the binomial actually represents the simplest type of probability it is natural to start from it and it is doubtless right to treat it or its limit as a part of any system; it must in fact be a special case of any more general type that may be evolved.

One can proceed either by building up a curve on assumptions which it seems natural to adopt or by taking a more complex series than the binomial (e. g. the hypergeometrical); and in either case an expression might be reached having greater generality than the binomial. But it must be remembered that the ultimate justification of any evolved formula rests, not so much on the accuracy of its mathematical developements, as in its breadth of application to statistics which may reasonably be described as « chance distributions ». Such application is, I think, an important test of the fundamental assumptions that were adopted in reaching the formula, for it must be admitted that the plausibility of one's initial statements would be a poor defence of a curve which broke down whenever it was put to a practical test.

The well known « probability curve » or « normal curve of error », $y = e^{-x^2}$, was, of course, a first step towards finding a simple frequency curve, but though it works well as a description of the binomial $(p + q)^n$ when p is approximately equal to q or when n is large, it is unsatisfactory in other cases. In actuarial work these cases frequently arise. At the ages attained by the majority of lives assured in any assurance office the rate of mortality or probability of a person dying in a year is small, and the frequency distribution giving the number of deaths happening in successive years out of 50 cases, say, when $q = \cdot 02$ and $p = \cdot 98$ would not be satisfactorily described by the normal curve of error. It is, of course, true in a sense that the normal curve is a « law of great numbers » but it is clear that if it can only deal with cases resting on such a basis it cannot have a large sphere of action in practical statistics and it can hardly be expected to be of value when one has to deal with series more like the hypergeometrical than the binomial.

It is the failure of the « normal curve » to describe the majority of cases that has led to the work of PEARSON, THIELE, CHARLIER, EDGEWORTH, BRUNS, KAPTEYN and others and the curves suggested by these writers are of considerable interest to all students of statistical mathematics. The present paper is an attempt to show how far some of these curves fit the statistics that arise in practice; how far, in fact, they graduate the rough figures obtained from the collected facts, and where they will break down.

Before proceeding, however to this point it will be necessary to mention our methods of curve fitting and to enumerate briefly the suggested types. We may also mention an old difficulty in practical work of the nature of that with which we are now concerned namely, that statistics are seldom obtained from strictly homogeneous material. This fact must be taken as one of the typical elements in practice and if a series can graduate in spite of a small amount of heterogeneity it is, from some points of view, all the more valuable in much of the work that comes to the hands of an actuary or statistician.

II.

Method of Moments.

In fitting the curves we shall in all cases use PEARSON's Method of Moments as it is a general method capable of being used with all the systems we shall examine and is known to give good results from the statistical point of view.

The method may be ontlined as follows:

If $y = f(x)$ be the equation to a curve which it is required to fit to a particular statistical distribution then the method of moments consists of equating the algebraic or trigonometric expressions for

$$\int f(x)\,dx \qquad \text{(the total frequency)}$$

$$\int f(x)\,x\,dx$$

$$\int f(x)\,x^2\,dx \qquad \text{etc.}$$

to the corresponding numerical values obtained from the particular statistical distribution with which we are dealing. The solution of these equations gives the constants in $y = f(x)$ and enables us to graduate the distributions under examination.

III.

Curves dealt with.

We may now summarize the curves with which we propose to deal in the following notes.

I) K. Pearson's system.

This system is derived from the equation

$$\frac{1}{y} \cdot \frac{dy}{dx} = \frac{x + a}{b_0 + b_1 x + b_2 x^2}$$

which was first given in the Philosophical transactions of the Royal Society, vol. 186 A. He there derived it by considering the slope relation of a hypergeometrical series.

The following are the types of curves resulting from the solution of the differential equation:

Type I . . . . $y_0\left(1 + \frac{x}{a_1}\right)^{\nu a_1}\left(1 - \frac{x}{a_2}\right)^{\nu a_2}$ with range from $-a_1$ to $+a_2$

Type II . . . . $y_0\left(1 - \frac{x^2}{a^2}\right)^m$ with range from $-a$ to $+a$

Type III. . . . $y_0\left(1 + \frac{x}{a}\right)^{\gamma a} e^{-\gamma x}$ with range from $-a$ to ∞

Type IV. . . . $y_0\left(1 + \frac{x^2}{a^2}\right)^{-m} e^{-\nu \tan^{-1}\frac{x}{a}}$ with range from $-\infty$ to ∞

Type V . . . . $y_0\, x^{-p}\, e^{-\frac{\gamma}{x}}$ with range from 0 to ∞

Type VI. . . . $y_0(x - a)^{q_2}\, x^{-q_1}$ with range from a to ∞

Type VII . . . $y_0\left(1 + \frac{x^2}{a^2}\right)^{-m}$ with rang from $-\infty$ to $+\infty$

Type VIII . . . $y_0\, e^{-\frac{x^2}{2\sigma^2}}$ with range from $-\infty$ to $+\infty$

(Normal curve of error).

It will be noticed that the last equation in this list comes at once from the fundamental differential equation when $b_1 = b_2 = 0$. The other types are reached with various values for b_0 b_1 and b_2, Pearson has given criteria based on the moments showing when each curve should be used.

II) T. N. THIELE's suggestions.

$$F(x) = A_0 \Phi(x) + A_3 \Phi'''(x) + A_4 \Phi^{IV}(x) + \cdots$$

where $\Phi(x) = \frac{1}{\sqrt{2\pi}\,\sigma} e^{-(x-b)^2/2\sigma^2}$ is given on p. 18 of THIELE's interesting *Theory of Observations* (London, 1903) (¹).

III) C. V. L. CHARLIER has developed and used the equation given above (THIELE) which he calls type A and has also taken a type B

$$F(x) = B_0 \psi(x) + B_1 \Delta\psi(x) + B_2 \Delta^2 \psi(x) + \cdots$$

$$\text{where } \psi(x) = \frac{e^{-\lambda} \sin \pi x}{\pi} \left[\frac{1}{x} - \frac{\lambda}{1!(x-1)} + \frac{\lambda^2}{2!(x-2)} - \cdots \right].$$

In the limit when x is an integer this form becomes $\frac{e^{-\lambda} \lambda^x}{x!}$. CHARLIER has devoted a considerable amount of work to these types of has dealt with them in a valuable series of memoirs in one of which (*Researches into the theory of Probability*, Lund 1906) he has given a number of numerical examples and has made many interesting and useful suggestions. BRUNS has also worked on Type A.

IV) F. Y. EDGEWORTH has used a modified form of Type A which he has derived by various methods in a paper published in the transactions of the Cambridge Philosophical Society 1905 (*Law of Error*). In a paper read before the Royal Statistical Society in 1906 as *The Generalised Law of Error* he has dealt with some further aspects and the question and has given details of the application with examples (²). The equation he found was

$$e^{-k_1 \frac{1}{3!}\left(\frac{d}{dx}\right)^3 + k_2 \frac{1}{4!}\left(\frac{d}{dx}\right)^4 - \cdots} \left[\frac{1}{\sqrt{2\pi}\,\sigma} e^{-\frac{x^2}{2\sigma^2}} \right].$$

(¹) The subject had previonaly been discussed by THIELE in *Forelaesninger over Almindelig Iagttagelselslaere*. Copenhagen 1889.

(²) Edgeworth had previonsly (1899) suggested other methods; for instance « the method of translation », which has recently been advocated by J. C. KAPTEYN in much the same form. It is not proposed to deal with this method on the present occasion.

We may now proceed to examine the graduation capacities of (1) the PEARSON-type (2) the THIELE — BRUNS — CHARLIER curve which we shall for brevity call Type A (3) the CHARLIER Type B (4) the EDGEWORTH curve.

IV.

Numerical Examples.

EXAMPLE I.

(Symmetrical curve not capable of satisfactory graduation by the normal curve of error).

Observations	PEARSON'S Type II	Type A	EDGEWORTH	Normal Curve
11	14	15	16	20
116	109	106	106	95
274	286	284	285	270
451	433	437	436	456
432	433	437	436	456
267	285	283	284	270
116	109	106	106	95
16	14	15	16	20

In this case all the curves except the normal give excellent graduations. We have not used type B because CHARLIER apparently only adopts it when Type A is unsuccessful. He does not give a statistical criterion to show when A or B should be used and it is difficult to see how such a criterion can be evolved. The solution of his Type A does not lead to imaginary quantities when Type B should have been used, in the way that PEARSON'S Type I (e. g.) does when it is inapplicable. In reaching Type A and the EDGEWORTH graduations we have used the terms involving A_4 and k_2 respectively.

EXAMPLE II.

(A distribution which is not markedly skew).

Observations	PEARSON'S Type III	Type A	EDGEWORTH
3	4	5	4
20	17	22	17
38	42	47	42
63	59	60	59
51	53	50	53
29	33	27	32
21	15	13	15
4	5	4	6
0	1.4	1	2
1	0.4		1

In each case 3 moments have been used; i. e. we have omitted the A_3 and k_2 terms in Type A and EDGEWORTH. The observations and EDGEWORTH graduation are taken from EDGEWORTH's paper *The Generalised Law of Error.* Type A is the least successful

EXAMPLE III.

(A distinctly skew distribution).

Observations	PEARSON's Type I	Type A	Type B	EDGEWORTH
—	—	— 2	—	1
—	—	4	—	9
—	2	15	12	30
64	67	38	64	64
116	116	71	104	102
140	138	108	129	130
145	139	137	134	135
134	128	148	128	130
106	110	135	116	111
82	89	108	93	92
72	69	78	73	73
49	51	54	53	53
37	35	37	36	36
25	24	27	25	20
13	15	18	14	10
10	9	12	10	4
5	5	7	5	—
2	2	4	2	—
0.4	1	2	1	—

This example is abstracted from Biometrika, vol. V, p. 209. PEARSON's figures come from his *Chances of Death* and EDGEWORTH's from his *Generalised Law of Error.* Clearly PEARSON's Type I is the best and Type B the next best graduation. We do not think CHARLIER would use Type A in such a case. In fitting his Type B there are however many difficulties owing to the fact that he gives us four approximate methods of application; this is an objection which may be surmounted in the future but makes Type B awkward at present. The other point to be noticed in these Graduations are the negative frequency in Type A of the 40 cases in EDGEWORTH's graduation which have no cases corresponding to them in the data. EDGEWORTH however has remarked that he only aims at the main body of the curve and does not much concern himself with the tails, but one cannot help feeling that the main body must be understated if the tail possesses an excess of 40 out of 1000 cases.

Example IV.

(J. shaped curve).

Observations	Pearson	Type B
133	136.9	134.9
55	48.5	51.6
23	22.6	22.5
7	9.6	9.5
2	3.4	2.9
2	.8	.6

The type B curve is given by Charlier in *Researches into the theory of probability* and Pearson gave his graduation in the Phil. Trans. paper already cited. The type B curve gives a slightly better graduation but the agreement is close in both cases. Type A and Edgeworth's curve would be unsuitable.

Example V.

(Series which is nearly symmetrical).

Observations	Pearson Type IV	Type A	Edgeworth
10	6	4	3
13	16	14	10
41	49	46	34
115	135	126	110
326	321	306	298
675	653	637	662
1113	1108	1108	1164
1528	1535	1563	1603
1692	1712	1753	1747
1530	1522	1548	1510
1122	1074	1075	1024
611	604	589	571
255	274	256	263
86	102	92	104
26	32	29	37
8	8	7	12
2	2	2	2
1	1	1	1
1	—	—	—

Example VI.

(Distribution having two maxima).

Data	Pearson's Type II	Type A	Edgeworth
10	3	26	4
78	96	74	34
193	191	156	135
286	261	262	270
303	304	354	363
291	319	390	390
303	304	354	363
286	261	262	270
193	191	156	135
78	96	74	34
10	3	26	4

This is an imaginary example giving a double-humped distribution. It was formed from Charlier's type A by putting $A_3 = 0$ and $A_4 = \cdot 09$; the tables given by Charlier then enabled us, by taking suitable differences, to form the series

$-4, \quad -19, \quad -53, \quad -76, \quad +103, \quad +783, \quad +1929, \quad +2855, \quad +3026, \quad +2912$ etc.

Negative frequencies, wich are meaningless, were discarded and the data cutdown and graduated. The interesting feature is that Type A from which the data were formed gives a poor agreement. This is due to the negative frequencies and the integration for moments from $-\infty$ to $+\infty$. Negative frequencies are somewhat objectionable in themselves; they are still more objectionable when they influence curve fitting to the large extent shown in this example.

The only way I can suggest at present for overcoming the difficulty of the limits of integration is that a normal curve should be calculated and the ratios of the original figures to those of this normal curve could then be graduated by $a + bx + cx^2 + \cdots$. Any limits could be assigned but the process would appear arbitrary and would mean that Charlier's expansion into $\Phi(x)$ and its differential coefficients was discarded or, at any rate, concealed.

Example VII.

We have remarked that there is a difficulty in choosing a solution to Type B but one can compare its graduation power with those of other formulae by an alternative method. In his *Researches into the theory of probability* Charlier gives a table which enables us to see the values that can arise with Type B and it is interesting to abstract a few of these in order to see its possible range of application. We have already noticed that a J shaped curve can be produced and we can now glance at the less extreme abnormalities. For comparison I have added examples of PEARSON's Type III though it must not be supposed that either set is meant to give the closest agreement with the other that it would be possible to make; they have merely been, taken to give an idea of the range of application

Type B			Pearson's Type III		
I	II	III	I	II	III
368	111	45	387	63	31
368	244	140	386	279	149
184	268	217	160	285	230
61	197	224	47	189	218
15	108	173	15	102	160
3	48	107	4	49	101
1	18	55	1	21	56
—	6	25	—	9	29
—	2	10	—	3	14
—	—	3	—	—	6
—	—	1	—	—	3
—	—	—	—	—	1

V.

Conclusions.

The few examples we have given will be of help in bringing out the comparison of the types of curves with which we have been dealing.

The PEARSON-type curves will graduate satisfactorily all the examples we have taken but cannot reproduce the double hump of our imaginary data (Example VI). They will graduate symmetrical, slightly skew and very skew distributions and also J and U shaped distributions. They have been fitted in very various circumstances and are certainly satisfactory from the point of view of agreement. The arithmetic involved is however often heavy and there are no auxiliary tables such as those given by CHARLIER for Type A; the curves are however the most useful of those now considered.

Type A gives numerically the least work but it does not graduate satisfactorily very skew nor J and U shaped distributions and it has therefore a comparatively small vogue. If however it is combined with Type B as CHARLIER suggests, J shaped and skew distributions, can be graduated. We have found some difficulty in applying Type B, for CHARLIER does not give one much help in deciding which of his four methods of fitting should be followed in a particular case, and we feel that the graduation capacity of this type may be greater than our trials with it justify us in thinking at present. It would clearly be impossible to improve on its graduation in Example IV but Example III and two examples given by CHARLIER in his *Researches into the theory of Probability* are less fortunate. As however CHARLIER has, we gather, some further work in hand in connection with Type B it will be well to wait with interest for this and merely content ourselves with mentioning the difficulties we have found in the hope that he may be able to remove them.

EDGEWORTH's curve can, roughly speaking, graduate the same distributions as Type A.

We may now refer to two difficulties in connection with EDGEWORTH's curve and with Type A respectively which have already been mentioned. In Example III we found that 40 out of 1000 in EDGEWORTH's graduation have no observations corresponding to them and we remarked that it seemed a large excess; the reproduction of the exact number of observations is not only of practical necessity but is assumed by the method of moments which EDGEWORTH himself uses. If therefore a large number of cases falls outside the observations altogether we must either say that the total frequency is not reproduced or that the frequencies are misplaced; in either case the main body must be artificially reduced below the amount shown in the original data. In slightly skew distributions the frequencies are satisfactorily reproduced and many of the graduations of such material are excellent but the method can hardly be considered satisfactory as a general formula until some method of overcoming the difficulty mentioned above has been found.

The difficulty in connection with Type A is the large part that negative frequencies play in some of the less symmetrical graduations. If one gets a negative frequency has one overstated the positive frequencies? Of course, the defence of such negatives is that further terms of the series would put it right, but it is hard to see how one is justified in basing much argument on constants derived from the higher moments which have large, almost overwhelming, probable errors. It is also unsatisfactory that a curve cannot reproduce itself even approximately and the disappointing result of our example VI makes one wonder if it would not be well to consider such cases as relating to heterogeneous material and therefore more suitable for representation by two or more superimposed curves ([1]). If one could integrate CHARLIER's Type A or EDGEWORTH's curve from $-a$ to ∞ instead of from $-\infty$ to ∞ one could doubtless get over the difficulties to some extent, but, failing that, it would seem necessary to limit the range of applicability to the less abnormal distributions.

([1]) We are doubtful if it is statistically possible ever to produce a double hump with Type A or EDGEWORTH's curve if the ordinary $-\infty$ to ∞ integration is performed, because the relative values of the second and fourth moments required by the coefficient in the formula would seem impossible.

In putting forward these notes which show, I think, that of the curves considered here those of Karl Pearson are the most useful in practical work, I wish to express the hope that others may investigate the relative capacities of various curves from the point of view of graduation. I would suggest that an extensive investigation of such a kind would not only enable the statistician to appreciate the relative merits of alternative systems, but might also, by pointing to the failures in practice, indicate the weak places in the initial assumptions from which the curves were evolved, and so help the mathematician studying the theories of error to see the lines on which it is most likely that practical results will be obtained.

G. BOHLMANN

DIE GRUNDBEGRIFFE DER WAHRSCHEINLICHKEITSRECHNUNG IN IHRER ANWENDUNG AUF DIE LEBENSVERSICHERUNG

Die Aufgabe, die sich der vorliegende Artikel stellt, ist:

« Ein System von Annahmen und Sätzen aufzustellen, aus denen die Rechnungsregeln der Lebensversicherung folgen ».

Die Fragestellung ist also einerseits aus dem Erfahrungsgebiete des « Aktuars » gegriffen, bietet aber anderseits, wie ich hoffe, durch ihre Beziehungen zur allgemeinen Wahrscheinlichkeitslehre gerade auch für den reinen Mathematiker Interesse. Zum ersten Male habe ich ein derartiges System von Annahmen und Sätzen in meinem Encyklopädieartikel über Lebensversicherung (1) vom Jahre 1901 kurz zusammengestellt, dessen Entwurf dem Pariser internationalen Kongress der Aktuare vom Jahre 1900 vorgelegt wurde. Es handelt sich also hier um eine genauere Darlegung und Begründung des dort skizzierten Standpunktes, und ich ergreife um so lieber die Gelegenheit dies zu tun, als gerade neuerdings in einer Dissertation von U. Broggi (2) der auf die allgemeine Wahrscheinlichkeit bezügliche Teil der Aufgabe von einem Gesichtspunkt aus behandelt ist. Diese Arbeit hat mir Veranlassung gegeben, mein obenerwähntes System von Annahmen und Sätzen noch einmal durchzuprüfen und an einigen Stellen, die der Kundige leicht bemerken wird, zu verbessern. Im Wesentlichen aber habe ich den in meinem Encyklopädieartikel eingenommenen Standpunkt beibehalten, nach dem in der *Definition* der Wahrscheinlichkeit das Schema der günstigen und möglichen Fälle ganz aufgegeben wird.

Dagegen gebe ich darin Herrn Broggi vollständig Recht, dass eine mathematische Begründung der Wahrscheinlichkeitsrechnung durch eine logische Analyse des Ereignisbegriffs ergänzt werden muss. Es ist dies eine Aufgabe für den Philosophen, speziell für den Vertreter der formalen Logik, die sich vermutlich dank der modernen Entwickelung dieser Disciplin mit ganz anderer Schärfe und Sicherheit jetzt in Angriff nehmen liesse als es in früheren Zeiten möglich war.

(1) *Encyklopädie der mathematischen Wissenschaften*, Leipzig 1898-1904, Bd. I, Teil 2, Artikel I D 4*b*.

(2) U. Broggi, *Die Axiome der Wahrscheinlichkeitsrechnung* (Göttingen 1907).

Dass im Anfang der folgenden Arbeit und gelegentlich später die Wiederholung sehr bekannter Dinge nicht immer vermieden werden konnte, liegt in der Natur der Aufgabe. Wir bitten daher den Leser dieses zu entschuldigen. Andererseits sind öfters, wo es sich nicht um den systematischen Aufbau, sondern um Beispiele handelte, schon im allgemeinen Teil Fragen aus der Lebensversicherung oder verwandten Gebieten zur Illustration herbeigezogen.

ERSTES KAPITEL.

Grundlagen der allgemeinen Wahrscheinlichkeitslehre.

§ 1.

Ein einzelnes Ereignis.

1. Definition und Addition der Wahrscheinlichkeiten. — Von den Ereignissen oder Tatbeständen, die wir ins Auge fassen, postulieren wir, dass ihnen eine durch eine Zahl messbare Wahrscheinlichkeit zukommt, welche die im Folgenden aufgestellten Forderungen erfüllt.

Axiom I. Die Wahrscheinlichkeit dafür, dass das Ereignis E eintritt (kurz «die Wahrscheinlichkeit von E») ist eine positive Zahl p, die E zugeordnet ist.

Axiom II. p ist 1, wenn das Eintreten von E gewiss ist.

Axiom III. Das Eintreten von E_1 und das von E_2 (kurz «E_1 und E_2») mögen sich ausschliessen. Ist dann p_1 die Wahrscheinlichkeit von E_1, p_2 die Wahrscheinlichkeit von E_2, so ist

$$p_1 + p_2$$

die Wahrscheinlichkeit, dass entweder E_1 oder E_2 eintritt.

Satz I. Ist q die Wahrscheinlichkeit, dass E nicht eintritt (kurz die Wahrscheinlichkeit von «Nicht-E»), so ist

$$p + q = 1.$$

Nicht-E, das kontradiktorische Gegenteil von E, wird in der Folge durch E' bezeichnet. Da in der Gleichung von Satz I weder p noch q negativ sind, so folgt:

Satz II. Die Zahl p liegt immer zwischen 0 und 1.

Ist E unmöglich, so ist E′ gewiss, also $q = 1$, also $p = 0$. Es folgt daher:

Satz III. Ist ein Ereignis unmöglich, so ist seine Wahrscheinlichkeit 0.

Axiom II und Satz III lassen sich nicht umkehren (Nr. 3).

Wiederholte Anwendung von Axiom III führt zu:

Satz IV. Es seien:

$$E_1, E_2, E_3 \ldots$$

eine endliche Zahl von Ereignissen, die sich gegenseitig ausschliessen, und

$$p_1, p_2, p_3 \ldots$$

die zugehörigen Wahrscheinlichkeiten. Dann ist

$$p_1 + p_2 + p_3 + \cdots$$

die Wahrscheinlichkeit, dass entweder E_1 oder E_2 oder E_3 oder eins der übrigen Ereignisse eintritt.

2. Das Schema der günstigen und möglichen Fälle. — Es seien

$$E_1, E_2, \ldots E_m$$

m sich ausschliessende Ereignisse oder « Fälle », von denen einer eintreten muss. Das Ereignis E, dessen Wahrscheinlichkeit p zu bestimmen ist, möge dann eintreten, wenn einer der Fälle

$$E_1, E_2, \ldots E_g$$

eintritt (günstige Fälle), dagegen dann nicht, wenn einer der Fälle

$$E_{g+1}, E_{g+2} \ldots E_m$$

eintritt. Ist p_k die Wahrscheinlichkeit von E_k, so liefert Satz IV der Nr. 1:

$$p_1 + p_2 + p_3 + \cdots + p_g = p$$

$$p_1 + p_2 + p_3 + \cdots + p_m = 1.$$

Die Hypothese der sogenannten « Gleichmöglichkeit » besteht dann darin, dass man die Wahrscheinlichkeiten p_k als einander gleich annimmt. Dann liefert die letzte Gleichung:

$$p_1 = p_2 \ldots = p_m = \frac{1}{m}$$

und die vorletzte

$$p = \frac{g}{m}.$$

Es ergiebt sich also nach unserem Standpunkte als Folgerung:

Satz V. Hat man m sich ausschliessende und alle Möglichkeiten erschöpfenden Fälle, und setzt man diese als gleich «möglich» oder «wahrscheinlich» voraus, so ist die Wahrscheinlichkeit eines Ereignisses E, dass durch das Eintreten von g dieser Fälle charakterisiert ist, gleich dem Quotienten $\frac{g}{m}$ der günstigen und möglichen Fälle.

3. **Wahrscheinlichkeiten im einfach ausgedehnten Continuum.** — Wir denken uns auf einer Graden die Punkte (x) durch ihre Entfernungen x vom Nullpunkt bestimmt und nehmen an, die Wahrscheinlichkeit, dass (x) zwischen zwei gegebenen Punkten (a) und (b) liegt, sei eine Funktion von a und b allein:

$$\Phi(a, b).$$

Diese Funktion kann — auch abgesehen davon, dass ihre Werte zwischen 0 und 1 liegen müssen — nicht willkürlich gewählt werden. Sei, um die Ideen zu fixieren, $a < b$, und $c > b$ ein dritter Punkt der Graden. Dann folgt aus Axiom III:

$$\Phi(a, c) = \Phi(a, b) + \Phi(b, c).$$

Hieraus folgt

$$\Phi(b, c) = \Phi(c) - \Phi(b),$$

wo $\Phi(x)$ nur noch von x abhängt. Ist umgekehrt diese Bedingung erfüllt, so wird dem Axiom III Genüge geleistet.

Für das Gebiet der Anwendungen, die wir hier im Auge haben, können wir — ohne der Allgemeinheit zu schaden — $\Phi(x)$ als differentierbar voraussetzen. Ist $\varphi(x)$ der Differential-Quotient, so kann dieser nicht negativ sein, und man gewinnt die bequeme Integraldarstellung:

$$\Phi(a, b) = \int_a^b \varphi(x)\, dx.$$

Daher wird die Wahrscheinlichkeit, dass (x) genau auf einen vorgeschriebenen Punkt (a) fällt:

$$\int_a^a \varphi(x)\, dx = 0,$$

obwohl dieser Fall logisch nicht unmöglich ist. Der Satz III der vorigen Nummer ist also nicht umkehrbar.

Ganz ähnlich kann man für das zweifach ausgedehnte Continuum aus dem Axiome III ableiten, dass die Wahrscheinlichkeit dafür, dass ein Punkt der Ebene (x, y) in einem gegebenen Rechteck G liegt, durch das Integral über dieses Rechteck

$$\iint_G \varphi(x, y)\, dx\, dy$$

gegeben ist und diese Darstellung wird durch die Grenzübergänge der Integralrechnung auf ein beliebig begrenztes Gebiet G ausgedehnt.

Ganz ebenso stellen sich die Betrachtungen für mehr als zwei Dimensionen. Wegen der prinzipiellen Grundlagen für Punktmengen, die weder endlich noch continuierlich sind — die wir im Folgenden nicht brauchen — verweisen wir auf U. Broggi's Dissertation.

§ 2.

Zwei Ereignisse.

4. Grundlegende Gleichungen [1]. — Sei $E_1 E_2$ das Ereignis, das durch das Eintreten von E_1 und E_2 charakterisiert ist. Alsdann sind die vier sich ausschliessenden und erschöpfenden Möglichkeiten zu unterscheiden:

$$E_1 E_2\,,\ E_1 E_2'\,,\ E_1' E_2\,,\ E_1' E_2'\,.$$

Wir nehmen an, dass ihnen durch Zahlen messbare Wahrscheinlichkeiten zukommen und bezeichnen diese bezw. durch

$$p(1,1)\quad,\quad p(1,0)\quad,\quad p(0,1)\quad,\quad p(0,0),$$

sodass $p(\alpha, \beta)$ die Wahrscheinlichkeit bedeutet, dass E_1 α mal und E_2 β mal eintritt $(\alpha, \beta = 0, 1)$. Zwischen den vier Grössen besteht im Allgemeinen nur *eine* Relation, die aus Nr. 1 folgt:

$$p(1,1) + p(1,0) + p(0,1) + p(0,0) = 1\,. \tag{1}$$

[1] Diese finden sich bereits bei Poincaré, *Calcul des probabilités*. Paris, 1896, p. 12 ff. Sie konnten des Zusammenhangs wegen hier nicht fortbleiben.

Ist daher p_i die Wahrscheinlichkeit, dass E_i, q_i die dass E'_i eintritt, also

$$p_i + q_i = 1 \qquad i = 1, 2$$

so lassen sich die $p(\alpha, \beta)$ im Allgemeinen nicht durch p_1 und p_2 allein ausdrüken, denn sonst genügten die $p(\alpha, \beta)$ allgemein noch einer zweiten Relation, die sich durch Elimination von p_1 und p_2 ergäbe. Wohl aber bestimmen sich umgekehrt p_1 und p_2 durch die p auf Grund der Nr. 1:

$$(2) \qquad \begin{cases} p_1 = p(1,1) + p(1,0) \quad , \quad q_1 = p(0,1) + p(0,0) \\ p_2 = p(1,1) + p(0,1) \quad , \quad q_2 = p(1,0) + p(0,0) . \end{cases}$$

Ein Ereignis wie $E_1 E_2$ heisst ein « zusammengesetztes Ereignis ». Wir sehen, und dies gilt auch für mehr als zwei Ereignisse:

Während die üblichen Darstellungen der Wahrscheinlichkeitsrechnung die Wahrscheinlichkeiten zusammengesetzter Ereignisse aus denen der einfachen Ereignisse berechnen, liegt im allgemeinen Fall die Sache vielmehr umgekehrt. Erst müssen die Wahrscheinlichkeiten der zusammengesetzten Ereignisse definiert sein, ehe man die der einfachen Ereignisse berechnen kann.

Der gewöhnliche Weg ist eben — wie bekannt — ohne Weiteres nur gangbar im Falle der « Unabhängigkeit » von E_1 und E_2, zu deren Definition wir uns jetzt wenden. Vorher bemerken wir nur noch, dass aus (2) folgt:

$$(3) \qquad p(1,1) \leqq p_1 \quad , \quad p(1,1) \leqq p_2 .$$

5. Unabhängigkeit. — *Definition I.* Sei p_1 die Wahrscheinlichkeit von E_1, p_2 die von E_2, $p(1,1)$ die von $E_1 E_2$, dann heissen E_1 und E_2 von einander unabhängig (im Sinne der Wahrscheinlichkeitsrechnung), wenn

$$(4) \qquad p(1,1) = p_1 p_2$$

ist.

Besteht Unabhängigkeit, so folgt aus den Gleichungen (2):

$$p(1,1) = p_1 p_2 \quad , \quad p(0,1) = q_1 p_2$$
$$p(1,0) = p_1 q_2 \quad , \quad p(0,0) = q_1 q_2 ,$$

also folgt:

Satz VI. Gleichzeitig mit E_1 und E_2 sind auch voneinander unabhängig E_1 und E'_2, E'_1 und E_2, E'_1 und E'_2.

Ferner gilt:

Satz VII. Die beiden Ereignisse E_1 und E_2 sind dann und nur dann voneinander unabhängig, wenn die Determinante

$$D = \begin{vmatrix} p(0,0) & , & p(0,1) \\ p(1,0) & , & p(1,1) \end{vmatrix} = p(1,1) - p_1 p_2$$

verschwindet.

Zum Beweis dieses Satzes genügt es zu zeigen, dass die Determinante D in die in dem Satze angegebene Form $p(1,1) - p_1 p_2$ gebracht werden kann.

Aus den Gleichungen (1) und (2) ergiebt sich aber:

$$p(1,1) - p_1 p_2 = p(1,1) \cdot \{p(0,0) + p(0,1) + p(1,0) + p(1,1)\}$$
$$- [p(1,0) + p(1,1)] \cdot [p(0,1) + p(1,1)] = p(0,0)\, p(1,1) - p(0,1)\, p(1,0).$$

Die soeben abgeleitete Form der Determinante D lehrt weiter, dass, wenn sie nicht verschwindet, wenn also Abhängigkeit zwischen E_1 und E_2 besteht, zwei wesentlich verschiedene Fälle zu unterscheiden sind, je nach dem Vorzeichen dieser Determinante.

Ist nämlich $D > 0$, so ist:

$$p(1,1) > p_1 p_2$$

d. h., die Wahrscheinlichkeit dafür, dass sowohl E_1 als E_2 eintritt, ist grösser als im Falle der Unabhängigkeit. Das Umgekehrte gilt natürlich, wenn $D < 0$ ist. Wir werden später bei Betrachtung des mittleren Fehlers sehen, dass der erste Fall zu übernormaler Dispersion führt, dagegen der zweite zu unternormaler Dispersion.

6. **Empirisches Kriterium zur Entscheidung über die Unabhängigkeit.** — Wir legen Wert auf die Möglichkeit, dass die Entscheidung über die Unabhängigkeit zweier Ereignisse — ein genügend grosses Beobachtungsfeld vorausgesetzt — empirisch erfolgen kann. Wir nehmen deshalb an, es könnten für unser Ereignispaar $(E_1 E_2)$ μ Beobachtungen angestellt werden und die Auszählung ergäbe, dass unter den μ Malen

n_{11} — mal die Kombination $E_1 E_2$
n_{10} — " " $E_1 E_2'$
n_{01} — " " $E_1' E_2$
n_{00} — " " $E_1' E_2'$

beobachtet sei. Dann ist

$$n_{00} + n_{01} + n_{10} + n_{11} = \mu.$$

Sonst lässt sich aber über die Zahlen n vor der Beobachtung nichts aussagen. Wir nehmen nun an, dass bei jeder Beobachtung die den vier Möglichkeiten entsprechenden Wahrscheinlichkeiten dieselben, in der vorigen Nummer bezeichneten

Werte haben, und die Wahrscheinlichkeiten p der einzelnen Beobachtungen von einander unabhängig seien ([1]). Dann wird in dem Ausdrucke ([2])

$$(5) \qquad F(x,y,z,u) = \{p(0,0)\,x + p(0,1)\,y + p(1,0)\,z + p(1,1)\,u\}^{\mu} =$$
$$= \sum_{(n)} \varphi(n_{00}, n_{01}, n_{10}, n_{11})\, x^{n_{00}} y^{n_{01}} z^{n_{10}} u^{n_{11}}$$

die Summe über alle logisch denkbaren Werte n zu erstrecken sein und dadurch die Funktion φ definiert. Es wird für das obige *spezielle* Wertsystem $(n_{00}, n_{01}, n_{10}, n_{11})$, das beobachtet ist, der zugehörige Wert von φ die Wahrscheinlichkeit angeben, die diesem Wertsystem zukommt. Wendet man nun die landläufigen in Nr. 3 meines oben erwähnten Encyclopädieartikels angeführten « Principien » an, nach denen die Theorie auf die Erfahrung angewandt wird, so ist

$$n_{00}\, n_{11} - n_{01}\, n_{10}$$

ein der Determinante D der vorigen Nummer nachgebildeter empirischer Ausdruck, den man in erster Annäherung mit seinen Erwartungswert

$$[n_{00}\, n_{11} - n_{01}\, n_{10}]^0 = \sum_{(n)} \varphi(n_{00}, n_{01}, n_{10}, n_{11})\,(n_{00}\, n_{11} - n_{01}\, n_{10})$$

identificieren wird. Diesen Erwartungswert findet man am einfachsten aus Gleichung (5), indem man beachtet, dass er gleich dem Ausdruck

$$(6) \qquad \frac{\partial^2 F(e^x, e^y, e^z, e^u)}{\partial x\, \partial u} - \frac{\partial^2 F(e^x, e^y, e^z, e^u)}{\partial y\, \partial z}$$

an der Stelle $x = y = z = u = 0$ ist. Es ergiebt sich so:

$$(7) \qquad [n_{00}\, n_{11} - n_{01}\, n_{10}]^0 = \mu(\mu - 1)\, D\,.$$

So lässt sich D empirisch näherungsweise bestimmen.

Der mittlere Fehler dieser Bestimmung:

$$M(n_{00}\, n_{11} - n_{01}\, n_{10}) = \sqrt{\sum_{(n)} \varphi(n_{00}, n_{01}, n_{10}, n_{11})\,[n_{00}\, n_{11} - n_{01}\, n_{10} - \mu(\mu - 1)\, D]^2}$$

([1]) Die später gegebene Definition der Unabhängigkeit der Wahrscheinlichkeiten von Gruppen von mehr als 2 Ereignissen wird hier — als der Sache nach bekannt — anticipiert.

([2]) Die sogenannte « erzeugende Funktion », deren Wichtigkeit hier zum ersten Male hervortritt.

wird ebenfalls durch Differentiationsprocesse aus der erzeugenden Funktions F berechnet. Es wird nämlich, wenn man den Process (6):

$$\Delta = \frac{\partial^2}{\partial x\, \partial u} - \frac{\partial^2}{\partial y\, \partial z}$$

zweimal ausgeführt:

$$\Delta\Delta F(e^x, e^y, e^z, e^u)_0 = \sum_{(n)} \varphi(n_{00}, n_{01}, n_{10}, n_{11})\,(n_{00}\, n_{11} - n_{01}\, n_{10})^2,$$

wo der Index 0 auf der linken Seite andeutet, dass nach der Differentiation $x = y = z = u = 0$ zu setzen ist. Hat man nun diesen Ausdruck berechnet, so findet man M aus:

$$M^2(n_{00}\, n_{11} - n_{01}\, n_{10}) = \sum_{(n)} \varphi(n_{00}, n_{01}, n_{10}, n_{11})\,(n_{00}\, n_{11} - n_{01}\, n_{10})^2 - \mu^2(\mu - 1)^2 D^2.$$

Es ergiebt sich so:

$$(8) \quad \begin{aligned} M^2(n_{00}\, n_{11} - n_{01}\, n_{10}) = {} & \mu^2(\mu - 1) \{ - D^2 + (q_1 - p_1)(q_2 - p_2) D + p_1 q_1 p_2 q_2 \} \\ & + \mu(\mu - 1) \{ 2 D^2 - (q_1 - p_1)(q_2 - p_2) D \}. \end{aligned}$$

Nach dem oft benutzten Theorem von Tchebycheff — Pizzetti [1] folgt also mit einer Wahrscheinlichkeit, die grösser als $1 - \frac{1}{\nu^2}$ ist:

$$\left| \frac{n_{00}\, n_{11} - n_{01}\, n_{10}}{\mu(\mu - 1)} - D \right| < \nu \cdot \frac{M}{\mu(\mu - 1)}.$$

Da nun für $\mu = \infty$ die rechte Seite den Limes 0 hat, so folgt:
Die Wahrscheinlichkeit dafür, dass

$$\frac{n_{00}\, n_{11} - n_{11}\, n_{10}}{\mu(\mu - 1)}$$

von D um weniger als eine vorgeschriebene Zahl ε abweicht, konvergiert unter den angegebenen Voraussetzungen mit unbegrenzt wachsender Zahl der Beobachtungen gegen 1.

Findet man also in einen gegebenen Falle, dass der empirische Ausdruck von

$$\frac{n_{00}\, n_{11} - n_{01}\, n_{10}}{\mu(\mu - 1)}$$

von null nicht mehr abweicht, als der mittlere Fehler erwarten lässt, so ist die

(1) Vergl. u. a. Math. Encyclop., Bd., I, p. 861 unten.

Hypothese der Unabhängigkeit in dem Falle empirisch als zulässig erwiesen. Praktisch wird allerdings dieses Kriterium wegen des beschränkten Umfangs des einschlägigen Materials oft versagen. So ist die Hypothese bei Versicherungen auf verbundene Leben stets stillschweigend gemacht, aber nie — was wohl auch schwerhalten dürfte — geprüft worden. Andererseits betrachtet man in der Invalidenversicherung für einen Aktiven eines gegebenen Alters die Wahrscheinlichkeiten der vier folgenden Fälle

$p_x^{aa} = p(0,0)$ —	Der	Aktive	überlebt dar Alter	$x+1$	als Aktiver
$p_x^{ai} = p(0,1)$ —	„	„	„ „	„	wird aber vorher invalide,
$p_x^{aa} = p(1,0)$ —	„	„	stirbt vor dem Alter	„	in der Aktivität,
$q_x^{ai} = p(1,1)$ —	„	„	„ „	„	wird aber vorher invalide.

Hier entspricht das Sterben im $x+1^{ten}$ Lebensjahre dem Eintritt von E_1, das Invalidewerdem im $x+1^{ten}$ Lebensjahre dem Eintritt von E_2. Das gesammelte statischeMaterial hat stets numerische Werte für die in Rede stehenden vier Wahrscheinlichkeiten ergeben, für welche die Determinante:

$$D = p_x^{aa}\, q_x^{ai} - p_x^{ai}\, q_x^{aa}$$

auch in rohester Annäherung im allgemeinen nicht null ist. Diese Verhältnisse sind nach der Natur der Sache im Voraus zu erwarten, einmal, weil das Eintreten der Invalidität die Sterblichkeit des Individuums markant affiziert, sodann, weil wir es hier mit zwei *gleichzeitig* wirkenden Ausscheideursachen zu tun haben.

Das Beispiel aus der Invalidenversicherung hat übrigens auch für die reine Lebensversicherung Interesse. Denn in der Dividendenberechnung berücksichtigen moderne Aktuare und moderne Tafeln (¹) auch die Häufigkeit des Verfalls. Würde diese sich also auch als mathematische Wahrscheinlichkeit herausstellen, so hätte man für die Versicherten eines gegebenen Alters x folgende vier Wahrscheinlichkeiten zu unterscheiden

$p(0,0)$	Der	Versicherte	erlebt das Alter	$x+1$	als Versicherter,
$p(0,1)$	„	„	„ „	„	hat aber die Police vorher aufgegeben,
$p(1,0)$	„	„	stirbt von dem Alter	„	als Versicherter,
$p(1,1)$	„	„	„ „	„	nachdem er die Police aufgegeb. hatte.

Formell werden also diese Wahrscheinlichkeiten genau wie die obigen vier bei der Invalidenversicherung gebildet. Die lebhaften Diskussionen über den Unabhängigkeits-

(¹) Vergl. z. B. J. Karup, *Die Reform des Rechnungswesens der Gothaer Lebensversicherungsbank* (Jena, 1903, p. 188 ff.).

begriff bei diesen Wahrscheinlichkeiten [1] haben also auch für jene eine Bedeutung. Man pflegt aber bei den Sterblichkeit und Verfall berücksichtigenden Tafeln dadurch das Schema bedeutend zu vereinfachen, dass man den Verfall in einem Versicherungsjahr auf das Ende oder den Anfang desselben verlegt, und zwar immer auf den dem wirklich beobachteten Zeitpunkt näherliegenden Termin.

7. Die Wahrscheinlichkeit bedingter Ereignisse. — *Axiom IV.* Es sei p_1 die Wahrscheinlichkeit, dass E_1 eintritt, $p(1,1)$ die, dass sowohl E_1 als E_2 eintritt, alsdann bezeichnet der echte Bruch $\frac{p(1,1)}{p_1}$ wieder eine Wahrscheinlichkeit, nnd zwar die Wahrscheinlichkeit, dass E_2 eintritt, wenn man weiss, dass E_1 eintritt. Bezeichnen wir diese mit $p(E_2 \text{ w. } E_1)$ und das entsprechende Ereignis kurz mit « $(E_2 \text{ w. } E_1)$ », so ist unser Axiom ausgedrückt durch die Gleichung:

$$p(1,1) = p_1 \,.\, p(E_2 \text{ w. } E_1). \tag{8}$$

Es möge darauf aufmerkasam gemacht werden, dass in diesem Axiom die Konjunktion « wenn » rein konditional ohne irgend eine Andeutung einer zeitlichen Reihenfolge zu verstehen ist.

Durch folgenden Satz gewinnt der zunächst rein formal definierte Unabhängigkeitsbegriff eine anschauliche Bedeutung:

Satz VIII. Die Ereignisse E_1 und E_2 sind dann und nur dann voneinander unabhängig, wenn die Wahrscheinlichkeit dafür, dass E_2 eintritt, wenn E_1 eintritt, gleich ist der Wahrscheinlichkeit dafür, dass E_2 eintritt, wenn E_1 nicht eintritt.

In der Tat wird, wenn man in der letzten Gleichung q_1 durch $1 - p_1$ ersetzt:

$$p(E_2 w E_1) - p(E_2 w E_1') = \frac{p(1,1)}{p_1} - \frac{p(0,1)}{q_1} = \frac{p(1,1) - p_1 [p(1,1) + p(0,1)]}{p_1 q_1} =$$

$$= \frac{p(1,1) - p_1 p_2}{p_1 q_1}.$$

Das Axiom IV dieser Nummer bildet mit den Axiomen I, II, III der Nr. 1 ein vollständiges System von Annahmen für die allgemeine Wahrscheinlichkeitslehre, soweit sie im Folgenden gebraucht wird.

Es möge in diesem Zusammenhange noch der folgende auf das gewöhnliche Schema der günstigen und möglichen Fälle bezügliche Satz angegeben werden, dessen Beweis sich von selbst versteht:

(1) Vergl. L. von BORTKIEWICZ's, Referat, Artikel I, D. 4ᵃ, p. 847 ff. (Encyklopädie der Mathematik, Bd. I, Teil 2).

Satz IX. Legt man ein Schema von günstigen und möglichen Fällen zu Grunde und nimmt man an, dass die durch Kombination der m möglichen Fälle von E_1 und der n möglichen Fälle von E_2 zunächst rein formal für das gemeinsame Eintreffen von E_1 und E_2 gebildeten $m.n$ möglichen Fälle gleich wahrscheinlich sind, so kann man die Gleichwahrscheinlichkeit der m möglichen Fälle von E_1 und der n möglichen Fälle für E_2 *folgern*, und es folgt dann ausserdem, dass die beiden Ereignisse E_1 und E_2 voneinander unabhängig sind.

§ 3.

Drei und mehr Ereignisse.

8. Die Unabhängigkeit dreier Ereignisse voneinander. — Betrachtet man statt zweier Ereignisse eine grössere Anzahl von solchen, so bieten sich neue Besonderheiten dar. Schon der Fall dreier Ereignisse lässt aber das Charakteristische des allgemeinen Falles erkennen. Wir bezeichnen analog wie in Nr. 4 mit $p(\alpha_1, \alpha_2, \alpha_3)$ die Wahrscheinlichkeit dafür, dass E_1 α_1 mal, E_2 α_2 mal, E_3 α_3 mal eintritt, wo α_i 0 oder 1 ist, je nachdem des Ereignis E_i nicht eintritt oder eintritt. Aus den Axiomen des § 1 folgt wieder:

$$\sum_{(\alpha)} p(\alpha_1, \alpha_2, \alpha_3) = 1, \tag{9}$$

wo die Summation über die acht Wertekombinationen (α) zu erstrecken ist.

Ferner wird, wenn p_1 die Wahrscheinlichkeit von E_1, q_1 die von Nicht — E_1 bedeutet:

$$p_1 = \sum_{(\alpha)} p(1, \alpha_2, \alpha_3)$$

und

$$q_1 = \sum_{(\alpha)} p(0, \alpha_2, \alpha_3)$$

und

$$p_1 + q_1 = 1.$$

Analoge Gleichungen gelten für p_2, q_2, p_3, q_3.

Ferner wird die Wahrscheinlichkeit p_{12}, dass sowohl E_1 als E_2 eintritt, gegeben durch

$$p_{12} = \sum_{\alpha} p(1, 1, \alpha).$$

Entsprechende Ausdrücke ergeben sich allgemein für die Wahrscheinlichkeit $p_{i,k}$ dafür, dass sowohl E_i als E_k eintritt. Demnach sind die Grössen p_i und $p_{i,k}$ durch die Werte der $p(\alpha_1, \alpha_2, \alpha_3)$ bestimmt.

Sollen nun die drei Ereignisse E_1, E_2, E_3 voneinander nnabhängig sein, so müssen sich die $p(\alpha_1, \alpha_2, \alpha_3)$ in bekannter Weise durch die Produkte der p_i und q_i ausdrücken lassen, sodass die acht Gleichungen bestehen:

$$(10)\quad \begin{cases} p(1,1,1) = p_1 p_2 p_3 \quad, & p(0,1,1) = q_1 p_2 p_3 , \\ p(1,1,0) = p_1 p_2 q_3 \quad, & p(0,1,0) = q_1 p_2 q_3 , \\ p(1,0,1) = p_1 q_2 p_3 \quad, & p(0,0,1) = q_1 q_2 p_3 , \\ p(1,0,0) = p_1 q_2 q_3 \quad, & p(0,0,0) = q_1 q_2 q_3 . \end{cases}$$

Die Addition aller acht Gleichungen ergiebt, dass aus ihrem Bestehen die Relation (9) von selbst folgt. Im Uebrigen können, wenn keine Unabhängigkeit besteht, die Grössen $p(\alpha_1, \alpha_2, \alpha_3)$ alle möglichen Werte zwischen 0 und 1 haben, wenn nur ihre Summe gleich 1 ist. In dem Gleichungssystem (10) werden also sieben dieser Grössen durch drei Parameter p_1, p_2, p_3 ausgedrückt, sodass $7 - 3 = 4$ Gleichungen zwischen den $p(\alpha_1, \alpha_2, \alpha_3)$ übrigbleiben, die die Unabhängigkeit der drei Ereignisse E_1, E_2, E_3 voneinander ausdrücken.

Bildet man, um diese vier Relationen zu finden und ihre Bedeutung zu verstehen, zunächst die Summe der ersten zwei Gleichungen des Systems (10), so findet man:

$$p(1,1,1) + p(0,1,1) = p_{2,3} = p_2 p_3 .$$

Damit die drei Ereignisse voneinander unabhängig sind, müssen also E_2 und E_3 und allgemein je zwei der drei Ereignisse voneinander unabhängig sein. Dies giebt im Ganzen drei Bedingungen, von denen die erste soeben hingeschrieben ist und die beiden anderen sich aus ihr durch cyklische Vertauschung ergeben. Da aber nach dem oben Gesagten zwischen den $p(\alpha_1, \alpha_2, \alpha_3)$ vier Gleichungen bestehen müssen, damit die drei Ereignisse voneinander unabhängig sind, so bleibt uns noch eine vierte Bedingung zu finden übrig, und diese ergiebt sich aus der ersten Gleichung des Systems (10), wenn man diese in die Form schreibt:

$$p(1,1,1) = (p_1 p_2) p_3 .$$

Diese Gleichung bedeutet, dass das Eintreffen von E_3 von dem gemeinsamen Eintreffen von E_1 und E_2 unabhängig sein muss.

Wir finden also:

Satz X. Damit die drei Ereignisse E_1, E_2, E_3 voneinander unabhängig sind, genügt es nicht, dass je zwei von ihnen voneinander unabhängig sind. Es muss vielmehr noch die vierte Bedingung erfüllt sein, dass E_3 von dem gemeinsamen Eintreffen von E_1 und E_2 unabhängig ist.

Auf diesen Umstand wird in den herkömmlichen Darstellungen der Wahrscheinlichkeitsrechnung gewöhnlich nicht aufmerkasam gemacht und es möge daher das Gesagte durch ein möglichst einfaches Beispiel aus der Lehre von den Glücksspielen erläutert werden, bei dem sich die Wahrscheinlichkeiten nach dem Schema der günstigen und möglichen Fälle definieren lassen.

9. **Beispiel.** — Es seien 16 Kapseln, die sich äusserlich durch nichts unterscheiden, in eine Urne gelegt. Von ihnen möge jede drei Kugeln enthalten, die der Reihe nach mit den Ziffern 1, 2, 3 numeriert sind, und von denen jede entweder weiss oder schwarz ist. Jeder Kapsel sei eine Charakteristik $(\alpha_1, \alpha_2, \alpha_3)$ zugeordnet, wo jedes α gleich 0 oder 1 ist, je nachdem die entsprechende Kugel schwarz oder weiss ist.

Es seien vorhanden:

Drei Kapseln mit der Charakteristik	$(1, 1, 1)$
„ „ „	$(0, 1, 0)$
„ „ „	$(0, 0, 1)$
„ „ „	$(1, 0, 0)$
Eine Kapsel „ „	$(0, 1, 1)$
„ „ „	$(1, 1, 0)$
„ „ „	$(1, 0, 1)$
„ „ „	$(0, 0, 0)$.

Alsdann ist die Wahrscheinlichkeit dafür, dass die gezogene Kapsel α_1 weisse Kugeln mit der Nr. 1, α_2 weisse Kugeln mit der Nr. 2 und α_3 weisse Kugeln mit der Nr. 3 enthält, gegeben durch

$$p(\alpha_1, \alpha_2, \alpha_3) = \frac{1}{8} \pm \frac{1}{16}$$

wobei auf der rechten Seite das $+$ oder $-$ Zeichen zu wählen ist, je nachdem die Anzahl der Einsen, die unter den drei Argumenten $\alpha_1, \alpha_2, \alpha_3$ vorkommen, ungerade oder gerade ist. Es ist daher immer

$$p(\alpha_1, \alpha_2, 1 - \alpha_3) = \frac{1}{8} \mp \frac{1}{16}$$

und daher die Wahrscheinlichkeit, dass α_1 weisse Kugeln Nr. 1 und α_2 weisse Kugeln Nr. 2 in der gezogenen Kapsel vorhanden sind:

$$p(\alpha_1, \alpha_2) = p(\alpha_1, \alpha_2, \alpha_3) + p(\alpha_1, \alpha_2, 1 - \alpha_3) = \frac{1}{4}.$$

Analoge Gleichungen folgen für das Kugelpaar (2, 3) und (3, 1) durch cyklische Vertauschung. Im Besonderen wird

$$p_{12} = p_{23} = p_{31} = \frac{1}{4}.$$

Daher wird die Wahrscheinlichkeit $p(\alpha_1)$, dass α_1 weisse Kugeln Nr. 1 in den Kapsel sind, gegeben durch

$$p(\alpha_1) = p(\alpha_1\,,0) + p(\alpha_1\,,1) = \frac{1}{2}.$$

Es wird also:

$$p_1 = q_1 = \frac{1}{2}$$

und analog:

$$p_2 = q_2 = p_3 = q_3 = \frac{1}{2}.$$

Es wird also:

$$p_{12} = p_1 p_2 = p_{23} = p_2 p_3 = p_{31} = p_3 p_1 = \frac{1}{4},$$

während

$$p(1\,,1\,,1) = p_1 p_2 p_3 + \frac{1}{16} = \frac{3}{16}$$

wird.

10. μ **Ereignisse.** — Im allgemeinen Falle von μ Ereignissen bedient man sich mit Vorteil der in der Wahrscheinlichkeitsrechnung auch sonst vielfach nützlichen *erzeugenden Funktion.* Es sei $p(\alpha_1\,,\alpha_2\,,\ldots\alpha_\mu)$ die Wahrscheinlichkeit dafür, dass E_1 α_1 mal, E_2 α_2 mal ... E_μ α_μ mal eintritt, wo jedes α den Wert 1 oder 0 hat, je nachdem man das Eintreten oder Nichteintreten des betreffenden Ereignisses verlangt. Dann ist das Wahrscheinlichkeitsschema durch die Koefficienten der folgenden « erzeugenden Funktion » gegeben:

$$E(x_1\,,x_2\,,\ldots x_\mu) = \sum_{(\alpha)} p(\alpha_1\,,\alpha_2\,,\ldots\alpha_\mu)\, x_1^{\alpha_1}\, x_2^{\alpha_2}\ldots x_\mu^{\alpha_\mu},$$

wo die Summation auf der rechten Seite über alle 2^μ möglichen Wertekombinationen (α) auszudehnen ist und die x unbestimmte Variable sind. Die p haben, ausser dass sie zwischen 0 und 1 liegen müssen, im Allgemeinen nur der einen Bedingung zu genügen, dass ihre Summe gleich 1 ist:

$$\sum p(\alpha_1\,,\alpha_2\,,\ldots\alpha_\mu) = 1\,. \tag{11}$$

Es sind also $2^\mu - 1$ Grössen p im Allgemeinen durch keine Gleichung miteinander verbunden. Die Gleichung (11) giebt für die erzeugende Funktion die Bedingung:

$$E(1\,,1\,,\ldots 1) = 1\,.$$

Im Uebrigen sieht man, dass die erzeugende Funktion linear in jeder einzelnen der Variablen x ist.

Ist das Wahrscheinlichkeitsschema, d. h. die erzeugende Funktion, gegeben, so ist auch die Wahrscheinlichkeit q_i von Nicht-E_i bestimmt.

Die μ Ereignisse heissen dann und nur dann voneinander unabhängig, wenn die erzeugende Funktion $E(x_1, x_2, \dots x_\mu)$ in μ relle positive Linear-Faktoren zerfällt:

$$E(x_1, x_2, \dots x_\mu) = \sum_{(\alpha)} p(\alpha_1, \alpha_2 \dots \alpha_\mu)\, x_1^{\alpha_1} x_2^{\alpha_2} \dots x_\mu^{\alpha_\mu} =$$

$$= (q_1 + p_1 x_1)(q_2 + p_2 x) \dots (q_\mu + p_\mu x_\mu).$$

Diese Gleichung ergiebt durch Gleichsetzung der Koeffizienten auf beiden Seiten die $p(\alpha_1, \alpha_2, \dots \alpha_\mu)$ ausgedrückt durch die Parameter $p_1, p_2, \dots p_\mu$. Da aber die Gleichung (11) von selbst erfüllt sein muss, so folgen durch Elimination der $p_1, p_2 \dots p_\mu$, $2^\mu - \mu - 1$ verschiedene Relationen zwischen den $p(\alpha_1, \alpha_2 \dots \alpha_\mu)$, durch welche die Unabhängigkeit der μ Ereignisse voneinander definiert ist.

Ohne das Hülfsmittel der erzeugenden Funktion definiert sich die Unabhängigkeit bei μ Ereignissen wie folgt:

Definition II. Die Ereignisse E_1, $E_2 \dots E_\mu$ mögen durch ein Wahrscheinlichkeitsschema charakterisierbar sein, sodass $p(\alpha_1, \alpha_2 \dots \alpha_\mu)$ die Wahrscheinlichkeit angiebt, dass E_1 α_1 mal, E_2 α_2 mal, $\dots E_\mu$ α_μ mal $(\alpha_i = 0, 1)$ eintritt. Ferner sei p_i die Wahrscheinlichkeit von E_i, q_i die von E_i', $(i = 1, 2 \dots \mu)$. Alsdann heissen $E_1, E_2 \dots E_\mu$ *voneinander* unabhängig (im Sinne der Wahrscheinlichkeitsrechnung), wenn die 2^μ Gleichungen bestehen:

$$p(\alpha_1, \alpha_2 \dots \alpha_\mu) = \prod_{i=1}^{\mu} p_i^{\alpha_i} q_i^{1-\alpha_i} \quad , \quad (\alpha_1, \alpha_2 \dots \alpha_\mu = 0, 1).$$

Es folgt unmittelbar:

Satz. XI. Damit μ Ereignisse $E_1, E_2 \dots E_\mu$ voneinander unabhängig sind, reicht es im Allgemeinen nicht aus, dass je zwei derselben voneinander unabhängig sind — was nur $\frac{\mu(\mu-1)}{2}$ Bedingungen ergäbe. Vielmehr ist notwendig und hinreichend, dass die folgenden $2^\mu - \mu - 1$ verschiedenen Relationen erfüllt sind:

1) je zwei der Ereignisse sind voneinander unabhängig,

2) das Eintreffen eines dritten Ereignisses ist von dem gemeinsamen Eitreffen eines Paares von zwei Ereignissen unabhängig,

3) das Eintreffen eines vierten Ereignisses ist von dem gemeinsamen Eintriffen einer Gruppe von drei Ereignissen unabhängig,

. . . .

$\mu-1$) Das Eintreffen des μ ten Ereignissen ist von dem gemeinsamen Eintreffen der $\mu-1$ übrigen unabhängig.

In diesem Satz werden gefordert:

Unter 1). (μ_2) Bedingungen,
" 2). (μ_3) "
" 3). (μ_4) "
. . . .
" $\mu-1$) (μ_μ) "

Summe: $(\mu_2)+(\mu_3)+\cdots+(\mu_\mu)=2^\mu-\mu-1$ Bedingungen.

11. Beispiele. — Zur Illustration weisen wir kurz auf das Schema der wiederholten Versuche hin, bei dem man ein bestimmtes Ereignis E ins Auge fasst und das Ereignis E_i mit dem Eintreten von E beim i ten Versuche identifiziert. Hier kommt es gewöhnlich nicht darauf an, bei welchem Versuche das Ereignis E eintritt, als vielmehr darauf, *wie oft* es unter μ Versuchen eintritt. Man wird daher in der erzeugenden Funktion $x_1=x_2=\cdots x_\mu=x$ setzen, wodurch die erzeugende Funktion die Gestalt annimmt:

$$E(x)=\sum_0^\mu{}_n\,\varphi_\mu(n)\,x^n$$

wo $\varphi_\mu(n)$ die Wahrscheinlichkeit bedeutet, dass E bei den μ Versuchen n mal eintritt. Setzt mau Unabhängigkeit voraus, so entsteht das Poisson'sche Schema:

$$E(x)=\sum_0^\mu{}_n\,\varphi_\mu(n)\,x^n=(q_1+p_1x)\quad(q_2+p_2x)\ldots(q_\mu+p_\mu x).$$

Setzt man ausserdem voraus, dass die Wahrscheinlichkeit bei jedem Versuche denselben konstanten Wert p hat, so entsteht im Besonderen das Bernoulli'sche Schema:

$$E(x)=\sum_0^\mu{}_n\,\varphi_\mu(n)\,x^n=(q+px)^\mu.$$

Betrachtet man dagegen das klassische Beispiel von einer Urne mit $2m$ schwarzen und weissen Kugeln, in der sich — wie wir hier der Einfachheit halber voraussetzen wollen — gleich viel weisse und schwarze Kugeln befinden, wo aber die gezogene Kugel nicht wieder in die Urne getan wird, so besteht nicht mehr Unabhängigkeit. Ist wieder μ die Anzahl der Ziehungen und $\mu\leqq 2m$, so ist die diesem Schema entsprechende erzeugende Funktion:

$$E(x)=\frac{1}{(2m)^{(\mu)}}\sum_0^\mu{}_n\,(\mu_n)\,m^{(n)}\,m^{(\mu-n)}\,x^n\,,\ \text{wo}\ m^{(n)}=m(m-1)\ldots(m-n+1)\,,\ m^{(0)}=1.$$

Diese lässt sich nicht mehr in reelle positive Linear-Faktoren zerlegen.

12. Der mittlere Fehler bei Abhängigkeit. — Betrachtet man μ Versuche und nennt α_i die Anzahl von Malen, die ein bestimmtes Ereignis E bein i ten Versuche eintritt, so ist das Wahrscheinlichkeitsschema durch die Funktion

$$p(\alpha_1, \alpha_2, \ldots \alpha_\mu)$$

gegeben, die die einer bestimmten Kombination der α zukommende Wahrscheinlichkeit bedeutet. Dis α sind natürlich wieder 0 oder 1. Die wahrscheinliche Anzahl von Malen, die E bei den μ Versuchen eintritt, wird dann definiert durch

$$\sum_{(\alpha)} p(\alpha_1, \alpha_2, \ldots \alpha_\mu) \quad (\alpha_1 + \alpha_2 + \cdots + \alpha_\mu).$$

Ist α_i^0 der wahrscheinliche Wert von α_i, so wird diese wahrscheinliche Anzahl von Malen, die E bei den μ Versuchen eintritt,

$$\alpha_1^0 + \alpha_2^0 + \ldots + \alpha_\mu^0 = p_1 + p_2 + \cdots + p_\mu, \tag{12}$$

wie man leicht durch Ausmultiplicieren findet. Dabei ist p_i die Wahrscheinlichkeit, dass E beim i ten Versuche eintritt.

Wir haben also:

Satz XII. Wir betrachten ein Ereignis E bei μ Versuchen und nennen p_i die Wahrscheinlichkeit, dass E beim i ten Versuche eintritt. Unabhängigkeit der μ Versuche voneinander werde aber in keiner Weise vorausgesetzt. Ist dann n Anzahl von Malen, die E bei den μ Versuchen eintritt, so ist ihr wahrscheinlicher Wert n^0 durch dieselbe Formel:

$$n^0 = p_1 + p_2 + \cdots + p_\mu \tag{12}$$

gegeben, die von dem (Poissonschen) Schema unabhängiger Versuche her bekannt ist.

Das Quadrat der mittleren Abweichung der Anzahl von Malen, die E bei den μ Versuchen eintritt, ist definiert durch

$$\mathrm{M}^2 = \sum_{(\alpha)} p(\alpha_1, \alpha_2 \ldots \alpha_\mu) \quad (\alpha_1 - \alpha_1^0 + \alpha_2 - \alpha_2^0 + \cdots + \alpha_\mu - \alpha_\mu^0)^2. \tag{13}$$

Diese Summe besteht aus μ Summen von Quadraten:

$$\sum_{(\alpha)} p(\alpha_1, \alpha_2 \ldots \alpha_\mu) \quad (\alpha_1 - \alpha_1^0)^2 + \sum_{(\alpha)} p(\alpha_1, \alpha_2 \ldots \alpha_\mu) \quad (\alpha_2 - \alpha_2^0)^2 + \cdots \tag{13a}$$

plus $\mu(\mu-1)$ Summen von Produkten:

$$(13\,b)\quad 2\sum_{(\alpha)} p(\alpha_1\ldots\alpha_\mu)\,(\alpha_1-\alpha_1^0)\,(\alpha_2-\alpha_2^0)+2\sum_{(\alpha)} p(\alpha_1\ldots\alpha_\mu)\,(\alpha_1-\alpha_1^0)\,(\alpha_3-\alpha_3^0)+\cdots$$

Das erste Glied in der Summe (13 a) wird

$$q_1(0-\alpha_1^0)^2+p_1(1-\alpha_1^0)^2=q_1p_1^2+p_1q_1^2=p_1q_1.$$

Es wird also (13 a):

$$(13\,a)\qquad p_1q_1+p_2q_2+\cdots+p_\mu q_\mu.$$

Die erste Summe in (13 b) wird, wenn $p(\alpha_1,\alpha_2)$ die Wahrscheinlichkeit bedeutet, dass E beim ersten Versuche α_1 mal, beim zweiten α_2 mal $(\alpha_1,\alpha_2=0,1)$, eintritt:

$$p(0,0)\,p_1p_2-p(0,1)\,p_1q_2-p(1,0)\,p_2q_1+p(1,1)\,q_1q_2.$$

Dabei ist q_i die Wahrscheinlichkeit, dass E beim i ten Versuche nicht eintritt $(i=1,2)$. Setzt man hierin $q_i=1-p_i$, so findet man für den Ausdruck (13 b) den Wert

$$(13\,b)\qquad \sum_{i\neq k}(p_{ik}-p_ip_k).$$

Mithin folgt durch Addition der in (13 a) und (13 b) gefundenen Ausdrücke als Wert von M^2 nach (13):

$$(14)\qquad M^2=\sum_1^\mu{}_i\,p_iq_i+\sum_{i\neq k}(p_{ik}-p_ip_k).$$

Hieraus folgt:

Satz XIII. Unter den Annahmen des Satzes XII ist die mittlere Abweichung $M(n)$ der Anzahl n von Malen, die E eintritt, von ihrem wahrscheinlichen Werte durch die Gleichung gegeben:

$$(14)\qquad M^2(n)=\sum_1^\mu{}_i\,p_iq_i+\sum_{i\neq k}(p_{ik}-p_ip_k).$$

Wir haben also denselben Wert wie bei *normaler Dispersion*:

$$M^2(n)=\sum p_iq_i$$

wenn nur *je zwei* der Versuche voneinander unabhängig sind, dagegen *übernormale* Dispersion

$$M^2(n)>\sum p_iq_i$$

wenn alle $p_{ik} > p_i p_k$ sind, wenn also das Eintreten von E bei einem Versuche sein nochmaliges Eintreten bei einem anderen wahrscheinlicher als im Falle der Unabhängigkeit macht. Endlich haben wir *unternormale* Dispersion

$$M^2(n) < \sum p_i q_i$$

wenn alle $p_{ik} < p_i p_k$ sind, wenn also das Eintreten von E bei einem Versuche sein nochmaliges Eintreten bei einem anderen weniger wahrscheinlich macht als im Falle der Unabhängigkeit.

Besonders einfach gestalten sich die obigen Formeln, wenn man annimmt, dass die p_i und p_{ik} für alle μ Versuche die gleichen Werte haben, also

$$p_i = p\,,\ p_{ik} = p_{12} \qquad (i \neq k)$$

setzt. Alsdann wird die wahrscheinliche Anzahl n^0 von Malen, die E bei den μ Versuchen eintritt, nach Formel (12) wie beim BERNOULLI'schen Theorem durch:

$$n^0 = \mu p \tag{15}$$

und die mittlere Abweichung durch

$$M^2(n) = \mu pq + \mu(\mu - 1) \quad (p_{12} - p^2) = \mu pq + \mu(\mu - 1)D \tag{16}$$

gegeben.

Bei der in Nr. 11 betrachteten Urnenziehung wird z. B., wie sich durch elementare Rechnungen ergiebt:

$$p = \frac{1}{2} \quad , \quad p_{12} = \frac{1}{4}\left(1 - \frac{1}{2m - 1}\right).$$

Mithin folgt

$$D = p_{12} - p^2 = -\frac{1}{8m - 4} < 0$$

und

$$M^2(n) = \frac{\mu}{4} - \frac{\mu(\mu - 1)}{4(2m - 1)} = \frac{\mu}{4}\left(1 - \frac{\mu - 1}{2m - 1}\right).$$

Es ergiebt sich hier also *unternormale* Dispersion, wie nach der Natur des Schemas auf Grund des oben Ausgeführten zu erwarten war, da das Ziehen einer weissen Kugel bei einer Ziehung, das nochmalige Eintreten dieses Ereignisses bei einer späteren Ziehung weniger wahrscheinlich macht, als bei einem Schema, wo Unabhängigkeit besteht.

Um auch für übernormale Dispersion ein Beispiel zu geben, nehmen wir den extremsten Fall, dass das Eintreten des Ereignisses E bei *einem* Versuch das Eintreten desselben bei jedem anderen Versuch gewiss macht. Dann wird, wenn p die Wahrscheinlichkeit von E ist, auch:

$$p_{12} = p$$

also

$$D = p_{12} - p^2 = pq > 0.$$

Es folgt aus (15) und (16):

$$n^0 = \mu p$$
$$M^2(n) = \mu pq + \mu(\mu - 1) pq = \mu^2 pq$$

oder:

$$M(n) = \mu \sqrt{pq}.$$

Man benerkt also, dass, wenn infolge Abhängigkeit der Ereignisse die Dispersion übernormal wird, der mittlere Fehler von n von derselben Grössenordnung (nämlich μ^1) wie der Erwartungswert von n werden kann. Dann wird aber die Approximierung der Wahrscheinlichkeit p durch die relative Häufigkeit $\frac{n}{\mu}$ illusorisch. Der bekannte Schluss beim Bernouilli'schen Schema:

« Die Wahrscheinlichkeit dafür, dass $\left|\frac{n}{\mu} - p\right| < \varepsilon$ wird, konvergiert mit unbegrenzt wachsendem μ gegen 1 » versagt hier vollständig.

ZWEITES KAPITEL.

Grundlagen der Lebensversicherungsmathematik.

§ 1.

Allgemeine Vorbemerkungen.

13. Formulierung der Aufgabe. — In meinem Encyklopädieartikel habe ich gezeigt — und ich glaube den dort gegebenen Ausführungen in dieser Richtung nichts hinzuzusetzen zu brauchen — dass sämtliche Rechnungsregeln und Resultate der Lebensversicherungsmathematik, einschliesslich der auf die Theorie des Risikos bezüglichen sich durch Anwendung der Begriffe « Wahrscheinlicher Wert » und « Mittlere Abweichung » aus dem Schema der Sterbenswahrscheinlichkeiten ergeben.

Dagegen bedarf dieses letztere Schema, wie ich es in dem genannten Artikel aufzustellen versucht habe, der näheren Begründung und Erläuterung. Dies soll in den §§ 2-3 dieses Kapitels geschehen. Von vornherein möchte ich dabei hervorheben, dass es sich dabei nicht um blosse Wiederholungen der allgemeinen Grundsätze des ersten Kapitels für diesen Fall handelt, sondern dass sich das Interesse vielmehr auf die Besonderheiten richtet, die bei den Sterbenswahrscheinlichkeiten gegenüber den allgemeinen Wahrscheinlichkeiten hervortreten.

14. Gesamtheit gleichartiger Risiken. — Logisches Schliessen allein, blosse Denkformen, die allein Gegenstand der abstrakten Wahrscheinlichkeitsrechnung sind, können nie eine Erfahrung, nie beobachtete Tatsachen ersetzen. Die Aufgabe ist nur die, solche Schemen logisch widerspruchsfrei und in zweckmässiger Form aufzustellen, sodass sie die Erfahrung einerseits nicht doctrinär zu anticipieren versuchen, andererseits die aus ihr gewonnenen Resultate in übersichtlicher Weise zusammenzufassen gestatten. Welche Gruppe von Risiken man daher hinsichtlich der Sterblichkeit als gleichartig zusammenfassen soll, kann nur die Erfahrung lehren. Die Erfahrung wird auch fortwährend uns dazu führen, unsere Auffassung in dieser Richtnng zu korrigieren und die Unterscheidungsmerkmale zu verfeinern. *Ein* Uebereinkommen aber müssen wir treffen, wenn auch mit der Ueberzeugung, dass ihm Willkürlichkeiten und Ungenauigkeiten anhaften. So ist auch mit wachsender Erkenntnis und mit der ungeheuren Vermehrung des verwertbaren Materials unsere Zeit sehr viel anspruchsvoller in den Anforderungen geworden, die sie an die Klassifizierung der Risiken stellt. Eine Definition der Gleichartigkeit von gewissen Risiken wird daher, weil die Erfahrung sie motiviert haben muss, immer etwas Relatives dem jeweiligen Stande der Erkenntnis Entsprechendes einschliessen. Nach den gegenwärtigen Anschauungen und Erfahrungen wird man als gleichartig betrachten, das heisst durch dieselbe Sterbenswahrscheinlichkeit messen, alle männlichen Risiken, die normal nach vollständiger ärztlicher Untersuchung auf den Todesfall versichert sind, denen man das gleiche Eintrittsalter zuschreibt und die den gleichen Zeitraum hindurch ununterbrochen bei einer Anstalt versichert gewesen sind. Das gleiche Eintrittsalter aber schreibt man, der Berechnung und Anwendung der Prämientarife entsprechend, allen Personen zu, die bei Eingehen der Versicherung mindestens $e-\frac{1}{2}$, aber weniger als $e+\frac{1}{2}$ Jahre alt waren. Die Versicherungsdauer dagegen wird in modernen Sterbetafeln scharf, wenn auch nicht nach Minuten und Sekunden, so doch nach Tagen gemessen und wer die Zeit t hindurch versichert gewesen ist, wird als $x=e+t$ Jahre alt gezählt. Alle dem Eintrittsalter e zugehörigen und die gleiche Zeit t hindurch versicherten Personen der oben bezeichneten Gesamtheit heissen dann gleichaltrig und $x=e+t$ zählt als das von ihnen erreichte Alter. Gleiche Alter werden natürlich hier nicht *gleichzeitig* erreicht.

§. 2.

Ein und zwei Individuen.

15. Die fingierte Absterbeordnung für 1 Individuum. — Aus den allgemeinen Betrachtungen des ersten Kapitels (Nr. 4) folgt, dass die auf 1 Individuum bezüglichen Axiome aus den für μ Individuen gemachten Annahmen logisch sich folgern lassen müssen. Trotzdem empfiehlt es sich wie im ersten Kapitel bei Ereignissen vorzugehen und erst die Axiomengruppe A_1 für 1 Individuum aufzustellen, dann die A_2 für zwei Individuen und erst dann die A_μ für μ Individuen. Es ist dann nachträglich zu zeigen, dass die Axiome A_1 in den A_2 und beide wieder in den A_μ enthalten sind. Entsprechende Axiome sollen gleiche römische Ziffern erhalten, die nach der Zahl der Individuen, auf die sie sich beziehen, durch Indices unterschieden werden mögen. Ein Individuum, das das Alter x erreicht hat, werde durch (x) bezeichnet. Analog bezeichnen wir später mit $(x_1, x_2 \ldots x_n)$ eine Gruppe von n Personen mit den Altern x_1 bezw. $x_2 \ldots x_n$. w sei ein Grenzalter, das niemand überlebt. Man kann es entweder der Erfahrung gemäss wählen oder ins Unendliche rücken lassen.

Axiom V_1 Ist e eine gegebene positive Zahl, so wird für alle Werte x, y, für die $e \leqq x \leqq y \leqq w$ ist, die Wahrscheinlichkeit, dass (x) Alter y erlebt, durch eine Zahl $p(x, y)$ gemessen, die von x und y abhängt.

Axiom VI. Die Wahrscheinlichkeit $p(x, w)$ dass (x) das Alter w erlebt, ist 0.

Dass wir dem Axiom VI nicht den Index 1 gegen, hat seine besonderen Gründe (Nr. 17).

Das Axiom V_1 hat — wie alle Axiome für *ein* Individuum — natürlich nur die Bedeutung, dass es eine Rechnungsregel bezeichnet, nach der man bei Gesamtheiten « gleichartiger » Risiken (Nr. 14) verfährt. Es soll dabei niemals über ein in Konkreto gegebenes physisches Individuum unmittelbar etwas ausgesagt werden.

Aus den Ueberlebenswahrscheinlichkeiten $p(x, y)$ — diese als bekannt vorausgesetzt — lassen sich mit Hülfe der Annahmen und Sätze des ersten Kapitels alle Sterbenswahrscheinlichkeiten des Individuums ermitteln. Ist $q(x, y \longmapsto z)$ die Wahrscheinlichkeit, dass (x) zwischen den Altern y und z stirbt und $x \leqq y \leqq z$, so folgt aus Nr. 1:

$$(17) \qquad q(x, y \longmapsto z) = p(x, y) - p(x, z).$$

Im Besonderen wird die Wahrscheinlichkeit q_x, dass (x) vor Erreichung des Alters $x+1$ stirbt, gegeben durch

$$q_x = q(x, x \longmapsto x+1) = 1 - p(x, x+1) = 1 - p_x,$$

wo p_x wie üblich die Wahrscheinlichkeit bezeichnet, dass (x) das Alter $x+1$ erlebt. In der Tat ist $p(x, x) = 1$ nach Axiom II der Nr. 1.

In Gleichung (17) muss die rechte Seite positiv sein, es ist also

$$\frac{p(x\,,z)}{p(x\,,y)} \leqq 1\,.$$

Aus Axiom IV (Nr. 7) folgt daher, dass

$$\frac{p(x\,,z)}{p(x\,,y)}$$

die Wahrscheinlichkeit bedeutet, dass (y) das Alter z erlebt. Es ist also

(18) $$\frac{p(x\,,z)}{p(x\,,y)} = p(y\,,z)\,.$$

Ist nun $p(y\,,z)$ eine Funktion von y und z allein, so kann man links x gleich einem speziellen Werte x_0 setzen. Alsdann ändert der Quotient auf der linken Seite seinen Wert nicht. Ist daher C eine willkürliche positive Konstante und wird

$$p(x_0\,,y) = Cl(y)$$

gesetzt, so ist $l(y)$ eine positive mit y nicht zunehmende Funktion von y, die für $y = w$ verschwindet. Es wird daher

(19) $$p(y\,,z) = \frac{l(z)}{l(y)}\,.$$

Die Funktion l heisst die « Zahl der Lebenden des Alters y ». Sie hat hier lediglich die Bedeutung einer rechnerischen Hülfsfunktion und braucht natürlich nicht ganzzahlig zu sein. Nennt man in (19) die Argumente $x\,,y$ statt $y\,,z$, so folgt:

Satz XIV. Ist $p(x\,,y)$ eine Funktion von x und y allein, so existiert eine positive nicht zunehmende Funktion $l(y)$ des Alters y, genannt die Zahl der Lebenden des Alters y, sodass

$$p(x\,,y) = \frac{l(y)}{l(x)}$$

wird.

Die Funktion $l(x)$ definiert die (fingierte) Absterbeordnung der Lebenden des Alters x.

Ist $l(x)$, wie wir annehmen, differentierbar, so folgt aus Nr. 3 die Existenz der Sterbensintensität

$$\mu_x = -\frac{l'(x)}{l(x)}$$

des Alters x.

§ 3.

Zwei Individuen.

16. Die fingierte Absterbeordnung für Paare. — *Axiom* V_2. Es seien e_1, e_2 zwei gegebene positive Zahlen, alsdann wird für alle Variablenpaare (x, y), die den Bedingungen

$$e_1 \leqq x_1 \leqq y_1 \leqq w \quad , \quad e_2 \leqq x_2 \leqq y_2 \leqq w$$

genügen, die Wahrscheinlichkeit dafür, dass (x_1) vor dem Alter y_1 und (x_2) vor dem Alter y_2 stirbt, durch eine Zahl

$$f(1, 1, x_1 \text{—} y_1 \quad , \quad x_2 \text{—} y_2)$$

gemessen, die von $x_1 y_1 x_2 y_2$ abhängt. Das Gleiche gilt allgemein von jeder der vier Wahrscheinlichkeiten

$$f(\alpha_1, \alpha_2, x_1 \text{—} y_1 \quad , \quad x_2 \text{—} y_2)$$

dass bei (x_1) und (x_2) in den Altersstrecken x_1 — y_1 und x_2 — y_2 α_1, und α_2 Sterbefälle stattfinden.

Lassen wir für den Augenblick bei den vier Funktionen die Argumente xy, die wir als gegeben betrachten, fort, so entsprechen die vier Wahrscheinlichkeiten

$$f(0, 0) \quad , \quad f(0, 1) \quad , \quad f(1, 0) \quad , \quad f(1, 1)$$

bezw. den Annahmen, dass in den Altersstrecken x_1 — y_1, x_2 — y_2

(x_1) überlebt	,	(x_2) überlebt
(x_1) „	,	(x_2) stirbt
(x_1) stirbt	,	(x_2) überlebt
(x_1) „	,	(x_2) stirbt.

Die Summe der vier f muss 1 sein (Nr. 1). Sonst folgt zwischen ihnen aus den bisherigen Annahmen keine weitere Gleichung. Nach Nr. 1 wird ferner durch das Schema des Axiom V_2 die Wahrscheinlichkeit $f(0, 0) + f(0, 1)$ bestimmt, dass (x_1) das Alter y_1 erlebt. Allerdings wird diese im Allgemeinen noch von x_2 und y_2 abhängen, was aber Axiom V_1, auf (x_1) angewandt, nicht ausschliesst. Analog wird $f(0, 0) + f(1, 0)$ die Wahrscheinlichkeit, dass (x_2) das Alter y_2 erlebt. Gilt also Axiom V_2 für das Paar (x_1, x_2), so gilt Axiom V_1 für (x_1) und (x_2) einzeln genommen. Axiom V_1 ist also in Axiom V_2 enthalten. Aus Axiom VI_1 und V_2 dagegen folgt als:

Satz XV_2. Die Wahrscheinlichkeit

$$f(0\,,0\;\;;\;\;x_1 y_1\,,x_2 - x_2 y_2)$$

dafür, dass (x_1) und (x_2) beim Alter y_1 und y_2 noch leben, ist 0, wenn y_1 oder y_2 gleich w werden.

In der Tat folgt auf Nr. 1:

$$0 \leqq f(0\,,0\;;\;x_1 - y_1\,,x_2 - y_2) \leqq p(x_1\,,y_1)\,.$$

Also folgt für $y_1 = w$:

$$0 \leqq f(0\,,0\;;\;x_1 - w\,,x_2 - y_2) \leqq p(x_1\,,w) = 0$$

oder

$$f(0\,,0\;;\;x_1 - w\,,x_2 - y_2) = 0\,.$$

Analog beweist man

$$f(0\,,0\;;\;x_1 - y_1\,,x_2 - w) = 0.$$

Dem Satz XIV_1 der vorigen Nummer entsprechend gilt für zwei Individuen:

Satz XIV_2. Jede der vier Wahrscheinlichkeiten des Axiom V_2:

$$f(\alpha_1\,,\alpha_2) = f(\alpha_1\,,\alpha_2\,;\,x_1 - y_1\,,x_2 - y_2) \quad , \quad (\alpha_1\,,\alpha_2 = 0\,,1)$$

sei eine Funktion von $x_1\,,y_1\,,x_3\,,y_2$ allein. Dann existiert eine positive, mit wachsenden Argumenten nicht zunehmende Funktion $l(x_1\,,x_2)$ von x_1 und x_2, genannt die Zahl der lebenden Paare der Alterskombination $x_1\,,x_2$, durch die sich die vier Funktionen f wie folgt ausdrücken:

$$f(0\,,0) = \frac{l(y_1\,.\,y_2)}{l(x_1\,,x_2)}\,,\; f(0\,,1) = \frac{l(y_1\,.\,x_2) - l(y_1\,.\,y_2)}{l(x_1\,,x_2)}\,,\; f(1\,,0) = \frac{l(x_1\,.\,y_2) - l(y_1\,,y_2)}{l(x_1\,,x_2)}$$

$$f(1\,,1) = \frac{l(x_1\,,x_2) - l(y_1\,.\,x_2) - l(x_1\,.\,y_2) + l(y_1\,.\,y_2)}{l(x_1\,,x_2)}$$

Zum Beweise führen wir zunächst die Bezeichnung

$$f(0\,,0)\;;\;x_1 - y_1\,,x_2 - y_2) = p(x_1\,,y_1\;;\;x_2\,,y_2)$$

ein. Dann folgt aus Axiom IV (Nr. 7) für beliebige $x_i \leqq y_i \leqq z_i$ $(i = 1\,,2)$.

Der Quotient:

$$\frac{p(x_1, z_1; x_2, z_2)}{p(x_1, y_1, x_2, y_2)} = p(y_1, z_1; y_2, z_2)$$

ist von x_1 und x_2 unabhängig. Man schliesst daraus wie bei Satz XIV (Nr. 16) auf die Existenz einer Funktion $l(x_1, x_2)$ von den in Satz XVI ausgesprochenen Eigenschaften für die

$$p(y_1, z_1; y_2, z_2) = \frac{l(z_1, z_2)}{l(y_1, y_2)}$$

wird. Schreibt man hierin wieder x für y, y für z, so wird die linke Seite $f(0,0)$ und es ergiebt sich die erste der vier Gleichungen (20):

$$(20^a) \qquad f(0, 0) = \frac{l(y_1, y_2)}{l(x_1, x_2)}.$$

Ferner geht:

$$f(0, 0) = f(0, 0; x_1 - y_1, x_2 - y_2))$$

für $x_2 = y_3$ in die Wahrscheinlichkeit über, dass (x_1) beim Alter y_1 noch lebt. Es ist also

$$(20^b) \qquad f(0, 0) + f(0, 1) = f(0, 0, x_1 - y_1, x_2 - y_2) = \frac{l(y_1, x_2)}{l(x_1, x_2)}.$$

Subtrahiert man von dieser Gleichung (20^a), so entsteht die zweite der Gleichungen (20). Analog wie (20^b) beweist man:

$$(20^c) \qquad f(0, 0) + f(1, 0) = f(0, 0, x_1 - x_1, x_2 - y_2) = \frac{l(x_1, y_2)}{l(x_1, x_2)}$$

und hieraus folgt durch Subtraktion von (20^a) die dritte der vier Gleichungen (20). Die letzte von ihnen ergiebt sich dann einfach aus

$$(20^d) \qquad f(0, 0) + f(0, 1) + f(1, 0) + f(1, 1) = 1.$$

17. Unabhaengigkeit bei Paaren. — Der Ausdruck (20^b) der vorigen Nummer:

$$(20^b) \qquad \frac{l(y_1, x_2)}{l(x_1, x_2)}$$

giebt die Wahrscheinlichkeit $p_1(x_1, y_1)$, dass (x_1) das Alter y_1 erreicht. Sie ist im Allgemeinen noch von dem Alter x_2 des zweiten Individuums abhängig. Die gewöhnliche Annahme ist, dass dies nicht der Fall ist. Man setzt dann eben Unabhängigkeit der Sterbenswahrscheinlichkeiten von (x_1) und (x_2) voraus. Das ist im Interesse der Einfachkeit der Rechnung sehr vernünftig, aber nichtsdestoweniger eine neue Hypothese. Es besteht hier eine vollständige Aequivalenz zwischen den folgenden beiden Axiomen, von denen das erste (VII_2) Unabhängigkeit im analytischen, das zweite (VIII_2) Unabhängigkeit im Sinne der Wahrscheinlichkeitsrechnung fordert, die aber beide nicht aus den früheren Axiomen folgen:

Axiom VII_2. Die vier Wahrscheinlichkeiten des Axioms V_2

$$f(\alpha_1, \alpha_2 ; x_1 - y_1, x_2 - y_2)$$

seien nur Funktionen von $x_1\, y_1\, x_2\, y_2$. Dann ist die Wahrscheinlichkeit, dass (x_1) das Alter y_1 erlebt, analytisch unabhängig von dem Alter x_2 des zweiten Individuums, das dem Alter x_1 des ersten entspricht.

Axiom VIII_2. Die vier Wahrscheinlichkeiten des Axioms V_2

$$f(\alpha_1, \alpha_2 ; x_1 - y_1, x_2 - y_2)$$

seien nur Funktionen von $x_1\, y_1\, x_2\, y_2$. Dann ist das Ereignis, dass (x_1) das Alter y_1 erlebt, im Sinne der Wahrscheinlichkeitsrechnung unabhängig von dem Ereignis, dass (x_2) das Alter y_2 erlebt.

In der Tat, gilt Axiom VII_2, so heisst dies, dass der Ausdruck (20^b) von x_2 nicht abhängt. Dann zerfällt $l(x_1, x_2)$ in zwei Faktoren:

$$l(x_1, x_2) = l_1(x_1)\, l_2(x_2), \tag{21}$$

von denen der erste nicht von x_2, der zweite nicht von x_1 abhängt. Dann wird aber

$$f(0,0) = p(x_1, y_1 ; x_2, y_2) = \frac{l(y_1, y_2)}{l(x_1, x_2)} = \frac{l_1(y_1)}{l_1(x_1)}\, \frac{l_2(y_2)}{l_2(x_2)},$$

$$f(0,0) + f(0,1) = p_1(x_1, y_1) = \frac{l(y_1, x_2)}{l(x_1, x_2)} = \frac{l_1(y_1)}{l_1(x_1)},$$

$$f(0,0) + f(1,0) = p_2(x_2, y_2) = \frac{l(x_1, y_2)}{l(x_1, x_2)} = \frac{l_2(y_2)}{l_2(x_2)}.$$

Also folgt

$$p(x_1, y_1 ; x_2, y_2) = p_1(x_1, y_1)\, p_2(x_2, y_2)$$

das ist die Behauptung des Axioms VIII_2.

Gilt umgekehrt Axiom VIII_2, so muss die Determinante D des Satzes VII (Nr. 5) verschwinden. Dies giebt:

$$(22)\qquad 0 = D = \begin{vmatrix} f(0,0), & f(0,1) \\ f(1,0), & f(1,1) \end{vmatrix} =$$

$$= \frac{1}{l(x_1, x_2)^2} \begin{vmatrix} l(y_1, y_2), & l(y_1, x_2) - l(y_1, y_2) \\ l(x_1, y_2) - l(y_1, y_2), & l(y_1, y_2) - l(x_1, y_2) - l(y_1, x_2) + l(x_1, x_2) \end{vmatrix}.$$

Diese Gleichung reduziert sich auf

$$\begin{vmatrix} l(y_1, y_2), & l(y_1, x_2) \\ l(x_1, y_2), & l(x_1, x_2) \end{vmatrix} = 0$$

das ist

$$(23)\qquad \frac{l(y_1, y_2)}{l(y_1, x_2)} = \frac{l(x_1, y_2)}{l(x_1, x_2)}.$$

Es muss also sein

$$l(x_1, x_2) = l_1(x_1)\, l_2(x_2)$$

und es folgt Axiom VII_2. Es gilt also:

Satz XVI_2. Die Axiome VII_2 und VIII_2 sind einander vollständig aequivalent.

Setzt man l als differentierbar voraus, so lässt sich derselbe Schluss auf folgende etwas übersichtlichere Art gewinnen:

Durch einfache Umformungen lässt sich die Bedingung (22) zunächst in die Form setzen

$$\begin{vmatrix} l(x_1, x_2), & \Delta_{x_2}\, l(x_1, x_2) \\ \Delta_{x_1}\, l(x_1, x_2), & \Delta^2_{x_1 x_2}\, l(x_1, x_2) \end{vmatrix} = 0.$$

Dabei bezeichnet

$$\Delta_{x_1} l(x_1, x_2) = l(y_1, x_2) - l(x_1, x_2), \quad \Delta_{x_2} l(x_1, x_2) = l(x_1, y_2) - l(x_1, x_2)$$

$$\Delta^2_{x_1 x_2} l(x_1, x_2) = l(y_1, y_2) - l(y_1, x_2) - l(x_1, y_2) + l(x_1, x_2).$$

Lässt y_1 nach x_1, y_2 nach x_2 hineinrücken, so folgt:

$$\begin{vmatrix} l(x_1, x_2), & \dfrac{\partial l(x_1, x_2)}{\partial x_2} \\ \dfrac{\partial l(x_1, x_2)}{\partial x_1}, & \dfrac{\partial^2 l(x_1, x_2)}{\partial x_1\, \partial x_2} \end{vmatrix} = 0$$

Es ist also

$$l \cdot \frac{\partial^2 l}{\partial x_1 \partial x_2} = \frac{\partial l}{\partial x_1} \cdot \frac{\partial l}{\partial x_2}. \tag{24}$$

Diese partielle Differentialgleichung hat aber zum allgemeinen Integral die Gleichung (21).

18. Empirische Ermittelung der Absterbeordnung von Paaren. — Denkt man sich einen grossen Bestand von Versicherungen auf zwei verbundene Leben gegeben, so kann man aus ihm, indem man die Axiome I-VI voraussetzt, ohne Zuhülfenahme des Axioms VII oder VIII für eine gegebene Alterskombination (x_1, x_2) die relative Häufigkeit bestimmen, mir der im nächsten Lebensjahre folgende vier Fälle beobachtet werden:

a) x_1 überlebt, x_2 überlebt,
b) x_1 überlebt, x_2 stirbt,
c) x_1 stirbt, x_2 überlebt,
d) x_1 stirbt, x_2 stirbt.

Man zählt zu diesem Zwecke einfach aus, bei wieviel Paaren des Beobachtungsmaterials jede dieser vier Möglichkeiten eintritt und dividiert die so für jeden dieser vier Fälle beobachtete Anzahl von Paaren durch die Gesamtzahl aller Paare, bei denen der erste Versicherte beim Alter x_1 und der zweite Versicherte beim Alter x_2 lebt. Eine solche Statistik liesse sich natürlich nur aus solchen Versicherungsarten ableiten, bei denen sowohl der erste als der zweite Tod von der Versicherungsgesellschaft beobachtet würden, wie dies z. B. bei den Renten bis zum zweiten Tod der Fall ist.

Die relativen Häufigkeit nun, die sich so für jede der obigen vier Möglichkeiten ergeben, stellen Näherungswerte für die entsprechenden Wahrscheinlichkeiten $f(0,0)$, $f(0,1)$, $f(1,0)$, $f(1,1)$ dar, deren Summe immer 1 ist und deren mittlerer Fehler aus der Anzahl der beobachteten Paare nach den üblichen Formeln gerechnet werden kann. Es wird sich so für die Determinante

$$\begin{vmatrix} f(0,0), & f(0,1) \\ f(1,0), & f(1,1) \end{vmatrix}$$

ein bestimmter Zahlenwert ergeben und wenn dieser mehr von 0 abweicht als sich auf Grund des mittleren Fehlers (Nr. 6) erwarten lässt, so wird für ein solches Material die Zulässigkeit der üblichen Formeln für die Berechnung der Prämien und Reserven mindestens zweifelhaft erscheinen. Es ist aber leicht einzusehen, dass man aus einem solchen Material direkt eine durch die Funktion $l(x_1, x_2)$ charakterisierte Absterbeordnung von Paaren empirisch ableiten könnte. Ebenso hat es keine Schwierigkeit mit Hülfe dieser Funktion $l(x_1, x_2)$ die für die Prämienberechnung und Reserveberechnung erforderlichen verallgemeinerten Formeln abzuleiten, bei denen die Sterbenswahrscheinlichkeiten der beiden zu einem Paare vereinigten Leben nicht mehr als voneinander unabhängig vorausgesetzt werden.

Praktisch wird allerdings dieses Kriterium für die Unabhängigkeit der Sterbenswahrscheinlichkeiten der beiden zu einem Paare vereinigten Leben kaum Anwendung finden können, weil das statistische Material gerade bei Versicherungen auf zwei verbundene Leben sehr beschränkt ist. Um so wichtiger ist die theoretische Einsicht, dass die Annahme des Unabhängigkeitsaxiomes VII oder VIII für die beiden zu einem Paare vereinigten Leben eine willkürliche Festsetzung ist, die keineswegs von den « Theorie » der Wahrscheinlichkeiten gefordert wird, sondern wohl nur deshalb gemacht wird, weil dadurch die Rechnungen bequemer werden und weil die gegenteilige Annahme — dass nämlich das Axiom VII nicht gilt — noch nicht bewiesen ist.

Etwas anders liegen die Verhältnisse bei Versicherungen auf einzelne Leben, weil hier, wie aus den folgenden Betrachtungen hervorgeht, eine Aufgabe des Unabhängigkeitsaxioms VII die Auffassung und Rechnung derartig komplicieren würde, dass dies praktisch auf die Unmöglichkeit hinauskäme, die Wahrscheinlichkeitsrechnung auf die Lebensversicherung anzuwenden. Jedenfalls setzen die üblichen Formeln der Lehrbücher für die Berechnung der Prämien und Reserven immer die Gültigkeit des Axiomes VII oder VIII auch bei Versicherungen auf einzelne Leben voraus, wie dies weiter unter gezeigt werden wird.

§ 3.

Drei und mehr Individuen.

19. Die fingierte Absterbeordnung für eine Gruppe von n Individuen. — *Axiom V_n.* Sind $e_1, e_2, \ldots e_n$ gegebene positive Zahlen, so werden für alle Werte $e_k \leqq x_k \leqq y_k \leqq w$ $(k = 1, 2, \ldots n)$ durch Zahlen gemessen die Wahrscheinlichkeiten:

$$f(\alpha_1, \alpha_2 \ldots \alpha_n ; x_1 - y_1, x_2 - y_2, \ldots x_n - y_n)$$

dafür, dass bei der Personengruppe $(x_1, x_2 \ldots x_n)$ bis zu den entsprechenden Altern $(y_1, y_2 \ldots y_n)$ beziehungsweise $\alpha_1, \alpha_2 \ldots \alpha_n$ Todesfälle stattfinden $(\alpha_i = 0, 1)$.

Die Bezeichnungsweise ist also die, dass x_k das Alter angiebt, das das k^{te} Individuum erreicht hat, und dass α_k die Anzahl der Sterbefälle angiebt, die bei diesem Individuum bis zum Alter y_k eintreten. Es ist daher jede der Zahlen α_k entweder 0 oder 1, je nachdem das betreffende Individuum die betreffende Altersstrecke überlebt oder in ihr stirbt. Es ergeben sich so 2^n Möglichkeiten, denen ebensoviele Wahrscheinlichkeiten:

$$f(\alpha_1, \alpha_2 \ldots \alpha_n)$$

— wir haben der Bequemlichkeit halber die Alter in den Argumenten nicht aufgeführt — entsprechen. Die Summe dieser f ist $= 1$.

Addiert man dagegen die 2^{n-1} Grössen f, bei denen $\alpha_1 = 0$ ist, während die übrigen α alle möglichen Werte durchlaufen, so ergiebt sich die Wahrscheinlichkeit $p(x_1, y_1)$, dass (x_1) das Alter y_1 erlebt. Analog ergeben sich für die entsprechenden Altersstrecken die Ueberlebenswahrscheinlichkeiten für die anderen Individuen der Gruppe. Es folgt also das Axiom V_1 aus dem Axiom V_n. Analog zeigt man, dass auch das Axiom V_2 in dem Axiom V_n enthalten ist.

Satz XV_n. Die Wahrscheinlichkeit $p(x_1, y_1; x_2, y_2; \ldots. x_n, y_n)$ dafür, dass $(x_1, x_2 \ldots x_n)$ sämtlich die entsprechenden Alter $y_1, y_2 \ldots y_n$ erleben, ist 0 sobald eine der Zahlen y gleich w wird.

Es folgt analog wie in Nr. 17 die Existenz einer fingierten Absterbeordnung für eine Gruppe von n Personen, d. h.: es gilt der Satz:

Satz XIV_n. Jede der 2^n Wahrscheinlichkeiten des Axioms v_n:

$$f(\alpha_1, \alpha_2 \ldots \alpha_n)$$

sei eine Funktion von $x_1, y_1; x_2, y_2; x \ldots x_n, y_n$ allein. Dann existiert eine positive Funktion $l(x_1, x_2 \ldots. x_n)$ der n Variablen $x_1, x_2 \ldots x_n$, die die Zahl der Lebenden der Gruppe von n Personen bei der Alterskombination $x_1, x_2 \ldots. x_n$ heisst. Diese nimmt mit wachsenden Argumenten nicht zu und verschwindet, wenn eines der Argumente unendlich gross wird. Mit ihrer Hülfe drückt sich die Wahrseheinlickeit $p(x_1, y_1; x_2, y_2; \ldots x_n, y_n)$, dass $x_1, x_2 \ldots x_n$ bezw. die Alter $y_1, y_2 \ldots y_n$ erleben, durch die Gleichung aus:

$$f(0, 0 \ldots 0) = p(x_1, y_1; x_2, y_2; \ldots x_n, y_n = \frac{l(y_1, y_2 \ldots y_n)}{l(x_1, x_2 \ldots x_n)}.$$

Der Beweis dieses Satzes bedarf keiner weiteren Ausführung. Natürlich drücken sich auch die anderen Wahrscheinlichkeiten $f(\alpha_1, \alpha_2 \ldots \alpha_n)$ unserer Gruppe ebenfalls durch die Funktion l aus, analog wie dies für $n = 2$ in Nr. 17 gezeigt wurde.

20. Unabhängigkeit bei Gruppen von n Individuen. — Bis hierher bietet der Schritt von $n = 2$ nach $n = n$ keine Eigentümlichkeiten, Schwierigkeiten oder Interesse. Dagehen tritt ein besonderes Moment in die Erscheinung, wenn wir uns zu den Axiomen VII_n und VIII_n wenden, die das Analogon der Axiome VII_2 und VIII_2 zu bilden haben. Im ersten Kapitel (Nr. 10) haben wir nämlich darauf aufmerksam gemacht, dass zur Unabhängigkeit mehrerer Ereignisse voneinander nicht ausreicht, dass je zwei derselben voneinander unabhängig sind. Bei den Axiomen der Lebensversicherungsmathematik kann man dagegen, wie wir sofort sehen werden, aus der Unabhängigkeit von je zwei der Ueberlebenswahrscheinlichkeiten bei einer Gruppe von n Individuen auf die Unabhängigkeit aller dieser Ueberlebenswahrscheinlichkeiten voneinander schliessen. Der Grund hierfür liegt in dem Parallelismus der

Axiome VII und VIII, nach denen man von einer Unabhängigkeit im Sinne der Wahrscheinlichkeitsrechnung auf eine Unabhängigkeit im analytischen Sinne und umgekehrt schliessen kann. Dabei hat die analytische Gestalt der Unabhängigkeitsbedingungen noch eine gewisse besondere Form. Wir stellen zunächst das Axiom auf, das für n Individuen dem Axiome VII_2 entspricht. Es lautet;

Axiom VII_n. Die 2^n Wahrscheinlichkeiten $f(\alpha_1, \alpha_2 \ldots \alpha_n)$ seien nur Funktionen von $x_1 y_1 x_2 y_2 \ldots x_n y_n$. Dann ist die Wahrscheinlichkeit, dass bei der Personengruppe $(x_1, x_2 \ldots x_n)$ das i^{te} Individuum das Alter y_i erreicht, analytisch unabhängig von den Altern x, die bei den übrigen Individuen der Gruppe dem Alter x_i entsprechen.

Dieses Axiom besagt offenbar, dass z. B. für das erste Individuum der Quotient:

$$\frac{l(y_1, x_2, \ldots x_n)}{l(x_1, x_2, \ldots x_n)}$$

von den Veränderlichen $x_2, x_3 \ldots x_n$ nicht abhängt. Es muss also die Funktion l $(x_1, x_2 \ldots x_n)$ in ein Produkt von zwei Funktionen zerfallen, von denen die erste $l_1(x_1)$ nicht von x_2 und die zweite $l_2(x_3, \ldots x_n)$ nicht von x_1 abhängt. Allgemeiner folgt, dass die Funktion $l(x_1, x_2, \ldots x_n)$ sich für jedes Wertepaar (x_i, x_k) in zwei Faktoren zerlegen lässt, von denen der erste nicht von x_i, der zweite nicht von x_k abhängt $(i \neq k)$. Es gilt nur der « Hülfssatz » [1], dass eine solche Funktion l in n Faktoren verfällt, von denen der erste nur von x_1, der zweite nur von $x_2, \ldots$ der letzte nur von x_n abhängt:

$$(a) \qquad l(x_1, x_2, \ldots x_n) = l_1(x_1)\, l_2(x_2) \ldots l_n(x_n).$$

In der That gilt der Hülfssatz für $n = 2$. Angenommen, er sei bereits für $n - 1$ Veränderliche bewiesen, so folgt:

$$(b) \qquad l(x_1, x_2, \ldots x_n) = m_1(x_1, x_n)\, m_2(x_2, x_n) \ldots m_{n-1}(x_{n-1}, x_n).$$

Lässt man x_n und x_{n-1} ihre Rolle vertauschen, so ist auch:

$$(c) \quad l(x_1, x_2, \ldots x_n) = \mathrm{M}_1(x_1, x_{n-1})\, \mathrm{M}_2(x_2, x_{n-1}) \ldots \mathrm{M}_{n-2}(x_{n-2}, x_{n-1})\, \mathrm{M}_{n-1}(x_n, x_{n-1}).$$

Setzt man die rechten Seiten von (c) und (b) einander gleich und x_n konstant, so wird:

$$(d) \quad \mathrm{M}_1(x_1, x_{n-1})\, \mathrm{M}_2(x_2, x_{n-1}) \ldots \mathrm{M}_{n-2}(x_{n-2}, x_{n-1}) = l_1(x_1)\, l_2(x_2) \ldots l_{n-2}(x_{n-2})\, m_{n-1}(x_{n-1}).$$

(1) Dieser wird weiter unten bei der Folgerung von Axiom VII_n aus VIII_n gebraucht. Die hier in Rede stehende umgekehrte Folgerung von VIII_n und VII_n würde ohne den Hülfssatz einfacher geschehen.

Dabei bedeutet $l_i(x_i)$ das was aus $m_i(x_i, x_n)$, $(i = 1, 2 \ldots n-2)$, $m_{n-1}(x_{n-1})$ das, was aus $m_{n-1}(x_{n-1}, x_n) : M_{n-1}(x_n, x_{n-1})$ wird, wenn man darin x_n konstant setzt. Setzt man diesen Wert aus (d) in (c) ein, so folgt für beliebige Variable $x_1, x_2 \ldots x_n$:

$$(e) \qquad l(x_1, x_2 \ldots x_n) = l_1(x_1)\, l_2(x_2) \ldots l_{n-2}(x_{n-2})\, l_{n-1}(x_{n-1}, x_n)$$

wo $m_{n-1}(x_{n-1})\, M_{n-1}(x_n, x_{n-1}) = l_{n-1}(x_{n-1}, x_n)$ gesetzt ist.

Da nur x_{n-1} und x_n der anderen Variablen gleichberechtigt sind, folgt (a) aus (e). Damit ist der ‚Hülfssatz' bewiesur.

Aus Gleichung (a) folgt für unsere Ueberlebenswahrscheinlichkeit $p(x_1, y_1; x_2, y_2; \ldots x_n, y_n)$ die Darstellung:

$$(21_n) \qquad p(x_1, y_1; x_2, y_2; \ldots x_n, y_n) = \frac{l_1(y_1)\, l_2(y_2) \ldots l_n(y_n)}{l_1(x_1)\, l_2(x_2) \ldots l_n(x_n)}.$$

Mithin sind die n Ueberlebenswahrscheinlichkeiten, die jedem Einzelnen der n Individuen unserer Gruppe entsprechen, v o n e i n a n d e r unabhängig (im Sinne der Wahrscheinlichkeitsrechnung), wenn die in Axiom VII$_n$ vorausgesetzte Unabhängigkeit (im Sinne der Analysis) besteht.

Parallel dem Axiom VII$_n$ ist nun das Axiom VIII$_n$, das lautet:

Axiom VIII$_n$. Die 2^n Wahrscheinlichkeiten $f(\alpha_1, \alpha_2 \ldots \alpha_n)$ des Axioms V$_n$ seien nur Funktionen von $x_1 y_1 x_2 y_2 \ldots x_n y_n$. Dann ist das Ereignis, dass in der Gruppe $(x_1, x_2 \ldots x_n)$ das i^{te} Individuum das Alter y_i erreicht, im Sinne der Wahrscheinlichkeitsrechnung unabhängig von dem Ereignis, dass irgend ein anderes Individuum der Gruppe, z. B. das k^{te}, das Alter y_k erreicht.

Wir wollen nun zeigen, dass die Axiome VII$_n$ und VIII$_n$ einander vollständig aequivalent sind. Zunächst ist klar, dass aus VII$_n$ das Axiom VIII$_n$ folgt, denn das erste Axiom hatte die Gleichung (21_n) zur Folge.

Es handelt sich also nur noch darum zu zeigen, dass auch umgekehrt aus dem Axiom VIII$_n$ das Axiom VII$_n$ folgt. Um dieses zu zeigen, wenden wir das Axiom VIII$_n$ z. B. auf das Paar (x_1, x_2) an, das sich für $i = 1$, $k = 2$, ergiebt. Dann schliessen wir in Nr. 17 auf die Gültigkeit der Gleichung (vergl. Gleichung (23) der Nr. 17):

$$\frac{l(y_1, y_2, x_3 \ldots x_n)}{l(y_1, x_2, x_3 \ldots x_n)} = \frac{l(x_1, y_2, x_3 \ldots x_n)}{l(x_1, x_2, x_3 \ldots x_n)}.$$

Hieraus schliesst man aber wieder, wie in Nr. 17, dass die Funktion $l(x_1, x_2 \ldots x_n)$ sich in ein Produkt von zwei Faktoren zerlegen lassen muss, von denen der erste nicht von x_2, der zweite nicht von x_1 abhängt. Diese Schlussweise, gilt für jedes Paar (x_i, x_k). Also folgt aus dem Hülfssatz auf voriger Seite, dass die Funktion $l(x_1, x_2 \ldots x_n)$ in ein Produkt von n Funktionen zerfällt, von denen die erste nur von x_1, die zweite nur von x_2, schliesslich die letzte nur von x_n abhängt ([1]). Daraus folgt:

Satz XVI. Die Axiome VII_n und VIII_n sind einander vollständig aequivalent.

Gleichzeitig ergiebt sich der merkwürdige

Satz XVII. Gelten die Axiome I-VI, so folgt aus der Unabhängigkeit der Ueberlebenswahrscheinlichkeiten je zweier Individuen unserer Gruppe die Unabängigkeit aller Ueberlebenswahrscheinlichkeiten dieser Gruppe *voneinander.*

21. Schlussbemerkung. — Aus den Annahmen des ersten Kapitels folgen die Formeln der Versicherungs-Lehrbücher. Umgekehrt folgen aus den Formeln dieser Lehrbücher die Annahmen des ersten und zweiten Kapitels. Als entscheidend hat sich dabei die Annahme von der Unabhängigkeit der Sterbens- und Ueberlebenswahrscheinlichkeiten herausgestellt. Diese lässt sich noch konkreter fassen: Nimmt jemand eine Versicherung auf sein (nicht auf verbundene) Leben, so ist seine Prämie nicht abhängig von der Höhe der Prämie, die ein anderer in demselben Jahr eintretender Versicherter zu zahlen hat. Diese selbstverständliche Forderung des praktischen Betriebes folgt aus dem Unabhängigkeitsaxiom VII, umgekehrt dieses aus ihr. Man nehme nur als eingegangene Versicherung eine reine Erlebensfallversicherung, die (x_1) gegen einmalige Prämie auf das Alter y_1 abschliesst. Die einmalige Prämie ist bis auf den Diskontierungsfaktor die Ueberlebenswahrscheinlichkeit $p(x_1, y_1)$.

Die Sätze der Theorie des Risikos im Besonderen sind daher auch nur eine logische Folge der für die Berechnung der Prämien und Reserven in den Versicherungs-Lehrbüchern abgeleiteten Sätze. Die Lehre vom Risiko lässt sich daher ganz wie diese Sätze « elementar », d. h. ohne wahrscheinlichkeitstheoretische Kenntnisse ableiten, indem man « naiv » mit der fingierten Absterbeordnung operiert. Im Besonderen ist der Satz von der Addition der Quadrate der mittleren Risiken (den Raedell als einem elementaren Beweise unzugänglich betrachtete) genau so eine unmittelbare Folge des Unabhängigkeitsaxioms wie der soeben betrachtete von der Addition der Prämien.

[1] Ein weiterer Beweis folgt aus den der Gleichung (24) der Nr. 18 analogen und aus ihr folgenden Differentialgleichungen:

$$l \cdot \frac{\partial^2 l}{\partial x_i \partial x_k} = \frac{\partial l}{\partial x_i} \frac{\partial l}{\partial x_k} \quad (i < k = 1, 2 \ldots n).$$

L. MARCH

UNE NOUVELLE STATISTIQUE INTERNATIONALE DE LA POPULATION.

OBSERVATIONS SUR LA COMPARAISON ET SUR LA TERMINOLOGIE DES STATISTIQUES

Depuis le milieu du siècle dernier, les statistiques internationales ont fait de grands progrès sous l'impulsion que leur ont donnée, d'abord les Congrès de statistique, puis l'Institut international de statistique créé en 1885. Comme elles peuvent aider à découvrir ce qu'il y a de général dans les relations numériques des faits qui intéressent directement l'homme et la vie sociale, comme aussi chaque peuple est intéressé à connaître les autres, dans un grand nombre de pays, les statistiques officielles font une part de plus en plus large aux tableaux internationaux.

Cependant, ces documents n'acquièrent toute leur valeur que si les méthodes sont rendues uniformes et si les termes qui servent de base aux comparaisons peuvent être ramenés à la même signification dans les differents pays. C'est peut-être la mission la plus importante de l'Institut international de statistique que de veiller sur cette uniformité indispensable.

Puisque, pour la première fois, le Congrès international de mathématiques comprend, dans sa section de mathématiques appliquées, des questions intéressant la science des Actuaires et la Statistique, il me semble utile, d'une part de signaler au Congrès des documents pouvant être utilisés pour l'application des théories, d'autre part d'appeller l'attention sur des éléments essentiels des comparaisons statistiques, dont l'expression peut donner lieu à de fausses interprétations.

I.

La Statistique générale de la France a introduit dans ses publications un grand nombre de tableaux propres à faciliter les comparaisons internationales, par exemple, dans son Annuaire statistique, dans les résultats des recensements.

L'ouvrage que je crois utile de présenter spécialement au Congrès a paru à la fin de l'année 1907 sous le titre : *Statistique internationale du mouvement de la population, d'après les registres de l'état civil; Résumé rétrospectif depuis l'origine des statistiques de l'état civil jusqu'en 1905.*

Cet ouvrage complète et met à jours les *Confronti internazionali* publiés en 1894 par M. L. Bodio.

On trouvera en tête du volume un exposé des procédés actuellement en usage dans tous les pays pour l'enregistrement et le dépouillement des mariages, des naissances et des décès. Actuellement, dans presque tous les pays, le dépouillement des actes de l'état civil est effectué par un Service central, grâce à l'usage de bulletins individuels d'état civil, système qui donne plus de confiance dans la valeur des résultats et permet une meilleure utilisation des documents originaux que le système du dépouillement local.

Pour certains pays, les tableaux partent du milieu du XVIIIe siècle. Ils sont groupés en trois parties et accompagnés d'un commentaire explicatif dans lequel on a rappelé les événements qui paraissent avoir eu le plus d'influence sur les mouvements enregistrés.

La première partie est consacrée au mouvement général de la population: état sommaire de la population, des mariages, des naissances, des décès, de l'excédent des naissances sur les décès. Les nombres proportionnels pour 10.000 habitants sont calculés ennée par année et par périodes décennales ou quinquennales.

Dans la seconde partie, les nombres de mariages et les nombres de naissances sont analysée suivant de nombreux caractères, étudiés en tenant compte du sexe et de l'âge.

Dans la troisième partie, les nombres de décès sont soumis à une semblable analyse. Cette partie renferme un grand nombre de tables de mortalité et de survie applicables à des Etat entiers ou à la population des grandes Villes.

On a indiqué le mode de construction de ces tables, on en a comparé les éléments et l'on a rapproché ces tables de celles qui ont été dressées, pour des têtes choisies, par le Compagnies d'assurances.

Enfin, d'autres tableaux fournissent des indications sur les décès causés par les principales maladies.

Le volume renferme ainsi de longues suites de nombres dont la valeur comparative, surtout pour les plus récents, paraît satisfaisante. Ces nombres sont susceptibles d'être soumis à l'analyse mathématique avec d'autant plus de fruit que les principales influences aux quels ils sont soumis sont des influences d'ordre physique.

II.

Dans la mise en oeuvre des résultats statistiques, il ne suffit pas d'être averti de l'origine des documents, et des méthodes suivant lesquelles ils ont été élaborés, il importe encore que les expressions et représentations dont on fait usage possèdent des significations précises et uniformes, et ne risquent pas d'égarer ceux qui utilisent les conclusions de l'analyse.

Les éléments essentiels des comparaisons statistiques sont les fréquences et les moyennes ; on a recours aussi aux réprésentations graphiques pour établir certaines relations. Il me paraît utile de proposer quelques précisions relativement aux modes usuels de comparaison et à la terminologie ordinaire.

Fréquences. — La méthode statistique intervient quand on veut mesurer, dans un ensemble, l'intensité d'un caractère, ou quand on compare des ensembles par rapport au même caractère, et que les parties de l'ensemble ne possèdent pas le caractère au même degré. On appelle alors fréquence d'un degré quelconque le rapport du nombre des parties correspondant à ce degré au nombre total des parties de l'ensemble ([1]).

En général les circonstances qui ont imprimé à plusieurs parties de l'ensemble, et au même degré, le caractère étudié nous sont inconnues. L'analyse statistique cherche à découvrir les plus importantes en comparant entre elles, sous différentes conditions, les fréquences observées. Comme base de comparaison on convient souvent de se reporter au schéma de combinaisons et de répétitions sur lequel est fondé le calcul des probabilités.

Mais une différence essentielle sépare la fréquence observée en statistique et la probabilité mathématique. En statistique, nous ignorons les circonstances initiales des faits observées ; notre connaissance peut tout au plus s'étendre à quelques parties de l'enchainement intermédiaire entre les conditions originelles et le résultat. Par exemple, nous ne connaissons pas les chances de mort des hommes qui entrent dans leur 30e année, et nous connaissons mal les raisons qui feront que certains seront frappés plutôt que d'autres dans le cours de cette 30e année.

Dans le schéma des probabilités les combinaisons et répétitions qui contiennent en puissance le résultat final sont complètement connues; seul le jeu du déclenchement qui fait apparaître certaines combinaisons demeure imperceptible en raison de l'exiguitè de son action.

L'accord d'une distribution de fréquences, observée en statistique, avec une distribution de probabilités n'implique donc qu'une analogie apparente entre l'enchainement des faits statistiques et la formation des probabilités. Pour l'ordonnance du travail du statisticien, cette analogie offre une grande utilitè puisqu'elle permet de sérier les recherches, de négliger provisoirement les variations imputables en apparence à des cas fortuits. Dans l'exposé des résultat il convient de ne pas laisser supposer que l'enchainement des faits étudiés est assimilable au schéma conventionnel que l'on a pris comme terme de comparaison.

Aussi serait-il opportun, en statistique, de renoncer à l'emploi du mot probabilité pour exprimer l'attente que fait naître la constatation d'une fréquence ; car, si, dans la théorie des probabilités, la convention sur laquelle repose cette attente isnpire une parfaite confiance, en statistique le degré de confiance que mérite cette attente est souvent modifié par l'étude des liaisons des faits, par les enseignements des sciences spéciales.

([1]) Le mot fréquence impliquant l'idée de répétition, il est logique d'éliminer de l'ensemble les parties qui ne sont pas susceptibles de posséder le caractère étudié.

D'ailleurs les applications du calcul seraient à peu près aussi commodes si l'on opérait sur des fréquences au lieu d'opérer sur des probabilités; les énoncés des propositions devraient être transformés, mais ils seraient plus rigoureux et éviteraient bien des critiques adressées aux anciens énoncés.

Par exemple, lorsque LAPLACE contestait le caractère accidentel des écarts du coefficient de natalité masculine observé à Paris, à Londres et à Naples, en assimilant la détermination du sexe à un tirage au sort, il s'exposait aux critiques que BERTRAND a adressées à son énoncé. Mais le statisticien a le droit de décider, obéissant à une convention justifiée par l'expérience, que les écarts dont il cherchera l'explication par une analyse ultérieure devront dépasser une certaine limite, en deçà de laquelle les écarts sont provisoirement regardés comme accidentels. Cette limite, l'analogie, d'accord avec l'expérience, engage à la fixer d'après une échelle de probabilité.

On se borne ainsi à faire appel à ce que M. EMILE BOREL a appelé la valeur pratique du calcul. L'ampleur théorique des propositions, leur autorité sur les esprits avides d'objectivité s'amoindrissent sans doute, mais la théorie s'etablit en meilleure harmonie avec le faits.

En mathématique on distingue les probabilités à priori et les probabilités à posteriori. Il serait parfaitement inutile de modifier cette terminologie car les mathématiciens ne peuvent se méprendre sur le sens véritable des termes. Dans les applications à la Statistique il ne paraît pas suffissant de substituer à la notion de probabilité à posteriori, qui, elle aussi repose sur une convention initiale, celle de probabilité statistique que suggère BLASCHKE. Pour que les personnes insuffisamment averties ne se méprennent pas sur la portée de ces applications, il semble préférable d'écarter complètement de l'analyse des résultats statistiques le terme *probabilité* et le mot *probable* entendu dans le sens mathématique.

Si l'on tient à exprimer un degré de confiance, il vaudrait mieux employer des expressions telles que *plausibilité* et *plausible*, la plausibilité embrassant tous les éléments actuels d'appréciation.

Moyennes. — Quand on veut comparer rapidement deux ensembles statistiques, on est amené à former, pour chacun d'eux, un coefficient unique susceptible de synthétiser l'intensité du caractère étudié, intensité qui n'est d'ailleurs pas uniforme. Puisque l'on a en vue une synthèse, ce coefficient doit être fonction des intensités particulières à toutes les parties; parmi l'infinité des fonctions possibles on choisit de préférence la plus simple, celle qui exprime l'intensité totale. Enfin, pour que ce coefficient ne dépende pas de la dimension de l'ensemble on rapporte l'intensitè totale au nombre des parties : le résultat est appelé moyenne arithmétique.

On fait aussi usage d'autres fonctions, ou comme on dit d'autres moyennes : géométrique, harmonique, quadratique, mediane, etc... ; je ne me propose pas de les comparer. Je veux simplement signaler que, dans le langage courant le mot moyenne a un tout autre sens que dans les sciences mathématiques et physiques où il correspond à la notion de centre de gravité.

A vrai dire, dans le langage courant, le mot moyenne a un sens assez vague, celui de terme intermédiaire entre le plus grand et le plus petit. Quand on cherche à préciser la notion, en examinant par exemple l'établissement des cotes sur les marchés publics, on constate que, le plus souvent, le mot moyenne est entendu dans le sens de valeur la plus fréquente.

Aux Halles centrales de Paris, par exemple, les mandataires qui cotent les ventes journalières de chaque denrée ne tiennent compte que des ventes opérées par grosses quantités. Ou bien il s'établit sur le marché un prix courant auquel la quantité offerte trouve aisément acquéreur: c'est ce prix qui est indiqué comme cours moyen; ou bien la demande n'est pas assez active pour qu'il en soit ainsi; les grosses quantités sont traitées à des prix divers et le prix moyen s'obtient simplement en formant la demi somme des prix extrêmes (demi somme que l'on décore du nom de moyenne mathématique).

On peut admettre que, dans ce dernier cas, les mandataires ont simplement pour but de parvenir le plus simplement et le plus vite possible à la fixation de la valeur courante. Le prix moyen coté aux Halles est donc autre chose qu'une moyenne arithmétique. Si les ventes par petites quantités étaient très importantes, comme elles s'opèrent généralement à des prix relativement élevés le prix moyen pourrait être très voisin du prix minimum.

A la Bourse des Valeurs, les conditions d'établissement de la cote sont un peu différentes. Le coteur ignore les quantités vendues; il inscrit simplement sur un registre, avant l'ouverture du marché, les prix auxquels chaque valeur est offerte. Puis, au cours du marché, il note les prix auquels se sont opérées les diverses transactions. A la fin, le cours moyen est calculé en formant la demi somme du prix le plus haut et du prix le plus bas.

Le chiffre ainsi obtenu est naturellement différent de la moyenne arithmétique et il serait également différent de la valeur la plus fréquente sans une circonstance grâce à laquelle il coïncide en fait avec cette valeur: la majeure partie des ordres sont donnés à l'avance au cours moyen et par conséquent le cours arbitré, comme il vient d'être dit, devient le cours auquel le plus grand nombre des titres ont été négociés.

De même encore quand des ouvriers estiment la moyenne des salaires, ou revendiquent un minimum de salaire, ce qu'ils visent c'est le salaire gagné par la majeure partie d'entre eux.

Au contraire les prix moyens calculés pour les marchandises importées dans un pays sont des moyennes arithmétiques.

Diverses expressions ont été proposées pour désigner, dans une série statistique, la valeur la plus fréquente: Lexis l'appelle la valeur normale, Pearson l'appelle le mode. Aucune des deux expressions n'est pleinement satisfaisante. Si le mot *normal* implique une règle générale, il fait naître aussi une idée de loi qui dépasse l'idée de fréquence. Le terme *mode* semble indiquer que la valeur la plus fréquente exprime la manière d'être de la série, ce qui n'est point tout-à-fait exact, plusieurs éléments étant nécessaires pour caractériser cette manière d'être.

Acceptons le mot normal [1], nous constaterons que la moyenne, telle qu'on l'entend dans le langage courant est, non pas la moyenne arithmétique, mais la valeur normale.

[1] S'il n'étaient pas sans grande utilité de créer un néologisme, les expressions valeur *pléistique, valeur plurale,* seraient plus exactes.

Conviendrait-il de modifier le langage scientifique pour le conformer au langage vulgaire?

Ce serait sans doute le meilleur parti si la valeur normale ou plurale pouvait être déterminée avec précision dans tous les cas. Mais il n'en est point ainsi. D'abord on n'est point tout-à-fait d'accord sur la question de savoir si, dans son estimation, il faut éliminer ou non les cas jugés exceptionnels. Puis, la ligne représentant une série de fréquences est parfois une ligne polygonale à dents plus ou moins nombreuses. S'il y a plusieurs dents à peu près de même hauteur, sera-ce la plus haute qui devra être regardée comme normale, bien que peut être elle ne soit la plus haute que par accident?

On convient donc de représenter la série des observations par une courbe continue à un seul sommet, sans écarter aucune observation supposée bien faite, conformément à la règle que s'imposent les physiciens. On admet alors que la position de ce sommet correspond à la valeur normale; ainsi cette valeur dépend de la nature de la courbe choisie et de la méthode d'ajustement.

Elle est différente, par exemple, suivant que l'on emploie comme courbe d'ajustement une courbe binomiale ou l'une des courbes de Pearson. Ce dernier auteur, qui a montré par de nombreux exemples combien sont fréquentes dans la nature et dans la société humaine les distributions dissymétriques, a indiqué une méthode conventionnelle uniforme propre à faire connaître, par l'application de règles fixes; la valeur normale. Malheureusement, sa méthode d'ajustement à l'aide du calcul des moments de plusieurs ordres, excellente dans une foule de cas, où la dissymétrie est assez forte, jusq'à un certain degré, a l'inconvénient de donner une importance excessive aux observations extrêmes. Par exemple, en appliquant son critérium à l'observation détaillée des revenus, le calcul conduit à une valeur normale tendant vers zéro, alors que les statistiques démontrent que cette valeur est loin d'être nulle et va en croissant.

Pour obtenir une meilleure approximation de cette valeur, il faut renoncer au critérium, choisir une autre courbe et alors on retombe dans l'arbitraire.

Il en résulte que jusqu'à présent, la valeur normale ou plnrale n'est pas fixée par une règle uniforme comme la moyenne arithmétique ; elle sera d'ailleurs toujours d'un calcul beaucoup moins simple. La moyenne arithmétique doit donc être préférée comme caractéristique uniforme du caractère de l'ensemble statistique.

Il y aurait quelque présomption à proposer une modification du langage ordinaire que la précision n'attire pas. Mais on peut demander que cette précision s'impose dans les travaux et publications statistiques. Dans ces travaux le mot moyenne devrait toujours avoir le sens de moyenne arithmétique; on désignerait sous le nom de valeur normale, ou plurale, la valeur la plus fréquente, et, quand il s'agirait de prix ou de cours, on substituerait aux expressions inexactes de prix moyen, cours moyen, des expressions plus correctes telles que prix courant, cours arbitré. On éviterait de la sort beaucoup de méprises auxquelles donnent lieu les discussions relatives aux moyennes.

Quételet, et beaucoup d'auteurs l'ont suivi, attachait une grande signification au cas particulier dans lequel la moyenne et la normale sont confondues. Pour lui il n'y a de moyenne véritable que dans ce cas. Il admettait que les erreurs des mesures physiques se distribuent symétriquement et, à son avis, la nature dans ses créations typiques opère suivant cette loi d'erreurs, vise un but dont elle ne s'écarte qu'accidentellement et indifféremment dans un sens ou dans l'autre.

Les mesures physiques ne suivent pas toujours la loi symétrique des erreurs; Bravais en a signalé des exemples á Quételet lui même ([1]). Mais surtout rien n'autorise à attribuer à la nature, par une sorte d'anthropomorphisme peu justifié, la tendence à ne s'écarter du type que suivant une loi uniforme. Les observations météorologiques, biologiques, sociales, aujourd'hui fort nombreuses, démontrent que dans la nature, les types, au sens où l'entendait Quételet, sont rares: ce sont presque des accidents.

Cependant, les observations typiques, ou à peu près typiques, sont assurément beaucoup mieux synthétisées que les autres par le calcul de la moyenne; elles satisfont mieux l'esprit parce qu'elles éveillent l'idée d'une tendance commune. D'autre part l'hypothèse que ces observations se conforment à peu près à la loi d'erreurs dispense à peu près de s'inquiéter de la répartition des faits autour de la moyenne. Mais il n'y a aucune raison de contester la valeur comparative de la moyenne arithmétique, ou doit seulement reconnaître que cette valeur est mieux représentative des faits quand la moyenne arithmétique est une *moyenne normale*.

Arrivons à un dernier abus du mot moyenne. Nous avons vu que pour caractériser la valeur moyenne d'une série de prix on se contentait souvent de former la demi somme des termes extrêmes. En réalité on n'obtient de la sorte qu'un indice commode de la véritable valeur de la moyenne. Il en est encore ainsi quand, au lieu de prendre la demi somme des prix extrêmes on divise la somme des prix par le nombre de ces prix.

De même qu'en physique le terme vitesse moyenne a un sens différent de celui de moyenne des vitesses, il ne faut pas confondre la moyenne des prix et le prix moyen. La première n'est qu'un indice, ce qui ne lui enlève pas d'ailleurs sa valeur comparative. Outre que souvent l'indice est trés voisine de la moyenne et peut la remplacer pratiquement, l'indice a parfois une valeure comparative spéciale d'une réelle valeur.

Par exemple si, à l'aide de tables de mortalité successives, on veut comparer l'état de la mortalité des adultes de 20 à 40 ans au moyen d'un coefficient synthétique, on peut adopter comme élément de comparaison le rapport du nombre des décès survenus entre 20 et 40 ans au nombre des individus de la génération de 20 ans. Mais la comparaison se fera sous un autre aspect, intéressant à d'autres égards, si l'on adopte comme élément de comparaison la moyenne des taux annuels entre 20 et 40 ans. Il en est de même des indices de comparaison des prix de diverses marchandises: suivant le but de ces comparaison l'indice de la moyenne peut être mieux appoprié au but que la moyenne proprement dite qui tient compte des quantités vendues. Des indices de ce genre sont donc fort utiles; il importe seulement que rien n'autorise à les confrondre avec les moyennes proprement dites.

([1]) On sait que les épreuves dites au hasard ne suivent pas toujours la loi des probabilités. D'après Pearson, la roulette de Monaco donne des séries cahotiques.

Variabilité comparative. — Pour comparer des faits variables on fait souvent usage de représentations graphiques. Il ne suffit pas en effet de rapprocher les moyennes et les écarts quadratiques.

On évite toute fausse apparence de l'allure des mouvements comparés en se servant d'échelles logarithmiques. On obtient d'ailleurs la même avantage plus simplement, et moyennant une représentation plus exacte de ces mouvements si, pour construire chaque courbe on se borne à substituer aux nombres observés leurs rapports à la moyenne d'une certaine série de ces nombres.

La juxtaposition des courbes permet de se rendre compte de l'accord ou du désaccord des mouvements ; la comparaison reste néanmoins un peu vague et imprécise. Pour lui donner la valeur d'une mesure, on calcule des coefficients moyens qui synthétisent l'accord des variations observées, en tenant compte ou non de l'importance de ces variations.

Un type de coefficient de ce genre a reçu de Fechner le nom de coefficient de dépendance. Un autre a été appelé par Pearson coefficient de corrélation.

Ces expressions ont l'inconvénient de laisser supposer que la grandeur du coefficient mesure effectivement la dépendance ou la relation plus ou moins étroite qui existe entre les faits comparés. Or il n'en est point ainsi. Le coefficient révèle simplement la concomitance des variations c'est pourquoi il semble plus correct de ne l'employer en statistique que comme *coefficient de covariation.*

*
* *

En résumé, les statistiques sociales s'enrichissent de documents de plus en plus nombreux, applicables à des catégories de population plus étendues et à de longues séries d'années.

Des progrès analogues dans le domaine des observations biologiques font que, sans parler des applications possibles dans la physique proprement dite, l'intervention de la méthode statistique s'étend à des documents plus nombreux et plus soigneusement recueillies.

Les applications des mathématiques à l'analyse de ces documents peuvent apporter l'ordre et la précision nécessaires et aider à orienter les investigations des statisticiens. Peut-être les théories auraient-elles besoin de quelques développements pour mieux s'adapter aux réalités, notamment en ce qui concerne les cas de probabilité variable, l'étude des ensembles concrets et limités, l'interpolation, etc.

Mais il importerait que, dans ces applications, dont les conclusions sont destinée au public, les modes de comparaison et la terminologie fussent uniformes et débarrassés aussi bien que possible des risques d'ambiguité.

D'après ce qui précède, les précautions suivantes semblent devoir être recommandées :

1° — Eviter le terme probabilité pour caractériser l'attente à laquelle donne lieu l'observation d'une fréquence. Indiquer quand on le peut, les limites conventionnelles entre lesquelles il est légitime d'admettre que cette fréquence peut varie. fortuitement.

2° — Réserver le terme valeur moyenne à la moyenne arithmétique ; on désignerait sous les noms de valeur normale, ou valeur plurale, prix courant, cours arbitré, indice de la moyenne, les rapports exprimés dans le langage courant sous les noms de : valeur moyenne, prix moyen, cours moyen.

3° — Dans les comparaisons de variations, si l'on a recours à la méthode graphique, choisir les unités de façon à assurer l'uniformité de comparaison ; si l'on calcule un coefficient synthétique de l'accord ou du désaccord des variations, éviter que son expression paraisse préjuger l'existence de liaisons entre les faits ; le considérer simplement comme coefficient de covariation.

F. DE HELGUERO

SULLA RAPPRESENTAZIONE ANALITICA DELLE STATISTICHE ABNORMALI

Il compito della statistica nelle sue varie applicazioni alle scienze economiche e biologiche non consiste solo nel determinare la legge di dipendenza dei diversi valori ed esprimerla con pochi numeri, ma anche nel fornire un aiuto allo studioso che vuole ricercare le cause della variazione e le loro modificazioni.

A questo scopo ben soddisfa la curva degli errori di osservazione o curva *normale*, tanto frequente nelle statistiche biologiche ed economiche, che esprime la variazione risultante da cause elementari di variazione infinitesime ed in numero infinito, indipendenti fra loro, facentisi equilibrio intorno alla media, od in una parola da cause *accidentali*. Soddisfano bene a questo scopo anche le curve dimorfiche che ci rivelano la eterogeneità del materiale studiato.

Invece le curve teoriche studiate dal PEARSON e dall'EDGEWORTH per la perequazione delle statistiche abnormali in un materiale omogeneo, mentre dànno con molta approssimazione la legge di variazione (meglio della curva normale perchè ne sono delle generalizzazioni), a mio avviso sono difettose in quanto si limitano a dirci che le cause infinitesime elementari della variazione sono *interdipendenti*. Nulla ci fanno sapere sulla legge di dipendenza, quasi nulla sulle relazioni colla curva normale che pure deve essere considerata come fondamentale.

Io penso che miglior aiuto per lo studioso potrebbero essere delle equazioni che supponessero una perturbazione della variabilità normale per opera di cause estranee.

Una tale ipotesi dal punto di vista biologico fu per la prima volta affacciata dallo GIARD (1) che interpretò la bimodalità della variazione della larghezza del *Carcinus moenas* e la lunghezza delle pinze nelle forficule come dovuta all'azione di parassiti che infettassero una parte del materiale studiato.

Molte e varie ipotesi possono farsi sulla legge di perturbazione della variabilità normale: io qui ne espongo due, l'una che corrisponde all'ipotesi dello GIARD, l'altra che suppone la legge di perturbazione lineare, ipotesi a mio avviso molto importante.

(1) GIARD A., *Sur certains cas de dédoublement des courbes de Galton dus au parasitisme et sur le dimorphisme d'origine parasitaire* (Comptes Rendus de l'Ac. des Sciences, Paris, volume CXVIII, p. 870, 1894).

I.

Curve dello GIARD.

Si abbia una popolazione distribuita normalmente secondo la legge

$$y = \frac{y_0}{\sigma\sqrt{2\pi}} e^{-\frac{1}{2}\left(\frac{x-b}{\sigma}\right)^2}$$

ed una causa perturbatrice, p. es. morbosa, affetti alcuni individui non lasciandoli raggiungere lo sviluppo x cui giungerebbero, ma li faccia invece figurare nella classe $(x - c)$. Se la causa perturbatrice ipertrofizzasse gli individui affetti, c sarebbe negativo.

La costante c misura l'effetto della causa perturbatrice sullo sviluppo dell'organismo e può dirsi *indice di atrofia* se positivo, di *ipertrofia* se negativo, in generale *indice di eterotrofia*.

Sia h la probabilità che ha un individuo di esser colpito dalla causa perturbatrice: se si tratta di una causa patologica può dirsi indice di *morbidità*.

Nella nostra trattazione supponiamo c ed h indipendenti da x. Inoltre poichè h esprime una probabilità deve essere $0 < h < 1$.

L'equazione della curva perturbata sarà allora

$$y = \frac{y_0}{\sigma\sqrt{2\pi}} e^{-\frac{1}{2}\left(\frac{x-b}{\sigma}\right)^2} - \frac{hy_0}{\sigma\sqrt{2\pi}} e^{-\frac{1}{2}\left(\frac{x-b}{\sigma}\right)^2} + \frac{hy_0}{\sigma\sqrt{2\pi}} e^{-\frac{1}{2}\left(\frac{x-b+c}{\sigma}\right)^2}$$

che può scriversi:

$$(1) \qquad y = \frac{y_1}{\sigma\sqrt{2\pi}} e^{-\frac{1}{2}\left(\frac{x-b}{\sigma}\right)^2} + \frac{y_2}{\sigma\sqrt{2\pi}} e^{-\frac{1}{2}\left(\frac{x-b_1}{\sigma}\right)^2}$$

avendo posto

$$(1 - h)y_0 = y_1 \ , \ hy_0 = y_2 \ , \ b - c = b_1 .$$

Dalle posizioni risulta che y_1 ed y_2 devon esser sempre positive, mentre b_1 è di segno contrario a b se l'origine si prende sul baricentro.

Si vede inoltre dalla (1) che abbiamo a che fare con una curva dimorfica risultante dalla somma di due curve normali aventi però la stessa deviazione normale. Per ricavare i valori dei cinque parametri y_1, y_2, b, b_1, σ si applicano perciò i metodi da me altrove [1] esposti per la risoluzione delle curve dimorfiche.

[1] HELGUERO F., *Per la risoluzione delle curve dimorfiche* (Memorie della R. Acc. dei Lincei, Roma, 1906).

Si procede in questo modo: Dai dati empirici si calcola la media $\mu'_1 = \frac{\mu_1}{\mu_0}$ e rispetto a questa i momenti $\mu'_2 = \frac{\mu_2}{\mu_0}$, $\mu'_3 = \frac{\mu_3}{\mu_0}$ e $\mu'_4 = \frac{\mu_4}{\mu_0}$, dove μ_0 è l'area.

Si risolve poi l'equazione trinomia di 3° grado in p_2:

$$p_2^3 + \tfrac{1}{2}(\mu'_4 - 3\mu_2'^2)p_2 + \tfrac{1}{2}\mu_3'^2 = 0\,. \tag{2}$$

Poi la

$$p_1 = -\frac{\mu'_2}{p_2}\,.$$

Le b e b_1 sono le radici della

$$b^2 - bp_1 + p_2 = 0. \tag{3}$$

Per b si deve prendere la radice maggiore se si tratta di atrofia, la minore se si tratta di eterotrofia.

Gli altri parametri son dati dalle formule

$$\sigma = \sqrt{p_2 + \mu'_2} \quad y_1 = -\frac{b_1\,\mu_0}{b - b_1} \quad y_2 = \frac{b\mu_0}{b - b_1} = \mu_0 - \mu_1\,.$$

Da queste si hanno

$$y_0 = \mu_0\;,\; h = \frac{y_2}{\mu_0}\;,\; c = b - b_1\,.$$

Così si ricavano $y_0\,, b\,, \sigma$ parametri della variazione ipotetica e c ed h parametri della perturbazione.

Perchè la statistica possa avere una tale interpretazione biologica, bisogna che sia $p_2 < 0$, poichè $p_2 = bb_1$. Perciò la (2) deve ammettere una soluzione reale e negativa che deve anche essere maggiore di $-\mu'_2$ perchè risulti σ reale. Questa condizione è anche sufficiente.

Essa può anche mettersi sotto altra forma. La (2) trinomia di terzo grado col termine noto positivo ha sempre una ed una sola radice reale negativa.

Perchè questa sia maggiore di $-\mu'_2$ dev'essere

$$-\mu_2'^3 - \tfrac{1}{2}(\mu'_4 - 3\mu_2'^2)\mu'_2 + \tfrac{1}{2}\mu_3'^2 < 0$$

ovvero

$$\mu'_2\mu'_4 > \mu_2'^3 + \mu_3'^2\,.$$

Per fare uso dei simboli noti (V. Davenport, *Statistical Methods*, p. 18), dividiamo per $\mu_2'^3$ e si ha

$$\frac{\mu'_4}{\mu_3'^2} > 1 + \frac{\mu_3'^2}{\mu_2'^3}$$

ovvero

$$\beta_2 - \beta_1 - 1 > 2 \quad \text{ponendo } \beta_0 = \frac{\mu'_4}{\mu'^2_2},\ \beta_1 = \frac{\mu'^2_3}{\mu'^3_2}.$$

È questa dunque la condizione necessaria e sufficiente perchè la curva sia suscettibile di una tale interpretazione biologica.

Per tracciare effettivamente la curva ci serviremo della sua equazione sotto la forma (1).

II.

Curve perturbate per selezione.

Supponiamo che sopra una popolazione distribuita colla legge normale

$$\frac{y_1}{\sigma\sqrt{2\pi}}\, e^{-\frac{1}{2}\left(\frac{x-b}{\sigma}\right)^2}$$

agisca una selezione sfavorevole alle classi più basse (o alle più elevate) tale che per ogni classe y vengano eliminati $y\varphi(x)$ individui, dicendo $\varphi(x)$ la probabilità che ha ogni individuo di essere colpito. Noi supponiamo $\varphi(x)$ funzione di x; poichè essa rappresenta una probabilità dovrà essere $0 < \varphi(x) < 1$.

Per ogni classe rimarranno allora $y - y\varphi(x)$ cioè

$$y(1 - \varphi(x)) \text{ individui.}$$

L'ipotesi più semplice che possiamo fare in $\varphi(x)$ è che sia funzione lineare di x.

$$\varphi(x) = A(x - b) + B.$$

Essa acquista il valore zero per $x_0 = b - \frac{B}{A}$ e il valore 1 per $x_1 = b + \frac{1 - B}{A} = x_0 + \frac{1}{A}$ che dovranno perciò cadere fuori del campo di variazione.

Sostituendo e ponendo

$$y_0 = y_1(1 - B) \quad , \quad \alpha = -\sigma\frac{A}{1 - B},$$

si ha l'equazione

$$y = \frac{y_0}{\sigma\sqrt{2\pi}}\left(1 + \frac{\alpha(x - b)}{\sigma}\right) e^{-\frac{1}{2}\left(\frac{x-b}{\sigma}\right)^2}.$$

Figurano in questa le costanti b e σ media e deviazione normale della variazione normale ipotetica, y_0 proporzionale al numero degli individui studiati ed $\frac{\alpha}{\sigma}$ che misura la deviazione dalla normalità che io dico perciò *coefficiente di abnormalità.* Esso è positivo o negativo secondo che la selezione colpisce di più gli individui delle classi basse o quelle delle classi elevate.

La curva così ottenuta ha un solo massimo (*unimodale*), asimmetrica, da una parte asintotica all'asse delle x, mentre dall'altra lo taglia alla distanza $-\frac{\sigma}{\alpha}$ dall'asse della variazione ipotetica.

Della grande importanza di queste curve mi riservo di parlare altrove e delle loro applicazioni alla economia e alla biologia, qui tratto solo del problema delle determinazioni dei parametri per mezzo dei dati empirici.

Il metodo che espongo è generale e può applicarsi qualunque sia il coefficiente di abnormalità.

Sia al solito l'equazione

$$y = \frac{y_0}{\sigma\sqrt{2\pi}}\left(1 + \frac{\alpha x}{\sigma}\right) e^{-\frac{x^2}{2\sigma^2}}$$

della quale vogliamo determinare i parametri y_0, σ, α e la posizione dell'origine rispetto al baricentro. Anche qui faremo uso dei momenti della curva empirica.

Poniamo

$$y_1 = y_0 \frac{\alpha}{\sigma};$$

l'equazione può scriversi

$$y = \frac{y_1}{\sigma\sqrt{2\pi}}\left(\frac{\sigma}{\alpha} + x\right) e^{-\frac{x^2}{2\sigma^2}}$$

e si annulla per $x = -\frac{\sigma}{\alpha}$.

Calcoliamone i momenti: supporrò α positivo, ma il procedimento sarebbe assolutamente analogo se α fosse negativo e le formule finali sono le stesse.

Indichiamo i momenti rispetto all'asse della variazione ipotetica con ν_n. Per trovarli dovremo servirci degli integrali:

$$\mathrm{I}_n = \frac{1}{\sigma\sqrt{2\pi}} \int_{-\frac{\sigma}{\alpha}}^{+\infty} x^n e^{-\frac{x^2}{2\sigma^2}} dx.$$

È facile avere una relazione ricorrente:

$$\mathrm{I}_n = \frac{\sigma}{\sqrt{2\pi}} \int_{-\frac{\sigma}{\alpha}}^{+\infty} x^{n-1} de^{-\frac{x^2}{2\sigma^2}} = \frac{\sigma}{\sqrt{2\pi}}\left(\frac{-\sigma}{\alpha}\right)^{n-1} e^{-\frac{1}{2\alpha^2}} + \frac{(n-1)\sigma}{\sqrt{2\pi}} \int_{-\frac{\sigma}{\alpha}}^{+\infty} x^{n-2} e^{-\frac{x^2}{2\alpha^2}} dx,$$

ponendo

$$\frac{1}{\sqrt{2\pi}} e^{-\frac{1}{2}\left(\frac{1}{\alpha}\right)^2} = z\left(\frac{1}{\alpha}\right)$$

si ha:

$$I_n = \sigma\left(-\frac{\sigma}{\alpha}\right)^{n-1} z + (n-1)\sigma^2 I_{n-2}.$$

In questo modo si riconducono tutte le I ad I_0 ed I_1. Calcoliamole:

$$I_0 = \frac{1}{\sigma\sqrt{2\pi}} \int_{-\frac{\sigma}{\alpha}}^{+\infty} e^{-\frac{x^2}{2\sigma^2}} dx = \int_{-\frac{1}{\alpha}}^{+\infty} \frac{1}{\sqrt{2\pi}} e^{-\frac{1}{2}t^2} dt,$$

che è funzione di $\frac{1}{\alpha}$; la indicherò con $I_0\left(\frac{1}{\alpha}\right)$.

$$I_1 = \frac{1}{\sqrt{2\pi}} \int_{-\frac{\sigma}{\alpha}}^{+\infty} e^{-\frac{x^2}{2\sigma^2}} d\,\frac{x^2}{2\sigma^2} = +\frac{\sigma}{\sqrt{2\pi}} e^{-\frac{1}{2\alpha^2}} = \sigma z\left(\frac{1}{\alpha}\right).$$

Le due funzioni I_0 e z sono ben note e ne sono state costruite delle tavole; cito quelle di W. F. Sheppard nelle quali si adotta il simbolo $\frac{1}{2}(1+\alpha)$ invece di I_0. Ho dovuto cambiare il simbolo in questo procedimento per non generare confusione.

Gli altri integrali I_n si ottengono facilmente:

$$I_0 = I_0\left(\frac{1}{\alpha}\right),$$

$$I_1 = \sigma z\left(\frac{1}{\alpha}\right),$$

$$I_3 = -\frac{\sigma^2}{\alpha} z + \sigma^2 I_0 = -\sigma^2\left(\frac{1}{\alpha} z - I_0\right),$$

$$I_2 = \frac{\sigma^2}{\alpha^2} z + 2\sigma^3 z = \sigma^3\left(\frac{1}{\alpha^2} + 2\right) z,$$

$$I_4 = -\frac{\sigma^4}{\alpha^3} z - 3\frac{\sigma^4}{\alpha} z + 3\sigma^4 I_0 = -\sigma^4\left\{\left(\frac{1}{\alpha^3} + \frac{3}{\alpha}\right) z - 3I_0\right\}.$$

Calcoliamo ora i momenti:

$$\nu_0 = y_1\left(\frac{\sigma}{\alpha} I_0 + I_1\right)$$

$$\nu_1 = y_1\left(\frac{\sigma}{\alpha} I_1 + I_2\right)$$

$$\nu_2 = y_1\left(\frac{\sigma}{\alpha} I_2 + I_3\right)$$

$$\nu_3 = y_1\left(\frac{\sigma}{\alpha} I_3 + I_4\right).$$

Da esse si ha sostituendo:

$$\nu_0 = \sigma y_1\left(\frac{1}{\alpha} I_0 + z\right)$$

$$\nu_1 = \sigma^2 y_1 I_0$$

$$\nu_2 = \sigma^3 y_1\left(\frac{1}{\alpha} I_0 + 2z\right)$$

$$\nu_3 = \sigma^4 y_1\left(3I_0 - \frac{1}{\alpha} z\right).$$

Dalla prima si ottiene y_1 in funzione degli altri parametri:

$$y = \frac{\nu_0}{\sigma} \frac{1}{\frac{1}{\alpha} I_0 + z},$$

e ricordando le posizioni fatte

$$y_0 = \nu_0 \chi_1(\alpha)$$

dove $\chi_1(\alpha) = \dfrac{\frac{1}{\alpha}}{\frac{1}{\alpha} I_0 + z}$ è funzione della sola α, pari, sempre positiva.

Dividendo ν_1, ν_2, ν_3 per ν_0 si ha:

$$\frac{\nu_1}{\nu_0} = \frac{\sigma I_0}{\frac{1}{\alpha} I_0 + z} = \sigma \frac{1}{\frac{1}{\alpha} + F}$$

$$\frac{\nu_2}{\nu_0} = \sigma^2 \frac{\frac{1}{\alpha} I_0 + 2z}{\frac{1}{\alpha} I_0 + z} = \sigma^2 \frac{\frac{1}{\alpha} + 2F}{\frac{1}{\alpha} + F}$$

$$\frac{\nu_3}{\nu_0} = \sigma^3 \frac{3I_0 - \frac{1}{\alpha} z}{\frac{1}{\alpha} I_0 + z} = \sigma^3 \frac{3 - \frac{1}{\alpha} F}{\frac{1}{\alpha} + F}$$

dove $F = \dfrac{z}{I_0}$ è una funzione dispari di α.

La prima ci fa conoscere la distanza del baricentro dalla media della variazione ipotetica; onde conoscendo il baricentro ed α, potremo trovare l'asse della variazione ipotetica posta a $-\sigma\chi_2(\alpha)$, dove

$$\chi_2(\alpha) = \frac{1}{\left[\frac{1}{\alpha} + F\right]}$$

è funzione dispari, avente sempre lo stesso segno di α.

Cerchiamo ora i momenti μ_2 e μ_3 rispetto al baricentro.

$$\mu_2 = \frac{\nu_2}{\nu_0} - \left(\frac{\nu_1}{\nu_0}\right)^2 = \frac{\left(\frac{1}{\alpha^2} + 2\frac{1}{\alpha}F + 2F^2 - 1\right)}{\left[\frac{1}{\alpha} + F\right]^2} = \frac{2\left[\frac{1}{\alpha} + F\right]^2 - \frac{1}{\alpha}\left[\frac{1}{\alpha} + F\right] - 1}{\left[\frac{1}{\alpha} + F\right]^2}\sigma^2$$

$$\mu_3 = \frac{\nu_3}{\nu_0} - 3\frac{\nu_1}{\nu_0}\frac{\nu_2}{\nu_0} + 2\left(\frac{\nu_1}{\nu_0}\right)^3 = -\sigma^3\frac{\frac{1}{\alpha}F\left[\frac{1}{\alpha} + F\right]^2 + 3F\left[\frac{1}{\alpha} + F\right] - 2}{\left[\frac{1}{\alpha} + F\right]^3}.$$

Dalla prima si ricava σ:

$$\sigma^2 = \mu_2\chi_3(\alpha), \quad \text{dove } \chi_3(\alpha) = \frac{\left[\frac{1}{\alpha} + F\right]^2}{2\left[\frac{1}{\alpha} + F\right]^2 - \frac{1}{\alpha}\left[\frac{1}{\alpha} + F\right] - 1}$$

è funzione pari di α, sempre positiva.

Elevando μ_3 a quadrato e dividendo per il cubo di μ_2 si elimina σ. Facendo uso della lettera β_1, già usata dal Pearson per indicare la stessa espressione abbiamo:

$$\beta_1 = \frac{\mu_3^2}{\mu_2^3} = \frac{\left\{\frac{1}{\alpha}F\left[\frac{1}{\alpha} + F\right]^2 + 3F\left[\frac{1}{\alpha} + F\right] - 2\right\}^2}{\left\{2\left[\frac{1}{\alpha} + F\right]^2 - \frac{1}{\alpha}\left[\frac{1}{\alpha} + F\right] - 1\right\}^3}$$

che è anch'esso funzione della sola α, sempre positivo.

Inversamente in questa formula potremo considerare α come funzione di β_1 che si ottiene dai dati empirici. Noto α avremo gli altri parametri mediante le formule già trovate.

$$\sigma^2 = \mu_2\chi_3(\alpha)$$
$$b = \mu_1 - \sigma\chi_2(\alpha)$$
$$y_0 = \nu_0\chi_1(\alpha)^2.$$

Le funzioni χ_1 e χ_3 sono sempre positive, χ_2 ha il segno di α, cioè il segno del momento terzo rispetto al baricentro μ_3. Delle funzioni $\chi_1, \chi_2, \chi_3, \beta_1$, la tabella dà i valori dei logaritmi per α da ·30 a 1·—.

Per $\alpha < \cdot 30$ la curva è così vicina alla normalità che la sua rappresentazione per mezzo di quella può considerarsi come soddisfacente.

Ecco il procedimento pratico per applicare la teoria svolta.

Dalla statistica si comincia col calcolare la media e rispetto a questa i momenti μ_2 e μ_3. Da questi si calcola $\beta_1 = \frac{\mu_3^2}{\mu_2^3}$.

Si cerca sulle tavole il valore di β_1 più vicino a quello trovato e così si ha α, a cui si dà per segno il segno di μ_3. Volendo un grande rigore si potrebbe interpolare in modo da ottenere per α un più preciso valore, ma nelle mie prove mi son convinto che si può senz'altro prendere per α il valore più prossimo.

Nello stesso tempo si osservano i valori delle funzioni χ_1, χ_2, ecc.

Trovato α si calcolano gli altri parametri mediante le formole

$$\sigma = \sqrt{\mu_2 \chi_3(\alpha)},$$

$$y_0 = \nu_0 \chi_1(\alpha).$$

L'asse della variazione normale ipotetica è posto a

$$b = \mu_1 - \sigma\chi_2(\alpha),$$

dove χ_2 ha il segno di α.

L'equazione riferita a quest'asse come origine è:

$$y = \frac{y_0}{\sigma\sqrt{2\pi}} \left(1 + \frac{\alpha x}{\sigma}\right) e^{-\frac{1}{2}\left(\frac{x}{\sigma}\right)^2}$$

III.

Applicazione ad alcune statistiche di salari.

Termino questo scritto applicando il metodo alla rappresentazione di due statistiche di salari per far vedere come possono confrontarsi statistiche analoghe.

I dati mi sono stati forniti dal dott. Mengarini che sta preparando una Memoria su questo soggetto: sono due statistiche degli « *Ouvriers à veine* » per gli anni 1896 e 1900 ricavate dal libro: *Statistique des Salaires dans les Mines de Houille*, pubblicato dalla Sezione di statistica dell'Ufficio del lavoro belga. (Bruxelles, Fourez, 1901).

I dati della prima curva sono:

Media a 4·1642 , $\mu_2 = 1{\cdot}8107$, $\mu_3 = {\cdot}5287$, onde $\beta_1 = {\cdot}047084$.

Il valore di α corrispondente è ·54.

Con questo troviamo:

$$\sigma = {\cdot}78725 \ , \ y_0 = 99{\cdot}329.$$

La media della variazione ipotetica è 3·7659.

Il limite è inferiore a 2·345.

L'equazione è:

$$y = \frac{99{\cdot}329}{{\cdot}76725\sqrt{2\pi}}\left(1 + {\cdot}54\,\frac{x - 3{\cdot}7659}{{\cdot}76725}\right)e^{-\frac{1}{2}\left(\frac{x-3{\cdot}7659}{{\cdot}76725}\right)^2}.$$

Per la seconda curva abbiamo:

$$\text{Media} = 6{\cdot}3534\ ,\ \mu_2 = 5{\cdot}5930\ ,\ \mu_3 = 2{\cdot}9326 \text{ onde } \beta_1 = {\cdot}049156.$$

Il valore di α più vicino è ·54.
Con questo troviamo:

$$\sigma = 1{\cdot}3485\ ,\ y_0 = 99{\cdot}329.$$

L'asse della variazione ipotetica è a 5·1667.
Il limite è inferiore a 3·4159.
L'equazione è:

$$y = \frac{99{\cdot}329}{1{\cdot}3485\sqrt{2\pi}}\left(1 + {\cdot}54\,\frac{x - 5{\cdot}1667}{1{\cdot}3485}\right)e^{-\frac{1}{2}\left(\frac{x-5{\cdot}1667}{1{\cdot}3485}\right)^2}.$$

Le curve sono tracciate nella figura, coi poligoni empirici. La differenza non è grande specialmente riflettendo all'enorme concentrazione del 35 % in una sola classe della prima statistica.

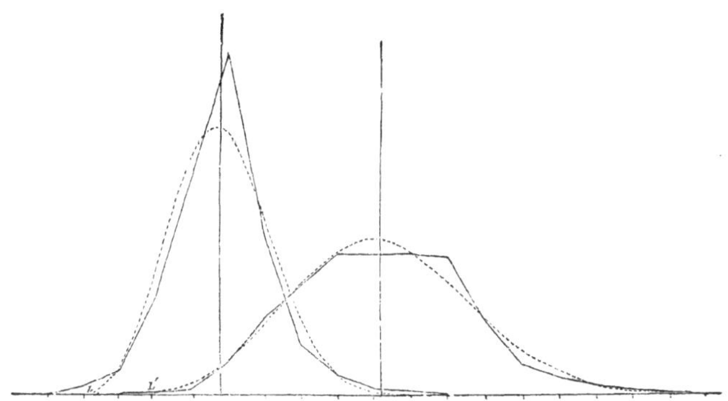

Statistiche dei salarî degli « Ouvriers à veine » delle Miniere di carbon fossile del Belgio.

Poichè le rappresentazioni sono abbastanza buone possiamo trarre la conclusione che la variazione dei salari considerati è quale ci darebbe una variabilità normale perturbata con una legge di selezione che colpisse di preferenza i salari bassi.

Naturalmente non basta questo per poter affermare l'esistenza di una causa perturbatrice; lo studio dettagliato del fenomeno in tutte le sue modalità deve controllare questa ipotesi.

Solo posso indicare quale potrebbe essere in generale una causa di selezione per le statistiche dei salarî: l'emigrazione alla quale si lasciano più facilmente trascinare gli operai meno retribuiti.

Riguardo alla abnormalità i coefficienti $\frac{\alpha}{\sigma}$ sono ·704 e ·400 onde si vede che essa è notevolmente diminuita in 4 anni, per quanto il valore di α sia rimasto costante.

TABELLA

α	$\log \chi_1(\alpha)$	$\log \chi_2(\alpha)$	$\log \chi_3(\alpha)$	β
·30	$\bar{1}$·9999854	$\bar{1}$·4769203	·0406982	·00358
·31	$\bar{1}$·9999772	$\bar{1}$·4910660	·0434899	·00433
·32	$\bar{1}$·9999659	$\bar{1}$·5047294	·0463532	·00519
·33	$\bar{1}$·9999509	$\bar{1}$·5179339	·0493820	·00616
·34	$\bar{1}$·9999308	$\bar{1}$·5306992	·0522639	·00725
·35	$\bar{1}$·9999048	$\bar{1}$·5430436	·0553039	·00845
·36	$\bar{1}$·9998720	$\bar{1}$·5549844	·0583818	·00977
·37	$\bar{1}$·9998314	$\bar{1}$·5665371	·0614946	·01121
·38	$\bar{1}$·9997818	$\bar{1}$·5777161	·0646353	·01276
·39	$\bar{1}$·9997227	$\bar{1}$·5885351	·0677959	·01440
·40	$\bar{1}$·9996522	$\bar{1}$·5990069	·0709697	·01615
·41	$\bar{1}$·9995697	$\bar{1}$·6091439	·0741514	·01801
·42	$\bar{1}$·9994749	$\bar{1}$·6189582	·0773351	·01996
·43	$\bar{1}$·9993665	$\bar{1}$·6284613	·0805150	·02201
·44	$\bar{1}$·9992431	$\bar{1}$·6376631	·0836849	·02413
·45	$\bar{1}$·9991052	$\bar{1}$·6465753	·0868421	·02633
·46	$\bar{1}$·9989504	$\bar{1}$·6552081	·0899820	·02860
·47	$\bar{1}$·9987790	$\bar{1}$·6635706	·0930998	·03093
·48	$\bar{1}$·9985911	$\bar{1}$·6716737	·0961941	·03333
·49	$\bar{1}$·9983845	$\bar{1}$·6795253	·0992591	·03577
·50	$\bar{1}$·9981605	$\bar{1}$·6871358	·1022952	·03825
·51	$\bar{1}$·9979352	$\bar{1}$·6945130	·1052979	·04078
·52	$\bar{1}$·9976560	$\bar{1}$·7016672	·1082694	·04335
·53	$\bar{1}$·9973751	$\bar{1}$·7086045	.1112034	·04594
·54	$\bar{1}$·9970744	$\bar{1}$.7153329	·1140987	·04855
·55	$\bar{1}$·9967553	$\bar{1}$·7218622	·1169581	·05118
·56	$\bar{1}$·9964170	$\bar{1}$·7281985	·1197790	·05384
·57	$\bar{1}$·9960582	$\bar{1}$·7343481	·1225579	·05651
·58	$\bar{1}$·9956801	$\bar{1}$.7403187	·1252972	·05918
·59	$\bar{1}$·9952826	$\bar{1}$·7461171	·1279958	·06185
·60	$\bar{1}$·9948640	$\bar{1}$.7517479	·1306503	·06452
·61	$\bar{1}$·9944276	$\bar{1}$·7572200	·1332698	·06719
·62	$\bar{1}$·9939721	$\bar{1}$.7625382	·1358412	·06986
·63	$\bar{1}$·9934972	$\bar{1}$.7677075	·1383744	·07252
·64	$\bar{1}$·9930036	$\bar{1}$.7727340	·1408667	·07517
·65	$\bar{1}$·9924912	$\bar{1}$.7776222	·1433175	·07781
·66	$\bar{1}$·9919618	$\bar{1}$·7823791	·1457318	·08045

α	$\log \chi_1(\alpha)$	$\log \chi_2(\alpha)$	$\log \chi_3(\alpha)$	β
·67	$\bar{1}$·9914120	$\bar{1}$·7870056	·1481001	·08305
·68	$\bar{1}$·9908453	$\bar{1}$·7915095	·1504309	·08564
·69	$\bar{1}$·9902611	$\bar{1}$·7958946	·1527226	·08822
·70	$\bar{1}$·9896599	$\bar{1}$·8001649	·1549790	·09078
·71	$\bar{1}$·9890418	$\bar{1}$ 8043245	·1571918	·09332
·72	$\bar{1}$·9884068	$\bar{1}$·8083770	·1593682	·09584
·73	$\bar{1}$·9877557	$\bar{1}$·8123265	·1615087	·09833
·74	$\bar{1}$·9870888	$\bar{1}$·8161765	·1636145	·10081
·75	$\bar{1}$·9864064	$\bar{1}$·8199307	·1656815	.10326
·76	$\bar{1}$·9857089	$\bar{1}$·8235921	·1677152	·10569
·77	$\bar{1}$·9849953	$\bar{1}$·8271266	·1697294	·10808
·78	$\bar{1}$·9842680	$\bar{1}$·8306474	·1716748	·11046
·79	$\bar{1}$·9835267	$\bar{1}$·8340488	·1736059	·11280
·80	$\bar{1}$·982707	$\bar{1}$·8373683	·1755022	·11513
·81	$\bar{1}$ 9820023	$\bar{1}$·8406107	·1773696	·11744
·82	$\bar{1}$·9812193	$\bar{1}$.8437762	·1792012	·11971
·83	$\bar{1}$·9804247	$\bar{1}$·8468696	·1810060	·12196
·84	$\bar{1}$·9796164	$\bar{1}$·8498909	·1827759	·12418
·85	$\bar{1}$ 9787965	$\bar{1}$·8528445	·1845192	·12638
·86	$\bar{1}$·9779649	$\bar{1}$·8557315	·1862326	·12855
·87	$\bar{1}$·9771214	$\bar{1}$·8585542	·1879172	·13070
·88	$\bar{1}$·9762665	$\bar{1}$.8613144	·1895735	·13282
·89	$\bar{1}$·9754015	$\bar{1}$·8640148	·1912040	·13492
·90	$\bar{1}$·9745250	$\bar{1}$·8666561	·1928060	·13698
·91	$\bar{1}$·9736386	$\bar{1}$·8692412	·1943828	·13903
·91	$\bar{1}$·9727422	$\bar{1}$·8717712	·1959331	·14105
·93	$\bar{1}$·9718364	$\bar{1}$·8742481	·1974591	·14305
·94	$\bar{1}$·9709204	$\bar{1}$.8766729	·1989597	·14502
·95	$\bar{1}$·9699957	$\bar{1}$.8790474	·2004352	·14696
·96	$\bar{1}$·9690623	$\bar{1}$·8813737	·2018885	·14888
·97	$\bar{1}$·9681212	$\bar{1}$·8836524	·2033171	·15077
·98	$\bar{1}$·9671697	$\bar{1}$·3858855	·2047247	·15265
‘99	$\bar{1}$·9662112	$\bar{1}$·8880739	·2061095	·15450
·100	$\bar{1}$·9652450	$\bar{1}$·8902190	·2074723	·15633

CH. LEMBOURG

L'ACTUAIRE, SA FONCTION, LES DEUX ASPECT DE CELLE-CI

La communication que je ferai au Congrès sera brève; je me bornerai à indiquer quels sont, dans l'ordre d'idées que je viens d'exposer, les sentiments de l'association à laquelle j'ai l'honneur d'appartenir.

Cette communication, dès lors, n'appelle pas la discussion.

A l'envisager matériellement, et tel qu'il se présente le plus souvent, le métier de l'actuaire consiste à fournir à des établissements financiers, surtout à des institutions d'assurance, des prix d'opérations et des valeurs de réserves. Sa besogne semble donc se résumer à des purs calculs.

Mais il faut remarquer que ces calculs ont pour base des lois supposées de fréquence, et un certain taux de l'intérêt. Dès lors l'actuaire doit se préoccuper de la valeur de ces lois de fréquence, et aussi du point de savoir si le temps d'intérêt adopté se réalisera. De sorte que le voilà porté aux études statistiques et économiques.

Ces études, il doit les entreprendre avec méthode c'est-à-dire faire en sorte de les appuyer sur des phénomènes mesurables.

On voit immédiatement que l'exercice de sa profession obligera l'actuaire à avoir recours aux mathématiques: il devra former, pour son usage, dans cette branche du savoir humain, une discipline particulière.

Je l'esquisse à grands traits.

I. — Elle consiste tout d'abord en une partie purement formelle, de calculs. Ceux-ci s'effectueront:

1) par des tables ou barèmes,
2) par des auxiliaires techniques (machines à calculer),
3) par des formules d'approximation (sommation-interpolation),
4) par des procédés graphiques d'approximation.

Jusqu'ici rien de bien spécial: comme tous les calculateurs (ingénieurs, astronomes) et autant qu'eux, il aura besoin de certaines ressources; en raison de ces besoins il créera, ou du moins il éprouvera le désir de créer un outillage plus parfait que l'outillage existant. Il aidera donc au progrès du calcul. Exemples: l'arithmomètre THOMAS qu'un assureur a fait connaître; les tables de logarithmes de F. THOMAN établies surtout en vue des calculs d'intérêt.

II. — Néanmoins, et toujours en vue de simplifier sa besogne, l'actuaire cherchera à représenter les lois de fréquence dont il fait usage par des fonctions analytiques. Les recherches qu'il entreprendra dans ce sens pourront le conduire à des résultats utilisables non seulement en actuariat, mais encore dans d'autres domaines, voire en mathématiques pures.

III. — Si les lois de fréquence étaient toujours connues ou admises sans conteste, et sans qu'il soit besoin de vérifier l'accord entre la base des calculs et l'expérience, la tâche de l'actuaire serait, somme toute, terminée dès qu'il aurait su établir ses formules et donné les moyens de les calculer. Mais il faut noter la nécessité, pour l'actuaire, de se rendre compte de l'hypothèse qu'il emploie, à savoir une de fréquence déterminée, ou une loi de corrélation déterminée. Dès lors il faudra qu'il devienne statisticien, qu'il sache employer les méthodes diverses d'ajustement, que même il en crée de nouvelles. Nous voyons donc s'étendre le domaine mathématique de l'actuaire qui n'est plus seulement un spécialiste du calcul.

Particulièrement ce domaine de l'ajustement est intéressant à explorer: évidemment il n'est pas exclusif à l'actuaire des Compagnies d'assurance, mais il n'appartient, au point de vue des applications, qu'à ceux qui recherchent, par l'observation des phénomènes réalisés dans une foule, des lois générales d'ordre biologique ou économique.

IV. — Ayant établi une loi de fréquence il y a lieu d'étudier sous quelles conditions l'institution d'assurance sera stable, et de déterminer l'importance des sommes qui, outre la réserve des primes, doivent garantir, dans une mesure correspondant à de raisonnables prévisions humaines, le fonctionnement de l'institution.

Dès lors naît la théorie du risque mathématique, où l'actuaire demandera au théorème de Bernouilli réponse aux questions qui le préoccupent.

Comme on le voit, peu à peu s'est formée une mathématique spéciale; dès à présent nous pouvons affirmer que cette mathématique spéciale constitue un corps de doctrine.

Mais il y a plus.

Comme je l'ai dit, l'étude des phénomènes d'ordre économique demandera à être faite à un point de vue mathématique. L'actuaire qui, pour la présentation de ses résultats, doit avoir envisagé ces phénomènes, est le mieux qualifié pour en entreprendre l'étude à ce point de vue. Les travaux de Walras, de MM. Pareto et H. Laurent montrent que tout n'est pas vain dans ce domaine.

Les lois de fréquence elles mêmes sont le plus souvent l'expression de phénomènes d'ordre biologique; l'actuaire pourra donc aider le biologiste dans certaines de ses recherches.

Il me sera aisé maintenant de définir la fonction, et l'ambition, de l'actuaire.

Par la force des choses il est spécialiste en matière de calculs financiers. Mais si, par le métier qu'il exerce, et par la formation que ce métier nécessite, l'actuaire est désigné pour servir les intérêts des assureurs par la fourniture de calculs précis, ou par un aiguillage intelligent, c'est-à-dire profitable, des affaires, il a surtout pour rôle néanmoins d'étudier les lois des ensembles par les procédés de la statistique:

il sera, par conséquent, l'auxiliaire indispensable du biologiste, de l'économiste, du politique, comme il est celui de la grande banque, comme il sera celui du grand commerce.

Son ambition scientifique est des plus hautes: il fera la physique mathématique des phénomènes de masse, il appliquera les formules de cette physique à la multitude des faits d'un même ordre, mais à cette multitude en tant que multidude. Dans une foule il pesera l'individu, s'il le peut, l'affectera des paramètres que cette pesée révèle, mais calculera un effet d'ensemble, car pour lui c'est l'action de l'ensemble qui compte. Sa pesée sera plus ou moins précise, et pour l'examen de l'élément dont il compose sa foule il aura besoin de l'aide de toutes les sciences d'observations, mais, en revanche, il leur fournira des lois que seul un ensemble révèle et qui préparent une synthèse.

Au point de vue productiviste, comme seul il est possesseur des lois suivant lesquelles un ensemble évolue, seul il sera capable de tracer la voie que doivent suivre les ensembles pour utiliser au maximum, dans un sens donné, la résultante de l'activité de ses éléments.

Ayant ainsi défini le métier de l'actuaire, dit son ambition, il sera aisé de montrer quels sont, au point de vue mathématique, les deux aspects de sa fonction. Encore une fois je serai très bref:

a) En vue de certaines nécessités pratiques l'actuaire fait des mathématiques. Il apparait donc aux mathématiciens comme un ingénieur d'une espèce particulière qui érige des constructions spéciales suivant les règles d'une architecture définie. En raison de ce but, il se pose des problèmes spéciaux mais dont il est aisé d'appliquer la solution à d'autres questions.

Il est à remarquer, en effet, que si un problème, même élémentaire, se traduit par une équation, une équation ne traduit pas qu'un seul problème. Si, pour l'interprétation des solutions d'un problème, il est nécessaire de tenir compte de la signification des paramètres il n'en est pas de même quand il s'agit de transformer purement et simplement l'équation. Il peut donc ainsi arriver, et il est arrivé, que des questions spéciales qui se sont posées aux actuaires leur ont fait trouver des solutions qui trouvent leur application à des problèmes d'un tout autre ordre.

Les actuaires, donc, qui se servent, pour l'exercice de leur métier, des mathématiques, sont donc à même de concourir pour leur part, eux aussi, et précisément à raison de leur métier, au progrès des mathématiques.

b) L'actuaire, en raison de sa formation mathématique, apportera dans la pratique de son métier des idées de généralisation, de rigueur et de correction. Il proposera hardiment, car il n'a pas le culte des formules compliquées, la substitution des solutions simples et générales, aux solutions immédiates, particulières et complexes: il orientera les opérations vers la clarté.

Et, confiant sans témérité dans les solutions qu'il propose, solutions qu'il croit justes parce qu'elles sont équitables et étudiées, il fera pratiquer l'assurance dans tous les domaines, aux conditions les meilleures, c'est à dire à un prix qui ne laisse à l'assureur que son bénéfice légitime, mais qui le lui laisse. Cette correction, cette rigueur seront avantageuses à la fois au public et à l'assureur.

C. GINI

SULLA REGOLARITÀ DEI FENOMENI RARI

In questa Nota mi propongo di esaminare se la regolarità dei fenomeni rari è maggiore o minore della regolarità dei fenomeni più frequenti.

Si consideri una massa di sn osservazioni, raggruppate in s categorie di n osservazioni ciascuna.

Sia A un fenomeno dotato di una probabilità p costante nelle s categorie ed indipendente nelle singole osservazioni dalla frequenza con la quale A si è avverato negli altri casi della stessa categoria.

La probabilità che, in una categoria di n osservazioni, A si avveri un numero di volte x è data allora dalla formula

$$\frac{n!}{x!(n-x)!}p^x q^{n-x}, \tag{1}$$

e il valore probabile dell'errore quadratico medio $\sqrt{\frac{\Sigma(p_i-p)^2}{s-1}}$ (dove $p_i = p_1, p_2, \ldots, p_s$ indica la frequenza di A nelle singole categorie) dalla formula

$$\sqrt{\frac{pq}{n}} \tag{2}$$

dove è $q = 1 - p$.

Qualche volta (ad esempio, nei giuochi di azzardo) è noto a priori che la probabilità dei fenomeni considerati è costante nelle varie categorie e nelle singole osservazioni di una stessa categoria. Si è allora autorizzati a prevedere, in base alla formula (1), la frequenza delle varie combinazioni e, in base alla formula (2), l'intensità dell'errore quadratico medio (*Applicazioni deduttive del calcolo delle probabilità*).

Ma molto più spesso mancano codeste cognizioni a priori. Si assume allora la costanza di p come un' ipotesi di lavoro. Si calcola la frequenza teorica delle varie combinazioni mediante la formula (1) (o formule da essa derivate) e l'intensità teorica dell'errore quadratico medio mediante la formula (2). Si confrontano poi queste quantità teoriche con le quantità effettive corrispondenti. In caso di coincidenza, si dice che la *dispersione* del fenomeno è *normale* e si conclude che l'ipotesi circa la costanza di p, da cui eravamo partiti, è formalmente esatta. Se gli errori effettivi sono invece più o meno forti dei teorici, si dice che la dispersione è *più che normale* o, rispettivamente, *meno che normale* (*Applicazioni induttive del calcolo delle probabilità*).

L'espressione

$$Q = \frac{\sqrt{\frac{\Sigma(p_i - p)^2}{s-1}}}{\sqrt{\frac{pq}{n}}}$$

viene assunta come *indice di dispersione*. $Q = 1$ è indice di dispersione normale; $Q > 1$ indice di dispersione più che normale; $Q < 1$ indice di dispersione meno che normale.

Si è misurata in questo modo la dispersione di molti fenomeni demografici raggruppati in categorie secondo anni o mesi o circoscrizioni territoriali. Tali i rapporti dei sessi nelle nascite e particolarmente nei nati vivi, nei nati morti, nei nati illegittimi, nei morti distinti in varie categorie di età; tali ancora i coefficienti di illegittimità, di nuzialità, di mortalità ecc.

Per i rapporti sessuali dei nati e talora per i rapporti sessuali dei morti e i coefficienti di mortalità, la dispersione è normale; per gli altri fenomeni, la dispersione è notevolmente più che normale.

In tutti questi casi p è abbastanza elevato: i fenomeni, cioè, di cui si esamina la dispersione, sono piuttosto frequenti.

Che cosa avviene per il caso in cui p sia piccolo, vale a dire per il caso di fenomeni rari?

Il von Bortkewitsch avrebbe riscontrato che, quando è piccolo il numero dei casi avveratisi e molto grande il numero delle osservazioni, la dispersione risulta costantemente normale o quasi normale (*Legge dei piccoli numeri*). Per i suicidî di bambini al disotto dei 10 anni, per i suicidî di donne, per gli infortunî sul lavoro seguiti da morte, per i decessi dei soldati in seguito al calcio di un cavallo, i valori di Q si mostrarono molto prossimi all'unità, variando fra 0.88 e 1.15 con una media di 1.04.

Del curioso fenomeno il Bortkewitsch dava la seguente spiegazione [1]. Il valore teorico $\sqrt{\frac{pq}{n}}$ dell'errore quadratico medio sta in ragione inversa di $\sqrt{n}$. Il valore empirico $\sqrt{\frac{\Sigma(p_i - p)^2}{s-1}}$ si può, invece, quando la dispersione è più che normale, scindere in due componenti: l'una, la *componente accidentale* che sta pure in ragione inversa di $\sqrt{n}$; l'altra, la *componente fisica*, a cui è dovuto l'eccesso di dispersione, che è indipendente da n. Si intende dunque come l'eccesso di dispersione $Q - 1$ debba andar crescendo col crescere di n e viceversa diminuire quanto più n diviene piccolo.

Vi era manifestamente in questo ragionamento un equivoco che ho altrove posto in evidenza [2]. Un fenomeno è raro non già perchè è piccolo il numero n delle os-

[1] Cfr. *Das Gesetz der kleinen Zahlen* (p. 31, 33 e 37).

[2] *La legge dei piccoli numeri* (Giornale degli Economisti, settembre 1907).

servazioni fatte, ma perchè è piccola la probabilità p, che si desume praticamente dal rapporto del numero dei casi, in cui il fenomeno si è avverato, ad n. Nelle applicazioni fatte dal BORTKEWITSCH il numero delle osservazioni era molto grande; piccolo era il numero dei casi avverati. La spiegazione data dal BORTKEWITSCH non regge.

E certamente vi è anche, nel metodo da lui seguito per confrontare la distribuzione teorica e la distribuzione effettiva degli errori, un'inesattezza.

Alla formula (1) egli sostituisce la formula seguente del POISSON:

$$\frac{K^x e^{-k}}{x!}$$

che è valida fin tanto che p sia molto piccolo, n molto grande e sia costantemente, nelle s categorie, $pn = K$. E l'errore quadratico medio viene misurato similmente sostituendo a pn la costante K.

Ma, nel fatto, il numero delle osservazioni, a cui si riferiscono i singoli termini di una serie demografica, non è mai costante. Il numero delle donne che si possono suicidare varia, ad esempio, di anno in anno. Il BORTKEWITSCH dunque esaminava la varietà di un rapporto tenendo conto delle variazioni di un solo termine, il numero dei casi avverati e trascurando le variazioni dell'altro termine, il numero delle osservazioni.

Quali effetti può esercitare, sull'indice di dispersione di una serie, il non tener conto delle variazioni del numero delle osservazioni?

Si intende come gli effetti debbano essere differenti secondo i casi.

Se il numero delle volte, in cui il fenomeno si è avverato, varia nei termini della serie corrispondentemente al variare del numero delle osservazioni fatte, la dispersione così calcolata sarà maggiore della dispersione calcolata correttamente. Facciamo un esempio. Esaminiamo la dispersione dei rapporti sessuali delle nascite della Nuova Galles del Sud nei venti anni 1885-1904. Se si suppone che il numero delle nascite sia nei singoli anni lo stesso, si trova che entro i limiti dell'errore probabile cadono 4 rapporti sessuali, anzi che 10 come dovrebbe avvenire secondo la teoria. Se si tiene conto, invece, di tali oscillazioni, si trova che, entro i limiti dell'errore probabile, cadono 9 rapporti sessuali, vale a dire che la dispersione è presso a poco normale.

Ma può darsi invece che il numero delle volte in cui il fenomeno si è avverato, non varii nei termini della serie corrispondentemente a quanto varia il numero totale delle osservazioni. Il numero delle osservazioni, poniamo, va rapidamente crescendo, mentre il numero dei casi, in cui il fenomeno si è avverato, non subisce che variazioni puramente accidentali. La frequenza del fenomeno varierà allora solo accidentalmente (e quindi la dispersione potrà essere normale) se si suppone costante il numero delle osservazioni; andrà invece diminuendo (e quindi la dispersione sarà più che normale) se si tiene conto del crescere del numero delle osservazioni. Pare che questo fosse il caso negli esempî addotti dal BORTKEWITSCH. Esaminando, infatti, la dispersione della probabilità che un suicidio si riferisca a un fanciullo di 10 anni (Prussia 1881-1893) si trova che l'indice di dispersione è $= 0.97$ quando si supponga che il numero dei suicidî rimane lo stesso nei varî anni considerati, ed è invece $= 1.06$ quando si tenga conto dell'aumento a cui questo numero andò soggetto. Questo risultato si spiega facilmente pensando che le cause che determinarono nei tempi recenti un aumento nel numero dei suicidî agirono quasi esclusivamente sulle persone adulte. Similmente, per la probabilità che un bambino fra i 6 e i 10 anni si suicidî (Prussia 1869-1883), si trova Q = 1,12, se si suppone che il numero dei bambini rimanga costante e Q = 1,15 se si tien conto dell'aumento a cui andò soggetto. Per la probabilità che un parto sia quadrigemino si trova Q = 1,005 (Prussia 1824-1874) se si suppone che il numero annuale dei parti sia rimasto costante e Q = 1,34 se si tiene conto del suo aumento.

È da ritenere che anche per gli altri fenomeni rari esaminati dal Bortkewitsch si sarebbe riscontrata una dispersione superiore a quella da lui trovata, qualora si fosse tenuto conto del variare del numero delle osservazioni. Conviene riconoscere, è vero, che la differenza non sarebbe stata molto forte; ma è da ricordarsi che gli esempî del Bortkewitsch si riferivano tutti a coefficienti di mortalità i quali spesso mostrano una dispersione normale anche quando il numero dei casi avverati è grande.

Rimaneva così impregiudicata la questione: se una dispersione normale o quasi normale costituisce una caratteristica costante dei fenomeni rari tale da potersi elevare a legge.

A risolverla, ho esaminato la dispersione di svariati fenomeni. La tavola seguente riporta i valori di p e di Q (1) per i coefficienti della mortalità complessiva e della mortalità per alcune cause di morte in Italia nei 13 anni 1893-1905.

Causa di morte	Valori di p	Valori di Q
Malattie dei vasi linfatici	$\frac{3,38}{1.000.000}$	8,9
Colera asiatico	$\frac{7,6}{1.000.000}$	55,8
Itterizia	$\frac{43}{1.000.000}$	2,1
Omicidio e conflitto con la forza pubblica	$\frac{44,8}{1.000.000}$	4,1
Suicidio	$\frac{61,7}{1.000.000}$	2,9
Vaiuolo	$\frac{66,2}{1.000.000}$	35,4
Meningite semplice	$\frac{467}{1.000.000}$	13,1
Pneumonite crupale e bronco-polmonite acuta	$\frac{2342}{1.000.000}$	18,4
Mortalità complessiva	$\frac{23022}{1.000.000}$	52,0

(1) p è in questi casi non una probabilità semplice, ma una probabilità media, risultante dalla media delle varie probabilità di morte nei varî gruppi di età. Se la proporzione degli esposti a morire delle varie classi di età fosse costante, la dispersione sarebbe minore che se p fosse una probabilità semplice. Se codeste proporzioni variano con dispersione normale, la probabilità p mostrerà la stessa dispersione che se fosse una probabilità semplice.

Per quanto il valore di p sia spesse volte piccolissimo, non si ha in nessun caso dispersione normale. Nemmeno si può asserire che le cause di morte più rare mostrino regolarmente una dispersione minore delle cause di morte più frequenti. La dispersione della mortalità complessiva risulta invece più alta della dispersione per la maggior parte delle singole cause di morte.

Passiamo ad altri esempî. Un padre morendo lascia frequentemente 0, 1, 2 o 3 figli; rarissimamente invece 17, 18, 19 o più figli. Ecco la dispersione di queste varie probabilità per la Nuova Galles del Sud nei singoli anni 1893-1905.

Padre con	p	Q
0 figli	0,12719	4,3
1 figlio	0,079459	3,2
2 figli	0.084136	4,1
3 »	0,082256	3,0
4 »	0,081081	2,5
17 figli	0,00063291	4,3
18 »	0,00038129	2,5
19 »	0,00054054	3,0
20 » e più	0,00065805	2,6

La dispersione è sempre più che normale e non risulta sensibilmente maggiore per i casi più frequenti.

Sono numerosi, in un'annata, i giorni piovosi; sono rari, specialmente in certe città, quelli di neve e di grandine. La dispersione risulta per fenomeni così diversamente frequenti sostanzialmente la stessa e sempre più che normale. M denota nella tavola seguente il numero annuo medio (1874-1904) dei giorni, in cui si ebbe precipitazione atmosferica, o neve o grandine.

Osservatorio di	Precipitazione atmosferica		Neve		Grandine	
	M	Q	M	Q	M	Q
Torino	108.3	1.98	9.8	1.54	2.6	1.28
Milano.	117.3	1.79	9.3	1.62	3.0	1.04
Firenze	116.4	1.66	2.7	1.87	4.0	1.16
Roma	112.8	2.09	1.8	1.13	6.0	1.38
Napoli.	112.6	1.64	0.7	1.32	3.9	1.96
Palermo	114.1	1.82	1.7	1.78	5.1	1.41

Altro esempio di fenomeni rari ci forniscono i parti quadrupli e i tripli; essi pure mostrano una dispersione più che normale per quanto minore di quelli dei parti doppî più frequenti. Nella tavola seguente, p indica la probabilità che un parto sia quadruplo o, rispettivamente, triplo, doppio, plurimo, in Prussia, negli anni 1824-74.

Parti	p	Q
Quadrupli	0.0000023955	1.34
Tripli	0.00013670	2.25
Doppî	0.011891	7.39
Plurimi.	0.012030	7.49

Esaminiamo infine la dispersione delle varie forme di suicidio in Italia per un periodo (1895-1902) in cui la frequenza dei suicidî si mantenne presso a poco costante.

Suicidio per	p	Q
Annegamento.	0.0000128	2.0
Armi da fuoco	0.0000147	1.3
Armi da taglio	0.00000245	1 5
Impiccamento	0.00001135	1.6
Precipitazione	0.00000545	1.1
Schiacciamento	0 00000197	1.3
Avvelenamento	0.00000445	1.2
Asfissia.	0.00000323	1.6
Altra causa o causa ignota.	0.00000593	2.1
Qualunque causa	0.0000623	1.2

La dispersione è leggermente più che normale, e generalmente più alta per le singole forme di suicidio, che per i suicidî complessivamente.

Possiamo così constatare:

I. *Una dispersione normale non è punto una caratteristica dei fenomeni rari.*

II. *Non si può asserire che i fenomeni più rari abbiano regolarmente una dispersione minore dei fenomeni più frequenti. Talora ciò fu riscontrato vero (parti quadrupli e tripli in confronto dei doppî); tale altra no (neve e grandine in confronto della pioggia; famiglie molto prolifiche in confronto di famiglie poco prolifiche; certe cause di morte in confronto di certe altre).*

Da un punto di vista teorico, si può dimostrare che la dispersione dei fenomeni frequenti è uguale, maggiore o minore della dispersione dei fenomeni più rari che li compongono, secondo che i fenomeni componenti mostrano nelle loro oscillazioni, indipendenza o, viceversa, concomitanza o compensazione [1]. Ciò spiega da una parte la maggiore dispersione della mortalità complessiva in confronto delle singole cause di morte, e dei parti plurimi in confronto dei parti quadrupli, tripli e doppî e dall'altra la minore dispersione del suicidio per qualunque causa in confronto delle singole forme di suicidio.

(¹) Cfr. per la dimostrazione il nostro articolo: *Su la legge dei piccoli numeri e la regolarità dei fenomeni rari.* Giornale degli Economisti, dicembre 1908. Cfr. pure *La regolarità dei fenomeni rari.* Ibidem, marzo 1908, nel quale però sono incorsi numerosi errori di stampa.

MILES M. DAWSON

NECESSARY CAUTIONS FOR THE GUIDANCE OF MATHEMATICIANS IN DEALING WITH ACTUARIAL PROBLEMS

Few vocations offer so good a field of usefulness, with financial rewards so remunerative, for the man whose training has been in pure mathematics only, as does that of an actuary. Yet it should not be forgotten that actuarial science is applied mathematics-applied in the field of finance where blundering application may introduce unsoundness, foster dishonesty and even induce ruin. Such may not so promptly, unerringly and crushingly react upon the mathematician as does the collapse of a certified structure under strain upon the reputation of an engineer; but they are on a par with one another, notwithstanding.

Given all the factors and the correct value of each, the result of an actuarial computation should be definite and reliable. This is true,notwithstanding that the calculus of probabilities is not exact; for the limits can be determined pretty accurately and the caution which should attend financial undertakings, indicates the safe course.

Merely to have mentioned the calculus of probabilities recalls to my mind that this Congress has assembled in the land where, in the sixteenth century CARDAN wrote, (before 1576, in which year he died) the first essay known to us upon probabilities, under the title, *De ludo aleae.* Presented as a mere idle study of the chances of gaming and as a subject of curious interest only, it stirred into activity the cortical convolutions of PASCAL and of so many worthy successors, that we now see this calculus become one of the most important handmaids of progress. It is now the means of cancelling for the individual those hazards of sea and land, of health and of life itself, because of which the Romans of old made sacrifice here to the fickle, inconstant goddess, Fortuna. We are also in the land where in Venice the first practical application of this calculus was made in marine underwriting about the fifteenth century.

This glimpse into the past emboldens one to hazard peering into the future by way of forecast, the more willingly because the formulae of probabilities are themselves in effect prophecies. Where we now meet, in October next convenes the eighth

International Congress of Workmen's Insurance, to discuss means whereby to push actuarial science into fields of broader usefulness—in advance, it must be acknowledged, of any such conquest of the fields already submitted to its dominion or any such preparation for the greater and more complex problem before us, as assures actuarial service of reliable excellence.

For it is coming to be apprehended that the affairs of men will never be conducted in a just or business-like manner, until wealth shall be the reward only of service of men and not to be had by fraud, by force or by fortune. The function of insurance, guided by skilled actuaries, is to forward the cause of protection against misfortune and, therefore, of substantial equalization of fortune, by means of insurance, annuities and pensions.

The purpose of this paper is to encourage all pure mathematicians who are free to enter upon this great emprise, to do so, and to hold up the blunders of such in the past, in simpler fields of actuarial activity, blunders not infrequently persistent to this day, as a warning to be circumspect not to impair the value of their work in the solution of the much more complex problems to come, by like negligence.

The good work in actuarial science, that which makes for clear insight, correct methods, soundness and reliability, is due to the mathematicians, as also the faulty work which has at times jeopardized the entire structure. The virtues and the faults have been theirs, alike.

As has been stated, the two sources of error have been (*a*) to omit essential factors of the problem and (*b*) to assign an incorrect value to one or another of the factors.

Omitting Essential Factors of the Problem.

The effect of omitting any factor of an actuarial problem which is necessary to a correct solution, may be to cause a problem to be solved most triumphantly, which is not the problem at all. It is the more dangerous for that reason; its very completeness and seeming inevitableness may be a snare.

Classic instances of these errors persist even to this day in the simplest computations of premiums and values.

The Computation of Life Insurance Premiums.

Experience has proved conclusively that in order that it may be safe and adequate, every life insurance premium must provide for the actual mortality risks, for the cost of procurement, for expenses of management, for contingencies and profits, and for costs of collection of premiums. The formula is:

$$(1) \qquad P'_{(x)} = \left(\frac{A_{(x)} + F}{a_{(x)}} + c + f_x\right)(1 + k).$$

In which

$A_{(x)}$ = the accurate, discounted value of the risks.
$a_{(x)}$ = the accurate, discounted value of the annuity.
c = a provision for expenses of management.
f_x = a margin for contingencies and profits.
k = a percentage added, in order to afford $\frac{k}{1+k}$ percentage of the gross premium for cost of collection.

It does not in the slightest degree, of course, impair the correctness of the foregoing formula, that:

(*a*) The provision for expenses of management may be included in k; or
(*b*) The provision for contingencies and profits may be included in k or in c; or
(*c*) May be concealed in $\frac{A_x}{a_x}$ by making use of too low a rate of interest or of redundant rates of mortality; or
(*d*) The provision for cost of procurement may be disguised by taking $\frac{A_x}{a_x}$ according to an ultimate table of mortality, though the lives are subjected to a medical examination.

The provisions, notwithstanding, must always be in the computation in some guise; else the premiums are inadequate.

It is profitable to transform formula (1) into an equation of the present values of outgo and income, as follows:

(2) $$[A_{(x)} + F + (c + f_x)\, a_{(x)}]\,(1 + k) = P'_{(x)}\, a_{(x)}.$$

This fulfills the fundamental requirement that at the outset, before the first premium is paid or the risk entered upon, the present value of the probabilities of financial outgo of all kinds and of financial income should precisely balance.

The Computation of Life Insurance Reserves.

At the end of one year, the provision for cost of procurement, if the cost is to be met when it is incurred, must have been realized and expended and, designating the balancing accumulation as ${}_1V_{(x)}$, we have the equation of present values of outgo and income (plus immediate resources), as follows:

$$[A_{(x)+1} + (c + f_x)\, a_{(x)+1}]\,(1 + k) = P_{(x)}\, a_{(x)+1} + {}_1V_{(x)}$$

$$\therefore {}_1V_{(x)} = [A_{(x)+1} + (c + f_x)\, a_{(x)+1}]\,(1 + k) - P'_{(x)}\, a_{(x)+1}.$$

And, generally,

(3) $${}_nV_{(x)} = [A_{(x)+n} + (c + f_x)\, a_{(x)+n}]\,(1 + k) - P'_{(x)}\, a_{(x)+n}.$$

This is obviously the true value of the policy at the end of n years; for

(*a*) It is precisely the sum, no more and no less, that will remain of premiums already paid if every assumed condition has been precisely realized; and

(*b*) It is precisely the sum, no more and no less, that will be required, together with future premiums, if every assumed condition is in future to be precisely realized.

Net Premium Formulas.

It is possible, of course, to discover by an analysis of the correct formula for computing a premium what is the net premium each year, e.g. the portion of each premium, not required to supply provisions for cost of procuremont, for expense of management, for contingencies and profit and for cost of collection, which portion is available, of course, solely to provide for the net risks, present and future.

To demonstrate what these net portions of the premiums are, recourse may be had to the initial equation of values of outgo and income, i.e. to formula (2), thus:

$$[A_{(x)} + F + (c + f_x) a_{(x)}](1 + k) = P'_{(x)} a_{(x)}.$$

Substituting for $P'_{(x)}$ in the foregoing, its value according to formula (1), we have:

$$[A_{(x)} + F + (c + f_x) a_{(x)}](1 + k) = \left(\frac{A_{(x)} + F}{a_{(x)}} + c + f_x\right)(1 + k) a_{(x)}.$$

$$A_{(x)} + F = \left(\frac{A_{(x)}}{a_{(x)}} + \frac{F}{a_{(x)}}\right) a_{(x)} = \left(P_{(x)} + \frac{F}{a_{(x)}}\right) a_{(x)}.$$

$$A_{(x)} = \left(P_{(x)} + \frac{F}{a_{(x)}}\right) a_{(x)} - F = P_{(x)} + \frac{F}{a_{(x)}} - F + \left(P_{(x)} + \frac{F}{a_{(x)}}\right) a_{(x)}.$$

Stated in words, instead of a formula, this is:

(*a*) The net premium the first year is the net level premium, increased by an annuity to spread the provision for cost of procurement over all the years and diminished by the cost of procurement.

(*b*) The net premium for each year after the first is the net level premium, increased by an annuity to spread the provision for cost of procurement over all the years.

That is in formulas:

(4) $${}^{1}P_{(x)} = P_{(x)} + \frac{F}{a_{(x)}} - F$$

(5) $${}^{1}P_{(x)} = P_{(x)} + \frac{F}{a_{(x)}}$$

The net premium policy value for the nth year may be found in like manner by recourse to formula (3), as follows:

$$\begin{aligned} {}_nV_{(x)} &= [A_{(x)+n} + (c + f_x)\,a_{(x)+n}](1 + k) - P'_{(x)}\,a_{(x)+n} \\ &= [A_{(x)+n} + (c + f_x)\,a_{(x)+n}](1 + k) \\ &\quad - \left[\frac{A_{(x)} + F}{a_{(x)}} + (c + f_x)\right](1 + k)\,a_{(x)+n}. \end{aligned}$$

Whence:

(6) $$ {}_nV_{(x)} = A_{(x)+n} - \left(P_{(x)} + \frac{F}{a_{(x)}}\right) a_{(x)+n}. $$

Inapplicable Net Premium Formulas.

The usual formula for the net premium, the first and every year, is:

$$P_{(x)} = \frac{A_{(x)}}{a_{(x)}}.$$

And for the so-called net premium value:

$$ {}_nV_{(x)} = A_{(x)+n} - P_{(x)}\,a_{(x)+n}.$$

These formulas have the merit, from the standpoint of mathematicians, of simplicity and directness; but they have been shown to be inapplicable to the problems involved in life insurance with level gross premiums.

Yet such problems are precisely what it is often affirmed that they are suitable to furnish a solution for, on the basis that a level gross premium implies of necessity a level net premium.

It has been shown that when all the elements of the problem are taken into account, the reverse is true, e.g., that a level gross premium implies of necessity a net premium lower the first year than in subsequent years, by the whole amount of the cost of procurement.

Origin and Evolution of the Net Premium Delusion.

It is very interesting to trace the beginnings and the development of the delusion of this net premium method of computing premiums and policy values and to consider what extraordinary, fortuitous conditions have in some countries enabled it to persist even to this day, embuttressed by ignorance, the selfish interests of companies and prostrate idolatry for formulas of pure mathematics. It is a history of achievement, though at the same time one of collossal failure, repeated at each stage, to get all of the essential elements into the equation from which the formula is adduced.

The first valuation formula was set forth about 1760 by Dr. RICHARD PRICE. Translated into the symbols of the International Congress of Actuaries, it was, as applied to an individual policy:

$$_nV_x = A_{x+n} - P'_x a_{x+n}.$$

The bracket ( ) about x is omitted, because he had no notion of the modern select table. He also proposed to value gross premiums, which, however, in the case of the Equitable Society, of London, the policies of which were the first to be valued, were also supposed to be net premiums. There was, therefore, no issue at that time between gross premiums and net premiums. There was also little reason for an issue, for the expenses of the Equitable Society were expected to be trifling, merely nominal; and there was a large margin for contingencies and expenses in the provisions for the risk according to the London mortality table upon which the Society's premiums were originally computed and, as it proved, even according to the Northampton table which, on Dr. PRICE's recommendation, was substituted.

When this substitution was made, a « loading » was introduced for the reason that the net premiums, much lower than those then in use, seemed to the actuary to require an addition for the purpose of security, for contingencies—not especially for expenses. This was the genesis of « loading », i. e. of any overt provision for any outgo, except the naked cost of the insurance, and it was added, professedly, in order surely to cover that cost. Therefore, up to the time when these rates were adopted and beyond, there was no recognized provision, corresponding to F, c, f_x or the percentage k in the complete formula for a premium; and then only f_x was provided for in the form kP_x.

Mathematicians soon worked out from the formula, representing Dr. PRICE's view of valuation, the following:

$$\Sigma V = \Sigma A - \Sigma P_a$$

in which ΣA is the sum of the present values of the future claims payable and ΣPa the sum of the present values of actual premiums receivable in future. That this was « the true value » was at that time and for more than half a century as clear as crystal, in fact irrefutable to the minds of the leading mathematicians who addressed themselves to the subject. This view for a time dominated the Institute of Actuaries; it was the orthodox opinion, resting on the high authority of the great actuarial mathematicians, W. S. B. WOOLHOUSE, from whose expressions of opinion as from those of his eminent compeer, F. G. P. NEISON, the following are quoted:

« The calculations of the commissioners [1], in the report alluded to, being based on a hypothesis of fictitious premiums, having no relation whatever to the society's

[1] Net premium valuation.

tables, or the premiums actually receivable, are necessarily fallacious, and may be regarded purely as a fabrication. It would therefore be a waste of time to enter on any discussion of them beyond the announcement of this undoubted fact ». — WOOLHOUSE.

« It is held that the whole of the premium is as completely and as entirely the property of the society as a part of it, and there is as much right to calculate on receiving the one as the other. A few years ago, two able papers were read before the Institute of Actuaries, by one of its leading members, insisting on a valuation of the gross premiums as being a correct way of proceeding, and that any other is merely dealing with a fiction, and not with fact ». — F. G. P. NEISON.

From this there was a revulsion to net premium valuation, which was anathema for a time. But the presence of large negative values, when gross premiums are valued, at first led to the establishment of the rule that such should be excluded and then to the argument that net preminms should be valued, which would certainly avoid negative values, since it sets out from the equation:

$$A_x = P_x a_x .$$

So that

$${}_0V_x = A_x - P_x a_x = 0 .$$

And the value cannot be less than ${}_0V_x$, whatever value be given « n » in ${}_nV_x$, because A_{x+n} steadily increases in value as n increases, while P_x is constant and a_x diminishes in value as n increases.

Theoretically, when P_x is valued, the « loading », i. e. $P'_x - P_x$ is the provision — and, indeed, must be the mathematical equivalent of the provision if the mortality is precisely according to the table — for F, c, f_x and the percentage k in our formula. And in the formulas for premiums, in vogue soon after net level premium valuation came into use, the provision was as per the following formula:

$$P'_x = (P_x + c)(1 + k).$$

It was explained, also, that, of course, either c or k could be zero. Indeed, under the usual rules of net level premium valuation, both c and k can be zero, without affecting, the value; which is increased only in case $P'_x < P_x$. In fact, I have personally known a very able actuary, under the obsession of the net level premium method, which is alone orthodox in his country, to insist upon valuing by $A_{x+n} - P_x a_{x+n}$, although the actual premium was much less than P_x and without charging as an additional value the present value of an annuity equal to the deficiency of the actual premium, i. e. $P_x - P'_x$.

It is scarcely less unwise, however, than to value policies with gross premiums of P_x by the formula, $A_{x+n} - P_x a_{x+n}$, which leaves no margin for cost of collection, expense of management or contingencies and profits.

Variations of the Net Premium Method.

At least as soon as the necessity that somehow and somewhere the elements, F, c, f_x and the percentage k be included in the premium, came to be understood, the utter inapplicability of the net level premium method was evident to certain able minds, as, for instance, to Dr. ADAM ZILLMER in Germany as early as 1863, to Dr. THOMAS BOND SPRAGUE in Great Britain at least by 1880, to EMORY MC CLINTOCK in the United States before 1895 and to T. B. MACAULAY of Canada by 1897.

But all of these eminent actuaries offered, as a substitute, only an arbitrary variation of the net level premium method, e. g. by valuing P_{x+1} instead of P_x.

It has been seen in the demonstration of the correct formula for the premium, in this paper, that ${}^{\tau}P_{(x)} = P_{(x)} + \frac{F}{a_{(x)}}$ is the true net renewal premium and that ${}^{1}P_{(x)} = {}^{\tau}P_{(x)} - F = P_{(x)} + \frac{F}{a_{(x)}} - F$ is the true net premium for the first year. But ${}^{1}P_{(x)}$ must not be less than $vq_{(x)}$. Therefore the largest value for F is found by substituting in the foregoing for ${}^{1}P_{(x)}$, this minimum value for it, $vq_{(x)}$:

$$ {}^{1}P_{(x)} = vq_{(x)} = P_{(x)} + \frac{F}{\mathrm{a}_{(x)}} - F = P_{(x)} + \frac{F(1 - \mathrm{a}_{(x)})}{\mathrm{a}_{(x)}} \therefore F\frac{a_{(x)}}{\mathrm{a}_{(x)}} = P_{(x)} - vq_{(x)} $$

$$ F = (P_{(x)} - vq_{(x)})\frac{\mathrm{a}_{(x)}}{a_{(x)}}. $$

Plainly in such case, there is no policy value at the end of the first year; the net renewal premium, therefore, must be $P_{(x)+1}$ and we have the following equivalent expression for the maximum value of F:

$$ F = (P_{(x)+1} - P_{(x)})\,\mathrm{a}_{(x)}. $$

The « $x+1$ » method of valuation, therefore, gives a correct maximum for F, manifestly the largest possible value for it, if the cost of procurement is to be paid from the first year's premium.

Cautions Concerning the Maximum Value of F.

When the policy is merely one of life insurance, the foregoing maximum value for F may stand, it would seem; for in the cases of term or whole life premiums, paid for life insurance, it cannot be said that in the contemplation of the purchasers any portion of the premium is earmarked, as it were, for investment.

But it is otherwise with the portions of premiums for limited premium life policies or endowment policies, which are consciously paid, over and above the full whole life premium, in the one case in order to prepay life premiums that would not otherwise fall due for, say, ten, fifteen or twenty years or in the other case, to cause the policy to mature as an endowment.

Sound finance does not permit of discounting installments of an investment, to be received in future, for the purpose of creating a fund for immediate distribution as profits or for immediate disbursement for expenses. Therefore, the largest value of F for all forms of policies with premiums exceeding the whole life premium at the same age is also:

$$F = (P_{(x)} - vq_{(x)}) \frac{a_{(x)}}{a_{(x)}} = (P_{(x)+1} - P_{(x)})\, a_{(x)} \qquad (7)$$

in which $P_{(x)}$ is the net level whole life premium and $P_{(x)+1}$ the same for a life $x+1$ years old and one year beyond the date of the last medical examination.

A Double Limitation of the Value of F.

If the provision for F is made in some other way as by a constant as in Great Britain and in some other countries or by using an ultimate mortality table in computing premiums as in the United States and in Canada, the maximum value for F is as per formula (7) or the provision employed in computing the premium whichever is the smaller. The well-established doctrine that the valuation must not bring out negative reserves fixes the controlling maximum value in any event at the net level premium for the policy less $vq_{(x)}$, but sound financial principles require that the controlling maximum be as per formula (7). In other words, the maximum according to that formula is of general, universal application whereas other maxima are only of limited application and must not in any event exceed that maximum.

With that fundamental principle firmly in mind, it must be acknowledged that taking F as a constant is advantageous in Great Britain where in the cases of all forms of policies as to which it is employed, the constant of ·01 of the sum insured, which is commonly taken, is less than the maximum value of F according to formula (7); and that where $P' = (P + c)(1 + k)$ as in the United States and Canada, P being taken by an ultimate table of mortality, the resultant maximum for F, $(P_x - P_{(x)})\, a_{(x)}$ for the whole life policy and the value of a similar expression suitably altered for other forms present advantages if not allowed when in excess of $(P_{(x)+1} - P_{(x)})\, a_{(x)}$, the universally applicable maximum.

The significance of $(P_x - P_{(x)})\, a_{(x)}$, P_x being by the ultimate table, with its corresponding valuation formula

$${}_nV_{(x)} = A_{(x)+n} - P_x\, a_{(x)+n}$$

viz: that the discounted salvages on mortality, caused by procuring the new lives and by sifting them out by medical examinations, are the measure for cost of procurement, renders it peculiarly well-adapted to guide a company's management in avoiding unprofitably extravagant cost of procurement. But, notwithstanding, it is but a particular case, falling under the general formula which is applicable, though there were no favorable medical selection or even though there were temporary adverse selection.

Stock or Non-Participating Policies.

All that has been said in this paper obviously applies to mutual or participating insurance, conducted for the benefit of policyholders, only. But how about stock or non-participating insurance? May not the shareholders pay more for cost of procurement thnn is liberated by the maximum in formula (7) and rely upon a larger f_x, for instance, to work it out?

Manifestly. But in such case, no more should be allowed in valuation than as per formula (7); that is, the minimum valuation should be by the formula:

$$V_{(x)} = A_{(x)+n} - P_{(x)+1}\, a_{(x)+n}\,.$$

if it is a life policy or by a formula allowing the same provision for F and suited to the form of policy. For the reason that, if the stockholders have relied upon an annual provision for the excess of F over the maximum by formula (7), they should get the advantage of this annual provision as it is realized and no more rapidly.

There is also the question whether on grounds of public policy a larger cost of procurement should be permitted by the State, in the case of stock or non-participating policies; but that is not a mathematical question.

In one case, at least, viz: when policies are sold for small weekly or monthly premiums, an initial expenditure far in excess of the first premiums collected is unavoidable and in that event, an advance, recovered from provisions in renewal premiums, is plainly indicated.

The Danger of Spurious Mathematical Equivalence.

It is well-known to actuaries that it is mathematically possible to compute a precisely adequate net level premium for a fixed life insurance benefit, payable in event of death at any moment after birth, i. e. $P_{(0)}$. But it is equally well-known that such could not be used in practice, because $P_{(0)} < P^{\,1}_{[0]\overline{1|}}$, that is, the net level premium would not cover the risk for the first year and there is no certainty that, even if funds were provided from some other source to make this good, premiums will be paid until such advances are made good. Therefore, while it is possible to have a gross level premium from birth, it must be at least equal to $P^{1}_{[0]\,\overline{1}|}$ and the net premium is the net premium for one year term insurance each year until $P_{(0)+n} > P^{1}_{(0)+n\,\overline{1}|}$ and thereafter is $P_{(0)+n}$.

Another classic instance of misleading or spurious mathematical equivalence in actuarial problems is this: It is entirely possible mathematically to compute the net single premium, payable at the end of the term of n years, to cover the insurance for the term of n years, i. e. in commutation symbols, $\frac{M_{(x)} - M_{(x)+n}}{D_{(x)+n}}$. But of course it is not practicable to pay the death-claims as they fall in, out of premiums which are not to be paid until the end of the term.

The fallacy, involved in the foregoing instances of spurious mathematical equivalents, is obviously present also in the following practice which has persisted in the United States and Canada to this day: Compute gross single premiums by the formula $(A + ca)(1 + k)$ or, more commonly, merely $A\ (1 + k)$, using an ultimate mortality table. Then reserve on the basis that the entire loading is available at once for expenses and profits.

Manifestly every element requisite to an annual premium is requisite here excepting the cost of collection. Therefore, the percentage k and the constant c, if also present, must represent c and f_x in the annual premium formula. The following is the correct formula for a whole life net single premium.

$$A'_{(x)} = A_{(x)} + F + (c + f_x)\,a_{(x)}. \tag{8}$$

From which, rougly equating with $A'_x = A_x(1 - k)$:

$$(c + f_x)\,a_{(x)} = kA_{(x)} \text{ and } F = A_x - A_{(x)}.$$

The element c will be required annually to cover expenses of management, precisely as if premiums were annual and to discount the provision for contingencies and profits, f_x, is neither safe nor conformable with sound financial principles. Yet by the spurious method referred to, the present value of both is treated as provision for immediate expenses and profits.

Another such practice in the United States and Canada is to exhaust during the term (m years) during which premiums are payable, the entire loading on limited-premium policies, leaving only $A_{(x)+m}$ to meet all elements of cost thereafter. These premiums are usually computed as follows:

$${}_mP'_{(x)} = {}_mP_x(1 + k) + k'P_x \text{ or merely} = {}_mP_x(1 + k)$$

the values being taken according to an ultimate table of mortality. The correct formula, remembering that there is no cost of collection beyond m years, is:

$${}_mP'_{(x)} = \left(\frac{A_{(x)} + F + (c + f_x)\,a_{(x)}}{a_{(x)+m}}\right)(1 + k).$$

Equating, it is seen that

$F = ({}_mP_x - {}_mP_{(x)})\ a_{(x)}$ and that all the other necessary elements of the loading are in kP_x per annum.

But, as before, there is the same necessity each year for a provision for expenses of management and for contingencies and profits after m years, as during that term. In other words there should be $A_{(x)+m} + (c + f_x)\ a_{(x)+m}$ on hand at the expiration of m years, instead of merely $A_{(x)+m}$.

These single premium and limited premium blunders are due to the application of the misleading net level premium method of valuation.

This divorcement of valuation from the facts has even resulted in the following extreme mathematical folly being put forward, viz: That the loading of the premiums of all policies, whatever the term of the insurance, whatever the nature of the insurance, whatever the premium-paying period, may properly be of the same present value and may properly be distributed through the different policy years in any manner, the valuation rigorously following this distribution.

As has been seen, the loading really comprises provisions for cost of procurement, F; for expenses of management, c; for contingencies and profits, f_x; and for cost of collection, the percentage k.

F may or may not be of the same value, without regard to the age of the policyholder, sort of policy, term of the insurance or premium-period. In countries where commissions are a percentage of the sum insured, it is a constant as to most forms of policies.

c also may be constant for all forms of policies and usually is; but as the policy should contribute to expense of management each year it is in force, the present value of this provision varies with the term of the insurance.

f_x also may be constant, though usually it is not; but the provision for contingencies and profits is also one which is necessary from year to year and its present value varies at least with the term if not also with the nature of the insurance.

k may or may not be the same percentage in every case; but, in any event, it is required for each year of the premium-paying period and its present value varies with that period.

Yet it was proposed that the sum of these present values might with propriety be the same for a one year term or endowment policy as for an annual premium whole life policy, to state the extreme cases: and also that the whole of these provisions might with propriety be « distributed » in any desired manner, wholly without regard to the necessities which cause them to be superimposed upon the pure risk premiums — e. g. might be exhausted as soon as possible in extravagance or dividends, might all be released in equal amounts each year or even might be husbanded until the very last years.

The false view that they were in any real sense mathematical equivalents in present value also deserves attention; for obviously when reduced to possession by collecting a single premium, the whole is realized while when « distributed » in whole life annual premiums, the probabilities of discontinuance affect the true present value most seriously.

The variations of F, c, f_x and k, both as to values and incidence, are necessarily limited. This has been seen both as to the value of F and the incidence of each of them. Practice indicates the limits of the other values by limiting the entire premium through competition. The theory that there is or should be unlimited freedom of « distribution », violates the very data of the problem to be solved and is tantamount to declaring that F may be swollen so as to absorb all or be reduced to zero, that f_x may be discounted and absorbed from the earliest premiums or be hoarded unexpended until near the end of the chapter, that c may be enlarged by including the whole in it or may be reduced to extinction and that k may receive all unto itself or be utterly disregarded. These things are accomplished very readily in a mathematical formula but are impossible in practice.

Rules For Determining the True Liability by Valuation

Valuation, if it is to reveal the true liability of the company for its outstanding policy obligations, must take into account all of the necessary elements of cost, which are yet to be met. Since the cost of procurement is assumed to have been met and covered at the outset, it need not be taken into account as a liability to be met in future and in consequence, the gross premiums receivable in future need not be reduced by the equivalent of this item to arrive at the amount of the same to be allowed in the valuation.

The full process of the valuation is to charge on the one side the present value of all future outgo, treating the provision for future profits and expenses, as a certain outgo, and to credit on the other side the full present value of all gross premiums receivable.

This process may be abbreviated into a « net premium valuation » formula, but only by cancelling the same items on both sides of the equation of value, which will give to be valued a lower net premium the first year and a higher net renewal premium thereafter than the net level premium in all cases when the gross premium is level and a level net premium only when the gross premium the first year is larger than the gross renewal premiums, by the full amount of the provision for cost of procurement.

Therefore, whenever F, c, f_x and the percentage k have all been fully and adequately provided for in the level gross premiums, the following net premium formula may safely be used in valuation, because precisely equivalent to an accurate gross premium formula:

$$ {}_{n}V_{(x)} = A_{(x)+n} - \left(P_{(x)} + \frac{F}{a_{(x)}} \right) a_{(x)+n} . $$

This formula reserves from future premiums the total provisions for expenses of management, contingencies and profits and cost of collection. For participating policies this tends to maintain rates of bonuses or dividends and for stock policies to assure reliable returns for stockholders.

If the gross premiums receivable are insufficient, however, to make provision on a minimum basis for the expenses of management and costs of collection and leave $P_{(x)} + \frac{F}{a_{(x)}}$ as the net premium, then obviously the formula, in net premium symbols, should be:

$$_{n}V_{(x)} = A_{(x)+n} - \frac{P'_{(x)} - c}{1 + k} a_{(x)+n}$$

in which c and the percentage k are such minimum provisions.

What Mortality Table or Tables Should Be Used in Valuation?

Obviously since valuations are usually made at the close of a fiscal year or of a calendar year — or, in any event, on a particular date in the same — and not at the close of the policy year, « n » in all these formulas has a fractional value, i. e is a fraction of a year or an integer and a fraction, except as to policies that chance to have been issued on the same day in previous years, as the date of valuation.

Suppose — because it is as good for the purpose as any other supposition — the valuation is at the close of business on December 31st.

Then, if we knew just the death rates among insured lives of each age on admission (x) in the first calendar year after entry, the second calendar year after entry, etc., we should have the very best possible mortality table to measure the value of $A_{(x)+n}$ and of $a_{(x)+n}$, giving to « n » in these formulas the significance, not of the exact duration for each policy, but merely of the number of December thirty-firsts that have elapsed since the policy was issued.

For the purpose of finding an average date of the moment of payment of claim, it will be sufficiently accurate to take June 30th in each case, i. e. to presuppose a uniform distribution of admissions throughout the calendar year. This will give an average value for n, as a duration, of $1/2$ years, $1\ 1/2$ years, etc. But since the mortality table measures the mortality rates by calendar years after the year of admission, that is not important. It is important, however, for the purpose of determining the interest to be used in computing the value of the reversion and of the annuity, which severally become approximately $A_{(x)+n}$ and $\overline{a}_{(x)-n}$ — the latter because June 30th is also taken as the day for payment of the annual premium. From this, however, $1/2\ \overline{A}_{(x)+n}$ must be deducted, since nothing is payable after the death.

It is clear that the true net premium is also by a select table — although the net premium by an ultimate table, P_x, may be taken because representing $P_{(x)} + \frac{F}{a_{(x)}}$ — and that this net premium must be by a policy year select table, corresponding as accurately as may be with the calendar year select table. The formation of the latter table from the data of insured lives is easy and the former may be derived from the same data, rearranged by policy years, or may be deduced approximately from the calendar year select table.

The Necessity of Employing Correct Values.

While most of this paper has been given over to warnings that in actuarial computations the mathematician must avoid omitting one or several of the essential factors of the problem, it is, of course, equally manifest that, even though he were to include all in his formula, he would go far astray if he assigned to them other than their true values.

Thus all of these factors, F, c, f_x and the percentage k, for instance, must be allowed on a basis which actually squares with the facts. Otherwise, to have included the symbols in the formula is a mere pretense.

They must, also, accord with the incidence of these various elements of outgo. Money cannot be disbursed before it has been collected; and it is neither sound finance nor a proper application of mathematics to proceed as if it could be.

The necessity for using a mortality table which shall be as nearly correct as possible, is also indicated. Mortality tables, deduced from insured lives, have been formed by three methods, known as aggregate, select and ultimate, respectively.

The aggregate method represents the annual deathrates according to ages attained among the lives insured without regard to the duration of the insurance.

The select represents the annual death-rates according to ages on admission and to duration of insurance.

The ultimate represents the annual death-rates, according to attained ages, among lives that have been insured long enough so that the fresh medical examination no longer affects the death-rates materially. Select tables are usually « topped off » by using ultimate tables, deduced from the same experience, for the years of duration beyond the period affected by fresh selection.

An aggregate table, deduced from the experience of the earlier years of a company would very nearly correspond with the portion of a select table, representing the mortality for the first years of duration. If deduced from a longer experience, it may be less affected. It will always be more affected, also, at the younger ages; and it will never be correct for a membership into which no new lives are introduced. Accordingly, it is not a proper table for any purpose; for such a table should bring out premiums and values, that will stand, without regard to whether there are new accessions or not.

The use of an ultimate table appears more reasonable, because making ample provision — in fact, more than ample in all cases except when there are no accessions to the membership. But we have seen that when the net premium P_x is by an ultimate table, it merely means that one of the provisions, F, c, f_x or the percentage k, has been more or less adequately made in the form of $(P_x - P_{(x)})\,a_{(x)}$. In other words, calling the net premium P_x by an ultimate table does not make the pure risk premium that level sum, but merely provides a loading which is available at the outset if valuation is by the select and ultimate formula

$$_nV_{(x)} = A_{(x)+n} - P_x\,a_{(x)+n}$$

or annually as released, if the valuation is by the ultimate formula

$$_nV_x = A_{x+n} - P_x\, a_{x+n}\,.$$

For the use of an ultimate table for the reversion and annuity only, the argument might be advanced that it is conservative; but in point of fact, it has never been employed in that way only, excepting after the period affected by fresh selection is considered to have passed.

The use of a select table is plainly indicated. It gives correct pure risk premiums and correct values, at all points, and if the computations take in all the essential factors it reserves the provisions in future premiums for the purposes for which they were intended. If there are many new entrants, it accommodates that; if there are none, it soon becomes the use of the ultimate section of the table in valuation for the reversion and annuity, which is right.

There are classical instances of the use of erroneous tables and of the consequences. The adoption of the Northampton table for computations of both insurances and annuities is a case in point. It was redundant and proved ruinously so, when applied to annuities. It is interesting to speculate what might have been the consequences upon the development of life insurance, had it shown too low, instead of too high death-rates.

The blunder of Mr. CHARLES ANSELL in putting out sickness rates, deduced from the experience of certain Highland Societies of Scotland, affords another classic instance. These rates proved to be lower than any other societies have experienced and the development of sickness insurance by responsible companies was retarded thereby in English-speaking countries for nearly a century.

The theory, therefore, which is sometimes advanced by mathematicians, that even when a nation or state desires to give to its citizens assurances as to the solvency of life insurance companies, it can properly permit the companies to value their policies by any mortality table, whether exhibiting too low or too high death-rates, must be dismissed along with the other theory that, under similar conditions, the companies may be permitted to make such provisions — or none at all — for F, c, f_x and the percentage k, as they may elect. Such freedom can, of course, be permitted in countries where the government assumes no responsibility for certifying solvency, requiring publicity only, to the end that patrons of the companies may judge of their methods and their condition. But, even when such freedom is permitted by law, the principles of actuarial science and of sound finance do not admit of a departure from the requirement that all these essential factors must be adequately provided for and that a select table, as nearly correct as possible, shall be used. The use of P_x by the ultimate section of the table, in the select and ultimate method of valuation, is, of course, not a departure from this; because it is merely used as a value for $P_{(x)} + \frac{F}{a_{(x)}}$, in order that $F = (P_x - P_{(x)})\, a_{(x)}$.

There is more to be said for the use of a rate of interest, lower than that which is likely to be realized. It is difficult to provide surely against a fall in returns upon investments, through f_∞, directly, while to employ a low rate of interest throughout does provide against it very definitely. It has been seen, also, to be a very satisfactory method of providing for stable bonuses or dividends in event the investment income keeps up. As a means of strengthening reserves voluntorily, therefore, it is without a rival.

But no argument is required to demonstrate that, while conservatism should be observed, it would not truly be a test of solvency, to value policy obligations by assuming a rate of interest, materially lower than the net rate which is likely to be realized.

It may be a poor pun, but it is a valuable truth, that the actuary should deal with the actual.

G. CASTELLI

L'INSEGNAMENTO DELLA MATEMATICA FINANZIARIA E ATTUARIALE
NELLE SCUOLE PROFESSIONALI ITALIANE

Questo Congresso non restringe l'opera sua al riassumere ed al discutere i grandi problemi della scienza, che, meglio di ogni altra, attesta la potenza logica dell'intelletto umano e la sociale utilità delle speculazioni e delle applicazioni di una dottrina, che non conosce confini nello spazio e nel tempo; ma con savio intendimento accoglie nel programma dei suoi lavori anche relazioni e quesiti di carattere didattico per concorrere in modo più diretto e più efficace all'educazione della gioventù e per agevolare un migliore assetto dell'ordinamento scolastico, in quanto s'attiene all'esposizione delle verità acquisite ed alla formazione dei maestri del domani.

Ho quindi ragione di sperare che possa essere opportuna qualche notizia intorno all'opera del Ministero di Agricoltura, Industria e Commercio del Regno d'Italia, intesa a promuovere nelle scuole professionali lo studio delle applicazioni della matematica alle questioni economiche ed alle funzioni tutte o pubbliche o private, che si esercitano sopra materie di credito e di previdenza.

Per tal modo il Governo dà prova d'intendere che fra i doveri dello Stato moderno vi è quello di far penetrare negl'istituti e nei costumi la legge infallibile dei numeri, che nel mentre rassegnano ed illustrano i fatti compiuti, dànno luce e consiglio per calcolare le probabilità dell'avvenire. La matematica per tal guisa, come la medicina col suo codice d'igiene sociale, si asside nelle aule del Governo e del Parlamento: dètta norme sapienti di legislazione e di amministrazione e rende sicuro e spedito il controllo sull'impiego del pubblico denaro.

*
* *

Fra i servizi del Ministero, che investono, con azione assidua e svariata, tutta quanta l'economia nazionale, uno dei più rapidamente progressivi è quello che concerne l'insegnamento industriale e commerciale. Nel 1886 si avevano 150 scuole professionali, fra commerciali, industriali, artistiche industriali (ripartite in tre gradi) e professionali femminili (ripartite in tre categorie) con 21120 alunni iscritti, mentre nel 1905 il numero delle scuole era salito a 315 e quello degli alunni a 49314. Le statistiche che si stanno apparecchiando per gli anni successivi ci faranno la gradita rivelazione di più notevoli progressi. Ad ogni modo queste poche cifre, relative agli anni estremi di un solo ventennio, sono abbastanza eloquenti, sì da rendere superfluo ogni particolare commento.

L'ordinamento scolastico si svolge rapido e sicuro, coordinato e predisposto al meraviglioso rinnovamento industriale e commerciale della nazione. Un consiglio superiore dell'insegnamento agrario, industriale e commerciale presiede alle funzioni amministrative, tecniche e didattiche dei molti e varî istituti pur conservando ad essi l'autorità e la forza di una ragionevole autonomia.

Sapendo di rivolgere il discorso a matematici eminenti, mi astengo da ogni argomentazione per dimostrare l'importanza fondamentale della loro scienza in un ordinamento scolastico, essenzialmente moderno, diretto ad elevare e ad intensificare la coltura dei giovani, che si apprestano alle lotte tecniche ed economiche del lavoro industriale e del traffico. L'aritmetica è guida e consigliera quotidiana nei negozi mercantili; la geometria è ausilio prezioso delle arti; la finanza e l'assicurazione hanno fondamento nella matematica e nella statistica; e questa, a sua volta, non può essere utilizzata appieno, se non quando sia adoperato abilmente quel prodigioso strumento d'invenzione, di critica e di elaborazione di dati sperimentali, che è la scienza delle quantità. Il Ministero ha dunque curato particolarmente la posizione, l'atteggiamento e la estensione di questa sovrana disciplina nei programmi dell'insegnamento professionale.

Dirò di più, contenendo il discorso, come sopra ho annunziato, nel campo delle questioni di statistica, di banca e di assicurazione, che la matematica dev'essere considerata quale mezzo potente di educazione economica generale, in quanto siano da essa illuminati e rinvigoriti non solamente i metodi riguardanti la produzione e la circolazione della ricchezza, ma pur quelli che conducono alla più acconcia distribuzione dei guadagni durante la vita dei singoli lavoratori, e regolano pertanto gli atti di risparmio e di assicurazione, i quali consentono di sperare componibili in sempre più alte armonie gl'interessi spesso antagonistici nei loro aspetti immediati, delle varie classi sociali. Alludo, in particolare, alla progressiva elevazione economica e morale, che ha radice nel risparmio, ed al nobile programma di solidarietà umana, che si attua col sistema delle assicurazioni sociali. Ora possiamo immaginare una energia di propaganda più illuminata ed efficace, una energia di progresso meglio orientata di quella, che irradia dalla scuola, centro di verità e di luce, collocato al di fuori e al di sopra dei partiti e delle fazioni?

***

Il Ministero ha concepito pertanto in tre gradi l'insegnamento della matematica applicata alla statistica, al credito ed alla previdenza.

L'insegnamento elementare nella quinta e nella sesta classe, e nelle scuole professionali di primo grado, deve dare ai giovanetti le essenziali e sicure nozioni di matematica applicata al lavoro ed ai negozi; deve, segnatamente, mostrare lo scopo e il funzionamento delle Casse di Risparmio, delle Società economiche di produzione, di consumo, di credito, delle Società di mutuo soccorso; diffondere, insomma, idee e precetti inestimabili di ordine, di morale, di parsimonia e di previdenza. Forme speciali del grado elementare debbono essere altresì le scuole reggimentali e le cattedre ambulanti di previdenza.

L'insegnamento medio deve rivolgersi in ispecie agli agricoltori, ai commercianti ed agl'industriali, agl'impiegati, ai cittadini tutti, che hanno coscienza di cooperazione sociale; deve scaturire da esso una più matura conoscenza della matematica applicata ai fatti della vita economica ed ai problemi sociali e costituire una propaganda di second'ordine.

L'insegnamento superiore, infine, è il coronamento necessario dell'edificio; esso riassume e riduce a sistema la scienza e la pratica nel duplice riguardo della preparazione professionale degli attuari e del progresso generale del sapere; vivifica il grado medio con la sua funzione di magistero, e, rivolgendosi, per la soluzione degli ardui problemi della statistica matematica, della economia sociale e delle finanze, ad un complesso sempre più esteso di giovani forze intellettuali, è causa del perenne, indefinito avanzarsi della scienza.

***

Questo vasto programma è attuato gradatamente nelle scuole commerciali di nuova istituzione e indirizzato con opportune riforme a più utili funzioni.

Nel qual proposito giova dare qualche notizia sull'evoluzione degl'istituti d'istruzione teorica e pratica, che anche in Italia sono predisposti al fine dell'espansione commerciale del paese.

Il grande favore che, da parte d'uffici, d'istituti commerciali, di famiglie e di giovani studiosi, incontrò la R. Scuola media di studî applicati al commercio in Roma indusse il Governo a istituire scuole simili in altre città, o a trasformare, giusta gli ordinamenti della Scuola di Roma, altre scuole commerciali più antiche. E così sorsero Scuole medie a Napoli, a Milano, a Bologna, a Brescia, a Palermo, a Bari, a Firenze, a Feltre, a Salerno, a Torino, dove fu istituita altresì la prima Scuola media femminile del commercio.

L'interessamento delle famiglie, la frequenza degli alunni, la bontà dei risultati, l'avviamento durevole e proficuo, che senza difficoltà ottengono i giovani licenziati da così fatte scuole, sono titoli più che sufficienti a dimostrare che questa istituzione, sinceramente italiana, è destinata a consolidarsi ed a prendere posto molto onorevole nel sistema dei nostri studî.

In tutte queste scuole inferiori e medie e nelle analoghe che via via sorgeranno, la matematica finanziaria ed attuariale è o sarà insegnata nei limiti, notevolmente estesi, di una trattazione elementare. Intanto la Scuola media di commercio di Napoli ha una Sezione speciale di matematica attuariale.

Il tipo recente di Scuola superiore è offerto dal R. Istituto di studi commerciali, aggregato con Decreto 5 novembre 1906, n. 591, alla R. Scuola media di commercio di Roma. Fin dal primo anno di vita esso ha dato, più che una semplice promessa, sicuro affidamento di vita prospera e d'influenza direttamente profittevole all'economia nazionale; nel corrente anno scolastico, 1907-8, il secondo dalla sua istituzione, raccoglie oltre a 250 allievi ripartiti nelle tre sezioni: attuariale, commerciale, coloniale.

È una scuola superiore centrale, che per un lato interessa le grandi amministrazioni pubbliche e le maggiori aziende private, e dall'altro assicura ordine, stabilità, sicurezza di funzioni a tutti gli uffici che si connettono col credito e con la previdenza o intendono a tutelare il lavoro italiano nelle competizioni doganali e nei rapporti dell'attività nostra col movimento dell'industria e del traffico.

Anzichè rappresentare la ripetizione di altri istituti superiori, che hanno acquistato titoli di alta bemerenza, si è aggiunto alla serie delle istituzioni professionali con personalità e fisionomia propria, con attribuzioni specialissime, corrispondenti a determinate necessità della vita moderna ed alla evoluzione progressiva della nostra legislazione.

Un'altra R. Scuola superiore di commercio è stata recentemente istituita in Torino, ove, per il notevole e confortante sviluppo dell'attività commerciale, sentivasi vivissimo il bisogno di un istituto di alti studi commerciali, teorici e pratici, per la formazione di personale idoneo a dare nuovo impulso alle intraprese economiche. Ed il Governo accolse e tradusse in atto la lodevole iniziativa, presa da uno speciale Comitato, composto di autorevoli e benemeriti cittadini, di istituire appunto in quella città una scuola superiore di commercio.

Sono condotte innanzi e felicemente le trattative tra il Ministero di Agricoltura, le amministrazioni locali e i consigli direttivi per dare un ordinamento nuovo e più proficuo alle scuole commerciali superiori di Venezia e di Genova. Quella di Bari è stata già saviamente ricostituita; e così potrà esplicare ancor meglio la sua azione benefica, soprattutto nelle provincie meridionali del Regno.

A Milano ha sede l'Università commerciale « Bocconi ». Così che in Italia l'istruzione commerciale superiore è degnamente rappresentata a Venezia, Genova, Milano, Torino, Roma, Bari. Napoli e Palermo dovranno, io credo, chiudere, forse in tempo non lontano ed onorevolmente, la serie di queste grandi istituzioni moderne.

*
* *

Quali siano gl'intendimenti dello Stato nell'insegnamento della matematica finanziaria ed attuariale, impartito nelle scuole medie, si rileva dalle disposizioni che qui appresso si riportano, contenute nello Statuto organico della R. Scuola media di commercio di Napoli.

« La Scuola di Napoli ha due Sezioni: la commerciale e l'attuariale. I corsi di « ciascuna Sezione si compiono in quattro anni.

« Le due Sezioni hanno comuni gl'insegnamenti e le esercitazioni seguenti:

« 1° Italiano; diritti e doveri. — 2° Nozioni di storia economica d'Italia; geo-« grafia commerciale. — 3° Istituzioni commerciali; nozioni di economia politica. — « 4° Elementi di diritto civile e di diritto commerciale. — 5° Computisteria e « ragioneria. — 6° Banco modello; funzionamento pratico di aziende mercantili,

« bancarie, di credito e di previdenza. — 7° Lingue estere: francese, inglese, tedesca « e spagnuola. — 8° Calligrafia, stenografia e dattilografia.

« Nella sezione commerciale l'insegnamento delle lingue estere è obbligatorio « per il francese, l'inglese ed il tedesco; nella sezione attuariale per il francese e « per una delle altre due lingue, inglese e tedesca.

« Il corso della lingua spagnuola è facoltativo.

« Saranno inoltre tenute nella Scuola conferenze sulla morale nell'acquisto della « ricchezza e sulla igiene applicata al commercio.

« Il corso della sezione commerciale comprende inoltre i seguenti insegnamenti « ed esercitazioni:

« 1° Matematica; merceologia (analisi e saggi delle merci); adulterazioni e sofi- « sticazioni. — 2° Studio degl'imballaggi. — 3° Legislazione doganale e trattati « di commercio e navigazione (esercitazioni pratiche sull'uso delle tariffe doganali e « sul calcolo dei dazi). — 4° Trasporti e legislazione relativa; servizi marittimi sov- « venzionati (esercitazioni pratiche sull'uso delle tariffe ferroviarie e sul calcolo dei « noli). — 5° Legislazione commerciale ed industriale; usi mercantili con particolare « riguardo al commercio marittimo.

« Nella sezione attuariale oltre gl'insegnamenti e le esercitazioni comuni alle « due sezioni, vengono impartiti i seguenti insegnamenti:

« 1° Matematica pura. — 2° Calcolo delle probabilità. — 3° Matematica finan- « ziaria. — 4° Matematica attuariale. — 5° Nozioni di diritto amministrativo, di stati- « stica e di scienza delle finanze. — 6° Legislazione sociale. — 7° Legislazione « degl'Istituti di credito e previdenza. — 8° Storia degl'Istituti di credito e pre- « videnza.

« Agli allievi della sezione commerciale, i quali abbiano superato, dopo il quarto « anno, l'esame di licenza, è rilasciato dal Ministro di Agricoltura, Industria e Com- « mercio il diploma che conferisce il titolo di perito commerciale. A quelli della « sezione attuariale viene conferito, dopo gli esami di licenza, il diploma di ragio- « niere attuario.

« Tali diplomi, oltre ad attestare della idoneità all'esercizio del commercio e « delle funzioni di attuario, sono titoli di ammissione senza esami, ai corsi delle « RR. Scuole superiori di Commercio del Regno; agli esami di concorso ai posti di « addetto commerciale di seconda classe presso i Consolati italiani; ed agli esami « di concorso agli assegni ed alle borse di pratica commerciale all'estero. Sono pari- « ficati, per tutti gli effetti di legge, ai diplomi di licenza da Scuola di egual « grado ».

La matematica finanziaria ed attuariale è insegnata nelle Scuole superiori di commercio di Venezia, Genova, Torino, Milano, Bari; ma solo in quella di Roma tale disciplina forma una facoltà e costituisce un sistema organico d'insegnamenti, che concorrono a creare la coltura e l'esperienza di chi si sente chiamato alla professione di matematico in servizio delle pubbliche amministrazioni e degl'Istituti di credito e di previdenza.

Ecco il programma degli studi superiori di matematica finanziaria ed attuariale, che si compiono in questa Scuola con l'intendimento di impartire l'istruzione teorica e pratica ai giovani, che intendono di dedicarsi a professioni ed impieghi di grande importanza nella vita moderna.

Il corso dura tre anni e comprende i seguenti insegnamenti fondamentali: matematica pura (analisi algebrica; geometria analitica; calcolo infinitesimale; calcolo delle differenze finite; calcolo delle probabilità); matematica finanziaria ed attuariale; ragioneria; diritto commerciale ed industriale; storia e legislazione degl'Istituti di credito e di previdenza; economia politica e scienza delle finanze; legislazione sociale; statistica demografica, industriale, commerciale; lingue estere.

Altri insegnamenti possono essere aggiunti con Decreto Ministeriale, su proposta del Consiglio Accademico e sentita la Giunta amministrativa e di vigilanza.

Il corso di matematica pura prende forma e contenuto dallo scopo scientifico della scuola e accoglie con relativa ampiezza le teorie, che sono particolarmente adeguate alla critica ed alla elaborazione dei fatti statistici, ai calcoli approssimativi, ai calcoli interpolatori, alla costruzione delle tavole numeriche.

Il corso di matematica applicata comprende:

a) le applicazioni alla statistica, cioè: la statistica metodologica, l'analisi qualitativa dei fatti, il rilevamento dei dati, la elaborazione conseguente, la teoria degli errori di osservazione, la frequenza di alcuni fatti demografici (mortalità, morbilità, invalidità), ecc.;

b) le applicazioni alle operazioni finanziarie, cioè: le operazioni di banca a breve scadenza, quelle di borsa, di cambio, quelle a lunga scadenza, ecc.;

c) le applicazioni alle assicurazioni, cioè: l'assicurazione sulla vita, l'assicurazione contro le malattie, l'invalidità, gl'infortuni, le assicurazioni speciali (disoccupazione, malattie, infortuni, invalidità e vecchiaia, vedove ed orfani, maternità, ecc.), l'assicurazione delle cose;

d) le applicazioni ad altre questioni di carattere frammentario o monografico, come l'equilibrio e il moto dei mercati, il commercio internazionale, il monopolio, i trasporti, l'estimo, ecc.

La distribuzione didattica delle materie matematiche sopra indicate nei tre anni di corso sarà in massima parte determinata dal concetto di scegliere costantemente, di preferenza nel campo della scienza attuariale, gli argomenti che valgono a illustrare le teorie di matematica pura.

Come si vede, nel nostro paese l'insegnamento della scienza attuariale progredisce rapidamente nelle varie forme, elementare, media e superiore. Se limitiamo l'esame alla forma superiore o universitaria, che implica le altre, noi dobbiamo riconoscere che ben pochi sono i paesi che ci hanno preceduto in questo indirizzo essenzialmente moderno di studi. Presso il celebre *Institute of actuaries*, che rappresenta e riassume le nobili tradizioni della scienza attuariale nel Regno Unito, le matematiche superiori sono state rese obbligatorie per tutti i candidati al titolo di membro, solamente a partire dal 1891. Anche l'*Institut des actuaires français* ha fissato da pochi anni un programma per gli esami di ammissione, nel quale è fatta larga parte alle matematiche superiori. Recentemente nel Seminario di Gottinga, in quello di Tokio, nella Università e nella Scuola tecnica superiore di Vienna sono stati iniziati corsi speciali di grado universitario. Un cospicuo posto nell'ordinamento generale degli studi ha assegnato l'Italia a questo importante ramo di alta coltura, istituendo una Scuola governativa autonoma, che, insieme e intorno alle matematiche, accoglie numerose materie economiche e giuridiche affini ed ausiliarie, e conferisce, alla fine del corso, il diploma di dottore in matematica finanziaria ed attuariale.

*
* *

Il Ministero di Agricoltura, Industria e Commercio, nel mentre riconosce di essere ben lontano dall'attuazione del suo programma, in ordine all'insegnamento della matematica, desidera e spera di ricevere conforto di sapienti consigli dagl' illustri cultori della scienza, convenuti in Roma per il IV Congresso internazionale.

L. LUIGGI

RAPPORTS ENTRE LES MATHÉMATIQUES ET L'ART DE L'INGÉNIEUR

Ce m'est un bien agréable devoir que de donner un cordial salut aux collègues Ingénieurs venus au Congrès de Rome; dans cette antique Cité, où l'art de l'Ingénieur eût ses origines.

Si les Egyptiens, les Assyriens, les Grecs furent de grands architectes et des artistes, les Romains furent essentiellement des Ingénieurs, et même de grands Ingénieurs. Leurs ponts, leurs acquéducs, leurs égouts; leurs routes merveilleuses; leurs canaux d'irrigation et de drainage; leurs temples, leurs thermes, leurs arcs de triomphe, si imposants et si grandioses, où la voûte — d'invention romaine — joue un rôle si important, appartiennent plus au domain de l'Ingénieur, comme nous le concevons aujourd'hui, qu'à celui de l'Architecte.

Et telle était l'importance que les Romains donnaient à ces ponts et à ces voûtes, qu'ils avaient réservé aux constructeurs de ponts en arc, un titre spécial, de *pontifex*; et même de *pontifex maximus* à celui, qu'aujourd'hui — avec beaucoup moins de poésie — nous appelons le « Directeur Général des ponts et chaussées ».

Mais je m'aperçois que le nom de Rome m'entraine hors de ma voie; je vous prie d'excuser cette digression et je reviens à l'objet de notre réunion.

C'est la première fois, je crois, que les Ingénieurs out l'honneur de participer à un Congrès de Mathématiques: et, je dois avouer, qu'ils n'y viennent pas sans quelque timidité, n'ayant nulle prétention d'y apporter des idées nouvelles, mais seulement l'intention d'exposer aux Mathématiciens, leurs doutes, leurs besoins, leurs désirs, et pour demander aide et conseil sur beaucoup de problèmes.

Nous nous rappelons, avec reconnaissance, que c'est aux Mathématiques que l'art de l'Ingénieur doit ces miracles de la construction qui font l'orgueil du siècle dernier, et qui s'appellent Barrages du Furens, de Vyrnwy, de Saint Rocque, du New Croton, de Urfthal; ponts en maçonnerie du Dee, de Morbegno, de Walnutstreet à Philadelphie, de Plauen, de Salcano; ponts métalliques du Douro, du Forth, de Brooklyn; tunnels du Mont Cenis, du St. Gothard, de l'Arlberg, du Simplon; canaux de Suez, de Manchester, de Kiel; tour Eiffel; navires comme le Great-Eastern, le Duilio, la Mauretania, et milles autres constructions merveilleuses que vous connaissez parfaitement.

Sans l'aide des Mathématiques, les problèmes posés à cette occasion auraient été inabordables; comme inabordables auraient été les problèmes de l'art de l'Ingénieur en relation avec la thermodynamique, l'électrotechnique, la technique des phares et une foule d'applications de la physique-mathématique. Sans une telle aide, l'Humanité n'aurait pas atteints aux progrès dont nous goutons aujourd'hui les bénéfices: entre autres, celui de nous rencontrer ici — gens de tout les pays, parlant de langues si différentes — et que les chemins de fer, les steamers, les automobiles ont facilement et commodément réunis dans le but élevé de l'avancement des Sciences Mathématiques considérées au point de vue de leurs applications aux besoins matériels des Peuples.

Mais nous attendons encore bien d'autres bénéfices des mathématiques appliquées aux constructions.

Et c'est ici que les doutes dont je vous ai parlé se présentent. Nous savons que les constructions si grandioses du siècle passé ne sont plus suffisantes aux besoins du XXème siècle. Des constructions bien plus importantes seront nécessaires; mais les méthodes de calcul, les formules employées jusqu'à présent, seront-elles encore suffisantes pour ces grandes constructions, ou bien: ont elles des limites et lesquelles?

Dans ces dernières années, les Ingénieurs, à côté de leurs triomphes, ont malheureusement dû compter aussi quelques désastres.

Des Barrages projetés avec les meilleures méthodes de calcul de l'époque, et très bien exécutés, ont subi des avaries graves, ou même se sont écroulés, entrainant des dommages matériels énormes et des pertes de vies humaines, encore plus déplorables; des navires, peut être trop longs par rapport à leurs dimensions transversales, se sont brisés sur des ondes hors de proportion avec les conditions usuelles; quelques ponts métalliques, et des toitures, en bon nombre, sont tombés; et tout récemment nous avons eu le désastre du Pont de Québec. Tout ces accidents peuvent avoir une cause matérielle, dans la conception du projet ou dans son éxécution, mais leur frequence nous fait supçonner qu'il pourrait y avoir quelque point faible dans les formules employées jusqu'ici; qu'elles pourraient bien n'être pas complètes, on bien, peut être, ne pas suffisamment tenir compte des facteurs, par exemple la chaleur, qu'on négligeait dans le passé, mais qui ont pourtant une valeur réelle dans les très grandes constructions d'aujourd'hui.

Comment devons nous reviser, corriger, compléter nos calculs pour les mettres en relation avec les besoins de l'avenir?

M. le Prof. CLAXTON FIDLER, de l'Université de Dundee, nous expose plus en détail — dans le Mémoire que j'ai l'honneur de vous présenter — beaucoup de ces points douteux.

Voyons nos nouveaux besoins. Les surprises bien désagréables des ponts métalliques qui ont une vie si courte, incitent à retourner autant que possible aux ponts en maçonnerie et d'adopter des arcs même de 120 ou 150 m. de corde; des raisons économiques conseillent la construction de barrages jusqu'à 100 m. de hauteur. La possibilité, grâce aux ciments Portland, d'avoir des mortiers capables de supporter des pressions allant jusqu'à 350 kgr. par cm.² comme, par exemple, au Pont de Plauen, nous encourage à tenter ces constructions si hardies.

Mais nos connaissances sur la distribution des efforts à l'intérieur de ces grandes masses de maçonnerie sont assez incertaines. La loi de MERY — connue usuellement sous le nom de loi du trapèze — et qui est très admissible pour des épaisseurs de mur modérées, ou lorsqu'on a des pressions de 6 à 8 kgr. par cm.², est elle encore admissible pour des épaisseurs de murs de 50 à 60 mètres et plus, ou bien des pressions de 20 à 30 kgr. par cm.²?

Les études de l'Ing. CASTIGLIANO ou du Prof. UNWIN, les observations directes de Sir BENJAMIN BAKER, les recherches récentes de MM. PEARSON et POLLARD de l'Université de Londres, de OTLEY, BRIGHTMORE, HILL, nous démontrent que les efforts ne varient pas selon une loi linéare; et que là où l'ancienne théorie, encore en usage, nous assure qu'il y a des compressions, l'expérience prouve qu'il peut y avoir des tensions, même très grandes.

Les grands maîtres de l'art, depuis GUILLEMAIN, BOUVIER, MAURICE LÉVY; jusqu'à CRUGNOLA, FTELEY, CERADINI, TORRICELLI, WEGMANN, INTZE, en abordant le problème, en apparence si simple, des barrages en maçonnerie, ne peuvent désormais cacher une certaine préoccupation à cet égard, et même de la timidité.

Mais quand nous voyons le Ministère des Travaux Publics de France conseiller de calculer les pressions *maxima maximorum* avec les deux méthodes différentes, de BOUVIER et de LÉVY, et d'adopter pour les assises successives celui des résultats qui est plus grand que l'autre, on comprend que cette timidité tient à la nébulosité qui persiste encore dans nos théories, même les plus simples; nébulosité qui devient encore plus épaisse quand on veut tenir compte des effets des variations de température dans les grandes masses de maçonnerie, et qui doivent être bien grandes sur des barrages long de 2 ou 300 m. avec des températures relativement basses du côté de l'eau et souvent très-hautes du côté aval exposé quelque fois aux rayons d'un soleil tropical, comme il arrive par exemple au barrage en arc de Barossa en Australie dont la variation de flèche avec la température peut atteindre jusqu'à 40 mm.

Et encore: comment devons nous interpréter les réserves que font les grands Constructeurs quand on leur demande des ponts en maçonnerie avec des arches, par exemple, supérieures à 60 m.? Et que devons nous penser quand nous voyons que cinq Ingénieurs seulement, RINALDI, MARRO, WEBSTER, SÈJOURNÉ, OMMENLANGE, ont eu le courage d'aller jusqu'à des arcs de 70, 72 m. 80, 84 à 90! ou quand nous écoutons de leur bouche, les préoccupations et les craintes qui ont éprouvées au moment du décintrage?

Evidemment on comprend que si nous nous arrêtons à des dimensions modestes, c'est parce que nous ne sommes pas bien sûrs de nos formules actuelles et n'osons pas les appliquer à des arcs de 100 ou de 150 m. de corde.

Il faut donc que Vous, les Mathématiciens, nous aidiez à réviser, perfectionner et compléter nos méthodes de calculation, dans le but d'arriver à éliminer toute cause d'incertitude ou de crainte.

M. le Prof. CANEVAZZI, de l'École des Ingénieurs de Bologne et M. le Prof. D'OCAGNE, de l'École des Ponts et Chaussées de Paris, exposeront bien d'autres difficultées sur lesquelles nous, les Ingénieurs, appelons toute votre attention et demandons vos précieux conseils pour les surmonter et les résoudre.

Avant de finir je dois encore vous manifester, Messieurs, une aspiration, un désir des Ingénieurs à l'égard de l'enseignement des mathématiques considérées du point de vue de leur application à l'art de bâtir.

Les élèves de nos Ecoles techniques font généralement leurs études avec les futurs adeptes des hautes mathématiques, ou bien sous la direction de Professeurs qui généralisent trop leurs méthodes d'études.

Les résultats, il est bien triste de devoir l'avouer, ne sont pas complètement satisfaisants.

Nous mettons dans les mains de nos élèves des outils très-puissants, comme ce sont les mathématiques, sans avoir la patience de leur apprendre pratiquement à s'en servir. De là l'empirisme, dont les conséquences sont quelque fois des désastres, mais qui causent toujours un gaspillage de matériel et d'argent, toutes les fois que les constructions s'écartent quelque peu de la routine ordinaire.

Voilà, Messieurs, un argument qu'on doit bien méditer, si nous voulons élever le niveau de la culture mathématique des Ingénieurs.

M. le Prof. Swain, du Technological Institute de Boston, vous présente à cet égard une Note sur la quelle je vous prie de porter toute votre attention.

Et je conclurai, Messieurs, en faisant deux voeux:

Le premier est que entre les Mathématiciens purs et les Ingénieurs-constructeurs il y ait plus de rapports, plus d'intimité; ou au moins qu'il y ait un trait d'union constitué par des Ingénieurs-Mathématiciens, exactement comme nous trouvons les représentants de la Physique-Mathématique entre ceux de la Physique expérimentale et ceux de la Mathématique pure.

Le deuxième voeu est, que, dans les différents pays, si bien représentés à notre Congrès, les adeptes des Mathématiques appliquées à la construction, veuillent bien examiner les méthodes de calcul adoptées dans leur pays, pour résoudre certains problèmes de grande importance pour tous les Ingénieurs, et qui sont résolus de manière différentes et pas toujours bien rationnelles (notamment à propos des grandes voûtes en maçonnerie, des grands barrages, des radiers des grands bassins de carénage, des murs de quai dans les ports à grandes marées et d'autres), et en faire au prochain Congrès l'objet de rapports, qui seraient discutés, de façon à preparer le choix des méthodes les plus satisfaisantes; et arriver ainsi a l'*unification des calculs de la stabilité des constructions*; exactement comme cela a déjà été fait pour beaucoup de questions relatives à l'unification des méthodes d'essai des matériaux employés dans les constructions.

Procédant ainsi, on arrivera à cette communion d'idées entre les Mathématiciens et les Ingénieurs, à cette union intime entre la Théorie et l'Experience, indispensable pour nous guider dans la solution des grands problèmes posés pour les constructions de l'avenir.

On pourra ainsi les resoudre en obtenant toute garantie de voir durer les oeuvres à travers les siècles, — comme jadis les *oeuvres des Romains*, — tout en réalisant une juste économie de matériaux et d'argent.

Ces grands problèmes se présentent spécialement dans le domaine de l'irrigation, déstinée à augmenter la production du sol au bénéfice des générations prochaines, et dans le domaine des transports, par eau et par chemins de fer, déstinés à rendre plus étroits les rapports et les liens de sympathie entre les Nations, entre les Peuples civilisés. Ce sont donc de problèmes du plus haut intérêt pour tous les Pays!

S. CANEVAZZI

LA MATEMATICA E L'ARTE DEL COSTRUTTORE IN ITALIA

Invitato a prendere la parola intorno ai servigi che la matematica rende alla tecnica professionale, riconosco ad un tempo l'onore fattomi e l'arduo compito che mi è stato assegnato. L'alta competenza degli ascoltatori da un lato, la vastità dell'argomento dall'altro, fanno questo assunto oltremodo difficile, nè saprei in quale maniera raggiungere l'intento, se le norme generali stabilite per questo Congresso non prevedessero molteplici conferenze, e non permettessero quindi di ridurre il campo di ognuna alla considerazione di una determinata disciplina, ed anche al solo sviluppo che questa può aver avuto in un periodo speciale per opera di benemeriti cultori della scienza. In conformità a questo concetto, io parlerò dell'applicazione della matematica all'arte del costruttore, prendendo specialmente in esame l'ultimo cinquantennio e limitandomi ad occuparmi soltanto dell'importante ed efficace contributo portato a questi studî da scrittori italiani.

Leonardo Salimbeni nel 1787 scriveva: « Quando la matematica non rivolge « la mira ad oggetto di pubblica utilità, infruttuose si rimangono le sue scoperte, non « servendo che a pascere la speculativa di pochi, ma se il contrario succeda, non può « dirsi quanto illumini quella scienza la pratica, ed oltre i confini la spinga, ai quali « per se stessa non sarebbe pervenuta giammai ». Gli ingegneri sono sempre stati convinti della verità di questa sentenza ed in tutti i rami d'applicazione, non appena in base ad osservazioni ed esperienze poterono enunciare qualche legge, questa ridussero in formula nell'intento di dedurne coll'indagine matematica nuovi veri e particolari relazioni, atte a risolvere i problemi della pratica. L'idraulica, la termotecnica, l'elettrotecnica, la scienza delle costruzioni, sono la prova manifesta di questo fatto, e dobbiamo solo alla matematica se queste materie dalla cerchia ristretta di una serie di regole sperimentali sono assurte alla dignità di scienze.

I costruttori medioevali erano indagatori tenaci e profondi, nè mai si abbandonavano al comodo sistema della consuetudine; disgraziatamente essi non ci hanno lasciato alcun scritto, che ci permetta di giudicare intorno ai metodi seguìti per determinare le forme eleganti delle loro mirabili costruzioni. Leonardo da Vinci, come a tanti altri argomenti, così anche alla resistenza dei materiali ha portato il contributo del suo portentoso ingegno, ma bisogna venire fino al secolo decimosettimo per trovare gli albori della scienza delle costruzioni. Galileo negli immortali suoi dialoghi applica pel primo l'analisi razionale allo studio di un solido incastrato ad un estremo, fondando ad un tempo la teoria della mensola e la scienza delle costruzioni. GALILEO considera anche il caso di una trave appoggiata agli estremi, e con intuito meraviglioso deduce metodicamente tutti i teoremi, che ora sono conseguenza notoria dell'espressione algebrica del momento elastico di resistenza a flessione. Si è rimproverato alle ricerche di GALILEO che il rapporto da lui fissato fra la resistenza a rottura per sforzo longitudinale e quella corrispondente alla rottura per sforzo trasversale non è esatto; rimane però sempre il fatto che tutti i teoremi da lui enunciati sussistono e sono confermati dalle ricerche posteriori, e che esso è il vero fondatore della scienza del costruttore. L'opera di GALILEO non rimase infruttuosa e la nuova via che esso aveva aperta fu premurosamente seguíta da eminenti scienziati in Italia ed all'estero. ALESSANDRO MARCHETTI, professore a Pisa, si occupava nel 1669 dei solidi di uniforme resistenza alla flessione, e si interessarono assai dei problemi relativi alla resistenza dei corpi il padre FABRI (1669), VINCENZO VIVIANI ed il suo continuatore padre GRANDI camaldolese (1693), il cui trattato è soprattutto rimarchevole per l'introduzione dell'uso della geometria nella risoluzione dei problemi proposti.

Occupati di questioni matematiche gli scienziati del secolo decimottavo trascurarono quelle riguardanti la resistenza dei corpi alla rottura e non è che sul finire di questo periodo che lo studio delle condizioni di equilibrio delle strutture costruttive è stato ripreso con rinnovellato ardore. Peraltro non può dirsi che in Italia tale importante branca della ingegneria sia stata lasciata in completo abbandono. Il problema dell'equilibrio della cupola di San Pietro, studiato dal padre BOSCOVICH nel 1742 in unione ai p. p. LE SUER e JAQUIER per ordine di BENEDETTO XIV, fornì al marchese POLENI l'occasione di eseguire una serie di esperienze sulla resistenza del ferro alla trazione. LORGNA (1763) si occupava della coesione delle murature e della loro resistenza alla spinta delle terre, FRISI (1777) dell'equilibrio delle cupole e delle volte, DELANGES (1779) della spinta delle terre e successivamente dei principî della statica per i tetti, per i ponti e per le volte (1803). Studî interessanti di statica delle costruzioni hanno fatto RICATI (1780), LAMBERTI (1781), ORSINI (1808), ed il prof. MASCHERONI di Pavia (1785). Nomineremo finalmente LEONARDO SALIMBENI che pubblicava nel 1787 un notevole trattato degli archi e delle volte in sei libri, nel quale l'uso della matematica è ampiamente applicato con singolare perizia, considerando l'azione delle forze trasmesse dai conci delle volte e quella dei loro momenti. L'opera magistrale di un compianto collega, la Biblioteca matematica italiana del prof. PIETRO RICCARDI, mi dispensa, senza incorrere nella taccia di oblioso, dal ricordare altri nomi; essa è una cronistoria esatta e completa della produzione scientifica italiana nel campo tecnico-matematico, e può essere consultata con grande profitto.

Non mi indugerò ulteriormente sull'opera di studiosi italiani in materia di resistenza dei materiali anteriore al 1850, poichè mi tarda di venire alla seconda metà del secolo decimonono, in cui l'attività italiana nello studio matematico per l'incremento della scienza delle costruzioni si manifesta con indiscutibile successo, stampandovi un'orma incancellabile. Si deve infatti a scienziati italiani l'applicazione della teoria dell'energia elastica e delle sue conseguenze alla risoluzione dei problemi costruttivi ed un forte contributo alla teoria geometrica dei sistemi elastici in equilibrio. Alcuni di questi nobili ingegni sono purtroppo scomparsi dalla scena del mondo e tutti noi rimpiangiamo la perdita di Menabrea, di Castigliano e di Cremona: gli altri, per la maggior parte, possono fortunatamente prestare ancora l'opera loro per l'incremento della scienza. Io non li indicherò personalmente per non offendere la modestia di eminenti colleghi ed amici carissimi, ma i loro nomi sono sulla bocca di tutti. Qui mi limito a formare il voto che essi siano per lungo tempo conservati alla patria, che altamente onorano.

L'Italia può vantare un gran numero di fisici apprezzatissimi, che si sono occupati della teoria matematica dell'elasticità con successo universalmente riconosciuto. I limiti fra questa scienza e la teoria della resistenza del materiale non sono così ben definiti perchè, seguendo l'esempio di un grande maestro, il prof. Eugenio Beltrami, gli allievi ed i continuatori di lui non abbiano fortunatamenle spesso sconfinato, portando vedute analitiche nuove e precisione matematica nel campo dell'applicazione. Mi sono imposto una legge e la seguo non facendo speciali citazioni, ma non posso tacere che un giovane scienziato ha pubblicato or son pochi mesi sul *Nuovo Cimento* un pregevolissimo studio sui progressi della teoria dell'elasticità in Italia. All'indicazione dello sviluppo delle nuove ricerche e successive semplificazioni delle soluzioni trovate, esso fa seguire copiose notizie bibliografiche, in guisa che il suo lavoro è riescito un importante capitolo di storia delle matematiche, utilissimo a quanti si interessano di questa materia. L'oggetto che ci siamo prefisso ci vieta di soffermarci maggiormente sopra questo argomento e ci fa apparire sufficiente averne fatto un breve cenno per l'eventualità di particolari ricerche prima di entrare nel campo pratico della scienza delle costruzioni.

Il generale Menabrea, in una Memoria presentata nel 1857 all'Accademia delle scienze di Torino, ed in altra letta nel 1858 all'Accademia delle scienze di Parigi, esponeva sotto il nome di principio di elasticità il teorema del minimo lavoro elastico di deformazione in un sistema in equilibrio, facendo anche vedere come questa proprietà poteva servire a determinare le reazioni incognite. Di questo argomento si erano occupati in precedenza Pagani, Mosotti e Dorna, ed in seguito se ne interessò ancora lo stesso Menabrea, presentando una nuova Memoria all'Accademia delle scienze di Torino nel 1868. Questo teorema però e l'uso che se ne può fare rimase ignorato agli ingegneri per parecchi anni e si deve all'ing. A. Castigliano se i concetti energetici penetrarono nella scienza delle costruzioni arrivando a servire di base pei calcoli usuali di resistenza. Questi nel 1873 e 1875, studiando le proprietà del lavoro elastico di deformazione, enunciava i teoremi sulle derivate del lavoro elastico di deformazione espresso in funzione delle deformazioni e delle forze esterne, che appunto portano il nome di teoremi di Castigliano, e presentava il principio di elasticità come corollario dei medesimi. Nel 1879 poi lo stesso Castigliano pubblicava la *Teoria dell'equilibrio dei sistemi elastici*, vero trattato di scienza delle costruzioni, fondato sui teoremi sopra ricordati, coll'aggiunta di esempî e moduli per la condotta degli ordinarî calcoli di stabilità per le opere usuali. In questo modo egli introdusse nella tecnica nuovi procedimenti di calcolo di facile applicazione, che vennero subito adottati, anche da grandi amministrazioni, come ad esempio la cessata Società ferroviaria dell'Alta Italia.

Le proprietà del lavoro elastico di deformazione e le questioni attinenti al medesimo sono state in Italia oggetto di molto studio fra i cultori della scienza delle costruzioni e della teoria matematica della elasticità, cosicchè nuovi teoremi vennero ad aggiungersi a quelli sopra ricordati. Basterà fra questi citare il teorema di Betti sulla reciprocità esistente fra le forze molecolari e le deformazioni corrispondenti a due diversi sistemi di forze applicate negli stessi punti e colle medesime direzioni, i teoremi di correlazione fra le forze esterne ed interne e gli spostamenti e deformazioni corrispondenti nelle stesse ipotesi di carico dianzi considerate e la deduzione conseguente del principio di Maxwell e del principio dei coefficienti unitarî di deformazione, che, applicato nel piano in via geometrica, conduce al tracciamento delle linee d'influenza rispetto alle deformazioni. L'insieme di questi teoremi, congiunti alle ipotesi fondamentali sulla deformazione delle travature forniscono nuovi metodi, diversi da quelli classici di Navier e di Bresse, pel calcolo dei sistemi di travi semplici, combinate o composte, per la determinazione delle reazioni sovrabbondanti, dei problemi impliciti e degli spostamenti di punti determinati. Questi nuovi metodi di calcolo dei sistemi resistenti, oltrechè in Italia, sono stati oggetto di studio per gli ingegneri anche all'estero, e specialmente in Germania, ma nel nostro paese è forse stato conservato più spiccato il carattere matematico, deducendo le proprietà dei sistemi elastici dalla combinazione dei teoremi delle velocità virtuali e del potenziale di elasticità con quelli puramente algebrici, caratteristici delle funzioni omogenee di 2° grado. A primo aspetto il metodo può sembrare più complesso, ma in realtà è filosoficamente più completo e soddisfacente. Didatticamente poi esso risulta estremamente semplice e quasi intuitivo qualora siano possedute le cognizioni che sono ordinariamente richieste per l'ammissione alle scuole d'applicazione per gli ingegneri.

Un corpo elastico in base alla sua definizione ed all'infuori di influenze esterne, cambiamenti di temperatura od altro, è per se stesso soggetto ad un sistema di forze interne, le quali ammettono un potenziale ed uno stato naturale di equilibrio. Se forze esterne o vincoli speciali impediscono al corpo di raggiungere tale stato, esso si costituisce in equilibrio conservando in se stesso latente un'energia potenziale, uguale al lavoro che le forze interne faranno per raggiungere lo stato naturale, qualora vengano a cessare le cause che agivano esternamente al corpo stesso: gli ingegneri sogliono chiamare questa energia latente col nome di lavoro di deformazione. Il costruttore deve sempre prendere in esame corpi elastici duri, cioè tali che le deformazioni contate dallo stato naturale di equilibrio, siano piccolissime rispetto alle dimensioni primitive. Questa circostanza permette di considerare le deformazioni stesse come quantità infinitesimali e per conseguenza di dimostrare che il lavoro elastico di deformazione è una funzione omogenea di 2° grado delle deformazioni, e che le sue derivate prime sono funzioni lineari senza termine indipendente ed uguali alle forze che mantengono il corpo in equilibrio. Tenute presenti le proprietà delle forme di 2° grado e delle loro trasformate, non che i principî della statica dei sistemi, si deducono immediatamente i teoremi fondamentali sopra ricordati, caratteristici dei sistemi elastici, e che trovano, o possono trovare, un uso continuo nella risoluzione dei problemi che si presentano al costruttore.

Entrare in maggiori particolari esorbiterebbe dal quadro che ci siamo tracciato; queste notizie sommarie però, congiunte all'osservazione che l'uso del calcolo differenziale ed integrale è indispensabile e continuo per la valutazione delle deformazioni e spostamenti elastici nelle travature, sono sufficienti a dimostrare quale grande e si può anche dire indispensabile sussidio sia l'analisi per l'ingegnere costruttore, tanto negli studî di ricerca, quanto in quelli di stabilità e di progetto.

Un illustre geometra, il prof. LUIGI CREMONA, intorno al 1870, volgarizzava in Italia l'uso dei metodi grafici nella risoluzione dei problemi costruttivi, dettando nel R. Istituto tecnico superiore di Milano splendide lezioni di geometria projettiva e di statica grafica. Non mi spetta di parlare qui del CREMONA come geometra, e neppure dell'opera sua come capo scuola e di quella dei suoi numerosi e valenti allievi. Debbo limitarmi a considerare unicamente in lui il professore, cui si deve l'introduzione in Italia della statica grafica. I procedimenti pel calcolo geometrico delle quantità e dei sistemi di forze, già prima integrati nel 1866 dal KULLMANN in un corso ordinato di lezioni per gli allievi del Politecnico di Zurigo, furono subito studiati in Italia con amore, e lo stesso CREMONA iniziava il movimento della produzione italiana in questa branca speciale dell'alta coltura tecnica pubblicando nel 1872 quella geniale concezione, che è la teoria delle figure reciproche nella statica grafica pel calcolo delle travature reticolari. Dopo di lui i suoi numerosi allievi professanti l'ingegneria si misero per la via già tracciata dal loro maestro, portando soprattutto la loro attenzione sulle questioni attinenti alla scienza delle costruzioni. Certamente le soluzioni geometriche dei problemi della statica delle costruzioni hanno avuto in Germania il loro maggiore sviluppo, ma si può asserire senza tema di errore, non esservi problema costruttivo, alla cui soluzione grafica gli studiosi italiani non abbiano contribuito efficacemente. L'equilibrio molecolare è stato studiato in Italia estendendovi il concetto cremoniano delle figure reciproche, e così pure è stato studiato l'equilibrio delle terre in base alle varie teorie in uso. Tanto in trattati completi di statica grafica o di scienza delle costruzioni, come in Memorie separate, sono state date in Italia eleganti soluzioni grafiche dei problemi relativi alle travature ad asse rettilineo, semplici o continue, agli archi elastici semplici o reticolati, a cerniere od incastrati alle loro estremità, e finalmente alle travature reticolari ed all'equilibrio delle murature e delle opere in cemento armato. Gli ingegneri italiani, impegnatisi in una nobile gara con eminenti cultori esteri della stessa scienza, hanno spaziato in tutto il vasto campo delle applicazioni costruttive e dovunque hanno portato o nuove considerazioni o semplificazioni importanti ai metodi di calcolo già proposti od in uso.

Da questi brevi cenni appare di quale utilità sia per l'ingegnere la matematica, tanto nella forma analitica quanto in quella geometrica. Un esame più particolareggiato non potrebbe essere racchiuso nella cerchia di una breve conferenza, e neppure sarebbe opportuno tentarlo, perchè questa prenderebbe allora, almeno parzialmente, il carattere di Memoria scientifica di ordine analitico, cosa che ci siamo proposti di evitare. Pei cultori della scienza delle costruzioni e delle materie affini, quanto è stato detto è sufficiente per poter apprezzare l'importanza della produzione scientifica italiana in relazione all'arte del costruttore. Qui ci basta poter asserire che il movimento intellettuale per cui da una serie di procedimenti empirici o professionali, basati sul criterio del confronto e dell'esperienza, l'arte del costruttore è assurta ad una serie di processi razionali, ordinatamente collegati fra loro, acquistando dignità di scienza, è stato possibile soltanto per l'introduzione dei metodi matematici nello studio delle condizioni di equilibrio dei sistemi resistenti. Se il problema di proporzionare le dimensioni di una struttura costruttiva alle forze che la sollecitano senza che gli sforzi interni e le deformazioni superino limiti determinati è ormai risoluto, ciò è avvenuto unicamente perchè l'esperienza e l'induzione matematica si sono date la mano, sorreggendosi reciprocamente.

Siamo poi lieti di poter aggiungere che la prima spinta data a questo alto progresso scientifico in Italia da GALILEO e dai suoi immediati successori, non è rimasta senza continuatori nel nostro paese. La produzione scientifica italiana relativa alla teoria della resistenza dei materiali può forse avere languito per qualche tempo, nel quale i maggiori e più importanti lavori sono stati fatti all'estero, ma nell'ultimo sessantennio un nuovo spirito di indagine ha animato i nostri ingegneri tanto nel campo scientifico quanto in quello sperimentale. Il pensiero dei teoremi e metodi di calcolo sopra ricordati, ci permette di poter affermare, traendone lieti auspicî per l'avvenire, che l'opera nazionale ha valso dapprima a fondare la scienza delle costruzioni e che in seguito, specialmente nell'ultimo sessantennio, ha contribuito efficacemente al suo progresso.

CENNI BIBLIOGRAFICI.

I due lavori citati:

Biblioteca matematica italiana del prof. PIETRO RICCARDI (Modena, tipografia dell'erede Soliani, 1870;

Progressi e sviluppo della teoria matematica dell'elasticità in Italia (Memoria del prof. ROBERTO MARCOLONGO, pubblicata nel *Nuovo Cimento*, anno 1907, mese di novembre, serie V, vol. XIV);

contengono copiosissime indicazioni bibliografiche, che troppo lungo sarebbe riprodurre, e che d'altra parte possono essere facilmente rintracciate da quanti si interessano allo studio della storia delle matematiche. Crediamo quindi sufficiente aggiungere soltanto l'elenco dei trattati di scienza delle costruzioni pubblicati in Italia nell'ultimo cinquantennio. Le Memorie, le monografie e gli studî riflettenti argomenti speciali o sono indicate nei due lavori sopra citati, o sono ricordate nei varî trattati, dei quali facciamo seguire l'elenco.

CURIONI GIOVANNI. *L'arte di fabbricare. Resistenza dei materiali e stabilità delle costruzioni* (Torino 1877, ed. A. F. Negro).

CHICCHI PIO. *Corso teorico pratico sulla costruzione dei ponti* (Torino 1886, ed. A. F. Negro).

CASTIGLIANO ALBERTO. *Théorie de l'équilibre des systèmes élastiques et ses applications* (Torino 1879, ed. A. F. Negro).

CANEVAZZI SILVIO. *Meccanica applicata alle costruzioni (Arte di fabbricare): Teoria generale della resistenza dei materiali — Statica delle costruzioni* (Torino 1891, ed. A. F. Negro).

CANEVAZZI SILVIO. *Ferrocemento* (Torino 1904, ed. Società editrice succ. A. F. Negro e C.).

CERADINI CESARE. *Meccanica applicata alle costruzioni* (Milano, Casa editrice dottor Francesco Vallardi).

SAVIOTTI CARLO. *La statica grafica* (Milano 1888, ed. U. Hoepli).

ALASIA CRISTOFORO. *Calcolo grafico ed applicazioni alla statica grafica* (Città di Castello 1899, ed. S. Lapi).

CAVALLI ERNESTO. *Cemento armato* (Napoli 1907, ed. Trani).

CROTTI FRANCESCO. *La teoria dell'elasticità nei suoi principî fondamentali e nelle sue applicazioni pratiche alle costruzioni* (Milano 1888, ed. U. Hoepli).

CRUGNOLA GAETANO (Pubblicazioni in volumi separati): *Dei tetti metallici.* — *Sui muri di sostegno delle terre e sulle traverse dei serbatoj d'acqua.* — *Sulla spinta delle terre e delle masse liquide* (Torino, ed. A. F. Negro).

GUIDI CAMILLO. *Lezioni della scienza delle costruzioni date nella R. Scuola d'applicazione per gli ingegneri in Torino* (Torino 1898, tip.-lit. Camilla e Bertolero di R. Bertolero editore).

JORINI ANTONIO. *Teoria e pratica della costruzione dei ponti* (Milano 1905, ed. U. Hoepli).

ZUCCHETTI FERDINANDO. *Statica grafica* (Torino, ed. A. F. Negro).

M. d'OCAGNE

LA TECHNIQUE DU CALCUL
CONSIDÉRÉE PRINCIPALEMENT AU POINT DE VUE DE LA SCIENCE DE L'INGÉNIEUR.

Dans toutes les applications des sciences mathématiques aux sciences techniques, la question du calcul numérique est d'une haute importance alors que, de fait, les mathématiciens de profession s'en soucient généralement fort peu. La mise en nombres des formules auxquelles conduisent leurs spéculations leur apparaît comme peu digne de retenir leur attention sollicitée par des objets plus élevés. Ils abandonnent aux techniciens le soin de cette besogne sans attrait, réservant tous leurs efforts pour les beaux problèmes que leur offre la théorie pure.

Or, si le mathématicien a raison — et cela ne saurait même pas faire question — de pousser toujours plus avant dans la voie de la théorie, sans même se soucier de son immédiate utilisation pour les besoins de la pratique, et si c'est même là la part la plus belle et la plus noble de sa mission, il aurait tort de se cantonner exclusivement dans ce rôle. Il lui appartient encore de rendre plus facile et plus rapide l'exécution des calculs numériques, en la soustrayant d'autre part, autant que possible, à toute chance d'erreur ; et c'est à juste titre que M. C. Runge voit, dans une telle discipline, une partie intégrante du domaine ouvert au labeur des mathématiciens (¹). Cette discipline sera classée parmi les mathématiques appliquées parce qu'elle n'intervient, en effet, qu'au moment où l'on passe aux applications, mais elle se rattache étroitement aux mathématiques pures dont, en réalité, elle constitue un prolongement logique.

A l'origine de tout calcul se rencontre l'opération fondamentale à laquelle, de proche en proche, se ramènent toutes les autres : le simple comptage s'effectuant unité par unité.

C'est à partir de cette opération fondamentale qu'ont été dressées, de proche en proche, toute les tables numériques d'où nous tirons les résultats de calculs dont nous avons besoin, car, pour nous, calculer numériquement, ce n'est jamais que faire une suite d'extraits de tables de résultats tout faits.

(¹) Jahresbericht der deutschen Mathematiker-Vereinigung, 1907, p. 497.

On a commencé par cataloguer les sommes, obtenues par comptage, des nombres, pris deux à deux, ce qui a fourni la table d'addition. Des applications répétées de celle-ci ont, à leur tour, donné naissance à la table de multiplication.

N'était l'infirmité de notre mémoire, il eût suffi de prolonger ces tables jusqu'à la limite des nombres pratiquement utilisables pour que les quatre opérations fondamentales de l'arithmétique se bornassent à un simple appel à la mémoire, sans le secours d'aucune règle particulière. Ces quatre règles, que l'on nous enseigne dès notre plus jeune âge, et qui finissent par nous apparaître comme l'essence même du calcul, n'ont d'autre but que de réduire la part dans laquelle il convient de faire intervenir notre mémoire au strict minimum en la bornant, tant pour l'addition que pour la multiplication, à ce qui concerne les données d'un seul chiffre. Mais, en somme, ce que nous faisons en appliquant ces quatre règles, ce n'est qu'une suite d'extraits des tables de résultats formés d'avance, tables que nous avons imprimées, une fois pour toutes, dans notre cerveau de façon à n'avoir pas besoin de les avoir constamment sous les yeux.

Nous pouvons d'ailleurs, lorsque les circonstances s'y prêtent, recourir, pour la multiplication et la division, aux tables, bien plus étendues que la simple table classique (improprement dite *de Pythagore* ([1])), qui se rencontrent en divers recueils.

Donner un procédé d'éxecution pour un calcul quelconque, c'est indiquer comment on en peut obtenir le résultat par une suite d'extraits effectués dans les tables d'addition et de multiplication. Mais, de même qu'après avoir obtenu la première de ces tables par simple comptage, on en a, par des applications répétées, déduit la seconde, on peut pousser plus avant dans la même voie en se servant de ces tables pour en construire d'autres répondant à de nouvelles opérations, et ainsi de suite.

Il est tout naturel d'assimiler ces tables successives aux appareils de levage, de plus en plus perfectionnés, qui se rencontrent sur nos chantiers. Au début de sa belle *Histoire de l'Architecture* ([2]), M. AUGUSTE CHOISY établit de façon lumineuse que les manoeuvres requises par l'emploi en construction des masses les plus formidables peuvent se ramener à l'emploi du simple levier... à la condition que le temps ni la main d'oeuvre ne soient comptés pour rien, ce qui était le cas chez les peuples primitifs dont le mégalithisme nous a conservé la trace.

Exactement de même, les calculs les plus compliqués se peuvent-ils résoudre en une suite d'extraits des seules tables classiques d'addition et de multiplication qui jouent un peu ici le rôle du levier.

Mais nous cherchons, de plus en plus, à économiser notre temps et notre travail ; c'est ce qui nous incite à perfectionner de plus en plus l'outillage de nos chantiers ; c'est ce qui, de même, nous pousse à multiplier les tables propres à réduire, de plus en plus, les opérations de calcul, c'est-à-dire les extraits à faire dans chaque cas, d'autres tables antérieurement obtenues.

« Que de découragement, s'écrie MENABREA ([3]), la perspective d'un long et aride

([1]) Voir, *Encycl. des sc. math.*, t. 1, vol. 4, pag. 212.

([2]) 2 vol. in 8° ; Paris, Gauthier-Villars, 1899.

([3]) Bibliothèque universelle de Genève, T. XLI, p. 352.

« calcul ne jette-t-elle pas dans l'âme de l'homme de génie qui ne demande que du « temps pour méditer et qui se le voit ravi par le matériel des opérations ! ».

Il va de soi — et c'est presque commettre un truisme que de le dire — que l'établissement d'une table nouvelle n'est avantageuse que si l'opération à laquelle elle correspond doit revenir fréquemment dans les applications. On n'aurait évidemment pas l'idée de dresser une table embrassant tout un ensemble de valeurs de données s'il s'agissait de n'avoir le résultat isolé de l'opération correspondante que pour un seul choix particulier de ces données.

Mais, lorsque l'opération est de celles qui reviennent souvent dans les applications, le bénéfice à retirer d'une table spéciale se montre clairement, et d'autant plus qu'en général la détermination d'une suite de résultats, correspondant à des valeurs des données croissant de façon régulière, comporte de très sensibles simplifications par rapport au travail qu'exigerait la détermination individuelle de tous ces résultats. L'exemple classique du calcul des tables de carrés et de cubes rend la portée de cette remarque immédiatement saisissable. Ce calcul, qui, pour chacun des nombres de la table, pris isolément, exigerait l'usage de la table de multiplication, s'effectue pour l'ensemble au moyen de la seule table d'addition, grâce à la considération des différences secondes ou troisièmes.

Construire des tables spéciales pour toutes les formules ou équations qui interviennent dans les applications, tel est, en fait, le moyen de venir en aide au technicien qui a besoin de recourir au calcul numérique. On est toutefois souvent arrêté dans cette tâche par la considération du travail requis par une telle construction étendue à tout le champ dans lequel, pratiquement, varient les valeurs des données. Les simplifications que comporte cet établissement ne sont pas, en effet, toujours aussi importantes que celles qui viennent d'être rappelées à propos des tables de carrés et de cubes ; il y a là une question d'économie de peine et de temps ; il s'agit d'apprécier si, vu l'usage qui doit être fait de la formule en question, il peut y avoir bénéfice à la réduire en table particulière au lieu d'en laisser rechercher le résultat, dans chaque cas, par des applications successives de tables déjà existantes (y compris les tables classiques d'addition et de multiplication). Mais on peut se heurter, d'autre part, à un obstacle qui, de prime abord, peut sembler infranchissable ; nous voulons parler de l'impossibilité de dresser des tables numériques à plus de deux entrées, d'où résulte l'obligation de ramener tout calcul numérique à une suite d'opérations ne portant pas chacune sur plus de deux variables.

Or, il est un moyen à la fois très facile et très général de supprimer radicalement ces difficultés, de rendre très simple et très expéditif l'établissement d'une table quelconque et, en même temps, d'y permettre l'extension du nombre des entrées ; ce moyen consiste à substituer aux tables numériques ordinaires des tables graphiques, *abaques* ou *nomogrammes*.

Il existe bien, sur les tables ordinaires, une sorte de relation de position entre les valeurs inscrites pour les données et la valeur inscrite pour le résultat : les premières figurant dans des cases disposées le long des bords du tableau, la dernière se trouve dans la case située à la rencontre de la colonne correspondant à celle de l'une des données et de la rangée correspondant à celle de l'autre. Mais cette relation de position n'a, à proprement parler, rien de mathématique. Il en va tout autrement sur les nomogrammes.

Ici, à chacune des variables intervenant dans l'équation représentée, on fait correspondre sur un plan un système d'éléments géométriques dépendant de cette variable en sorte qu'à chaque valeur particulière de celle-ci corresponde un élément particulier de ce système simplement infini et *vice versa*. La valeur de la variable correspondant à l'un de ces éléments en est dite la *cote*. Pour un choix convenable de ces éléments cotés, il existe entre eux une relation de position simple, susceptible d'une vérification immédiate, lorsque l'ensemble de leurs cotes respectives satisfait à l'équation proposée. On a ainsi une *représentation nomographique* de cette équation qui, on le voit immédiatement, peut tenir lieu de table numérique. De même, en effet, que, sur celle-ci, les valeurs des données définissent la rangée et la colonne à la rencontre desquelles est la case où doit se lire le résultat, de même, sur le nomogramme, les valeurs des données définissent certains éléments dans n-1 des systèmes représentés, et ces n-1 éléments par une certaine relation de position, d'une constatation immédiate, en déterminent, dans le $n^{\text{ième}}$ système, un autre dont la cote est le résultat du calcul cherché.

Outre la plus grande rapidité de construction et la possibilité d'un nombre d'entrées supérieur à deux, ces tables graphiques offrent encore l'avantage de se prêter à l'interpolation à vue, grâce à l'intercalation par la pensée, entre les éléments réellement figurés sur le plan, de ceux qui correspondraient à des cotes intermédiaires.

Mais, au point de vue mathématique, ces tables graphiques ou nomogrammes se distinguent des tables numériques ou barèmes par une différence essentielle ; c'est à savoir qu'un barème ne peut être établi que grâce à l'emploi de quelque autre barème préalablement existant (ne fût-ce que les tables classiques d'addition et de multiplication), tandis qu'un nomogramme s'appliquant à une relation parfois très compliquée, peut être obtenu directement sans qu'il soit besoin de passer par aucun intermédiaire. C'est ainsi, par exemple, que nous avons fait voir que les équations algébriques complètes des sept premiers degrés peuvent être résolues au moyen de nomogrammes entièrement constructibles à l'aide de projections d'échelles métriques.

Au point de vue pratique — et c'est là l'objet principal de la Nomographie — on doit s'efforcer de représenter les équations au moyen des relations de position les plus simples possibles entre éléments géométriques aussi simples que possible.

Les éléments géométriques les plus simples sont des points, dont la suite cotée constitue une échelle ; la relation de position la plus simple entre des points est l'*alignement*. Les nomogrammes les plus simples et les plus commodes seront donc ceux à *points alignés*, dont, depuis près d'un quart de siècle [1] nous n'avons cessé de poursuivre l'étude et dont, après l'avoir entièrement développée dans notre grand *Traité de Nomographie* [2], nous venons encore de reprendre, sous une forme nouvelle, la théorie détaillée dans nos récentes leçons de *Calcul graphique et Nomographie* [3].

(1) Notre premier Mémoire sur ce sujet a paru en 1884 dans les Annales des Ponts et Chaussées.
(2) Paris, Gauthier-Villars, 1899.
(3) Paris, Doin, 1908.

Il nous sera sans doute permis de constater que ce mode spécial de calcul est aujourd'hui utilisé, sur une vaste échelle, par les techniciens des spécialités les plus diverses ([1]).

Les nomogrammes, il est vrai, ne sont pas, comme les barèmes, susceptibles d'une approximation indéfinie, à tout le moins, ce qui est pratiquement le cas, lorsqu'on les réduit à des dimensions couramment maniables. Mais si rares sont les cas, vu l'objet poursuivi par le technicien dans ses calculs, où il a besoin d'une approximation conduisant à des nombres de plus de 3, voire de 4 chiffres, qu'en ce qui le concerne, ce mode de calcul apparaît comme d'un intérêt à peu près universel.

([1]) Voir à ce sujet nos articles dans la Revue générale des Sciences (T. IX, 1898, p. 116 et T. XVIII, 1907, p. 392).

M. d'OCAGNE

SUR LA RECTIFICATION GRAPHIQUE APPROCHÉE DES ARCS DE CERCLE

L'impossibilité, définitivement démontrée depuis les travaux d'HERMITE et de LINDEMANN, de construire *rigoureusement*, au moyen de la règle et du compas, un segment de droite de même longueur qu'un arc de cercle donné ne doit être entendue que dans le sens de la théorie pure. *Pratiquement*, si une construction permet d'obtenir un segment de droite dont la longueur ne diffère de celle de l'arc donné que d'une quantité inférieure aux erreurs considérées comme négligeables dans l'exécution des tracés, cette construction peut être employée couramment dans les applications. On admet généralement qu'il en est ainsi lorsque, pour le cas d'un très petit arc considéré comme quantité du 1er ordre, cette différence est une quantité du 5ième ordre, que nous représenterons par ε_5.

Voici, par ordre chronologique, quelques constructions offrant ce caractère:

I. *Construction de* SNELLIUS (*Cyclometricus*, Leyde, 1621). — Si le rayon AO

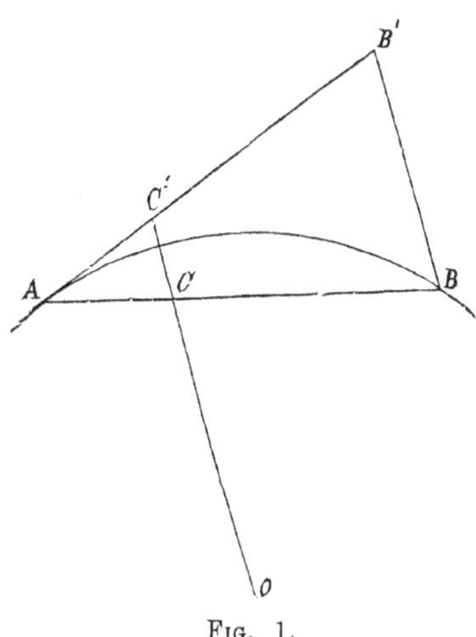

FIG. 1.

(fig. 1) était prolongé, au delà du centre O du double de sa longueur, il suffirait de joindre le point B à l'extrémité du vecteur ainsi construit pour obtenir sur la tangente en A le point B' tel que

$$AB' = \text{arc } AB - \varepsilon_5.$$

Nous ferons remarquer que, pour réduire les dimensions de l'épure, il suffit de mener par le centre O une parallèle à BB'; elle rencontre AB au point C tel que $AC = \frac{AB}{3}$; d'où la variante: joindre le centre O au point C, au tiers de AB, et mener par B la parallèle BB' à OC.

II. *Construction de* Huygens (*De circuli magnitudine inventa*, Leyde, 1654). — Si M est le milieu de l'arc AB (fig. 2) et si on porte sur AM les segments $MA_1 = AM$,

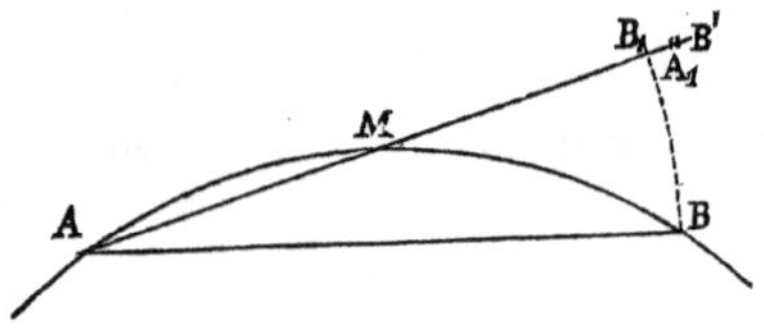

Fig. 2.

$AB_1 = AB$, $A_1B' = \frac{B_1A_1}{3}$, on a

$$AB' = \text{arc } AB - \varepsilon_5.$$

III. *Constructions de* Macquorn Rankine (*Philosophical Magazine*, 3e Série, Vol. 34, p. 284 et 381; Londres, 1867). — Si à partir de A, dans le sens extérieur au cercle, on porte sur le prologement de la corde, le segment $AD = \frac{AB}{2}$ (fig. 3),

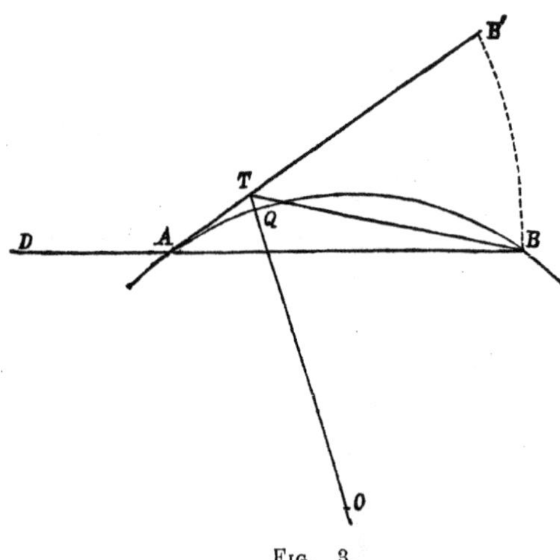

Fig. 3.

et si, de D comme centre, avec DB comme rayon, on décrit un cercle qui coupe en B' la tangente AT en A, on a

$$AB' = \text{arc } AB - \varepsilon_5.$$

Si, d'autre part, l'arc AQ est le quart de l'arc AB et si le rayon OQ coupe la tangente en T, on a aussi

$$AT + TB = \text{arc } AB + \varepsilon_5 .$$

En outre, la quantité

$$\frac{AB' + 4(AT + TB)}{5}$$

ne diffère de l'arc AB que d'une quantité du 7ème ordre.

IV. *Construction de J. VAN DEN BERG* (*Nieuw Archief voor Wiskunde*, T. IV, p. 200; Amsterdam, 1878). — Ayant abaissé de A sur le rayon OB la perpendiculaire AH (fig. 4), on tire la droite HI faisant, à l'intérieur de l'angle AHB un

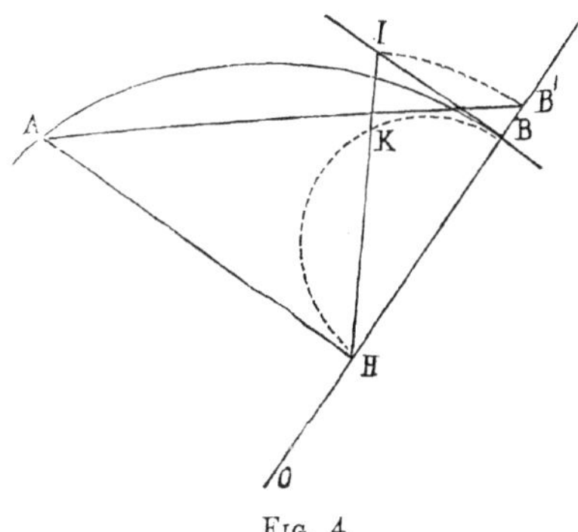

Fig. 4.

angle de 30° avec HB; cette droite coupe la tangente en B au point I, et on rabat le segment HI en HB′ sur HB, on a dès lors

$$AB' = \text{arc } AB - \varepsilon_5 .$$

Au reste, pour tirer HI il suffit, ayant décrit un demi-cercle sur HB comme diamètre, de prendre sur ce demi-cercle le point K dont la distance à B est égale au rayon $\frac{HB}{2}$.

V. *Construction de M. d'OCAGNE* (Nouvelles Annales de Mathématiques, 4e Série, T. VII, p. 1, Paris 1907). — Soient S le point de la corde AB tel que $AS = \frac{2}{3} AB$, S′ le point où la droite OS coupe l'arc AB; si l'on tire AS′, puis la parallèle BB′ à OS′ on a

$$AB' = \text{arc } AB + \varepsilon_5 .$$

Lorsque, dans une épure, on a à rectifier des arcs de cercle, par exemple dans le développement d'une surface conique ou cylindrique de révolution, on a généralement besoin d'effectuer ensuite la construction inverse pour reporter sur la surface certains points obtenus sur son développement. Autrement dit, il faut pouvoir *reporter sur un cercle donné, à partir d'un de ses points* A *pris pour origine, un arc* AB *de longueur donnée.*

Si la construction indiquée pour la rectification permet ce retour inverse (ce qui, au point de vue pratique, lui confère une supériorité sur laquelle il est inutile d'insister) nous disons qu'elle est *réversible.*

Or, on voit immédiatement que, parmi les six constructions reproduites ci-dessus (le N° III en comprenant deux distinctes) il n'en est que deux qui soient réversibles: la première et la dernière. Ce sont donc celles qui, dans l'exécution des épures, devront être préférées. Voici comment chacune d'elles se prête au tracé inverse:

1° Ayant, sur la tangente en A (fig. 1), porté le segment AB′ égal à la longueur donnée et pris sur ce segment le point C′ tel que $AC' = \frac{AB'}{3}$, on mène par B′ la parallèle B′B à la droite joignant le point C′ au centre O.

2° Ayant tracé la corde AS′ égale aux $\frac{2}{3}$ de la longueur donnée (fig. 5), et porté cette longueur en AB′ sur cette corde, on mène par B′ la parallèle B′B au rayon OS′.

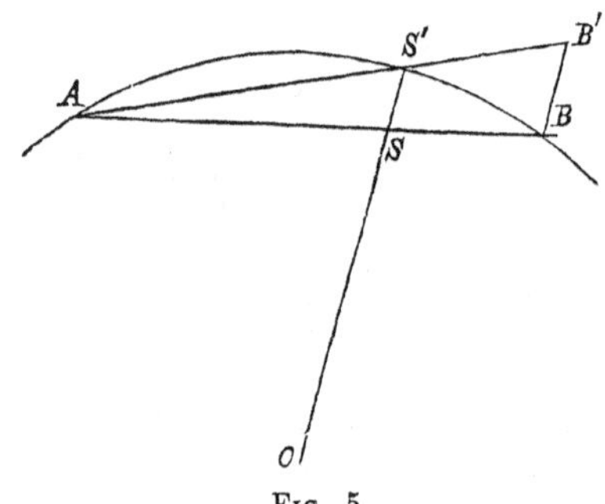

Fig. 5.

Or, si l'on compare les approximations obtenues au moyen de ces deux constructions on constate que celle de la seconde est très sensiblement supérieure à celle de la première.

Alors, en effet, que, pour celle-ci, l'erreur relative n'atteint la valeur de 0,0001 que pour un arc voisin de 35° et celle de 0,001 que pour un arc voisin de 65°, elle est environ 10 fois plus forte avec la première. Exactement, si nous posons

$$\varrho = \left| \frac{\text{arc AB} - \text{AB}'}{\text{arc AB}} \right|$$

on a, si ω est l'amplitude angulaire de l'arc AB, avec la première construction,

$$\text{pour } \omega = 35^\circ \quad , \quad \varrho = 0{,}00098216$$
$$\text{»} \quad \omega = 65^\circ \quad , \quad \varrho = 0{,}008312$$

avec la seconde,

$$\text{pour } \omega = 35^\circ \quad , \quad \varrho = 0{,}000096248$$
$$\text{»} \quad \omega = 65^\circ \quad , \quad \varrho = 0{,}00098619 .$$

D'autre part, si on représente graphiquement ces approximations, en portant en abscisses les amplitudes angulaires des arcs et en ordonnées les longueurs en parties du rayon, ce qui, pour un choix convenable des modules, donne pour la droite représentative des longueurs exactes la bissectrice OA de l'angle des axes (fig. 6) les lon-

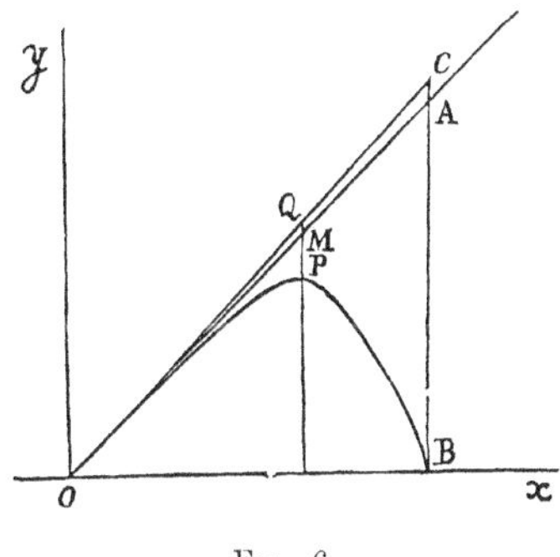

Fig. 6

gueurs fournies par la première construction sont représentées par la courbe OMB dont le point M le plus haut correspond à $\omega = 120°$, et qui coupe Ox pour $\omega = 180°$, tandis que celles que fournit la seconde sont données par la ligne OC; on a d'ailleurs, pour $\omega = 120°$, $MP = 0{,}3619$ tandis que $MQ = 0{,}0274$, et pour $\omega = 180°$, $AC = \pi - 3 = 0{,}1415$, tandis que $AB = \pi = 3{,}1415$.

Le seul examen de cette figure suffit à mettre en évidence la supériorité de la dernière construction par rapport à la première.

T. CLAXTON FIDLER

ON THE APPLICATION OF MATHEMATICS TO THE THEORY OF CONSTRUCTION

The Science of Mathematics is not confined to the treatment of Real Quantities or the attainment of useful ends; and whenever it is applied to a utilitarian purpose its problems are encumbered with unwelcome conditions which seem to hamper the free exercise of Pure Reason. I must therefore confess from the outset that I cannot venture to follow this Science in its higher flights of thought, and that my interest lies entirely in its *Application* to the real problems and useful purposes of Engineering.

Yet within these lower limits it has already rendered invaluable service. Modern engineering depends upon this Science for all its methods of precision, and derives from them much of the confidence which has enabled the engineer to venture upon such projects as the building of the Forth Bridge or the boring of the Simplon Tunnel.

In earlier times it is true that engineers have found reason to distrust the guidance of an imperfect Theory; but it is the constant task of Engineering Science to trace out such imperfections with the view of removing them, and for this purpose it must often undertake some « critique » of Applied Mathematics, reviewing the process of Application from a logical point of view.

While it is impossible that the processes of Pure Mathematics can contain any error, yet large errors may sometimes arise from a very small inaccuracy in some hypothetical assumption. Thus, for example, in the Science of Hydraulic Engineering, which honours Italy as its true birthplace, the single assumption of a « perfect fluidity » was enough in itself to throw all the deductions of Pure Hydrodynamics out of harmony with the known practical facts; and in consequence the hydraulician was compelled to fall back upon Empirical Data which could only be obtained from numerous experiments. And these labours recall to us the classical names of Torricelli, Michelotti and Venturi, along with that of Bernouilli and the hydraulicians of France and Germany, whose work will doubtless be carried forward by many other observers: — for the real value of the Empirical Method must always depend upon the *completeness* of its experimental research.

In like manner our knowledge of the « Strength of Materials » is derived very largely (although not wholly) from experiment: and here it is obvious that the empirical method contains not one but many sources of error. We use the Testing Machine for such Materials as Iron and Steel which are not homogeneous, and in doing so we implicitly assume that the test-piece represents the material of the actual structure, or at least represents it within certain estimated limits of deviation which are to be covered by the « Factor of Safety ».

But this is not all, for it is also known that the measured strength of the test-piece will depend upon the *Manner* of loading, while the manner of loading in the testing-machine is not the same as it will be in the actual structure. At the critical instant of fracture the equilibrium of the molecular forces may be threatened by certain internal stresses which are not measured by the external load: they are sometimes due to molecular vibrations or the dynamic action of moving masses; or again they may be due to some unequal distribution of stress arising from small irregularities in the form of the test-piece. And once more the ultimate effects of Time-under-load are not followed out in the testing-machine, although they have to be reckoned with in the structure.

All these imperfections were, in earlier times, covered by the use of a large Factor of Safety applied to all cases without distinction, but a more discriminating treatment has already been adopted by modern engineers; and further experiments will doubtless serve to eliminate some of the remaining ambiguities (1).

Thus, using a Factor which is reasonably adapted to each case, a « Safe Working Load » (or stress per square inch) is determined for each material, and it forms one of the Empirical Data in the Theory of Construction.

In proceeding to review the whole Theory, as it now stands, it will be easy to distinguish between its rational and its empirical methods, and to estimate its sufficiency for the practical purposes of « Safe Construction ». The errors which have just been mentioned belong wholly to the empirical side; and their extent is confined within such limits that engineering practice is already protected, or can be protected against them by a Factor of Safety; while the purely Mathematical reasoning is free from error within its own domain. Thus the Theory is competent to deal with a large group of questions with practical safety; but the greatest danger arises from its mis-application to a wider group of questions in which the Factor of Safety, fails to ensure its supposed object.

The component parts of the Theory of Construction may perhaps be described as follows:

a) Starting with the known external forces, the principles of Statical Equilibrium are applied to determine the unknown forces and to find the internal stresses in every member of the given structure. The same principles may also be used to

(1) For some years the Author has been engaged upon a long series of experiments with the view of analysing those known effects which have been attributed to the « Fatigue » of Iron and Steel.

examine the stability or instability of certain special structures such as arches or suspension-bridges. Up to this point the Theory is almost wholly rational if it excludes any assumption as to the local distribution of stress among the fibres or particles.

b) Here the Elasticity of the material comes into question, and some assumption is necessary for the framing of any Theory of Columns or of Beams, and for the calculation of internal stresses in all structures which are « Statically indeterminate » such as Continuons Girders. The problems of Elastic Deflection can be dealt with by successive Integration or by Graphic methods, but the results will always depend upon the assumed uniformity of the modulus within certain limits of stress. This assumption is known to be inaccurate, but the resulting errors may be very small in some calculations and much greater in others, according to the character of the problem. They are not very serious in the case of Continuous Girders of ordinary proportions, and they become insignificant when the buckling of a slender column is treated by the Euler Formula which reduces the question to one of molecular equilibrium. In the case of stouter columns the errors due to this assumption are far more serious, but here the observed *variations* of Modulus may be brought into the Theory and its results may be tested by experiment.

c) At this point we have to bring into consideration all that further mass of information about the Strength of Materials which has been obtained by experiment under all kinds of stress: and as mentioned above, the Empirical Method gives us the « Safe Working Stress » per square inch of section, as its ultimate contribution to our Theory.

d) In applying these various kinds of information to the usual purposes of the engineer, the first step is to calculate the stresses in each member of the structure, due to each and all of the given external forces; and thus to find the *greatest* stress that the member will have to endure under any possible combination of those forces.

At the same time the Safe Working Load or stress per square inch will (in modern practice) be separately determined for each case, with due regard to the manner of loading and the liability of buckling in each member.

By simple division it is then easy to determine the required sectional area for each member, and the member should then quite certainly be strong enough to resist safely the maximum calculated stress — safely, so far as concerns any possible fracture of the individual member.

e) When all this has been done carefully for each member in turn, it is sometimes assumed that *the whole structure will be safe;* but this mis-application of the Theory is based upon a fallacy, and it has been the most fruitful source of disaster.

Peraps the *First* Condition of Safety is that every member should be strong enough to resist the maximum stress; but this is only the *first* and not the only essential condition. It appears to be certain that the First Condition has been fully complied with in many bridges that have fallen, including the latest great American Cantilever at Quebec. Yet the fact remains that they have often collapsed without suffering the action of any abnormal forces: and their fall must be attributed to some instability of the *whole* structure and not to an inadequate sectional area in any of its parts. The Stability of the Whole Structure is therefore *another* condition of safety, which will depend not only upon the strength of the members but upon their place and arrangement in the general framework, upon their adaptation to *all the functions which are necessary for safety,* and therefore upon the whole character of the Design.

This mis-application of Theory has its clearest illustration in that system of competitive Bridge-design which originated in America, although American engineers have always protested against its dangerous consequences. Under this system the claims of safety are supposed to be guaranteed by the Rules of the Competition, but the Rules themselves are based upon same fallacy. They make no stipulation as to the form or character of the design, but take only the « Factor of Safety » the Column Formula and the Testing Machine as their guarantees for the safety of the whole structure.

If numerous failures have occurred under this system, the responsibility cannot fairly rest upon the Theory of Construction nor upon the designer. Any efforts on his part to ensure a greater degree of stability are not only uncalled for but are almost excluded by the stress of competition.

But while the responsibility rests upon the inadequate Rules, it would be difficult, or perhaps impossible to frame any others that could be trusted with such onerous duties:

1. The stability of the whole and of every part must be a necessary condition and it would be a question of equilibrium having reference to every one of all the possible movements or deformations in each of the three principal planes. This would work out to an infinity of detail.

2. If the structure, and every part, is perfectly braced in each plane, every member of such framework that is essential to stability must be designed with a strength that shall be adequate *for that duty,* even though the maximum calculated stress should be zero — as it often is. Here the Factor of Safety fails entirely.

3. In other members the maximum calculated stress will be an exceedingly small quantity, and the sectional area prescribed by the present Rules would have reference only to the indefinitely small stress and no reference to the larger demands of stability. In such a case the structure may possibly stand, but would fall (like a house of cards) upon the application of the slightest force from an unexpected quarter, and cannot be called safe.

4. The designer working under the present Rules will always be careful to make due provision for the *highest* while he may overlook the consequences of the *lowest* stresses.

Thus the diagonal ties forming the web-system of a cantilever may be designed to act only in tension, and the requisite strength *of each tie* may be ensured by giving it the sectional area prescribed by the Rules. But when the tensile stress falls nearly or quite to zero, the very absence of stress creates a new freedom of movement in one direction, which would threaten the equilibrium of *other members* — inviting in fact a buckling of the lower boom, which would be fatal to the stability of the whole structure. Thus the bridge might collapse under the passage of a rolling load *owing to the absence of stress* in these members, or it might fall like the Quebec Bridge during the process of erection (1). In any such case stability depends upon the form and character of the design, but cannot be ensured by merely increasing the sectional area of the ties.

But these remarks can only serve to illustrate some of the deficiencies in the Rules, and to point out a few among the many contingencies which the engineer has to consider in his defensive warfare with the Forces of Nature.

The Theory of Construction, so far as it is written, will always be a useful and a very necessary guide in meeting the First Condition of Safety, and it may go still further in examining any given questions relating to Stability: but the word Safety is a comprehensive negative implying the exclusion of *every* kind of danger that can reasonably be apprehended.

It may be doubted whether anything is to be gained by an attempt to compass such an end by a set of written rules which should dispense with the exercise of human reason and careful thought. In Engineering as in Mathematics a living Science cannot consist of dead rules.

(1) Vide Notes on the Erection of Cantilever Bridges. Procedings of Inst. C. E. Session 1907-08.

G. F. SWAIN

SOME OBSERVATIONS REGARDING THE VALUE OF MATHEMATICS TO THE CIVIL ENGINEER AND ON THE TEACHING OF THAT SUBJECT TO CIVIL ENGINEERS

It is with some hesitation that I respond to the request with which I have been honored, to present a paper before this Congress, for I feel that I can submit little if anything which is new or especially interesting. During the course of a long experience as an engineer and as a teacher, however, I have become strongly impressed with the idea that the value of mathematics and its function in the education of the engineer are in many cases misunderstood, and that some improvement might be made in the methods of teaching it, and I therefore venture to present these ideas for whatever they may be worth.

With reference to the value of mathematics as a part of a liberal education there as been considerable discussion and some difference of opinion, as all mathematicians are no doubt aware. It has perhaps generally been considered that mathematics is an important part of any scheme of education and that it is very valuable as a means of mental training. By some it has been considered as one of the most effective means of training the mind, while others have considered it of little value. Probably the most remarkable and powerful attack on the value of mathematics in itself is that which was made by Sir WILLIAM HAMILTON (1) in an article published in the Edinburgh Review just seventy-two years ago, in which be maintained that of all the subjects in the usual curriculum there is none which cultivates a smaller number of intellectual faculties or cultivates them in a more inadequate and partial manner. No one will, of course, deny the value of mathematical training up to a certain point, including arithmetic, geometry and the elements of algebra. It is the value of the study of the subject carried far beyond this point and into its higher branches, *and for its own sake*, which is the subject of discussion. Without attempting to make so sweeping a statement as that of Sir WILLIAM HAMILTON, my reflections and observations have led me to agree with him as to the *small value of mathematical*

(1) Not Sir WILLIAM ROWAN HAMILTON, the inventor of Quaternians, but Sir WILLIAM HAMILTON the metaphysician and philosopher.

training when considered simply as a study in itself and without reference to its applications. Or, to put it in another way, I believe that almost its only value lies in its applications, and not in the study as an exercise of the mind. Let me allude briefly to this aspect of the subject.

It is commonly supposed that the study of mathematics teaches men to reason logically. My observation convinces me that the study of mathematics is less efficient in training the reasoning powers than the study of most branches of natural science, or of political economy, or of many other non-mathematical subjects; and that students trained in mathematics are not as a rule more accurate reasoners than men with little mathematical training who have been practiced in other lines. A study of the lines of eminent men will, I think, confirm this view. LOUIS AGASSIZ, for instance, was certainly an accurate reasoner, and yet he is said to have been lacking in mathematical ability. Even the study of history, it seems to me, affords as good a training of the reasoning powers, unless it is made the mere memorizing of names and dates; and the study of language and rethoric, which train the mind to observe the precise meaning of words, is in my opinion calculated to produce as good reasoners as the study of mathematics, since so many logical errors arise from a confusion of the meaning of terms. Certainly the study of the law, which is not a mathematical subject, is one of the best means of gaining the power of logical thought. At all events, my own observations convince me that young men who have studied the higher mathematics have not *thereby* gained as a rule the power of accurate reasoning.

Mathematics certainly does not train the observation, neither does it train the imagination, except in the branches of geometry, descriptive geometry, and projective geometry, which should be emphasized, in my view, in any curriculum.

Sir WILLIAM HAMILTON admits that there is one faculty which it does train, namely, that of continuous attention, but I have been unable to reach the conclusion that it does even this better than other studies.

Mathematics has been defined as the science of the direct or indirect measurement of quantity, and it was divided by COMTE into Geometry, Calculus (or Analysis) and rational Mechanics. The latter branch would today hardly be included in the field of pure mathematics, so that we may say that it consists of Geometry and Analysis.

Geometry is as old as the history of man. It could be cultivated before man possessed even a system of numerals, and when figures had to be drawn with sticks on the sand. Analysis is very different; it is a machine, a discovery, an invention, a very powerful tool for performing varied operations based upon assumed data. Into one end of this mathematical machine are put the data, and the machine then proceeds to grind out the result, by a rigidly fixed series of operations, whether this result be true or false. Further, Geometry is concrete; the mind perceives the steps of a demonstration and grasps the results as they are reached. These results are intelligible to the mind, and are not expressed abstractly by means of formulae. Analysis, on the other hand, is abstract, and the concrete meaning of the steps of a demonstration is frequently lost sight of, while sometimes no concrete perception is possible.

Now it seems to me that the difficulty with mathematics as a mental training arises largely from the preponderant attention given to analysis, and to the lack of concreteness of mathematical ideas and processes as ordinarily taught. The tremendous power of the mathematical machine is undoubted, but the continued study of the machine itself, i. e., of the mathematical processes, leads the mind to a failure or an inability to pay due attention to the data upon which the machine is to be used, and the particular use which the machine is to be put to in dealing with those data. The machine will perform many operations, it is multiplex in its faculties; and each one of its operations involves a hard and fast, cast-iron method of logical deduction, with no opportunity for the consideration of questions of *quality* (as distinguished from quantity), or for the exercise of logical discrimination between fine shades and meaning or slight differences in the data.

While the mathematical processes, therefore, are examples of logical deduction, they lack the elasticity of ordinary reasoning regarding actual things. Continued training in these processes, therefore, may easily unfit the mind for reasoning on ordinary questions in which mathematical accuracy is impossible, or for dealing with practical questions in which the most important matter is the quality of the data rather than the mathematical process itself. Perhaps this may be expressed by saying that mathematical reasoning is concerned mainly with the deductions from premises which are absolutely fixed; while ordinary engineering reasoning is concerned quite as much with the premises as with the reasoning, and an error of judgment in regard to the premises is quite as fatal as an erroneous use of the mathematical process. With the engineer, indeed, the premises are often if not generally the most important part of the problem; while the mathematician pays much less attention to them. For him they are either facts mathematically true in themselves, and not open to discussion, or they are at all events assumed as correct without question. The mathematical process in itself, then, does not train the mind in the discovery of many of the subtle differences and errors which may thus creep into the line of reasoning. The mathematical demonstration is so rigid that it tends to compress the mind into a groove, especially since it so often happens that during the process the separate steps are not perceived by the mind and in many cases cannot be perceived in their true meaning. The equations are manipulated and transformed according to fixed and true mathematical laws, but while this is being done the perceptive powers of the mind are held abeyance.

It is generally thought that the study of mathematics trains to accuracy, since the mathematician demands an exact result and is not satisfied with an approximation. This is doubtless true, yet it would seem that in this respect arithmetic, for which everybody concedes the necessity, is the most effective branch of the subject. Analysis, or algebra, is simply a universal language, and trains no mere in accuracy then any other language. Yet the very accuracy developed by mathematical study is apt to prove a fictitious accuracy in dealing with practical problems based upon uncertain data, and here the mathematician is very apt to show his lack of practical knowledge, by working out results to more figures than are warranted by the data.

For these reasons it often happens that the best mathematicians make the poorest engineers, and, instead of rising to responsible positions, continue to hold subordinate positions where they make the computations for abler men who supply the data and tell them what is wanted.

Testimony is not wanting that the views thus far given have been shared by many eminent men, some of them themselves mathematicians. For instance, the following are referred to by Sir WILLIAM HAMILTON:

« GOETHE says, in a letter to ZELTER: 'This also shows me more and more distinctly what I have long in secret been aware of, that the cultivation afforded by the Mathematics is, in the highest degree, *one-side and contracted*. Nay, VOLTAIRE does not hesitate somewhere to affirm: j'ai toujours remarqué que la géométrie laisse l'esprit où elle se trouve ».

D'ALEMBERT says: « We shall content ourselves with the remark, that if mathematics (as is asserted with sufficient reason) *only make straight the minds which are without a bias*, so they *only dry up and chill the minds already prepared for this operation by nature* ».

BALLIET, the biographer of DESCARTES, records the following: « It was now a long time, since he had been convinced of the *small utility* of the Mathematics, especially when studied on their own account, and not applied to other things. There was nothing, in truth, which appeared to him *more futile* than to occupy ourselves with simple numbers and imaginary figures, as if it were proper to confine ourselves to these *trifles* (bagatelles) without carrying our view beyond. There even seemed to him in this something *worse than useless*. His maxim was, that *such application insensibly disaccustomed us to the use of our reason*, and made us run the danger of losing the path which it traces'. ...' In a letter to MERSENNE, written in 1630, M. DESCARTES recalled to him that *he had renounced the study of mathematics for many years*; *and that he was anxious not to lose any more of his time in barren operations of geometry and arithmetic, studies which never lead to anything important'*... We have observed that, after having studies these sciences to the bottom, *he had renounced them as of no use for the conduct of life, and solace of mankind'* ».

PASCAL says: « The cause why certain observant minds are not mathematical, is, because they are wholly unable to turn themselves towards the principles of mathematics; *but the reason why there are mathematicians void of observation, is, that they do not see what lies before them; and that accustomed to the clear and palpable principles of mathematics, and only to reason after these principles have been well seen and handled, they lose themselves in matters of observation, where the principles do hot allow of being thus treated. ... Thus it is rare, that mathematicians are observant, or that observant minds are mathematical:* because mathematicians would treat matters of observation by rule of mathematics; and make themselves ridiculous by attempting to commence by definitions and by principles, — a mode of procedure incompatible with this kind of reasoning ».

GIBBON affirms: As soon as I understood the principles, I relinquished for ever the pursuit of the mathematics; nor can I lament that I desisted *before my mind was hardened by the habit of rigid demonstration, so destructive of the finer feelings of moral evidence*...

DUGALD STEWART declared: « In the course of my own experience *I have never met with a mere mathematician who was not credulous to a fault:* credulous not only with respect to human testimony, but credulous also in matters of opinion; and prone, on all subjects which he had not carefully studied, to repose too much faith in illustrious and consecrated names... »

And HAMILTON himself affirms: « *Mathematical language, precise and adequate, nay absolutely convertible with mathematical thought, can efford us no example of those fallacies which so easily arise from the ambiguities of ordinary language*; its study cannot, therefore, it is evident, supply us with any means of obviating those illusions from which it is itself exempt ».

« *Mathematics afford us no assistance, either in conquering the difficulties, or in avoiding the dangers which we encounter in the great field of probabilities wherein we live and move* ».

The mathematician, as already noticed, is exclusively engrossed with the deduction of inevitable conclusions, from data passively received; while the cultivators of the other departments of knowledge, mental and physical, are for the most part, actively occupied in the quest and scrutiny, in the collection and balancing of probabilities, in order to obtain and purify the facts on which their premises are to be established ».

Even JOHN STUART MILL, in his reply to Sir WILLIAM HAMILTON, does little more than assert that the latter himself knew nothing of mathematics — a method of argument far from convincing. For the rest, he tacitly admits many of the claims of Sir WILLIAM HAMILTON. For instance, he says:

« Inasmuch as abstract science in general, and mathematics in particular, afford no practice in the estimation of conflicting probabilities, which is the kind of sagacity most required in the conduct of practical affairs, it follows that, when made so exclusive an occupation as to prevent the mind from obtaining enough of this necessary practice in other ways, it does worse than not cultivate the faculty — it prevents it from being acquired, and *pro tanto* unfits the person for the general business of life ».

« The resolution of a common equation can be reduced to almost as mechanical a process as the working of a sum in arithmetic. The reduction of the question to an equation, however, is no mechanical operation, but one which, according to the degree of its difficulty, requires nearly every possible grade of ingenuity...

« Applied mathematics in its post-Newtonian development does nothing to strengthen, and very much to correct, these errors *provided the applications are studied in such a manner that the intellect is aware of what it is about, and does not go to sleep over algebraical symbols* ».

Is not the great trouble with the advanced and too elaborate study of mathematics that the mind is very apt to « go to sleep over algebraical symbols? ».

But this has been pursued perhaps quite far enough. Let it only be said that in what has preceded we have had no desire to detract in the slightest from the great use of mathematics, and its tremendous power in enabling us to attack the problems of science. And further, there is no question as to the desirability or even the necessity of a knowledge of the elementary parts of mathematics, which find their application in daily life.

If there is any truth in the proceeding arguments, the conclusion which they seem to abundantly justify is this, — that mathematics should be looked upon as a *tool*, and *not as an end in itself*, and that it is only by teaching and studying it as a tool that its study will be of benefit; and this I believe to be an undeniable truth. Especially is this important for the engineer, who is engaged in construction, and who is daily occupied with practical problems. Nobody can deny that the knowledge of this tool and the ability to use it promptly, easily and properly, is of immense importance to the engineer, whether civil, mechanical, electrical, mining, or in any other branch of the profession.

With reference to the amount of mathematical knowledge which the engineer requires, I believe it is comparatively limited. Speaking from a somewhat long experience in practice and teaching, I believe that the structural, railroad, or hydraulic engineer needs only an acquaintance with the subject through the elementary principles of the calculus; and even the calculus and analytical geometry may be so seldom used that they will soon become rusty, leaving, as a main reliance, arithmetic, geometry, algebra, and trigonometry. For this reason, the fundamental principles of analytical geometry and of the calculus should be studied so thoroughly and their applications so well enforced that they will make a permanent impression upon the mind, leaving out the more advanced and less used portions. The theoretical electrician needs some knowledge of differential equations, and the geodesist needs the theory of least squares, but the civil or mechanical engineer rarely or never requires either of these branches.

I believe, then, that every one except those who desire to become professional mathematicians should, in the study and use of mathematics, keep constantly in mind that it is studied and used as a tool. How can this best be done, and how can the subject be best taught to engineers? I will venture a few words on this point, with due modesty, since many who will hear these remarks can give much better advice.

First and most important of all, the subject should be taught *concretely* and *not abstractly*, and emphasis should be laid upon concrete points of view. Of the two branches of mathematics, geometry and analysis, geometry is concrete and analysis abstract; and it seems probable that one great reason for the poor results of much mathematical teaching is over-emphasis of analysis. At all events, it is certainly true that many students who have pursued advanced mathematical studies, are at the end almost incapable of applying them to simple practical problems. I have great sympathy with the geometrical point of view, and believe that analysis should be interpreted geometrically wherever possible. Moreover, every equation is an intelligible sentence; but unfortunately it is frequently not interpreted, and the student does not perceive its meaning, so that in this way his mind loses its perception of the meaning of the process, and becomes involved in a maze of algebrical expressions.

While analysis is abstract, therefore, if the steps taken are interpreted it may lose some of its abstractness, or at all events may be concretely perceived. It is a perversion of mathematical teaching, in my opinion, to demonstrate equations which are to be taken bodily and values substituted, if the case is one which can be grasped concretely. The student who studies in this way fails to realize that algebraical language, — i. e. general language, is necessary when writing a book and stating general principles, but that when studying a special problem there is no need of general language, and the problem should be put in particular language at once. Let me give an example of what I mean.

In a book on the theory of structures we find the following treatment of the method of determining the stress in a bar of a roof truss.

Referring to the figure, the angle α is first computed to be about 63° 26′.

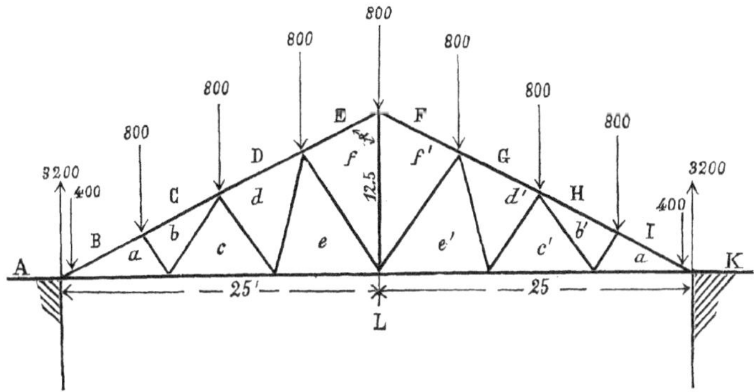

The angle between the vertical and the parallel bars *ab*, *cd*, *ef*, is then computed as 33° 41′; that between the vertical and *bc* as 33° 41′ and for *de* 12° 31′.

Taking, for instance, the apex BC, we have angles with the vertical C*b* = 63° 26′ and its cosine is minus, because the piece C*b* lies in the second quadrant (according to a convention adopted), and its sine is plus for the same reason. The book continues:

« Calculation, - Remembering, then, always to take the sines and cosines with their proper signs in the general formulae for the algebraic sum of the vertical and horizontal components, and also recollecting that upward forces are positive and downward forces negative, we can proceed to the calculation.

The numerical values of the sines and cosines are easil foundy to be as follows:

« For the upper hays, $\begin{cases} \text{Cos } \theta = 0.44724 \\ \text{Sin } \theta = 0.98441 \end{cases}$ lover bays $\begin{cases} \text{Cos } \theta = 0 \\ \text{Sin } \theta = 1 \end{cases}$

braces parallel to ab, $\begin{cases} \text{Cos } \theta = 0.83212 \\ \text{Sin } \theta = 0.55460 \end{cases}$

for bc $\begin{cases} \text{Cos } \theta = 0.83212 \\ \text{Sin } \theta = 0.55460 \end{cases}$ de $\begin{cases} \text{Cos } \theta = 0.97625 \\ \text{Sin } \theta = 0.21672 \end{cases}$

« We hare now ready to apply our principles ».

The joint at the abutment is first solved and then the joint AB, which may be given as an example of the method of treatment adopted.

« Here we have for the algebraic sum of the vertical components

$$(c) \qquad W_2 + Ba \cos \theta_{Ba} + Cb \cos \theta_{cb} + ab \cos \theta_{ab} = 0$$

and for the horizontal components,

$$(d) \qquad Ba \sin \theta_{Ba} + Cb \sin \theta_{cb} + ab \sin \theta_{ab} = 0 .$$

« Inserting in equation (c) the value of $Ba \cos \theta_{Ba}$ as found from the previous joint AB, we have, after substituting value of Cb from (d), and reducing,

$$(3) \qquad \text{strain in } ab = \frac{W_2 \sin \theta_{cb}}{\sin \theta_{ab} \cos \theta_{cb} - \cos \theta_{ab} \sin \theta_{cb}} = \frac{W_2 \sin \theta_{cb}}{\sin (\theta_{ab} - \theta_{cb})} .$$

In the same way we find from equation (d),

$$(4) \qquad \text{strain in } Cb = - \frac{Ba \sin \theta_{Ba}}{\sin \theta_{cb}} - \frac{W_2 \sin \theta_{ab}}{\sin (\theta_{ab} - \theta_{cb})} .$$

Inserting numerical values, we have

$$\text{strain in } ab = - \frac{-800 \,.\, 0.89441}{\sin (33^\circ\, 41' - 116^\circ\, 34')} = \frac{-715.528}{-0.99230} = +720 .$$

« Hence ab is in compression (Observe, that the angles θ_{ab} and θ_{cb} are reckoned as shown in the figure. Thus $\theta_{cb} = 116^\circ\, 34'$).

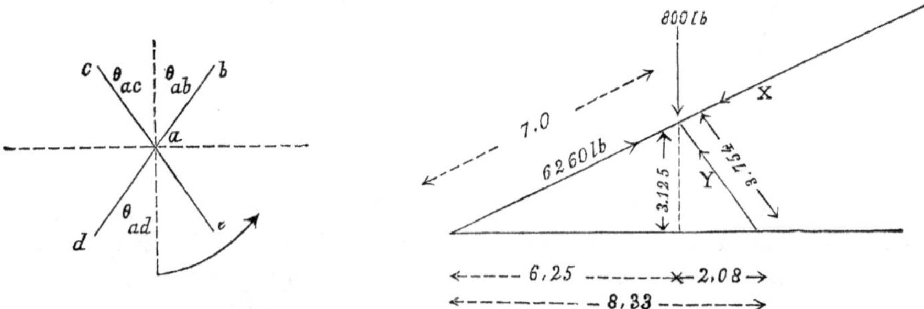

« We have in like manner

$$\text{strain in } Cb = +6260 - \frac{-800 \,.\, 0.55460}{-0.99230} = +6260 - 447 = +5813 \text{ Ibs}.$$

« Hence Cb is in compression ».

The proper method of computing this joint, we venture to say, is as follows: We sketch the joint, put on the dimensions, place the known forces on the figure, including the stress on Ba, which has been found from the previous joint, assume the direction of the other forces to be all toward the joint, or compressive, and write at once the equations $\Sigma H = 0$ and $\Sigma V = 0$, as follows.

$$\sqrt{6.25^2 + 3.125^2} = 7.0$$
$$\sqrt{2.08^2 + 3.125^2} = 3.754$$

$$\Sigma H = 0 \text{ gives us; } 6260 \frac{6.25}{7} - X \frac{6.25}{7} - Y \frac{2.08}{3.754} = 0$$

$$\Sigma V = 0 \text{ gives us; } 6260 \frac{3.125}{7} - X \frac{3.125}{7} + Y \frac{3.125}{3.754} - 800 = 0 .$$

Multiplying the second equation by 2, and subtracting the first from it, we can write at once

$$\frac{8.33}{3.754} = 1600$$

and by the slide rule, $Y = +720$, or compression. From the first equation we then write at once

$$X = 6260 - 720 \frac{2.08}{3.754} \cdot \frac{7.0}{6.25} = +5813, \text{ comp.}$$

This in the simple, concrete way of solving this problem. The mind perceives each step, and is using common sense all the time.

The first method, quoted, seems to us the very perversion of mathematics.

But if analysis is abstract in itself, the first portion of most mathematical problems, as they present themselves in actual life, i. e. the *formulation of the problem*, is generally concrete. More attention should be focussed upon this part of the instruction and less upon the mathematical machine. It may not be the case in Europe, but I believe it to be true in America, that in much of the mathematical instruction little attention is paid to the formulation of the problem, and this lack of training alone will account for much of the inability of the pupils to attack new problems themselves.

Another fault which may be found with mathematics is that it too often overloads the *memory*, for many mathematical students endeavor to memorize formulae instead of grasping and seeing the principles. Now, the memory is a limited faculty, and every fact put into it renders it necessary to exclude other facts; it is like a box which can only hold a fixed number of objects, although, of course, its capacity may be increased by training. But a general principle, if once seen, can be applied to an infinite number of cases, and if really perceived, in its general form, it is retained not by an exercise of memory, but is perceived again whenever the exciting causes, or the preliminary thoughts, are the same. This applies of course, to other subjects than mathematics, yet my experience indicates that the study of mathematics is a fertile cause of abuse of the memory. In the suggested solution of the roof truss given above no memory whatever is needed — no conventions, no trigonometry — nothing but the knowledge that ΣH and $\Sigma V = 0$, and of the properties of similar triangles.

Further, too little attention is now paid, in America at all events, to mental arithmetic. Ask a student in engineering, who has completed the calculus, to tell you at once the square of 20.75 and he will stare at you in astonishment; yet if he had once grasped the true meaning of the binomial theorem he could perform the operation in his head without difficulty. Too much reliance is placed upon pencil and paper.

Of course the usual and well-known pedagogical principles apply to the teaching of mathematics as of all other subject. Yet I will venture to record here the opinion that the lecture system is not well suited to teach mathematics to engineers, and that the Socratic method of question and answer, or crossexamination, is here especially necessary, in order to make the student think, and to prevent him from falling into the mechanical and rule-of-thumb methods which are so easily acquired in this subject.

The best results in mathematical teaching to engineers will, I am confident, be obtained if the mathematical teachers are themselves engineers, or at least sufficiently acquainted with engineering to *appreciate the problems* which engineers have to solve, and the point of view which they must take. It is not necessary that they should be themselves engineers, if they have sufficient acquaintance with the subject to possess this point of view. This, however, would seem very necessary if mathematics is to be taught and studied not for itself, but as is here advocated, as a tool; for how can the use of a tool be well taught except by one who himself knows how to use it and what uses it is to be put to, beyond its mere mechanical manipulation?

PARTE III

COMUNICAZIONI

Sezione IV

QUESTIONI FILOSOFICHE, STORICHE, DIDATTICHE

F. ENRIQUES

MATEMATICHE E FILOSOFIA

All'inizio dei nostri lavori, nella sezione filosofica di questo Congresso, consentitemi di esprimere il voto che la discussione valga a chiarire le rispettive posizioni del nostro pensiero, sicchè possiamo mutuamente comprenderci.

Dico espressamente « comprenderci », non « convenire nelle medesime conclusioni ». Infatti, le divergenze di vedute che separano in generale i filosofi, non sono suscettibili di essere composte, come le controversie scientifiche, mercè un più rigoroso accertamento della verità. Non sono questioni di fatto, o almeno non soltanto questioni di fatto, quelle che distinguono le scuole filosofiche: sono interessi e sentimenti diversi, estetici e pratici, che servono di base a differenti criterî di valutazione. Tra i quali una riunione di filosofi non può essere chiamata a pronunziare una scelta, ma che essa sola può discriminare e spiegare, ponendo in luce i motivi delle differenze colla discussione critica.

Ora questa intesa, che costituisce insieme una condizione ed un risultato del progresso filosofico, diventa fortunatamente più facile per noi che, nel campo di una scienza precisa come le matematiche, troviamo il comune fondamento alle nostre speculazioni. Fondamento, diciamolo pure, magnifico; imperocchè da questa base sorsero ognora nella storia i pensatori più grandi, da CARTESIO a LEIBNIZ, a KANT; filosofi che prolungando in una veduta universale alcune intuizioni tratte dalle matematiche, s'incontrarono soprattutto coi rappresentanti delle scienze della vita nell'alta contesa per il dominio degli spiriti.

***

Per comprendere la posizione assunta nella speculazione dai pensatori matematici, parmi necessario tener presente il concetto che essi si formarono della propria scienza, in rapporto alla sua evoluzione storica.

Agli inizî della matematica moderna, la teoria non si distingue dall'applicazione, nè l'intuizione dalla logica. Oggetto immediato della speculazione è il tentativo di *spiegare* le leggi della natura come rapporti quantitativi: da questo punto di vista l'analisi s'identifica col problema cosmologico, ed il pensiero matematico si confonde collo sforzo gigantesco ond'ebbero origine i grandi sistemi metafisici del secolo decimosettimo.

Si può dire in un certo senso che NEWTON chiude questo periodo eroico, dando un assetto positivo alla Meccanica e all'Astronomia. Infatti, nel sistema newtoniano si riconosce un concetto filosofico nuovo della spiegazione scientifica, la quale non appare più come una costruzione immaginativa, esclusivamente razionale e *a priori* della realtà fisica, ma come una costruzione, che pur movendo da alcune intuizioni presupposte, accoglie ipotesi non intuitive sulla base dell'osservazione e dell'esperienza.

I meravigliosi sviluppi della teoria newtoniana e le conferme così precise e brillanti che essa ricevette, venivano ad orientare il movimento del pensiero in un senso nuovo: parendo ormai stabilito il programma della spiegazione definitiva del mondo, si proseguiva da un lato quell'ordine di ricerche che ha costituito la Fisica-matematica moderna, avanti la scoperta della conservazione dell'energia; d'altro lato una ricerca critica, concernente le condizioni e i limiti della conoscenza umana, sorgeva a prendere il posto del problema cosmologico nella speculazione dei filosofi.

E la critica della conoscenza fu infatti, per KANT, la critica della sistemazione newtoniana; quelle che il filosofo pose come intuizioni *a priori*, condizioni necessarie di ogni scienza, furono, a dir vero, le intuizioni presupposte di NEWTON; tali lo spazio e il tempo assoluto, l'invarianza della massa (sostanza), il postulato della causa.

D'altra parte, come gli sviluppi dell'Astronomia e della Fisica newtoniana integravano con ipotesi proprie i principî meccanici, mettendo capo all'osservazione e alla esperienza, così KANT ammise il carattere sperimentale di ogni costruzione scientifica che s'inquadri negli schemi *a priori* dell'intuizione umana.

* * *

Abbiamo visto come il problema cosmologico e il problema della conoscenza si riattacchino successivamente allo sviluppo storico delle matematiche facente capo a NEWTON.

Per comprendere l'atteggiamento assunto dai pensatori matematici durante il secolo decimonono, occorre tener presenti le condizioni generali dello sviluppo scientifico che caratterizzano questo periodo e trovano la loro espressione più chiara nella *classificazione delle scienze*, proposta dalla filosofia positiva di A. COMTE.

L'avvento del particolarismo, tendente ad una rigida differenziazione dei problemi e dei metodi entro campi di ricerca ben definiti, si accompagna ad una differenziazione propria delle matematiche; le matematiche pure si distinguono dalle applicazioni.

In conseguenza, lo schema del procedimento fisico, si concreta nella forma logico-sperimentale che ci è ormai familiare.

La parte che in questo schema viene assegnata alle matematiche tende a ridursi ognor più alla trasformazione delle ipotesi, che l'istrumento analitico ha l'ufficio di elaborare avvicinandole alle esigenze pratiche della verifica sperimentale.

La Matematica pura si svolge per astrazioni successive dai problemi che hanno per oggetto la trasformazione accennata, in un campo illimitato di ricerche teoriche: e poichè a queste presiede un criterio supremo di bellezza, il pensiero tende ad appagarsi ognor più nella contemplazione artistica del suo oggetto, come in qualcosa di compiuto.

Questo concepimento statico della scienza, elimina la veduta di quanto si riferisce all'acquisto delle ipotesi, e conduce ad un'ultima distinzione degli elementi onde resultava in principio l'edificio matematico. Come all'epoca di NEWTON, l'esperienza si distaccò dall'intuizione e dalla logica, così ora l'intuizione viene distinta dalla logica, e sembra esulare dal campo proprio della Matematica pura, la quale appare così, allo spirito dei filosofi, una costruzione sistematica, cui si vuole conferire armonica perfezione in ogni sua parte, ponendo a base un opportuno ordinamento delle proposizioni primitive e derivate.

Di qui il problema logico, tanto dibattuto ai nostri giorni fra i pensatori matematici; di qui ancora alcune vedute generali e caratteristiche della speculazione moderna: l'arbitrarietà delle ipotesi, e la possibilità di soddisfare alle esigenze economiche del sapere scientifico.

Ma nel discorso che precede ho posto in rilievo soltanto un aspetto della evoluzione del pensiero filosofico nel campo matematico. È facile convincersi che il procedere delle matematiche verso l'astratto, cioè il purificarsi di una dottrina che trae origine da elementi diversi, d'esperienza, d'intuizione e di logica, condurrebbe ad esaurire in breve il progresso della ricerca, se questa non attingesse ognora nuovi impulsi, dalla realtà fisica circostante e dalla visione immaginativa che ne vien suscitata.

Perciò, accanto al matematico che tende a consolidare in forma logica gli acquisti fatti, troviamo l'investigatore di campi sconosciuti, disposto a sacrificare i desiderati estetici del purismo, e perfino le esigenze di una costruzione logica rigorosa, per chiarire comunque, coll'intuizione creatrice, le vie oscure dell'ignoto.

Il secolo decimonono non ha visto soltanto stabilire sopra un fondamento aritmetico le basi incrollabili dell'analisi pura, ma ben anche ha visto allargarsi il quadro dei problemi antichi coi concetti sorti dalla prospettiva, dalla gnomonica, dal piegamento della carta. E questi concetti, intendo la Geometria proiettiva e l'*Analysis situs*, ha visto pure inaspettatamente recar nuova luce alle questioni più ardue della teoria delle funzioni.

Perciò l'atteggiamento del pensiero riguardante l'aspetto statico delle dottrine, nella loro purezza astratta, non può esaurire il campo della filosofia matematica all'ora presente.

Sorge di fronte alla veduta statica una veduta dinamica della Scienza, e quindi al problema logico si contrappone il problema psicologico.

Non credo d'ingannarmi affermando che i diversi indirizzi speculativi che oggi traggono origine dalle Matematiche, si lasciano in qualche modo riattaccare a questi due aspetti fondamentali della nostra scienza, dove taluno contempla di preferenza ciò che è acquisito: « la teoria logicamente formata », altri ciò che diviene: « la storia ».

Due oggetti diversi della volontà scientifica costruttrice, congiunti a diversi sentimenti estetici e pratici, porgono così una base naturale alla distinzione delle scuole, che si moltiplicano poi in una varietà di atteggiamenti più larga, relativamente alle correnti di pensiero promananti da altri campi di studio.

Così parmi avere illustrato il concetto espresso al principio del mio discorso. E piacemi conchiudere auspicando ad un elevato dibattito, fra le più opposte ed irreducibili tendenze, poichè dal punto di vista della Storia e della Psicologia, tutte le finalità diverse appaiono ugualmente, se pure parzialmente, giustificate; e sopra il contrasto delle idee filosofiche s'innalza verso l'avvenire il progresso della Scienza!

G. HESSENBERG

ZAEHLEN UND ANSCHAUUNG

Die grossen Erfolge, von denen die Untersuchungen über die allgemeinsten Grundlagen des Zahlbegriffs begleitet gewesen sind, haben vielfach zu der Ueberzeugung geführt, dass die Lehre von den Zahlen ein Kapitel der reinen Logik sei; dass ihr nicht nur die Ableitung der formalen Eigenschaften der Zahlen aus einfachsten Postulaten, sondern auch die unmittelbare Folgerung ihrer Existenz aus der Definition gelungen sei. Der unverkennbare Gegensatz zwischen Geometrie und Arithmetik führt dann leicht dazu, die Geometrie den Erfahrungswissenschaften zuzuweisen und den Raum für einen Gegenstand von Laboratoriumsversuchen zu halten. Wenn auch neuerdings die Reaktion gegen diese Auffassung wieder schärfer hervortritt, wenn vor allem die Bedeutung und das Vorhandensein unbewiesener Forderungen in der Mengenlehre sich allgemeine Anerkennung verschafft, so bleibt doch vielfach die Ansicht bestehen: es müsse bei weiterer Vertiefung und Verallgemeinerung der Grundlagen die Verwandlung der Zahlenlehre in ein Kapitel der reinen Logik erreichbar sein.

Wenn ich mich dieser Ansicht nicht anschliessen kann, so liegt es mir doch fern, den grundlegenden Untersuchungen ihre Bedeutung abzusprechen. Vergleichen wir etwa die klassischen Dirichlet'schen Beweise der kommutativen und associativen Eigenschaften der Addition und Multiplikation mit den modernen Dedekind'schen Induktionsbeweisen und weiterhin die Begründung des Induktionsverfahrens durch die Kettentheorie und deren Zurückführung auf die evidenten mengentheoretischen Grundbegriffe, so werden wir den Fortschritt in den neueren Untersuchungen kaum verkennen können. Dass aber eine *Ueberschätzung* eines solchen Fortschrittes genau so gut eine Verkennung seiner Bedeutung enthält, wie eine *Unterschätzung*, das bedarf keiner besonderen Betonung; und die Erfahrungen der letzten Zeit lehren uns, dass nur zu leicht mit der Erkenntnis zuvor übersehener Mängel statt des fehlerhaften Teiles das ganze Gebäude unnötigerweise wieder bis auf seine Fundamente abgetragen wird, zum grossen Bedauern derjenigen, die solche Fehler von vornherein erkannt und über ihre Stelle Klarheit gewonnen hatten. Nur eine Verkennung der Kettentheorie kann zum Beispiel dazu führen, sie als Begründung des Induktionsschlusses zu verwerfen; die Berufung auf die Intuition als Quelle dieses Schlussverfahrens dagegen schreibt der Anschauung eine Bedeutung zu, die ihre Kompetenz überschreitet, und verzichtet nicht nur auf eine Begründung, die fälschlich die Anschauung glaubte ausgeschaltet zu haben, sondern zugleich auf die wertvollen Kriterien, die jene Begründung als notwendige und hinreichende Bedingungen für die Zulässigkeit des Induktionsschlusses aufgedeckt hatte.

Um die Rolle der Anschauung klarzustellen, bedürfen wir nicht durchweg philosophischer oder psychologischer Argumentationen. Wir können durch Prüfung von Tatsachen, die jedem Mathematiker geläufig sind, ein gutes Teil Klarheit gewinnen. Die Unterscheidung reiner Existenzbeweise von sogenannten Konstruktionsverfahren ist an Beispielen leicht zu verstehen; sie ist neuerdings in mengentheoretischen Diskussionen von Wichtigkeit geworden und einer der bedeutendsten Fortschritte der Mengenlehre, der Beweis des Wohlordnungssatzes, beruht wesentlich auf dieser Unterscheidung; er wird da, wo er noch verkannt wird, meist als Konstruktionsverfahren angegriffen, obwohl er ausdrücklich den Anspruch ablehnt, ein solches zu sein, selbst dann, wenn durch das Auswahlpostulat nicht nur die Existenz, sondern auch die Konstruierbarkeit einer Menge gefordert wäre, die mit jedem Element einer Menge teilfremder Mengen genau ein Element gemein hat.

Der von Herr Hamel erbrachte Beweis der Existenz unstetiger Lösungen der Funktionalgleichung $f(x+y)=f(x)+f(y)$ bewahrt den Charakter eines reinen Existenzbeweises auch dann, wenn es möglich wäre, eine Wohlordnung des Kontinuums herzustellen.

Allgemein sind wohl weitaus die meisten Beweise für die Existenz von Funktionen, die gegebenen Bedingungen genügen, *keine* Konstruktionsverfahren. Die Theorie der Integralgleichungen liefert zahlreiche Beispiele, die Existenz der Integrale von Differentialgleichungen nicht minder. Auch der Fundamentalsatz der Algebra lässt sich so beweisen, dass er ein Konstruktionsverfahren nicht enthält, und im Gegensatz dazu beruht der Cantor'sche Existenzbeweis transzendenter Zahlen auf einem ausgesprochenen Konstruktionsverfahren.

Betrachten wir nun im einzelnen die Theorie der Reihe der natürlichen Zahlen. Welche Definition der Zahl dabei auch zu Grunde gelegt wird, — vielfach wird eine solche überhaupt nicht oder aber so verschwommen gegeben, dass sie von vornherein als unwesentlich ausscheidet, — stets läuft die Theorie auf eine reine Theorie des Cantor'schen Ordnungstypus Omega hinaus. Und in der Tat bestehen ja für jede Menge dieses Typus Beziehungen, welche sämtliche formalen Eigenschaften der Addition, Multiplikation u. s. w. besitzen. Die Definition der Potenz lautet: $a^1=a$, $a^{m+1}=a^m.a$, und es wird bewiesen, dass sie eindeutig für jeden Wert beider Argumente den Funktionswert festlegt.

Ist diese Definition ein Konstruktionsverfahren? Wir können sie so auffassen. Es ist z. B. die Million als sechste Potenze von 10, d. h. als zehnfaches der fünften Potenz definiert. Das zehnfache von a ist nach Definition das Neunfache, vermehrt um a, dieses das Achtfache, vermehrt um a u. s. f. Die Vermehrung um 10 ist eine Vermehrung um neun, deren Resultat um 1 vermehrt wird. Die Vermehrung um 1 bleibt mehr oder weniger Grundoperation. Sie bedeutet in der Zahlenreihe den Uebergang zum nächsten Element, und sind die Zahlen als Cardinalzahlen von Mengen definiert, so ist die unmittelbar folgende Zahl durch die Vermehrung um ein Element definiert.

Wollen wir hiernach 10^6 konstruieren, so haben wir $10^5 . 10 = 10^4 . 10 . 10$ u. s. f. zu bilden; diese Produkte sind wieder in Summen von Zehnen und diese in Summen von Einen zu verwandeln. *Die « Konstruktion » besteht also darin, dass bis zu einer Million gezählt wird.*

Es fragt sich aber, ob diese Art der Konstruktion ohne « Anschauung » möglich ist, und ich glaube, diese Frage ist unbedingt zu verneinen. Und wer sich an der Grösse der gewählten Zahl stösst und etwa findet, dass sie überhaupt nicht mehr anschaulich ist, der mag den Begriff der Zahl 2×3 rein logisch definieren. Es ist $2 \times 3 = (2 \times 2) + 2 = (2 \times 1 + 2) + 2 = (2 + 2) + 2 = ((2 + 2) + 1) + 1$ u. s. f. $= 1 + 1 + 1 + 1 + 1 + 1$. Um diese Definition hinzuschreiben, muss ich bis sechs zählen können, und dasselbe muss von dem verlangt werden, der sie auf ihre Richtigkeit nachprüft.

Rein logisch muss ich von einer Menge von sechs Elementen verlangen, dass ich sie *unterscheiden* kann; wie ich das mache, ist dem Logiker gleich; sind die sechs Elemente auch bloss gedacht, ununterscheidbar darf ich sie nicht denken. Die Zweideutigkeit der Behauptung, es werde von den Unterschieden « abstrahiert », ist wiederholt betont worden, sehr scharf von Frege. Ich abstrahiere wohl von der Art, auf die ich die Unterscheidung gründe, nicht aber von der Tatsache ihrer Möglichkeit.

Vergleichen wir damit das Verfahren des Geometers, der von den Punkten seiner Geraden verlangt, dass sie alle von einander verschieden und unterscheidbar zu denken sind, und dass die Menge aller dieser Punkte nach einem logisch scharf bestimmten Ordnungstypus geordnet sei. Die Methode der Unterscheidung ist in Arithmetik und Geometrie wohl grundverschieden, aber worauf es hier in beiden Fällen ankommt: sie ist logisch nicht zu fassen und ist auch für die rein logische Theorie der Ordnungstypen irrelevant. Gegenstand der rein logischen Theorie ist nur der Ordnungstypus und das aus ihm folgende System der Relationen der Elemente zueinander. Die Konstruktion eines Elementes aus definierenden Relationen, seine Individualisierung, ist nicht Gegenstand dieser Theorie und kann es gar nicht werden. Die Theorie schaltet also die Intuition so wenig aus, wie sie durch sie ersetzt werden kann.

Man wird nicht behaupten dürfen, dass das, was wir hier Konstruktion nannten, bis ins einzelne mit dem übereinstimme, was Kant als *Konstruktion in reiner Anschauung* bezeichnet hat. Im Gegenteil, da zu Kant's Zeiten die Zergliederung der Elementarbegriffe noch gar nicht so weit fortgeschritten war, wie es der heutige Stand der Wissenschaft zeigt, werden Unterschiede sich mühelos aufzeigen lassen. Wesentlich ist aber dabei die Frage, ob der von Kant behauptete anschauliche Gehalt der mathematischen Erkenntnis sich verflüchtigt hat oder ob er nicht vielmehr, dem schärferen Stand der Zergliederung entsprechend, heute mit grösserer Schärfe nachweisbar ist. Dass ich die Frage in diesem zweiten Sinne glaube beantworten zu müssen, und aus welchen Gründen, war meine Absicht, hier klarzulegen.

P. BOUTROUX

SUR LA RELATION DE L'ALGÈBRE À L'ANALYSE MATHÉMATIQUE

Qu'est-ce au juste que l'analyse mathématique et en quoi se distingue-t-elle de l'algèbre? Voilà une question qu'il eût été inconvenant de poser devant les mathématiciens du siècle dernier: car, apparemment, les fondateurs de la science contemporaine s'imaginaient savoir de quoi ils parlaient. Aujourd'hui, nous ne saurions être aussi affirmatifs. Quelle variété de réponses n'obtiendrions-nous pas, en effet, si nous demandions à chacun des membres de ce Congrès une appréciation sur le rôle de l'Analyse! C'est que, de l'aveu de tous, la tâche des mathématiciens est devenue particulièrement délicate. Plus encore que de résoudre des problèmes, on leur demande d'en poser, et cela ne laisse pas que d'être embarrassant. Prenons pour exemple la théorie des fonctions. Elle est évidemment susceptible de s'engager dans une infinité de voies différentes; nous pouvons imaginer une foule de questions qui s'y rattachent. Cependant, parmi ces questions, il faut que nous choisissions arbitrairement celles que nous étudions, sûrs d'avance que si notre choix paraît judicieux à une moitié du monde savant, il sera jugé artificiel par l'autre moitié. Une orientation précise, et qui s'impose à tous, voilà ce qui fait défaut à la science théorique de nos jours. — C'est pourquoi nous éprouvons de plus en plus le besoin de nous recueillir un instant au seuil de nos travaux, pour chercher à mieux comprendre l'objet et la portée des efforts qu'on nous demande.

Un fait est certain: c'est que l'Analyse n'était originairement qu'un prolongement de l'Algèbre. Mais, en se développant, elle s'est de plus en plus opposée à la science du calcul. Aujourd'hui, on peut se demander si elle n'a pas le devoir de s'en séparer radicalement, sous peine de dégénérer en une encyclopédie informe ou en une entreprise aussi vaine que celle des Danaïdes de la légende.

***

Reportons-nous, tout d'abord, aux origines de l'Analyse mathématique, c'est-à-dire à la science d'il y a trois cents ans.

L'algèbre du XVIIe siècle se présente comme une méthode de calcul qui procède indirectement de DIOPHANTE ([1]). Elle se décompose ([2]) en *algèbre vulgaire* ou *nombreuse* (algèbre des anciens) et *algèbre* ou *logistique spécieuse* (algèbre nouvelle), cette dernière opérant sur des lettres et ayant par suite une portée universelle ([3]). L'algèbre spécieuse est une science analytique, en réalité sinon en apparence ([4]), car l'analyse est, pour l'algébriste, la méthode d'invention ([5]) « tandis que la synthèse est la méthode de doctrine » (méthode d'exposition). Aussi DE BILLY qualifie-t-il l'analyse moderne la *doctrina analytica* et BACHET de *subtilissimus analysta*. De même NEWTON, dans son *arithmétique universelle*, fait du mot « analyse » un synonyme exact d'« algèbre » lorsqu'il oppose à l'Arithmétique vulgaire, où le calcul se fait avec des nombres, l'Analyse où le calcul s'opère sur des lettres. Et ainsi, c'est encore de l'algèbre que pense faire NEWTON, lorsqu'il édifie la théorie des développements en séries et la méthode des fluxions: ces doctrines ne sont pour lui qu'une « Analyse » perfectionnée: quicquid vulgaris Analysis per æquationes ex finito terminorum numero constantes (quando id est possibile) perficit, hæc per æquationes infinitas semper perficiet. D'où ce nom d'*Analyse infinitésimale*, consacré définitivement par EULER ([6]), qui s'est transmis jusqu'à nous, et qui signifie historiquement: *Algèbre de l'infini*.

Notons en passant que LEIBNIZ avait des mathématiques modernes une conception un peu différente. Pour lui aussi Algèbre et Analyse ne font qu'un [« ce que nous appelons l'Algèbre ou l'Analyse » dit-il quelque part]. Mais le calcul intégral, — premier échantillon de la science combinatoire universelle (caractéristique universelle) que LEIBNIZ rêvait d'instituer, — est, à ses yeux, théorie synthétique [« duæ sunt methodi, synthetica seu per artem combinatoriam et analytica ([7]) ». « Algebra et combinatoria differunt apud me ut Analysis et Synthesis » ([8])]. Et l'on doit tout particulièrement regarder comme synthétique la méthode des développements en séries, fondement de la théorie des fonctions: « l'opération synthétique la plus générale consiste dans la construction d'une série au moyen d'une table ou d'une loi de formation connue » ([9]).

Ce fut, cependant, la terminologie de NEWTON et d'EULER qui l'emporta, et à bon droit, sans doute, car la théorie des fonctions mathématiques ne fut, pendant fort longtemps, qu'une généralisation du calcul algébrique. « On appelle fonction d'une ou plusieurs quantités, dit LAGRANGE (*Théorie des fonctions analytiques*) toute

([1]) Voir, par exemple, l'Introduction de DE BILLY à l'édition des *Oeuvres de Diophante*, annotées par Fermat (en particulier le chapitre *Diophantum in plurimis Fermatius superat*).

([2]) Cf. HÉRIGONE, *Cours mathématique*, 1635; OZANAM, *Dictionnaire mathématique*, 1691, etc.

([3]) Cf. les Cartésiens, p. ex. SCHOOTEN *Principia matheseos universalis*, 1651.

([4]) « Artifex geometra, dit VIÈTE, quanquam Analyticum edoctus, illud dissimulat, et tanquam de opere efficiendo cogitans, profert suum syntheticum problema et explicat ».

([5]) Cf., p. ex., OZANAM, op. cit.

([6]) *Introduction à l'Analyse infinitésimale*.

([7]) Cité p. COUTURAT, *La Logique de* LEIBNITZ, p. 178.

([8]) Ibid., p. 512.

([9]) Ibid., pag. 270.

expression de calcul dans laquelle ces quantités entrent d'une manière quelconque. Le mot *fonction* a été employé par les premiers analystes pour désigner en général les puissances d'une même quantité. Depuis on a étendu la signification de ce mot à toute quantité formée d'une manière quelconque d'une autre quantité. « Les fonctions représentent les différentes *opérations* qu'il faut faire sur les quantités connues pour obtenir les valeurs de celles que l'on cherche, et *elles ne sont proprement que le dernier résultat de ce calcul* ». (*Leçon sur le calcul des fonctions*). Ainsi l'Analyse est un calcul, et elle ne se distingue de l'Algèbre que parce qu'elle « répète une infinité de fois » [1] les opérations de cette dernière.

Telles sont les vues qui furent universellement adoptées durant plus de deux siècles. La théorie des fonctions n'a été et n'est encore, pour beaucoup d'analystes, que l'étude des développements en séries de Taylor. Il est vrai que certains savants partent d'une définition moins explicite de la fonction. Ainsi fait Cauchy qui prend pour point de départ certaines conditions de continuité et montre que les fonctions satisfaisant à ces conditions sont représentables par des séries de Taylor. Ainsi font Riemann et, tout récemment, Baire et Lebesgue pour les fonctions de variables réelles. Mais, à vrai dire, le travail d'analyse extra-algébrique auquel se sont livrés ces savants, pourrait être regardé comme un travail préparatoire. En quoi consiste-il en effet? On part d'une notion de fonction discontinue convenablement restreinte (par des considérations sur l'*oscillation*, sur l'ensemble des points de discontinuité, etc.), et, en analysant cette notion, on obtient une représentation algébrique des fonctions que l'on a en vue (développements en séries de fonctions continues, en séries de Fourier, en séries trigonométriques de Lebesgue, etc.). On pourrait donc soutenir que la théorie des fonctions n'est, proprement, qu'un ensemble de calculs portant sur les diverses formes de représentation algébrique connues (ces formes de représentation devenant d'ailleurs de plus en plus nombreuses).

Quel crédit faut-il accorder à cette opinion? Après avoir reconnu qu'historiquement elle est fondée, il peut sembler téméraire de la vouloir juger: peut-être est-il permis cependant de poser ici un point d'interrogation.

***

Se proposer comme but une étude systématique des expressions algébriques convergentes, n'est-ce pas s'assigner une tâche absolument indéterminée? Nous n'en voulons pour preuve que l'impossibilité où se trouvent les analystes de donner une définition satisfaisante des fonctions transcendantes. Nous ne saurions plus, en effet, nous contenter d'affirmer, comme Euler, que les fonctions transcendantes résultent de la combinaison d'une infinité d'opérations. Accepterons-nous alors cette définition de Mac Laurin [2]: « Les fonctions transcendantes sont celles dont la nature ne peut s'exprimer que par des équations transcendantes, c'est-à-dire qui contiennent des expressions différentielles? » — Non: cette définition est trop étroite et trop arbitraire.

(1) Euler, *Introduction à l'analyse infinitésimale.*

(2) *Traité d'Analyse,* Part II, Sect. II.

Identifierons-nous la notion de fonction avec celle d'un ensemble de séries de TAYLOR se déduisant les unes les autres par la méthode du prolongement analytique? — Cela n'est plus permis aujourd'hui, et, d'ailleurs, cela nous conduirait à donner de la *transcendance* une définition tout aussi verbale que celle que nous critiquons chez EULER. Tenterons-nous donc de définir les fonctions par des considérations analogues à celles que nous trouvons chez RIEMANN, LEBESGUE et BAIRE? En ce cas nous nous attelons à une besogne sans fin: car, quelles que soient les fonctions discontinues que nous envisagions, il existera toujours des fonctions *plus discontinues*, fonctions qu'une science construite *à priori* n'a aucune raison de rejeter.

Mais, dira-t-on, personne ne songe à édifier une théorie qui embrasse *toutes* les fonctions. On nous demande seulement d'étudier celles qui jouent un rôle dans la science appliquée, et nous ne devons élargir les définitions consacrées par l'usage que lorsque les besoins de la Mécanique et de la Physique viennent à l'exiger. — Alors, dans quelques vingt ans d'ici, l'Analyse ne sera plus qu'un gros dictionnaire enseignant le maniement des formules dont les physiciens peuvent se servir.

Non pas, répliqueront quelques mathématiciens artistes. Il est vrai que toute science présuppose un choix. Mais ce choix s'impose de lui-même, car les analystes devront toujours donner la préférence aux fonctions et aux formules qui jouissent de propriétés remarquables. — En ce cas, l'Analyse n'est plus qu'un musée de curiosités.

Et ainsi, peu à peu, une impression se dégage: c'est que, si elle doit vraiment se confondre avec l'étude des expressions algébriques, l'Analyse est une science parfaitement vaine. Mais, en réalité, l'Analyse est tout autre chose que ce que nous venons de dire: en la regardant comme un prolongement de l'Algèbre, nous avons pris pour la fin ce qui n'est que le moyen.

En lui-même, en effet, le maniement des formules est sans valeur; et, s'il y a découverte en Analyse, c'est seulement au moment où l'analyste *reconnaît* qu'il existe une loi mathématique pouvant être exprimée par telle ou telle formule. Qu'est-ce, par exemple, que la théorie des fonctions? Ce n'est pas une construction qui serait condamnée d'avance à n'être jamais achevée. C'est l'effort que nous faisons pour analyser, pour représenter sous forme concrète et maniable une notion dont, avant toute science, nous avons l'intuition: la notion de correspondance entre variables. Cette notion, le savant la prend pour point de départ, et il la creuse, cherchant à en exprimer le contenu et à la traduire dans la langue de l'algèbre. En d'autres termes, le but poursuivi par l'analyste n'est point d'ajouter quelques pierres à l'immense édifice de la science, mais de parvenir à une compréhension, de plus en plus complète, de plus en plus intime, des lois ou correspondances mathématiques. L'algèbre, ou science du calcul, n'est, en somme, qu'un instrument. Comme le physicien fait de la physique avec les mathématiques, l'analyste fait de l'analyse avec l'algèbre.

Peut-être estimera-t-on qu'il n'y a là qu'une question de point de vue et de préférences personnelles. Il est possible: mais de ces préférences dépend l'orientation future de la science.

Encore une fois, ferons-nous métier d'architecte ou d'observateur? La réponse n'est point indifférente. Revenons, en effet, à l'exemple de la théorie des fonctions. La partie la plus achevée de cette théorie est, sans contredit, celle qui porte sur certaines classes remarquables de fonctions dont la facture (d'ailleurs semblable à plus d'un titre) se complique progressivement: fonctions trigonométriques, elliptiques, modulaires, fuchsiennes. D'où, pour le mathématicien synthétiste, une tâche tout indiquée, qui consiste à façonner, à son tour, quelques modèles nouveaux de fonctions. Bien différent sera le but poursuivi par le mathématicien analyste (au sens vrai du mot). Ce dernier voudra, par dessus tout *savoir*, voudra forcer, coûte que coûte, le secret des fonctions qui sont restées jusqu'ici rebelles à nos efforts. Peu lui importera que son étude le conduise à des formules barbares, ou même à un résultat négatif. Il regarde les vérités mathématiques comme des faits et il ne se permet pas de juger les faits.

N'avons-nous pas raison de voir, entre les deux points de vue que nous venons de définir, une opposition radicale? Et cette opposition n'est-elle pas, précisement, celle que l'on peut établir entre la synthèse et l'analyse? Mais que les termes sont décevants! Car voici maintenant que j'appelle *Synthèse* l'algèbre ou « analyse » du XVIIe siècle, et *Analyse* la science que Leibniz regardait comme éminemment synthétique.

MAX SIMON

HISTORISCHE BEMERKUNGEN ÜBER DAS CONTINUUM, DEN PUNKT UND DIE GERADE LINIE

Ueber Punkt und Gerade sprechen heisst im Grunde nichts anderes als die beiden Probleme behandeln, welche durch den Begriff Continuum gesetzt werden, nämlich Resolutio et Compositio Continui, Analysis und Synthesis « τοῦ συνεχοῦ ». Aristoteles hat diese Probleme ausdrücklich als solche formuliert, nachdem die Eleaten, insbesondere Zeno, und Demokrit, der letzte erreichbare Urheber der Differentialrechnung, auf spezielle Fälle dieser Probleme gestossen waren. Beide Probleme sind durchaus mathematisch, wenn anders die Mathematik beansprucht werden darf als Wissenschaft der Trennung und Verknüpfung und ihrer Ordnungen.

Die Rücksicht auf die Zeit verbietet mir jede systematische Behandlung, historisch möchte ich bemerken, dass das grösste Verdienst um die Klärung des Begriffs Continuum, des Mathematisch-Unendlichen und der Verwandten, Galilei gebührt; aus Galilei's reifstem Werke, den *Discorsi*, citiere ich:

« In hac et aliis similibus objectionibus adversario satisfacere possumus dicendo non solum non duo sed nec decem nec mille indivisibilium quantitatem divisibilem posse componere, sed *bene* infinita ». Immer wieder sagt Galilei, dass nicht das Experiment die logische Synthese bestätigt, sondern diese es ist, der sich jede Erfahrung fügen muss. Galilei hat zugleich auch das Wesen des mathematischen Begriffes Unendlich erfasst als *frei* von jeder sinulichen Unendlichkeit.

Discorsi p. 43 (Leydener Ausgabe) heisst es: « Die Resolution der Linie in ihre Unendlich vielen Punkte (partes non quantas) ist ebenso leicht wie die Division in ihre endlichen Teile unter einer Bedingung: Et haec est ne a me postules ut tibi ab invicem ista puncta *separem*, eaque tibi super hac charta distincte ostendam singula ».

Und *Discorsi* 31 liest man: « Das Continuum ist ins Unendliche teilbar, deshalb können diese Unendlich-vielen Teile keine Grösse haben, denn eine unendliche Zahl von Grössen giebt eine Erstreckung in's Unendliche ». Es folgt die wichtigste Stelle: « Gerade darum weil die Teilung in Teile, welche Grösse haben, continuierlich fortgesetzt werden kann, ergiebt sich die compositio continui ex infinitis partibus non quantis, d. h. aus Differentialen.

Man sieht, wie klar der unsterbliche Mann den realisierenden Charakter des Differentials erkannt hat, das eine rein *intensive* Grösse ist, aber eben deshalb die extensive continuirliche Gröss durch unendliche Häufung, durch das *Integral* realisiert, d. h. erkennbar macht. Man sieht auch wie eng Galilei an die Hellenen anschliesst und wie er auch hier mit dem ihm ebenbürtigen Lionardo da Vinci zusammentrifft, welcher sagt: « Ogni quantità continua intellettuamente è divisibile in infinito ».

Bolzano ist von Galilei in den « *Paradoxien des Unendlichen* », jener für Weierstrass und G. Cantor fundamentalen Schrift, stark beeinflusst während auf geometrischem Gebiet und auch sonst Bolzano von Leibniz abhängig ist.

Ich komme nun zu der Arithmetisierung der Linie, denn der Punkt, sowohl der des Raumes « *στιγμή* », wie der der Zeit, das « *τὸ νῦν* », ist schon von den Pythagoräern mit der Einheit « *μονάς* » identificiert. — Der Versuch das Continuum mit der an sich diskreten Zahl in Connex zu bringen, scheint seltsamer als er ist. Zunächst liefert die physikalische und psychische Bewegung (sodann Farben-und Tonspectra) Continua; die Bewegung überträgt den ununterbrochenen Fluss des in Raum und Zeit Beweglichen auf Raum und Zeit selbst. Es handelt sich nun darum diese von der Anschauung gegebene Continuität logisch nachzuconstruieren. Die Logik fordert, dass nach Erwerb des Hilfsbegriffs (notion auxiliaire) Raum der Körper sich nur in einer Bahn bewegen kann, die vor, in und nach der Bewegung existiert, und daher habe ich s. Z. diese Leistung der Kategorie Raum, dass sie es ist, welche uns die Continuität liefert, als eine ihrer fundamentalsten angesprochen. Der Raum überträgt die Continuität durch Vermittelung der Bewegung auf die Zeit und zwar kommt äussere und innere Bewegung in Betracht, denn das Einheitsbewusstsein des Intellects begleitet beständig die wechselnden Erlebnisse. Von diesem Gesichtspunkte aus kann man den Marburger Neuplatonikern das Kategorische des Continuitätsbegriffs gern zugestehen.

Wenn nun von der Natur der Satz des Aristoteles « natura non facit saltus » unbezweifelt gilt, so musste die Mathematik notwendig folgen, denn ihre Aufgabe ist es aus Wahrnehmungen durch Mass und Zahl Naturerkenntnis zu schaffen; es musste versucht werden auch die Zahl continuierlich zu machen. Sobald man die verworrene Vorstellung des Continuums als eines Haufens von Punkten, Strichen etc. schärfer erfassen wollte, also die Vorstellung zergliedern um sie zu componieren, war man zu einer ins Einzelne gehenden abzählenden Trennung der Elemente gezwungen, die durch die Zahl bewirkt werden musste. Hierbei zeigte sich nun zwar sofort die Unzulänglichkeit der Zahl als Ordinalzahl und Cardinalzahl das Continuum zu erschöpfen, aber man hatte im Zählen und der Zahl Sonderung und Verknüpfung und so die Möglichkeit die beiden Probleme des Continuums wenigstens in Angriff zu nehmen; und um den *Versuch zu wagen* es aller sinnlichen Unterscheidungsunfähigkeit der einzelnen Elemente zum Trotz logisch durchzuführen, bot sich die dritte Wurzel der Zahl, die Relativität. Mit ihrer Hilfe gelang es schon in praehistorischer Zeit durch Schöpfung der Brüche der ersten Haupteigenschaft des Continuums gerecht zu werden, die von G. Cantor Ueberalldichtigkeit genannt, schon von Parmenides und Zeno erkannt wurde, während sie P. Dubois-Reymond in seiner curiosen Funktionentheorie als Pantachität nachentdeckte.

Schon PLATON (vgl. seine Wissenschaftslehre im Theätet z. B. 185 und 186) erklärte, dass alle Erkenntnis in der von Relationen beruhe und sagt ibi 185 D dass in diesem Begriff der Verknüpfung das Wesen der Arithmetik und Geometrie bestehe. Es bedarf der Lectüre des Theon Smyrnäos nicht um zu begreifen wie sonderbar einem antiken Platoniker die immer noch herrschende Ansicht anmuten würde, sie hätten die Brüche und Irrationalzahlen nicht als Zahlen angesehen. Deckt sich doch die Euklidisch-Eudoxische Definition des Streckenbruches wörtlich mit der WEIERSTRASS'schen Definition der allgemeinen Zahl.

Die Pythagoräer, diese nie hoch genug zu wertenden Geisteshelden, schufen die Irrationalzahl nicht unbewusst wie die Inder, sondern völlig klar über die Tragweite. G. CANTOR hat mit bewunderungswertem Scharfsinn durch Einführung des Begriffs der Höhe kurz und bündig gezeigt, dass auch die algebraische Irrationalzahl der Hellenen keinen Fortschritt für die Abbildung des Continuums im Einzelnen bedeute und erst die allgemeine Reihenzahl den Körper der reellen Zahlen zu einer perfecten Menge mache. Die CANTOR'sche Einführung der Irrationalzahl hat alle übrigen geschlagen, weil sie die Codification des gesunden Menschenverstandes ist, der nach NAPOLEON dem Grossen zuletzt stets Recht behält; CANTOR hat den Begriff der Irrationalzahl, den nicht nur ein ARCHIMEDES, sondern den jeder Schulknabe hat, zur wissenschaftlichen Höhe erhoben. Aber wenn CANTOR und seine Anhänger glaubten, dass Zeit und Raum vom Ordnungstypus Θ, vom Körper der reellen Zahlen, ihre Continuität empfangen, so muss ich dem auch hier wiedersprechen und befinde mich dabei in der guten Gesellschaft Herrn VERONESE's.

Abgesehen davon, dass die Continuität der geraden Linie durch einen einzigen Akt des Intelekts erfasst wird, während die der Zahl einen infinitären Process und seinen Grenzabschluss erfordert, kommt auch die CANTOR'sche Lehre vom arithmetischen Continuum nicht ohne Sprung aus. Der Sprung liegt darin, dass seine Definition der Irrationalzahl durch die Fundamentalreihe, insbesondere die Definition der Gleichkeit mittelst der Nullreihe die Continuität schon voraussetzt. Die unzähligen Fundamentalreihen, welche dieselbe Zahl definieren, definieren eine unendlich kleine Strecke, bezw. ein Element des selbst von der Mächtigkeit $\aleph$ ist. Der Vorwurf des Zirkelschlusses den CANTOR (Annalen 46) gegen den ausgezeichneten italienischen Mathematiker in Folge eines Missverständnisses der abgekürzten Ausdrucksweise erhoben hat, lässt sich gerade für den Gleichheitsbegriff gegen ihn erheben. Für meine Ansicht citiere ich aus VERONESE's Fundamentalwerk (Ausgabe Schepp) p. 56 Note: « Ein Punktsystem kann niemals, wenn der Punkt als Zeichen der Trennung gedacht wird, im absoluten Sinn das ganze intuitive Continuum geben, weil der Punkt keine Teile hat ».

Meine Herren, schon ARISTOTELES bewies, dass andrenfalls die Seite eines Quadrates gleich der Diagonale wäre. Für praktische Zwecke ausreichend stellt schon die Rationalzahl das Continuum dar. VERONESE fährt fort: « Das geradlinige Continuum ist niemals aus seinen Punkten, sondern aus Strecken zusammengesetzt, welche die Punkte zu je zweien verbinden und welche selbst ebenfalls continuirlich sind ». Derselbe Satz findet sich auch in meinen « *Elementen der Geometrie mit Rücksicht auf die absolute Geometrie* » von 1890, und noch etwas früher und zwar wiederholt bei ARISTOTELES.

Weiter sagt VERONESE: « Auf diese Weise wird das GEHEIMNIS der Continuität von einem gegebenen bestimmten Teil auf einen beliebig kleinen unbestimmten Teil der Geraden zurückgedrängt, welcher immer noch continuirlich ist, in welchem es aber nicht gestattet ist, mit unserer Vorstellung einzudringen ». In diesem GEHEIMNIS ist dann im Grunde der Fundamentalbegriff der Grenze verborgen. Diese Grenze nannte ich l. c. das Differential.

Ich komme nun auf die HILBERT'schen Stetigkeitsaxiome. Die Hilbertschen Grundlagen sind ein anerkanntes Meisterwerk deduktiver Logik, anders steht die Frage, was sie für die geometrische Geometrie bedeuten, die Geometrie der reinen Auschauung im Sinne KANT's und PLATONS, wo reine Auschauung dasjenige bedeutet, was die Vernunft rein bei sich selbst *sieht.* Es ist gewiss interessant, dass man für die linearen Congruenzaxiome das Congruenzzeichen interpretieren kann durch « gleichgefärbt », aber bei der gänzlichen Unbestimmtheit der « gewissen Beziehungen », zwischen, gleich, congruent, Gebiet (Satz 6), Strecke, sagt B. RUSSEL mit Recht: « Diese Geometrie ist eine Wissenschaft, von der man niemals weiss, wovon man spricht ». Logisch kann man ja fordern, was man will, z. B. es wird verlangt sich an seinem eignen Schopf aus dem Sumpf zu ziehen, aber mit Ausnahme von Münchhausen hat dies noch Niemand realisiert. Will man die Axiome und Sätze der freien Geometrie räumlich deuten, so kann man den Raumbegriff nicht entbehren. Ich werde der Versuchung auf die Lehre vom Raum einzugehen nicht erliegen, aber ich will doch bemerken, dass der schwerste Fehler KANT's meines Erachtens die Verwechselung der Kategorie Raum mit dem Constructionsraum des Geometres ist, und dass ich die KANT'sche transcendentale Aesthetik als einen Rückschritt gegen LEIBNIZ betrachte.

Von den beiden Stetigkeitsaxiomen HILBERT's hört das erste auf den Namen des ARCHIMEDES, Beweis genug, dass es etwa von EUDOXOS oder, was mir nach dem EPHODION mehr einleuchtet, von DEMOKRIT herrührt, da es ARCHIMEDES selbrt in der Quadratur der Parabel älteren Mathematikern vindiciert. Das zweite von HILBERT Vollständigkeitsaxiom genannt, ist logisch unantastbar, aber der Schluss des § 17 zeigt deutlich, dass es auch wieder nur die arithmetische Continuität begründet und somit gelten die früheren Einwände. Und für die wirkliche Geometrie wird durch Axiom II gar nichts bewiesen. Die Continuität unseres Raumes, des Raumes, von dem GAUSS sagte: « wir müssen in Demut gestehen, dass er auch ausser unserer Logik eine Realität hat », liegt eigentlich schon in dem Axiom von der continuirlichen Gleichförmigkeit des Raumes, dass die Bewegungsmöglichkeit als Gesammtheit der Lagen sichert, und da ist es merkwürdig, dass es sich erreichbar zuerst bei dem Autor findet, der die Bewegung geleugnet hat.

In *περὶ φύσεως* des *Parmenides* heisst es (DIELS Fragmente der Vorsocratiker)

αὐτὰρ ἐπεὶ πεῖρας πύματον, τετελέσμενον ἐστὶ
πάντοθεν, εὐκύκλου σφαῖρης ἐναλίγκιον ὄγκωι
μέσσοθεν, ἰσοπαλὲς πάντηι τὸ γὰς οὔτετι μεῖζον
οὔτε τι βαιότερον πελέναι χρεόν εστι τῆι ἢ τῆι.

« Aber da es eine letzte Grenze giebt, so ist er von allen Seiten abgeschlossen, ähnlich dem Körper der wohlgerundeten Kugel, von der Mitte aus über all an

Kräften gleich, denn da darf es hier oder dort nichts geben, was mehr oder weniger wäre. Hier haben wir also den *endlichen* kugelförmigen RIEMANN'schen RAUM und das Axiom von der Gleichförmigkeit.

Ich gehe zu Punkt und Gerade über und verweise der Kürze halber auf frühere Publikationen: Elemente der Geometrie von 1890; Zu den Grundlagen der nichteuklidischen Geometrie 1891; Euklid 1901; Methodik und Didaktik 1908 (*Baumeister* IX, 2. Aufl.).

Kein Begriff der Mathematik hat mehr Kopfschütteln verursacht als der des Punktes; bekannt ist die Definition des als Physiker wie als Humorist gleich bedeutenden LICHTENBERG: « Der Punkt ist ein Winkel, dem man die Schenkel ausgerissen hat ». Hierbei ist eigentlich nur das Reissen zu bemängeln. Gelegentlich erkläre ich meinen Schülern: Stellt Euch vor, Ihr machtet einen Punkt und in der Feder wäre keine Tinte.

Interessant scheint mir, dass der weltgeschichtliche Gegensatz zwischen PLATON und ARISTOTELES (zwischen dem reinen Idealismus und dem Idealismus auf realistischer Grundlage) sich auch in der Auffassung der Punktes wiederspiegelt. Bei PLATON ist der Punkt die *ἀρχὴ γραμμῆς*, der Ursprung, das Differential, der Linie; bei ARISTOTELES die *μονὰς θέσιν ἔχουσα*, oder wie LEIBNIZ in Euklidis *Πρῶτα* sagt: « Punctum est cujus pars nulla est » addendum est: situm habens. Der Punkt unterscheidet sich von der Eins dadurch, dass er LAGE hat, die specifische Differenz beider Disciplinen.

Der Begriff der LAGE ist aus der ANSCHAUUNG durch Anwendung des Grenzbegriffs erwachsen, und dass HILBERT diesen Anteil der Anschauung am Punkt der Geometrie nicht berücksichtigt hat, das macht seine Grundlagen, so hoch sie an sich zu werten sind, für die Geometrie unfruchtbar.

Wiederholt betont ARISTOTELES, dass zwei Punkte, und wären sie noch so nahe, durch den Abstand getrennt sind. Charakteristica geometrica 11 findet sich bei LEIBNIZ eine wörtliche Uebereinstimmung mit ARISTOTELES. Nachdem in N. 10 gesagt ist: « Der Punkt drückt im Raum das aus, was am meisten limitiert ist, die einfache Lage oder den Ort, sagt er « dass durch 2 Punkte sofort ihr Abstand mitgesetzt ist ». Auffallend ist die Nichtberücksichtigung der *Richtungsbeziehung*; hervorzuheben, dass LEIBNIZ den Punkt durchaus nicht rein negativ als ohne Länge, Breite, Tiefe definiert, sondern als Maximum des Limitierten nach allen Dimensionen und hier wieder mit KANT (Reflexionen II, p. 201, Erdmann) zusammentrifft; nur dass LEIBNIZ wiederum der Klarere ist.

Indem ich für meine Auffassung des Punktes als Grenzbegriff auf die Festschrift für Kummer verweise, füge ich nur noch hinzu, dass ich die *Einheit des Bewusstseins* psychologisch als das Fundament der Monade der Zeit wie des Raumes halte.

Die vielumstrittene Definition der Geraden des EUKLID ist unvollständig, aber sie wird ergänzt durch die Postulate 1 und 2, zusammen definieren sie die Gerade als eine unterschiedslose (*ἐξ ἴσου*) und unendliche continuirliche Grösse (Postulat 2), die durch 2 ihrer Punkte eindeutig bestimmt ist (Postulat 1). Von den vielen Definitionen der Geraden bei LEIBNIZ bemängelt LEIBNIZ selbst die in der Analysis Geometrica propria, die Gerade als Symmetrielinie der Ebene, er bemerkt: « Wenn

Iemand zweifelt, ob die Ebene so geteilt werden kann, ist es vielleicht besser die Gerade als Schnitt zweier Ebenen zu definieren ». Aber abgesehen von diesem Zweifel wäre die Erklärung nicht eindeutig, da die Sinuslinie z. B. dieselbe Eigenschaft hat, und ferner die Symmetrie schon Abstand und Lot voraussetzt. Bei Gerhardt V 185, 3 findet sich auch schon die Definition, welche sich bei GAUSS, HELMHOLTZ, WEIERSTRASS findet, aber auch schon bei PROCLOS. Auch die von BOLYAI und LOBATSCHEFFSKI gegebene der Geraden als Symmetrieort dreier Punkte (FOURIER 1790) geht auf LEIBNIZ zurück.

Das Archimedische Axiom der Geraden als geodätischer Linie, für Anfänger immer noch die zweckmässigste Definition, hat der in der Blüte der Jahre der Wissenschaft entrissene B. KERRY von dem Begriff der Länge und damit vom Zirkelschluss befreien wollen. Er definierte die Gerade als Linie kleinsten Kraftmasses und wies wie PROCLOS und FREYCINET auf den Esel, der sein Futter sucht, hin. Aber das Agens hier ist nicht die Kraft und ihre Schätzung, sondern das Bewusstsein der Richtung, welches auch den Hund lehrt, seinem Herrn richtig vorauszulaufen bis zum nächsten Kreuzweg.

Richtung und Abstand sind die beiden Constituenten der geraden Linie, für diese beiden irreducibeln Grundbegriffe verweise ich auf p. 11 und 12 meiner Festschrift für KUMMER. Richtung ist eine der intensiven Grössen, welche durch die Kategorie Bewegung mitgesetzt sind, allerdings liegt in ihrem Wesen zunächst nur die Gleichmässigkeit, und um die Gerade vom Kreise zu trennen genügt es nicht mit LEIBNIZ zu sagen: « Die Gerade ist die Linie, in der jeder Teil dem Ganzen ähnlich ist », denn das gilt vom Kreise gerade so wie die Gleichung AB + BC = AC, sondern es mus entweder die Strecke selbst in der innern Anschauung gegeben werden oder es muss das Axiom der Gleichförmigkeit des Raumes heraugezogen werden und axiomatisch gefordert werden, dass unter den unzähligen Richtungen, die von A ausstrahlen und damit auch von *B*, nur einmal die Richtung *AB* vorkommt; man vgl. auch BOLZANO's Betrachtungen von 1808. Am citierten Ort habe ich darauf hingewiesen, dass es die Zeit ist, welche Abstand und Richtung sondert.

Was die Bestimmtheit der Geraden durch 2 Punkte betrifft, so findet sich schon bei ASSMANN im Anschluss an GIORDANO BRUNO, den ASSMANN genau gekannt hat, die RIEMANN'sche Hypothese der Auflösung der Curven in geradlinige Elemente. ASSMANN meint dann ganz scharfsinnig für die Gerade sind eigentlich nicht 2 Punkte, sondern 2 consecutive mensurae minutissimae nach GIORDANO BRUNO nötig. Hier liegt aber doch eine Verkennung der Grundeigenschaft der Geraden als Linie gleicher Richtung vor, das eine Element, das z. B. Kreis und Tangente gemein haben, bestimmt die Richtung und damit die Gerade. Dass die Gerade durch *irgend* 2 Punkte bestimmt ist, liegt von diesem Gesichtspunkt aus daran, dass die intensive Grösse von jeder extensiven Beziehung frei ist.

Hochansehliche Versammlung, es scheint mir mehr als fraglich, ob wir diese subtilen Fragen ohne Zirkelschluss beantworten können oder richtiger ausgedrückt, es scheint nicht möglich die Resultate einer schier unendlichen Geistesarbeit in bestimmte Sätze zu formulieren.

F. BERNSTEIN

UEBER DIE AXIOMATISCHE EINFACHHEIT VON BEWEISEN

Eines der sachlich bedeutungsvollsten Momente, in denen der philosophische Charakter der Mathematik in Erscheinung tritt, ist dieses: dass sie imstande ist, über die Gewinnung ihrer Einzelresultate hinaus, über die Methode als solche Rechenschaft zu liefern.

Hierher gehören die bekannten Unmöglichkeitsbeweise z. B. der für die Aufgabe der Quadratur des Zirkels, hierher gehören vor allem moderne Untersuchungen, welche von der Erforschung der axiomatischen Grundlagen der Geometrie ihren Ausgangspunkt nahmen. Seit dem Emporkommen der syntetischen Geometrie hat man sich bemüht, gewisse Beweise « rein » d. h. unter Ausschliessung gewisser Hilfsmittel zu führen, die nach dem Gefühl der Forscher etwas der Sache Fremdes hatten. Diese vom subjektiven Gefühl inspirierte Tendenz, die gelegentlich zu einer Art der Exklusivität gegenüber abweichenden Bestrebungen geführt hat, besitzt ihren objektiven sachlichen Hintergeund, der in dem Augenblick klar zu Tage trat, als die Frage nach der *Möglichkeit* « reiner » Beweise formuliert wurde, formuliert in der Form, ob gewisse Sätze mit gewissen axiomatischen Hilfsmitteln beweisbar seien, oder nicht. Es ist D. Hilbert, welcher nach vielen bedeutenden Vorarbeiten anderer, zum ersten Male in ganz prinzipieller Form diesen Sachverhalt zum Ausdruck gebracht hat und es bedeutet sein Schlusswort der « Grundlagen der Geometrie » in historischer Hinsicht das Ende der Schulgegensätze auf dem Gebiete der Geometrie, welche das 19te Jahrhundert durchziehen.

Diese Wirkung hat sich weder bisher, auf die Geometrie allein beschränkt, noch wird dies wie mir scheint künftig der Fall sein. Jede subjektive Exklusivität (z. B. etwa die gegen den Gebrauch transfiniter Zahlen in mathematischen Beweisen) gehört in ihrer Subjektivität einer historisch überwundenen Epoche an; an ihre Stelle muss die tiefere wenn auch schwierigere Bemühung treten jeweils zu entscheiden, ob bei den gewählten axiomatischen Grundlagen, der Gebrauch irgend welcher Hilfsmittel, (z. B. transfiniter Zahlen) entbehrlich ist, oder nicht.

In der Ersetzung des Subjektivismus der Schule durch die Objektivität einer Ersforschung der Methode, besteht eine der leitenden Entwicklungstendenzen der heutigen Mathematik.

M. H. Es ist meine Absicht Ihnen heute von einer Untersuchung zu sprechen, die unter meiner Anregung entstanden, ein Beitrag nach dieser Richtung liefert. Man hat sich historisch nicht nur bemüht, « reine » Beweise zu geben, sondern vor allem hat man nach *einfachen* Beweisen gestrebt. In dem Wunsch, den objektiven Charakter dieser Bemühung zu extrahieren, griff ich nach einem Beispiel, dessen Alter ein gewisse Wahrscheinlichkeit dafür zu bieten schien, dass der Prozess der Abklärung in dieser Hinsicht einigermassen vollendet sei, nämlich nach dem Beispiel des Pythagoräischen Lehrsatzes. Wir legen, um für die Behauptung, wie für den Beweis die nötige Bestimmtheit zu gewinnen, ein bestimmtes Axiomensystem zu grunde. Ohne andere Möglichkeiten des Vorgehens auszuschliessen, greifen wir ein für den Beweis besonders charakteristisches Axiom, das der ebenen Kongruenz, heraus und definieren die Zahl der Anwendungen desselben als Maass der Einfachheit des Beweises, sodass wir als den *axiomatisch einfachsten* Beweis denjenigen bezeichnen, der die geringste Anzahl der Anwendungen dieses Axioms erfordert. Ueberdies wollen wir, um die Frage weiter zu vereinfachen, nur diejenigen Beweise vergleichen, welche auf der einfacheren Flächengleichheit durch Addition kongruenter Stücke nicht der durch Subtraktion, beruhen.

Die Anzahl der Anwendungen des ebenen Kongruenzaxioms wird hier identisch mit der Anzahl der Dreiecke, aus denen die beiden als gleich zu erweisenden Figuren zusammen gesetzt werden und der einfachste Beweis ist derjenige, der die Minimalzahl von Dreiecken benutzt. Unter den historisch bekannten Beweisen hat der des AN-NAIRIZI (900 n. Chr.) die kleinste Zahl, nämlich *sieben*. Die Vermutung, dass sieben die wahre Minimalzahl sei, wurde durch eine auf meine Anregung ausgeführte Uutersuchung des Herrn HANS BRANDES, die als Hallenser Dissertation erschienen ist, bestätigt. Es ist also nicht möglich aus weniger als sieben Dreiecken simultan beide Figuren, das Hypothenusenquadrat und die beiden Kathetenquadrate aufzubauen. Hierbei handelt es sich wohlgemerkt um Beweise, welche die beiden Figuren in allgemeiner Lage und mit beliebig veränderlichem Kathetenverhältnis voraussetzen. Es gibt eine endliche Anzahl singulärer Kathetenverhältnisse, welche eine weitere Reduktion der Zahl gestatten.

In bezug auf alle weiteren Einzelheiten der z. T. nicht ganz einfachen Untersuchung sei auf die ausführliche Arbeit des Herrn BRANDES verwiesen und nur noch folgendes bemerkt. Die hier eingeschlagene Richtung der Untersuchung ist keineswegs die einzige. Man könnte nicht nur die Subtraktionsbeweise in gleicher Art untersuchen, sondern ebenso die Reduktion bezüglich anderer Axiome vornehmen. Eine etwas andere Fragestellung hat Herr E. MAHLO erledigt, in dem er gezeigt hat, dass ein Beweis mittelst lauter einander ähnlicher Dreiecke nicht zu führen ist.

Endlich sei nicht unterlassen, darauf hinzuweisen, dass diese Untersuchungen sich mit den Fragen der Geometrographie des Herrn LEMOINE insoweit berühren, als auch für die bisher empirisch betriebene Geometrographie in solcher exakten Untersuchung über die *wahre* Minimalzahl die Richtung einer fruchtbaren Weiterbildung liegen dürfte.

A. PASTORE

SULLA NATURA EXTRALOGICA DELLE LEGGI DI TAUTOLOGIA E DI ASSORBIMENTO NELLA LOGICA MATEMATICA

Prima di Leibniz la Matematica e la Logica vivevano in due campi disparati e lontani. Poi, in seguito alle geniali intuizioni di quella vasta mente di filosofo e di matematico, la Logica si avvicinò risolutamente alla Matematica, e l'avvicinamento progressivo continuò per opera di successori i quali scoprirono le numerose e feconde analogie donde trasse origine la Logica matematica. Questo indirizzo ha già una vasta letteratura che qui è inutile esporre.

Ciò premesso, sorge naturale la domanda: dove ci porterà questo lento ma continuo avvicinamento dei due calcoli? Notiamo subito che, contro la tesi della loro fusione definitiva, si oppone un gruppo di ragioni che ha, per lo meno, il vantaggio della tradizione. È noto infatti che quasi tutti i matematici, che contribuirono maggiormente al progresso del calcolo logico, si fanno un dovere di introdurre un sistema speciale di segni per trattare le interessanti questioni relative alla Logica deduttiva, pur riconoscendo che questa fa parte delle scienze matematiche, e malgrado la grande analogia presentata dalle operazioni fondamentali dei due campi. E si capisce che i loro sforzi sono ispirati dal desiderio di impedire una fusione possibile dei due calcoli, che, a prima giunta, ha l'apparenza d'una confusione.

Frattanto si presenta un fatto nuovo. Indipendentemente dalle aspirazioni accennate, tanto il calcolo matematico quanto il calcolo logico, intesi a perfezionare i proprj metodi, vanno sempre più assumendo un carattere di estrema generalità, in cui alla crescente purezza formale delle nozioni si accompagna il crescente rigore deduttivo dei ragionamenti. Ciò significa che i due calcoli, malgrado le loro presunte differenze, funzionano in realtà come due sistemi ipotetico-deduttivi, intimamente congiunti nell'impiego d'un procedimento comune.

Questo fatto, il quale si può considerare come un acquisto recente, è tanto grave e inaspettato che impone la necessità di elencare e discutere colla massima brevità (e quindi efficacia) tutte le ragioni che attualmente si adducono per impedire il riconoscimento dell'identità fondamentale dei due calcoli.

Mi limito ora ad osservare che la ragione più forte si ricava dall'affermazione che alcune operazioni fondamentali del calcolo logico non hanno le corrispondenti nel calcolo matematico o differiscono notevolmente nelle loro proprietà. Per esempio, si afferma che le proprietà espresse dalle seguenti identità, in generale

$$aa = a \ , \ a \cup a = a$$

pel prodotto e per la somma, non hanno le corrispondenti in Algebra numerica (1), sebbene di queste formole si faccia continuo uso nell' Algebra della logica, la quale, priva così dei multipli e delle potenze, riceve una semplificazione enorme rispetto all' Algebra numerica (2). La legge rappresentata da queste formole fu dal Jevons (3) chiamata *the law of simplicity*, da altri la legge di tautologia (4); da questa deriva la legge di assorbimento (5)

$$a(a \cup b) = a \ , \ a \cup (ab) = a \, ,$$

e un gruppo vastissimo di conseguenze che costrinsero il calcolo logico a diffondersi

(1) G. Boole [*The calculs of logic* (Cambridge and Dublin math. Journal, 1848, V. III, pp. 183-198); *An investigation of the laws of thought, on which are founded the mathematical theories of logic and probabilities* (London, Walten et Maberly, 1854)] afferma che le due equazioni

$$aa = a \quad | \quad a + a = a$$

sono caratteristiche del calcolo logico. La sua dottrina ebbe gran seguito nella scuola inglese, scozzese e americana. Nel '72 Robert Grassmann affrontando, con criterj originali, questo argomento, pubblicò le sue ricerche nella Wissenschaftlehre oder Philosophie, Stettin. È noto che egli divide la matematica in quattro rami distinti: 1) la « Begriffslehre » (logica); 2) la « Bindelehre » (teoria delle combinazioni); 3) la « Zahlenlehre » (aritmetica); 4) l' « Ausdehnungslehre » e riduce le proprietà caratteristiche di queste quattro discipline ai diversi modi coi quali si connettono fra loro eguali elementi. (Verknüpfungsarten gleicher Stiften) nella « Fügung » (addizione) e nella « Webung » (moltiplicazione) di tali elementi, come mostra il prospetto seguente;

$$\left.\begin{matrix} e+e=e \\ ee=e \end{matrix}\right\} (1) \quad \left.\begin{matrix} e+e=e \\ ee \neq e \end{matrix}\right\} (2) \quad \left.\begin{matrix} e+e \neq e \\ ee=e \end{matrix}\right\} (3) \quad \left.\begin{matrix} e+e \neq e \\ ee \neq e \end{matrix}\right\} (4).$$

G. Peano [*Calcolo geometrico secondo l'Ausdehnungslehre di Grassmann, preceduto dalle operazioni della logica deduttiva* (Torino, Bocca, 1888)], dichiara che le operazioni riferite, le quali sono fondamentali al calcolo logico, non hanno le corrispondenti nel calcolo logico. In « F_2 N 1 » [*Logique mathématique* (Turin, Bocca, 1897, p. 35)] nota che la proprietà della moltiplicazione logica espressa dalla P42 ($a = aa$) rende le formule logiche più semplici che le algebriche.

(2) L. Couturat, *L'Algèbre de la logique* (Paris, Gauthier-Villars, Ed. 1905, p. 13).

(3) W. S. Jevons, *The principles of science, a treatise on logic and scientific method* (London, 1883).

(4) A. Nagy, *Fondamenti del calcolo logico* (Napoli, 1890, Pellerano); *Principj di logica esposti secondo le dottrine moderne* (Torino, Loescher, 1892). A p. 47 e segg. di quest'opera la legge di tautologia viene indicata in generale coll'espressione seguente:

$$\Pi a = a \quad | \quad \Sigma a = a \, .$$

(5) E. Schröder chiama le due equazioni: $a = a + ab$, $a = a(a + b)$ « Absorptions gesetz ». Cfr. *insup.* Nagy, *Principj* ecc., p. 48, e *Fondamenti* ecc., p. 3; Couturat, op. cit., p. 13.

con relativa lentezza e fecero sì che anche le applicazioni della Matematica alla Logica pura siano ancora oggidì avversate da troppi logici e matematici.

Lo scopo della presente comunicazione è di portare un contributo diretto alla tesi dell' identità fondamentale dei due calcoli:

1° dimostrando che tutte le apparenti dimostrazioni che furono date finora di tali leggi si riducono ad una mera trasformazione descrittiva di concetti, cioè sono logicamente insussistenti;

2° riconoscendo che la concezione stessa di queste leggi assunte come primitive o ha natura extralogica o non può essere pensata come compatibile col principio fondamentale dell' identità;

3° indicando le più elementari applicazioni che vengono suggerite in conseguenza.

I.

Esaminiamo in primo luogo le dimostrazioni, limitandoci a citare le più importanti, per amore di brevità.

Giova ricordare che l'autorità della tesi tautologica rimonta a LEIBNIZ il quale dichiarò esplicitamente: « *repetitio ejusdem literae in eodem termino est inutilis* » (1) quanto al prodotto, e « *si idem secum ipso sumatur nihil constituitur novum, seu* A + A ∞ A » (2) quanto alla somma.

In seguito quasi tutte le scuole di logica matematica: l'inglese (HAMILTON, BOOLE, CLIFFORD, JEVONS, VENN, ecc.), l'americana (HALSTED, PEIRCE), la tedesca (SCHRÖDER, H. e R. GRASSMANN, FREGE), l'italiana (PEANO, NAGY, BURALI-FORTI, ecc.), la francese (COUTURAT), la russa (PORETZKY), accettarono questi principj. Tutte le dimostrazioni poi che furono escogitate si riducono, a quanto mi risulta, malgrado la deplorevole anarchia di notazioni, alle due forme seguenti, riprodotte, con poche modificazioni, dai varj autori (3).

Nella prima forma (4) si dimostra, in primo luogo, la Proposizione

[1] $$a \supset aa \,,$$

al quale scopo prima si moltiplicano fra loro le due deduzioni $a \supset a$ e $a \supset a$; quindi si compongono secondo le nota formola di Composizione:

$$a \supset b \,.\, a \supset c : \supset : a \supset bc \,,$$

quindi si deduce la Ths.

In secondo luogo, in virtù della definizione dell'eguaglianza, da

$$aa \supset a \,.\, a \supset aa \,,$$

(1) LEIBNIZ, *PhilS.*, t. 7, p. 224. Cfr. PEANO, F_2 N3, pp. 14, 41.

(2) Id., Mss. *Phil.* VII, p. 3.

(3) Vedi p. es. il COUTURAT che, in op. e loc. cit. ripete la stessa dimostrazione del PEANO, ma adoperando la relazione d'inclusione col segno $<$.

(4) G. PEANO, F_2N1: P31: $a \supset aa$ [Hp . P21 . P21 . $\supset$. $a \supset a \,.\, a \supset a$. Cmp . $\supset$. Ths.
P42: $a = aa$ [P23 $\cap$ P31 . $\supset$. P.]. La P23 è: $a, b \,\varepsilon\, K \,.\supset .\, ab \supset a$.

in cui la $aa \supset a$ è tratta da $ab \supset a$), per $(a|b)$, si deduce la proposizione tautologica

[2] $$a = aa .$$

E analogamente si ragiona per la somma.

Quanto infine alla legge di assorbimento

$$a(a \cup b) = a \ , \ a \cup (ab) = a$$

si capisce che la sua sorte dipende dalle formole di Cmp e di Smp che furono già impiegate precedentemente e saranno esaminate fra poco.

Ora si vede che la dimostrazione della [1] è subordinata alla condizione che si possa sostituire $(a , a , a \mid a , b , c)$ nella formola del Cmp

$$a \supset b . a \supset c : \supset : a \supset bc ,$$

affinchè le due deduzioni $a \supset a$ e $a \supset a$ si possano comporre per la deduzione della Ths. Ma è chiaro che tale sostituzione (di termini tutti eguali ad un dato termine a nella formola del Cmp che contiene termini differenti) non si può fare perchè, con essa, l' Hp diventerebbe

$$a \supset a . a \supset a$$

da cui, in virtù della

$$aa \supset a$$

già posta antecedentemente; e per la sostituzione, in questo caso, legittima $(a \supset a|a)$ non si ricava che

$$a \supset a .$$

Dunque la tesi

$$a \supset aa$$

cade senza rimedio, e con essa la sua corrispondente per la somma, e tutto il sistema delle conseguenze legate alla legge di tautologia.

Ma c'è ancora un'altra prova contraria alla validità di codesta dimostrazione. Infatti, non solo non si può fare la sostituzione riferita nella forma del Cmp, ma neppure si può ricorrere al principio di composizione per dedurne la Ths della tautologia, perchè, rigorosamente parlando, la proposizione del Cmp non è che la stessa proposizione tautologica mascherata. Invero non si bada che la formola del Cmp la quale esprime che « se si hanno due deduzioni colla medesima Hp e per Ths il prodotto logico delle due Ths » implica già un ὕστερον πρότερον, vale a dire costituisce un appello manifesto a quella convenzione la quale esprime che « ripetendo più volte la medesima Hp non si ottiene mai altro che la medesima Hp ».

In una parola è necessario supporre già la validità di quella legge che si cerca in seguito di dimostrare, perchè la vera formola del Cmp non è questa

$$a \supset b \,.\, a \supset c : \supset : a \supset bc,$$

ma quest'altra

$$a \supset b \,.\, a \supset c : \supset aa \supset bc,$$

la quale si ottiene moltiplicando membro a membro la deduzione $a \supset b$ per la deduzione $a \supset c$ e dice propriamente che « dal prodotto delle Hp si deduce il prodotto delle Ths ».

Nella seconda forma [1] la proposizione

[1] $$a \supset aa$$

non è dimostrata, ma è posta immediatamente come Pp. E allora dalla affermazione simultanea

$$a \supset aa \,.\, aa \supset a,$$

in cui la p. $aa \supset a$ è ottenuta per la sostituzione $(a|b)$ nella Pp. $ab \supset a$, si deduce la Ths.

[2] $$a = aa$$

Ora anche qui si comprende che la dimostrazione del principio tautologico è logicamente insussistente, perchè la sua validità è subordinata alla Pp. [1] nella quale è giocoforza supporre già la validità di quel principio che si cerca in seguito di dimostrare.

Infatti, poichè in nessuna deduzione la Ths può essere maggiore dell'Hp (la vecchia logica esprimeva questo canone con la nota legge: « latius hos quam praemissae conclusio non vult »), segue che ponendo $a \supset aa$ noi sappiamo già che aa non può essere maggiore di a. Inoltre, poichè la deduzione $a \supset aa$ (« da a si deduce a ed a ») implica già ad evidenza come un caso particolare che « da a si deduce a », segue che aa non può essere minore di a. Ciò posto, segue di necessità che ponendo $a \supset aa$ resta già posto $a = aa$.

Questo significa, in altri termini, che anche qui la Pp $a \supset aa$ non è che la stessa proposizione tautologica mascherata.

Concludendo, si può affermare che le ordinarie dimostrazioni della proprietà tautologica sono, in sostanza, un puro complesso di convenzioni descrittive e può ritenersi che qualunque altra dimostrazione escogitabile sia, in ultima analisi, riducibile a tale significato.

[1] C. Burali-Forti, *Logica matematica* (Milano, Hoepli, 1894, p. 11; Pp2. $a \supset aa$; pag. 15 P2. $aa \supset a$; pag. 45 P44. $a = aa$ [Pp2. P2 : $\supset$: P44].

II.

Ed ora passiamo al secondo punto. Ho detto che alcuni autori accettano il principio tautologico senza dimostrazione, cioè come un postulato. Per chiarezza di critica gioverà ancora distinguere questi autori in due gruppi.

Taluni si appoggiano evidentemente sopra una giustificazione che trascende la natura e i limiti della logica pura. È questo il caso tipico di S. Boezio il quale fondandosi su questo criterio « velut si dicam sol sol sol, non tres sol effecerim sed uno toties praedicaverim » (1) dà un tuffo nella teologia e nell'ontologia proponendosi di corroborare l'ardua tesi della Trinità, ed è pure il caso di tutti i sostenitori della logica a fondamento ontologico. È chiaro che il loro ragionamento si riduce a questo. L'oggetto esteriore non si moltiplica anche se noi lo pensiamo molte volte di seguito; dunque neanche si moltiplica il concetto, vale a dire ciò che corrisponde nella nostra mente ad un oggetto considerato come un reale ontologico esterno. Ma chi non vede che qui si confonde il campo logico col campo ontologico, perchè si pretende che ciò che vale ontologicamente valga anche logicamente? Questo principio può interessare solo dal punto di vista della celebre questione capitale della Scolastica che chiede: se ai concetti (generici) corrisponda un reale ontologico e di qual natura esso sia, e come si comporti cogli individui (2). Dunque il principio tautologico non è posto che per ragioni extralogiche, chiamando — per comodità — extralogico tutto ciò che non è logico (alogico, illogico, metalogico, ontologico, gnoseologico, psicologico, glottologico, ecc.).

Altri, credendo di potersi valere dell'ampia libertà conceduta alla scelta delle Pp, pongono esplicitamente il principio tautologico come un postulato, senza aggiungere alcuna giustificazione al riguardo.

Ora è della massima importanza il ricordare che solo fino ad un certo punto si può dire che la scelta delle Pp è arbitraria. Infatti da un sistema ipotetico deduttivo qualunque si deve sempre pretendere che le sue Pp siano non contraddittorie e indipendenti e conducano a risultati esclusivamente formali e necessarj.

Ma queste condizioni bastano a radiare il principio tautologico da qualsivoglia calcolo logico che non voglia sacrificare il principio di identità ($a = a$). Infatti, ponendo $aa = a$ si affermano relativamente identiche due quantità logiche fra cui passa un'innegabile diversità di contenuto e di estensione, che si può provare nel modo seguente.

Noi ammettiamo come condizione indispensabile alla purezza del calcolo logico che l'unico vero e proprio oggetto logico è il concetto il quale, per essere, non ha bisogno di esistere, perchè non ha bisogno d'altro che d'essere pensato. Da ciò risulta che,

(1) Boetius, *De Trinitate* etc., § 3. Cfr. Peano, F2 N1 . P42.

(2) Porfirio, *Isag.* Cap. 1. *αὐτίκα περὶ γενῶν τε καὶ εἰδῶν, τὸ μὲν εἴτε ὑφεστῆκεν εἴτε ἐν μόναις ψιλαῖς ἐπινοίαις κεῖται, εἴτε ὑφεστεκότα σώματά ἐστιν, ἢ ἀσώματα, καὶ χωριστὰ ἢ ἐν τοῖς αἰσθητοῖς, καὶ περὶ ταῦτα ὑφεστῶτα, παραιτήσομαι λέγειν, βαθυτάτης οὔσης τῆς τοιαύτης πραγματείας καὶ ἄλλης μείζονος δεομένης ἐξετάσεως.*

ponendo *aa*, sebbene il concetto del primo *a* sia identico al concetto del secondo *a*, tuttavia gli oggetti logici, cioè i concetti di cui si tratta, sono innegabilmente due, e quindi il concetto della loro affermazione simultanea è irreducibile al concetto semplice di *a* se non vogliamo smarrire i due concetti dell'unità e della moltiplicità che sono fondamentali a qualunque calcolo. Se questa distinzione fra *a* e *aa* non può esser fatta dalla sensibilità e nella realtà oggettiva esteriore, prima di tutto non è richiesta dalla logica pura, in secondo luogo è sempre fatta dalla e nella ragione, alla quale, durante l'affermazione simultanea, son presenti due oggetti logici e non uno, perchè tutte le volte che noi pensiamo un concetto, il concetto è (¹).

Ogni concetto è un pensato e ogni pensato concettuale tante volte è quante volte si pensa, indipendentemente dal fatto che ad esso corrisponda o no verun oggetto reale esistente fuori del pensiero. Del pari tutte le operazioni che si possono compiere in qualsivoglia calcolo non sono altro che rapporti ideali, vale a dire ancora certi pensati fra certi altri pensati ai quali dagli spiriti coltivati nelle scienze astratte non si deve imporre limite alcuno. L'aver sempre presente una sola identità reale o un *flatus vocis* tutte le volte che noi evochiamo il concetto in diversi nessi moltiplicativi, non costituisce una sola identità logica dei molteplici concetti corrispondenti che vengono predicati nello stesso tempo, perchè solo questi predicati astratti sono i veri e proprj oggetti logici, dei quali si deve occupare la logica pura. Dunque fra *a* ed *aa* passa una diversità concettuale ed operativa assoluta e pensare come vero l'opposto di questo pensiero sarebbe un negare assurdamente la validità universale del principio di identità a cui si connettono naturalmente tutte le operazioni possibili d'ogni calcolo.

Ciò è tanto vero che, indipendentemente dalla possibilità operativa di cui farò cenno fra poco, l'adozione del principio non tautologico implica una *semplice estensione* delle condizioni in cui le operazioni del calcolo possono compiersi attualmente, stando al carattere esclusivamente formale degli enti e delle relazioni possibili, in armonia col principio d'identità.

Dunque il principio tautologico non resta giustificato logicamente in nessuna maniera, nè come derivato nè come primitivo.

III.

Vediamo ora di renderci conto di alcune applicazioni suggerite dalla presente ricerca. Anzitutto un doppio compito si impone:

1° sgombrare il terreno della logica deduttiva dalle proprietà extralogiche che riescono a paralizzarla;

2° sviluppare il calcolo logico in ordine alla possibilità delle nuove operazioni.

(¹) G. Peano, *Super theorema de Cantor-Bernstein.* Estr. dal t. XXI (1906) dei Rendiconti del Circolo Matematico di Palermo, p. 6: « Nos cogita numero, ergo numero es ». L'importanza logica e filosofica di questo principio necessario a stabilire la purezza d'ogni calcolo e sufficiente a troncare ogni inutile disquisizione metafisica è enorme, ma non sentita a bastanza da tutti i cultori delle scienze pure.

Si capisce che il primo compito porta ad uno studio abbastanza facile.

Invece il secondo condurrà necessariamente ad un vasto campo di applicazioni intorno alle quali non sembra facile portare un apprezzamento adeguato finchè non saremo in grado di raccoglierne e di ordinarne i risultati.

Le applicazioni più elementari sembrano le seguenti:

a) in primo luogo restano modificate le definizioni del prodotto e della somma logica coll'adozione della coppia di equazioni

$$aa \neq a \quad , \quad a + a \neq a$$

esprimenti in generale proprietà analoghe a quelle della moltiplicazione e dell'addizione matematica;

b) in secondo luogo, al posto della legge di assorbimento pel prodotto si sostituisce la proprietà distributiva anche nella forma

$$a(a + b) = a^2 + ab;$$

c) in terzo luogo si rende possibile l'introduzione delle potenze e dei multipli nel calcolo logico, col doppio vantaggio di trattare in maniera più rigorosa e corretta i problemi logici già risolti per altra via, e di aprire nuovi e più vasti campi di ricerche all'analisi logica.

Ma non posso ora proseguire il racconto degli speciali acquisti conseguibili in tale ordine di idee, riservandomi di svilupparli in altro lavoro. Noterò solo che per tal modo vengono distrutte le più forti ragioni tecniche contrarie alla tesi dell'identità fondamentale dei due calcoli, perchè calcolo logico e calcolo matematico si presentano ormai come due insiemi che possiedono le medesime proprietà fondamentali; quindi, sulle traccie del Russell (¹), del Huntington (²) e del Couturat (³), è ovvio identificarli puramente e semplicemente dal punto di vista formale (⁴).

(¹) B. Russell, *The Principles of Mathematics* (t. I, Cambridge, University Press, 1903); *Sur la Logique des relations, avec des applications à la théorie des séries* (ap. Revue de Mathém. di G. Peano, t. VII, pp. 115-147. Turin, 1902). Le magistrali ricerche del Russell, compiute dal nuovo punto di vista della Logica delle relazioni e coll'impiego della Logica matematica del Peano, costituiscono una ricostruzione logica di tutta la matematica pura. Molto opportunamente il Couturat nel suo prezioso resoconto, citato qui sotto nella nota (³) ne ha fatto rilevare l'importanza grandissima. Si può ripetere con lui che, grazie alle ricerche del Russell il collegamento della teoria degli insiemi, scoperta da G. Cantor e da altri matematici, al calcolo logico, è ormai un fatto compiuto.

(²) Huntington, *Note on the definitions of abstract groups and fields by sets of independent postulates* (ap. Transact. of t. American Mathem. Society, t. VI, pp. 181-193, 1905). Quest'opera contiene la dimostrazione del carattere logico della teoria dei gruppi di Sophus Lie, studiata dal punto di vista della Logica delle relazioni.

(³) L. Couturat, in *Les principes des Mathématiques* (Paris, F. Alcan, 1905) tratta profondamente e con grande chiarezza i rapporti fra la Logica e la Matematica; tutta l'opera è destinata a giustificare la tesi dell'identità fondamentale della Logica e della Matematica.

(⁴) Queste considerazioni ci lasciano intravedere l'utilità derivabile dall'introduzione della veduta del Pluecker nell'apprezzamento teorico della Logica e della Matematica. Già l'Enriques

***

Le cose più importanti che ho esposto in questa Comunicazione si riducono in sostanza alla dimostrazione della natura extralogica delle leggi di tautologia e di assorbimento nel calcolo logico. Ciò significa che una vera e propria dimostrazione di queste leggi finora non la possediamo e non la possederemo tanto presto; il che però non toglie il pregio dei risultati conseguiti dalla Logica matematica; soltanto ci obbliga a riconoscere che è un puro arbitrio descrittivo affermare che l'addizione e la moltiplicazione logica godano realmente delle proprietà speciali espresse dalle leggi surriferite, a differenza di quanto avviene in Matematica. Abbiamo veduto come da tale fatto risulti possibile l'introduzione nella Logica matematica di un gruppo di nuove nozioni e di nuove operazioni, universalmente respinto da LEIBNIZ ai giorni nostri, il cui retto uso è peraltro intimamente collegato con quello delle nozioni e delle operazioni fondamentali di tutti i calcoli che vanno gradatamente unificandosi sotto il cielo comune della deduzione nel senso più esteso della parola.

E ciò basti a porre in luce il molto che resta ancora da fare per tale via.

nei suoi *Problemi della Scienza* (Bologna, Zanichelli, 1906, p. 165) ha rilevato l'interesse logico e matematico di cotesta veduta che porge un principio di trasformazione delle teorie basato appunto sul loro valore formale. Allo stesso risultato si arriva utilizzando la teoria del PETROVITCH [*La mécanique des Phénomènes fondée sur les analogies* (Paris, Gauthier-Villars, Ed. 1906)] il quale presenta sotto una forma insieme abbastanza semplice e abbastanza generale il fecondo concetto della rappresentazione schematica d'un gruppo d'analogia, e colla proposta del fenomeno tipico astratto eleva lo studio dei sistemi particolari naturali e razionali alla pura ricerca delle relazioni logico-matematiche generali tra le cause e gli effetti, i principj e le conseguenze. Tutte queste teorie sono dominate dallo spirito comune della teoria dei modelli e costituiscono oramai una nuova branca della filosofia della natura e della scienza. In *Teoria della Scienza: Logica, Matematica e Fisica* (Torino, Bocca, 1903); *Logica formale dedotta dalla considerazione di modelli meccanici* (Torino, Bocca, 1906); *Del nuovo spirito della Scienza e della Filosofia* (Torino, Bocca, 1907), ho tentato di rendere famigliari in Italia l'importanza logica e filosofica e le applicazioni della moderna teoria dei modelli dovuta all'alta mente di ENRICO RODOLFO HERTZ.

GINO LORIA

LE TRADIZIONI MATEMATICHE DELL'ITALIA

O Italiani! - non obliate giammai, che il primo passo a produrre uomini grandi sta nello onorare i già spenti.

G. Mazzini.

I.

Signori,

Solevano i nostri proavi ne' giorni di maggiore letizia, in tutte le ricorrenze per qualche ragione memorabili, negli anniversari di date gloriose radunarsi a ricordare i nomi ed i fatti più famosi della loro storia, non mossi da un sentimento di « misero orgoglio di un tempo che fu », ma col nobile scopo di tributare una giusta riconoscenza a chi aveva illustrata la patria. In tali circostanze gli elmi e le corazze che già protessero gli eroi più illustri, le lancie e le spade che essi maneggiarono da valorosi, tutti i preziosi cimeli religiosamente conservati, solevano venir tolti dai reliquari ed esposti alla venerazione universale, con la ferma fede che lo spettacolo del culto generale tributato a gloriosi defunti avesse il magico potere di far risorgere l'antica virtù in giovani petti.

A tale costumanza, inspirata da sensi elevati di filiale gratitudine, sia concesso a me d'uniformarmi in questo giorno che l'Italia segna « albo lapillo », in cui per la prima volta Roma accoglie e festeggia i matematici di tutto il mondo qui convenuti per dare una novella conferma dell'essere la scienza UNA come la verità. E, nel mentre porgo il più cordiale « benvenuto » a tutti coloro che ebbero il volere ed il potere di accettare il nostro invito, mentre volgo un affettuoso pensiero al Nestore degli storici della matematica (¹), che non osò affrontare i disagi di un lungo viaggio, mentre con memore cuore penso ad un altro nostro illustre compagno di lavoro (²), cui il gelido tocco dell'ala della morte vietò di venir qui ad aiutarci

(¹) M. Cantor.
(²) P. Tannery.

col suo autorevole consiglio; chiedo siamo permesso di presentare alla Sezione un primo saggio degli studi da me istituiti da molto tempo nell'intento di proseguire l'opera magistrale di GUGLIELMO LIBRI, evocando il ricordo delle persone e delle opere grazie a cui la mia patria, malgrado le sue condizioni politiche incessantemente variabili, ma sempre tristissime, riuscì a serbar sempre accesa e risplendente la face della ricerca matematica.

II.

Non crediate però, Signori, che io, lasciandomi trascinare dall'entusiasmo pel mio tema o da vanagloria nazionale, faccia risalire le origini della matematica italiana a PITAGORA, ad ARCHITA, ad ARCHIMEDE; non lo farò — malgrado l'esempio datomi da un illustre storico della nostra letteratura (1) — perchè l'Italia meridionale e la Sicilia, non solo furono sedi di fiorenti colonie elleniche, ma erano abitate da popolazioni la cui intima affinità con i Greci è, a tacer d'altro, dimostrata dalla lingua che esse parlavano, la quale si accosta assai più al sacro idioma dell'Ellade che ai dialetti usati nel resto d'Italia.

D'altronde chi ignora la nessuna parentela intellettuale fra il popolo greco e quello di cui l'itala gente è la continuatrice diretta? Se in filosofia la Grecia divenne ad un tempo suddita e maestra di Roma, in matematica dominatori e schiavi rimasero totalmente estranei gli uni agli altri; sicchè i Romani, paghi di avere al loro servizio agrimensori capaci di misurare le terre conquistate ed architetti in grado di eternare nel marmo la gloria delle loro armi, superbi di aver saputo compiere la riforma del calendario, limitavansi a dichiarare per bocca di Cassiodoro « tolle saeculo computum; et omnia ignorantia caeca complecitur » (2), ma riguardavano come sterili fantasticherie le opere immortali dei grandi geometri della Grecia. Lungi dall'adoperarsi a prolungare od almeno spianare le vie aperte da ARCHIMEDE ed APOLLONIO, sembra che essi siansi proposti il non nobile còmpito di stendere il velo dell'oblio su quanto questi avevano prodotto, elevando un argine granitico contro il quale l'onda fresca e limpida dell'antico sapere matematico dovette fatalmente frangersi; e gli è soltanto quando, sotto la pressione e gli urti ripetuti dei barbari, quell'argine malaugurato crollò, che gli *Elementi* di EUCLIDE cessarono di essere, come erano stati durante la dominazione romana, il libro dei sette suggelli.

Ecco perchè noi Italiani andiamo bensì superbi di proclamarci discepoli di PITAGORA ed ARCHIMEDE, ma non ci sentiamo di accampare diritti ad esserne considerati gli eredi legittimi, gli unici continuatori, riconoscendo onestamente che come tali possono, al pari di noi, riguardarsi tutti i popoli presso cui la Geometria è tenuta nel debito onore.

(1) Alludesi qui al TIRABOSCHI.
(2) *De artibus ac discipl. lib. litt.* (ed. Garetii, p. 578).

III.

Escluso che la grande famiglia dei matematici italiani abbia avute le proprie origini a Crotone, a Taranto, a Siracusa o qui in Roma, ne consegue la necessità di farla cominciare in quel periodo di seconda giovinezza dell'umanità, in cui, al diradarsi della caligine medioevale, tramontava per sempre l'impero della forza e dell'ignoranza. Del resto sette secoli di storia sempre onorevole e spesso gloriosa non son forse sufficienti a rendere illustre una famiglia, anche se come capo-stipite di essa sta, non un guerriero onusto di allori conquistati alle Crociate, ma un modesto mercante, il quale, essendosi convinto nel corso de' suoi viaggi in Oriente, che « l'aritmetica pitagorica a confronto dell' Indiana è un delirio », giudicò suo dovere di recare in patria, non solo stoffe variopinte ed inebbrianti profumi, ma una cosa ben più preziosa, l'arte del conteggio?...

Col *Liber Abaci*, pubblicato nel 1202 da LEONARDO FIBONACCI PISANO, comincia, o Signori, la letteratura matematica italiana. Esso riuscì a diffondere in tutta Europa, non soltanto l'Aritmetica decimale, ma anche i fondamenti dell'Algebra; sicchè la mia patria — come, verso il 1000, per merito di GUIDO d'Arezzo aveva cominciato a divenir maestra nell' arte del canto; come con PLATONE Tiburtino traduttor d'*Albategno*, aveva additato all'Europa quale doviziosa fonte di sapere fossero le opere arabe; come con GHERARDO CREMONESE, traduttore dell'*Almagesto*, aveva cominciato a richiamare l'attenzione degli studiosi sulla scienza greca — con LEONARDO PISANO somministrava un ausilio di inesauribile potenza tanto alla ricerca matematica quanto alle transazioni commerciali.

Nè a ciò si limitano le benemerenze di LEONARDO PISANO; chè con la sua *Practica geometriae* egli ha dato l'esempio di una ripresa della ricerca geometrica e con il suo *Liber quadratorum* « scoprì » (per dirla con le parole immaginose di un Orientale [1] « nuovi porti e terre nuove nel pelago immenso diofanteo ». Venute, grazie alla illuminata munificenza di BALDASSARE BONCOMPAGNI, le opere del FIBONACCI in dominio di tutti, i moderni vi ravvisarono i germi della teoria delle frazioni continue ascendenti, misurarono i pregi della serie numerica che oggi porta appunto il nome dell'illustre PISANO e vi trovarono occasione e stimolo ad importanti investigazioni di aritmetica superiore [2].

Chi ha presente la rapidità con cui ai dì nostri tutte le idee vengono conosciute, accolte, assimilate e svolte, sarà indotto a supporre che LEONARDO sia stato capo di una schiera d'investigatori intenti ad applicare e diffondere le nuove idee di cui egli erasi fatto messaggiero. Ma chi considera le condizioni politiche ed intellettuali dell'epoca di LEONARDO, non si stupirà se non meno di tre secoli abbiano dovuto tra-

(1) ABULFARAGIO, citato da G. B. GUGLIELMINI nel suo *Elogio di Lenardo Pisano*.

(2) Cfr. le *Recherches sur plusieurs ouvrages de Léonard de Pise et sur diverses questions d'arithmétique supérieure*, pubblicate da E. LUCAS nel t. X (1877) del Bullettino di bibliogr. e storia ecc.

scorrere prima che l'Italia vedesse nascere chi fosse degno di raccoglierne e sapientemente amministrare la pingue eredità; tre secoli — il Trecento, il Quattrocento, il Cinquecento — che occupano un posto cospicuo nella storia generale della cultura, ma in cui l'umanità fu assorbita da cure ben diverse dalla ricerca matematica.

IV.

Ed invero, Signori, la gloriosa epoca dei Comuni fu un periodo in cui l'arte occupò tutte le menti e infiammò tutti i cuori; appunto allora DANTE, PETRARCA e BOCCACCIO elevarono il volgare eloquio alla dignità di lingua, facendogli raggiungere una purezza ed una perfezione che i posteri cercarono indarno di accrescere. D'altra parte, gli è nella seconda metà del Trecento che GIOTTO iniziava la fulgida serie di pittori ed architetti a cui l'Italia è debitrice del suo incontrastabile primato in quelle che SETTEMBRINI chiamava « arti mute », serie che doveva poco dopo annoverare il BRUNELLESCHI, MICHELANGELO e RAFFAELLO, LEON BATTISTA ALBERTI e LEONARDO DA VINCI ognuno dei quali, non solo vergò sulla tela o nel marmo una nuova strofe dell'eterno inno ispirato all'umanità dalla contemplazione del Bello, ma collaborò alla redazione delle leggi razionali della prospettiva, per apprendere le quali ABERTO DURERO intraprese uno dei suoi viaggi in Italia.

A tale periodo d'intensa produzione artistica originale segue un non breve lasso di tempo in cui l'Italia, travagliata da guerre sanguinose e da discordie intestine, quasi sentisse orrore e ribrezzo pel mondo presente, si volse allo studio del passato. « Lo scoprimento di un libro » (osserva uno storico reputatissimo) [1] « per poco non si rimirò come la conquista di un regno. I viaggi a tal fine intrapresi, le liti e le inimicizie nate per occasione de' codici, ci fan vedere fin dove possa giugnere l'amor della gloria, e un'emulazione ch'è lodevole, finchè si contiene entro giusti confini e non passa a divenir fanatismo... Quasi tutti gli autori classici ritrovati furono in Italia, o, se altrove, dagl'Italiani; quasi tutti furono col confronto di varj codici dagli Italiani emendati come allor poteasi meglio; quasi tutti furono per la prima volta pubblicati in Italia; e in Italia, prima che altrove, si videro quelle copiose e splendide biblioteche che sono anche al presente oggetto di meraviglia a chi le rimira ».

A questo movimento generale degli spiriti, che nella storia va notoriamente sotto il nome di Umanesimo, non rimasero spettatori indifferenti coloro che s'interessavano alle scienze esatte. A convincersene basta ricordare le traduzioni di antichi matematici greci compiute presso di noi nel Cinquecento: EUCLIDE edito dallo ZAMBERTI, PROCLO da FRANCESCO BAROZZI, ERONE da BERNARDINO BALDI. Ma coloro che riuscirono sopra tutti eccellenti in siffatti lavori, sono FRANCESCO MAUROLICO e FEDERICO COMMANDINO, i quali, col riporre in circolazione idee e metodi ingiustamente dimenticati, col facilitarne l'intelligenza mediante geniali commenti e nuove applicazioni, fecero scorrere nuovi torrenti di sangue caldo per le membra intorpidite della Geometria.

(1) TIRABOSCHI, *Storia della letteratura italiana* (t. VI, Venezia, 1795, p. 108).

A tali brillanti prove di ben intesa attività intellettuale vanno aggiunte quelle somministrate dal moltiplicarsi e fiorire delle nostre Università, la cui rinomanza fu tale che, dopo il Rinascimento, l'Italia divenne l'agognata mèta dei pellegrinaggi delle personalità più cospicue. Già fin da prima che nascesse LEONARDO FIBONACCI, IRNERIO aveva gettato basi indistruttibili alla fama dell'Archiginnasio bolognese e le autorità successivamente preposte a quel grande istituto si adoperarono e riuscirono a continuarne ininterrottamente le tradizioni gloriose; e quale altra scuola può competere con una che vide fra i propri discepoli NICOLÒ COPERNICO, che, appunto mentre eıa scolaro a Bologna, con la amica e fedele scorta di DOMENICO MARIA NOVARA, iniziò quegli studi sul corso degli astri che dovevano determinare la rovina del sistema tolemaico [1] e dall'insegnamento del celebre ellenista ANTONIO URCEO trasse quella famigliarità col greco che gli permise di penetrare nell'intimo del concetto che gli antichi si erano formati della struttura del cosmo?...

Con Bologna dividono la gloria di avere annoverato fra i propri alunni il padre della moderna astronomia gli « Studi » di Ferrara e Padova; quello destinato a condurre una vita stentata e tribolata fra due vicini ultrapotenti, questo [2] che, dopo avere contato fra i propri maestri personalità eminenti quali PIETRO D'ABANO, BIAGIO PELACANI e PROSDOCIMO DE' BELDOMANDI, accolse nel collegio dei proprî insegnanti stranieri illustri quali GIORGIO PURBACH ed il Regiomontano (GIOVANNI MÜLLER); coll'ammetterveli i Riformatori di quel celebre studio precorsero i loro tempi, giacchè affermarono, sotto la forma più solenne, come la scienza non conosca confini politici o distinzioni di nazionalita!.

V.

Al pari di certi corsi d'acqua che, ad un tratto, diffondendosi in un vasto terreno paludoso, sembrano, a chi li contempla da lungi, aver perduto per sempre aspetto e dignità di fiume, mentre poi, più innanzi, radunate le acque disperse riprendono il loro corso vivace e giocondo; così delle dottrine aritmetiche e geometriche di cui LEONARDO PISANO si fece e fu apostolo, per circa tre secoli si perdono traccie sicure. La storia ha bensì scritti nelle sue pagine i nomi di PAOLO DAGOMARI [3] (la cui singolare perizia nell'arte del calcolo, anche se non fosse stata eternata dal Boccaccio, risulterebbe dal sopranome « dell'abaco » conferitogli dai contemporanei) di BIAGIO DA PARMA, di RAFFAELE CANACCI e di altri minori; ma l'esatta determinazione dell'opera da essi compiuta, nonchè l'eventuale scoperta di altri che ebber sino ad oggi la sorte nemica, è un problema tuttora insoluto a cui gli studiosi dovrebbero

(1) Cfr. alcune significantissime parole del RETICO riferite dal TIRABOSCHI, op. cit., T. VI, p. 367.

(2) A. FAVARO, *Le matematiche nello studio di Padova dal principio del secolo XI alla fine del XVI* (Nuovi Saggi dell'Accademia di Padova t. IX, Parte I, 1880, pp. 1-91); *Galileo Galilei e lo studio di Padova* (t. I, Firenze, 1883, Cap. IV); *Die Hochschule Padua zur Zeit des Coppernicus* (Thorn, 1881); Bullettino-Boncompagni, T. XI, 1878, p. 319, e T. XII, 1878, p. 1.

(3) Cfr. Bullettino-Boncompagni t. XVI, p. 679.

affrettarsi a dedicare le loro fatiche. La storia ricorda invece come, dopo la metà del secolo XV, il *Liber abaci* minacciando di venir sepolto in un deplorevole oblio, esso sia stato surrogato da un'altra opera egregia, dovuta ad un monaco che scrisse circa nel momento in cui la scoperta d'America inaugurava una nuova èra della storia universale. La *Summa* di Fra LUCA PACIUOLO — forse libro di testo per le lezioni di chi, con eleganza moderna, direbbesi fosse titolare d'una cattedra ambulante di matematica — e le altre opere dello stesso matematico, scritte in lingua volgare, valsero a democratizzare una scienza che fino allora era rimasta privilegio, quasi monopolio di pochi eletti.

Con la pubblicazione della *Summa* (e forse per effetto di essa) l'Algebra italiana inizia il suo splendido cammino ascendente e lo prosegue poi con tale gloria e sì grande velocità da vincere il « record » su tutte le altre nazioni, onde LEIBNIZ non esitò a dichiarare « essere l'algebra quasi totalmente parto degli Italiani ». E con pieno fondamento lo disse; chè gli è nella prima metà del secolo XVI che, per opera di SCIPIONE FERRO, NICOLÒ TARTAGLIA, GEROLAMO CARDANO e LUDOVICO FERRARI, con la risoluzione delle equazioni cubiche e biquadratiche, la teoria delle equazioni letterali toccava l'ultima Tule a cui, per quanto concerne le formole di risoluzione, può giungere senza invadere il campo trascendente. Le pubbliche disfide, che ebbero appunto per tema preferito questioni risolubili mediante questioni del terzo grado o del quarto; le vive ed ostinate dispute, che esse provocarono fra i geometri del tempo, le clamorose avventure romanzesche di cui questi furono protagonisti, attrassero l'attenzione del gran pubblico sopra le scienze esatte, sicchè si può dire esser queta un'epoca (l'unica forse che ricordi la storia!) in cui l'Algebra sia stata la scienza di moda.

Con RAFFAELE BOMBELLI e PIETRO ANTONIO CATALDI, il secondo dei quali giustamente famoso per la prima scoperta delle ordinarie frazioni continue, l'Algebra italiana manda ancora due lampi di fulgida luce e poi, per più di un secolo, spossata ed esausta, con un sonno riparatore si appresta a nuove battaglie, a nuove vittorie.

Ma, o Signori, appunto nel corso di questo fecondo secolo XVI, alcuni matematici italiani, con alla testa GIAMBATTISTA BENEDETTI e FEDERICO COMMANDINO, stringevano con gli artisti una sorta di società in accomandita per dare un assetto definitivo alla prospettiva, che un nostro esimio pittore, PIER DELLA FRANCESCA aveva prima tentato di erigere sopra basi razionali; l'immortale scoperta del « punto di concorso » fatta da GUIDOBALDO DEL MONTE sullo scorcio del secolo XVI, chiude ben degnamente il primo periodo della storia della prospettiva ed inaugura quello che non a torto venne considerato per il periodo aureo di siffatta disciplina; e i sei libri che ad essa dedicò il grande matematico pesarese, costituiscono una delle gemme più preziose della nostra letteratura scientifica e formarono un coronamento degno del secolo di TARTAGLIA e CARDANO [1].

[1] Credo opportuno aggiungere qui come in quest'epoca abbia vissuto anche l'eruditissimo BERNARDINO BALDI, autore d'un grande numero di buone biografie di matematici (alcune delle quali vennero ai dì nostri pubblicate dal BONCOMPAGNI nel suo Bullettino) e di una *Cronica dei matematici*, che viene tuttora consultata con profitto e citata con onore.

VI.

Nel secolo successivo, come notò un nostro sommo letterato (¹), la scienza fu il grande affare dell'Italia. Addì 17 agosto 1603 vennero gettate le basi dell'Accademia dei Lincei e meno di cinquant'anni dopo vide la luce l'Accademia del Cimento, l'una e l'altra sostanzialmente diverse da quelle che allor fiorivano in ogni angolo d'Italia, giacchè mentre queste avevano per unico scopo di promuovere la poesia, quelle posero come loro programma le investigazioni di matematica e di fisica (²). In quel secolo il bastone di maresciallo dei cultori delle scienze esatte venne per ispontaneo universale consenso conferito a GALILEO GALILEI, il quale, ispirandosi ai liberi sensi che prepararono la tortura ed il rogo a GIORDANO BRUNO, TOMMASO CAMPANELLA e GIULIO CESARE VANINI, spiegò il vessillo della rivolta contro l'autocratica dominazione di Aristotile. Grazie a lui la Meccanica, nelle varie sue diramazioni, trovò la via che doveva guidarla a glorioso porto e l'Astronomia, arricchita di fatti nuovi dianzi insospettati, potè aspirare alla promozione da semplice scienza sperimentale a disciplina fisico-matematica, che KEPLERO e NEWTON dovevano poco dopo accordarle.

È inutile, o Signori, che io qui mi dilunghi a descrivere le migliorie di sostanza, d'indirizzo, di forma di cui tutte le scienze positive gioirono per opera del metodo sperimentale consigliato da GALILEO con la grazia suaditrice della parola e con la forza irresistibile dell'esempio; nè, data l'immensa diffusione delle sue opere, fa mestieri che io faccia risaltare lo splendore del suo sistema di esposizione; basti dire che, per effetto di esse, l'Italia acquistò, quello che dianzi le mancava, uno stile scientifico, elegante e preciso ad un tempo. Ciò che va eziandio esplicitamente ricordato è la straordinaria influenza che il grande fiorentino esercitò con la voce e con gli scritti, la quale fu tale che durante il secolo XVII tutto il movimento scientifico italiano fu governato da uomini di alto intelletto che si proclamavano ed erano discepoli di GALILEO.

Fra questi emergono: BONAVENTURA CAVALIERI, EVANGELISTA TORRICELLI e GIOVANNI ALFONSO BORELLI.

Il primo conseguì i pinnacoli della fama per avere inventato quel « metodo degli indivisibili » che gli guadagnò da GALILEO il nome di « secondo Archimede » (³) e che anche oggi viene fruttuosamente invocato ogniqualvolta si vogliano risolvere elementarmente questioni relative a quadrature di aree piane e cubature di solidi non limitati da superficie non tutte piane; che la rinomanza del CAVALIERI non abbia tardato a varcare i confini d'Italia, è indiscutibilmente dimostrato dall'esser egli stato scelto come arbitro in una controversia scientifica insorta tra il LONGO-

(¹) G. CARDUCCI, *Opere*, T. XVI, p. 82.

(²) È noto che il nome di Accademia venne in Italia usato per la prima volta quando, per volere di Cosimo de' Medici, Marsiglio Ficino fondò una società intesa a rinnovare la filosofia di Platone.

(³) V. una lettera scritta da GALILEO a FULGENZIO MICANZIO in data: Arcetri, 26 luglio 1636.

MONTANO ed il PELL ([1]). Il secondo, sommo tanto quale fisico quanto come matematico, fu a ragione proclamato dal MERSENNE « primus observator vacui » ([2]) e precedette il ROBERVAL nella scoperta di quell'utilissimo « metodo delle tangenti » che di consueto viene attribuito a quest'ultimo ([3]); la sua fama, già grande in vita, si accrebbe per la postuma pubblicazione di alcune sue ricerche e conseguirà indubbiamente le proporzioni che merita con l'edizione delle sue opere complete che Faenza deliberò per commemorare degnamente il prossimo quarto centenario della nascita del più illustre de' suoi figli. Il terzo, infine, oltrechè essere stato geometra egregio ed erudito coscienzioso, ispirandosi forse alle osservazioni fatte da LEONARDO DA VINCI sul volo degli uccelli, affrontò l'arduo ma bellissimo problema di stabilire le leggi della meccanica del corpo umano; e con tal successo ne venne a capo, che la teoria da lui proposta fu subito giudicata così utile ai medici che nell'Università di Montpellier venne fondata una cattedra da cui essa doveva venir insegnata ([4]); nè crediate, o Signori, che la teoria borelliana debba collocarsi fra le inutili anticaglie, chè appunto da essa prese le mosse il prof. FISCHER, il quale, come è noto, ai dì nostri si dedicò con tanto impegno e tanta genialità al medesimo soggetto ([5]).

E come potrei, parlando della scuola galileiana, non consacrare una parola di lode a VINCENZO VIVIANI, sommo nell'arte, omai tramontata per sempre, di divinare le antiche opere perdute, la cui mondiale rinomanza valse a lui in vita una delle otto pensioni accordate a dotti stranieri da Luigi XIV e dopo morte un bellissimo elogio da parte di Fontenelle? ([6]).

I metodi d'investigazione geometrica proposti ed applicati da CAVALIERI e TORRICELLI, alla costituzione dei quali sembra non sia rimasto estraneo lo stesso GALILEO ([7]), vennero subito magistralmente svolti da tre uomini che gli stranieri andarono a gara di onorare e che realmente basterebbero da soli alla gloria di un secolo; sono: MICHELANGELO RICCI, STEFANO DEGLI ANGELI, GUIDO GRANDI. Se la fama di cui godettero presso i loro contemporanei di tutto il mondo civile è di gran lunga superiore a quella che seppero conservare fra i posteri gli è che, appunto nel periodo di loro attività scientifica, venivano a maturità quei fecondi procedimenti d'indagine con cui LEIBNIZ e NEWTON provocarono una « instauratio ab imis fundamentis » di tutta la scienza matematica e prepararono l'avvento dell'analisi moderna. Il mirabile formalismo leibniziano fece porre il metodo degli indivisibili nel museo degli strumenti fuor di moda, onde le opere in cui questo trovasi applicato

([1]) JACOLI, *Notizia sconosciuta relativa a B. Cavalieri*, nel T. II (1868) del Bullettino Boncompagni.

([2]) Veggansi a questo proposito i significantissimi articoli di F. MATHIEU sopra *Pascal et l'expérience de Pui-de-Dôme*, nei fascicoli 1° e 15 aprile e 1° maggio 1906 della Revue de Paris.

([3]) JACOLI, *E. Torricelli ed il metodo delle tangenti detto Metodo di Roberval*, nel T. VII (1874) del Bullettino Boncompagni, p. 256 e seg.

([4]) TIRABOSCHI, op. cit., T. VIII (Venezia 1796), p. 198.

([5]) Cfr. il T. IV dell'*Encyklopädie der math. Wissenschaften*.

([6]) *Eloges des académiciens* (La Haye, MDCCXL), T. I, pp. 29-46.

([7]) G. B. C. DE' NELLI, *Vita e commercio letterario di Galileo Galilei* (Losanna 1792, pp. 491-493).

furono ben presto considerate come scritture che avevano fatto il loro tempo; ma io sono convinto che, quando sorgerà l'alba invocata del giorno in cui qualche benemerito investigatore si disporrà a dare alla geometria infinitesimale sintetica quella forma rigorosa e soddisfacente che la farà collocare fra i più sicuri strumenti geometrici, dopo di avere meditato sopra le opere di ARCHIMEDE e CAVALIERI, chiederà, non indarno, ispirazione ed ammaestramento agli scritti, oggi dimenticati, del RICCI del DE ANGELI, del GRANDI (¹).

VII.

È un fatto degno di nota (e di cui non sarebbe difficile di indicare una spiegazione) che l'Italia, mentre rimase spettatrice pressochè passiva a lo spuntare ed il fiorire della geometria analitica cartesiana, al contrario prese un posto onorevole fra le nazioni che coltivarono i nuovi metodi spuntati quasi simultaneamente in Inghilterra ed in Germania. Ed infatti a GABRIELE MANFREDI devesi l'integrazione delle equazioni differenziali omogenee del primo ordine con due variabili indipendenti, nonchè quella prima trattazione metodica di tutte le equazioni differenziali del primo ordine che valse a colmare la deplorevole lacuna esistente nella letteratura matematica per la brusca interruzione al primo volume dell'*Analyse des infiniment petits* del marchese DE L'HOPITAL (²). Inoltre JACOPO RICCATI efficacemente promosse lo studio delle equazioni differenziali d'un ordine superiore al primo, legando il proprio nome ad un'importantissima classe di equazioni del secondo ordine. Finalmente GIULIO CARLO DE' FAGNANI, immortalandosi con genialissimi studi intorno alla rettificazione della lemniscata, tracciò le prime linee di una grande teoria in cui EULERO e LEGENDRE, ABEL e JACOBI dovevano raccogliere larga messe di allori (³).

Questi tre geometri appartengono a famiglie illustri, non soltanto per nobiltà di natali, ma anche per aver dati altri nomi all'elenco dei matematici italiani. Tali sono EUSTACCHIO MANFREDI, astronomo di grido e geometra i cui contributi alla

(¹) Dopo di avere segnalati questi progressi fatti dalla Geometria nella direzione tracciata dal grande siracusano, avrei dovuto (se non me ne avesse distolto il desiderio di riuscir breve) fare onorevole menzione di un teorema e di un metodo appartenenti alla geometria di posizione, dovuti ad un geometra italiano del secolo XVII e che grazie ad una rivendicazione operata da MICHELE CHASLES (*Aperçu historique*, Note VII) son destinati ad attraversare i secoli portando seco il nome di chi ebbe l'abilità e la fortuna di scoprirli. Alludo a quel teorema fondamentale della teoria delle trasversali che porta il nome di GIOVANNI CEVA ed alle ingegnose considerazioni cinematiche da lui usate per stabilirlo, nelle quali non è difficile ravvisare un preludio al « calcolo baricentrico » del MÖBIUS.

(²) Cfr. il mio articolo sopra *Il giornale de' letterati d'Italia di Venezia e la Raccolta Calogerà*, ecc., nel t. IX (1899) delle Abhandlungen zur Geschichte der Mathematik.

(³) « Bei dieser Gelegenheit habe ich auch einen für die Geschichte der Mathematik ungemein wichtigen Tag gefunden, den welchem unsere Akademie EULER aufforderte das von FAGNANI übersandte Werk zu prüfen, ehe man dem Verfasser antwortet. Aus dieser Prüfung ist die Theorie der elliptischen Functionen entstanden ». Così scrisse JACOBI a P. H. FUSS il 24 ottobre 1847; v. Bibliotheca mathematica, III Reihe, Bd. 8, 1908, p. 255; cfr. anche p. 263.

prospettiva son di quelli non destinati a perire; VINCENZO e GIORDANO RICCATI, il primo dei quali, oltre ad essere un reputato ed originale espositore dell'analisi infitesimale, passa per inventore della teoria delle funzioni iperboliche (1); e GIANFRANSCESCO ONOFRIO FAGNANO che, con alcune interessanti ricerche di calcolo integrale, si dimostrò figlio non degenere dell'autore delle *Produzioni matematiche.*

Ove la discrezione ed il pensiero della via lunga che ancora ci resta a percorrere non mi inducessero, o Signori, a ricordare esclusivamente le personalità di primo ordine, terrei qui parola anche di quegli Italiani che con i fatti dimostrarono come la Geometria, dopo il trionfo dei nuovi calcoli, sia stata vinta ma non doma. Tuttavia nessuna considerazione può ragionevolmente distogliermi dal ricordare qui con onore quel GIROLAMO SACCHERI, che, dopo esser stato per un secolo e mezzo sepolto in un'ingiusta dimenticanza, venne esumato da un religioso dei nostri giorni (2) e segnalato da EUGENIO BELTRAMI come un remoto precursore di LOBATSCHEWSKY e BOLYAI, come un pioniere della geometria non-euclidea, a torto trascurato dai moderni (3).

Interposto, direbbesi, fra la nobile schiera degli analisti ed il gruppo di geometri italiani del secolo XVIII si asside GIANFRANCESCO MALFATTI, dei cui lavori, veramente ottimi, siami lecito ricordare soltanto le ricerche sopra le equazioni di 5° grado e la così detta « risolvente di MALFATTI » a cui esse condussero (4), ed il bel problema di geometria elementare da lui concepito e risoluto ed al quale numerose ed eleganti ricerche posteriori fecero acquistare straordinaria importanza ed immensa notorietà (5).

VIII.

Tutto ciò, Signori, sta a dimostrare come, malgrado le incessanti sanguinose guerre, di cui le contese per la successione di Spagna fecero teatro per un metà del secolo XVIII la mia misera patria, gl'Italiani abbiano continuato a subire l'ineffabile fascino che i numeri e le figure esercitano su tutti coloro che una volta ne intravidero la sovrumana bellezza. Ma nel secolo stesso in cui GIAMBATTISTA VICO creava una nuova scienza (la Filosofia della Storia) e GOLDONI dava vita alla commedia nazionale, in cui PARINI s'illustrava nella satira ed ALFIERI nella tragedia, in cui GALVANI e VOLTA scoprivano nell'elettricità l'agente fisico dell'avvenire, in quel secolo meraviglioso il mondo assistette al sorgere in Piemonte un astro di prima grandezza de-

(1) CANTOR, *Vorlesungen über Geschichte der Mathematik* (t. IV, 1908, p. 411).

(2) Il P. ANGELO MANGANOTTI.

(3) Rendiconti della R. Accademia dei Lincei, 1889.

(4) Veggasi a questo proposito l'assennatissimo esordio alla Memoria del BRIOSCHI: *Sulla risolvente di Malfatti per le equazioni del quinto grado* (Annali di Matematica, t. V, 1863; oppure *Opere di F. Brioschi,* t. II, p. 39).

(5) Un ricco elenco dei lavori sul problema di MALFATTI si trova nel t. IX, 1876, del Bullettino Boncompagni; sarebbe utile renderlo completo con la lista dei lavori posteriori sul medesimo tema.

stinato a contendere ad Eulero la gloria di dare il proprio nome all'èra che lo ammirò intento al suo portentoso lavoro; se è superfluo io dichiari di alludere a Giuseppe Luigi Lagrange, è, per converso, necessario che esponga, almeno in compendio, le ragioni per cui ritengo assolutamente inaccettabile l'opinione secondo cui quel gran genio sarebbe una gloria francese, opinione che, manifestata da Delambre (1), abbracciata dall'Arago (2) ed accettata da J. A. Serret, venne accolta al di là dell'Alpi con compiacenza evidente.

Ora, per determinare qual grado di solidità posseggano le basi di questa tesi, ricordiamo che il creatore del calcolo delle variazioni nacque a Torino il 25 gennaio 1736 da un tesoriere di guerra del Re di Sardegna e dalla figlia di un medico di Cambiano, cioè da genitori sulla cui nazionalità non può nascere dubbio alcuno. È vero che la famiglia Lagrange era oriunda francese; ma, sin dal 1672, il bisavolo del grande matematico era già siffattamente naturalizzato in Italia che, oltre essere capitano di cavalleria nell'esercito piemontese, disimpegnava importanti e delicate missioni affidategli dal Duca di Savoia Carlo Emanuele II e sceglieva come propria sposa una dama appartenente a cospicua famiglia romana. Orbene se — tale essendo la genealogia di Lagrange — sia legittimo considerarlo per un francese domiciliato in Italia, lo dica chi ricorda, ad esempio, come i discendenti di Giandomenico Cassini, che Luigi XIV volle presso di sè ad illustrare la sua corte ed il suo regno, già sin dalla seconda generazione si riguardarono e furono ritenuti francesi; lo dica anche chi ha presenti le attuali disposizioni delle leggi civili in vigore attualmente in Italia ed in Francia, secondo le quali viene considerato come cittadino italiano il figlio di chi in Italia risiede da un decennio (3) e come cittadino francese ognuno sia nato da padre nato in Francia (4).

Se poi quell'opinione trova la propria ragione nel fatto che l'illustre matematico, non potendo trovare in un regno di recente formazione quelle condizioni materiali e morali presentategli prima da Federico II e poi da Luigi XVI, accettò l'ospitalità offertagli da la Francia dopo la Germania, ci sembra non si tenga abbastanza conto della facilità che avevano gli artisti, i letterati, gli scienziati nei secoli scorsi di lasciar la patria per entrare al servizio di principi mecenati, ai quali non bastava la gloria dell'armi (5). Inoltre, ammettendo che il cambiamento di residenza significhi cambiamento di nazionalità, si giungerebbe a conclusioni strane, assurde, inaccettabili quali sarebbero il far di Pitagora un italiano, di Eulero un russo e di Steiner

(1) *Notice sur la vie et les ouvrages de M. le Comte J. L. de Lagrange*, riprodotta in testa al t. I delle *Oeuvres de Lagrange*, t. I (Paris, 1867).

(2) Cfr. Bullettino Boncompagni, t. VI, 1873, p. 542.

(3) Art. 8 del Codice civile italiano.

(4) Legge del 7 febbraio 1851: « Est français tout individu né en France d'un étranger qui lui même y est né ».

(5) Si osservi anche che i genitori del sommo geometra non lo seguirono all'estero; sicchè quando l'esercito francese occupò nel 1795 il Piemonte, il ministro degli affari esteri incaricò il ben noto letterato Pier Luigi Ginguéné, commissario del Direttorio a Torino, di presentare gli ossequi del governo francese al vecchio Lagrange ormai nonagenario; così narra E. de Beaumont nel t. XXXVIII, p. cxiii dei Mém. de l'Institut de France.

un prussiano; ed io son certo che, ove quella massima fosse stata universalmente accettata, il REGIOMONTANO non avrebbe accettata la cattedra offertagli dallo « Studio » di Padova, GIOVANNI BERNOULLI mai sarebbe divenuto lustro e decoro dell'Università di Groninga ed AGOSTINO CAUCHY sarebbesi sdegnosamente rifiutato di occupare nell'Ateneo torinese la cattedra di Fisica matematica istituita nel 1832 da Carlo Alberto, appunto per assicurare i mezzi di sussistenza al sommo analista proscritto dalla sua patria (¹).

Se, finalmente, a quella conclusione si giunse considerando che i lavori di LAGRANGE sono nella massima parte (ma non nella totalità, come asserì il DELAMBRE) in lingua francese, si osservi, con un illustre storico della letteratura italiana (²), come « gl'Italiani che dalla battaglia di Torino a quella dell'Assietta (1707-1747) respinsero sempre le armi francesi, non seppero e non poterono respingere le mode, i libri, le opinioni che venivano di Francia: la quale, essendo più forte nel pensiero, dominò col pensiero. La civiltà comune d'Europa doveva svolgersi in una lingua comune, che fosse facile ed analitica come la filosofia del tempo, entrante come la donna, piena di spirito e di vezzi; e questa lingua fu la francese, che venne parlata nelle corti di Madrid, di Vienna, di Berlino, di Pietroburgo e di Torino ». La lingua francese essendo stata nel secolo XVIII una vera e propria lingua universale, quale illazione può mai trarsi dall'esser essa stata usata di preferenza da LAGRANGE?...

Notate poi, o Signori, come la leggenda della nazionalità francese di LAGRANGE (a somiglianza di tutte le leggende!) siasi andata formando soltanto dopo la morte di lui; chè egli mai ha dimenticata la terra che lo vide nascere e questa mai ha cessato di considerarlo come uno dei suoi figli di cui andava giustamente orgogliosa. Sorta, infatti, la Società italiana delle scienze, il LAGRANGE vi fu inscritto in qualità di *membro nazionale* (³); e quando, verso il 1780, ALESSANDRO ZORZI, con la valida scorta del MALFATTI, stese il piano d'una *Enciclopedia italiana*, consimile a quella pubblicata in Francia da DIDEROT e d'ALEMBERT, fu subito rivolto invito a LAGRANGE di collaborarvi e se tale invito non potè venir accettato, gli è soltanto a cagione delle gravi occupazioni dell'illustre direttore dell'Accademia di Berlino (⁴). D'altra parte, l'Accademia delle scienze di Parigi, la quale elesse il LAGRANGE « associé étranger » sin da quando egli trovavasi al servizio del Re di Prussia, al suo arrivo nella capitale della Francia, pur volendo accordargli il diritto di voto e non potendo inscrivere un non-francese nella categoria dei propri membri, creò, apposta per lui, il grado di « pensionnaire honoraire » e così implicitamente dichiarò

(¹) Cfr. Bullettino Boncompagni, t. IV, 1871, p. 375.

(²) L. SETTEMBRINI, *Lezioni di letteratura italiana*, t. III, Napoli 1876, p. 6.

(³) Cfr. Bullettino Boncompagni, t. VI, 1873, p. 139.

(⁴) Bullettino Boncompagni, t. VI, 1873, p. 129 e 139. Come ulteriore prova dell'avere gli Italiani sempre riguardato il LAGRANGE come un connazionale può considerarsi il fatto che alla sua morte il conte G. SCOPOLI, direttore generale della P. I. del Regno d'Italia, ordinava fosse « invitato un professore della Facoltà matematica in ognuna delle tre Università a voler recitare un elogio di questo celeberrimo matematico »; di tali orazioni la più meritatamente nota è l'« Elogio di LUIGI LAGRANGE recitato nell'Aula Magna della R. Università di Padova li XV Giugno MDCCCXIII » da PIETRO COSSALI e subito stampato a Padova con dedica al Vicerè BEAUHARNAIS.

non trattarsi di un profugo ritornato ai patri lari. Che più? Scoppiata la rivoluzione francese LAGRANGE stava per essere espulso, per effetto della legge contro gli stranieri votata il 16 ottobre 1793 e tale dolore gli fu risparmiato soltanto grazie all'intervento di un fedele amico, il noto chimico GUYTON DE MORVEAU, che, per ottenere un'eccezione a di lui favore, fece valere certi studi sui projettili che egli andava facendo (1).

Gli è soltanto dopo la scomparsa di LAGRANGE che la Francia sentì un insopportabile dolore per non vedere ascritto fra i propri figli chi potè contrastare ad EULERO il grado di corifeo dei matematici del secolo XVIII; e, considerando la desinenza del suo nome, la lingua che egli mostrò di avere caramente diletta ed il lungo soggiorno da lui fatto a Parigi, in un impeto di tenerezza, gli concesse « post mortem » la cittadinanza che non avevagli accordata in vita; quel sentimento è titolo d'onore tanto per chi lo ha provato quanto per chi ebbe il potere di suscitarlo; ma non può nè deve annebbiare il freddo giudizio dello storico imparziale. Il quale però dovrà riconoscere che, se sette città si contesero l'onore di aver dato i natali ad OMERO, è ben naturale che due nazioni possano disputarsi l'onore d'inscrivere nel Pantheon delle proprie glorie colui che inaugurò la propria carriera scientifica inventando il « calcolo delle variazioni », che da giovane seppe riuscir vittorioso d'importanti questioni poste a concorso dall'Accademia di Parigi, che non fu inferiore ad EULERO nella teoria dei numeri e lo superò nella teoria delle equazioni algebriche (2), che diede all'applicazione dell'algebra alla geometria la sua forma definitiva (3) e verrà venerato dai posteri più remoti come creatore della meccanica analitica. Sicchè se egli non è secondo ad alcuno dei matematici del secolo XVIII, è senza contrasto il più grande geometra che abbia prodotto l'Italia.

IX.

Errerebbe chi ritenesse avere io così finito di delineare o colorire il quadro delle benemerenze che seppe acquistarsi l'Italia di fronte alle scienze esatte nel secolo meraviglioso che antiprecede l'attuale. Pur tacendo di PAOLO FRISI il quale, benchè dipintoci da un contemporaneo « come colui che dragona da generale dei matematici italiani » (4), benchè abbia ottenuti in vita tutti gli onori a cui uno scienziato può aspirare (5), appare oggigiorno come una di quelle fame passeggiere che non resistono all'esame spassionato dei posteri — vanno ricordati GIULIO MOZZI, scopritore di un fondamentale teorema di cinematica, ed un gruppo di meccanici, delle cui opere è da

(1) Bullettino Boncompagni, t. XII, 1879, p. 819.

(2) PIERPONT, *Lagrange place in the theory of substitutions* (Bulletin of the American math. Soc., t. I, p. 196 e seg.).

(3) Veggasi la mia comunicazione: *Pour une histoire de la géometrie analytique* nelle Verhanl. des III Mathem. Kongresses, Leipzig, 1904.

(4) Così il MALFATTI in una lettera al LORGNA; v. Bullettino Boncompagni, t. VI, 1873, p. 121 e t. IX, 1879, p. 493.

(5) Cfr. A. FAVARO, *Sette lettere inedite di G. L. Lagrange al P. Paolo Frisi* (Atti della R. Accademia di Torino, t. XXXI, 1895).

augurarsi che il prof. Marcolongo voglia darci completa quella storia che egli ha egregiamente iniziata (1). Nè va dimenticato Lorenzo Mascheroni, poeta elegante e matematico di grido, che, con le sue ottime note al *Calcolo integrale* di Eulero, si affermò analista profondo (2) e con la sua famosissima *Geometria del compasso* riprese in modo originale un ordine di idee in cui eransi distinti i suoi conterranei dell'epoca di Cardano e preparò gli studi di Brianchon e Servois sulla geometria della riga e quelli di Poncelet e Steiner sulla risoluzione delle questioni geometriche del secondo grado. E poi sul finire del secolo XVIII che un medico modenese intuì la ragione per la quale erano state frustrate le speranze, per lunghi secoli nutrite, di giungere alla risoluzione algebrica delle equazioni letterali del quinto grado e sforzandosi di stabilirla in modo irrecusabile, si pose in prima linea fra i cultori della teoria delle sostituzioni. Paolo Ruffini, come di regola accade a coloro che precorrono i loro tempi, non conseguì in vita tutta la gloria che gli spettava (3); ma oggi, dopo che il « teorema di Ruffini » venne dimostrato da Abel e da altri, dopo che la teoria delle sostituzioni è divenuta accessibile a tutti, si è misurato al giusto tutto il valore delle sue mirabili intuizioni. A questo trionfo della giustizia ha contribuito possentemente il prof. Burckhardt con un suo magistrale lavoro (4), che gli valse, oltre l'ammirazione dei competenti, la perenne gratitudine degli Italiani, della quale siami lecito farmi interprete in questa occasione solenne. L'Italia, grazie ad una felice iniziativa del prof. Bortolotti, si appresta, auspice il Circolo matematico di Palermo, ad elevare al Ruffini un monumento imperituro, facendo un'edizione completa delle sue opere.

Ancora molto rimarrebbe a dire da chi volesse fare un resoconto completo della produzione matematica italiana nel secolo XVIII; si dovrebbe, ad esempio, accennare ad un famoso trattato di analisi vergato da mano femminile (5) ed al risveglio delle scienze esatte nel Regno di Napoli cagionato dalla voce saviamente ammonitrice di Nicola Fergola; nè si potrebbe passar sotto silenzio la fondazione, per opera del Lorgna, della prima accademia scientifica nazionale, la quale, porgendo il mezzo per un fecondo scambio d'idee fra i geometri disseminati per tutta la penisola, rese possibile si potesse parlare di una « matematica italiana » assai prima che la mia patria avesse conseguita l'agognata unità politica.

Ma quello che, in questa Sezione del Congresso, non può nè deve venir passato sotto silenzio è che Pietro Cossali, con due immortali volumi dedicati alla storia

(1) Bollettino di bibliografia e storia delle sc. matem. t. VIII, 1905 e t. IX, 1906.

(2) Si ricordi che nella teoria degli integrali euleriani s'incontra una « costante di Mascheroni ».

(3) « Di somma importanza e profondità », scrive il Franchini (*La storia dell'algebra e dei suoi principali scrittori sino al secolo XIX;* Lucca 1827, p. 103) « sono le produzioni del cav. Ruffini; ma per la massima parte scritte in un gergo analitico insopportabile »; giudizio tanto più significante in quanto proviene da persona che si adoperò a diffondere le idee del Ruffini.

(4) *Die Anfänge der Gruppentheorie und Paolo Ruffini* (Abhadl. zur Gesch. der Mathematik, VI Heft, Leipzig 1892). Ne esiste una traduzione italiana dovuta al prof. Pascal. Cfr. anche l'articolo di J. Pierpont, *Zur Geschichte der Gleichung des V Gudes* (Monatshefte f. Mathemat. u. Physik, t. VI, 1895, p. 68).

(5) Allusione a Maria Gaetana Agnesi.

dell'Algebra italiana nella sua epoca di splendore massimo, diede forse il primo esempio di un'esposizione critica delle vicende di una scienza positiva e somministrò un imperituro modello agli storici della Matematica; in sua lode che cosa, o Signori, potrei aggiungere a quanto ne scrisse un giudice di difficilissima contentatura come il NESSELMANN [1] e dopo che il COSSALI fu acclamato e riconosciuto ispiratore e duce di una valorosa falange di studiosi di vaglia, nella quale brillano GIAMBATTISTA VENTURI, GUGLIELMO LIBRI e BALDASSARE BONCOMPAGNI?...

X.

Fra gli sconvolgimenti intestini della Francia, che ebbero per tragico epilogo la morte di Luigi XVI, venne concepita e fra i fiumi di sangue che bagnarono la Francia all'epoca del Terrore, vide la luce la nuova disciplina che, da un lato doveva surrogare, assorbendole, la prospettiva dei pittori e la stereotomia degli architetti e, d'altro lato, doveva mutare la geometria di EUCLIDE ed APOLLONIO in una disciplina totalmente nuova.

Ora le idee ed i metodi d'un rivoluzionario come MONGE non potevano per fermo sperare di venir accolte col meritato favore dalle nazioni che appunto allora erano in guerra con la Francia pel trionfo dei principî legittimisti: onde parecchi anni dovevano passare prima che la Germania e l'Inghilterra accordassero alla Geometria descrittiva l'ingresso entro i loro confini. Ma l'Italia, che, dalle nuove idee innovatrici, agitantisi nel seno della nazione sorella, sperava di trarre i mezzi e le forze per franger le catene del suo secolare servaggio; l'Italia che, pel tramite di FABBRONI, FRANCHINI, MASCHERONI, suoi rappresentanti nella « Commissione internazionle del metro », aveva stabilite relazioni oltremodo cordiali coi più cospicui scienziati francesi ed in particolare con MONGE; l'Italia che erasi affrettata ad inviare alcuni de' suoi figli da natura chiamati ad alti destini, come GIAMBATTISTA GIORGINI e GIOVANNI PLANA, ad istruirsi in una scuola che, non appena fondata, era giustamente assurta alla più alta rinomanza; l'Italia che da secoli aveva dimostrata una perenne spiccata attitudine per le ricerche puramente geometriche, fu la prima nazione a fare ai metodi di MONGE le più festose accoglienze. Non solo si diede a tradurre le lezioni di quel celebre geometra; ma, per mezzo di VINCENZO FLAUTI [2], vi fece considerevoli aggiunte di sostanza e vi diede aspetto più conforme ai classici e, poco dopo, per opera di GIUSEPPE TRAMONTINI [3], vi apportò una notevole migliorìa con la metodica applicazione del cambiamento dei piani di proiezione, cioè con l'introduzione di quell'artificio che sì fiera tempesta doveva far scatenare quando TEODORO OLIVIER se ne fece paladino presso i propri connazionali. Più tardi la patria mia — auspice GIUSTO BELLAVITIS [4] — doveva stringere in più intimo connubio la Geometria descrittiva

(1) *Die Algebra der Griechen* (Berlin, 1842, p. 25).

(2) *Geometria di sito sul piano e nello spazio* (Napoli, 1808).

(3) *Trattato teorico-pratico delle projezioni grafiche.* (Modena, 1912-13).

(4) *Lezioni di geometria descrittiva.* (Padova, 1851). A proposito di quest'opera il TERQUEM

con il multiforme concetto di « trasformazione geometrica », nel frattempo pervenuto a completa maturità; e con LUIGI CREMONA, doveva collegare armonicamente il metodo della proiezione centrale al metodo di MONGE, con criteri analoghi a quelli che GUGLIELMO FIEDLER rese vittoriosi in tutto il mondo, mediante un trattato giustamente famoso.

« Rebus sic stantibus », si potrà forse dire, o Signori, esser l'amor di patria che mi fa velo all'intelletto quando io dai fatti precedenti mi credo autorizzato a concludere che all'Italia spetti il primo posto fra le nazioni che contribuirono al trionfo delle idee di MONGE?...

Giova qui aggiungere non esser questo che uno degli aspetti di una più vasta e complessa opera scientifica che, nel secolo XIX, fece considerare l'Italia come la vessillifera della Geometria pura. Se a tale risultato contribuirono parzialmente GAETANO GIORGINI, il primo scopritore del complesso lineare di rette, e GIUSTO BELLAVITIS, l'inventore del « metodo delle equipollenze », nella sua totalità è dovuta all'azione altamente benefica esercitata da LUIGI CREMONA, il quale, dopo di essersi assimilati i nuovi metodi d'indagine geometrica inventati in Francia da MONGE, CARNOT, PONCELET ed in Germania da MÖBIUS, STEINER, PLÜCKER ne mise in luce e ne accrebbe il potere, aggiungendo nuove ubertose provincie al vasto impero della Geometria. Sia perenne gloria a Lui, non solo pei nuovi veri di cui gli siamo debitori, ma anche per la fiorente scuola di cui fu organizzatore e capo, scuola in cui brillarono ETTORE CAPORALI e RICCARDO DE PAOLIS, ahimè! troppo presto rapiti alla scienza ed alla patria, in cui tuttora altri brillano, i cui nomi io pronuncierei con la debita riverenza, ove non mi fossi imposto (per ragioni che è superfluo dichiarare) il vincolo di non parlare di chi è ancor valido sulla breccia; ma, in generale, si può asserire che tutti coloro i quali, in questi ultimi cinquant'anni, coltivarono la Geometria al di quà delle Alpi, salutano in LUIGI CREMONA il loro padre ed autore.

---

scrisse le seguenti parole (Nouv. Ann. de mathém., t. XII, 1853, p. 106) che noi Italiani non possiamo leggere senza commozione e gratitudine:

« L'Italie s'est toujours montrée, dans la région intellectuelle, au premier rang; c'est elle qui nous a ouvert les trésors de l'antiquité littéraire et scientifique. Combien ne devons-nous pas au seul COMMANDIN? La malheureuse péninsule (*Italia! Italia!*) conserve son illustre nationalité au moins dans les travaux de l'esprit. Pour s'en convincre, en ce qui concerne les sciences exactes, il suffit de parcourir le recueil mensuel que publié à Rome, le célèbre professeur BARNABA TORTOLINI, collection qui gagne chaque jour en intérêt par les savantes communications des BONCOMPAGNI (Balthazar), BRIOSCHI, CHELINI, GENOCCHI, SECCHI, TARDY, TORTOLINI, VOLPICELLI, etc. On y trouve l'annonce avec éloge d'un nouveau Traité de géométrie descriptive par M. GIUSTO BELLAVITIS de Bassano, professeur de cette science à l'Université de Padoue. On dit que l'auteur a suivi une nouvelle méthode qui *non è nè copia nè imitazione di verun'altra.* L'ouvrage est divisé en cinq livres qui traitent avec un ordre et une clarté admirables, des points, des droites, des plans, des lignes et surfaces courbes, des intersections, des contacts et de la courbure des lignes surfaces, et toujours sous un point de vue général, évitant les cas particuliers qui ne peuvent jamais épuiser un sujet aussi bien qu'un petit nombre d'idées générales »,

XI.

Nè devesi credere che l'attività geometrica spiegata dall' Italia nel secorso decorso abbia fatto sì che essa rimanesse spettatrice incuriosa ed indifferente ai portentosi progressi che andava facendo l'analisi.

Infatti, Giovanni Plana (¹) — pensatore oggi quasi dimenticato, ma che ai contemporanei apparve (per usare le frasi incise sulla sua tomba) « astronomus, physicus, matematicus nulli sui temporis secundus » — importò nella terra ove nacque Lagrange le teorie che aveva apprese a Parigi e svolgendole ed applicandole egregiamente seppe tesserne il più entusiastico elogio. Coadiuvato da Felice Chiò ed Angelo Genocchi egli accese al piè dell'Alpi un vivace focolare di studi matematici, che, grazie ad abili vestali, tuttora vampeggia, illumina, riscalda.

Un secondo importante centro di ricerche analitiche si stabilì a Pavia (²) per merito di Gregorio Fontana (³), il quale « contribuì non poco a diffondere in Italia la conoscenza di alcune dottrine matematiche ». L'opera da lui inaugurata venne proseguita da Pietro Paoli, i cui numerosi ed ottimi lavori rivelano « forse più che in ogni altro geometra italiano del suo tempo, una cognizione profonda, completa e famigliare dell'analisi matematica, condotta al punto in cui trovavasi allora per opera di Eulero, di Lagrange, di Laplace, di Monge, ecc. ». Degno di succedere al Paoli si dimostrò Vincenzo Brunacci « che contribuì moltissimo ad elevare fra noi il livello dell'insegnamento matematico, sia colle proprie lezioni, sia colle riforme da lui provocate nell'ordinamento degli studi ». Discepolo del Brunacci e poi suo collega fu Antonio Bordoni, uno dei più profondi e geniali cultori della Matematica in genere ed in particolare dell'analisi applicata alla Geometria. « Quest'ultimo ramo di scienza (osserva il Beltrami), inaugurato nella sua odierna larghezza da Monge, è stato dal Bordoni trattato con evidente predilezione e con grande novità ed eleganza nelle sue *Lezioni di calcolo*, e gli ha fornito argomento ad interessantissime ed originali ricerche, nelle quali è difficile dire se brilli maggiormente per l'acume dei concetti o per il magistero dell'analisi, quasi sempre mantenuta nelle vie lagrangiane. Questi lavori assicurano al Bordoni una riputazione duratura; nè sarà difficile allo storico imparziale della scienza il trarre positivi argomenti di priorità in favore di lui, specialmente rispetto alla dottrina delle coordinate curvilinee che d'ordinario si attribuisce a Gauss ». L'opera scientifica del Bordoni attende ancora il suo sto-

(¹) Cfr. E. de Beaumont, *Eloge historique de Jean Plana*. (Mém. de l'Acad. des Sciences de l'Institut de France, t. XXXVIII, 1873).

(²) Le parole virgolate sono tolte da alcune notizie scritte dal Beltrami ed inserite nella I parte delle *Memorie e documenti per la storia dell'Università di Pavia* (Pavia, 1878).

(³) Del Fontana il Franchini scrisse: « Letterato insigne, matematico celebre ed autore di moltissime produzioni, ove non sappiamo se più debbasi lodare la facile venustà dello stile o la spontanea novità delle speculazioni (*Saggio sulla storia della matematica*, Lucca 1821, p. 27).

rico ([1]); ma quanto già se ne conosce autorizza a considerar lui come capo della nobile coorte di cultori che la geometria differenziale trovò in Italia e nella quale (per non ricordare che i defunti) brillano per luce propria GASPARE MAINARDI, DELFINO CODAZZI, EUGENIO BELTRAMI, ERNESTO CESÀRO. Alla scuola pavese, come discepolo diretto del BORDONI, appartiene anche « last but not least », FRANCESCO BRIOSCHI, della cui vasta e duratura azione scientifica io non tenterò di tessere l'elogio, chè la figura di lui appare così colossale agli occhi di tutti che è vano sforzarsi di accrescerne l'imponenza collocandola sopra un piedestallo!

Il trasferimento del PAOLI dall'Ateneo di Pavia a quello di Pisa ebbe per risultato un notevole risveglio degli studi matematici, non soltanto nell'Università illustrata da GALILEO, ma anche in tutta la Toscana. In conseguenza venne istituita una terza sede di investigazioni analitiche e fisico-matematiche, alla cui imperitura rinomanza provvidero OTTAVIO FABRIZIO MOSSOTTI, ENRICO BETTI e (perdonatemi quest'infrazione che mi permetto ad una regola da me sempre osservata, in favore di un sommo tuttora vivente!) ULISSE DINI, nomi destinati a venir sempre ricordati accanto a quelli di GALOIS e WEIERSTRASS ed a cui si deve se l'Italia è oggi considerata come maestra nella teoria matematica dell'elasticità.

XII.

I nomi che son venuto sin qui ricordando sono certamente molti e potranno da taluno esser giudicati soverchiamente numerosi; ma tali per fermo non sembreranno a chi riflette alle omissioni a cui mi ha costretto il desiderio di non abusare della pazienza di chi mi fa l'onore di ascoltarmi; sicchè mi assale il tormentoso dubbio che taluno non mi saprà perdonare di non aver fatto menzione di persone che molti dei presenti ricorderanno con affetto di amici o devozione di discepoli; tali sono DOMENICO CHELINI, maestro insuperato nella Geometria analitica e nella Meccanica; BARNABA TORTOLINI ([2]), grazie a cui la matematica italiana venne in possesso di un esclusivo suo organo; GIUSEPPE BATTAGLINI, efficace ed originale diffonditore dei più elevati metodi algebrico-geometrici nelle provincie meridionali; FELICE CASORATI, analista finissimo, a cui solo un malvaggio capriccio del caso vietò di legare il proprio nome ad alcuni fondamentali teoremi dell'analisi moderna. E come potrei io non riconoscere il mio torto per non avere celebrate le vittorie che gli Italiani ottennero nelle ricerche astronomiche nei secoli che corrono da GALILEO GALILEI a GIOVANNI SCHIAPARELLI?

([1]) Il compianto prof. CASORATI scrisse una briografia del BORDONI che presentò al BRIOSCHI in occasione di un suo giubileo; se essa esiste tuttora fra le carte lasciate da l'uno o l'altro di quegli illustri analisti serebbe desiderabile renderla di pubblica ragione.

([2]) È forse noto a pochi come, sin dal 1828, il VIESSIEUX, notissimo per avere fondata una nostra celebre rivista letteraria, progettasse la pubblicazione di *Annali delle scienze matematiche, fisiche e naturali* e come GIUSEPPE MAZZINI si adoperasse « toto corde » per l'effettuazione di tale disegno senza però riuscirvi: veggasi il t. I degli *Scritti editi ed inediti di Giuseppe Mazzini* (Imola, 1906).

Ma queste ed altre probabili lacune nel bilancio, che ho tentato presentarvi del patrimonio matematico dell'Italia, non possono lasciar nascere alcun ragionevole dubbio sopra la solidità dell'azienda.

Non appena dissipata la caligine, che, nell'Età di mezzo, gravò come una cappa di piombo sopra tutta l'umanità, l'Italia si pose subito alla testa delle nazioni in cui le scienze esatte son tenute nella debita considerazione e poi, attraverso a vicissitudini politiche così lunghe e tremende da fiaccare le fibre più robuste, malgrado la somma di energia spesa per conseguire l'agognata indipendenza nazionale, ad onta dell'attivo interesse costantemente dimostrato per tutte le manifestazioni dell'arte, se non sempre seppe conservare saldo in pugno lo scettro che avevale affidato LEONARDO PISANO, non lasciò passare alcun secolo senza aggiungere qualche pietra al mirabile edificio che i matematici andavano assiduamente elevando; sicchè presso di noi non si riscontra alcun sintomo di quel fenomeno, avvertito dal MANSION nella matematica belga (1), che la dominazione straniera sia stata insormontabile ostacolo allo svolgimento del pensiero matematico.

Nè devesi pensare che i sentimenti ostili degli oppressi verso gli stranieri dominatori abbian trasformate le Alpi in una barriera che le idee matematiche fossero incapaci di valicare. Alle relazioni agro-dolci fra i discepoli di GALILEO ed i contemporanei di CARTESIO, succedono quelle francamente amichevoli attestate dalla collaborazione dei RICCATI e dei FAGNANO agli *Acta eruditorum* di Lipsia. Ai rapporti veramente fraterni fra scienziati francesi e scienziati italiani all'epoca napoleonica, fanno riscontro le accoglienze oneste e liete che da noi ricevettero JACOBI e BORCHARDT (2), STEINER e DIRICHLET; e come potrei passar sotto silenzio il soggiorno in Pisa e la stretta amicizia con ENRICO BETTI di BERNARDO RIEMANN, di cui la mia patria conserva tuttora i resti mortali? (3) Le numerose ristampe e versioni in italiano di opere giustamente famose dovute a francesi, tedeschi ed inglesi confermano come presso di noi la scienza stesse al di sopra di ogni competizione di parte (4); onde non devono giudicarsi come isolati ed insignificanti gli spettacoli offerti dal MOSSOTTI, dal BETTI, dal CREMONA, i quali, reduci dall'aver combattuto per la redenzione della patria a Curtatone, a Montanara, a Venezia, deposte le armi, riprendevano lo studio delle opere con cui, appunto allora, la Germania stava conquistando l'eccelsa posizione che attualmente occupa nelle scienze esatte.

(1) *Esquisse de l'histoire des mathématiques en Belgique* (Revue des questions scientifiques, Janvier 1907).

(2) Cfr. Atti della quinta unione degli scienziati italiani tenuta in Lucca nel settembre del MDCCCXLIII, Lucca 1844, pp. 475 e 500.

(3) Dei viaggi e soggiorni in Italia di JACOBI, STEINER e RIEMANN esistono traccie indelebili nelle loro opere, fra cui trovansi lavori scritti nella lingua di Dante.

(4) Senza pretendere di dar qui un'enumerazione nemmeno approssimativa di tal pubblicazioni, mi limito a ricordare la ristampa fatta a Venezia degli *Acta eruditorum*, e quelle del *Calcolo differenziale* di EULERO e degli *Elementa matheseos universalis* del WOLF; fra le traduzioni citerò il *Calcolo infinitesimale* del MARIE e la *Dottrina degli azzardi* del DE MOIVRE (entrambe con note del FONTANA), il *Saggio sulla storia delle matematiche* del BOSSUT ed il noto *Dizionario delle scienze matematiche* del MONTFERRIER.

Ai dì nostri la scienza si sforza di cancellare le distinzioni di nazionalità, affermando il suo carattere internazionale e si accinge a nuovi trionfi contemperando il principio della divisione con quello della concentrazione del lavoro: le accademie, da locali divenute nazionali, si stringono in un fascio pel conseguimento d'intenti di generale interesse; ed alle opere individuali, fatiche preferite dei nostri maggiori, succedono grandi imprese collettive, frutto del lavoro concorde di specialisti sparsi in tutto il mondo civile. Tuttavia, in certi giorni memorabili, è ben lecito ad ogni popolo riandare al proprio passato e misurare le proprie forze. Oggi è per l'Italia una di tali storiche date; essa dalle glorie del passato trae i più lieti auspici per l'avvenire; e, contando i maestri ancora intenti ad opere feconde ed i numerosi discepoli, ormai maturi per prenderne il posto, pensa con gioja, fiducia ed orgoglio che le sue tradizioni più volte secolari saranno per essere continuate; ed i combattenti per la ricerca del vero incuora alle lotte incruenti, ritemprandoli nella coscienza d'una eterna missione, ripetendo le parole del suo poeta:

Chinatevi al lavoro, o validi omeri;
schiudetevi a gli amori, o cuori giovani;
impennatevi a i sogni, ali de l'anima;
irrompete a la guerra, o desii torbidi;
ciò che fu torna e tornerà ne i secoli.

H. G. ZEUTHEN

SUR LES RAPPORTS ENTRE LES ANCIENS ET LES MODERNES PRINCIPES DE LA GÉOMÉTRIE

Dans l'excellente analyse des Principes de la Géométrie contenue au 1er cahier du Tome III de l'Encyclopédie, l'auteur a eu l'obligation de rendre compte avant tout de la reconstruction moderne du fondement logique de la Géométrie qui s'est montrée nécessaire ou du moins souhaitable, malgré l'exactitude que depuis l'antiquité on attribue tout particulièrement à cette science. En même temps il était naturel de donner des aperçus historiques sur les principes qu'on avait pris autrefois pour points de départ. Cependant dans une telle mention accessoire, s'attachant aux différentes pierres de la construction moderne, on n'évite pas de faire tort aux principes anciens. Chacun des deux fondements de la géométrie est un entier où chaque pierre a sa place déterminée; mais cette place est différente dans les deux constructions: souvent une pierre est dans l'une appuyée sur ce qu'elle porte dans l'autre, et on ne comprend la différence des formes qu'on lui donne qu'en ayant égard aux destinations respectives.

En n'apprenant la connexion que pour les nouveaux principes, on manque le point de vue nécessaire pour juger de la valeur de la forme antérieure des mêmes principes.

En même temps la possibilité logique de différents fondements de la géométrie est reconnue soit par les anciens soit par les modernes. En effet, les uns et les autres commencent par faire des postulats, qui peuvent être plus ou moins utiles, mais entre lesquels, en tout cas, il faut choisir. La différence du choix amenera d'elle-même une grande différence entre les constructions, entièrement logiques, qui en prennent leur point de départ, ce qui n'empêche pas que l'une emprunte quelque pierre à l'autre; mais elle n'en peut faire usage qu'après en avoir adapté la forme à son propre but.

Voilà ce qu'on doit avoir sous les yeux pour juger bien de la logique et de l'exactitude des anciens géomètres, non seulement de ceux de l'antiquité: les Viète, les Fermat, les Huygens, les Newton, s'appuyaient encore sur les mêmes principes avec la conscience de leur valeur logique, et encore Leibniz y avait réfuge, lorqu'il s'agissait d'assurer logiquement des résultats obtenus. Il est vrai qu'au 18e siècle les excellents moyens de faire facilement de grandes et nouvelles conquêtes pour les mathématiques ont créé une routine qui faisait partiellement oublier le véritable fondement logique de ces principes; mais l'habitude de s'y appuyer s'est conservé jusqu'à nos jours, et ils font encore la véritable base de l'enseignement élémentaire et de celui qu'on donne par exemple aux ingénieurs de nos écoles polytechniques parce que les subtilités des principes modernes ont égard à des cas qu'on ne rencontre pas dans cet enseignement. Alors, en s'appuyant de fait sur les anciens principes on devrait en faire voir la connexion et la valeur logique qu'ils ont toujours, bien entendu si on les attache à leurs propres points de départ. Et il ne nuira nullement à la logique des futurs mathématiciens professionels d'apprendre aussi ce fondement plus simple, quand même ils en auront besoin encore d'un autre pour la construction des théories plus hautes. Seulement ils doivent apprendre à distinguer bien les deux fondements d'après leurs points de départ, ce qu'on fait beaucoup mieux en les apprenant bien tous les deux qu'en n'en apprenant que l'un, sans pouvoir éviter pourtant d'en rencontrer l'autre dans la littérature — ou dans l'enseignement qu'on doit donner plus tard à une école polytechnique.

Immédiatement je parle des principes de la Géométrie; mais avec eux des principes anciens de la Mathématique entière; car la modification moderne des principes est précisément celle qui s'est introduite par ce que M. Klein a appelé l'arithmétisation des mathématiques. Autrefois la forme exacte des mathématiques, c'était précisément la géométrie; un géomètre était un savant et « mathématicien » n'était que le nom d'un calculateur routiné. On avait raison alors; car l'exactitude est là où sont les formulations précises et générales, et alors c'était dans la géométrie. Cette généralité de la géométrie est exprimée dans ces paroles de Regiomontanus: La Mathématique, science des grandeurs, se divise en deux parties, savoir la géométrie et l'arithmétique, suivant que la grandeur traitée est continue ou numérique. C'est une expression correcte de l'ancienne position de la géométrie. Elle explique les points de vue qu'on avait pris en construisant dans l'antiquité le fondement logique de la géométrie.

La nécessité d'un fondement logique s'est présentée par la découverte des quantités incommensurables, due aux Pythagoriciens. On voyait qu'il existe des quantités dont il est impossible d'exprimer le rapport par des nombres entiers. Presque en même temps Zénon a montré d'un autre point de vue, par ses célèbres paradoxes, l'impossibilité de parvenir par des divisions aux parties infinitésimales dont devaient se composer les grandeurs continues. En bon Grec il en prit la conséquence, et niait l'existence du continu, l'existence du mouvement. C'était une position pratiquement insoutenable. Les géomètres doivent précisément s'occuper des quantités continues, et comme on ne pouvait y parvenir par l'intermédiaire des quantités discrètes, exprimables par des nombres entiers, il fallait renoncer à cet intermédiaire et reconnaître immédiatement l'existence du continu. Vû l'impossibilité de le représenter par des nombres, on n'avait pour le représenter que l'espèce la plus simple de quantités continues: la longueur variable d'une droite. Alors les opérations mathématiques, pour être exactes, devaient prendre la forme de constructions géométriques bien définies, la multiplication, par exemple, celle de la construction d'un rectangle, suivie, s'il y en avait besoin, de la transformation de ce rectangle en un autre à côté donné, l'extraction de la racine $\sqrt{2}$, celle de la construction d'un triangle, rectangle et isoscèle; l'expression de $(a+b)^2$ prenait la forme d'une décomposition d'un carré en deux carrés et deux rectangles égaux, et la solution générale d'une équation du second degré s'exécutait par une transposition de ces mêmes figures.

Sans doute, exécutées par le compas et la règle, ces opérations auraient encore le même caractère d'approximations que les calculs numériques: mais l'essentiel n'était pas l'opération avec ces instruments, qui ne sont pas même nommés par Euclide, c'était la description formelle des opérations à exécuter avec des droites et des cercles bien définis. Cependant il ne faut pas chercher les véritables définitions de ces lignes et des opérations à faire dans les « définitions » d'Euclide, qui ne disent que peu de chose, mais dans ses postulats et axiomes — de même qu'on le fait dans les principes modernes de la géométrie.

Il y a quelques-uns des principes modernes de la géométrie qu'on n'y trouve pas formellement exposés mais que néanmoins les anciens emploient expressément, nous pourrons dire consciemment, dans leurs démonstrations. Cela ne doit pas nous étonner pour les postulats de consécution des points d'une droite ou d'un cercle; car la notion de grandeurs continues, dont on commence par supposer l'existence, implique déjà la consécution ordonnée des points. On regrette plus de n'y trouver pas les autres postulats de l'analysis situs. La notion d'une aire limitée par un contour fermé, et les faits qu'une droite indéfinie passant par un point de cette aire, de même qu'un trajet quelconque joignant un point intérieur a un point extérieur, doivent rencontrer le contour, sont fort utilisés par Euclide sans être attachés a aucun énoncé formel d'un postulat. Seulement il glisse le postulat qu'une circonférence de cercle est un tel contour fermé dans la définition du cercle. Même le postulat fondamental de l'ancienne géométrie, le postulat de mouvement ou de transposition n'est énoncé qu'indirectement dans l'axiome disant que les grandeurs congruentes sont égales. L'existence de figures qui se peuvent superposer là est supposée. Hors de cette application principale à la comparaison des grandeurs, Euclide emploie du reste le moins possible une telle superposition. Il est nécessaire d'en faire usage dans la démonstration d'un seul des théorèmes sur l'égalité de triangles; mais Euclide l'évite dans les autres.

La formulation des autres postulats nécessaires pour utiliser dans un plan la droite et le cercle est plus précise. On postule qu'une droite indéfinie soit déterminée par deux points ou par un morceau de la droite, un cercle par le centre et un point, et que deux droites d'un plan se rencontrent dans des circonstances ordinaires. En renvoyant à un postulat exprès — le 5e, souvent appelé le 11e axiome — la condition suffisante de cette intersection, Euclide fait voir qu'il ne regarde pas cette suffisance comme un théorème démontrable. Son énoncé exprès du postulat de la géométrie Euclidéenne signale déjà la possibilté de la géométrie hyperbolique. Euclide s'en approche beaucoup plus que ceux qui ont après lui cru démontrer son postulat.

Pour la comparaison des grandeurs ces postulats constructifs ne suffisent pas. Euclide les supplée donc par ses axiomes ou « notions communes » qui assurent précisément cette comparaison de grandeurs. Il y énonce l'égalité de deux quantités égales à une même, ou composées par addition ou soustraction de quantités égales, l'égalité de grandeurs congruentes et que l'entier est plus grand qu'une partie. On a ainsi le moyen de comparer entre eux les segments de droites, les angles, les aires, et les volumes. Ce sont ces axiomes qui contiennent la véritable définition de ces grandeurs. On en réalise la comparaison sans faire usage de nombres. La géométrie fondée sur ces axiomes est donc également applicable aux grandeurs commensurables et aux grandeurs incommensurables. Qu'elle est fertile, voilà ce que montre Euclide, en composant ses quatre premiers livres sans avoir besoin d'autre supposition, et notamment sans faire encore usage du postulat faussement attribué à Archimède, qu'il va introduire ensuite.

En effet, à la longue la géométrie ne pouvait pas se passer de l'aide des rapports numériques, mais comment donner à cette aide une forme générale et applicable aux quantités variant d'une manière continue? Zénon avait reconnu que par la division en des parties de plus en plus petites on n'atteint jamais à ce but. Il en résulte qu'un nouveau postulat est nécessaire pour franchir cette limite des applications des nombres. Eudoxe inventait la forme si simple de ce postulat: une quantité peut être répétée un assez grand nombre de fois pour dépasser une quantité quelconque de la même espèce. C'est au même postulat qu'on donne encore un rang éminent entre les principes modernes de la géométrie, mais en l'appelant le postulat d'Archimède. Il me semble pourtant que plus on admire la manière dont ce postulat touche au but, plus on a l'obligation de le rapporter à son véritable auteur, qu'Archimède cite expressément.

C'est ce postulat, « lemme », qui permettait aux grecs de construire une théorie générale des proportions embrassant les quantités incommensurables aussi bien que les quantités commensurables. Il leur permettait aussi de mesurer les aires et les volumes qu'on ne peut pas composer par addition et soustraction d'un nombre fini de parties égales. Et bien entendu cela se fait d'une manière absolument exacte. Jusqu'à quel point les Grecs savaient apprécier cette exactitude, cela se montre d'une manière curieuse par le fait suivant: on regardait comme non existant les découvertes faites avant Eudoxe par des considérations infinitésimales plus vagues. Nous savons par l'ouvrage d'Archimède que M. Heiberg vient de retrouver, que déjà Démocrite connaissait les volumes d'une pyramide et d'un cône; mais d'un autre ouvrage d'Archimède nous voyons qu'il n'était permis de regarder qu'Eudoxe comme l'auteur de ces mêmes théorèmes: car seulement lui avait su les démontrer rigoureusement, ce qui ne devient possible que par son postulat. Voilà de rigueur! C'était comme si nous n'attribuerions l'invention du calcul différentiel qu'à Cauchy; car seulement lui a su définir précisément les quantités infiniment petites.

C'est en vérité la méthode exacte des limites qu'a créée Eudoxe, et qu'après lui Euclide et Archimède utilisent avec une sureté complète. Ils réitèrent même souvent la formulation charactéristique: rendre une différence plus petite que toute quantité donnée. En faisant un emprunt à cette terminologie les géomètres du 16e siècle les Grégoire de St. Vincent, les Pascal et les Wallis montrent seulement qu'ils connaissaient leurs maîtres antiques beaucoup mieux que ne le font les mathématiciens de nos jours.

Pour les anciens et pour les modernes le postulat d'Eudoxe est le pont qui réunit l'étude des quantités continues à celle des quantités discrètes; mais il y a pourtant une différence essentielle entre l'usage qu'on fait de ce passage. Prenant le point de départ arithmétique de notre temps, on ne reconnaît l'existence du continu qu'après y être atteint par l'intermédiaire dudit postulat. Les anciens, qui avaient dû étudier les quantités continues avant d'avoir franchi ce pont, avaient déjà admis l'existence de tous les deux domaines qu'il réunit. Il leur permet donc seulement de transporter des vérités démontrées pour l'un à l'autre, ce qui devenait alors plus utile pour l'application de la géométrie à l'algèbre que réciproquement.

Cette différence amène aussi quelque différence à la manière d'employer la méthode. $\sqrt{2}$ était par exemple déjà quelque chose pour les anciens, pas un nombre, car ils ne reconnaissaient que les nombres rationnels, mais le rapport d'un segment bien construisable à un autre. En faisant usage du postulat d'Eudoxe on pouvait ensuite démontrer que d'autres segments avaient le même rapport. L'aire d'un cercle ou une autre aire limitée par un contour donné était déjà pour eux une grandeur existante, et on n'avait pas besoin d'une intégration ou de quelque autre opération continuée à l'infini pour la définir. Sa comparaison avec des aires limitées par des droites avait été rendue possible par les axiomes d'Euclide. Il suffit donc pour démontrer une approximation indéfinie à l'aire du cercle, de montrer que la différence entre son résultat et l'aire du cercle peut être rendue plus petite que toute grandeur donnée, et non pas comme à présent de démontrer la convergence analytique de l'opération vers une limite inconnue et définie seulement par l'opération elle-même.

On dit, par exemple, souvent en parlant de l'approximation connue de Viète:

$$\sqrt{\frac{1}{2}}\sqrt{\frac{1}{2}\left(1+\sqrt{\tfrac{1}{2}}\right)}\sqrt{\frac{1}{2}\left(1+\sqrt{\tfrac{1}{2}\left(1+\sqrt{\tfrac{1}{2}}\right)}\right)}\cdots,$$

qu'il ne démontre pas la convergence de ce produit infini; mais pour Viète, qui se servit consciemment du fondement logique des anciens, sa convergence vers la limite bien définie $\frac{2}{\pi}$ était une conséquence immédiate du fait démontré rigoureusement par Euclide que la différence d'un cercle et d'un polygone inscrit régulier peut être rendue plus petite que toute grandeur donnée.

Pour ceux qui font usage des anciens principes la substitution d'une aire à nos intégrales rend superflu de démontrer explicitement que la valeur de $\lim \Sigma f(x)\Delta x$ est indépendente des rapports des différences Δx, si seulement elles s'approchent toutes de zéro. Fermat savait bien se servir de cet avantage.

Dans leurs calculs d'aires et de volumes les anciens pouvaient donc regarder les grandeurs à déterminer comme existantes indépendemment de notre faculté de les trouver; mais il en est tout autrement pour les longueurs et aires de lignes et surfaces courbes. Les principes d'Euclide ne donnent aucune existence immédiate à ces quantités, et il est impossible de les comparer à la longueur d'une droite ou à une aire plane, sans donner par des postulats nouveaux et exprès des règles pour cette comparaison. Archimède a vu cette nécessité aussi clairement qu'on le voit aujourd'hui, et il a formulé d'une manière simple et logique les postulats nécessaires, dont il se sert ensuite d'une manière aussi claire et logique. Il n'a donc nullement mérité, qu'en oubliant le second de ses postulats, ainsi que leur application, et les postulats analogues sur les surfaces courbes, on en a interprété le premier comme une définition de la droite: le plus court chemin entre deux points. Fort illogique au moment où l'on ne sait pas du tout ce que c'est que la longueur d'une ligne courbe!

Ce qui permet à Archimède de la calculer ce sont deux postulats (il les appelle λαμβανόμενα):

Le premier est celui qu'on a pris faussement pour la définition d'une droite. Le deuxième est: De deux lignes tracées entre les mêmes points, et qui tournent leur convexité du même côté, la ligne externe est la plus grande. Voilà une véritable base d'un calcul des longueurs courbes. En reprenant de tels calculs Fermat, ainsi que Neil et van Heuraet, ont expressément recours aux mêmes principes, qui ne sont nullement une invention des temps les plus modernes.

Pour base de son calcul d'une surface courbe Archimède prend les postulats suivants:

Une surface plane est plus petite qu'une surface courbe de même périmètre (ce qui n'est pas une définition du plan!); et

De deux surfaces courbes limitées au même contour plan et qui orientent leur convexité du même côté, la surface externe est la plus grande.

Ces derniers exemples montrent combien les anciens ont pris sérieusement la tâche de formuler expressément les suppositions qui font le point de départ de leurs recherches. Ils montrent en même temps qu'en reprenant la même tâche les modernes ont été, souvent sans le remarquer, conduits à reprendre les mêmes chemins où les anciens les ont précédés.

Le temps me défend de multiplier ces exemples et aussi d'appliquer ici à plusieurs principes anciens la critique nécessaire pour en faire ressortir le noyau sain. Si j'en aurais eu de plus, j'aurais été tenté à donner un aperçu sur le développement historique de l'exactitude mathématique; mais une tâche pareille serait trop grande pour une communication à un Congrès.

DAVID EUGENE SMITH

THE GANITA - SĀRA - SANGRAHA OF MAHĀVĪRĀCĀRYA

We have so long been accustomed to think of Pataliputra on the Ganges and of Ujjain over towards the western coast of India as the ancient habitats of Hindu mathematics, that we experience a kind of surprise at thinking that other centers equally as important existed among the multitude of cities of that great empire. In the same way we have known for a century, thanks chiefly to the labors of such scholars as COLEBROOKE and TAYLOR, the works of ARYABHAṬA (1), BRAHMAGUPTA, and BHASKARA, and have come to feel that to these men alone are due the noteworthy contributions to native Hindu mathematics. Of course a little reflection shows this conclusion to be an incorrect one. Other great schools, particularly of astronomy, did exist, and other scholars taught and wrote and added their quota, small or otherwise, to make up the sum total. It has, however, been a little discouraging that native scholars under the English supremacy have done so little to bring to light the ancient material known to exist, and to make it known to the Western world. This neglect has not been owing to the absence of material, for Sanskrit manuscripts are known, as are also Persian and Arabic and Chinese and Japanese, that are well worth translating, from the historical standpoint. It has rather been owing to the fact that it is hard to find a man with the requisite scholarship, who can afford to give his time to what is necessarily a labor of love.

It is a pleasure to be permitted to announce to this Congress the fact that such a man has been found, and that through his labors we are in due time to have new light upon the subject of Oriental mathematics, as known in another part of India and at a time about midway between that of ARYABHAṬA and BHASKARA and two centuries later than BRAHMAGUPTA. The learned pandit, M. RANGACHARYA, professor of Sanskrit in the Presidency College at Madras, Curator of the Library of Oriental Manuscripts, and Registrar of Books in the Department of Education, some time ago became interested in the work of MAHĀVĪRĀCĀRYA, and has now completed about two thirds of the translation. Having given some attention to the works of the Hindu

(1) Another scholar in India, G. B. KAYE, Esq., is now making a careful study of ARYABHATA.

scholars in my search for mathematical material in the East, I have Professor RANGACHARYA's permission to make this treatise known at this time, perhaps a year or two in advance of its publication.

MAHĀVĪRĀCĀRYA probably lived in the court of one of the old Rāshṭrakūṭa monarchs who ruled over what is now the kingdom of Mysore, and whose name is given as Amoghavarsha Nripatuṅga. He ascended the throne in the first half of the ninth century A. D., so that we may roughly fix the date of the treatise in question as about 850.

There are four or five manuscripts of this author's work known, three of the oldest being in Madras. Two transcripts of old manuscripts are in other cities, one of them being in Mysore. All of these are in Sanskrit, but all are written in the Kanarese characters used in Mysore in MAHĀVĪRĀCĀRYA's time. One has annotations in Devanagari characters, although the Mysore copy which I have seen has them in Kanarese. In the edition that Professor RANGACHARYA is preparing the Sanskrit will be given in Devanagari characters, with variant readings from the different manuscripts, and there will be a carefully annotated English translation.

The work itself, entitled *Gaṇita - Sāra - Saṅgraha*, consists of nine chapters, of which six have been translated. The first is introductory, and contains seventy stanzas on Terminology. It opens, as is usual with Oriental treatises, with an invocation, in this case apparently to the author's patron deity: « Salutation to Mahāvira, the Lord of the Jinas, the protector (of the faithful), whose four infinite attributes, worthy to be esteemed in (all) the three worlds, are unsurpassable (in excellence). I bow to that highlyglorious Lord of the Jinas, by whom, as forming the shining lamp of the knowledge of numbers, the whole of the universe has been made to shine ». This is followed by « An appreciation of the Science of Calculation » of which I venture to quote three stanzas: « In all those transactions which relate to worldly, Vedic or (other) similar religious affairs, calculation is of use. In the science of love, in the science of wealth, in music and in the drama, in the art of cooking, and similarly in medicine and in things like the knowledge of architecture: in prosody, in poetics and poetry, in logic and grammar and such other things, and in relation to all that constitutes the peculiar value of (all) the (various) arts; the science of computation is held in high esteem ». The terminology relates chiefly to the measures used, the names of the operations, numeration, and negatives and zero. Of the operations with numbers, eight are given, addition (except in series) and subtraction (even with fractions) being omitted as if presupposed. One interesting feature is the law relating to zero, which is stated thus: « A number multiplied by zero is zero, and that (number) remains unchanged when it is divided by, combined with, (or) diminished by zero »: That is, the law known to BHASKARA, of dividing by zero, is not here recognized, division by zero being looked upon as of no effect. The laws of multiplication by negatives is stated, and the imaginary number is thus disposed of: « As in the nature of things a negative (quantity) is not a square (quantity), it has therefore no square root ».

The second chapter treats of arithmetical operations the first being multiplication, and this being followed by division, squaring, square root, cubing, cube root, summation (of series, in which is included some treatment of arithmetical and geometrical progressions), and *Vyutkalita* (that is, the summation of a series after a certain number of initial terms, *iṣṭa*, have been cut off).

Chapter III treats of fractions, following the same order as Chapter II. The most noteworthy feature is that relating to the inverted divisor, which is set forth as follows: « After making the denominator of the divisor its numerator (and *vice-versa*), the operation to be conducted then is as in the multiplication (of fractions) ». It is curious that this device, which from another source we know to have been used in the East, became as it were a lost art until rediscovered in Europe in the sixteenth century. (See the writer's *Rara Arithmetica*, Boston, 1908, p. 233).

Chapter IV consists of miscellaneous problems in fractions which, however, include certain questions involving quadratic equations. For example:

« One-fourth of a herd of camels was seen in the forest; twice the square root (of that herd) had gone on to mountain slopes; and three times five camels (were), however, (found) to remain on the bank of a river. What is the (numerical) measure of that herd of camels? ». This evidently requires the finding of the positive root of the equation $\frac{x}{4} + 2\sqrt{x} + 15 = x$, or, in general, the solution of an equation of the type $x - (bx + c\sqrt{x} + a) = 0$, the rule for which is given. The chapter also contains various other types of equations involving some knowledge of radical quantities.

Chapter V relates to the Rule of Three, simple and compound, direct and inverse, with applications to interest, barter, and mensuration.

Chapter VI is entitled « Mixed Problems », and is interesting from the considerable use made of rules that would now be expressed in algebraic formulas, particularly with reference to the various computations of interest and to the solution of indeterminate equation.

Of the latter a single example may suffice to show the nature of the problems. « Into the bright and refreshing outskirts of a forest, which were full of numerous trees with their branches bent down with the weight of flowers and fruits, trees such as *jambu* trees, lime trees, plantains, areca palms, jack trees, date palms, *hintala* trees, palmyras, *punnāga* trees, and mango trees — (into the outskirts), the various quarters whereof were filled with the many sounds of crowds of parrots and cuckoos found near springs containing lotuses with bees roaming about them — (into such forest outskirts) a number of weary travellers entered with joy. (There were) sixty-three (numerally equal) heaps of plantain fruits put together and combined with seven (more) of those same fruits, and these were equally distributed among twenty-three travellers so as to have no remainder. You tell me now the numerical measure of a heap of plantains ». Problems of this sort are solved by a process of calculation known as *Vallikā-Kuttīkāra*, a kind of division or distribution employing a creeper-like chain of figures, and the patience shown by Professor Rangacharya in interpreting the long and complicated rule will strike the reader of this work as worthy of the highest praise.

A complex *kuttīkara*, known as *Sakala-kuttīkara*, is also given, an example of which is as follows: « A certain quantity multiplied by six, then increased by ten, and then divided by nine, leaves no remainder. Similarly, a certain other quantity multiplied by six, then diminished by ten, and then divided by nine, leaves no remainder. Tell me quickly what these two quantities are which are to be multiplied (by the given multiplier here) ». The case has no new interest, however, since it resolves itself into two simple problems, $\frac{6x+10}{9} =$ integer, and $\frac{6x-10}{9} =$ integer, instead of the problem $\frac{ax+by}{c} =$ integer. Cases, however, of the type

$$ax + by + cz + dw = p$$
$$\Sigma a = n$$

are given, and others involving several variables.

A single example will suffice to show their general nature: « Four merchants who had invested their money in common were asked, each separately, by the customs officer what the value of the commodities was, and indeed one eminent merchant among them, deducting his own investment, said that it was twenty-two; then another said that it was twentythree; then another, twenty-four; and the fourth said that it was twenty-seven, each of them deducting his own invested amount. O friend, tell me separately the value of the commodity owned by each ».

Chapter VII, not yet translated, treats of geometric problems, both with relation to practical applications and approximate results, and also from the accurate scientific standpoint.

Chapter VIII deals with mensuration, and principally with the common Hindu topic of « excavations », and the final chapter (IX) treats of the primitive trigonometry known in India by the name of « shadow problems ».

Such is a brief outline of the work. It is sufficient, however, to show that we shall have, in Professor RANGACHARYA's labors, the most noteworthy single contribution to the history of Hindu mathematics that has been made for nearly a century. What light it shall throw upon the relation of BHASKARA's *Lilavati* to works of his predecessors, upon the relation of the schools of Pataliputra and Ujjain to each other and to that of Mysore, upon the knowledge of Greek mathematics in the East, and upon the state of algebra in India at about the time that AL-KHOWARAZMI was writing his *Al-jebr w'al-muqabala* in Baghdad, it is impossible as yet to say.

It is on these accounts quite as much as for the details of the work itself that its appearance, perhaps in 1909 or 1910, will be awaited with interest. If its publication shall also have the effect of stimulating other Oriental scholars, such as India continues to produce, to make known to the West the sealed books of the East, the world will be still more Professor RANGACHARYA's debtor [1].

(1) The writer desires not only to record his personal indebtedness to Professor RANGACHARYA for information relative to MAHĀVĪRĀCĀRYA's work, but also to his able assistant in the Library of Oriental Manuscripts at Madras, R. RAMASWAMI, B. A., (vernacular, Munshi) whose many courtesies, including the furnishing of valuable information relating to mathematical manuscripts, he will always remember with gratitude.

PIERRE DUHEM

SUR LA DÉCOUVERTE DE LA LOI DE LA CHUTE DES GRAVES

La loi fondamentale de la chute des corps est la suivante: Lorsqu'un corps tombe en chute libre, sa vitesse croît proportionnellement à la durée de la chute.

Les anciens savaient que la chute des graves était accélérée; mais il ne paraît pas qu'ils aient connu la loi suivant laquelle ce mouvement s'accélérait. D'autre part, on sait que la loi précédemment formulée se trouve très nettement indiquée, et à plusieurs reprises, dans les manuscrits de Léonard de Vinci; rien ne laisse soupçonner, d'ailleurs, la voie par laquelle il était parvenu à reconnaître cette vérité; l'avait il trouvée de lui même? l'avait il tirée de ses lectures? il ne nous en dit rien.

Nous voudrions montrer ici comment certaines idées, émises au Moyen-Age, avaient pu lui suggérer cette découverte.

Pendant très longtemps, les philosophes et les géomètres ont borné les ambitions de leur analyse à l'étude du mouvement uniforme; bien qu'ils connussent l'existence de mouvements dont la vitesse varie d'un instant à l'autre, ils ne tentaient pas de préciser la loi de cette variation; en particulier, il semble bien que l'on puisse parvenir à une époque avancée du Moyen-Age sans trouver, dans les écrits des géomètres, la définition du mouvement uniformément varié. Jean de Meurs n'en parle aucunement dans le traité *De mobilibus et motis*, qui est le premier traité du livre IV de son *Opus quadripartitum numerorum*, achevé le 13 novembre 1343; Bradwardin n'en parle pas davantage en son *Tractatus de proportionalitate motuum in velocitate*, qui doit être à peu près contemporain du traité de Jean de Meurs, puisque Bradwardin est mort en 1349.

En revanche, la notion de mouvement uniformément varié se trouve nettement définie dans les ouvrages d'Albert de Saxe, qui enseigna à l'Université de Paris de 1351 à 1361.

En ses *Quaestiones subtilissimae in libros de Caelo et Mundo* (In lib. II quaest. 14) (¹), Albert fait une étude extrêmement remarquable du problème de la chute accélérée d'un grave.

(¹) Cette question capitale n'a pas été reproduite dans les deux éditions d'écrits d'Albert de Saxe, de Thémon et de Jean Buridan que Georges Lockert a données à Paris, en 1516 et en 1518.

Il remarque d'abord que cette proposition: Le mouvement devient plus intense vers la fin, peut s'entendre de diverses manières. Selon un premier sens, le mouvement (et par ce mot ALBERT, comme tous ses contemporains, entend l'*intensitas motus*, c'est à dire ce que nous nommons la *vitesse instantanée*) peut croître en devenant double, triple, quadruple, ... Selon un second sens, il peut croître de telle manière qu'à sa valeur première s'ajoute la moitié de cette valeur, puis la moitié de cette moitié, etc. En langage moderne, on dirait que les accroissements de vitesse peuvent suivre une progression arithmétique, ou qu'ils peuvent suivre une progression géométrique de raison fractionnaire.

La loi ainsi formulée par ALBERT DE SAXE comme loi possible de la chute des graves n'est pas la proportionnalité de la vitesse à la durée de la chute; c'est la proportionnalité de la vitesse à l'espace parcouru. On sait que cette loi avait séduit GALILÉE en sa jeunesse et qu'il en a, plus tard, démontré l'absurdité. Mais on doit remarquer qu'en l'analyse d'ALBERT, l'*extensio secundum tempus* est, constamment, mise en parallèle de l'*extensio secundum distantiam*; la concision seule de son exposé l'a, sans doute, empêché de signaler comme également recevable la proportionnalité de la vitesse au temps de chute; l'attention d'un lecteur intelligent pouvait se porter sur cette dernière loi, aussi bien que sur la loi formellement énoncée.

Le passage que nous venons d'étudier a donc fort bien pu suggérer à LÉONARD DE VINCI la découverte de la véritable loi de la chute des graves. Nous avons établi (1), en effet, que le grand peintre devait bon nombre de ses opinions scientifiques aux *Quaestiones in libros de Caelo et Mundo* d'ALBERT DE SAXE qu'il a formellement citées.

La *Question* d'ALBERT DE SAXE a pu influer également sur les recherches de divers autres mécaniciens de la Renaissance, car le livre qui la contenait a joui, à cette époque, d'une grande vogue. Si on laisse de côté les deux éditions données à Paris en 1516 et en 1518, éditions qui ne renferment pas la *Question* dont il s'agit, celle ci se trouve dans les *Quaestiones subtilissimae in libros de Caelo et Mundo* éditées à Pavie en 1481, à Venise en 1492, 1497 et 1520.

En outre, vers la fin du XVe siècle, le parisien PIERRE TATARET rédigea un petit manuel de philosophie intitulé: *Clarissima singularisque totius philosophiae necnon metaphysicae Aristotelis expositio* ou encore *Commentationes in libros Aristotelis secundum Subtilissimi Doctoris Scoti sententiam.* La vogue de ce résumé fut extrême; les éditions qui en furent faites étaient dejà au nombre de sept en l'an 1500; elles continuèrent à se multiplier pendant le premier tiers du XVIe siècle. Or ce manuel reproduit textuellement (2) le passage d'ALBERT DE SAXE que nous venons d'analyser.

L'opinion selon laquelle la vitesse de chute d'un grave croîtrait d'une manière uniforme soit avec le chemin parcouru, soit peut-être avec le temps écoulé, était

(1) P. DUHEM, *Études sur Léonard de Vinci*, Première Série, I: *Albert de Saxe et Léonard de Vinci* (Paris, 1906).

(2) TATARET, Op. cit., *De Caelo et Mundo* (lib. II, tract. II, circa finem).

donc émise, dès le milieu du XIVe siècle, à l'Université de Paris; vers l'an 1500, elle se trouvait grandement vulgarisée par les nombreuses éditions du *De Caelo* d'Albert de Saxe et du manuel de Pierre Tataret. Cette opinion, qui fut sûrement connue de Léonard de Vinci, a pu lui suggérer les énoncés que nous relevons dans ses manuscrits.

Ces énoncés nous paraissent incomplets. Quelle est la variable indépendante à laquelle sont rapportées les valeurs de la vitesse dont Albert fait mention? Son silence à cet égard provient de ce qu'il suppose son lecteur au courant de la Science de son temps, et la connaissance de cette Science nous permet de suppléer à ce silence. Lorsque les scolastiques du XVIe siècle traitaient de l'intensité d'une propriété quelconque (*intensio formae*), ils la regardaient comme fonction de l'extension (*extensio*) de la même propriété; dans le cas du mouvement, ils distinguaient deux sortes d'extensions, l'extension selon le chemin parcouru (*extensio secundum distantiam*) et l'extension salon la durée (*extensio secundum tempus*).

Les énoncés abrégés d'Albert doivent donc s'entendre ainsi:

Lorsque l'on fait croître suivant une progression arithmétique soit les chemins parcourus par le grave, soit les durées de chute, on peut supposer ou bien que les valeurs de la vitesse croissent suivant une progression arithmétique, ou bien que les accroissements successifs de ces valeurs suivent une progression géométrique de raison moindre que l'unité.

Pour fixer son choix, Albert invoque à titre d'axiome une proposition qu'il regarde comme l'expression de la pensée d'Aristote: Si un grave était placé infiniment loin du centre du Monde et si on le laissait tomber, la vitesse de ce grave croîtrait au delà de toute limite alors qu'il approcherait du centre, mais elle ne deviendrait pas infinie avant qu'il n'eût atteint ce point.

Fort de cette axiome, Albert exclut les lois de chute de la seconde forme, car, selon ces lois, la vitesse du mouvement ne pourrait croître au delà de toute limite.

Une considération du même genre lui permet d'exclure certaines autres lois que l'on pourrait proposer; on pourrait imaginer que la vitesse crût en progression arithmétique alors que les accroissements successifs du temps formeraient une progression géométrique de raison $\frac{1}{2}$, ou alors que les accroissements successifs de l'espace suivraient une semblable progression.

Ces hypothèses, en effet, assigneraient à la vitesse de chute une valeur infinie avant la fin du mouvement, quelque petite que soit la durée de ce mouvement ou quelque petit que soit l'espace parcouru, ce qui est faux: « *Nam tunc sequeretur quod quilibet motus naturalis qui per quantumcunque tempus parvum duraret, vel quo quantumcunque parvum spacium pertransiretur, ad quemcunque gradum velocitatis pertingeret ante finem. Modo est falsum* ». La finesse avec laquelle Albert a su découvrir l'impossibilité de telles lois et la précision avec laquelle il l'a signalée sont bien dignes de remarque.

Il faut donc entendre, ajoute-t-il que l'intensité du mouvement du grave devient double, triple, etc., dans le sens suivant: Quand un certain espace a été parcouru, ce mouvement a une certaine intensité (vitesse); quand un espace double a été parcouru, la vitesse est double; quand l'espace parcouru est triple, elle est triple, et ainsi de suite. Cette supposition s'accorde avec la proposition attribuée à ARISTOTE: « *Et ideo tertia conclusio intelligitur quod intenditur per duplum, triplum etc., ad istum intellectum, quod quando ipso pertransitum est aliquod spatium, est aliquantus, et quando ipso est pertransitum duplum est in duplo velocior, et quando ipso pertransitum est triplum spatium est in triplo velocior, et sic ultra. Et ad istum intellectum vadit auctoritas Aristotelis*... ».

G. PITTARELLI

LUCA PACIOLI USURPÒ PER SE STESSO QUALCHE LIBRO DI PIERO DE' FRANCESCHI?

Al Congresso storico internazionale, che si tenne in quest'alma città nell'aprile del 1903, io feci una Comunicazione intorno al trattato *De prospectiva pingendi* di PIER DE' FRANCESCHI da San Sepolcro, accennai all'accusa lanciata dal VASARI a LUCA PACIOLI, d'essersi costui appropriato del trattatello de' cinque corpi regolari scritto da PIERO, e promettevo di ritornare sull'argomento.

Il VASARI formula l'accusa con queste gravi parole (¹): « Fu Piero, come si è « detto, studiosissimo dell'arte, e si esercitò assai nella prospettiva, ed ebbe buonis- « sima cognizione di Euclide; in tanto che tutti i migliori giri tirati nei corpi rego- « lari egli meglio che altri geometri intese, ed i maggiori lumi che di tal cosa ci « siano, sono di sua mano: perchè maestro Luca dal Borgo, frate di S. Francesco, che « scrisse dei corpi regolari di geometria, fu suo discepolo; e venuto Piero in vec- « chiezza ed a morte, dopo aver scritto molti libri, maestro Luca detto, usurpandoli « per sè stesso, gli fece stampare come suoi, essendogli pervenuti quelli alle mani dopo « la morte del Maestro ».

Sì fatta accusa diede origine ad un processo. Il prof. GUSTAVO UZIELLI, studioso delle cose di PAOLO POZZO TOSCANELLI e di LEONARDO DA VINCI, nelle *Ricerche* intorno a questo (pag. 442 e segg.) (²), riporta i nomi degli accusatori e degli avvocati: egli si schiera tra questi e dopo alcune considerazioni dichiara *assolto il Pacioli dall'accusa di plagio verso il De' Franceschi, e chiuso il processo* (pag. 451).

Il VASARI estende l'accusa di plagio ai *molti libri scritti da Piero*. In verità, questi molti si riducono a due: al *De prospectiva pingendi* e al trattatello *De quinque corporibus regularibus*. Il primo fu pnbblicato in due grossi volumi, testo e Atlante, il 1899 a Strassbourg, dall'editore Heitz, per cura del dott. Winterberg, che ne rivide il testo secondo il codice palatino di Parma, scritto in volgare, e vi aggiunse la traduzione tedesca; il secondo è inedito, ed è un codice latino della Vaticana, fondo urbinate, n. 632, carte 68, del qual codice fu data notizia la prima volta dal Deunistonn, nella sua opera: *Memoirs of the Duker of Urbin*, 1851.

(¹) VASARI, *Le vite* (ed. del Sansoni, curata da G. Milanesi, 1878, tomo II, pp. 487-488).
(²) *Ricerche intorno a Leonardo da Vinci* (Torino, E. Loescher, 1896).

L'accusa, dunque, va considerata rispetto alla *prospectiva* e rispetto al *libellus* (de quinque corporibus). Quanto alla prima sono anch'io convinto che Luca non se l'approprio; poichè, tra l'altro, così nella *Summa de Arithmetica* come nella *Divina proportione*, egli ne parla come di cosa non sua, appresa anzi dal suo conterraneo Piero, che chiama *pittore sublime e monarca della pittura*, e del quale, pur non dichiarandosi espressamente discepolo, si confessa studioso ed ammiratore, come artista e come matematico (1).

Ma quanto al *libellus*, la cosa muta. Per la *prospectiva* il Pacioli fa come da compilatore: *feci degnissimo compendio*; pel *libellus*, al contrario, ei non fece che tradurlo in italiano e dedicarlo a Pier Soderini come libro suo!

Il prof. Uzielli (pag. 443), si fa questa domanda: *Ma, in realtà, è il Libellus del Pacioli identico a quello del De' Franceschi?* Dopo alcune testimonianze di altri e alcune considerazioni sue, conclude: *no.* Io riapro il processo e concludo: *sì.*

Gli argomenti recati dall'Uzielli si riducono in sostanza alle testimonianze contrarie di Egnazio Danti, che nella prefazione de' suoi commentarî alle due regole della prospettiva pratica del Vignola, dice: *sì come fece* (per i corpi regolari) *Pietro del Borgo, se ben F. Luca gli stampò poi sotto suo nome*, e dello Jordan (2) che da un confronto del *Libellus* di Piero, coi luoghi corrispondenti nella *Divina proportione* di Luca, conclude che questi tradusse letteralmente; e alla testimonianza favorevole del Winterberg (3), il quale ha riconosciuto che *parecchie proposizioni date in modo errato dal De' Franceschi, sono dimostrate in modo corretto dal Pacioli*. Sono parole dell'Uzielli, il quale dopo ciò, ovvero *his fretus*, dà l'assoluzione al frate francescano.

In verità l'aver Luca dimostrato in modo corretto alcune proposizioni che Piero avrebbe dimostrato in modo non esatto, non prova la non reità del primo: questi avrebbe fatta una traduzione con correzioni, ma non dice punto nè che la sua sia una traduzione, nè che il testo originale sia del pittore, anzi, contrariamente a ciò che dice l'Uzielli, dà il libro come suo. Egli sopprime la bella e affettuosa e storicamente importante dedica al duca Guidobaldo scritta da Piero in latino, e la sostituisce con quella a Pier Soderini, scritta pure in latino, dicendo così: *Ideo novum hoc opus quod jampridem parturiebam tibi uni dicare constitui!*

Di qualche altro mutamento, non sostanziale, dirò appresso.

La nostra biblioteca della Facoltà di scienze possiede della *Divina proportione* l'edizione di Venezia del 1509, appartenuta già allo Chasles, la quale per più giorni io portai alla biblioteca Vaticana per fare i confronti col *Libellus* di Piero. Io vorrei aver qui quel bel codice legato in marrocchino rosso, e leggerlo, mentre un altro potrebbe guardare il libro di Luca: il plagio risulterebbe evidentissimo. Non potendo dare a me il piacere di mostrarvi il codice, permettetemi che io vi dica qualche cosa del mio confronto; ma sarò brevissimo per non abusare della vostra

(1) *Summa de Arithmetica* (Venetiis 1494, a tergo della pag. 68, e nella dedica al duca Guidobaldo); *Divina proportione* (Venezia, 1509, parte I, c. 23 *r*).
(2) Jordan M., in Jahrb. der K. preuss. Kunstsammlung, vol. II (1880) pp. 115, 116, 118.
(3) Winterberg, *Repertorium für Kunstwissenschaft* (vol. V, 1882, pp. 33-41).

indulgenza. Vi domando però di credermi, che il confronto lo feci minuto, e vi mostro dodici pagine della mia scrittura fitta, riguardante il soggetto.

È debole la difesa fatta dal WINTERBERG, perchè a luoghi che nel PACIOLI si trovano corretti, possono contrapporsi luoghi dove invece il Pittore dice e fa giusto e il Frate no.

Esempî: Pag. 8 *r*. di LUCA, casus 50 che corrisponde al 51 di PIERO, il raggio di un circolo di superficie 28 sarebbe, secondo LUCA $\sqrt{372}$, mentre PIERO dà il valore giusto $\sqrt{352}$. — Pag. 9 *r*: il casus 1 di Luca corrisponde al casus 2 di Piero; ma il primo dice che la superficie di un tetraedro regolare il cui asse è 4 è $\sqrt{728}$, mentre l'altro la dà in $\sqrt{1728}$, ch'è giusto.

Tutte le intestazioni che in PIERO sono in rosso mancano in LUCA.

Spesso il primo è più esatto del secondo negli enunciati.

Prendiamo, per es., nel *Tractatus secundus* i casus 9, 10, 11 di LUCA, ai quali corrispondono i casus 10, 11, 12 di PIERO. Il primo parla del corpo *quattro base triangulare equilatero*, mentre i problemi si riferiscono a un tetraedro qualunque; e il secondo infatti non adopera punto l'aggettivo *equilatero*. Senza poi dire che questo aggettivo è, in LUCA, in contraddizione anche con le figure, poichè le basi sono triangoli aventi i lati 13, 14, 15 (triangoli molto adoperati a quell'epoca, perchè l'area, le altezze, le proiezioni delle altezze sui lati sono numeri razionali), e poichè l'ultimo problema si può formulare per una piramide qualunque, come appunto fa PIERO.

Altra differenza, lieve, è che LUCA pone numeri astratti, PIERO numeri concreti: avambraccia, braccia, ecc.

Veniamo alla terza parte, al *Tractatus tertius*. PIERO la fa precedere da una piccola introduzione, che LUCA pone come conclusione della seconda parte. Ma anche qui egli traduce male. Dice il pittore: « Sit igitur spera cujus axis ulnas 12 occupet. veluti habes in ultima XIII Euclidis ubi demonstratur speram omniam quinque corpora continere quae regularia sunt... »; e dice bene. Traduce il frate: « Adunqua sia la spera che il suo axis sia 12 . si commo tu ai nell'ultima del 13 de Euclide che si demostra nel semicirculo dela spera contenere tucti li cinque corpi regulari, ecc »; e, come si vede, traduce male.

Nel casus 2 la figura del cubo dal quale si ricava quella del tetraedro regolare è fatta meglio in PIERO: in LUCA la retta condotta per G nella facce GBCH dovrebbe passare pel vertice opposto C e non vi passa. E poichè parlo di esattezza nelle figure, faccio osservare che nella figura rappresentante il dodecaedro e l'icosaedro interno (reciproco questo del primo, come diremmo oggi), LUCA (pag. 17 della *Divina proportione*) fa cadere tre vertici di questo su tre lati di quello, mentre PIERO le disegna molto più giustamente e con giusta intelligenza del vero: non per niente era pittore, e che pittore!

Ammettendo pure col WINTERBERG che alcuni pochi calcoli siano corretti in LUCA, io devo dichiarare che feci e rifeci una grandissima parte dei calcoli indicati o fatti da PIERO, e tutti li trovai giusti.

Lasciando LUCA nella condanna che, dopo ciò che vi ho detto, gli avrete certamente inflitta, aggiungo brevemente qualche cosa del contenuto del codice Vaticano.

Lo stesso pittore ce ne dà notizia a principio, presso a poco così: il primo trattato (traduco io liberamente) abbraccia le figure piane, irregolari e regolari; il secondo ragiona dei poliedri regolari; il terzo descrive quei corpi che si possono inscrivere (collocari) in altri, per es. nella sfera, ecc. E benchè egli nella dedica a GUIDOBALDO affermi che il fine suo è quello di rendere aritmetico ciò che è geometrico in EUCLIDE, pure egli va più in là: risolve veri e proprî problemi che conducono ad equazioni di 2° grado o a riducibili a queste, richiamando alcune regole come si davano allora.

Le principali equazioni sono le seguenti, con le radici positive che ne dà l'autore:

$4x+60=x^2$	radice	10
$4x-x^2=3$	"	3
$4x=\frac{2}{9}x^2$	"	18
$2x^2=(x+6)^2$	"	$6+\sqrt{72}$
$x^2\sqrt{2}=\sqrt{32}$	"	2
$x(10-x)=12$	"	$5\pm\sqrt{13}$
ecc.		ecc.

Ecco un problema che conduce a un sistema: Determinare il lato l, la diagonale d di un pentagono regolare e il raggio r del circolo circoscritto, supposta fra i tre segmenti la relazione

$$d^2+l^2-4r^2=20\,.$$

L'autore aggiunge le altre due relazioni, perfettamente giuste,

$$d(d-l)=l^2 \quad , \quad \frac{4r^2}{l^2}=\frac{16}{10-\sqrt{20}}$$

e risolvendo il sistema trova

$$d^2=50+\sqrt{500} \quad , \quad l^2=50-\sqrt{500} \quad 4r^2=80\,.$$

Ecco un altro esempio curioso: l'area di un quadrato moltiplicata per la diagonale, dà 500: trovare il lato.

Si deve avere

$$x^3\sqrt{2}=500\,.$$

Di qui

$$2x^6=250000 \quad , \quad x^6=125000=5^3.10^3,$$

onde

$$x^2=50\,.$$

L'autore conosce anche il modo di rendere razionale il denominatore di una frazione, e l'artificio di passare un coefficiente sotto ad un radicale con elevarlo a quadrato. Del rapporto della circonferenza al diametro conosce il limite superiore $3\frac{1}{7}$ e un limite inferiore $3\frac{1}{8}$. Conosce il metodo delle figure simili e lo applica alla risoluzione dei problemi.

Tutto questo e l'altro che potrei aggiungere, mostra quanta fosse stata la dottrina nell'Algebra del tempo e nella Geometria di EUCLIDE posseduta dal nostro Pittore. Un pittore, signori miei! Ma già questo avveniva nel XV secolo, nel secolo dei Brunnelleschi, de' Ghiberti, degli Alberti, che vide morire PIERO e nascere LEONARDO in Italia e ALBERTO DÜRER in Germania.

Nè minor maraviglia reca il fatto che le conoscenze matematiche di questi grandi erano per loro fonte di diletto o dolce sprone allo spirito. Dice invero il Nostro nella sua citata dedica al duca di Urbino ch'egli compose il *Libellus* all'ultimo di sua età acciocchè l'ingegno non intorpidisse per l'inerzia (ne ingenium inertia torpesceret); e LEONARDO cotanto si beava della meccanica, da chiamarla *il paradiso delle scienze matematiche, perchè con quella si viene al frutto matematico.*

A voi certo piacerà veder posta in così alto loco, nientemeno in paradiso, la nostra scienza da un sommo italiano, artista e scienziato insieme; e in grazia di ciò mi perdonerete ch'io abbia sostenuta l'accusa contro un uomo che fu certo matematico celebre e benemerito, e fu amico di quel sommo!

A. GUTZMER

UEBER DIE REFORMBESTREBUNGEN AUF DEM GEBIETE DES MATHEMATISCHEN UNTERRICHTS IN DEUTSCHLAND

Der ehrenvollen Aufforderung des Organisationskomites des gegenwärtigen Kongresses, über die Reformbestrebungen auf dem Gebiete des mathematischen Unterrichts in Deutschland zu berichten, habe ich nicht ohne Zögern entsprochen. Denn grade das Gebiet des Unterrichts an den unteren und mittleren Lehranstalten, das für viele von Ihnen vielleicht das allergrösste Interesse besitzt, ist mir aus eigener Erfahrung nicht bekannt. Demgemäss habe ich meiner Zusage gleich die Bemerkung beigefügt, dass ich mich nicht auf den sogenannten Mittelschulunterricht beschränken würde, und diese Bemerkung will ich zur Vermeidung von Missverständnissen auch jetzt sogleich vorausschicken. Ich werde also keineswegs auf schultechnische Einzelheiten eingehen, auch nicht auf die lehrplanmässige Verteilung des Unterrichtsstoffes auf die einzelnen Schularten oder Klassenpensen.

Dieser Standpunkt wird mir auch durch die ganze Natur der gegenwärtigen deutschen Reformbestrebungen vorgeschrieben. In der Tat wird jeder, der den Blick über die Fragen der täglichen Unterrichtsarbeit erhebt, zugeben müssen, dass die Reformbewegung auf dem Gebiete des mathematischen Unterrichts über den Rahmen der höheren Lehranstalten hinausgewachsen ist, und dass nur dann eine wirkliche Besserung herbeigeführt werden kann, wenn — wie das schon ein Redner in Heidelberg andeutete — « der Zusammenhang nach unten und oben hin, nach den Vorschulen und den Hochschulen beachtet wird ». Es geht nicht an, nur eine Art von Lehranstalten ins Ange zu fassen und die bessernde Hand anzulegen; vielmehr muss die *Gesamtheit der Fragen des mathematischen Unterrichts* erörtert werden, und wir müssen ferner die Reformen des mathematischen Unterrichts mit denen der naturwissenschaftlichen Fächer zu einer höheren Einheit zusammenfassen. Das überaus lebhafte pädagogische Interesse unserer Zeit hat, wie überall so auch ganz besonders in Deutschland eine solche Fülle von Wünschen, Anregungen, Vorschlägen und Forderungen gezeitigt, dass es unmöglich ist, alles zu verwirklichen. Eine weise Selbstbeschränkung muss eintreten, wir müssen aus der erdrückenden Fülle der Wünsche dasjenige herausheben, was zur Zeit Aussicht und in erster Linie Anspruch auf Verwirklichung hat; ich möchte das als eine vernünftige Realpolitik bezeichnen. Oder wenn ich mich eines andern Bildes bedienen darf, so handelt es sich nach meiner Auffassung darum, aus der Mannigfaltigkeit der eine ungeordnete Bewegung darstellenden Einzelwünsche eine geordnete Bewegung zu organisieren und vor allem die Hauptlinien der Reform festzulegen.

Ein solcher Versuch, die Reformbestrebungen auf mathematischem und naturwissenschaftlichem Gebiet zu organisieren, ist von der Gesellschaft Deutscher Naturforscher und Aerzte unternommen worden, indem sie im Jahre 1904 eine Unterrichtskommission von 12 Mitgliedern verschiedener Berufe einsetzte, die den Auftrag erhielt, die Gesamtheit der Fragen des mathematischen und naturwissenschaftlichen Unterrichts einer eingehenden Erörterung zu unterziehen und abgeglichene Vorschläge auszuarbeiten.

Diese Unterrichtskommission hat in dreijähriger Tätigkeit bestimmte Vorschläge entworfen und in ihrem kürzlich erschienenen « Gesamtbericht » [1] der weitesten Oeffentlichkeit unterbreitet. Da die Arbeit dieser Kommission unmittelbar nach dem Heidelberger Kongress einsetzte und eben beendet ist, so glaube ich mich heute im wesentlichen auf eine kurze Schilderung der hauptsächlichsten Züge der Kommissionsvorschläge beschränken zu sollen. Gleichzeitig meine ich, auf diese Weise der Absicht der Kongressleitung am besten zu entsprechen. Die wichtigsten Einzelfragen des mathematischen Unterrichts sind ja in der pädagogischen Sektion des Heidelberger Kongresses dargelegt und behandelt worden, und man darf wohl ohne Uebertreibung sagen, dass seitdem das Interesse der Fachkreise und der Schulverwaltungen in Deutschland, so weit es sich um den mathematischen und naturwissenschaftlichen Unterricht handelt, ganz überwiegend den Reformvorschlägen der Unterrichtskommission zugewendet gewesen ist, mit andern Worten, die Arbeiten der Unterrichtskommission stellen im wesentlichen *die* Reformbestrebungen auf dem Gebiete des mathematischen Unterrichts in Deutschland seit dem letzten internationalen Kongresse dar. Es scheint mir daher innerlich berechtigt, dass ich mich heute auf diese Arbeiten in der Hauptsache beschränke.

Worin bestehen nun die erstrebten Reformen? Was bringen sie Neues? Diese Fragen mögen vor dieser internationalen Korona nur ganz im allgemeinen beantwortet werden.

Zunächst negativ: Die Vorschläge stellen nichts absolut Neues dar; sie sollen und wollen keinen Königsweg zur Mathematik bilden; weder soll die Zahl der mathematischen Unterrichtsstunden wesentlich geändert werden noch sind grundstürzende Umwälzungen der Klassenpensen vorgenommen worden. Die Vorschläge passen sich also den historisch gewordenen äusseren Bedingungen nach Möglichkeit an, sie wollen keine Revolution, sondern eine Evolution herbeiführen helfen.

In positiver Hinsicht regen die Vorschläge an, den Schulunterricht von manchem « Ballast » zu befreien, namentlich von allem, was nur den Zweck der Erzielung einer Routine hat oder nur damit beherrscht werden kann; es gehört hierher der bisweilen übermässige Kultus geometrischer Konstruktionsaufgaben, deren Lösung besondere

[1] *Die Tätigkeit der Unterrichtskommission der Gesellschaft Deutscher Naturforscher und Aerzte.* (Im Auftrage der Kommission herausgegeben von A. GUTZMER, Leipzig, 1908).

Kunstgriffe erfordert, die ermüdenden formalen Rechnungsübungen mit komplizierten Ausdrücken, das wochen- und monatelange Berechnen von trigonometrischen und anderen Aufgaben nach bestimmten Schematen u. dgl. m. Auch die zu früh einsetzenden übertriebenen Anforderungen an abstrakte Beweisführung wünscht die Kommission gemildert zu sehen; der Unterricht soll sich mehr noch als bisher schon der allmählichen geistigen Entwicklung der Schüler anpassen. Die Definition neuer Begriffe soll so vorbereitet werden, dass sie gewissermassen dem innern Bedürfnisse des Schülers entsprechen, auch soll der Zusammenhang mit dem übrigen Lehrstoff der Schule stärker als bisher betont werden. Dadurch werden die allgemeinbildenden Momente der Mathematik in den Vordergrund gerückt werden, und es wird möglich sein, die Schüler für ihr Leben auszustatten mit einer Einsicht in die Bedeutung der Mathematik für die exakte Naturerkenntnis und die gegenwärtige Kultur überhaupt. Es handelt sich also bei der Mathematik im deutschen Unterrichtswesen hauptsächlich um eine *innere* Reform.

Hierfür liegen schon viele Ansätze vor, und man muss anerkennen, dass es seit langem hervorragende Lehrer gibt, die sich in ihrem Unterricht nach der bezeichneten Richtung bewegt haben und bewegen. Immerhin scheint dies noch nicht die Regel zu sein, obwohl die Preussischen Lehrpläne von 1901 und die zugehörigen methodischen Bemerkungen ganz von dem Geiste der vorstehenden allgemeinen Ausführungen getragen sind.

Mit besonderem Nachdruck hat die Kommission drei Forderungen allgemeiner Art erhoben, die bei ihren Vorschlägen wesentlich sind; es sind dies die *Stärkung des räumlichen Anschauungsvermögens*, die *Berücksichtigung der Anwendungen* und vor allem die *Erziehung zur Gewöhnung des funktionalen Denkens.*

Was zunächst den letzteren Punkt betrifft, so ist er für die Reformvorschläge durchaus charakteristisch und *von zentraler Bedeutung*; die systematische Durchführung dieser Forderung der Erziehung zur Gewohnheit des funktionalen Denkens ist das Neue, das die Kommissionsvorschläge für den mathematischen Unterricht bringen. Es darf aber nicht verschwiegen werden, dass die Einführung dieser Aufgabe in die Schule vereinzelt zu Bedenken Veranlassung gegeben hat. Bald heisst es, die Zeit reiche dafür nicht aus, es sei das eine neue Belastung, bald wird gesagt, diese Aufgabe rage über den Rahmen des Schulunterrichts hinaus. Im grossen und ganzen aber haben sich die Anhänger des in Rede stehenden Vorschlags gemehrt. Durch die Arbeiten von Lesser [1], Schmidt, Schulke u. a. ist gezeigt worden, dass und auf welchem Wege es möglich ist, das von der Kommission vorgeschlagene Ziel zu erreichen. Jedenfalls glaubt die Kommission, nicht eine neue Belastung, sondern eine *Erleichterung* herbeizuführen. Für den Lehrer wird freilich der neue Unterricht anfangs manche Unbequemlichkeit mit sich bringen, da es gilt, vielfach eigene Wege zu suchen und zu finden und nicht Pfade zu wandeln, die seit Jahrhunderten ausgetreten sind.

Ein Missverständnis ist manchem insofern begegnet, als er glaubte, es handle

[1] Die näheren Literaturangaben findet man im Literaturverzeichnis, S. 307 ff. des Gesamtberichts.

sich um den Funktionsbegriff, dessen Aufbau und Ausschöpfung den Inhalt der modernen Analysis bildet. Das ist selbstverständlich nicht entfernt die Meinung der Kommission. Vielmehr ist nur eine propädeutische Einführung des Funktionsbegriffs gemeint, unter ausgiebiger Heranziehung graphischer Methoden und in der naiven Auffassung etwa, die die Mathematiker des 18. Jahrhunderts hatten. Selbstverständlich muss dieser Unterricht mit viel Takt erteilt werden, damit sich nicht falsche Vorstellungen in den Köpfen der Schüler einnisten. Der feinere Ausbau des Funktionsbegriffs wird naturgemäss dem Universitätsstudium vorbehalten bleiben müssen.

Ein anderer Einwand besagt, dass der Funktionsbegriff nicht zur Elementarmathematik gehöre, und es werde durch Heranziehung dieses Begriffs ein neues und fremdes Element in den Schulunterricht getragen, das den eigentlichen Zweck des mathematischen Schulunterrichts, nämlich die formale und logische Durchbildung, zu beeinträchtigen geeignet sei. Darauf ist zu erwidern, dass es keine allgemein anerkannte Definition der Elementarmathematik im Gegensatz zur höheren Mathematik gibt. Es wäre, nebenbei bemerkt, vielleicht eine nicht uninteressante Aufgabe zu untersuchen, wie sich dieser Begriff der « Elementarmathematik », der schon manches Unheil gestiftet hat, geschichtlich entwickelt und welche Wandlungen er im Laufe der Zeit erfahren hat. Das Entscheidende dürfte doch wohl nicht der Stoff sondern die Behandlungsweise sein, und so wie wir in der neueren Zeit die Grundfragen der Elementargeometrie von hohem wissenschaftlichen Standpunkt zu behandeln gelernt haben, so ist doch auch andererseits eine Reihe von Fragen und Methoden der höheren Mathematik so durchgebildet, dass sie unbedenklich der sogenannten Elementarmathematik zugerechnet werden können und sicher dem Verständnis der Schüler leichter zugänglich sind als gar manche Teile der alten Elementarmathematik. Von hier aus ist keine ernste Schwierigkeit zu erkennen. Und dass ferner die logische Durchbildung bei der Entwicklung des Funktionsbegriffes, in dem angegebenen Sinne verstanden, Einbusse erleiden sollte, dafür ist noch kein stichhaltiger Grund beigebracht worden. Im Gegenteil wird diese wichtige Aufgabe des mathematischen Schulunterrichts nur gefördert und erleichtert werden, zum mindesten dadurch, dass der Unterricht an Interesse für die Schüler gewinnen wird. Und zudem überwiegt wohl heute die Meinung, dass der formale Bildungswert der Mathematik zwar gewiss als wichtig, aber nicht als die Hauptsache anzusehen ist. Der Kürze wegen möchte ich in dieser Beziehung auf die Heidelberger Verhandlungen verweisen.

Mit der Gewöhnung zum funktionalen Denken wird der Schüler unserer höheren Lehranstalten auch dazu befähigt werden, die allerelementarsten Begriffe der Differential- und Integralrechnung aufzunehmen. Was in Frankreich in viel weiterem Umfange sich als durchführbar erwiesen hat, das sollte unter andern historischen Bedingungen doch mindestens bis zu einem gewissen Grade bei uns möglich sein. Aber das ist ein Punkt, über den die deutschen Lehrer noch nicht völlig einig sind. Die Macht der geschichtlichen Tradition ist in Deutschland sehr gross, und alles, was unternommen wird, soll mit wissenschaftlicher Gründlichkeit geschehen. Man übersieht dabei leicht, dass es psychologisch verschiedene Grade der Gründlichkeit gibt, die alle je nach dem geistigen Stande gleichen Wert haben. Selbstverständlich kann es sich nicht darum handeln, eine Differentialrechnung den Schülern aufzubürden, die dem höchsten erreichten wissenschaftlichen Standpunkte angepasst ist; wohl aber sollte es möglich sein, die allerersten infinitesimalen Begriffe in naiver Auffassung an der Hand der graphischen Darstellungen einfachster Funktionen zu entwickeln, damit auch der eine Ahnung von dem geistigen Lebensinhalt und der Gedankenarbeit eines Mathematikers und von der Bedeutung der höheren Mathematik gewinnt, der nicht mehr mit Mathematik in abstracto in seinem späteren Leben zu tun hat. Gar beweglich war es, als mir u. a. kürzlich ein in Deutschland sehr bekannter und hochgeschätzter Theologe sagte, es müsste doch im Rahmen der Schule möglich sein, den Abiturienten eine primitive Vorstellung zu geben von dem, was Differentialrechnung ist; es gehöre doch eigentlich zur allgemeinen Bildung zu wissen, was die verschiedenen Wissenschaften treiben. Klingt das nicht, wie eine herbe Anklage gegen unsern Schulbetrieb? Die Meinung der Kommission ist es jedenfalls, dass die allerersten Begriffe der Infinitesimalrechnung den Abschluss der mathematischen Schulstudien bilden sollten. Ich will der knappen Zeit wegen, die mir zur Verfügung steht, darauf verzichten, tiefer in diese Frage einzudringen, und ich begnüge mich damit, nachdrücklich auf die Schrift von F. Klein, *Vorträge über den mathematischen Unterricht an den höheren Schulen*, bearbeitet von R. Schimmack, Teil I, Leipzig 1907, zu verweisen, die für das Verständnis der mathematischen Reformvorschläge in Deutschland ganz wesentlich ist.

Wenden wir uns zu der *Stärkung des räumlichen Anschauungsvermögens*, so muss zugegeben werden, dass dessen Ausbildung in der Schule lange vernachlässigt worden ist. Es wird dies allseitig betont und beklagt, und so mancher hat in seinem Berufe darunter zu leiden gehabt. Seit einigen Jahrzehnten haben die Lehrerkreise dieser wichtigen Sache ernste Aufmerksamkeit geschenkt, auch haben neuerdings die Schulverwaltungen vielfach dem Bedürfnis Rechnung zu tragen gesucht; gleichwohl muss noch manches geschehen. Wir folgen ja nur klassischen Spuren, von denen u. a. die wunderbaren Baudenkmale dieses schönen Landes zeugen, wenn wir immer wieder die Förderung des räumlichen Vorstellungsvermögens verlangen. Das von mathematischem Standpunkt geeignete Hilfsmittel ist ein guter darstellendgeometrischer Unterricht, der meines Erachtens mit dem stereometrischen Unterricht verbunden sein sollte. Dabei wird es die Kunst des Lehrers sein, den Schüler die Konstruktionen aus dem Raum heraus gewinnen zu lassen, damit nicht ein schematisches Zeichnen nach Regeln eintritt.

Im Verein mit der besseren Ausbildung des räumlichen Anschauungsvermögens, der Gewöhnung zum funktionalen Denken und der Kenntnis der ersten Anfänge der Infinitesimalrechnung werden die *Anwendungen* ganz besonders dazu angetan sein, die allgemeine kulturelle Bedeutung der Mathematik in das richtige Licht zu setzen. Leider sind die Anwendungen der Mathematik im mathematischen Schulunterricht bei uns lange Zeit vernachlässigt worden; deshalb hat sich auch der Verein zur Förderung des mathematischen und naturwissenschaftlichen Unterrichts seit seiner Begründung bestrebt, in dem bezeichneten Sinne zu wirken, und es ist bekannt, welchen hervorragenden Anteil F. Klein an dieser Bewegung genommen hat. Die volle Bedeutung der Forderung, dass die Anwendungen der Mathematik mehr betont werden möchten, ist namentlich für den Fremden schwer zu verstehen; sie wird erst aus der geschichtlichen Entwicklung unseres mathematischen Unterrichts völlig klar. Denn bis gegen Ende des 18. Jahrhunderts wurden auf Schule und Universität auch in Deutschland die Anwendungen ausgiebig berücksichtigt, aber unter der Vorherrschaft des Formalismus trat vor etwa 100 Jahren eine Rückwirkung ein, indem die Anwendungen als etwas minderwertiges betrachtet und bald ganz aus dem gesamten mathematischen Unterricht von Schule und Universität entfernt wurden. Die Mathematiker der damaligen Zeit standen überhaupt dem Problem der Jugendbildung ohne Verständnis und Interesse gegenüber, und so wollte es das Verhängnis, dass bei der Neuregelung des höheren Schulunterrichts zu Beginn des 19. Jahrhunderts die mathematischen Lehrer den Aufgaben der Zeit nicht gewachsen waren und eine günstige Gelegenheit zu wirklichen Reformen verpassten. Es lebte jenes mathematische Geschlecht, das LICHTENBERG mit beissendem Spott charakterisierte, indem er schrieb, es verlange « sehr oft der sogenannte Mathematiker für einen tiefen Denker gehalten zu werden, ob es gleich darunter die grössten Plunderköpfe gibt, die man nur finden kann, untauglich zu irgend einem Geschäft, das Nachdenken erfordert, wenn es nicht unmittelbar durch jene leichte Verbindung von Zeichen geschehen kann, die mehr das Werk der Routine, als des Denkens sind ». Indem die Reformvorschläge den Anwendungen der Mathematik das Wort reden, knüpfen sie an glänzende Zeiten ([1]) der Vergangenheit an; sie suchen eben die Mathematik möglichst nach allen ihren so überaus zahlreichen Beziehungen zu andern Gebieten schon in der Schule zur Geltung zu bringen. Freilich kann das nur in verhältnismässig geringem Umfange geschehen, es muss deshalb in den Schulunterricht etwas von dem Geiste einziehen, der aus dem CANTOR'schen Worte spricht: « Das Wesen der Mathematik liegt in ihrer Freiheit ». Dazu ist aber nötig, dass mehr Spielraum für die Entfaltung der Persönlichkeit des Lehrers gelassen wird, und dass nicht gar zu viel Vorschriften über die Unterrichtsdetails gegeben werden. In dieser Beziehung sind die Preussischen Lehrpläne von 1901 mit den Kommissionsvorschlägen in ziemlich weitem Umfange im Einklang.

Das sind in allgemeinen Umrissen die leitenden Gesichtspunkte unserer Reformvorschläge für den mathematischen Unterricht an den deutschen höheren Lehranstalten.

Ich wende mich nun noch kurz zu den weiteren Vorschlägen, die sich auf die *wissenschaftliche Ausbildung der künftigen Lehrer der Mathematik* beziehen. Auch hier ist zum vollen Verständnis und zur richtigen Würdigung eine Kenntnis der historischen Entwicklung und eine Einsicht in die gegenwärtige Lage der Dinge erforderlich. Zeit und Ort gestatten nicht, weiter auszuholen, und so sei nur kurz daran erinnert, dass wir uns in Deutschland der akademischen Studienfreiheit erfreuen, die wir einerseits als ein ganz besonders kostbares Gut betrachten und behüten, die aber andererseits auch mancherlei Schwierigkeiten hervorruft. Die Kommission will diese Freiheit nicht beschränken; ihre Vorschläge für die wissenschaftliche Ausbildung der Lehrer sind daher anzusehen als Ratschläge für die Studierenden und

([1]) Ich erinnere nur an CHR. WOLF, den ersten Professor publicus ordinarius matheseos der Universität Halle, der für die Mathematik einschliesslich ihrer Anwendungen eintrat und ihre Bedeutung für die Kultur der damaligen Zeit kräftigst betonte. Vgl. CONRAD H. MÜLLER. *Studien zur Geschichte der Mathematik, insbesondere des mathematischen Unterrichtes an der Universität Göttingen im 18 Jahrhundert.* Abh. z. Gesch. d. math. Wiss. Bd. 18, S. 51-143, 1904.

als eine Mahnung [1] an die Dozenten, in der Spezialisierung nicht zu weit zu gehen und bei den Vorträgen und Uebungen den künftigen Beruf der Studierenden nicht aus dem Auge zu verlieren. Daneben suchen sie bei möglichster Anlehnung an die in den meisten deutschen Staaten geltende Prüfungsordnung für das höhere Lehramt auf eine zeitgemässe Weiterbildung der Examensbestimmungen hinzuwirken. Ich darf von den von uns ausgearbeiteten Vorschlägen, die in der Hauptsache auf F. Klein zurückzuführen sind, nur die allgemeinen Gesichtspunkte hervorheben, ohne auf Einzelfragen einzugehen.

Festgehalten wird in den Vorschlägen an dem Grundsatz, dass die Universitäten denjenigen Studierenden, die sich dem Lehrberuf zu widmen beabsichtigen, eine wissenschaftliche Fachbildung und eine allgemeine philosophische Durchbildung gewähren sollen. Es gehört hierzu auch eine Kenntnis der wissenschaftlichen Pädagogik. Dagegen soll die praktische pädagogische Ausbildung — wie bisher in Preussen — erst nach der Vollendung der wissenschaftlichen Studien beginnen.

Der mathematische Studiengang soll sich in zwei Stufen aufbauen. Die erste umfasst die sogenannten *generellen* Studien, die von jedem mathematischen Studenten zu absolvieren sind, die zweite die *speziellen* Studien, bei denen der Einzelne nach Neigung und Anlage sich individuell weiter entwickeln kann, indem er entweder tiefer in ein spezielles Gebiet vordringt oder seine Kenntnisse mehr nach der Breite in andern Unterrichtsfächern erweitert. Die angewandte Mathematik soll normaler Bestandteil der mathematischen Studien sein, weil von ihr der Lehrer in seinem Berufe meist den unmittelbarsten Nutzen haben wird. Das ganze Studium der reinen und angewandten Mathematik soll vom ersten Semester an durch Seminare und Praktika ergänzt und belebt werden.

Dies das allgemeine Prinzip der Vorschläge.

Von den speziellen Forderungen will ich nur einiges erwähnen. Insbesondere sollte der künftige mathematische Lehrer mit den vielseitigen Anwendungen seines

[1] Es sei an dieser Stelle auf die ausgezeichneten und beherzigenswerten Ausführungen hingewiesen, die Diels über Hochschulbildung im 1. Bande der « *Kultur der Gegenwart* » veröffentlicht hat. Er stellt treffend die Gefahren der « Ueberwissenschaftlichkeit » und der « Unterwissenschaftlichkeit » einander gegenüber und fährt dann fort: « Daher wäre es richtiger, wenn die Universität selbst sich auf ihren Doppelzweck besänne und in ihrem Unterricht selbst in ausreichendem Masse für die praktischen nicht minder wie für die theoretischen Bedürfnisse der Studierenden sorgte. Die Universitätspädagogik, die man möglichst wenig im Munde führen und möglichst ausgiebig zur Anwendung bringen sollte, verlangt, dass die Studierenden in organischer Weise sich ihre Kenntnisse aneignen und im methodischen Fortschreiten vom Leichteren zu dem Schwereren, von den Elementen zu den Höhen der Wissenschaft emporsteigen. Diese Stufenfolge zu organisieren, aber ohne die kostbare Studienfreiheit irgend anzutasten oder Zwangskollegien einzuführen, sollte die Hauptaufgabe der Fakultäten oder in der vielgespaltenen philosophischen Fakultät der Vertreter der einzelnen Gruppen sein. Es handelt sich dabei nicht bloss um sogenannte Studienpläne, die z. B. in den historischen Disziplinen recht farblos ausfallen müssen, sondern um sorgfältig erwogene, auf Jahre hinaus vorbedachte Vortragszyklen, und vor allem um systematisch abgestufte Uebungskurse, die zwischen den Hauptvertretern eines Faches und den Vorstehern der betreffenden Fachinstitute und Seminarien vereinbart werden müssen. Wo die Professoren diese praktische Seite nicht genügend ins Auge fassen, wo sich banausisches Schmarotzertum (genannt « Einpauker ») neben der staatlichen Organisation breit machen, darf von normaler Konstitution der Universitätsverhältnisse nicht die Rede sein ».

Faches vertraut werden, er soll gut rechnen und gut zeichnen lernen, die Grundzüge des das moderne Kulturleben immer mehr durchdringenden Versicherungswesens ebenso wie die Sprache des Ingenieurs kennen lernen; auch sollte er sich hinreichende Kenntnisse der Astronomie und Uebung in der Orts- und Zeitbestimmung aneignen. Schliesslich wird es als ein selbstverständlicher Wunsch erscheinen, dass in einer Zeit, in der durch die grossen und bahnbrechenden Arbeiten von GAUSS, BOLYAI, LOBATSCHEWSKIJ, RIEMANN, KLEIN, HILBERT u. a. unsere Kenntnis der Grundlagen der Geometrie weit über den Stand der griechischen Geometer emporgehoben worden ist, der künftige Lehrer, der in seinem Leben nahezu ausschliesslich Elementargeometrie zu unterrichten berufen ist, eine Uebersicht über diese neuen Errungenschaften erhält. Es ist das wichtiger als dass er ein entlegenes Spezialgebiet kennen lernt, das für seine allgemeine mathematische Ausbildung und die wissenschaftliche Vorbereitung auf seinen Beruf nicht entfernt gleiche Bedeutung besitzt.

Ich bin am Schlusse meiner Darlegungen. Zurückblickend erkennen wir, dass die Reformvorschläge sich für die höheren Schulen und für die Ausbildung der künftigen Lehrer gewissermassen in entgegengesetzter Richtung bewegen. Sie werden daher, so hoffen wir, an ihrem Teile dazu beitragen, die Entfremdung und die Kluft zwischen Schule und Hochschule zu beseitigen und das etwas gestörte Gleichgewicht beider Arten von Unterrichtsanstalten herbeizuführen.

Erwähnen muss ich noch, dass die Reformbewegung in Deutschland über den Kreis hinausgegriffen hat, den unsere Vorschläge zunächst berücksichtigen. Ich führe hier nur an, dass auch die Volks- und Fortbildungsschulen sowie die mannigfachen Arten von Fachschulen und die Lehrerseminare nach einer Reform des mathematischen und naturwissenschaftlichen Unterrichts drängen, und dass die Frage lebhaft ventiliert wird, wie weit die Technischen Hochschulen zur wissenschaftlichen Ausbildung der Oberlehrer mitwirken sollen. Es sind das alles äusserst wichtige und ernste Fragen, die sich zwar noch in dem Stadium der Diskussion befinden, die aber doch mehr und mehr der Klärung und Ordnung entgegengehen. Ein Teil dieser Dinge wird auf der diesjährigen Versammlung der Gesellschaft Deutscher Naturforscher und Aerzte zu Cöln im grösseren Kreise erörtert werden.

Wiederholt betonte ich, dass die Reformbewegung, zu deren Träger und Organ sich die Unterrichtskommission gemacht hat, an die historisch gegebenen Bedingungen anknüpft. So mag es kommen, dass Fragen, die bei uns noch der Erledigung harren, in andern Ländern bereits eine glückliche Lösung gefunden haben und umgekehrt. Pädagogische Reformen lassen sich eben nicht von einem Tage zum andern durchführen; ihre Erprobung und Einführung erfordert oft ein Menschenalter. Das wird bei der Beurteilung stets zu beachten sein.

Endlich noch ein Wort. MACH hat die Wissenschaft als eine Oekonomie des Denkens erklärt; entsprechend möchte ich einen guten Unterricht als eine *Oekonomie der Unterweisung* bezeichnen. Indem wir in der Kommission die Gesamtheit der Fragen des mathematischen und naturwissenschaftlichen Unterrichts einer abwägenden und abgleichenden Erörterung unterzogen, wurden wir von selbst genötigt, unsere Vorschläge, von denen ich ein Exemplar hiermit auf den Tisch des Hauses zu legen mich beehre, gemäss diesem Prinzip der Oekonomie zu gestalten.

C. GODFREY

THE TEACHING OF MATHEMATICS IN ENGLISH PUBLIC SCHOOLS FOR BOYS

1. The present paper refers to conditions prevailing in England only, to the exclusion of Scotland, Ireland and Wales.

2. The term « public school » has, in England, a rather special meaning. A public school is generally understood to be an endowed secondary school of fair size, educating boys of the upper and middle classes, independent of state control except in so far as its income is supplemented from public funds. Public schools may be either boarding schools or day schools, but most of them belong to the former category.

Other classes of Secondary schools exist, such as the unendowed day schools maintained by local taxation; these are increasingly numerous and important, and in many cases compete victoriously with the weaker endowed schools of the neighbourhood. These schools differ from public schools in that their educational policy is controlled in the main by a government office, the Board of Education.

3. The public schools monopolize the education of the upper classes of this country. They have always prided themselves on their freedom from external control; each school is governed by its own governing body and headmaster, and generally the latter is allowed to have a free hand.

This apparently complete freedom is tempered by the following causes. In the first place, many public schools find it advisable to accept pecuniary help from the state, and this entails inspection by the Board of Education. The richest and most important schools, however, are able to dispense with this aid. Of late years there has been a disposition on the part of the leading schools to submit their work voluntarily to inspection.

Secondly, it must be admitted that, in spite of this independence, these schools are not really free; the instruction given is determined mainly by a variety of public examinations, such as the Scholarship examinations of the Colleges at the Universities of Oxford and Cambridge, the preliminary examination for certificates of proficiency conducted by the Universities, the examinations for entrance to the Army conducted by the Civil Service Commissioners. The status of a school in the eyes of the public, and its power of attracting pupils and paying its way, depend largely on the success it can shew in these various competition. Few reforms can be accomplished unless the examining authorities approve, e. g. the study of Greek is compulsory for all boys aspiring to a degree at the Universities of Oxford or Cambridge, and the public schools are in effect compelled to teach Greek to all such boys. It wille be seen that the action of examining bodies has been all-powerful in the recent history of mathematical teaching in this country.

The present paper refers to the conditions prevailing in these public schools, and some account will now be given of their organization for mathematical teaching.

4. A public school is divided into « forms » or classes; the classification is determined mainly by proficiency in literary subjects such as Greek, Latin, English, History, Geography, Scripture Knowledge. These subjects are taught by the form master.

For purposes of mathematics, a group of forms constitutes a « block », and the boys in this block are redistributed into « sets » according to their proficiency in mathematics. A school of 400 may be divided into 4 blocks; and a block of 100 boys may form from 4 to 6 sets, the number of boys in a mathematical set varying from 25 to 15. The reasons for this system of redistribution for mathematics are (1) the « form master » does not generally possess an expertknowledge of mathematics. (2) the boys in a given form are always found to differ too widely in their mathematical ability and attainments, to be taught together without re-distribution.

The number of hours given to class-teaching in mathematics is 4-7 weekly, with 1 or 2 hours of preparation out of school. Many schools have a « Modern » department in which the place of Greek is taken by German and additional mathematics and science. A large proportion of the time in class is spent by the boys in working exercises on paper, the master going among them and giving help when it is needed.

All the different branches of mathematics are commonly taught in the same class by the same master; but in a few schools a different arrangement exists, and boys are grouped in one system of classes for Algebra and Arithmetic, and in another system for Geometry.

It may be stated here that a similar scheme of rearrangement is not unusual for the teaching of modern languages and science respectively.

5. During the last 2 years at School, between the ages of 17 and 19, there is a strong tendency for boys to specialize, the subject chosen for special study being generally one of the following: Classics, Mathematics, Science, Modern Languages, History. This early specialization is the result of the policy of the College authorities at Oxtord and Cambridge, who award Scholarships for excellence in one subject; e. g. a boy who shewed fair proficiency in both classics and mathematics would not stand a chance against another boy who was really good at one subject only. (In some cases, however a scholarship can be won for a combination (1) of mathematics and some physical science, (2) of classics and history). The consequence of this is that a candidate for a classical scholarship will often drop all mathematical and scientific work at the age of 17. Similarly a promising mathematician will often pass the last 2 years of his school life with little or no literary instruction, thoug it is only fair to say that there is a great difference between one school and another in this respect. In any case, the competition between schools for scholarship success tends to defeat the attempts of those teachers who believe that instruction should be on broad lines till the end of the school period.

6. Before trying to indicate the standard attained in the various mathematical subjects, it may be well to say a word about the considerable changes that have taken place in mathematical teaching during the recent years, changes that have overturned may landmarks and altered the standards of attainment in various directions.

7. Every subject of instruction may be viewed in two lights, according as it is appreciated for its utilitarian or for its disciplinary value. Perhaps teachers are apt to fix their attention on the latter aspect, while the general public regard the former as more important. It is not necessary to labour the point that a one-sided view is mistaken in either case. Possibly it could be maintained that almost every subject of instruction found its way into the curriculum for the sake of its practical utility; and that teachers, discovering a disciplinary way of presenting the subject, are inclined to retain it on this ground long after some change of circumstance has destroyed its practical value.

However this may be, it would seem that 10 years ago mathematics was regarded in public schools solely as a mental gymnastic. This exaggerated stress defeated its own object, as boys could hardly be induced to take an interest in a subject taught from motives that were to them foolishness. Good teachers felt the need of changes that would bring a breath of fresh air into the class-room and put more actuality into their work. But little change was possible; the existing system was stereotyped by the public examination papers; and it was clear to all that, though the times were ripe for change, no change would come till some wave of public opinion should carry examiners and teachers together to a new position.

8. The needful impulse came from the engineering profession. The times had gone by when engineers despised mathematics and relied on common sense and intuition combined with a large factor of safety. Nowadays they say that their young men cannot know too much mathematics, provided that it is mathematics of the right kind. The new epoch has been marked by the rise of a successful department of engineering at the university of Cambridge, a department whose graduates readily find openings on leaving the university.

The engineers, then, were ready to value mathematical teaching in schools; but they complained that the teaching actually given was not on practical lines. Matters came to a head at the Glasgow meeting of the British Association in 1902, when Professor J. Perry, professor of mechanics at the Royal College of Science in London, made an attack upon the existing state of things.

9. As an outcome of this movement, various committees were formed in which the views of the practical men and the schoolmasters were compared. It was found that substantial agreement was possible on most points. Schoolmasters realized that useful subjects could be made as educational as the conventional futilities that had come to be identified with school mathematics. Just as advanced research in pure

mathematics gains in dignity and purpose by a close connection with the problems offered by the physicist, and on the other hand may become aimless and unreal when divorced from its applications; so school mathematics found its salvation in a renewed alliance with the countless applications suggested by modern industrial life.

The Universities and most other examining bodies consented to alter their regulations and papers so as to fall in line with the new views. A fresh situation was thus created for all teachers and students of mathematics; and it is perhaps possible at the present date to review the gains or losses arising therefrom.

10. Arithmetic. This subject has won its way but slowly to a respectable position in English schools. It was regarded at one time solely as a handmaid to money reckoning and commerce. The time was spent, busily but unprofitably, in mastering the complexities of the British system of money, weights and measures. Arithmetic was not taught in its proper relation to other branches of mathematics. Financial questions took up too much time; and, as might be expected, these often became singularly unreal in the hands of the schoolmaster. A more serious evil was the host of special and tricky problems that cumbered the course. Any problem set in a public examination was pounced upon by the texte book writers and elevated into a type, with a chapter of its own, to be solved by special and ingenious methods. Thus we find in current text-books chapters on pipes filling and emptying baths, races and games of skill, cows grazing on a field of uniformly grazing grass.

The subject naturally fell into contempt and it was observed that at the age of 18 boys were quite unable to make any useful application of arithmetic and were even ignorant of the decimal system. What arithmetic boys had learned was useless in practical life; and, depending on a collection of special tricks rather than on a few simple principles, it was equally useless as an educational training.

So undignified had the subject become that competent mathematicians neglected it at school and were often almost helpless in the presence of figures and numerical results. Never by any chance were numerical data or illustrations introduced into Geometry. It was very unusual to meet with any demand for numerical work in the papers on advanced mathematics set at the universities. The result of this in that the knowledge of the mathematician trained under this system is almost entirely *qualitative*: it would seldom occur to him to apply any *quantitative* test to his work, unless his subsequent experience has been such as to correct the effects of early training.

11. The aim of recent reforms in arithmetic has been (1) *Destructive*, to simplify the subject, to rid it of unnecessary special rules and devices, to omit artificial types of problems whose original interest has evaporated, to lay less stress on financial arithmetic.

(2) *Constructive*, to insist on accuracy and facility in the simplest operations with integers and decimals, to insist on perfect comprehension of decimal notation and the metric system, to bring home to the pupil what an extremely small number of separate principles and rules he has to master and that, for the rest, he may rely on his common sense.

12. Some of the best teachers are inclined to emphasize the study of the *theory* of arithmetic e. g. to lay stress on rigorous proofs of fundamental operations with vulgar fractions, to examine minutely the degree of approximation arising from a given series of calculations, etc. Others hold that, while these studies are doubtless worthy of passing mention, they are for the most part a good deal too difficult for a thorough treatment at this stage; they would prefer to postpone them till the pupil has gained more maturity and learned a fair amount of algebra.

13. The use of 4 figure logarithm tables is coming into fashion. Ten years ago the only tables found in the mathematical classroom were those of 7 figures which were used in the solution of triangles. These were not handy enough and the boy never had enough practice to use logarithms with confidence. The science teachers however had discovered the practical usefulness of 4 figure tables and complained that they had to do the work of their mathematical colleagues in teaching the use of logarithms. This is ceasing to be true; it is found that boys of 14 can be taught to use 4 figure tables willingly and with comprehension; the range of possible operations has been widened considerably thereby.

14. Under the heading of arithmetic it is convenient to refer to two cognate matters, *the importance of numerical work in all subjects* and the introduction of *laboratory work* into mathematical teaching.

The importance of numerical work in all subjects. The excision of useless matter from the arithmetic course might conceivably have had this disadvantage, that the pupil would thereby lose opportunity of practising numerical manipulations. This danger has been avoided by the free use of numerical work in other branches, more especially in geometry and trigonometry. In every branch stress is laid on the necessity of rough numerical checks. The movement will be traced later on under the various headings; here it is enough to point out that it leads to (1) facility in numerical operations, (2) a more vivid realization of the results thus illustrated.

15. Laboratory work in mathematics. Many schools now arrange that boys of 13-15 shall take, as part of their mathematics, a course of experimental work in the laboratory. During this course they are taught to measure and weigh (incidentally learning to realize the advantages of the decimal notation), to determine the surfaces and volumes of actual objects, to determine densities and specific gravities, to discover the simpler laws of hydrostatics, etc. Perhaps the actual store of knowledge gained during this course is not great; but there is little doubt that it suggests a practical and workmanlike view of mathematics, and that it satisfies the need for coordination between brain, eye and hand which many teachers believe to be inherent in the nature of the British boy.

16. Plane Geometry. The most striking changes have taken place in the teaching of Geometry. Five years ago the universities and most other examining bodies demanded EUCLID's sequence of propositions. EUCLID's actual proofs were not demanded; but no proof was accepted that violated EUCLID's logical sequence.

This had long been found to be a trying restriction. It seemd probable that EUCLID's sequence could be improved upon in some respects. But the most serious aspect of the case was this, that the restriction consecrated and stereotyped a lifeless style of teaching. A keen teacher found his hands tied. There was little room for originality or freshness of presentation. No doubt much sound teaching was given; but the mass of schoolmasters were content to ask for a more or less intelligent memorizing of proofs. They regarded the solving of exercises or « deductions » as beyond the boy's powers. The constructions were very rarely performed with actual instruments. A great proportion of the boys were unfamiliar with the concepts about which they were expected to reason; e. g. it was not unusual to find that a boy had been through EUCLID's Book 2 (areas of rectangles) without distinguishing between « rectangle » and « right angle ».

17. The reforming party held that a more vivid realization of the shapes and properties of geometrical figures was necessary before these properties could profitably be made the subject of strict logical treatment. The logical training obtainable from Geometry they valued no less than did the conservatives. But they urged that, if the logic is to be more than mere word-play, an interested familiarity with the subject matter must come first.

Let us take as an illustration the theorem of Pythagoras about the squares on the sides and hypotenuse of a right-angled triangle.

The old view of geometry teaching was as follows: Here is a remarkable fact. We will shew the class that it is possible to start from the very simplest principles, to argue by steps that will convince the most ignorant, and finally to arrive at this astonishing result. The new school of thought, admitting the necessity and the value of the above proceedings, maintained that more was needed. It is necessary, they said, not only to astonish and conquer by the force of pure logic, but also to give power and mastery and the capacity of applying this weapon of logic to new conquests. In the case of Pythagoras theorem, the desire or a logical proof may not arise till the pupil has been conviced in other ways that the facts are as stated. He should measure the sides and calculate the squares, he should verify the equivalence by dissecting and fitting together (and perhaps by weighing). Moreover, the facts should not be stated crudely as a subject for verification; the matter should rather be presented in such a way that the boy may have a chance of thinking ahead of the teacher and anticipating the discovery. In every way he should be encouraged to lead rather than to follow.

18. Geometry, in fact, was conceived to be a suitable subject for experiment. To experiment in geometry, a child must learn to draw and measure with sufficient accuracy. He may experiment in other ways too; e. g. by cutting and folding paper, by using square-ruled paper, transparent paper, string, wooden blocks, etc. But he can hardly progress far without a fair amount of skill in handling simple drawing instruments.

For this reason then, in order to experiment, he must be provided with graduated ruler, protractor (for measuring angles), compasses, and set-square (for drawing perpendiculars and parallels).

For another reason, too, these instruments must be provided. Problems of construction are unmeaning unless it is specified what instruments are allowed. The problem of trisecting a given angle is solvable if a straight edge is allowed on which a given length may be marked. But the problem is not solvable by means of the instruments allowed by EUCLID. Problems of costruction, then, cannot be undertaken intelligently unless the learner understands these instrumental restrictions; and he is not likely to understand the restrictions unless he actually handles and uses the legitimate instruments.

Again, geometrical instruments satisfy the child's need for bodily activity. He thinks better if he is using his fingers. Ideas are suggested to him by the action of drawing figures. His attitude becomes active instead of passive.

19. Arguments such as the above were used to justify the use of instruments in the classroom. And of course it was not forgotten that geometrical drawing has a utilitarian value in many professions, e. g. in engineering, architecture, navigation, and in military work. Under the old system the instruction in geometrical drawing had been divorced from the study of theoretical geometry, to the detriment of both studies. It was frequently taught as a branch of the fine arts rather than as mathematics. One result of this has been an exaggerated respect for artistic finish and « inking-in »; but the worse feature was that « geometrical drawing » came to be identified with a vast collection of special and unrelated rules; the educational value of the subject had sunk to zero.

20. The teachers' demand for a freer and more experimental system of geometry teaching sprang from the belief that a more intimate knowledge of Geometry would increase its value as a logic-training subject. On the other hand, the engineers and other outside critics cared little for logical training, but greatly desired that their students should have some knowledge of geometrical facts, which was admittedly not given by the existing system.

21. However different the ultimate objects in view, the demand for definite change was too urgent and unanimous to be resisted. The universities remodelled their schedules of examination. The University of Cambridge set the tone of the reform by (1) requiring the use of instruments (2) accepting any proof of a theorem which should « appear to the Examiners to form part of a systematic treatment ». It published a modest list of theorems and constructions which were to be considered fundamental. The list omitted many of the less useful and interesting propositions of EUCLID's treatise. The second book of EUCLID (areas of rectangles) was recognized to be unsuitable for formal logical treatment; its chief propositions were introduced as « geometrical illustrations of algebraic identities ».

An important step was taken in admitting « proofs which are only applicable to commensurable magnitudes ». EUCLID's treatment of proportion is strict and covers all magnitudes, commensurable or incommensurable. It is of the greatest interest to a mature mathematician, and might suitably form part of a university course; though for this purpose a more modern treatment of incommensurables might possibly be preferred. But EUCLID's theory was a stumbling block to beginners; and indeed, as generally taught in English Schools, it was unintelligible, since Book 5 was always omitted. The university decided that the theory of similar figures might be studied in schools without attacking prematurely the much more difficult theory of incommensurables.

Hypothetical constructions were allowed; e. g. in proving the equality of the base angles of an isosceles triangle, it was considered legitimate to use the bisector of the vertical angle, even though a ruler and compass construction for this bisector might not have been given and proved at this stage. An existence theorem is, in fact, assumed; viz that an angle has a bisector. The choice of any particular method for drawing the bisector is not considered relevant to the discussion.

22. The change of regulations released a volume of pent-up energy. Every enthusiast felt that he might now teach geometry in his own way. Numerous text-books were produced, embodying every shade of opinion. As was to be expected, many of the new developments were extravagant and had no permanent effect. In particular, there was temporarily a tendency to overemphasize the practical and experimental side of the work. But it was soon realized that this would make the subject invertebrate, that there must be a certain element of severity in every school study, and that for purposes of general education geometry must still stand or fall by the logical training it gives. The most widely used of the new text-books did not differ from Euclid in their method of setting out and combining theorems. As for the experimental work, some books confined this to an introduction, while others preferred to allow experiment and theory to develop side by side. In all cases, constructions were expected to be done practically with instruments; and numerical data and illustrations were used freely. As regards sequence of theorems, no system has found favour that can be called revolutionary; there has been no bold cutting adrift from the Euclidean tradition. Among the variations from Euclid adopted by different authors are the following: (1) A rearrangement of the earlier theorems into the order-angles at a point, parallel lines, angles of triangles and polygons, congruent triangles. (2) The presentation of the theorems relating to areas of triangles, parallelograms and polygons rather in the light of mensuration rules than of geometrical theorems.

23. As to the effects of all these changes on education, perhaps it is still too soon to give a final opinion. The transitional period is still on us. No doubt boys find geometry a much more interesting subject than they used to. The have more practice in solving exercises for themselves; they no longer find this a hopeless undertaking. They are able to *see* more in a geometrical figure. They have gained a sense of power, and can easily be induced to take up little bits of research work for themselves, e. g. in plotting loci or in devising mechanical models to illustrate various points.

On the other hand, much less time can be given to writing out formal propositions; and there is some reason to think that boys have lost something of their power of expressing geometrical reasoning in words. Doubtless this is a fault that will correct itself in course of time; and perhaps it is as well that the stereotyped Euclidean language should give place to a more individual wording, even at the cost of some initial loss in accuracy. At one stage of the movement there seemed to be a danger that experimental verifications would be taken for proofs; but the distinction has been emphasized so repeatedly that perhaps this particular reproach can no longer be aimed at the new methods.

24. Geometry in three dimensions. The position of this subject in schools is still unsatisfactory. It does not form part of the geometry demanded for the preliminary examinations of Oxford and Cambrige, nor is it suggested here that it could with advantage be included in these schedules.

When a boy has covered the elementary course of plane geometry, he has presumably received an adequate training in logical method, in so far as this can be given by geometrical studies. If he goes on to the Geometry of three dimensions (Solid Geometry) the first object should be to gain the power of realizing mentally the relations of figures in space; he must learn to « think in space ». Few of the boys who used to study EUCLID's Book XI gained this power; and for this reason one can hardly regret that nowadays this book is hardly read at all in schools.

For many years an attempt was made by the Science and Art Department (now merged in the Board of Education) to encourage the study of solid geometry. Public examinations were held in the so-called *Descriptive Geometry* (¹) i. e. the representation of solids by means of plan and elevation, and by perspective projections. The same body used to examine in plane Geometrical drawing; and, unfortunately, the examination system succeeded in reducing both studies to mere collections of special tricks, often taught by teachers who had received no mathematical training. The attempt ended in failure; and the effect on public schools was null, as these schools made no use of the department's examinations.

25. A satisfactory course of instruction in three-dimensional geometry should include:

(1) The determination of the surfaces and volumes of the elementary solids.

(2) A discussion of the relations of points, lines and planes in space. This should be comparatively informal, and freely illustrated by all kinds of devices such as string and cardboard models, stereoscopic views, dissected solids etc. Much of it might be worked in incidentally during the plane geometry course e. g. when parallel and perpendicular lines *in plano* are before the class, it is very profitable to discuss parallel and perpendicular lines and planes in space. Indeed, should not the very earliest geometry teaching deal first with concrete solids, and then pass on to abstractions such as points and lines?

(3) A course of the really fundamental constructions in descriptive geometry. Probably this course if taught intelligently would do more than any other to cultivate the power of thinking in space.

No accepted or standard course exists which embodies these features. University-trained mathematical teachers are as a rule quite ignorant of descriptive geometry. This repreach will gradually disappear, as descriptive geometry is required in the new honours course at Cambridge: in the meantime, it is to be hoped that this subject will gradually win its way in public schools.

26. Algebra. The reform of geometry teaching was accompanied by some activity on the side of algebra. Many teachers and examiners held that the teaching

(¹) This is the *Geometrie Descriptive* of MONGE: and must not be confounded with the descriptive or non-metrical geometry of CHASLES and other writers.

had laid too great stress on manipulative skill, at the expense of intelligent study of the why and wherefore. Certainly much time was spent in working out long graduated sets of exercises on factors, equations, fractions etc. There was a kind of rebellion against this practice, and teachers sought to lighten the « toil » by introducing graphs, logarithms tables and other interesting matters at a comparatively early stage.

All this had a decidedly stimulating effect. It is a revelation to a boy to learn that a function of a variable may be associated with a curve; that he can solve equations, extract roots, etc. by graphical methods.

Following the usual law, the reform went too far. Some teachers and text-books were not content to touch lightly on graphs, immensely suggestive as this is for a boy of 13. They enlarged the subject until it amounted to a premature attack on analytical geometry. There was a certain tendency to abandon analytical in favour of geometrical and graphical methods. The laborious working of algebra exercises was cut down more and more, until there was a danger that the boys would become helpless in dealing with the most straight-forward algebraic expressions.

The pendulum is now swinging in the opposite direction. If its oscillations can be damped in time, we may hope to settle down to a system which gives reasonable skill in quite straightforward manipulation, and at the same time sets graphical work in the true position it should occupy in elementary teaching.

27. To speak frankly, it is not easy to determine the exact function of algebra teaching in a secondary education. It may be admitted that the conception of algebra as a generalized arithmetic is of great educational value. If a boy can be made to see that a single algebraic formula is a kind of portmanteau, into which are packed an infinite number of arithmetical data-if this can be brought home to him, he has gained one of the most fruitful ideas that his mathematical education can give. This alone would justify the teaching of algebra, and this end can be attained without giving any great amount of time to exercises in manipulation.

The above is an example of what may be called the *ideas* of algebra. Everyone is the better for acquiring these ideas. The majority of public school boys will never have occasion in their after life to make any direct use of the mathematics they learn at school: for this large class one is tempted to think that the *ideas* should suffice, together with the minimum of manipulative practice that will suffice to make these ideas intelligible.

For those, on the other hand, who will have to *use* mathematics in after life, the case is very different. For them algebra is an indispensable tool, a key to unlock the armoury. Without facility in handling algebraic expressions their path will indeed be thorny. They cannot shirk the drudgery of exercise-working: and for the mathematician, as for the musician, skill comes only as the reward of long and strenuous practice, practice which is perhaps of slight value in itself, and only desiderable for the sake of the end in view.

The above distinction between the amateur and the professional student of algebra is perhaps of small practical value in England; the fact being that, in the main, the object of English education is the passing of examinations. Examinations can test skill, but not ideas; hence it follows that all English boys tend to be taught as if they were destined to make practical use of mathematics in their after life.

28. Plane Trigonometry. This subject is now introduced at an early stage in many schools, say at 13-15 years of age. It is held that every school boy ought to be able to learn some trigonometry as an extension of his geometry.

This early introduction has become possible through the practice of laying increased stress on what may be called *numerical trigonometry*. A introductory course of numerical trigonometry deals with the sine, cosine and tangent of acute angles; the graphical determination of these functions; the use of Tables; the solution of right-angled triangles, and of practical problems depending on them; this work being closely related to the drawing to scale which now forms part of geometry teaching. Other triangles are solved by splitting them into right-angled triangles.

Treated in this way, the beginnings of trigonometry present no difficulties. The feasibility of the work at this stage seems to depend on

(1) A very gradual advance, and presentation of difficulties one at a time; e. g. to use logarithmic sines at this stage would lead to confusion.

(2) The postponement of what may be called *algebraic* trigonometry i. e. the manipulation of expressions containing trigonometrical functions.

The solution of practical problems is often based on observations made by the pupils with a simplified form of theodolite.

When the elements have been thoroughly digested, it is found that progress on the ordinary lines is fairly rapid.

29. Mechanics. Including *Statics* and *Kinetics*.

There is no uniform practice as to which of these subjects is to be taken first. The graphical movement of late years, however, has tended to set statics in the earlier place.

The best usage nowadays bases statics upon an experimental course in the laboratory, or mathematical workshop. Here the pupil establishes the parallelogram of forces; the laws of moments; of friction etc., and learns about the principles of work by experiments on a variety of simple machines. Subsequently or simultaneously he goes through a course of graphical statics; which is gradually combined with the analytical treatment for which the pupil's work in trigonometry has been preparing him. All this can be done at the age of 15-16.

If this course is adopted, kinetics come later. It is not easy to arrange experimental work in this subject; and the teaching is for the most part merely theoretical. The average boy seems to find kinetics much more difficult than statics; and perhaps trigonometry and statics will for some time form the limit of the mathematical studies of most boys in public schools.

30. Advanced school mathematics. Boys who intend to take up mathematical studies at the universities are expected to make some headway in the following subjects - modern geometry, analytical geometry, the geometry of the conic sections treated both geometrically and analytically, higher algebra, trigonometry, mechanics, differential and integral calculus.

Modern Geometry. Includes the geometry of the triangle, the properties of pole and polar, and of coaxal circles, inversion, reciprocation, orthogonal and conical projection etc.

Geometrical conics. Is a subject to which great and perhaps exaggerated importance has been attached in English schools. This may be due to the fact that NEWTON was compelled to throw his principia into a geometrical form, his contemporaries being unable to appreciate the method of fluxions by which his results were attained.

Analytical Geometry. Mainly of the straight line, circle and conic sections. Here again the conic sections bulk very large, they are studied in great detail, and the finished schoolboy mathematician is expected to attain considerable skill in the application of such methods as trilinear coordinates. The modern tendency is to try to reduce the treatment (both analytical and geometrical) of the conic sections to its true proportion; and to spend longer time on the more fruitful methods of the calculus.

Higher Algebra. A miscellaneous and unscientific category, covering summation of series, convergency, continued fractions, theory of numbers, inequalities, probability, theory of equations etc. This catalogue of subjects might be startling if it were not explained that only elementary and isolated propositions are studied.

Higher Trigonometry. A species of algebra usually classified by schoolmasters as a separate subject. Complex numbers first make their appearance at the introduction of this subject. This earlier work boys find very attractive; later on the treatment of infinite expansions and products tends to become laborious, and many teachers think that the pressure of examinations over-emphasizes this section of the work.

Differential and Integral Calculus used to be regarded as the coping-stone of school mathematics. But there is a strong movement at the present day in favour of an early use of the calculus. Perhaps it is hardly ascertained as yet how early this may be attempted; but it has been proved that a slight knowledge of differentiation and integration simplifies and generalizes the study of analytical geometry and kinetics; subjects to which tradition assigns an earlier place.

31. In order to make the information of the present paper as definite as possible, two appendices are given, namely:

APPENDIX 1. The regulations of the Previous Examination in mathematics for the degree of Bachelor at the University of Cambridge. This examination (or its equivalent) must be passed as a preliminary to the further examinations for every degree at Cambridge. It is very commonly taken by boys at the end of their school life, and just before going up to the University. It may be regarded as defining the minimum amount of mathematics which is considered necessary for a liberal education by the Cambridge authorities. Needless to say, a boy who is intending to specialize in Mathematics or Engineering - or even in Physical Science-will generally have read far beyond the limits laid down by this schedule.

APPENDIX 2. The scheme of mathematical teaching at a leading pubblic school.

APPENDIX I

SCHEDULE OF MATHEMATICS REQUIRED IN THE PREVIOUS EXAMINATION OF THE UNIVERSITY OF CAMBRIDGE

GEOMETRY

The paper in Geometry shall contain questions on Practical and on Theoretical Geometry. Every candidate shall be expected to answer questions in both branches of the subject.

The questions on Pratical Geometry shall be set on the constructions contained in the annexed Schedule A, together with easy extensions of them. In cases where the validity of a construction is not obvious, the reasoning by which it is justified may be required. Every candidate shall provide himself with a ruler graduated in inches and tenths of an inch, and in centimetres and millimetres, a set square, a protractor, compasses, and a hard pencil. All figures should be drawn accurately. Questions may be set in which the use of the set square or of the protractor is forbidden.

The questions on Theoretical Geometry shall consist of theorems contained in the annexed Schedule B, together with questions upon these theorems, easy deductions from them, and arithmetical illustrations. Any proof of a proposition shall be accepted which appears to the examiners to form part of a systematic treatment of the subject; the order in which the theorems are stated in Schedule B is not imposed as the sequence of their treatment.

In the proof of theorems and deductions from them, the use of hypothetical constructions shall be permitted. Proof which are only applicable to commensurable magnitudes shall be accepted.

SCHEDULE A.

Bisection of angles and of straight lines.

Construction of perpendiculars to straight lines.

Construction of an angle equal to a given angle.

Construction of parallels to a given straight line.

Simple cases of the construction from sufficient data of triangles and quadrilaterals.

Division of straight lines into a given number of equal parts or into parts in any given proportions.

Construction of a triangle equal in area to a given polygon.

Construction of tangents to a circle and of common tangents to two circles.

Simple cases of the construction of circles from sufficient data.

Construction of a fourth proportional to three given straight lines and a mean proportional to two given straight lines.

Construction of regular figures of 3, 4, 6 or 8 sides in or about a given circle.

Construction of a square equal in area to a given polygon.

SCHEDULE B.

Angles at a Point.

If a straight line stands on another straight line, the sum of the two angles so formed is equal to two right angles; and the converse.

If two straight lines intersect, the vertically opposite angles are equal.

Parallel Straight Lines.

When a straight line cuts two other straight lines, if

(i) a pair of alternate angles are equal,

or (ii) a pair of corresponding angles are equal,

or (iii) a pair of interior angles on the same side of the cutting line are together equal to two right angles,

then the two straight lines are parallel; and the converse.

Straight lines which are parallel to the same straight line are parallel to one another.

Triangles and Rectilinear Figures.

The sum of the angles of a triangle is equal to two right angles.

If the sides of a convex polygon are produced in order, the sum of the angles so formed is equal to four right angles.

If two triangles have two sides of the one equal to two sides of the other, each to each, and also the angles contained by those sides equal, the triangles are congruent.

If two triangles have two angles of the one equal to two angles of the other, each to each, and also one side of the one equal to the corresponding side of the other, the triangles are congruent.

If two sides of a triangle are equal, the angles opposite to these sides are equal; and the converse.

If two triangles have the three sides of the one equal to the three sides of the other, each to each, the triangles are congruent.

If two right-angled triangles have their hypotenuses equal, and one side of the one equal to one side of the other, the triangles are congruent.

If two sides of a triangle are unequal, the greater side has the greater angle opposite to it; and the converse.

Of all the straight lines that can be drawne to a given straight line from a given point outside it, the perpendicular is the shortest.

The opposite sides and angles of a parallelogram are equal, each diagonal bisects the parallelogram, and the diagonals bisect one another.

If there are three or more parallel straight lines, and the intercepts made by them on any straight line that cuts them are equal, then the corresponding intercepts on any other straight line that cuts them are also equal.

Areas.

Parallelograms on the same or equal bases and of the same altitude are equal in area.

Triangles on the same or equal bases and of the same altitude are equal in area.

Equal triangles on the same or equal bases are of the same altitude.

Illustrations and explanations of the geometrical theorems corresponding to the following algebraical identities:

$$k(a+b+c+\cdots) = ka+kb+kc+\cdots,$$
$$(a+b)^2 = a^2+2ab+b^2,$$
$$(a-b)^2 = a^2-2ab+b^2,$$
$$a^2-b^2 = (a+b)(a-b).$$

The square on a side of a triangle is greater than, equal to, or less than the sum of the squares on the other two sides, according as the angle contained by those sides is obtuse, right, or acute. The difference in the cases of inequality is twice the rectangle contained by one of the two sides and the projection on it of the other.

Loci.

The locus of a point which is equidistant from two fixed points is the perpendicular bisector of the straight line joining the two fixed points.

The locus of a point which is equidistant from two intersecting straight lines consists of the pair of straight lines which bisect the angles between the two given lines.

The Circle.

A straight line, drawn from the centre of a circle to bisect a chord which is not a diameter is at right angles to the chord; conversely, the perpendicular to a chord from the centre bisects the chord.

There is one circle, and one only, which passes through three given points not in a straight line.

In equal circles (or, in the same circle) (i) if two arcs subtend equal angles at the centres, they are equal; (ii) conversely, if two arcs are equal, they subtend equal angles at the centres.

In equal circles (or, in the same circle) (i) if two chords are equal, they cut off equal arcs; (ii) conversely, if two arcs are equal, the chords of the arcs are equal.

Equal chords of a circle are equidistant from the centres; and the converse.

The tangent at any point of a circle and the radius through the point are perpendicular to one another.

If two circles touch, the point of contact lies on the straight line through the centres.

The angle which an arc of a circle subtends at the centre is double that which it subtends at any point on the remaining part of the circumference.

Angles in the same segment of a circle are equal; and, if the line joining two points subtends equal angles at two other points on the same side of it, the four points lie on a circle.

The angle in a semicircle is a right angle; the angle in a segment greater than a semicircle is less than a right angle; and the angle in a segment less than a semicircle is greater than a right angle.

The opposite angles of any quadrilateral inscribed in a circle are supplementary; and the converse.

If a straight line touch a circle, and from the point of contact a chord be drawn, the angles which this chord makes with the tangent are equal to the angles in the alternate segments.

If two chords of a circle intersect either inside or outside the circle the rectangle contained by the parts of the one is equal to the rectangle contained by the parts of the other.

Proportion: Similar Triangles.

If a straight line is drawn parallel to one side of a triangle, the other two sides are divided proportionally; and the converse.

If two triangles are equiangular their corresponding sides are proportional; and the converse.

If two triangles have one angle of the one equal to one angle of the other and the sides about these equal angles proportional, the triangles are similar.

The internal bisector of an angle of a triangle divides the opposite side internally in the ratio of the sides containing the angle, and likewise the externally.

The ratio of the areas of similar triangles is equal to the ratio of the squares on corresponding sides.

ARITHMETIC.

A knowledge of recurring decimals and of the process of extracting cube root shall not be required.

The use of algebraical symbols and processes shall be permitted.

ELEMENTARY ALGEBRA.

Addition, subtraction, multiplication and division; simple equations; fractions; highest common factor, lowest common multiple; quadratic equations; solutions of two simultaneous equations, one at least being linear; simple graphs; problems requiring the classes of equations specified; simple questions on fractional indices; the nature and simple properties of logarithms to the base 10, with easy applications of fourfigure tables; ratio and proportion; arithmetic progression, finite geometric progressions.

DAVID EUGENE SMITH

THE TEACHING OF MATHEMATICS IN THE SECONDARY SCHOOLS OF THE UNITED STATES

Object of this Paper.

In accepting the kind invitation of your Committee to present before the Educational Section of this International Congress a paper upon the Teaching of Mathematics in the Secondary Schools of the United States, I do this with five distinct objects in view. First: To set forth briefly the historic influences that have tended to make our mathematics in the West what it is at present; Second: To speak of the present status of the subject; Third: To mention the influences now at work to mould the secondary mathematics of the future; Fourth: To consider some of the resulting suggestions now being made to change the present curriculum; Fifth: To suggest a few questions that International Congresses of this nature might profitably consider through the medium of committees representing the leading educational countries.

Historical influences.

That territory of the Western World now known as the United States of America, and called by its citizens, perhaps with undue assumption yet with pardonable brevity, America, was colonized chiefly by the French, Dutch, Spanish and English. Before education assumed very definite form, however, the dominant spirit of the Anglo-Saxon had asserted itself to such an extent that the best part of our country was under British rule and subject to British influences. It therefore came about that Harvard University, founded in 1636, William and Mary in 1693, Yale in 1701, Princeton in 1746, and Columbia in 1754, were all based more or less upon the English models of the 17th and 18th centuries. Naturally too the elementary and secondary schools took on the characteristics of those of England, with such variations as local conditions demanded. The first secondary school planned for America was a Latin grammar school in Virginia, and the first one actually developed was a similar one in Boston in 1635, others soon following in various towns of New

England. Even the Dutch settlers in New Amsterdam (the present New York) opened a school of this same character in 1659. It will thus be seen that the early secondary schools were classical in nature, profoundly influenced by the Humanism of the Reformation, and little given to the development of mathematics. This was, in general, the situation when, owing to the greatest mistake that England ever made in her colonial policy, she lost control of her most valuable western territory, and the United States came into being. She had already, however, made her influence felt in mathematics, and we have by no means broken entirely away from it. In particular the American arithmetic was framed upon English models, a reprint of HODDER's book (1719) being the first work of this kind to appear in New England, and GREENWOOD's textbook (1729), the first purely American product, being based upon COCKER and HODDER. As a result, and also because of the influence of the common language, the American arithmetics have, until very recently, closely resembled the English type.

In geometry the same tendency was manifest. Early wedded to EUCLID, the English schools paid no attention to solid geometry, so that even today, although EUCLID as a textbook has long since been abandoned in America, none of our colleges on the Atlantic coast require solid geometry for entrance to the arts course.

In algebra our textbooks have always been based upon English models, and they are so today in spite of all of the many Continental influences, — and the same may be said for trigonometry.

In analytic geometry our treatises are largely the Conics of APOLLONIUS, modified it is true by the Cartesian treatment, but still embodying essentially the ancient sequence. In the calculus, it was only two generations ago that our college students worked in « Fluxions », the Newtonian influence having endured until that period.

Thus it is that our elementary and secondary mathematics were early influenced almost entirely by England, and that they took on those characteristics which, like all popular features, are not easily changed.

The separation from England, however, and particularly the second war (1812), led our young men to go to France, and later to Germany, rather than to England for their higher training. The result of all this was that the more advanced mathematics took on a Continental aspect. Fluxions changed to the Calculus, even EUCLID gave way to LEGENDRE, conics became analytic geometry in name and treatment, although retaining its Apollonian limitations. Instead of advanced mathematics meaning the application of the calculus to mechanics, as seemed to be the Cambridge tendency, advanced pure mathematics began to call American students to France and still more to Germany. The latter country opened her universities to our young men more freely than France, and much more so than England, so that for the past quarter of a century German mathematics has nearly dominated the higher field. Göttingen has been our mathematical Mecca and Berlin our Medina, while Paris and Cambridge have, not altogether fortunately for the world, exercised a relatively small influence in the great West.

It will not do to dwell longer on these historic influences of countries or of schools. I wish, however, before I leave the topic to say a word as to the historic influence of different peoples upon American mathematics. America, I need hardly tell you, is the world's present meeting ground. Once all roads led to Rome; now many of them lead to America. Nearly a million immigrants come to our shores every year, and are assimilated into our body politic.

Of aliens or of alien parentage, we have in the United States four or five times as many Englishmen as Liverpool, five or six times as many Germans as Berlin, nearly twice as many Irish as all Ireland, about as many Scotchmen as Edinburgh and Glasgow combined, three times as many Italians as Rome, and so for various other nationalities. These immigrants are not in general from the learned class, but they have energy, vitality, and a desire that their children shall have an education. They may not bring with them the mathematics of their various lands, but they accomplish two most important things for us: First, by crossing blood they make a cosmopolitan race of enormous energy; and Second, they give to the American of today a blood-sympathy with the work of every country under the sun, and a mental tendency to look to other countries than England for educational models. And this brings me to my second topic, the present status of secondary mathematics in America.

The Present Status of Secondary Mathematics in America.

It is often thought that the United States, made up of some fifty state and territorial governments, with no centralized power in educational matters, must be without any uniformity in its schools. Such, however, is not the case. While the schools in the older portions of the country are more conservative in some respects, and while the wealthier sections have better trained teachers and more elaborate equipment as a rule, there is such a constant interchange of teachers and ideas, and there is such an influence exerted by organizations like the National Educational Association and by the large textbook publishing houses, that the essential features in the teaching of mathematics do not vary particularly from one part of the country to the other.

In general the children attend public schools, more than ten times as many being enrolled in the public elementary schools and more than four times as many in the public secondary schools than in the private. Moreover the public schools are growing much more rapidly than the private, and except in large cities the latter are hardly representative of American education.

The course usually consists of eight years in the elementary school (often, in the cities, with some preliminary kindergarten work), four years in the high or secondary school, four years in the college (leading to the bachelor's degree), and three additional years in the university for the degree of doctor of philosophy. Of our total school population only $4\frac{1}{4}$ % are in the high schools, and 1.4 % in higher institutions of all kinds, less than 0.6 % being in colleges and universities.

It will thus be seen that while we have over 17,000,000 persons attending school, the number in college is relatively small.

In general, taking the country as a whole, it may be said that the work in mathematics is about as follows:

Elementary School. Years I-VIII inclusive. 5 recitations per week. In the primary years, about 20-30 minutes each; in years V-VIII, 45 minutes each. Arithmetic, with mensuration. In the last two years the linear equation with one unknown is used as an aid to arithmetic.

High (Secondary) School.

IX	4 or 5 recitations per week.	Algebra.
X	" " "	Geometry.
XI	" " "	Algebra and Geometry.
XII	Elective.	Algebra, Geometry and Trigonometry.

College.

XIII	3 recitations per week.	Algebra, Geometry and Trigonometry.
XIV	Elective.	Analytic Geometry and Calculus.
XV	"	Advanced Calculus.
XVI	"	Advanced or applied mathematics.

University.

XVII	"	(Master's degree).
XVIII	"	
XIX	"	(Doctor's degree).

Many schools attempt to introduce some constructive or other form of concrete geometry into the work of the elementary classes, but the effort has not as yet resulted in any thing better than a more rational teaching of the elementary mensuration that has always had place in our curriculum.

I come now to the nature of the mathematical work in the secondary schools.

a. *The Students.* It must be born in mind that a great majority of the secondary schools in the United States are coeducational, practically all save in some of the cities. Boys and girls study the same mathematics and in the same classes. In the larger cities of the East, and in the private schools, this is not the case, and there is a slight tendency in favor of separating the sexes.

b. *The teachers.* The absolute freedom given to woman in America, her desire to be self-supporting, her willingness to work for a relatively low salary, and the better financial returns that other professions and vocations offer to men, have brought about an unfortunate condition with respect to teachers. While the woman is usually a better elementary teacher than the man, and while at the salaries now paid in America a secondary school can get a better woman than man, the best men teachers of algebra and geometry are better than the best women. The undesirability of having women in charge of pupils throughout their entire course is recognized, and in the cities every effort is made by the school authorities to bring men into the secondary work in mathematics. With the natural increase in population of our country there will come less opportunity for men in other lines, and a reaction against the undue feminization of the schools, already manifest, will become more pronounced.

c. *The curriculum in detail.* The following is a brief statement of the New York City curriculum, a fair exponent of the work in other parts of the country:

Year IX. Algebra, 5 periods (45 minutes each) a week. Fundamental operations; linear equations with one and several unknowns; indices; surds; complex numbers; quadratics with one and two unknowns; graphs of equations.

Year X. Geometry, 4 periods a week. Substantially the first four books of EUCLID's or LEGENDRE's geometry, studied from some modern textbook. At least 300 exercises in plane geometry. Geometric drawing.

Year XI. Geometry and Algebra, 3 periods. Plane geometry completed, covering substantially the ground of EUCLID and LEGENDRE, with exercises. Algebra through proportion, indeterminate equations, progressions, combinations, and the binomial theorem proved for positive integral exponents and used for others.

Year XII. Elective, 4 periods. Plane trigonometry and logarithms, or a review of mathematics, in the first half year. Solid geometry, higher algebra, and spherical trigonometry, or a review of mathematics, in the second half year.

d. *The influence of the colleges.* This curriculum is essentially what is demanded by the colleges, generally privately endowed institutions chartered by the various states, and all seeking to maintain a fairly uniform set of requirements. These colleges all admit students by their own examinations, most of them accept tests imposed by the College Entrance Board (a private cooperative committee made up of representatives of various colleges), and a large number admit on certificates from secondary schools of high standing. The result is quite the same, the colleges demanding practically the course above outlined, and forcing the schools to offer it. For better or for worse the course stands, although a very small percent of pupils complete it, and a still smaller percent ever goes to college.

Influences at Work to Mould the Secondary Mathematics of the Future.

But this state of affairs is not to endure with us. A comparison of the educational literature of the past with that of the present shows that there has never been in America such a period of protest, of measuring each step of the curriculum, of experiment, and of the study of the history of teaching, as the present. The secondary education of the country is on the eve of no small change, and the influences at work and the probable results may well occupy our attention as I bring this communication to a close.

a. *Influence of the elementary work.* The past ten or fifteen years have seen the work in arithmetic as greatly revolutionized as it was when the Pestalozzian influence reached America seventy-five years ago. This change has been brought about because of two consideration: (1) A growing interest in the psychological development of the child, resulting in a study of his mental aptitudes in the successive school years. (2) A growing interest in the real demands of business life, resulting in the substitution of modern applications for those of a remote past. This change has shown itself in the recent curricula and in the textbooks which have of late appeared. The work is now universally arranged on the basis of a conservatively drawn spiral, so that a child meets important topics two or more times, with increasingly difficult problems. Furthermore, without having any less abstract number work, the concrete problems are those that appeal to his interests, that represent genuine American conditions, and that relate to the life about him. The result has been a healthier attitude towards this subject on the part of pupils, teachers, and parents, and the question has naturally been raised as to whether it is possible to effect a similar reform in secondary mathematics.

b. *Foreign influences.* The study of foreign systems is also having a great influence on the present discussion. The continual stream of young men to German universities, the extensive study of European schools on the part of our educational leaders, the critical studies of curricula from all parts of the world that appear in the annual reports of the United States Commissioner of Education, and the dissemination of this knowledge by our higher institutions for the training of teachers, — all this is constantly bringing us in close touch with the world's best work. In my own clesses last year I had students reporting upon the excellent curriculum in the Bulgarian gymnasium, upon the MÉRAY movement in France, upon the latest Prussian curricula, upon the work of the Italian ginnasio, and upon similar topics relating to other countries. Not an important change is made in any secondary courses in Europe that is not at once discussed in the leading teachers associations in America, and not a theory is strenuously advocated, like that of Professor PERRY of London, that does not receive serious attention in the New World. The result of all this continued inquiry into the best that other lands have to offer is a constant examination of our own work to see wherein it is capable of improvement. It is not particularly to our credit that this should be so; it is merely the force of circumstances, the result of the seething of mixing bloods in a new human reservoir.

c. *Commercial influences.* The American has, until the present time, been content to exploit his own country, to gather in the wealth of her virgin fields and forests, and to take the product of her easily worked mines. But now the country is filling up and we have, within a generation, become a manufacturing people and have begun to look abroad for markets. The commercial spirit is rampant, and in the schools the constant question is asked, *Cui bono*? Hence the mathematics of the secondary schools is being continually called to account; its claims are being analyzed, and its results are being compared (with no common unit of measure, it is true) with the time devoted to the subject. This does not mean that mathematics is looked upon as purely utilitarian, for every one agrees that it has a high disciplinary value *per sè*, but it means that there is a healthy demand for the substitution of that which has greater value for that which has less. In the matter of applications it means, to use a phrase from which I have often preached to teachers, that « Whatever pretends to be practical should really be so », an idea that touches the keynote of an important present movement in America.

d. *Psychological influences.* There is another influence that is bound strongly to mould the future, and that is the intense study of practical psychology. Teachers are asking why the human mind should be asked to comprehend certain exceedingly abstract principles of geometry before the much easier parts of trigonometry are mastered; why the intricacies of advanced algebra are required before the simpler parts of the calculus are presented; and why, in general, there should be the conventional and accidental barriers maintained between algebra and geometry, geometry and trigonometry, and algebra and the calculus. I do not mean that these questions are not capable of answer, but that we are doubting whether it is a sufficient answer to say « Laissez faire ».

e. *Scientific influences.* There is also the influence that natural science is bringing to bear upon mathematics. Since our subject is needed in physics, physics is held to be especially joined with it, and extremists are not wanting who would go so far as to link the two together at every step. Out of this agitation, still in its crude and extreme phase, not a little good will come.

f. *The dogma of thoroughness.* Whether it be British conservatism that is at the bottom of the case, or some mistaken desire to exhaust every step before the next is taken, it sometimes seems that in no other country save England is the dogma of thoroughness so much in evidence. Our geometry is much more hair-splitting that that of Germany, although we do not produce so good geometers; our algebra covers many more details that the ordinary French textbook, yet we do not produce so good algebraists; and our trigonometries are quite as thorough as those of any other country save England, and yet our students are not particularly brilliant in this field, save only when they apply it to engineering. Whether this is a justifiable state of affairs may seriously be questioned. Educators are, therefore, asking if better results may not be attained by greater area and less depth, by introducing some plane trigonometry in place of part of the extensive treatment of plane geometry, and of giving a little insight into the calculus in lieu of part of algebra, just as curve tracing (graphs) is now introduced to give a slight notion of analytic geometry.

Suggestions of Change in the Curriculum.

Out of all of the discussion relating to secondary mathematics in the United States come numerous suggestions of change. I propose to summarize these, merely as showing some of the tendencies. I shall set forth a course that embodies many current ideas, although one that has been recommended by no body of teachers and adopted by no school. Its purpose is merely to provoke discussion and to show some of the views of a rather advanced line of educators in America. It is arranged for five years, the last year of the elementary school and the four years of the secondary school.

YEAR VIII. Mathematics I. Required. Boys and girls together. 5 periods per week.

General view. Transition from special to general forms. A combination of algebra, concrete geometry and arithmetic. Algebra the basis for the arrangement of the course.

Detailed view.

1. Algebraic formulas.
   (*a*) Application to mensuration, always leading to a formula to be manipulated like an equation. Simple work in square root to follow later in the year.
   (*b*) Application to business customs, as in interest, discount, and commissions.
   (*c*) Applications to statistics. Graphic representations with squared paper, both when the formula is given and when only the statistics are known.
   (*d*) The notation of simple functions, as that interest on a given principal at a given rate is a function of the time; that the area of a circle is a function of the radius, etc.
   (*e*) Sufficient simple experimental work to show the law of the lever, with its formula. This may reasonably lead to introducing other simple formulas of physics, without experiment, to show certain uses of algebra. E. g., the formula for the strength of a steel beam.
   (*f*) In the numerical evaluation of functions, as in $c = 2\pi r$, to introduce the slide rule and the check of 9's and 11's. The underlying principles of the checks may be postponed until Mathematics V (*b*) is studied. The metric system used now and in all subsequent work in which science problems are involved.
2. Linear equations with one unknown.
   (*a*) Applications to problems of arithmetic, with a discussion of the advantages or disadvantages of the algebraic symbolism.
   (*b*) Application to mensuration as before.
   (*c*) Mathematical recreations, bringing out the game element.
3. Algebraic functions and the fundamental operations.
   (*a*) Apply the work as much as possible to the formulas studied above.
   (*b*) Factoring, using geometric correspondence where it is helpful. Comparison with arithmetic. Apply this work to solving easy quadratics, including applications.
   (*c*) Fractions, reviewing at the same time the principles of and practice with numerical fractions.

4. Linear equations with two unknowns.
   (*a*) Applications to arithmetic.
   (*b*) Also to mensuration as above.
   (*c*) The recreation phase considered.

YEAR IX. Mathematics II. Required. Boys and girls in separate classes, with the possible proviso that girls may elect to enter the classes for boys. 5 periods per week.

General view. Elementary algebra through quadratics with one unknown, combined as closely as possible with the first three books of plane geometry, each presupposing Mathematics I, and building directly upon it. No definite allotment of hours to either as related to the other subject is to be made for the year, but this is to be regulated by the teacher as experience shows to be necessary. This should be the final required course for the girls. The concrete geometry now passes into the demonstrative. The correspondence between algebra and geometry is to be emphasized. The practical applications of each subject are to be made as real as possible. It is recognized that the success of the course depends upon the teacher's ability at this point to use the existing textbooks on algebra and geometry in the spirit here suggested. Textbooks combining algebra and geometry are not to be expected in the immediate future, even if they are to be desired (which is still doubtful). It is probable that the time will be divided about equally between algebra and geometry. Five hours may be given to each every two weeks, alternating day by day, or, preferably, each lesson should include both topics. The field is a new one, and this is one of the points for serious experiment.

Detailed view.

1. Book I of plane geometry, the book propositions being limited to those required in the recent syllabi.
   (*a*) Use of the protractor; drawing to scale. Machanical drawing begun in the art and manual training courses and applied to this work now and throughout the rest of the course. The construction of simple instruments for angle measure. Primitive methods of measuring distances based on Book I.
   (*b*) Mensuration whenever advantageous.
   (*c*) Original exercises, with a beginning of generalization whenever practicable. E. g., derive the laws of the equilateral triangle from those of the isosceles; consider the rectangle with respect to the parallelogram; consider the exterior angles of the various forms of the triangle.
   (*d*) Experiment upon the relation of solid geometry to plane, guided by MÉRAY and DE PAOLIS, carrying the work only so far as is positively advantageous.

2. In connection with the above, and related to it as far as possible, there should be a brief review of the operations on algebraic functions, with applications when they can be found, and a review of linear equations with one and two unknowns

in the same spirit. The graph of linear equations with two unknowns, for the purpose of bringing out the meaning of 'linear' and 'simultaneous' and incidentally of picturing roots in general. Graphic solutions of train problems as related to this work.

3. Book II of plane geometry (Euclidean sequence), treated only briefly as illustrating familar algebraic forms. E. g., $a(b+c)$, $(a+b)^2$, and a few similar forms, should be taken up as matters of interest during the class period. It is intended that there shall be not strict geometric treatment of this book.

4. Book III of plane geometry, omitting generalizations that are too difficult for this year. Relate the work to the quadratic, particularly in the applied problems.

5. Algebraic problems involving quadratics that relate to the geometry of this year, and (as far as possible) to other work of this class. E. g., if manual training can offer any problems, or if any simple mechanical laws can be illustrated to the class, advantage should be taken of this work.

6. As far as possible, the applications of geometry and algebra should be selected, for the boys, from mechanics, mensuration, and commercial life; for the girls, they should relate to designing, and to the domain of domestic arts and sciences as far as can reasonably be arranged. For the girls particularly, the work given in a book like BECKER's *Geometrisches Zeichnen* is very valuable.

7. When the laws of exponents are taken up, logarithms should be introduced and tables thenceforth used practically, as the slide rule has already been used. Comparison of these two aids to calculation. Each should be used whenever numerical computations are involved, as in evaluating expressions involving radicals.

YEAR X. Mathematics III. Required for boys; elective for girls. Separate classes. 5 periods per week.

General view. Elementary algebra completed, through quadratics with two unknowns, and variation. Plane geometry completed, condensed as in Mathematics II. Mechanical drawing continued in connection with applied work. The trigonometry of the plane triangle in connection with similar figures. Practical mensuration of plane and solid figures, with the help of trigonometry. The use of the transit. Solid geometry combined with plane as far as reasonable.

Detailed view.

1. Algebra through quadratics with two unknowns. Graphic work to illustrate the following:

(*a*) The nature of the roots (imaginaries entering in pairs, etc.).

(*b*) Number of roots to be expected.

(*c*) The three forms of the conics (the names being given).

2. The study of variation to include not an undue amount of simple experimental work in physics, together with related problems in mensuration. The regular work in physics this year to be related as closely as possible to this work.

3. Plane geometry completed. Ratio and proportion taken up for algebra and geometry at the same time. Limits and incommensurable cases considered only incidentally, no attempt being maade at strict proofs.

4. Similar figures to lead to the trigonometry of the plane triangle. Use of simple instruments to be constructed by the class, such as the 'riga', 'baculus', 'quadrans', 'speculum', etc., followed by the use of the transit and plane table. Computations in mensuration and physical problems to be performed both by the slide rule and by logarithms.

5. The mensuration of solid geometry.

6. As far as possible, problems for the boys should relate to business, machanics, physics, and practical applications to the mensuration of land and buildings; those for the girls (in their elective course) to Domestic Economy, including designing, sanitation and civic questions that touch the home.

Year XI. Mathematics IV. Elective for both boys and girls. Separate classes preferred. 5 periods per week.

General view. A course leading to mechanics and physiography and introducing the spherical triangle, the elements of analytic geometry and curve tracing generally.

Detailed view.

1. Relation of the work to physics. The work in physics this year is usually of a laboratory nature. The teachers of mathematics should be in constant touch with this work with a view to securing problems and to supplying the necessary mathematics at the proper times.

2. Mechanics should enter into the applied work as extensively as possible. Mechanical drawing continued as heretofore. and the ability secured to read a working drawing.

3. The course in physiography often given in the 12th school year should be transferred to this year and brought into close relation to this course. Study of simple map projections, and the applications of trigonometry and geometric drawing to physiography. Determination of latitude by observation of the sun and the polar star. Computation of local time and of longitude. Computation of great-circle arcs from given latitudes and longitudes. All this should be the objective work in the study of the spherical triangle.

4. Analytic geometry. The fundamental theorems relating to the conics, this course being, like the work in elementary geometry, condensed as much as possible. The study of curves used in mechanics and physics, with applications to such matters as the catenary corrections in steel taping.

5. A review of the essential theorems of geometry and trigonometry. Approximation formulas, such as Simpson's rule for areas.

6. Practical field work with the transit.

Year XII. Mathematics V (*a*). Elective for both boys and girls. Separate classes preferred. First half year (see also Mathematics V, b., below). 4 periods per week. Prerequisite, Mathematics IV.

General view. A half year of work in the calculus and its applications, with practical work in the use of the transit and with abundant applications to mechanics. It is possible that a parallel culture course for girls may be arranged, involving the elements of mathematical and descriptive astronomy.

Detailed view.

1. The elements of differential and integral calculus, with practical applications to mechanics. Such cases in mensuration as have thus far been treated rather unsatisfactorily should now be clearly understood; e. g., SIMPSON's rule.

3. Field work in the use of the transit. Railway curves, simple bridge-building problems and other applications of trigonometry and the calculus.

3. Applications for the work of V (*b*), as in the laws or probabilities and least squares.

Mathematics V (*b*). Required for boys, elective for girls. Separate classes. 3 periods per week throughout the year. Prerequisite, Mathematics III.

General view. Commercial arithmetic. A thorough course, 3 periods per week for the entire year, embodying all the commercial arithmetic needed by a man entering business. To include as far as possible a review of Mathematics I, II, III, and to cover all the common business applications of today. Elements of bookkeepping. All obsolete and non-utilitarian matter to be eliminated. For the girls, particular attention to the arithmetic of the various branches of Domestic Economy, including household accounts and investements, and household chemistry.

Detailed view.

1. Computation. Review of the slide rule and logarithms. Calculating machines explained and their uses set forth. The underlying principles of the checks of casting out 9's and 11's.

2. Theory of investments. The practical questions of compound interest, annuities, and investments in stocks and bonds.

3. Banking and exchange.

4. The simplier parts of the mathematics of statistics. Possibly the method of least squares with practical applications to science.

5. The construction and use of practical tables, such as interest, wage, exchange, temperature, longitude, tax, etc.

6. A brief treatment of the theory of fire and life insurance, involving the first principles of probability.

7. Fundamental principles of commission, brokerage, discounts, and other business customs.

I should add that some such course is now under contemplation in the Horace Mann School of Observation, Teachers College, Columbia University, New York City.

Questions for the Considerations of such Congresses as this.

And now, in closing, I should like to express the hope that these International Congresses may add to their already great value as clearing houses of thought, by sometime investigating, through committees, a few questions relating to secondary education. Countries cannot be uniform in their curricula, their school systems, nor their methods of teaching, but the influence of a Congress like this might greatly help many who are earnestly seeking to improve the teaching of mathematics. Some of the questions that might profitably be considered are the following:

1. What have been the results of attempting to remove the barrier between such topics as algebra and geometry, or to teach the two simultaneously, and are we prepared as yet to make any recommendation in this matter?

2. What have been the results of attempting to teach demonstrative geometry before algebra? If they have been favorable, what is the nature of the geometry best adapted to this apparently psychological sequence?

3. What is the opinion of impartial observes of ihe work of the MÉRAY geometry in France and of works like that of DE PAOLIS in Italy, as to the union of plane and solid geometry?

4. What is done in the various countries as to the union of plane geometry and trigonometry?

5. What is being done to advantage in the introduction of the elementary ideas of the calculus into the work in secondary algebra?

6. What is the safe minimum of Euclidean geometry, the calculus, and mechanics?

7. What is the safe relation to be established between secondary mathematics and physics?

8. What position should the secondary schools take with respect to the nature of applications and the relations of applied to pure mathematics?

9. What should be the relative nature of the courses in the secondary schools for those who do not intend to proceed to the universities, and for those who do intend to do so? In other words, of finishing and preparatory courses?

These questions, and others like them, are occupying the serious thought of American teachers. As we have always turned to Europe for conservative but helpful suggestions, so some of us would be glad if this Congress might deem it advisable to appoint international committees, corresponding in any of the four languages admittes to these deliberations to consider matters of this kind. An agreement is not essential, but the interchange of views and suggestions could not fail to by very helpful (1).

(1) This suggestion was carried out by the Congress, a Commission on the Teaching of Mathematics being appointed, to report in 1912.

R. SUPPANTSCHITSCH

L'APPLICATIONS DES IDÉES MODERNES DES MATHÉMATIQUES A L'ENSEIGNEMENT SECONDAIRE EN AUTRICHE

Nous avons en Autriche principalement deux espèces d'écoles secondaires: les « *Gymnasien* » et les « *Realschulen* » (¹). Les premières ressemblent aux collèges français division A et aux sections A et B du second cycle, les autres aux lettres correspondantes B, C et D. Mais le programme des Mathématiques et de la Physique est presque le même dans ces deux écoles, excepté la géométrie descriptive, qui est réservée aux « Realschulen ». On y enseigne ou plutôt on y enseignait les Mathématiques dites élémentaires, ainsi que la géométrie analytique plane jusqu'aux sections coniques, sans insister sur l'équation générale du second degré.

Or, dès que la France nous a donné un exemple célèbre par la réorganisation de l'enseignement secondaire, on a songé aussi chez nous à un nouveau programme dont on fait, à présent, des expériences dans certaines écoles.

En effet, nous sommes obligés de donner aux jeunes gens une instruction, qui leur permette de comprendre la vie moderne si compliquée et de jouer, eux aussi, leur rôle dans ce milieu si mouvementé.

A cet égard il y a, je pense, deux buts à atteindre. Il faut développer l'intuition naturelle et inspirer aux jeunes âmes le respect de la vérité, deux propositions un peu contradictoires.

On ne développe pas l'intuition en la supprimant par des démonstrations Euclidiennes ou par un traitement trop rigoureux des principes de l'Arithmétique. On ne doit point insister sur des démonstrations de choses absolument naturelles.

En conséquence, il est nécessaire de commencer par le raisonnement primitif qui ne concerne que les objets matériels et qui leur substitue plus tard des notions exactes propres aux transformations purement logiques. Nous y sommes aidés en Autriche par la division de l'enseignement secondaire en deux parties, que je veux

(¹) Le ministre de l'instuction publique a creé par son arrêté du 8 août 1908 les « *Realgymnasien* » intermédiaires entre les « *Gymnasien* » et les « *Realschulen* ».

appeler l'*initiation*, les quatre premières classes, et l'*enseignement*, les trois ou quatre autres. Dans l'enseignement le programme demande qu'on repète, mais plus scientifiquement, les parties déjà traitées dans l'initiation. Cette division n'est guère due aux délibérations mentionnées, elle est historique. Nous en profitons, dans nos expériences, pour enseigner aux garçons de dix à quatorze ans l'Arithmétique et la Géométrie élémentaire d'une manière parfaitement intuitive, en partant de choses pratiques qui intéressent les élèves de cet âge.

Entre la dernière classe de l'initiation et la première de l'enseignement il y a eu, jusqu'à présent, une grande discontinuité qui faisait échouer de nombreux élèves. Nous ne voulons pas l'éliminer absolument, et il y aura toujours des élèves qui ne pourront réussir que dans l'initiation, mais pour atténuer cette discontinuité nous ne voulons plus conserver des méthodes soi-disant rigoureuses qui ont été employées soigneusement jusqu'à présent, dans les classes de l'enseignement. En recourant également à l'intuition, dans les parties plus difficiles, nous arrivons, de temps en temps, à des démonstrations plus satisfaisantes; mais le but principal nous reste toujours, qui est: la faculté du jeune homme de savoir se servir des notions acquises et aborder un problème quelconque, sans être trop gêné par des scrupules philosophiques.

De cette manière nous gagnons assez de temps pour pouvoir donner aussi aux élèves quelques notions des fonctions et de la dérivée. Ici, nous ne faisons point de définitions ou de démonstrations atithmétiques. Le graphique des fonctions simples nous suffit pour en tirer les propriétés principales et les plus nécéssaires, en même temps, pour les futurs médecins, économes, bref, pour toutes les personnes, qui auront à faire avec des grandeurs soumises à une variation continue. On ne veut point, naturellement, former seulement des mathématiciens, on s'adresse, au contraire, surtout à ces élèves, qui ne rencontront plus tard point des mathématiques dans leurs études supérieures.

Pour établir la dérivée j'ai commencé, par exemple, par la notion de la pente d'une droite, et de la pente approximative d'une courbe. Cette dernière était du reste toujours une parabole:

$$y = ax^2 + bx + c.$$

J'ai examiné d'abord par des exemples spéciaux la signification géométrique du symbole:

$$y_1 - y/x_1 - x$$

ou bien:

$$y_1 - y/h = 2ax + b + ah.$$

Les élèves déjà familiarisés avec ce symbole comprenaient facilement qu'il fût très utile de donner à ce quotient *par définition* pour $h = 0$ la valeur $2ax + b$, et voilà la dérivée d'une telle fonction démontrée sans la notion des limites. Je n'ai pas fait allusion à celles-ci qu'en traitant les séries géométriques. Dans ce cas, il y a peu d'esprits qui ne puissent rien concevoir, surtout quand on s'explique d'abord géométriquement à l'aide d'exemples comme: $1 + \frac{1}{2} + \frac{1}{4} + \frac{1}{8} + \cdots$

Si les élèves sont très intelligents, on considère encore quelques fonctions plus difficiles, en établissant leurs dérivées par la notion des limites; mais je ne trouve pas que cela soit indispensable.

Car — et je reviens au second point — à côté du développement de l'intuition il faut aussi inspirer aux jeunes gens le respect de la vérité. Rappelons nous les belles paroles de M. Tannery (*Leçons D'Algèbre et D'Analyse*, p. VI):

« Le respect de la vérité est la première leçon morale, si non la seule, qu'on puisse tirer de l'étude des sciences ».

M. Tannery y demande aussi que l'enseignement soit absolument sincère, de manière qu'on avertisse toujours le lecteur quand on laisse à côté certains raisonnements trop difficiles. Cela va très bien pour les élèves assez avancés déjà pour comprendre les leçons de M. Tannery, un peu aussi pour ceux de la seconde division de nos écoles. Et c'est surtout pour cela que je recommande des réserves quant à la dérivée.

Cependant, je vais expliquer tout à l'heure encore un moyen, qui me semble bien plus propre à ce but et à démontrer, que nulle chose n'est plus subtile, plus sécrète que la verité, qui s'éloigne au fur et à mesure que nous espérons nous y approcher.

On s'est servi de l'intuition des élèves pour leur enseigner les idées grossières du corps, du plan, etc., plus tard on a transformé ces idées logiquement, pendant qu'elles devenaient plus nettes, c'est-à-dire, on a traité la géométrie pure.

Enfin, on ne termine pas l'enseignement des Mathématiques sans donner des exemples des nombreuses applications de la science. C'est là justement où l'on doit, comme je le pense, avertir les jeunes gens que ces lois si nettes dans la théorie, ne sont, en réalité, qu'une approximation, plus ou moins propre à substituer à la vérité une image simplifiée, tandis que celle-là reste inaccessible à nos esprits bornés. Mais il n'est point suffisant de leur montrer les difficultés de la mesure des longueurs, des aires, etc., j'ai insisté, au contraire, sur le fait général que les notions primaires, les définitions, les axiomes n'ont dans la nature aucune réalisation possible et que l'on ne s'en sert que par un principe d'utilité.

J'ai trouvé parmi des jeunes gens de 17 à 20 ans quelques uns qui comprenaient tout cela excessivement bien, mais même les autres y avaient un grand intérêt qu'on chercherait en vain en traitant des problèmes subtiles, mais sans importance générale. Et voilà la chose la plus curieuse que j'ai apprise par mes éléves: Les commençants ont aussi un certain goût pour les questions générales et pour celles à la mode dans le monde scientifique. On n'a qu'à développer cet intérêt et l'on sera surpris de la rapidité des progrès faits même par des élèves qui détestaient, jusqu'à lors, les mathématiques.

C'est, pour ainsi dire, l'esprit du siècle, qui s'agite dans les jeunes âmes.

Mais pour ne pas aller trop loin, on doit choisir soigneusement les questions pareilles, qu'on veut traiter; car il faut non seulement stimuler l'esprit, mais aussi le nourrir.

En résumé, j'espère qu'en Autriche les expériences actuelles finiront par nous convaincre d'une manière générale qu'il ne faut pas insister sur le programme invétéré lorsqu'on veut que les jeunes gens aient, en sortant, le goût des sciences et la faculté de comprendre la vie moderne.

Mais nous avons encore à surmonter une grande difficulté. Nous n'avons pas, jusqu'à présent, comme les maîtres français en ont, des livres à l'usage des écoles, inspirés par des idées modernes. Et c'est pour cela que nos expériences doivent durer probablement encore quelque temps pour aboutir à une réorganisation définitive [1].

[1] La réorganisation définitive est établie, sur ces entrefaits, en Autriche par les nouveaux programmes de 1909.

G. VAILATI

SUGLI ATTUALI PROGRAMMI PER L'INSEGNAMENTO DELLA MATEMATICA NELLE SCUOLE SECONDARIE ITALIANE

Un esame critico dei programmi di matematica attualmente vigenti nelle scuole secondarie italiane, è reso particolarmente interessante dalla imminenza di provvedimenti legislativi miranti a dare un nuovo assetto ai varî rami di esse, e a introdurre, in questi, nuovi soggetti e nuovi metodi di insegnamento.

Nonostante la ragionevole libertà che, dai nostri ordinamenti scolastici, è concessa agli insegnanti, sia per quanto riguarda il modo di svolgere i programmi prescritti, sia per quanto riguarda la diversa importanza o il diverso posto da assegnare alle singole parti di essi, pure la struttura dei programmi, specialmente in quanto esercita la sua influenza su quella dei libri di testo, è da porre tra le circostanze che maggiormente contribuiscono a determinare il carattere e l'indirizzo dell'insegnamento matematico nelle nostre scuole secondarie.

Per ciò che riguarda l'*Algebra*, è, per es., difficile attribuire ad altra causa che non sia l'ordinamento dei relativi programmi, il fatto che, nella maggior parte dei libri di testo adoperati nelle nostre scuole, non si arriva alla trattazione anche più elementare delle equazioni di primo grado, se non passando attraverso a una lunga serie di capitoli dedicati alle operazioni sui polinomi (non è esclusa la divisione), ai numeri negativi, e a ogni altra specie di « generalità » sul calcolo letterale.

I risultati di un primo insegnamento dell'algebra impartito secondo un tale indirizzo, non è da stupire se non riescono molto soddisfacenti.

Invece di riconoscere, nei segni e nei metodi dell'algebra, dei semplici mezzi per giungere con maggior speditezza e facilità a risolvere questioni aritmetiche, proponibili e risolubili anche indipendentemente da ogni loro espressione in formule, gli alunni hanno l'impressione di trovarsi davanti a delle difficoltà di ordine superiore, a delle questioni del tutto nuove e non aventi alcun rapporto con altre di cui si siano prima occupati.

Anche quando sono in grado di penetrare il significato delle regole e delle manipolazioni di formule che imparano materialmente ad effettuare, è ben raro che essi riescano a vederne o a immaginarne la utilità e lo scopo. Si disorientano, si impazientano, si annoiano, si irritano, e finiscono troppo spesso per prendere in odio l'algebra e i suoi simboli al punto che, quando passano poi nei corsi superiori, allo studio di quelle scienze nelle quali, come per es. nei varî rami della fisica, la conoscenza dell'algebra dovrebbe trovare la sua più proficua applicazione, essi si sentono inclinati a riguardare l' impiego di essa piuttosto come un impedimento che non come un aiuto per l'enunciazione o la rappresentazione dei più semplici rapporti di dipendenza o di connessione tra i fenomeni, o delle leggi fisiche più elementari.

***

Ciò che si è detto sopra a proposito del posto attribuito, negli abituali programmi d'algebra, ai primi esercizî di risoluzione delle equazioni di primo grado, è da ripetere anche per il caso delle equazioni di secondo grado.

L'insegnante che si facesse un dovere di seguire l'ordine indicato, per es., nei programmi del primo biennio dei nostri Istituti tecnici, dovrebbe astenersi dal proporre agli alunni problemi esigenti la risoluzione anche della più semplice equazione numerica di secondo grado a radici intere, prima di avere svolto innanzi a loro l'intera teoria delle operazioni sui numeri irrazionali e averli addestrati al calcolo dei radicali e magari anche a quello dei numeri immaginarî.

Un siffatto ordinamento dei programmi è da attribuire, tanto in questo caso come in quello precedentemente considerato, a una medesima causa. Si è creduto che le nozioni fondamentali relative alla risoluzione delle equazioni non potessero nè dovessero essere impartite se non sotto forma sistematica, prendendo cioè le mosse dal caso più generale, e determinando la « formula di risoluzione » da assoggettare poi a una discussione, portante a distinguere tutti i casi che possono presentarsi a seconda dei valori che si facciano assumere alle lettere in essa contenute.

È un procedimento questo che dovrebbe sembrare poco meno assurdo di quello di chi volesse, per esempio, far precedere la trattazione delle equazioni di secondo grado a quella delle equazioni di primo grado, col pretesto che dalle formule generali corrispondenti alle prime, quelle riguardanti le seconde possono derivare come casi particolari ponendo eguale a zero il coefficiente del quadrato dell'incognita.

I risultati di un insegnamento dell'algebra impartito in conformità a tali disposizioni dei nostri programmi, sono perfettamente analoghi a quelli che, nelle nostre scuole, si ottengono dall' insegnamento predominantemente grammaticale delle lingue antiche e moderne.

E allo stesso modo come per l'insegnamento delle lingue si va sempre più riconoscendo la convenienza e la necessità di ricorrere al cosidetto « metodo diretto » — consistente nel far precedere, invece che seguire, allo studio della grammatica e all'inculcazione delle regole, graduati esercizî di conversazione e di traduzione, eseguiti sotto la guida, e dietro l'esempio dell' insegnante — così anche per l'algebra non si dovrebbe tardare, se non fosse altro, a provvedere a che l'insegnante trovasse nei programmi un incoraggiamento e non un ostacolo a ordinare le sue lezioni in modo da mettere al più presto possibile l'alunno in immediato contatto colle questioni e coi problemi, alla cui soluzione si applicano le cognizioni teoriche che mano mano gli vengono impartite.

A impiegare i segni di operazione, le parentesi, ecc., gli alunni dovrebbero venir condotti — e al più presto possibile — non per la via di regole o definizioni astratte, ma mediante copiosi e ben scelti esempî dell'applicazione di tali segni alla rappresentazione di calcoli numerici effettuati o da effettuare, e all'enunciazione di problemi, e delle condizioni a cui devono soddisfare le quantità in essi domandate.

L'uso delle lettere per indicare le quantità incognite è un espediente, al quale l'alunno può essere indotto a ricorrere quasi spontaneamente nei suoi sforzi di formulare nel modo più semplice e conciso i problemi che gli vengono proposti.

Ben diverso invece è il caso per l'impiego delle lettere nelle identità, o nelle espressioni algebriche, dove esse stanno per indicare numeri da scegliere ad arbitrio. Le formule di questo genere non possono acquistare interesse per gli alunni se non dopo che gli esercizî sul calcolo e la trasformazione delle espressioni, o equazioni, contenenti soltanto dati numerici, abbiano fatto sorgere in loro il desiderio di enunciare in modo generale le proprietà delle operazioni, di cui essi hanno così già imparato a giovarsi per semplificare e accelerare i calcoli numerici.

Tra i presupposti indispensabili per qualunque miglioramento in questa direzione, è da porre questo: che gli esami cessino di essere concepiti come doventi consistere in saggi di recitazione di questa o di quella parte delle teorie indicate nei programmi, e assumano invece la forma di vere e proprie prove pratiche, nelle quali l'alunno venga invitato a porre in opera le attitudini e le conoscenze che ha acquistate, applicandole alla trattazione di determinate questioni: alla risoluzione di equazioni, al calcolo o alla semplificazione di espressioni ecc.

*
* *

Per ciò che riguarda la *Geometria* un primo punto fondamentale, nel quale mi sembra che gli attuali programmi delle nostre scuole secondarie siano bisognevoli di essere migliorati, è quello della connessione, che essi trascurano affatto di stabilire, tra l'insegnamento elementare della geometria e gli esercizî di disegno.

È necessario che in essi venga più chiaramente riconosciuta e sanzionata la necessità, di far precedere lo svolgimento sistematico della geometria, nello stadio superiore della scuola secondaria, da un insegnamento preliminare nello stadio inferiore, destinato a rendere noti e famigliari agli alunni i *fatti* geometrici, alla cui spiegazione, o dimostrazione, essi verranno poi condotti ad applicare il ragionamento deduttivo.

Il carattere che converrebbe fare assumere a questo primo insegnamento della geometria, non mi sembra sia completamente caratterizzato col denominarlo semplicemente, come spesso si fa, come un insegnamento *intuitivo*. Esso dovrebbe infatti essere non solo *passivo* ma anche *attivo*, e operativo, diretto cioè a sviluppare non solo le attitudini contemplative ed osservatrici degli alunni, ma anche quelle che entrano in giuoco nella costruzione delle figure e nei paragoni tra esse e le loro varie parti, mediante misure, scomposizioni, movimenti, mediante insomma tutti quei procedimenti che possono condurre a constatare e a verificare quelle proprietà di esse, che formeranno in seguito oggetto di analisi e di dimostrazione.

E neppure vi è ragione di stabilire una separazione recisa o un contrasto tra questa prima trattazione, per così dire sperimentale, della geometria, e quella « razionale » più adatta allo stadio superiore della scuola secondaria.

Il passaggio dall'una all'altra può, e dovrebbe, effettuarsi per gradi, applicando anzitutto il ragionamento deduttivo non già a dimostrare proposizioni che agli alunni appaiano già abbastanza evidenti, o della cui verità essi si siano già convinti per via di diretta constatazione, ma piuttosto a ricavare, appunto da queste ultime, altre proposizioni che essi ancora non conoscano e che essi possano poi facilmente verificare ricorrendo agli stessi mezzi.

Così essi impareranno a vedere nella deduzione un mezzo per « economizzare » le esperienze, o le verifiche, per giungere cioè senza il sussidio di queste, a *prevedere* il risultato di date misure o costruzioni sulle figure o sui loro elementi. Il procedimento di dimostrazione apparirà allora ad essi avere uno scopo e un'utilità, come mezzo di scoperta e di acquisto di nuove cognizioni.

A vedere poi nei procedimenti di dimostrazione anche un mezzo per spiegare e rendersi ragione di proprietà geometriche già a loro note, essi verranno condotti naturalmente, di mano in mano che, per mezzo del disegno o di altre operazioni di confronto tra le figure, essi verranno a prender conoscenza di verità geometriche che, appunto per non essere immediatamente evidenti, appariranno loro come bisognevoli di venire spiegate coll'aiuto di considerazioni atte a mettere in chiaro come e perchè esse si verifichino.

Un altro mezzo efficace e al quale non si dovrebbe trascurare di ricorrere per coltivare negli alunni l' interesse e la fiducia nel ragionamento deduttivo, è quello di non limitarsi, almeno nel caso delle proposizioni più importanti, a dare, di ciascun teorema, una sola dimostrazione, mostrando, invece, come, a una stessa conclusione, si possa giungere prendendo diversi punti di partenza e procedendo per diverse vie.

Quanto più diverse queste vie saranno, e quanto più eterogenee le premesse su cui tali diverse dimostrazioni verranno a fondarsi, tanto più il confronto dei diversi casi gioverà a destare negli alunni il senso della coerenza logica delle varie parti della geometria, e dell' intima connessione e solidarietà che sussiste tra esse.

***

Per ciò che riguarda la portata che, sui metodi di insegnamento delle varie parti della matematica nelle scuole secondarie dovrebbe essere concessa ai risultati delle più recenti ricerche sulla logica matematica e sui principî della geometria, un pregiudizio, che mi sembra da combattere, è quello che consiste nel credere che tali risultati giustifichino o autorizzino delle trasformazioni del metodo di insegnamento nel senso di una maggiore astrazione o « teoricità », in confronto a quanto si fa ora ordinariamente.

A convincere del nessun fondamento di tale opinione o preoccupazione, mi basterà qui solo un accenno alle varie direzioni nelle quali gli studî ai quali ho sopra alluso, relativi ai fondamenti della matematica e all'analisi dei processi di ragiona mento che essa impiega, manifestano invece una tendenza affatto opposta: la tendenza cioè a sfrondare e ad emancipare l'insegnamento secondario di una quantità di inutili sviluppi e di esigenze inopportune, facendogli assumere un carattere assai più svelto, assai più pratico, assai più intimamente connesso colle applicazioni concrete.

Il difetto infatti che si può spesso rimproverare agli autori dei nostri libri di testo, di volere nelle prime pagine insistere troppo a definire concetti o parole, anche quando ciò non giova affatto per dare all'alunno un concetto più chiaro del loro significato, tale difetto, dico, trova piuttosto un freno che non un incoraggiamento nelle considerazioni svolte dai logici matematici, sull'assurdità di voler tutto definire e sulla necessità di prendere le mosse, in qualsiasi trattazione, da un certo numero di concetti o termini non definiti, o definiti soltanto « implicitamente », cioè semplicemente col chiarire il significato delle frasi in cui essi compaiono.

Lo stesso è da dire della analoga, e non meno dannosa tendenza, a volere, fin dal principio, dimostrare ogni proposizione che sia capace di essere dimostrata, senza tener conto che in un primo insegnamento non è nè necessario nè conveniente adoperare, per la scelta dei postulati, o delle proposizioni da assumere senza dimostrazione, gli stessi criterî che si possono e devono seguire nelle ricerche e nelle analisi più avanzate sui fondamenti della geometria.

Anche qui le ricerche sulla indipendenza dei postulati, sulla loro portata, sulla loro compatibilità, ecc., ponendo in piena luce quanto siano imperfette, dal punto di vista di tale analisi, le trattazioni ordinariamente seguìte, non escluse quelle che riproducono l'esposizione di EUCLIDE, contribuiscono a far apparire tanto più assurda, e incompatibile colle esigenze didattiche inerenti a un insegnamento secondario, qualunque pretesa di cominciare l'insegnamento razionale della geometria con una elaborazione logicamente completa dei suoi principî.

Le stesse ricerche contribuiscono anche a fare apparire tanto più chiaro all'insegnante che ciò che si chiama il « rigore » di una dimostrazione geometrica è una qualità che dipende non dal numero, o dalla natura, delle presupposizioni o dei postulati di cui in essa si fa uso, ma piuttosto dal modo in cui questi vi si trovano impiegati. Una dimostrazione nella quale si faccia uso di ipotesi, o di premesse, più numerose, o anche affatto differenti da quelle che in altre sono adoperate, non cessa per questo di potere essere logicamente corretta, e di poter contribuire, come tale, a educare e a coltivare l'attitudine degli alunni, a ragionare in modo preciso e rigoroso. Per questo fine si richiede soltanto che ogni ipotesi, o postulato, a cui in ciascuna dimostrazione è fatto appello, sia chiaramente riconosciuto e formulato in modo esplicito, qualunque siano del resto le ragioni che possono avere indotto ad assumerlo tra i punti di partenza della trattazione. Nulla impedirà poi che in un corso superiore di studî, quelle stesse proposizioni che prima hanno funzionato da ipotesi o da punto di partenza delle dimostrazioni, vengano, alla loro volta, ad apparire come conseguenze di altre ammissioni o ipotesi più semplici, e così via, finchè si arrivi a far dipendere l'intera catena delle dimostrazioni da proposizioni soltanto che non possono essere ulteriormente dedotte o ridotte le une alle altre. A ciò si deve arrivare in fine, e non mai in principio di uno studio ben ordinato della geometria.

Un'altra direzione in cui è da sperare che le recenti ricerche, di indole logica o storica sui principî della geometria, esercitino qualche influenza per il miglioramento dei programmi e dei libri di testo, delle nostre scuole secondarie, è quello che riguarda l'*applicazione dell'algebra alla geometria*.

L'opinione, largamente diffusa, che il ricorrere alle notazioni dell'algebra per rappresentare fatti o relazioni geometriche, costituisca quasi una contaminazione o un attentato alla purezza della trattazione di Euclide, si dimostra sempre più incompatibile colle nostre cognizioni sullo sviluppo della geometria greca: cognizioni che ci conducono per esempio a riconoscere nella teoria delle proporzioni, esposte nel Libro V degli Elementi di Euclide, e nei teoremi sulla « applicazione » delle aree, i caratteri di una vera e propria « algebra », della quale i geometri greci facevano, nelle loro dimostrazioni, un uso affatto analogo a quello che, dai matematici moderni, si fa delle operazioni dell'algebra, nelle trattazioni di geometria analitica.

Solo un concetto ristretto e inadeguato della « nostra » algebra conduce a credere che le interpretazioni o applicazioni geometriche delle sue formule non possano effettuarsi se non attraverso alla considerazione dei numeri e delle misure corrispondenti agli enti geometrici — segmenti, angoli, aree, ecc. — che in esse si trovano indicati dalle lettere: come se per esempio un'equazione di secondo grado — ridotta naturalmente a forma omogenea — non potesse sempre essere intesa, oltre che come una richiesta di determinare numeri che soddisfino a una data condizione, anche come una richiesta di determinare segmenti tali, che tra certi rettangoli o quadrati costruiti con essi e con altri segmenti dati, sussista una data relazione.

E oltre che dell'applicazione dell'algebra alla geometria pare a me, nell' insegnamento secondario, non si dovrebbe trascurare di trar profitto anche di quelle che potrebbero qualificarsi come applicazioni della geometria all'algebra. Si pensi per esempio quanto più facilmente l'alunno riconoscerebbe il senso e la portata di una proposizione come questa: che « la media geometrica di due numeri positivi non può mai superare la loro media aritmetica », quando gli si facesse osservare che, in un circolo avente per diametro la somma di due segmenti, la prima è rappresentata dal raggio, e l'altra invece dalla metà di una corda.

Abituare fino dal principio l'alunno a riconoscere le condizioni necessarie e sufficienti perchè una data espressione o equazione possa interpretarsi come esprimente una costruzione o un problema geometrico, è certo da porre tra i mezzi più efficaci per bene prepararlo a concepire poi chiaramente il significato delle formule in cui, più tardi, i segni dell'algebra saranno da lui adoperati per esprimere proposizioni di meccanica o di fisica.

Ciò mi condurrebbe a occuparmi di un'ultima questione molto discussa al presente, se cioè convenga far posto nell' insegnamento secondario ai concetti di derivata prima e seconda e ai concetti fondamentali del calcolo infinitesimale. Nell'esprimere un'opinione decisamente favorevole a tale introduzione, mi permetto di rimandare, per ciò che riguarda le ragioni che ad essa mi inducono, all'esposizione che di tali ragioni ho già avuto occasione di fare in una precedente circostanza (1).

(1) V. Atti del Congresso della Società Italiana delle Scienze, Parma, settembre 1907.

R. MARCOLONGO

UN TRATTATO INEDITO DI MECCANICA DI VINCENZO DE FILIPPIS

ANTERIORE ALLA « MÉCANIQUE ANALYTIQUE » DI LAGRANGE

Nelle numerose pubblicazioni sulla storia della breve e gloriosa repubblica Partenopea del 1799, si parla spesso di due matematici, vittime della feroce reazione borbonica degli ultimi del '99; cioè di VINCENZO DE FILIPPIS e di NICOLA FIORENTINO. Di quest'ultimo e del suo opuscolo: *Saggio sulle quantità infinitesime e sulle forze vive e morte* (1782), si è già occupato il carissimo amico prof. G. VIVANTI nella XXVI sezione del 4° volume della *Storia delle Matematiche* del CANTOR (1). Non credo riusciranno prive del tutto d'interesse alcune notizie intorno ad un'opera inedita di meccanica del DE FILIPPIS.

Non mancano anzitutto notizie sulla vita del DE FILIPPIS; chè tutti coloro che dal COLLETTA in poi si occuparono della repubblica Partenopea, parlano a lungo di lui che di quella repubblica fu ministro dell'interno. Le riassumeremo brevemente (2).

Il DE F. nacque in Tiriolo, pittoresco paese della Calabria poco lungi da Catanzaro, ai 4 aprile 1749; studiò sotto il SALADINI che aveva in Napoli uno studio rinomato (3) e poi in Bologna. Nel 1787 fu nominato professore nelle R. Scuole di

(1) *Die Grundlagen der Infinitesimalrechnung*, s. 661.

(2) Queste notizie sono tratte in massima parte da: M. D'AYALA, *Vite degl'Italiani benemeriti della libertà e della patria* (Torino, Bocca, 1883, pp. 218-221; *Albo illustrativo della Rivoluzione Napoletana del 1799* a cura di B. CROCE, G. CECI, M. D'AYALA, S. DI GIACOMO (Napoli, Morano, 1899); e finalmente da molti lavori del prof. AMODEO, per es. *Gli Istituti d'istruzione e scientifici in Napoli intorno al 1800*; *Dai fratelli DI MARTINO a VITO CARAVELLI*, pubblicati negli Atti dell'Accademia Pontaniana.

Si parla pure di DE FILIPPIS, sulla scorta di documenti originali, in un opuscolo di GAETANO CAPASSO, *Un ministro della Repubblica partenopea* (Parma, Tipogr. Pellegrini, 1887); ed in un articolo dal titolo: *Un ministro impiccato* (Giornale Napoletano della Domenica, anno 1882). Ma non siamo riusciti a poterlo consultare.

(3) Così almeno afferma il prof. AMODEO, basandosi, crediamo, sull'autorità del NAPOLI-SIGNORELLI, *Vicende della cultura nelle Due Sicilie* (Napoli 1784).

Da lettere dirette al DE F. dal CANTERZANI e i cui originali abbiamo consultati, risulta che intorno al 1771 e fino all'agosto 1773 il DE F. era alunno nel Real Collegio Ancarano, in cui il PALCANI ed il PALADINI erano lettori.

Catanzaro ed ebbe tra i suoi allievi GIUSEPPE POERIO. Benchè nulla avesse dato alle stampe era stimato matematico valoroso, sicchè fu fatto socio della R. Accademia di Scienze e Belle Arti (1779). Nel 1793 ritiravasi a vita privata in Tiriolo.

Le sue idee liberali lo avevano già fatto segno alle prime persecuzioni del 1795 ([1]). Fondata la repubblica Partenopea (1799), fu dei 25 del potere esecutivo; presidente della Giunta deputata a esaminare il libro delle casse pubbliche di entrata e finalmente ai 25 aprile sostituì il CONSORTI nel ministero delle cose interne. Caduta la repubblica e fatto prigioniero dal Ruffo, dalla Giunta di Stato fu condannato alla forca e morì il 28 novembre ([2]).

I discendenti del DE F. vivono ancora a Tiriolo e conservano numerosi manoscritti dell'antenato e la numerosa e scelta libreria raccolta pazientemente e con grave dispendio. Il DE F. era ben al corrente colle pubblicazioni italiane e straniere del suo tempo e possedeva e studiava le opere di d'ALEMBERT, EULER, LAGRANGE, RICCATI, FRISI, MOZZI, ecc. Gli editori dell'Albo già citato, hanno riprodotto da un quadro ad olio che si conserva in Tiriolo, l'effigie del DE F.; hanno pubblicato un brano di una lettera a lui diretta da SEBASTIANO CANTERZANI, segretario dell'Istituto di Bologna ed una parte della prefazione che l'A. aveva preparato per il suo libro di Meccanica. Recentemente il prof. G. B. CARUSO, dell'Istituto Tecnico di Catanzaro, pubblicò una lettera del DE F. al CANTERZANI intorno ai terremoti di Calabria del 1783 e 1789 ([3]), e diè, insieme a molte notizie sul DE F., un elenco di tutti i manoscritti che ancora di lui si conservano dagli eredi. Debbo alla cortesia delle pronipoti sig^ne^ RAFFAELLA e BERENICE DE F. e del prof. CARUSO se io ho potuto esaminare i manoscritti che riguardano la meccanica e le numerose lettere originali dal CANTERZANI dirette al DE F. ([4]).

([1]) Le lettere del CANTERZANI, di cui diremo più innanzi, conservate dagli eredi, terminano col dicembre 1790. Mancano quindi quelle dell'epoca più travagliata pel DE F. Merita di esser notato però che in una lettera del 1777 il CANTERZANI, in risposta a opinioni espresse dal DE F. scrive: « mi dispiace, che ella non abbia trovato alla corte quello spirito, che desiderava; ma mi « consolo nello stesso tempo, che ella sia abbastanza filosofo per non inquietarsene ».

([2]) Nel libro recente del prof. SANSONE, *Gli avvenimenti del 1799 nelle Due Sicilie* (Nuovi documenti, Palermo, 1901, p. 258), sono pubblicate tutte le sentenze di quella feroce ed inumana Giunta. Il DE F., ai 25 ottobre:

« per essere stato uno dei membri del Corpo legislativo, per avere esercitato la carica di « Ministro dell'interno nel numero dei rappresentanti, per aver violato il Monastero di S. Maria « Maddalena dei Pazzi, con aver da quel luogo armata mano cacciata fuori una donzella, e data « in preda alle lascivie d'un prete, convinto a voti uniformi, è stato condannato a morir sulle forche « colla confisca dei beni, condanna di memoria, ed essendo degli 80, la Giunta, giusta il solito, « ne ha sospesa l'esecuzione ». Ma S. M. si degnò presto « *di lasciar correre le sentenze* ».

([3]) *De' Terremoti della Calabria ultra nel 1783 e 1789* (Catanzaro, 1905). Vedi dello stesso prof. CARUSO, *In Commemorazione dei martiri della Repubblica Partenopea nati nella Calabria ulteriore seconda* (Catanzaro, 1899).

([4]) Queste lettere, scientificamente poco importanti, sono notevolissime sotto altri aspetti e per la storia della cultura in Italia. Riguardano per lo più notizie di libri commissionati al CANTERZANI, e pei quali occorre attendere anni prima che arrivino alla lontana Tiriolo; notizie di matematici italiani ed esteri, ecc. Sono in tutto 33 quelle conservate e vanno dal 1771 al dicembre 1790; le prime dirette al DE F. quando era alunno nel R. Collegio Ancarano di Bologna; le altre

Questi manoscritti si compongono di quattro fascicoli, ognuno composto di fogli staccati e di altri fascicoletti; quello segnato col n. 4 ha per titolo: *Appunti di matematica e di meccanica*; il 2°, numero 5, contiene: 1) *scritti di fisica*, 2) *scritti di meccanica*; un altro, n. 6, s'intitola semplicemente: *Meccanica* e finalmente l'ultimo, n. 7, s'intitola: *Statica*. Vi ha poi un grosso volume rilegato in carta pecora, assai ben scritto e conservato. Nel dorso e sulla copertina porta il n. 8 e l'elenco di ciò che contiene; cioè: 1. *Problemi di matematica*; 2. *Meccanica*; 3. *Dinamica*; 4. *Catalogo delle opere di Eulero*. Nella pagina interna porta scritto semplicemente: *Zibaldone* e poi segue effettivamente una serie di problemi parte in latino e parte in italiano; qualche teorema noto sull'attrazione delle sfere, buon numero di fogli in bianco e finalmente: *Elementi di Meccanica. De' principj della Meccanica.* Libri tre di VINCENZO DE FILIPPIS. A questo volume sono annessi altri due fogli separati che contengono la prefazione dell'opera. I fascicoli numerati 4, 5, 6, 7, contengono gli stessi argomenti e gli stessi capitoli del volume 8, parola per parola, salvo qualche lieve aggiunta.

Il DE F. aveva preparato per la stampa il libro della Meccanica, la cui redazione è certamente anteriore alla pubblicazione della *Mécanique analytique* di LAGRANGE, edita, com'è noto, nel 1788. Ne fa fede, oltre la prefazione di cui diremo tra breve, un brano di lettera che il CANTERZANI scrisse al DE F. da Bologna il 12 settembre 1783 e pubblicato già nell'Albo citato, a pp. 23-24:

« Sono persuasissimo, che il suo trattato di statica, e di meccanica debba essere « interessantissimo, e il vedrò con sommo piacere: non saprei però dirle se alcuno « l'abbia prevenuta nell'idea di dedurre il principio delle velocità virtuali da quello « dell'equivalenza, poichè io tengo poco dietro alle questioni critiche della meccanica « contento del metodo di M^r^ d'ALEMBERT, il quale mi pare sommamente naturale, « e spedito. Forse il Conte VINCENZO RICCATI potrebbe averla prevenuta: ma Ella « avrà i di lui dialoghi su la forza viva (¹), e quando in essi non vi sia nulla, credo « che si possa sperare, che nissuno abbia per anco battuta la sua strada ».

Il DE F. stesso poi, nella prefazione, dice:

« Sono già molti anni che è nato questo libro, e che io composi a solo fine di « istruire qualche amico vago di vedere i principj della meccanica rigorosamente « dimostrati. Ma conscio della mia debolezza, e rispettoso del pubblico quanto mai,

---

a Napoli o a Tiriolo. A proposito delle difficoltà, veramente incredibili, di procurarsi libri esteri, il CANTERZANI dice: « *Gran cosa, che cotesti libri oltramontani di cose matematiche siano tanto rari in Italia, e tanto difficili da procacciarsi!* ». Il CANTERZANI vuol essere informato di ciò che avviene in Napoli e parla spesso dell'ANGIULLI, di VITO CARAVELLI e dal canto suo informa il DE F. delle novità letterarie italiane e nella lettera del 12 settembre 1783 lo richiede di una descrizione « *sensata e filosofica* » dei terremoti calabresi. Gli parla con entusiasmo degli opuscoli analitici di PIETRO PAOLI e a proposito della Mécanique analytique di LAGRANGE (7 febbraio 1789) dice che « *per quanto ho potuto giudicare dall'occhiata che gli ho data, è un capo d'opera, ma per renderla utile bisognerebbe accompagnarla con un comento* ».

(¹) Allude all'opera: *Dialogo di VINCENZO RICCATI della compagnia di Gesù dove ne' Congressi di più giornate delle forze vive e dell' azioni delle forze morte si tien discorso* (Bologna, 1749).

« e vivendo lungi dalla capitale, nella solitudine di una villetta con pochi libri e « senza poter consultare tutti gli autori che di siffatta materia han trattato; non « ardiva di darlo alla luce per giusto timore di non dover ancor io contribuire al- « l'infinita noja che deve venire da tanta moltiplicità di libri o cattivi, o inutili o « superflui, che l'invenzione della stampa ha dato occasione di nascere. Anzi da che « seppi (1) che il sig. DE LA GRANGE, sovrano maestro nelle scienze che dipendono « dal calcolo, era per dare fuori una sua meccanica, ne aveva deposto affatto il « pensiero. Ma avendo di poi la sua egregia opera diligentemente letta, ho trovato « che il suo scopo è stato più tosto di estendere l' uso de' principj meccanici più « che gli altri non han fatto, che di dimostrargli con maggior rigore; anzi ho tro- « vato che egli sia contento di quelle dimostrazioni, che io forse per la grossezza « del mio ingegno, ho creduto insufficienti ed oscure. Senza che la sua opera non « ammettendo figure benchè le supponga e facendo uso de' calcoli difficili più sublimi « con una certa disinvoltura e brevità propria degli espertissimi nel mestiere, non « può essere ben capita se non se dai dotati di una forza non ordinaria di fantasia; « e dagli iniziati nei più reconditi ed alti misteri dell'analisi. Le quali doti non « trovandosi se non in pochi, senza un largo commentario dee la sua opera riputarsi « poco utile alla gioventù ».

L'opera è adunque anteriore al 1788 e composta all' incirca verso il 1783; quanto abbiamo riferito spiega già che lo scopo del DE F. non è quello di scrivere un trattato completo, ma piuttosto di esaminare i fondamenti dei principî della Scienza e dedurne, per via elementare, le conseguenze più notevoli.

Nella stessa prefazione egli si schiera subito contro coloro che gettano qualche dubbio sulla evidenza dei principî e contro coloro che tutto vorrebbero ridotto e dimostrato coll'esperienza.

Mancava, come manca tutt'ora, una dimostrazione generale del principio delle velocità virtuali; LAGRANGE stesso nella prima edizione della sua classica opera e dieci anni prima della dimostrazione di FOURIER, riguardava tal principio come una specie di postulato (2). Non è certo di poco momento notare un primo tentativo nel DE F. E sempre nella prefazione egli dice:

« Mi venne in pensiero di cercare di dedurre il famoso principio dell'equilibrio « detto il principio delle velocità virtuali, o come altri lo chiamano principio delle « azioni, dal principio della equivalenza, principio che pur si deve a Galileo e che « è il solo principio di cui abbiamo una dimostrazione rigorosa e veramente geometrica; « e così fornire quel principio della somma evidenza, che dalle dimostrazioni che di- « rettamente ne sono state da celebri autori prodotte, non mi pareva di aver conse- « guita abbastanza; il che essendomi felicemente riuscito in tutta la sua estensione, « mi rivolsi alle leggi del moto, che vanno sotto il nome di leggi galileiane perchè, « dal gran Galileo, prima d'ogn'altro scoverte e colla esperienza dimostrate, e con-

(1) Sarà stato molto probabilmente informato dal CANTERZANI.

(2) Anche nella 2ª edizione (1815), *Ouvres complètes*, t. XI, 2ème Section, dice ancora: « qu'on peut par conséquent regarder comme une espèce d'axiome de Mécanique » il principio dei lavori virtuali.

« fermate con molti e diversi esempi; le quali poichè altra certezza non avevano « per l'addietro ottenuta che la fisica, e quella che loro potea procurare una indu-« zione, di avere le medesime sempre condotto al vero; cercai perciò col solo di-« scorso metafisico di dimostrarle ».

Osserva ancora che la dimostrazione delle leggi meccaniche data da alcuni valentuomini è fondata sull'uso del metodo delle flussioni e se questo può essere permesso per coloro che « *queste quantità infinitesime trattano alla maniera leibniziana* » non può assolutamente valere per coloro che seguono il metodo di Newton che si fonda appunto sulle leggi della meccanica.

La cose dette, spero, concilieranno qualche interesse alla presente comunicazione; ed io passo senz'altro ad esaminare quelle parti dell'opera del de F. che più sono interessanti e, presumo, erano già pronte per la stampa; la quale forse, per i gravi rivolgimenti politici, non ebbe più luogo.

***

L'opera consta di tre parti che egli denomina: *Del moto in generale; Della potenza*, ossia *Della Statica o scienza degli equilibrj* e finalmente *Della Dinamica*.

La prima parte corrisponde, rudimentalmente, alla moderna cinematica. Dopo una serie di definizioni su spazio assoluto e relativo, sulla misura del tempo; egli tenta una dimostrazione di ciò che oggi chiamiamo postulato della continuità del moto: « ogni corpo che o con moto assoluto o relativo si trasferisce in un altro « luogo deve passare per tutti i luoghi intermedj ». La considerazione del moto equabile lo conduce al concetto generale di velocità; ed egli si indugia anche a considerare le curve della *scala delle velocità e dei tempi*, cioè i diagrammi delle velocità e degli spazi. Infine enuncia e giustifica la legge d'inerzia; ma tutto il capitolo nulla presenta di originale e di notevole.

Assai più interessante è la seconda parte, destinata alla statica.

« Gli principj statici riduconsi specialmente a quattro. Il primo che presentossi « alla mente de' Fisici è quello che viene compreso sotto il nome di principio del-« l'indifferenza. A cui successe il principio della leva, ossia degli Antichi. A quali, « ne' tempi più recenti si aggiunse il terzo chiamato principio dell'equivalenza ed « ultimando: il quarto che principio delle velocità virtuali e da alcuni principio « delle azioni si appella ».

Il principio della indifferenza cioè che *se le potenze sono eguali e costituite ritrovansi nelle medesime circostanze staranno in equilibrio*, fondato sul principio della ragion sufficiente è poco fecondo nella scienza degli equilibri; e però si trovò il secondo principio della leva. Su questo il de F. osserva:

« La verità di un tal principio conosciuta per via dell'esperienza non essendo « che fisica non potè contentare pienamente l'animo de' Filosofi, i quali perciò si « rivolsero a dimostrare questo principio con verità metafisiche e geometriche. Il « primo tra questi fu Aristotele, il quale nel suo libro della meccanica ne diede « una dimostrazione metafisica, ma poco accurata. Alla quale per grande intervallo « deve anteporsi quella che dopo ne diede Archimede nel suo famoso libro degli « equiponderanti, cercando dedurre questo principio da quello dell'indifferenza colle

« sole geometriche e metafisiche verità; quale dimostrazione neppure è ferma abbastanza onde possa tra i teoremi geometrici o metafisici annoverare ».

Il DE F. critica adunque (e non è certamente il primo) ARCHIMEDE e coloro che più o meno lo hanno seguito; perchè in tutte le dimostrazioni date del principio della leva « generalmente supponesi i corpi equilibrati in un punto premere il punto stesso con una forza eguale all'aggregato di tutti i pesi; lo che non è così evidente che non possa dubitarsene, nè dubitandosene si potrà altrimenti dimostrare che colla esperienza. Onde sempre rimarrebbe a dire che questo principio fosse sperimentale ». Egli passa quindi ad esaminare la dimostrazione data dal MACLAURIN [1] e finalmente quella del FONCENEX [2], che egli ragionevolmente trova complicata e così poco naturale « che si discosta assai da quella che si sarà tenuta o potrebbe tenersi dagli inventori di detto principio ». Ma il DE F. non ne espone nessuna per minuto e passa invece al terzo principio della equivalenza ossia della composizione delle forze. Le dimostrazioni di NEWTON, VARIGNON, ERMANNO, MACLAURIN, quella della dinamica di d'ALEMBERT, fondate su concetti di movimento « debbono, egli dice, riputarsi poco esatte; poichè pare che escludendo la Statica ossia scienza degli equilibrj il moto, dalle leggi di questo debbano i suoi principj indipendentemente dimostrarsi ». Nè certamente avrà tenuto presente (o forse conosciuto) quella di GIOVANNI BERNOULLI fondata sull'equilibrio della leva angolare, perchè, come si disse, egli non riteneva rigorose le dimostrazioni sulla leva [3]. Egli infine segue la dimostrazione di d'ALEMBERT [4], che è a sua volta una riduzione di quella di DANIELE BERNOULLI [5].

In un punto però il DE F. si discosta dal BERNOULLI e da d'ALEMBERT. Infatti dopo aver ricercato la risultante di due forze eguali, egli passa in modo assai semplice al caso di due forze ortogonali e poi al caso di due forze qualunque, con un procedimento che ancora oggidì da molti vien seguito. Però il caso generale, giova avvertirlo, è trattato meno semplicemente che in BERNOULLI [6].

Questa parte si chiude con la riduzione delle forze applicate ad un sistema rigido « a due equivalenti, una delle quali sia normale ad un dato piano preso a piacimento e l'altra giaccia sul piano medesimo; delle quali poi in un caso di equilibrio deve essere sì l'una che l'altra eguale a zero ». Composizione ben nota

(1) *Exposition des découvertes philosophiques de M. le Chev. NEWTON* (edizione francese, 1749), libro 2°, Cap. 3°, pp. 156 e seg.

(2) Mélanges de Philosophie et mathém. de Turin (1760-61), p. 305.

(3) I. BERNOULLI, *Opera omnia*, t. IV, p. 253 (1742).

(4) *Opuscules mathématiques* (t. I, p. 169, Paris, MDCCLXI).

(5) *Examen principiorum mechanicae et demonstrationes geometricae de compositione et resolutione virium* (Commentarii Academiae Imperialis Petropolitanae, t. I, pp. 126-142, 1726). Questa dimostrazione semplificata dal d'ALEMBERT e dal RICCATI è stata l'origine delle innumerevoli dimostrazioni statiche della legge del parallelogrammo. Dopo quella del FONCENEX, in cui si fa uso di equazioni funzionali, si ebbero, collo stesso principio, altre di d'ALEMBERT. Vedi: *Histoire de l'Académie R. de Paris* (pour 1769, p. 285) e gli *Opuscules mathém.* (t. 6, p. 360, 1773); in queste ultime il d'ALEMBERT ricerca direttamente la forza risultante di altre due ortogonali.

(6) Il DE F. fa la stessa dimostrazione che trovasi in POISSON, *Traité de Mécanique* (Paris, 1833, vol. I, pp. 50-51).

di più forze concorrenti con un procedimento curioso; considera cioè tutte le forze i cui spazi sono di accesso e poscia quelle i cui spazi sono di recesso per rispetto ad un moto minimo; alle prime sostituisce due forze sole, mentre compone tutte le altre e così si riduce al caso di tre. E così pure fa, valendosi del teorema della proiezione di una spezzata poligona, pel caso di tre forze complanari e poi per un numero qualsivoglia di forze, usufruendo della riduzione a due forze ortogonali. Il moto minimo dei punti di applicazione che è stato supposto rettilineo, può anche supporsi circolare; dopo di che il DE F., enunciato il teorema in generale, conclude: « questo principio è stato dimostrato prescindendo dal principio evidentissimo del- « l'equivalenza. A me è parso che il dedurlo da quello fosse l'unico mezzo di pro- « curargli quel grado di evidenza che dimostrandolo d'altro modo non potrà mai avere del resto e comune a quei tempi e che trovasi anche minutamente esposta nel famoso « *Discorso matematico* di G. MOZZI [1].

Il DE F. passa infine a chiarire e ad esporre il quarto principio chiamato delle velocità virtuali oppure delle azioni. Delle azioni, perchè, secondo alcuni, il prodotto della potenza per lo spazio percorso dal punto di applicazione misura l'*azione* della potenza stessa.

Comincia col dimostrare un lemma geometrico, con soverchio lusso di casi e sottocasi; consiste in questo: considera un parallelogrammo e da un punto del suo piano conduce le normali ai due lati contigui e alla diagonale; tenuto conto della regola dei segni; chiamando spazi di accesso gli spazi positivi contati dal vertice ai piedi delle normali, e spazi di recesso gli altri; l'A. enuncia il teorema che i prodotti dei lati per i rispettivi spazi di accesso è eguale al prodotto della diagonale per il relativo spazio di accesso. Con altre parole e con veste moderna ciò significa che vale la proprietà distributiva del prodotto scalare. Osserva poscia che se tre potenze complanari e concorrenti in un punto O sono tali che è vera la proprietà accennata rispetto ad un punto n del piano, le tre potenze non sono in equilibrio; bisogna che tale proprietà abbia luogo anche per ogni altro punto n', non appartenente alla On per concludere l'equilibrio; supponendo allora che l'equilibrio non abbia luogo e attribuendo al punto O un moto minimo (spostamento virtuale) egli viene a dimostrare che se la somma dei lavori virtuali è nulla, come ora diremmo noi, l'equilibrio delle tre potenze deve sussistere. Passa quindi al caso « e che pur si richiede ad un principio universale di una scienza così vasta e così « necessaria quanto è la Statica ».

Il DE F. dunque riconosce la universalità del principio e, almeno pei sistemi di forze applicate a corpi rigidi, ne dà una dimostrazione lunga e non semplice e non molto generale e perspicua facendo troppa astrazione dal corpo o sistema rigido; ma sufficiente peraltro e consona all'indole dei suoi tempi. Siamo ben lungi dalla dimostrazione di FOURIER e da quelle successive di LAGRANGE; ma, specialmente la prima,

[1] *Discorso matematico sopra il rotamento momentaneo dei corpi*, del Cav. GIULIO MOZZI, Patrizio Fiorentino. In Napoli MDCCLXIII. Tale libro era anche posseduto dal DE F. Vedi una mia Nota: *Notizie sul « Discorso matematico e sulla vita di GIULIO MOZZI* [Bollettino di bibliografia e storia delle scienze matematiche, anno VIII, pp. 1-8 (1905)].

non fu nè conosciuta, nè apprezzata; tanto che il PRONY nella « Nouvelle Architecture Hydraulique », Paris, 1790, v. I, art. 140, p. 62, dice che: « Il n'existe pas de démonstration générale directe de ce principe »; e molti e molti anni dopo GIROLAMO SALADINI credeva ancora necessaria una dimostrazione geometrica del principio e ne tentava una, la quale, in fondo, non considera che il caso delle forze applicate ad uno stesso punto; e lo stesso dicasi di quella alquanto più ampia, generale e chiara del FOSSOMBRONI [1].

Il DE F. ritiene GALILEO primo autore del principio delle velocità virtuali e osserva che il GALILEO propose questo principio come « una proprietà generale dell'equilibrio e quasi come un'assioma meccanico. Il quale però tale non è ». Ed aggiunge:

« I filosofi che sono venuti dopo GALILEO han cercato dimostrare questo principio « o per induzione facendo vedere che in molti casi conduce a risultati veri, il che « suppone un altro principio rigorosamente dimostrato per cui si sappiano quelli risul- « tati esser veri, ovvero il dimostrano per via dell'esperienza. Ma la dimostrazione « per induzione è poco esatta quando non comprende tutti i casi possibili; ed un « principio sperimentale non può dirsi veramente principio mecanico, cioè di una « scienza capace di evidenza matematica ».

Le pagine seguenti sono dedicate all'esame della dimostrazione del principio delle veloc. virt. fondata sulle condizioni di equilibrio del vette (leva) e sulla misura dell'azione di una potenza, tema sempre all'ordine del giorno tra i filosofi e meccanici della fine del secolo XVIII. La misura dell'azione come prodotto della potenza per lo spazio, è originata, secondo certi autori, dal seguente raziocinio:

« La potenza esercita la di lei azione per un tempo e per uno spazio. Dunque « potrebbe egualmente andare che ella replicasse i suoi impulsi in ragione del tempo « e dello spazio. Nel primo caso la di lei azione varia in ragion composta della « potenza e del tempo; nel secondo della potenza e dello spazio. La prima non può « esser vera perchè non mantiene l'eguaglianza necessaria dell'azioni contrarie nel- « l'equilibrio. Dunque dee aversi per vera la seconda che cosiffatta eguaglianza pre- « cisamente contiene. E perchè codesta eguaglianza la conserva universalmente non « lo spazio percorso dal punto cui è la potenza applicata; ma sì bene quello per cui « fassi l'accostamento o il discostamento dal centro della potenza, come l'esperienza « dell'equilibrio del vette dimostra, per questo devesi misurare l'azione ». Il DE F. critica molto bene ed acutamente un siffatto modo di ragionare e arriva alla conclusione netta che tutte le ipotesi fatte, « perchè non vengono da conoscenza che si abbia « della natura della potenza, o del modo come ella agisca, nè da altra ragione intrin- « seca, che anzi par che sia indifferente a poter esser vera più tosto l'una che l'altra:

(1) *Memoria sul principio delle velocità virtuali* del Cavaliere VITTORIO FOSSOMBRONI, aretino, uno dei quaranta della Società italiana, socio dell'Istituto di Bologna, ecc. Firenze MDCCXCVI. Tale Memoria, anteriore a quella di FOURIER, contiene una prefazione o discorso storico-critico, pp. 3-29 e poi consta di due parti pp. 31-191, nella prima delle quali, con molta prolissità, è considerato il caso dei corpi rigidi. — G. SALADINI, *Sul principio delle velocità virtuali* (Mem. dell'Istituto Nazionale Italiano, t. II, par. 1ª, pp. 399-420, Bologna, 1808).

« dovrà concludersi che noi siamo assolutamente all'oscuro riguardo alla vera ed assoluta misura dell'azione della potenza ».

E però cadono tutte le dimostrazioni fondate sopra un vizioso giro di parole.

* * *

È facile rintracciare la fonte dei ragionamenti confutati con molta chiarezza dal DE F.

Vi ha infatti un piccolo libro che egli non cita mai, ma che ha evidentemente letto e studiato ed è il: *Discorso intorno agli equilibrj* di VINCENZO ANGIULLI stampato a Napoli il 1770 ([1]). Molte frasi, alcune espressioni e definizioni sono tolte da questo libro: p. e. quelle di *spazio di accesso* e di *recesso* adoperate dal DE F. Tutto quanto dall'ANGIULLI è esposto (numero XXXIV) a proposito del principio dell'indifferenza è riassunto quasi con le stesse parole dal DE F. e così pei successivi numeri fino al n. XXXVIII. Ma quanto il DE F. si discosti dall'ANGIULLI, apparirà dal seguente brano. L'ANGIULLI vuol stabilire la vera causa dell'equilibrio: « È cosa « evidente, egli dice a p. 15, e alla natura dell'equilibrio sommamente conforme, « che l'equilibrio dipenda da una qualche eguaglianza, la quale mancando, il moto « tosto debba seguire. Questa eguaglianza non può ammettersi tra le potenze; perchè le « potenze quantunque eguali, non sempre trovansi in equilibrio, nè sempre segue moto, « benchè le potenze siano disuguali. Deve dunque la detta uguaglianza ammettersi « tra altre quantità, le quali benchè non siano le potenze stesse, devono però alle « potenze in qualche maniera appartenere, giacchè alle potenze l'equilibrio appartiene. « Ma non vi sono altre quantità, che alle potenze appartengano, che le di loro azioni. « Dunque non potendosi costituir la causa dell'equilibrio nell'eguaglianza delle po- « tenze, altro a dir non resta, che l'equilibrio dipende dall'eguaglianza delle azioni

([1]) *Discorso intorno agli equilibrj* di VINCENZO ANGIULLI, Dottor di Filosofia, Accademico dell'Istituto delle Scienze di Bologna, Accademico Clementino nella stessa Città, e Professore di Matematica nella Real Accademia della Nunziatella di Napoli. In Napoli MDLCCX. L'opera, di pp. 1-168, è dedicata al ministro TANUCCI. Dell'ANGIULLI si parla anche in una lettera del CANTERZANI; pare che il DE F. aspirasse a succedere all'ANGIULLI.

Il libro dell'ANGIULLI, oggidì del tutto dimenticato — ne fa cenno l'AMODEO nella sua Memoria: *Dai fratelli Di Martino* ecc., p. 44, nota (1) — contiene altre sviste; p. e. la dimostrazione della legge del parallelogramma è errata. Si diffonde molto nell'applicare il principio delle azioni alla ricerca delle condizioni di equilibrio delle macchine semplici e dell'equilibrio dei fluidi.

L'ultimo capitolo (VIII) tratta del *Metodo con cui trattar si possono le curve d'equilibrio col principio delle azioni.* L'A. ispirandosi ai metodi di EULER, con ragionamento poco chiaro ed esatto, riduce tal problema a quello della ricerca della curva di data lunghezza che ha il centro di massa più basso o più alto; trova ancora l'equazione della catenaria omogenea pesante valendosi del metodo diretto e studia infine le proprietà della catenaria.

È anche singolare che le conoscenze storiche dell'ANGIULLI e del DE F. siano un po' più complete di quelle di LAGRANGE, il quale non nomina ARISTOTELE e attribuisce il principio della leva ad ARCHIMEDE.

Nelle lettere del CANTERZANI si parla spesso ancora di VITO CARAVELLI: ma nessun giovamento può aver ricavato il DE F. dai suoi *Elementi di matematica* composti per uso della. R. Accademia militare ecc... Napoli, 1770-1772, di cui gli ultimi volumi trattano in modo pedestre la *Dinamica e Statica* (vol. VIII) e *Idrostatica e Idraulica* (vol. IX).

« delle potenze stesse ». E con questo modo così convincente, egli giunge al principio che: « le potenze saranno in equilibrio qualora trovansi in tali circostanze co- « stituite, che se nascesse un moto infinitesimo, le diloro infinitesime azioni sareb- « bono uguali e contrarie ». E dopo aver fatto la solita escursione nella famosa disputa tra cartesiani e leibniziani a proposito della misura della azione, egli giunge al *principio delle azioni.*

L'operetta non mi pare al certo notevole; è però strano lo spirito di critica verso ARCHIMEDE e tutti coloro che hanno tentato dimostrare il principio della leva ed in ciò anche il DE F. segue l'ANGIULLI; il quale, p. 33, dice che dalle varie dimostrazioni « altro non apparisce, che gl'inutili sforzi fatti da' meccanici per rendere il principio della leva della somma evidenza fornito ». E dopo aver parlato del postulato su cui in sostanza si fondano le varie dimostrazioni aggiunge: « Sicchè « fuor d'ogni dubbio esser il principio degli Antichi un principio sperimentale, cioè « di fisica evidenza soltanto dotato ».

Tutta la Statica del DE F. adunque, tenuto conto del tempo in cui fu scritta, dello ambiente in cui viveva l'A., ci pare degna di qualche considerazione [1]. Egli colpisce giusto volendo veder chiaro nelle leggi statiche sbarazzando il terreno da frasi vuote di senso; è perfettamente nel vero volendo ricondurre, almeno per i sistemi rigidi, il principio dei lavori virtuali a quello della composizione delle forze. E si resta anche più colpiti ed ammirati pensando che l'A. viveva in un remoto paese perduto tra i monti calabresi e ben lungi da qualsivoglia centro scientifico. Se la sua Statica fosse venuta alla luce, lo storico del principio dei lavori virtuali avrebbe dovuto tener conto dei tentativi fatti prima e dopo FOURIER e non avrebbe certamente taciuto di questo del DE F. benchè assai difettoso, e benchè l'A. ritenga ingenuamente, con molti dei suoi coetanei, che tutto possa essere ridotto a rigorosa dimostrazione geometrica e rifugga quasi di fare costante appello alla esperienza. Ma opere e lavori imperfetti di oscuri lavoratori non debbono nemmeno essere trascurati, nè sfuggire alla considerazione dei posteri: essi meglio forse delle opere imperiture dei grandi maestri, servono a farci conoscere lo stato della scienza di un dato periodo; rivelano sempre più il graduale ma lento svolgimento delle idee, tentativi a mano a mano più felici; ci fanno meglio apprezzare il significato, l'importanza dell'opera di un sommo e, nel nostro caso, servono a farci sempre più ritenere fondamentalissima per la meccanica, la comparsa dell'opera del sommo LAGRANGE, che segna invero un'êra nuova.

* * *

Gli stessi difetti, forse maggiormente accentuati, si riscontrano nel terzo libro della sua opera, dedicato alla Dinamica e che, nella quasi totalità non tratta che della dinamica del punto libero. Nelle carte non c'è nulla che accenni al concetto di massa; l'A. lo suppone ben noto e chiaro ed espone una serie di lemmi che deb-

(1) Il volume e i quaderni manoscritti del DE F. contengono ancora varî altri capitoli sui baricentri, sull'equilibrio delle macchine semplici, ecc. che non presentano nulla d'interessante.

bono condurlo alle leggi del moto determinato da forze costanti: così ed es.: se due potenze A e B poste nelle stesse circostanze producono lo stesso effetto sulla stessa massa m sono eguali; lo stesso effetto produce la potenza P sulla massa mn che la potenza $\frac{P}{m}$ sulla massa n, poste nelle medesime circostanze, ecc.; per poter poi concludere che poste le masse eguali o la stessa ed i tempi eguali o gli stessi, le potenze sono nella ragione delle velocità, col solito ragionamento e considerando il caso delle velocità commensurabili ed incommensurabili; e che se le masse sono uguali ed eguali le velocità, saranno le potenze in ragion inversa dei tempi e infine che se le potenze sono alle masse proporzionali accelerano egualmente nello stesso tempo le masse cui sono applicate e fanno loro percorrere spazi eguali.

Dopo questa introduzione egli tratta del moto equabilmente accelerato, in cui il mobile in tempi eguali acquista eguali gradi di velocità; cioè quello che conviene ad una potenza costante. Notiamo un'osservazione del DE F. « Questa verità, egli dice, « che nel moto proveniente da potenza costante le velocità sieguano la ragion dei « tempi, fu prima di tutti scoverta dal gran GALILEO, e quasi contemporaneamente « dal BALIANI, esaminando il moto naturale dei gravi, cioè il moto prodotto dalla « gravità che si suppone costante. In quei tempi regnava presso molti l'opinione che « le velocità seguissero la ragione de' spazi. La quale fu dal GALILEO riprovata « falsa ed impossibile... ». E parlando poscia della controversia da ciò originata e delle ricerche di FERMAT, egli dice che questi in sostanza asserì « cosa non diversa da quella che il GALILEO promosse e provò, benchè non così rigorosamente » (1).

Dunque il DE F., seguendo evidentemente il RICCATI (2), rende giustizia a BALIANI, di poi quasi dimenticato, ma non esita ancora a dichiarare poco rigoroso il ragionamento del GALILEO, benchè, naturalmente, esatta la conclusione.

(1) Il ragionamento errato di GALILEO fu invece ritenuto assai ingegnoso da MONTUCLA: *Histoire des Mathématiques* (Nouv. édition, Paris, a. VII, t. II, p. 196).

Su tale questione vedi anche la Nota di G. B. FAVARO, *Una critica di G. PLANA ai Dialoghi Galileiani delle Nuove Scienze* (Atti Acc. di Torino, v. XXXIX, pp. 643-651, 1903-1904) e E. MACH, *La Mécanique. Exposé historique et critique de son développement* (Paris, 1904, pp. 123 e 243).

(2) Mi par certo che il DE F. dovesse conoscere: *De Principj della Meccanica.* Lettere di VINCEZO RICCATI al P. VIRGILIO CAVINA, professore delle matematiche in Cagliari di Sardegna. In Venezia, MDCCLXII; di cui è anche parola in una lettera del CANTERZANI. In queste lettere il RICCATI non soltanto rende giustizia al BALIANI, ma ad un altro italiano ancora. Infatti nella prima lettera in cui tratta dell'inerzia dei corpi, dice, p. 4: « GIUSEPPE BALLO in una operetta stampata in Pa« dova l'anno 1635, c'ha per titolo *Dimostrazione del moto naturale dei corpi,* per quanto io sappia « è stato il primo, ch'abbia sostenuto la vera sentenza, cioè che il corpo conserva in perpetuo il « movimento, che ha, quando non v'abbia una ragione, che lo minori o l'accresca. Di questo prin« cipio si sono pure serviti i due sommi uomini GALILEO e CARTESIO seguiti concordemente da tutti « i matematici fioriti dappoi ».

Il libro di BALLI (o BALLO) GIUSEPPE da Palermo (1557-1640) ha per titolo; *Demonstratio de motu corporum naturali.* Patavii 1635. (Vedi MAZZUCCHELLI, *Gli scrittori* ecc., t. II, par. I, p. 187; RAMBELLI, *Intorno alle invenzioni e scoperte italiane,* Modena, 1844, p. 382).

Nella esposizione delle leggi del moto uniformemente accelerato, egli segue il MACLAURIN [1], e parte da questo teorema che lo spazio percorso in un dato tempo è media aritmetica tra gli spazi che si descriverebbero nello stesso tempo dai moti che si hanno nel principio e nel fine di questo tempo, teorema che dimostra in via diretta ma laboriosa. Da qui deduce che se LR e RS sono due spazi percorsi dal punto M con moto uniform. accelerato in tempi eguali che si succedono l'uno all'altro immediatamente, nel tempo che M descrive LS col suo movimento avrebbe descritto uno spazio eguale ed LS col moto che ha in R continuato equabilmente; e quindi, subito si deduce, se in L la velocità è nulla; lo spazio percorso con moto uniform. accelerato è la metà dello spazio percorso in un tempo eguale colla velocità (movimento) acquistata in tutta questa accelerazione e continuato equabilmente. Di qui, com'è noto, si passa agevolmente alle formule del moto unif. accelerato rettilineo ed alla legge che regola le potenze costanti agenti nella direzione del moto e infine a quella delle potenze variabili, ma sempre in direzione del moto. Volendo passare al caso del moto libero in generale, egli (non essendo partito dalle leggi di NEWTON) deve dimostrare che la legge della composizione delle forze è valida anche in dinamica. E ciò fa in un capitolo successivo in cui molto chiaramente giunge alle equazioni del moto nella forma di MACLAURIN; mentre generalmente nei trattati del tempo è piuttosto delle formule di EULER che si fa uso. Però il DE F. non fa alcuna applicazione delle dette formule.

I movimenti *necessari*, cioè il moto di un punto vincolato a restare su di una curva o su di una superficie piana, formano oggetto di un nuovo capitolo, in cui l'A. si attiene alla Meccanica di EULER. In tutto il resto, anzi in tutta l'opera, mancano quasi sempre le illustrazioni, le più semplici applicazioni; ma, lo abbiamo detto già, scopo dell'A. non era di scrivere un trattato completo o di promuovere le applicazioni della meccanica; ma sì quello di esporre *rigorosamente* e *chiaramente* i principi stessi.

La fine immatura del DE F., così colto e notevole pei suoi tempi, non permise la pubblicazione dell'operetta. Salvata per le cure pietose dei parenti memori e devoti, non credemmo fare opera vana togliendola, anche per poco, dall'oblio e notando ciò che certamente l'avrebbe almeno fatta apprezzare dai suoi contemporanei.

[1] *A Treatise of Fluxions* (Edinburgh, 1732).

H. FEHR

LES MATHÉMATIQUES DANS L'ENSEIGNEMENT SECONDAIRE EN SUISSE

1. Il est réjouissant de constater qu'à l'heure actuelle, dans les principaux pays, l'enseignement scientifique fait l'objet d'études approfondies en vue d'une meilleure adaptation des plans d'études et des méthodes aux besoins de la vie économique et de la science moderne. D'importantes réformes sont proposées; elles intéressent également les divers degrés de l'enseignement. Les savants ont compris dès le début qu'ils ne devaient pas rester étrangers à ce mouvement dont ils seront les premiers à utiliser les bons résultats. Le comité du Congrès a donc été bien inspiré en provoquant une série d'études similaires sur l'enseignement mathématique dans les principaux pays.

Je veux essayer de donner ici un aperçu très bref de ce qui se fait en Suisse. La tâche n'est pas aussi simple qu'on pourrait l'imaginer à première vue, car on se trouve en présence, non pas d'un type unique d'écoles, mais d'établissements variant d'un canton à un autre. En Suisse l'instruction publique est en effet du ressort des cantons, au nombre de vingt-deux. Si j'ajoute que dans plusieurs d'entre eux l'organisation est municipale, vous comprendrez que la plus grande diversité règne chez nous dans les plans d'études ou tout au moins dans l'organisation des études.

Les inconvénients d'un pareil système sont minimes à côté des avantages qu'offre une organisation qui permet de tenir compte, dans la mesure du possible, des intérêts régionaux. Cette grand indépendance des autorités scolaires facilite considérablement l'étude et l'accomplissement de réformes, d'autant plus qu'une grande liberté d'initiative est généralement laissée au corps enseignant. Moins il y a de rouages purement administratifs, plus les progrès sont faciles à réaliser. On ne sera donc pas surpris de constater que des demandes de réformes faisant encore l'objet de nombreuses démarches dans les grands pays, ont reçu satisfaction depuis longtemps en Suisse. Ainsi, pour ne donner qu'un exemple, je signalerai le fait que dans plusieurs gymnases scientifiques [1] la première initiation au calcul différentiel figure au programme depuis plus d'un demi-siècle.

[1] Ainsi à Bâle, l'Ecole réale supérieure a été prolongée d'une classe en 1856-57 avec le programme suivant: Algèbre supérieure, 2 heures; Géométrie analytique, 2; Calcul différentiel et intégral 2; Mécanique 4; Géométrie descriptive 4; Minéralogie 2; Histoire des découvertes 1 (V. *Geschichte der obern Realschule zu Basel*, 1905).

Le temps nécessairement très limité accordé à chaque communication m'oblige de restreindre le plus possible le sujet. Je me bornerai à vous montrer la place qui est faite aux mathématiques dans nos gymnases. Toutefois, avant d'aborder cette question, il est indispensable de jeter un coup d'œil très rapide sur l'organisation même des établissements secondaires.

2. Les écoles moyennes conduisant aux études supérieures, portent des noms divers suivant les cantons: *Collège, Gymnase, obere Realschule, Kantonsschule.* C'est cette dernière dénomination qui est la plus répandue dans les cantons de langue allemande.

Examinés au point de vue de leur organisation extérieure, ces établissements présentent des différences assez notables. On y trouve généralement *deux cycles.* Le premier cycle est de 3 ou 4 ans et forme le *collège ou gymnase inférieur;* le second cycle comprend 4 ans (ou 4 ans $^1/_2$ dans certains cantons); les élèves y entrent à l'âge de 14 ou 15 ans.

Les gymnases se divisent en 2 ou 3, quelquefois même 4 *sections,* suivant les langues étrangères qui y sont enseignées. Nous laisserons de côté la section commerciale que l'on trouve dans plusieurs établissements. Dans quelques villes l'école de commerce forme en effet une section de l'Ecole cantonale, par exemple à Zurich, Berne, Lucerne, Aarau, Bâle, St-Gall.

Les *deux grandes sections,* communes à tous les gymnases sont:

a) *la section classique,* qui conduit à toutes les Facultés universitaires (et à l'Ecole polytechnique fédérale moyennant un complément d'études mathématiques); les branches spéciales sont le Latin, le Grec et la Philosophie.

b) *la section technique* ou *industrielle,* qui conduit plus particulièrement aux carrières scientifiques, techniques ou industrielles. Elle porte des noms différents suivant les villes: à Aarau et à Genève, c'est la *section technique,* à Berne l'*école réale* (*Realschule*), à Bâle l'*obere Realschule,* à Zurich, Frauenfeld et St-Gall l'*Industrieschule,* dans les cantons de Vaud et de Neuchâtel c'est le *Gymnase ou la section scientifique,* etc.

Les élèves qui sortent de cette section sont admis directement aux Facultés des Sciences et des Lettres, à la Faculté technique de Lausanne et à l'Ecole polytechnique fédérale.

Le Gymnase de Genève possède encore deux autres sections:

c) la *section réale,* créée en 1886, qui comprend, à côté de l'étude des langues modernes, celle du latin. Elle correspond à peu près à la section *Latin-sciences* en France et au *Realgymnasium* allemand. Une section analogue a été créée à Zurich en 1905. L'examen de sortie donne accès à toutes les Facultés universitaires.

d) la *section pédagogique,* qui prépare les candidats à l'enseignement primaire et qui, en outre, conduit aux Facultés des Sciences et des Lettres (pour les lettres modernes et les sciences sociales). L'enseignement scientifique est le même que dans la section réale.

A la fin du Gymnase les élèves obtiennent, après examen, un *diplôme de maturité* qui porte le nom de la section correspondante.

3. Passons à l'*organisation des études mathématiques*. Dans plusieurs établissements celles-ci se répartissent sur *deux cycles;* le premier cycle correspond au Gymnase inférieur et a pour but de fournir une *première initiation* à l'Algèbre et à la Géométrie. Dans cette première étude, qui est déjà précédée d'une première préparation fournie par l'Ecole primaire, l'enseignement de la Géométrie est basé uniquement sur la méthode intuitive, le maître a recours à la superposition et à la décomposition des figures; les élèves sont appelés à faire des constructions à l'aide des instruments, notamment des exercices simples sur des lieux géométriques.

Le *temps consacré* à l'Arithmétique et à l'introduction à l'Algèbre et à la Géométrie est généralement de 4 heures par semaine.

Sans doute cette période d'initiation n'existe pas dans tous les établissements. d'une manière également complète, mais partout où elle a été appliquée elle a donné d'excellents résultats. Il me paraît inutile d'insister ici sur la nécessité de faire précéder l'étude théorique des mathématiques d'un enseignement intuitif dans lequel on familiarise les jeunes élèves avec les figures géométriques et leurs propriétés les plus simples et avec l'emploi de la règle et du compas dans la résolution des problèmes élémentaires. En procédant ainsi les maîtres n'ont fait que suivre la voie tracée par Pestalozzi, qui devait nécessairement laisser de nombreux disciples parmi ses compatriotes, dont le plus illustre est sans doute le grand géomètre Steiner. Une nouvelle impulsion vient d'être donnée à cet enseignement d'initiation, tout au moins dans les milieux où il n'avait pas encore obtenu son plein développement, par M. Laisant, l'un des fondateurs de nos Congrès, grâce à son récent livre sur l'*Initiation mathématique* (¹).

4. Examinons maintenant quel est le *but* et le *plan d'études de l'enseignement mathématique dans la division supérieure des gymnases*. Si l'on parcourt les divers programmes, on constate que l'on a généralement reconnu qu'à côté du rôle qu'exercent les mathématiques sur le développement logique de la pensée chez l'élève, il y avait à tenir compte de l'importance des mathématiques dans la vie journalière et dans l'étude des phénomènes de la nature.

Je citerai le texte suivant du but de l'enseignement mathématique de la Kantonsschule de Zurich (Programme 1907, section classique):

« *Lehrziel* ». « Fertigkeit im numerischen Rechnen, besonders auch im Kopf-
« rechnen, und Gewandheit in der Auflösung von Aufgaben des bürgerlichen Lebens.
« Erziehung zu klarem, logischem Denken und Ausbildung des räumlichen Anschauungs-
« vermögens. Einsicht in die mathematische Behandlungsweise von Fragen des prak-
« tischen Lebens und einfachen gesetzmässigen Erscheinungen der Natur ».

Dans le programme de la section réale cette dernière partie a été complétée comme suit:

« Erwerbung der Fähigkeit, Aufgaben des praktischen Lebens, der Natur und
« der Technik auf mathematischem Wege behandeln und lösen zu können ».

(¹) 4me édition, Paris-Genève, 1908, prix: 2 frs.; traduction allemand par Schicht, Leipzig-Wien, 1908; traduction italienne par G. Lazzeri, Firenze, 1908. Il y a aussi une traduction polonaise.

Pour atteindre ce but les gymnase accordent une large place aux considérations empruntées aux sciences appliquées. Ainsi dans plusieurs établissements (classiques et industriels) l'enseignement des notions de Trigonométrie sphérique est suivi d'un cours de Géographie mathématique ou de Cosmographie. Dans les section industrielles des principaux gymnases le dessin technique comprend, dans les dernières classes, une série de leçons de levé de plans avec de nombreux exercices pratiques sur le terrain.

Quant au temps affecté à l'enseignement mathématique, il est généralement de *4 heures*, dans les *section classiques*, et *de 6 a 8 heures* (quelquefois même dix heures dans la dernière classe) dans les *sections industrielles.*

Le plan d'études des sections classiques comprend l'Algèbre, la Géométrie, la Trigonométrie, la Géométrie analytique, la Cosmographie.

Dans les sections industrielles ces mêmes branches sont étudiées d'une manière plus approfondie; on y trouve en outre les éléments de l'Algèbre supérieure et du Calcul différentiel et intégral et la Géométrie descriptive.

5. L'étendue des programmes de ces différentes branches présente quelques différences lorsqu'on passe d'une ville à l'autre. C'est surtout dans le domaine de la Géométrie que l'on trouve une plus grand variété. Les gymnases de la Suisse orientale accordent généralement une place plus grande aux notions empruntées à la Géométrie moderne.

Mais tous les programmes ont nécessairement une partie commune, un minimum, correspondant aux prescriptions de deux Commissions fédérales. En effet, bien que les écoles moyennes ne dépendent que de l'administration cantonale ou municipale, le Gouvernement fédéral exerce cependant une certaine influence, et indirectement un contrôle, sur les études secondaires supérieures dans les sections classiques et industrielle. Cela provient de ce qu'en Suisse les carrières médicales sont soumises à un diplôme fédéral. Il a été institué des *examens fédéraux de maturité pour les candidats aux professions médicales.* Les diplômes cantonaux peuvent être jugés équivalents, s'ils sont délivrés par des écoles dont l'organisation et le programme garantissent une bonne préparation aux études universitaires. A cet effet le Conseil fédéral fait dresser une liste des écoles moyennes suisses dont les certificats de sortie sont reconnus comme certificats de maturité.

Le programme fédéral exigeant la connaissance du latin, avec le grec comme branche facultative, les *gymnases classiques ou réaux* doivent nécessairement en tenir compte dans le plan d'études. Il constitue pour eux un minimum qui est généralement dépassé.

Voici le texte du *programme fédéral de maturité pour les candidats aux professions médicales*, en ce qui concerne les Mathématiques et la Physique.

MATHÉMATIQUES. — *a*) *Algèbre.* Opérations algébriques. Equations du premier et du deuxième degré à une et à plusieurs inconnues. Logarithmes. Progressions arithmétiques et géométriques. Intérêts composés et annuités. Eléments de la théorie des combinaisons et du calcul des probabilités. Binôme de Newton avec exposants entiers.

b) *Géométrie.* Planimétrie, stéréométrie, trigonométrie plane. Habileté dans la construction de figures géométriques. Géométrie analytique plane: point, ligne droit, cercle; théorie élémentaire des sections coniques (formes d'équations les plus simples). Application de la théorie des coordonnées à la représentation graphique de fonctions analytiques simples et de fonctions élémentaires de quantités physiques et mécaniques.

Physique. — Propriétés générales des corps solides, liquides et gazeux. Lois principales du son, de la lumière, de la chaleur, du magnétisme et de l'électricité.

Eléments de géographie physique. *(Programme du 6 Juillet 1906).*

C'est là le minimum des connaissance mathématiques que fournissent les gymnases classiques en Suisse. Vous constatez qu'il contient la *Géométrie analytique*, qui est du reste enseignée depuis longtemps dans le Gymnase classique avant même que le programme fédéral en fit mention. On y trouve aussi les applications à la représentation graphique de fonctions simples. Cette dernière partie a été ajoutée en 1906. Ces notions se trouvaient déjà implicitement comprises dans l'enseignement de la géométrie analytique; il s'agissait surtout de les développer en tenant compte des besoins modernes des sciences appliquées. L'*Association suisse des professeurs de mathématiques* l'a reconnu sans peine en adoptant à l'unanimité les thèses que j'ai eu l'honneur de lui soumettre en Décembre 1904 et dont voici le texte (1):

I. *En raison de leur importance et de leur portée, la notion de fonction et les problèmes fondamentaux qui s'y rattachent appartiennent au programme de l'enseignement mathématique des écoles moyennes.*

II. *Quant à l'étendue et à la méthode on devra, d'une part, se borner aux notions fondamentales, et à leurs applications typiques les plus simples, et, d'autre part, éviter un exposé purement abstrait.*

Sur la proposition de M. le professeur Suter il a été ajouté un troisième vœu, adopté également à l'unanimité:

III. *Il est désirable que dans l'enseignement secondaire supérieur, notamment dans les gymnases, une plus grande place soit accordée au développement historique des mathématiques.*

6. Le programme ci-dessus se retrouve donc nécessairement dans le programme des gymnases qui doivent en tenir compte dans l'élaboration de leur plan d'études. Chaque établissement étant libre de fixer son *programme détaillé*, on trouve une grande variété dans les programmes. En général le programme fédéral est dépassé ou tout au moins traité d'une façon très large. Ainsi les uns accordent une place importante aux notions de la géométrie moderne et à l'étude synthétique des sections coniques. La Stéréométrie comprend quelquefois des notions de Géométrie descriptive (par ex. Frauenfeld) et cette façon plus large d'envisager la stéréométrie devrait être adoptée dans tous les établissements n'ayant pas un enseignement proprement dit de Géométrie descriptive. Plusieurs gymnases (par ex. Berne, La Chaux-de-Fonds, St-Gall) font suivre la Trigonométrie plane des éléments de Trigonométrie sphérique et de ses applications simples à la Géographie mathémathique. Quelques programmes mentionnent encore des équations cubiques, les notions sur les nombres complexes et les

(1) *Der Funktionsbegriff im mathematischen Unterricht der Mittelschule.* (Vortrage gehalten in der Vereinigung der Mathematiklehrer an schweizerischen Mittelschulen am 17. Dezember 1904. Traduction française dans l'enseignement mathématique, 7e année. *La notion de fonction dans l'enseignement mathématique des écoles moyennes*, pp. 178-187 ,1905).

équations en général, (par ex. Berne, La Chaux-de-Fonds), ou les séries (Berne). La notion de fonction avec représentation graphique figure explicitement dans la plupart des programmes; quelques-uns ajoutent les premières notions de calcul différentiel et intégral (par ex. Frauenfeld, Schaffhouse).

Nous ne ferons pas ici une étude comparée complète des divers programmes. Ce qui précède montre suffisamment qu'en Suisse les mathématiques occupent une bonne place dans les établissements classiques. Personne ne conteste chez nous que les mathématiques appartiennent à l'ensemble des connaissances qui forment la culture générale indispensable à toutes les carrières libérales et chacun reconnaît que les éléments que l'on enseigne dans les gymnases sont à la portée de tout cerveau normalement constitué. La légende de la bosse des mathématiques, pour ce qui est des éléments, tend de plus en plus à disparaître.

7. Si nous passons maintenant aux *sections scientifiques* (industrielles ou techniques) nous constatons qu'ici aussi il y a un programme minimum que doivent avoir parcouru les élèves qui entrent à l'Ecole polytechnique fédérale (Zurich). Le Conseil de l'Ecole établit une liste des gymnases scientifiques dont le diplôme de maturité dispense des examens d'admission. Ce programme comprend les objets suivants concernant les mathématiques:

Les éléments d'Algèbre (y compris les notions sur la théorie des équations et les séries), la Géométrie à deux et à trois dimensions, la Trigonométrie plane et sphérique; la Géométrie analytique à deux dimensions avec des notions sur la Géométrie analytique à trois dimensions, la Géométrie descriptive. Les éléments de la théorie du mouvement et de la mécanique des corps solides, liquides et gazeux.

Voici, à titre d'exemple, comment ces branches ont été réparties dans le plan d'études de quelques gymnases.

Bâle: Obere Realschule. (Durée 4 ans $^1/_2$; âge d'admission: 14 ans révolus).

Classe I. Arithmétique et Algèbre jusqu'aux équations du premier degré à plusieurs inconnues (3 h.) — Géométrie; planimétrie et commencement de la stéréométrie (3 h.) — Dessin géométrique (2 h.).

Classe II. Algèbre: Puissances entières et fractionnaires, logarithmes. Equations du second degré (3 h.) — Géométrie, Stéréométrie (2 h.) — Dessin géométrique (2 h.).

Classe III. Algèbre: Progressions. Intérêts composés, annuités, applications aux calculs des assurances. Analyse combinatoire. Déterminants (3 h.) — Géométrie: Trigonométrie plane et sphérique (3 h.) — Dessin géométrique avec travaux pratiques sur le terrain (2 h.).

Classe IV. Algèbre: La loi du binôme. Séries. Nombres complexes. Résolutions des équations du degré supérieur, équations transcendantes (2 h.) — Géométrie analytique (2 h.) — Géométrie descriptive (2 h.) — Dessin géométrique, épures de Géométrie descriptive (2 h.).

Classe V. (1 semestre). Algèbre: Eléments du Calcul différentiel avec applications simples à la Géométrie et à la Physique (3 h.) — Géométrie analytique à 3 dimensions (3 h.) — Géométrie descriptive (2 h.); épures (2 h.).

Les *éléments de mécanique* font généralement partie du programme de Physique (Bâle, Zurich, Genève, etc.); toutefois dans quelques gymnases ils sont enseignés par le professeur de mathématiques et figurent au plan d'études pour 1 à 2 h. par semaine pendant 1 à 2 ans. (Lausanne, La Chaux-de-Fonds), etc.

On retrouve ce programme avec plus ou moins de développement dans les divers gymnases. Pour donner une idée exacte de l'ampleur avec laquelle il est traité, nous reproduisons ici le programme détaillé du *Gymnase de Zurich* (section industrielle) en conservant le texte original.

Zurich; *Industrieschule.* (Durée des études: 4 ans $^1/_2$; âge d'admission: 14 ans révolus).

Mathematik. — I. Kl. 6 St. *Rechnen.* Repetition der gewöhnlichen und Dezimalbrüche, des Dreisatres und seiner Anwendung auf die bürgerlichen Rechnungsarten. Teilbarkeit ganzer Zahlen. Ausziehen der Quadratwurzel aus dekadischen Zahlen. Verhältnisse und Proportionen. Uebungen im Kopfrechnen. — *Arithmetik.* Einführung der allgemeinen und der negativen Zahlen. Die vier Grundoperationen mit allgemeinen rationalen Zahlen und Ausdrücken. Sätze über Quadratwurzeln aus Produkten und Quotienten. — *Algebra.* Gleichungen des ersten Grades mit einer Unbekannten. Textgleichungen, insbesondere aus dem bürgerlichen Rechnen und der Planimetrie. — *Planimetrie.* Verschiebung Drehung, Messung. Die Lehre von den Winkeln und den Parallelen, die allgemeinen Sätze über das Dreieck, das Parallelogramm und das Trapez. Zentrale und axiale Symmetrie. Vergleichung, Verwandlung, Teilung und Messung der Flächen. Rechtwinklige Koordinaten. Sätze über Winkel, Sehnen und Tangenten des Kreises, Berechnung der Bogen und Sektoren. Die Lehre von den proportionalen Strecken und der Aehnlichkeit und deren Verwendung zur Untersuchung von Dreieck und Kreis. Teilverhältnis und harmonische Teilung. Die drei Flächensätze des rechtwinkligen Dreiecks, die Winkelhalbierenden, Schwerlinien und Höhen des Dreiecks. Konstruktion fundamentaler algebraischer Ausdrücke (Dimension). Verhältnis ähnlicher Flächen.

II. Kl. 6 St. — *Rechnen.* Ueberschlagsrechnungen im Kopf. Die Kubikwurzel. Abgekürzte Operationen. Rechnen mit begrenzter Genauigkeit. — *Arithmetik.* Potenzen und Wurzeln mit positiven und negativen, ganzen und gebrochenen Exponenten. Begriff der irrationalen, imaginären und komplexen Zahlen. — *Algebra.* Die linearen Gleichungssysteme mit mehreren Unbekannten. Uebungen im Ansetzen und Lösen von Textgleichungen, aus dem bürgerlichen Leben, der Arithmetik, der Geometrie und der Mechanik. — *Ebene Trigonometrie* (im Sommer). Funktionen spitzer Winkel. Auflösung des rechtwinkligen Dreiecks. Anwendungen auf die regulären Vielecke und die Berechnung von π, auf praktische Geometrie, Stereometrie und Physik. Die einfachsten Sätze zur Auflösung des allgemeinen Dreieks Funktionen stumpfer Winkel. — *Stereometrie* (im Winter). Einführende Anschauungen. Allgemeine und spezielle Lage der drei Raumelemente. Winkel und Abstände, dreierlei Symmetrie. Unendlich ferne Raumelemente. Eigenschaften von Zylinder-, Kegel-, Kugelflächen und ihren Tangentialebenen. Berechnung von Oberfläche und Volumen des geraden Prismas. Das Prinzip der Volumenvergleichung. Volumen von vollständingen und schief abgeschnittenen Prismen und Zylindern, von Pyramiden, Kegeln und ihren Stumpfen, von Kugeln und Kugelteilen, von Prismatoiden. Gewichtsberechnung bei technisch wichtigen Formen.

III. Kl. 6 St. — *Rechnen.* Interpolierendes Rechnen mit Zahlen- und graphischen Tabellen. Logarithmisches Rechnen mit fünfstelligen Tabellen. — *Arithmetik.* Potenzen mit irrationalen Exponenten. Die Lehre von den Logarithmen und ihrer Anwendung auf Arithmetik, Geometrie, Physik und Exponentialgleichungen. Arithmetische und geometrischen Progressionen. Näherungs- und Grenzwert bei fallenden geometrischen Reihen. Zinseszins-, Amortisations- und Rentenrechnung. Die Elemente der Lebensversicherung. Das numerische und das graphische Rechnen mit komplexen Zahlen. Der Moivresche Lehrsatz. — *Algebra.* Lineare diophantische Gleichungen. — *Ebene Trigonometrie* (im Sommer). Allgemeingültige Definitionen und Additionstheoreme. Gebrauch der Logarithmen und des Hilfswinkels. Zusammenhang der trigonometrischen Sätze. Anwendungen auf Vermessungen. Stereometrie und Physik. — *Neuere Geometrie* (im Winter). Potenz und Potenzlinien in bezug auf den Kreis. Harmonische Gruppen und Linealkonstruktionen. Polarität in bezug auf den Kreis. Aehnlichkeitscentra und Axen von Kreisen. Uebersicht der planimetrischen Konstruktionsmethoden.

IV. Kl. 6 St. im Sommer, 5 St. im Winter. — *Arithmetik.* Die gemeinen Kettenbrüche. Kombinatorik. Binomischer Lehrsatz für positive ganze Exponenten. Mathematische und empirische

Wahrscheinlichkeit und Anwendungen. — *Algebra.* Die Auflösung der Gleichungen des dritten Grades. Die Zahl der Wurzeln und die Wurzelfaktoren der algebraischen Gleichung. Auflösung numerischer Gleichungen durch Näherung. — *Analysis.* Begriff, graphische Darstellung und Einteilung von Funktionen. Stetigkeit, Null-, Maximal- und Minimalstellen, Grenzwerte. Das Tangentenverfahren zur Bildung der abgeleiteten Funktion. — *Sphärische Trigonometrie* (im Sommer). Sphärik. Sphärische und räumliche Koordinaten. Die Auflösung der speziellen Dreiecke. Die Hauptsätze für das allgemeine Dreieck. Die Lösung der Grundaufgaben und die Flachenberechnung. Anwendungen auf Stereometrie, darstellende Geometrie und Geographie. — *Mathematische Geographie.* Beobachtungen an den scheinbaren täglichen Fixsternbewegungen. Horizont- und Aequator- Koordinaten. Die scheinbare jährliche Bewegung der Sonne. Geographische und nautische Ortsbestimmung. — *Koordinatengeometrie* (im Winter). Recht- und schiefwinklige und polare Koordinaten, Transformationen, Gerade Linie und Kreis.

V. Kl. 6 St. (im Sommer). — *Algebra.* Begriff und Summe von konvergenten Reihen. Die einfachsten Konvergenzkriterien Die Entwicklung der Elementarfunktionen in Potenzreihen. Berechnung und Zusammenhang dieser Funktionen. — *Koordinatengeometrie.* Die Parabel. Gemeinsame Definition der Kegelschnitte. Die Zentra.kegelschnitte. Die zentralen, fokalen und Flächeneigenschaften. Geometrische Oerter zweiten Grades.

Buchhaltung. — I. Kl. 1 St. im Sommer; 2 St. im Winter. — Zins- und Diskontrechnung. Zahlungsverkehr. Wechsel und Scheck nach dem schweizerischen Obligationenrecht und in ihren wichtigsten volkswirtschaftlichen Funktionen. Bankverkehr und Kontokorrente. Entwicklung der Grundsätze der doppelten Buchhaltung und Erklärung der wichtigsten Bücher. Durchführung eines einmonatlichen Geschäftsganges eines industriellen Betriebes nach der amerikanischen Form.

Alle schriftlichen Arbeiten sind sauber und gefällig auszuführen.

Geometrisches Zeichnen.

Die Zeicheninstrumente, insbesondere die Reisszeuge, unterliegen der Kontrolle des Fachlehrers und werden am besten und am biligsten nach seinem Rate angeschafft.

I. Kl. 2. St. — Uebungen im exakten und gewandten Gebrauch der Zeicheninstrumente. Einfache Situationspläne. Konstruktionsaufgaben im Anschluss an den geometrischen Unterricht: Bestimmen von Dreiecken und Vierecken, Flächenverwandlungen und -teilungen, Kreisaufgaben, geometrische Oerter, Methoden der Bewegung und Abbildung.

II. Kl. 2 St. — Im Sommer: Konstruktionsaufgaben zur Fortsetzung der Planimetrie, insbesondere der Lehre von der Aehnlichkeit. Graphische Darstellungen von Funktion. Zeichnen von Kurven als Oerten, insbesondere von Kegelschnitten. — Im Winter: Darstellung von einfachen stereometrischen Formen in schiefer Parallelprojektion. Ausführung der Aufgaben der konstruierenden Stereometrie. Herstellung von Schnitten, Netzen, Modellen. Symmetriekonstruktionen. Konstruktion von Ellipsen als schiefen Kreisprojektionen. Konstruktionen geometrischer Oerter.

Darstellende Geometrie. — III. Kl. 3 St. im Sommer, 4 St. im Winter. — *Kotierte Normalprojektion.* Die Lösung von Aufgaben mittelst des umgelegten Differenzdreiecks. Darstellung von Raumgebilden, besonders von ebenen Figuren. Schichtenlinien. Um- und Aufklappungen um Hauptgeraden. Lehre vom Dreikant und von den Polyedern. Normale und schiefe Affinität. Die Ellipse als affine Figur des Kreises. — *Konjugierte Normalprojektionen.* Die Zweitafelprojektion der Raumelemente einfacher Objekte im ersten Quadranten. Ableitung neuer Projektionen mittelst Transformation und Drehung. Schnitt- und metrische Aufgaben. Raumelemente in allen vier Quadranten.

IV. Kl. 3 St. im Sommer, 4 St. im Winter. — Die Lösung der Grundaufgaben durch Transformation und Drehung. Die Darstellung der Zylinder- Kegel- und Kugelflächen und ihre Benutzung als Oerter. Hyperboloid, Schraubenlinien und -Flächen, Rotationsflächen. Das Dreitafelsystem. Querschnitte und Durchdringungen von Polyedern. Selbstschatten und ebene Schlagschatten. Durchdringungen von Polyedern, Zylindern, Kegeln und Kugeln. Abwickelungen. Technische Anwendungen. Schattenkonstruktionen.

V. Kl. 3 St. im Sommer. — Ebene Schnitte von Pyramidenmänteln und kollineare Verwandtschaft. Kollineare Konstruktion von Kegelschnitten. Hauptbegriffe der geometrischen Perspektive. Perspektivische Darstellung nach Massen.

Physik. — Der Unterricht wird sowohl experimentell als mathematisch durchgeführt. — II. Kl. 2 St. im Sommer, 3 St. im Winter- Einleitendes über Aufgabe und Methode der Physik. Längen- und Zeitmessung. Mechanik der festen Körper: Begriff von Geschwindigkeit, Beschleunigung, Kraft, Masse, Gewicht, Arbeit und Energie. Bewegung bezw. Gleichgewicht unter dem Einflusse einer oder mehrerer Kräfte. Der Wurf. Die Maschinen. Die Wage. Bewegung unter dem Einflusse einer beliebigen Zentralkraft. Das Sonnensystem.

III. Kl. 2 St. im Sommer, 3 St. im Winter. — Energie rotierender Körper. Der Kreisel. Das Pendel. Elastizität. Der Stoss. Mechanik der flüssigen Körper. Das spezifische Gewicht. Kapillarität. Diffusion. Osmose. Hydrodynamik. Wasserkräften. Wasserräden. Mechanik der gasförmigen Körper: Kinetische Gastheorie. Der Luftdruck. Anwendungen des Luftdruckes. Pumpen. Molekularerscheinungen in Gasen. Wellenlehre: transversale und longitudinale Schwingungen. Interferenz. Reflexion und Brechung. Stehende Schwingungen. Resonanz. Akustik: Die Erregung, Fortpflanzung und Wahrnehmung des Schalles. Optik: die Ausbreitung des Lichtes im Raume. Die Reflexion des Lichtes.

IV. Kl. 3 St. im Sommer, 2 St. im Winter. — Die Brechung des Lichtes. Die Dispersion. Achromasie. Die optischen Erscheinungen der Atmosphäre. Spektralanalyse. Fluoreszenz und Phosphoreszenz. Das Auge und das Sehen. Die optischen Instrumente. Interferenz und Beugung. Polarisation und Doppelbrechung. Wärme: Thermometrie. Ausdehnung der festen, flüssigen und gasförmigen Körper. Kalorimetrie. Aenderung des Aggregatzustandes. Hygrometrie. Wärmeleitung und Wärmestrahlung. Wärmequellen. Wärme und Arbeit. Die Grundgesetze der Elektrostatik. Das elektrische Potential. Kapazität. Kondensatoren. Das elektrostatische Masssystem. Der Magnetismus: Magnetische Feldstärke und Kraftlinien. Das magnetische Kraftfeld der Erde.

Physikalisches Praktikum im Winter: 2 St. in Halbklassen alle 14 Tage: Längenmessungen. Prüfung einer Wage. Dichtebestimmungen. Elastizitätsmodul. Schallgeschwindigkeit aus Staubfiguren. Krümmungsradius und Brennweite einer Linse. Brechungsexponent, Spektralanalyse und Wellenlänge eines Lichtstrahles.

V. Kl. 2 St. Die galvanische Elemente. Der elektrische Strom. Das magnetische Feld eines elektrischen Stromes. Elektromagnetismus. Das Biot- Savart'sche Gesetz. Das Ohm'sche Gesetz und die Kirchhoff'schen Sätze. Das elektromagnetische Masssystem. Elektrolyse. Die Polarisation und die Akkumulatoren. Stromenergie und Wärme. Glühlicht und Bogenlicht. Thermoelektrizität. Die Induktionsströme. Das Gesetz von Lenz. Selbstinduktion. Foucaultströme. Induktionsapparate. Entladungserscheinungen in verdünnten Gasen. Die dynamoelektrischen Maschinen. Telephon und Mikrophon. Elektrische Schwingungen. Teslaströme. Elektrische Wellen. Funkentelegraphie.

8. Il y aurait maintenant encore une série de questions à développer ici en vue de donner un tableau complet de l'organisation des études mathématiques dans les gymnases suisses. Il serait intéressant d'avoir quelques indications sur les méthodes d'enseignement et tout particulièrement sur l'enseignement de la Géométrie, sur l'emploi des modèles mathématiques, sur l'usage des manuels, sur la part accordée aux exercices et aux problèmes dans les leçons et dans les examens, etc. Ici encore la plus grande liberté est laissée au corps enseignant et l'on constate de grandes différences lorsqu'on passe d'un gymnase à un autre.

Je me suis borné à faire un tableau de la place accordée aux mathématiques. Ce n'est pas le lieu ici de l'accompagner d'une étude critique qui s'adresserait plutôt à quelques établissements qu'à l'ensemble des écoles moyennes. Car il y a évidemment des lacunes plus ou moins grandes dans quelques gymnases. Ainsi, en Géométrie, on n'accorde pas toujours une place assez large à la Stéréométrie et à la Géométrie pratique, tandis que la Trigonométrie est quelquefois trop développée. Dans plusieurs gymnases on néglige par exemple l'étude du prismatoïde, dont la formule du volume donne lieu à des généralisations remarquables. D'autre part il serait désirable de donner une courte étude synthétique des sections coniques, en partant du cône de révolution, en la plaçant avant l'étude analytique.

Quant à la préparation du corps enseignant, elle varie d'un canton à un autre; il en est de même des exigences de l'Etat, qui ne sont pas toujours assez élevées. L'organisation des études pour les candidats à l'enseignement est encore insuffisante aussi bien dans les universités qu'à l'Ecole polytechnique fédérale. Sous ce rapport il conviendrait d'examiner avec soin les conseils que donne le rapport (1) de MM. Klein et Gutzmer (Dresde 1907).

Cette diversité dans la préparation est peut-être même une force stimulante, car le corps enseignant, dans son ensemble, est à la hauteur de sa mission. Il a conscience que l'enseignement mathématique est perfectible. Aussi est-ce avec le plus grand intérêt qu'il suit les discussions et les efforts qui se font dans les pays voisins.

(1) Reproduit dans l'Enseignement mathématique du 15 janv. 1908, pp. 5-49.

F. S. ARCHENHOLD

UEBER DIE BEDEUTUNG DES MATHEMATISCHEN UNTERRICHTES IM FREIEN IN VERBINDUNG MIT REFORMVORSCHLAEGEN FUER DEN LEHRGANG

Gelegentlich der Aufgabe, die ich als Dozent der Humboldtakademie mir gestellt hatte, den mathematischen Elementarunterricht zu vereinfachen, bin ich zu einer neuen Methode des Unterrichts gelangt, die sich sowohl in bezug auf schnelle Bewältigung des Lehrstoffes, wie auch in bezug auf Steigerung des Interesses der Schüler von dem alten bisherigen Wege vorteilhaft unterscheidet. Ich möchte anregen, diese Methode auch auf den Elementarunterricht der Schüler zu übertragen. Gerade in der Mathematik ist ein Misserfolg des ersten Unterrichts von so nachhaltigem Schaden, wie bei keinem anderen Unterrichtsfach. Ein Schüler, der den ersten Definitionen nicht hat folgen können, ist für immer aus dem Sattel gehoben. Bei den meisten andern Fächern ist es für den weiteren Verlauf des Unterrichts von unwesentlicher Bedeutung, ob beispielsweise im geographischen Unterricht ein Schüler bei dem Unterricht über Europa unaufmerksam war, wenn er dem Unterricht über Asien wiederum folgt, so wird er diesen Teil für sich lernen können. Wenn beim Zoologischen Unterricht die Aufmerksamkeit des Schülers bei der Durchnahme eines der Säugetiere gering war, so kann er durch erhöhte Aufmerksamkeit bei den Reptilien ganz wohl diesen Teil der Zoologie verstehen. Wenn ein Schüler im Geschichtsunterricht die römische Geschichte mangelhaft gelernt hat, so hindert ihn das nicht, bei der Geschichte des Mittelalters ein vorzüglicher Schüler zu werden, wenn er auch nicht alle Teile pragmatisch verstehen wird. Wer aber auf der Unterstufe des mathematischen Unterrichts versagt, bleibt für immer ein schlechter Schüler in der Mathematik. Trotz aller späteren Bemühungen der Eltern klagt der Schüler, dass er dem mathematischen Unterricht nicht folgen kann. Aus diesem Grunde müssen wir mit grösster Gewissenhaftigkeit eine Methode ausfindig machen, die den Schüler von Anbeginn an fesselt und die an Vorstellungen anknüpft, welche wir mit der Erfahrung auch des unbegabtesten Schülers verbinden können. Die kleinen Kinder lernen nicht sprechen, indem sie einzelne Buchstaben lernen, sondern gleich ganze Worte. Erst später, in einer höheren Stufe des Unterrichts, werden die Worte in ihre Buchstaben zerlegt. In dem bisherigen mathematischen Unterricht wird aber ein Weg eingeschlagen, der den Kindern zuerst die einzelnen Buchstaben der Mathematik vorlegt, aus den Buchstaben werden Silben gebildet und erst aus den Silben die Wörter. Wer kann von einem Knaben verlangen, dass er den mathematischen Buchstaben und Silben schon ein so grosses Interesse entgegenbringt, dass er die Schwierigkeiten des Unterrichtes überwindet. Wie können wir verlangen, dass jemand ein Interesse hat für einen spitzen, stumpfen, erhabenen Winkel, für einen Scheitel, Gegen- und Wechselwinkel, wenn diese Begriffe für ihn tot bleiben und nicht durch Gegenstände aus der Natur oder aus seiner Erfahrung belebt werden. Alle die Pappmodelle und Anschauungsmittel, welche für den mathematischen Unterricht erdacht sind, bilden nur einen Notbehelf. Sie sind geboren aus dem berechtigten Wunsche des Lehrers, dem Schüler zu helfen, damit er sich bei diesen Begriffen etwas denken kann. Aber diese künstlichen Modelle bleiben zumeist ebenso interesselos für den Schüler, wie die Begriffe selbst, im Gegenteil sie rufen in ihm das Gefühl wach, dass es notwendig ist, erst Modelle zu schaffen, um wenigstens eine Anwendung der mit so grosser Mühe gelernten Begriffe zu ermöglichen.

Wenn wir aber den Schüler hinausführen in die freie Natur und aus der Natur heraus die Begriffe der verschiedenen Winkel ableiten, so erreichen wir dadurch, dass der Schüler nicht nur Interesse für die abgeleiteten, sonst trockenen Begriffe der verschiedenen Winkel erhält, sondern mit dieser neuen Methode sind gleichzeitig zwei andere Vorteile verbunden. Erstens lernt der Schüler schon auf der Unterstufe das, was der Naturforscher immer tun soll, nämlich' aus der Beobachtung heraus Begriffe und Gesetze ableiten, er lernt sehen. Der zweite grosse Vorteil ist, dass der mathematische Unterricht im Freien stattfindet, also auch gleichzeitig eine Erfrischung für den Schüler, eine hygienische Bedeutung für ihn gewinnt. Der Schüler muss sich auf den Unterricht freuen und es wird sich zeigen, dass mit dieser Methode ein weit grösserer Stoff bewältigt werden kann.

Um hier nur einige Beispiele anzuführen erwähne ich, dass jeder Gegenstand im Freien geeignet ist, uns den Begriff der verschiedenen Winkel klar zu machen. Ein Baum, ein Haus, ein grosser Stein, eine Wolke am Himmel, Sonne, Mond und Sterne, ein aufsteigender Luftballon, ein vorbeimarschierender Mann, etc. Ich stelle einen Schüler einem Baume gegenüber, lasse ihn die Spitze und den Stamm anvisieren, die beiden Linien, welche er von seinem Auge zu den beiden Punkten des Baumes zieht, werden einen bestimmten Winkel miteinander bilden. Von der Höhe des Baumes wird es abhängen, wie dieser Winkel sich verändert, wenn ich den Schüler auf den Baum zumarschieren lasse oder ihn rückwärts gehen lasse. Der Winkel wird aus einem spitzen im ersteren Falle zunächst ein rechter, alsdann ein stumpfer. Wenn ich das Auge am Horizont entlang streifen lasse, so kann ich durch Visur auch die erhabenen Winkel darstellen. Den Begriff des Nebenwinkels kann ich durch jede Strasse, die in einem beliebigen Winkel in eine andere grosse Strasse läuft, illustrieren. Den Begriff der Gegenwinkel, Wechselwinkel, kann ich unter Zuhülfenahme zweier paralleler Strassen, die durch eine Strasse durchschnitten werden, aus der Natur beleben, und kann dann unschwer die Notwendigkeit der Ableitung der Sätze den Schüler erkennen lassen. Wenn ich mir nun einen Apparat schaffe, der so hergestellt ist, dass zwei Schenkel sich um ein Scharnier drehen, welches ich festschrauben kann und welches eine Oeffnung für das Auge trägt, und wenn ich dann weiter neben diesen beiden Schenkeln eine Kreiseinteilung anbringe, bei der die einzelnen Gradstriche durch Sprossen dargestellt sind und diese Vorrichtung nicht nur senkrecht aufstellen, sondern auch so drehen kann, dass sie gegen den Horizont jeden Winkel einnehmen kann, so habe ich gleichzeitig ein Mess-Instrument und kann nun die Grösse der verschiedenen Winkel durch die Schüler abschätzen lassen und die Winkel gleichzeitig bestimmen, die zwei verschiedene Gegenstände miteinander bilden, seien es zwei Fensterkreuze in verschiedenen Etagen, sei es die Spitze eines Baumes mit der Spitze eines andern Baumes, sei es der Winkel, den zwei Sterne miteinander bilden, oder am Tage die Sonne mit dem Horizont. Wie interessant wird der Unterricht, wenn ich die Schüler erst die Grösse der Winkel schätzen lasse, die die Stämme zweier Bäume miteinander bilden und dann eine diebezügliche Messung vornehmen lasse. Es wird dem Schüler dann die Notwendigkeit der Einführung eines Winkelmasses vor Augen geführt. Hierbei ist es gleichgültig, ob ich den rechten Winkel in 90 oder 100 Teile eingeteilt habe. Wenn ich den Apparat so einrichte, dass er sich nach der anderen Seite hin in derselben Ebene bewegen lässt, so kann ich damit am besten den Scheitelwinkelbegriff lehren und gleichzeitig Gegenstände in der Natur aufsuchen, die solche Scheitelwinkel miteinander bilden. Wenn sich bei der Schätzung der Winkel das Bedürfnis herausgestellt hat, eine Winkelteilung zu schaffen, dann wird man auch gleichzeitig auf den Begriff des Durchmessers eines Kreises kommen können und das Bedürfnis entstehen lassen, aus dem Umfang eines Kreis den Durchmesser desselben abzuleiten und umgekehrt. So kann ich den Umfang eines Baumes direkt messen, aber nicht leicht seinen Durchmesser. Ich muss schon möglichst bald Aufgaben mit den Schülern lösen, die die mathematischen Begriffe beleben. Wenn ich beispielsweise die Schüler an einen kleinen Kreis führe und zwei Punkte, deren Verbindungslinien durch den Kreis hindurchgehen in ihrer Entfernung zu messen aufgebe, so wird sich leicht die Bedeutung des Scheitelwinkels an der Lösung dieser Aufgabe zeigen lassen. Die verschiedensten Dreiecke muss ich wiederum durch Punkte in der freien Natur, die sich leicht finden lassen, demonstrieren. Wenn man vielleicht einwenden-würde, man brauche ja alsdann nur einen Leitfaden über niedere Geodäsie herzunehmen, um eine solche Methode zu haben, so ist dabei zu bemerken, dass bei jeder Geodäsie auch vorher die mathematischen Begriffe abgeleitet sind.

Nach der von mir hier in Anwendung gebrachten Methode sollen die mathematischen Begriffe hergeleitet werden aus der Natur durch Lösung von Aufgaben. Wenn es auch Lehrer gibt, die einmal in dem einen oder anderen Falle es schon so machten, so habe ich kein methodisch durchgeführtes Lehrbuch gefunden und auch in den pädagogischen Werken, auch nicht bei Friedrich Reith, « Anleitung zum mathematischen Unterricht », Darlegungen gefunden, die eine solche Methode erwähnen. Es würde nicht nur von grösstem Vorteil für den Schüler sein, wenn eine solche Methode in den mathematischen Unterricht eingeführt würde, sondern es würde die Mathematik dadurch sich bald die Stellung in dem Lehrplan unserer Schulen erringen, welche ihr eigentlich zukommen sollte. Es würden auch mit der Einführung dieser Methode alle die verflachenden Notbehelfe verschwinden können, welche mathematische Sätze lehren ohne strenge Beweise gleichzeitig durchzuführen. Was ich verlange ist, dass bevor die mathematischen Sätze streng abgeleitet werden, der Schüler bekannt werden soll mit den Begriffen, die bei der Herleitung der mathematischen Sätze nötig sind. So wird der Punkt, die Linie, der Winkel, das Dreieck und die andern mathematischen Begriffe sich in der Vorstellung des Schülers poetisch verweben mit dem, was er in der freien Natur erschaut hat, er wird die Natur auf Grund einer ihm lieb gewordenen Methode der Anschauung mit ganz andern Augen betrachten und alsdann mit viel grösserer Freude mit seinem Verstande den Reiz der mathematischen Logik in sich nachwirken lassen. Wenn ein solcher Schüler in seinem praktischen Beruf, sei es als Ingenieur, als Landmesser, als Astronom, als Architekt Aufgaben gegenübersteht, wie sie die Natur bietet, so wird er sie mit viel grösserem Geschick lösen und viel schneller sich die nötigen Hilfsmittel verschaffen können, als ein Schüler, der nach der alten Methode die Sätze der Mathematik wohl völlig begriffen hat, für den aber die Anwendungen immer nur etwas Fremdartiges gehabt haben. Es wird dann auch der Fall eintreten, dass ein Schüler, der in seinem späteren Leben berufsmässig die Mathematik nicht weiter zu pflegen hat, doch noch sich gern mit mathematischen Aufgaben beschäftigen und den Fortschritten der Mathematik folgen wird.

J. ANDRADE

QUELQUES OBSERVATIONS PSYCHOLOGIQUES
RECUEILLIES DANS LES ENSEIGNEMENTS SCIENTIFIQUES D'INITIATION

I.

Avant d'exposer quelques faits précis et les idées que j'y rattache, je crois utile de bien marquer le sens que j'attache au mot *initiation.*

J'entendrai par *initiation* tout effort nouveau demandé à l'esprit dans un domaine où il pénètre pour la première fois; et je me servirai de cette désignation quel que soit d'ailleurs l'âge du sujet. Quelques auteurs ont, au contraire, réservé le mot d'initiation à toute première culture de l'enfant. Pour éviter tout malentendu j'ai cru devoir préciser le sens sous lequel j'emploie ce mot d'initiation.

II.

Parmi les quatre faits que je vais décrire, trois se rapportent à des observations pédagogiques recueillies sur des sujets de 13, 14 et 17 ans, je pourrais presque dire sur trois *patients* de notre enseignement secondaire français.

Le quatrième fait montre une influence bien inattendue de l'enseignement secondaire sur l'enseignement professionnel.

Pour la brièveté de cet exposé, je désignerai par des lettres les sujets observés.

III.

Observation du sujet A

(Recueillie en 1888).

A, âgé de treize ans, élève de 4eme, écoute attentivement une leçon sur le cas d'égalité des triangles; il avoue ingénument qu'il ne comprend pas ces transports de figures les unes vers les autres; son maître insiste pour tâcher de découvrir son idée de derrière la tête.

« Eh bien, voilà, — répond l'enfant — Comment donc êtes vous sûr que le « triangle $A\ B\ C$ que vous portez vers le triangle $A'\ B'\ C'$..., comment êtes vous sûr que « *ce triangle ne casse pas* pendant le voyage? ».

Inutile de vous raconter la suite par le menu: le professeur qui racontait la géométrie de LEGENDRE à ses élèves, fût, par cette confidence d'enfant, invité à se mettre à l'étude de la géométrie naturelle, il y fit d'ailleurs quelques progrès.

IV.

Observation du sujet B

(Recueillie en 1908).

Le sujet B, encore un élève de 4eme, est un gros garçon, très calme, qui trouve presque toujours les problèmes qu'on lui donne, mais qui, dit-il, « *ne sait pas mettre en phrases comment la solution lui est venue* »; il a l'œil et les doigts intelligents; quand une serrure dans la maison est dérangée, ses parents s'adressent à lui et il fait fort bien le serrurier.

Il apprend aussi la géométrie, mais il me demande à quoi servent tous « *ces règlements des dessins* » car c'est ainsi qu'il appelle la géométrie.

Or, un jour de cet hiver, le gamin est venu me trouver, prodigieusement *inquiet*, un paquet de dessins sous son bras.

Le petit serrurier préparait avec son frère un « *bobsleigh* »; vous savez qu'on nomme ainsi une *luge* ou glissoire destinée à descendre les pentes sur la neige, mais armée d'un cadre patin dirigeable à la main.

« Avec tous ces dessins, me dit-il, il m'arrive une drôle d'histoire! »

Et il m'expliqua, que, *pour imiter* l'axe incliné du volant des automobiles, il avait creusé un trou incliné dans la charpente; mais ayant voulu, comme d'habitude, préparer un petit modèle, il s'étonnait *perplexe*, de ne pouvoir produire le glissement plan d'une rondelle liée à l'axe, mais oblique à l'axe.

« Et pourtant me disait-il, en colère, dans ma géométrie les angles ont l'habitude « *de tourner* autour de *leur sommet* ».

Alors, je montrai à cet enfant, l'abat-jour d'une lampe, il *sentit* alors qu'une droite peut engendre un cône; sa colère se dissipa mais il me dit avec une sérieuse résignation:

« *Moi, je croyais que les droites qui tournent doivent toujours* former quelque chose *de plat* ».

Et il renonça à sa rondelle liée a l'axe et glissant sur le plan des supports.

V.

Observations du sujet C candidat au baccalauréat.

1° C, âgé de 17 ans, comprend les mathématiques quand on les lui explique lentement.

En physique, on lui a parlé pour la première fois de la résultante de deux forces représentée par la diagonale du parallélogramme qui a pour côtés contigus les deux segments représentatifs des forces composantes.

Il croit avoir compris, passe aux forces parallèles, il comprend encore ; mais, ici je suis laisse la parole :

« Après avoir compris celà *en physique*, voilà qu'on va revoir celà autrement, « en *mathématiques!* notre professeur nous apprend qu'on a encore changé nos pro- « grammes, et qu'il faut qu'il aille *au galop*.

« Il nous parle alors du *moment linéaire*, et il appelle *équivalents* deux sy- « stèmes de Vecteurs qui ont un même Résultant de translation et même moment « linéaire par rapport à un point. Il nous annonce alors qu'il va nous montrer que « le choix de ce dernier point est indifférent.

« Tout celà sera peut-être joli, mais je croyais avoir compris les systèmes équi- « valents de forces en physique. Et voilà qu'en mathématiques, je ne comprends plus !

« Et d'abord vecteurs et forces ce n'est donc pas la même chose? »

2° Pour comble de disgrâce, ce brave garçon, pas plus sot qu'un autre, croyez le bien, après s'être dégoûté des mathématiques enseignées *au galop*, s'est aussi dégoûté de la Physique entrevue à travers le baccalauréat, voici à quelle occasion.

Après un petit échec au baccalauréat il raconte :

« En voilà une bien bonne qui m'arrive !

« Dans mes leçons sur les unités électriques comparées, il y a un facteur π « multiplié par une puissance de 10 ; notre professeur de physique nous l'avait d'abord « expliqué ; puis après une visite de l'inspecteur général il nous a dit : — Eh bien « non ! décidément il y a contre-ordre, n'expliquez pas la signification de ce facteur ; « retenez le simplement par coeur.

« C'est ce que j'ai fait.

« Mais alors, Vlan ! au bachot, je tombe sur un examinateur qui me demande : « — Connaissez vous ici la signification du facteur π — ; Je lui réponds : — Je l'avais « d'abord comprise à peu près, mais depuis la dernière visite de M. l'inspecteur gé- « néral, nous sommes dispensés de la comprendre.

« Je ne sais plus où j'en suis. Oh, ma tête, ma tête ! »

VI.

Observation D.

Il y a quelques années, en faisant un cours de mécanique appliquée à l'horlogerie, j'avais observé que la plupart des anciens élèves d'une école professionnelle étaient gênés quand un raisonnement utilisait les constructions géométriques à trois dimensions.

Je fis part de mon étonnement au directeur de cette école professionelle et je lui demandai :

« N'ont ils pas appris à l'école le Veme livre de la géométrie de Legendre? »

Le directeur, grand artiste et homme d'esprit me répondit :

« Bah ! le cinquième livre, je ne l'ai jamais appris ; pour faire nos programmes, « j'ai pris dans les programmes des lycées les premiers éléments, ceux qui m'avaient « jadis suffi à moi-même ».

Evidemment le 5ème livre de LEGENDRE par son numéro d'ordre était chose lointaine, donc superflue, dans les souvenirs que mon interlocuteur avait conservés des programmes très surannés, il est vrai, de nos lycées.

Pourtant, le très grand artiste qui avait découpé ces programmes était, en cette occasion, un mauvais éducateur, car si son intuition, son génie même avaient suffi pour suppléer à ce qu'il n'avait jamais appris, il avait tort de compter que la même intuition ou le même génie viendraient au secours de tous ceux qui, systématiquement ignoreraient ce que lui-même avait ignoré à l'école : la géométrie de l'ajustage.

VII.

Quelques conclusions à propos des faits psychologiques qui précèdent.

L'observation **A** et l'observation **B** nous montrent avec une pleine évidence la nécessité de placer, au début même de la géométrie, la sensation du corps solide, et la notion des rotations précisée par l'étude du dièdre, c'est à dire la compréhension nette de l'identité du glissement plan sur un point de ce plan avec la rotation exécutée autour d'une droite perpendiculaire à ce plan.

L'observation **D** corrobore ces conclusions avec une grande force.

Nous indiquerons ici brièvement les faits que l'on peut ainsi grouper dans le premier livre de la géométrie naturelle : Le triangle, le dièdre, la symétrie, les trièdres et leurs images sphériques, le dallage de la sphère.

Ces faits (six ou sept leçons tout au plus) forment ce que j'ai appelé la géométrie de l'ajustage, en souvenir de l'observation **D** rapportée plus haut.

Le second livre de la géométrie sera consacré au phénomène de la similitude et aux propriétés métriques de l'espace euclidien.

Le troisième livre sera consacré à la mesure des étendues.

Soit en tout quinze leçons : une soixantaine de pages tout au plus, pour la géométrie élémentaire et fondamentale exigible d'un bachelier.

Faut il aller plus loin dans la réforme de la géométrie élémentaire ?

Je réponds nettement : *Non, en ce qui concerne l'enseignement secondaire* ; et je vais motiver ma réponse.

VIII.

Le but de l'enseignement secondaire.

Le but de l'enseignement secondaire a été excellemment défini par M. MARCEL PREVOST dans ses *Lettres à Françoise*.

C'est un enseignement destiné à donner, pour la vie, des notions simples mais solides, en-dehors de toute spécialisation.

Toute réforme qui le fortifie en le simplifiant répond à la poursuite de ce but ; à l'heure actuelle la réforme la plus urgente consiste à faire disparaitre cette funeste distinction d'une géométrie plate et d'une géométrie de l'espace.

Mais défions nous, dans cet enseignement *de tutelle*, de l'encyclopédie superficielle ; et proclamons nettement que l'enseignement secondaire n'est pas du tout une préparation aux mathématiques spéciales.

Je me refuse donc à placer dans l'enseignement secondaire la théorie *complète* des vecteurs si intéressante qu'elle me paraisse ; je me refuse également à faire pour les débutants une simplification *factice* de la notion de groupe.

Ces jeux d'esprit sont fort loin des nécessités de l'enseignement d'initiation.

Ils seront, au contraire, à leur place dans un enseignement mathématique plus spécialisé, même à ses débuts.

A l'égard de l'observation de **C** je crois devoir demander ici des réformes qui ont déjà été reclamées par les esprits les plus divers.

Les programmes véritables d'une éducation scientifique devraient être, non l'oeuvre aveugle des Bureaux, mais l'oeuvre vivante d'une coopération harmonieuse entre les maîtres d'une même maison d'éducation.

Exemple : lors qu'un maître de physique se plait à exposer les images vectorielles de MAXWELL en électricité il serait indispensable *qu'en cet instant* l'élève soit *déjà* très familiarisé par son maître de mathématiques avec les notions variées de la géométrie orientée.

L'enseignement, ne l'oublions pas, doit avant tout, être organisé pour les élèves ; l'initiation peut être profonde mais un maître qui a fait vraiment le tour de la science qu'il enseigne, sait ce qui importe avant tout et ce qui peut être résolument écarté.

Ayons le courage de le reconnaitre : l'enseignement en surface est condamné par la faillite de notre grotesque baccalauréat.

En matière d'éducation comme en matière de science l'à-peu-près est au dessous de tout.

A. CONTI

SULL'INIZIAZIONE ALLE MATEMATICHE

E SULLA PREPARAZIONE MATEMATICA DEI MAESTRI ELEMENTARI IN ITALIA

Secondo la vigente legislazione scolastica, la grande maggioranza dei fanciulli accede, in Italia, alla scuola media governativa all'età di dieci anni, dopo aver frequentato, dai 3 ai 6 anni d'età, un *giardino d'infanzia*, e dai 6 ai 10 anni le prime quattro classi della scuola elementare: nessuno può essere ammesso alla prima classe delle scuole medie pubbliche, se non dopo aver conseguito il « *diploma di maturità* », per ottenere il quale occorre aver superato un esame a cui è di speciale preparazione il programma svolto nelle prime classi elementari.

Una buona disposizione legislativa ([1]) aveva sancito che niuno potesse essere ammesso all'esame di maturità se non all'età di 10 anni compiuti, ma una leggina successiva ([2]) tolse questa limitazione, e così anche dei fanciulli di 8 o 9 anni sono dichiarati « maturi », e in un vero stato di « acerbità » sono sottoposti al lavoro della scuola media e a tutto il sovraccarico che è ancora una caratteristica di questa scuola italiana, per la cui riforma studia già, da più di due anni, una Commissione Reale appositamente istituita. Come possa avvenire che fanciulli di età inferiore ai 10 anni siano già preparati a sostenere l'esame di maturità è facilmente spiegato: non hanno frequentato *tutte e quattro* le classi elementari delle scuole pubbliche, perchè fanciulli d'età inferiore ai 6 anni non sono ammessi, per legge ([3]), alla prima classe, onde tutta o gran parte della loro *iniziazione* si è formata in scuole private, generalmente dette *asili infantili*, a proposito dei quali può ancora ripetersi col Paolini: ([4]) « la cieca e funesta frenesia di *far presto* ha per tal guisa sconvolto il buon « senso delle famiglie, da far loro dimenticare, disconoscere anzi apertamente, che « in fatto di coltura il far bene giova assai più che il far presto. Nel che trovando « consenzienti insegnanti di scarsa coscienza, infrangono ogni onesto limite d'età ed « elevano ad istituzione in onta alla legge la rovinosa scuola precoce, tarlo roditore

([1]) Art. 141 del Regolamento-legge per gli esami approvato con R. D. 13 ottobre 1904.

([2]) Del giugno 1905, per iniziativa dell'on. Sanarelli.

([3]) Legge 13 novembre 1859.

([4]) Paolini Eugenio Paolo, *Istruzioni e programmi per i Giardini d'Infanzia e pel coordinamento ad essi del corso inferiore elementare secondo la Circ. Ministeriale n. 786 del 17 settembre 1885*. Ditta G. B. Paravia, 1886.

« d'ogni più solido organismo cerebrale, aberrazione non saprei se più fatale al fisico « o al morale delle giovani generazioni ».

È doloroso a dirsi ma vero: molti asili infantili italiani non sono altro che delle *scuole precoci* pei bambini che, per legge, non sono ancora ammessi alla scuola elementare pubblica, e che ciò possa avvenire è pure facilmente spiegato, attesochè per gli Istituti infantili, la legislazione scolastica italiana è ancora addirittura embrionale; nel vigente *Regolamento generale per l'istruzione elementare* è contenuto soltanto un articolo (Art. 226) così espresso: « I Municipi, gli enti morali, i pri« vati e le private associazioni possono aprire istituti di educazione infantile in lo« cali riconosciuti salubri e convenienti. Le persone preposte a tali istituti devono « possedere titoli comprovanti la loro idoneità all'ufficio. *Speciali istruzioni mini« steriali determineranno i limiti, i programmi ed i metodi per gli istituti infan« tili* ». Ma *queste speciali istruzioni*, promesse già da 13 anni *non sono mai venute*; inoltre, se è vero che dopo il riordinamento delle Scuole Normali, ossia fino dal 1896, e dopo la conseguente istituzione del *diploma di maestra giardiniera*, questo avrebbe dovuto, e dovrebbe, essere il diploma d'idoneità all'ufficio di maestra d'asilo infantile, è altresì vero che le maestre fornite del diploma predetto « sono « poco disposte a prestar servizio negli asili d'infanzia a cagione della scarsità degli « stipendî; e così, vista l'indeterminatezza delle disposizioni regolamentari, i Provve« ditori agli Studi sono costretti a permettere che vengano preposte agli istituti in« fantili anche persone munite della sola patente di maestra elementare » (1) e anche persone che hanno appena la licenza elementare!

Ed è in questi istituti e sotto gli ammaestramenti che possono esser dati da persone che, sovente, non hanno nemmeno la licenza normale, è in tali condizioni che si compie la prima *iniziazione* alla matematica! tralasciando pure la considerazione di coloro — e non sono pochi — i quali giungono alla scuola media senza aver frequentato tutte e quattro le classi di una scuola elementare pubblica, rimane il fatto che la gran maggioranza dei fanciulli, che segue regolarmente la scuola elementare pubblica, passa anteriormente due o tre anni in un asilo infantile: asili infantili, giardini d'infanzia ve ne sono dapertutto e in numero grandissimo, ma solo la minima parte di essi, meno di cento, quelli annessi alla dipendenza delle scuole normali governative, è alla dipendenza del Ministero della Pubbllca Istruzione, mentre tutti gli altri asili, a centinaia sparsi ovunque, sono sotto una vigilanza, molto limitata, del Ministero dell'Interno, donde un'altra prova manifesta del poco interessamento che ancora è preso in Italia per l'iniziazione dell'istruzione e dell'educazione infantile (2).

Può pertanto ripetersi col Paolini (3): « Finchè mancava l'istituzione dell'asilo,

(1) Tullio Fontana, *Manuale di legislazione scolastica* (Ditta G. B. Paravia, 1905).

(2) Gli on. Boselli e Credaro nel brevissimo tempo durante cui presiedettero al Ministero della P. I. prepararono un disegno di legge sugli Istituti infantili, ma troppo presto le vicende politiche tolsero dal Ministero della P. I. questi due illustri parlamentari la cui abilità e la cui tenacia davano sicuro affidamento che avrebbero saputo condurre in porto il loro disegno di legge e legare così i loro nomi ad una delle più belle e delle più urgenti leggi di cui abbisogni l'Italia.

(3) L. cit.

« forza era convergere con gli sforzi educativi nella scuola elementare; ma ora che « l'asilo ha preso un rilevante sviluppo e favorisce o *pregiudica* l'azione successiva « della scuola, ragion vuole che si disciplini l'asilo stesso, sì che serva di *razionale* « preparazione alla educazione ».

« Il vaut bien mieux s'adresser à un élève ne sachant rien qu'à celui qui ayant « été mal enseigné, a pu être ainsi détourné de l'enseignement qu'il s'agit de lui donner » ([1]). Così l'illustre LAISANT fin dal 1899 nella sua interessantissima conferenza mai abbastanza apprezzata e i cui principî, con ottimo pensiero ed in forma magistrale, furono poi svolti dal LAISANT stesso in quell'aureo libretto: *Initiation Mathématique*, che già meritò la fortuna e l'onore di due edizioni in francese e di una traduzione in italiano ([2]) e che ebbe il plauso e l'incoraggiamento universale.

Un movimento generale si è andato manifestando in questi ultimi tempi a favore dell'introduzione nell'insegnamento secondario, di concetti matematici che finora, stando ai programmi, furono ritardati fino all'Università: « l'insegnamento deve raggiungere il fine saviamente assegnatogli da ERNESTO RENAN, quello cioè di rendere tutti partecipi, se non dell'odierno lavoro scientifico, almeno dei risultati di « tale lavoro; e per raggiungere od almeno avvicinare tale scopo devonsi anzitutto « introdurre nel piano dell'istruzione secondaria, al più presto possibile, almeno alcune di quelle idee generali, che intervenendo di continuo ed efficacemente nelle « teorie matematiche moderne, possono dirsi costituirne il midollo spinale » ([3]); tali, ad esempio, i concetti di funzione, di corrispondenza, di trasformazione, gli elementi della geometria analitica, i concetti fondamentali del calcolo infinitesimale...

E a questo si giungerà presto, è ormai lecito affermarlo; male però vi si giungerà se, ripetendo l'errore altra volta commesso, si riformerà da un lato senza preoccuparsi del resto dell'edificio, che, quando sia modificato in una sua qualsiasi parte, vuol esser tutto riveduto, allo scopo di accertarsi se le sue condizioni statiche perdurino o se abbiano invece bisogno d'una corrispondente modificazione in altre parti: così nel 1904 con la legge Orlando (legge n. 407 concernente *provvedimenti per la scuola e pei maestri elementari*) si riformò la scuola elementare creando la scuola popolare di sei anni, e questa scuola è ormai un fatto compiuto essendo stata istituita anche la sesta classe in tutti i più importanti Comuni, ma, per quanto un apposito capoverso dell'art. 8 della citata legge ORLANDO ne facesse obbligo al Governo, non si riformarono, *nè vi si pensò ancora affatto*, le scuole normali, onde esiste la scuola popolare di sei anni ma non esistono maestri adatti ad essa, nè la scuola normale, così com'è ancora costituita, può assolutamente dare dei maestri con una preparazione adeguata al nuovo assetto della scuola popolare, nè a mio avviso all' insufficienza della scuola normale può interamente riparare la scuola

([1]) *L'éducation fondée sur la science* par C. A. LAISANT. Paris, 1905 (2ème édition, Félix Alcan, éditeur) pag. 4.

([2]) *Initiation mathématique.* Ouvrage étranger à tout programme, dédié aux amis de l'Enfance par C. A. LAISANT (avec 97 figures), Paris, Librairie Hachette (1ère édition 1906, 2ème édition 1907). Tradotta in italiano da G. LAZZERI nel 1908 (Firenze, G. Barbèra, editore).

([3]) GINO LORIA, *Programmi del passato e programmi per l'avvenire.* Conferenza tenuta a Milano il 22 aprile 1905 (cfr. Bollettino dell'Associazione Mathesis dell'anno 1905).

pedagogica, di recente creazione, quand'anche tale scuola sia sapientemente organizzata e diretta.

Urge dunque rivolgere l'attenzione verso la prima scuola, verso il primo insegnamento, verso l'iniziazione: « dans l'enfance, lorsque ses cases sont encore vides, « le cerveau enregistre tout et retient à peu près tout. *Mais plus tard, lorsque ses « cases sont remplies, il devient difficile d'y faire des surcharges.* Ce n'est pas qu'il « ne soit encore possible d'acquérir des connaissances nouvelles et de les emmaga-« siner dans l'encéphale. Mais il arrive alors ce qui arrive avec une armoire bondée: « on ne peut y placer un objet nouveau qu'à la condition d'y faire un vide en en « retirant un des objets qui y avaient été antérieurement placés. Ainsi en va-t-il de « notre mémoire. Arrivés a une certaine période de l'existence, nous sommes encore « capables de modifier notre bagage intellectuel; nous ne pouvons plus guère l'ac-« croître. Nous ne fixons une idée nouvelle qu'en oubliant une idée ancienne. Toute « acquisition est liée à une perte equivalente; et c'est ce que nous exprimons tous « en répétant sans cesse que nous sentons notre mémoire décliner à mesure que nous prenons des années ». Così il NAQUET nella sua magistrale prefazione alle conferenze del LAISANT sull'*Éducation fondée sur la science*, testè ricordate (1).

Ma si affaccia sovente la domanda: è mai possibile dare ad un fanciullo delle nozioni di matematica, senza assicurarsi se egli ha quelle *attitudini speciali* all'uopo richieste? A cui, non in questa sede può sorger dubbio sulla risposta da darsi: è ormai assodato che nell'affermare la necessità di queste speciali attitudini si commette una grande esagerazione e si cade in un vero equivoco. Si esagera in omaggio alla leggenda formatasi nelle scuole e nelle famiglie, leggenda diffusa all'estero cosicchè il LAISANT può dire: « l'algèbre passe, dans les familles pour la chose la plus dif-« ficile, la plus compliquée et la plus abstruse que l'on puisse imaginer » (2), e non meno diffusa in Italia ove, ad esempio, a far coraggio a taluno per uno studio qualsiasi a cui attenda, dicesi frequentemente: *non è mica algebra!*

E si equivoca in quanto si confonde fra le qualità intellettuali necessarie a chi intenda divenire dotto, in modo speciale, in matematica e quelle sufficienti per assimilare quell'insieme di cognizioni matematiche, elementari, di fondamento alla cultura generale di tutti, e tali da essere facilmente acquistate da chiunque abbia un cervello normale.

« Che per la matematica occorra l'intelligenza e non basti la memoria, d'accordo; « ma quando l'insegnante non esiga, specialmente nei fondamenti, una troppo minuta « analisi e una critica troppo sottile, che appartengono più alla filosofia che alla ma-« tematica, lo sviluppo intellettuale richiesto per comprendere la nostra scienza, nella « sua parte elementare, non può essere superiore a quello che è necessario per ogni « deduzione logica... Chi è capace di dedurre: *da quello vien questo, dopo quel-« l'altro vien quest'altro* ha capacità anche per gli elementari ragionamenti della « matematica » (3).

(1) Op. cit., Pe XVIII.

(2) Conferenza citata. Cfr. l'*Éducation fondée sur la science*, pag. 18.

(3) E. NANNEI, Relazione sulle « *Cause del poco profitto che fanno nello studio della matematica i giovani delle scuole medie* » [*Atti del III Congresso fra i professori di matematica delle*

Ed il LAISANT nella sua *Initiation mathématique*: (¹) « il existe en toute ma- « tière un fond général de connaissances utiles, nécessaires même à tout le monde, « et d'une acquisition facile, pour tout être dont le cerveau n'est pas atteint d'une « tare. L'ensemble de ces connaissances, *grâce à l'initiation préalable*, peut être « assimilé en un temps beaucoup plus court que celui qu'on y consacre dans l'ensei- « gnement habituel... Tout enfant peut, qu'il soit doué ou non d'une manière spé- « ciale, s'assimiler l'ensemble de ces connaissances, de même qu'il peut arriver à lire « et écrire avec correction sinon avec élégance... ».

Un'iniziazione dunque, *ma un'iniziazione razionale*: in essa, sopratutto, il segreto per evitare il manifestarsi di una specie di *idiosincrasia* per tutto ciò che abbia sapore matematico e sfatare la vieta leggenda, e destare fin dai primi anni un gusto vero e proprio, un interessamento, per gli elementi almeno, e sopratutto pel metodo d'indagine, caratteristico della nostra disciplina. Ma sia un'iniziazione razionale, inspirata a quei principî generali, che affermati fin da PLATONE (²) ed ARISTOTILE e pur da CICERONE e da QUINTILIANO, ebbero poi magistrale svolgimento da quei grandi pedagogisti, che si chiamarono FRÖEBEL, PESTALOZZI, LA CHALOTAIS, VITTORINO DA FELTRE, e particolarmente per la matematica, sia inspirata a quei criteri, attenendosi ai quali il LAISANT nell'opera già più volte rammentata, ha dimostrato luminosamente come sia possibile far penetrare nella mente del fanciullo i più fondamentali concetti matematici, con un metodo costantemente giocoso, *mai facendo appello alla memoria, mai obbligando il fanciullo a delle astrazioni che sono delle vere torture intellettuali,* ma piuttosto dicendogli: *fa' questo, fa' quest'altro, e adesso osserva, vedi, tocca... e poi scomponi pur tutto, e torna a rifare o questo giuoco o un altro, finchè tu senta di divertirti*; *appena ti sopraggiunga la stanchezza, la noia, passa a tutt'altro giuoco!* Così, e non altrimenti, il fanciullo, prima ancora di saper leggere e scrivere, si sarà formato un concetto assai chiaro del numero con quegli stessi bastoncelli che fan parte del comune materiale didattico per l'insegnamento col metodo fröbeliano; bastoncelli che, associati fra loro a mazzetti, a fasci, a scatole, a cassette ecc., fissano nella mente infantile il concetto delle unità dei differenti ordini di cui è composto un numero, e permettono di rappresentare in modo concreto dei numeri abbastanza grandi, *con gli elementi rappresentativi della loro unità, tutti esistenti sotto gli occhi del bambino.* Oggi invece, anche in giardini d'infanzia annessi a scuole normali governative, anche in giardini retti da maestre

---

scuole medie italiane promosso dall'Associazione Mathesis. Editi a Torino dalla Tip. degli Artigianelli, nel 1904].

(¹) Op. cit., 1ª ed. francese, a pag. 157.

(²) « Diceva PLATONE che nei primi anni della vita infantile bisognava allontanare tutte le « cause che potevano generare l'umor triste, che, dai tre ai sei anni i bambini dovevano giuocare « sotto la vigilanza di alcuni magistrati addetti all'educazione e chiamati pedagoghi. Più tardi « ARISTOTELE affermò che gli adulti dovevano, coi giuochi, iniziare i fanciulli alle serie funzioni « della vita. Anche CICERONE disse che non bisognava impedire, ma svolgere la viva tendenza dei « bambini, ai giuochi. QUINTILIANO affermò che a lui non piacevano punto i bambini che non ave- « vano voglia di giuocare » (Dal volume di AMALIA DE ROSA: *FEDERICO FRÖBEL e il suo sistema d'educazione.* Napoli, 1896, tip. PAGNOTTA).

giardiniere senza dubbio colte e piene di buone attitudini e di buova volonta si dànno, per esempio, in mano al bimbo 10 bastoncelli e gli si dice di contare da uno a dieci, senza fargli comporre separatamente i gruppi di uno, di due, di tre... bastoncelli; e, quel ch'è peggio, con questi stessi 10 bastoncelli si dice al bimbo: quando sei arrivato a 10 ricomincia dal primo e prosegui dicendo undici... e così via, anche fino a 20, anche fino a 30... e il bimbo — anzi spesso il coro dei bimbi — conta 20, conta 30... conta 100 e ha sempre dinanzi a sè 10 bastoncelli soltanto e non si persuade, nè può davvero persuadersi, come mai con quegli stessi 10 oggetti sia arrivato a 20, a 30... a 100! Questo non è metodo fröbeliano davvero!... Questo è seminare dell' idiosincrasia, dell'avversione per tutto ciò che sappia di numero e di matematica!

Già coi bastoncelli, associati a mazzetti (a dieci a dieci), a fasci (di dieci mazzetti ognuno) possono i bimbi comporre numeri fino a 999 e far delle addizioni e delle sottrazioni in una forma che è ancora di vero giuoco, in quanto consiste nel muovere ora in un senso ed ora in un altro dei mazzetti, dei bastoncelli, nel formare nuovi mazzetti, nuovi fasci, nel disfare qualche mazzetto, qualche fascio; e con bastoncelli, o meglio ancora con dei piccoli chicchi di grano, con dei semi, con dei fagioli i nostri bimbi possono comporsi la cosiddetta tavola pitagorica ed incominciare ad acquistare la pratica di tutte le operazioni fondamentali, pur non sapendo ancora nè leggere nè scrivere, nè conoscendo ancora le *cifre* comunemente usate per la rappresentazione dei numeri. Già fissato un primo concetto di numero, apparirà assai spontaneo che anzichè continuare a fare uso soltanto di bastoncelli, che costituiscono un materiale piuttosto ingombrante per numeri d'una certa grandezza, si faccia appello alle nozioni familiari di moneta e di scambio fra monete di diverso valore: adoperando, pei numeri minori di *cento* delle monete da 10 centesimi e da 1 centesimo come rappresentanti della diecina e dell'unità e, tanto pei numeri minori di 100 quanto per numeri maggiori, dei gettoni di diverso colore, si intratterranno i bimbi in altri giuochi, durante i quali daccapo comporranno agevolmente dei numeri ed eseguiranno delle addizioni e delle sottrazioni senza incontrar difficoltà alcuna, e delle prime moltiplicazioni e divisioni, nei loro più elementari casi.

Per la Geometria, la prima iniziazione sarà pure agevolmente compiuta e sapientemente diretta quando si dica al bimbo di guardare attorno a sè: lo circondano dappertutto corpi che, colla forma loro complessiva e con quella delle loro parti valgono a destare i più elementari concetti geometrici di retta, di piano, di figure piane, con contorno rettilineo, di cerchio, di poliedro, di corpo rotondo di rotazione; *nel disegno e nella carta quadrettata,* se a quadretti piccoli specialmente, sta uno dei maggiori ausilii per questo primo avviamento alla geometria; la *piegatura della carta*, il cosiddetto *ritaglio geometrico* sono altri ottimi mezzi ausiliarî per questo primo avviamento.

Per le figure geometriche solide non è certamente col solo disegno che devono istillarsi i primi concetti nelle tenere menti infantili: bisogna condurre i bimbi stessi a costruirsi le principali figure poliedriche. Nè si obietterà che perciò si richiedano delle abilità manuali particolari; ciò potrebbe dirsi se si pensasse soltanto alla costruzione di tali figure col cartone, col fil di ferro, colla creta, ma si può far uso di mezzi anche più semplici e maggiormente alla portata dei bimbi dai quattro ai sei anni: dei cubettini di sughero, forati da parte a parte in corrispondenza al centro di ciascuna faccia, e dei bastoncelli soliti, di quelli che, a mazzi, fan parte del materiale per l'insegnamento col metodo fröbeliano; ed ecco quanto basta — è il giuochetto *The wood and cork worker,* in vendita sotto marca inglese, presso i principali negozî di giuocattoli — per formare, in brevissimo tempo molti solidi geometrici, regolari e irregolari, il cui numero e la cui varietà dipendono dal numero e dalla lunghezza dei bastoncelli e dalla quantità dei cubetti di sughero messa a disposizione del bimbo.

Beninteso che questo metodo giocoso deve proseguire fino a che il fanciullo non entri nella scuola media: non è soltanto nel Giardino d'infanzia che l'iniziazione matematica deve esser condotta coi criterî precedentemente spiegati, deve bensì proseguire per tutto il corso elementare, ove invece — in Italia e anche all'estero, in Francia certamente come è affermato dal Laisant [1] — i fanciulli sono oppressi da un vero e proprio studio, e costretti, in massima parte, ad un tormentoso lavoro mnemonico, e inceppati da un formalismo, secondo il quale tutti i calcoli devono esser fatti seguendo *certe determinate disposizioni e soltanto quelle,* formalismo da cui, specialmente, deriva che la scuola, troppo spesso, sopprima o indebolisca attitudini spontanee di agilità e prontezza intellettuale, diguisachè, sovente, in confronto agli alunni delle nostre scuole, con maggiore sicurezza e con maggiore rapidità, vengano effettuati dei calcoli, anche complicati, da persone analfabete. E per la geometria, quante sono le scuole elementari ove i fanciulli sono condotti a persuadersi *con delle effettive constatazioni*, delle più notevoli proprietà delle figure geometriche? anche quando si tratta della trasformazione delle figure piane, così agevolmente spiegabile con un po' di carta ed un paio di forbici!

Ma è doveroso constatare che se, purtroppo, è questo ancora l'indirizzo prevalente nella scuola elementare italiana, tale non dovrebbe mantenersi ove i maestri elementari *potessero e sapessero* attenersi più fedelmente allo *spirito* delle istruzioni che accompagnano gli ultimi programmi per le scuole elementari approvate con R. Decreto 29 gennaio 1905.

Vero è peraltro che alla bontà dei *criteri generali* di queste istruzioni ai programmi, non corrisponde altrettanta bontà da parte dei programmi e neppure delle istruzioni stesse, là dove il legislatore è entrato nei particolari, essendovi pure qualche grosso errore, tuttora lasciatovi, quantunque ne sia stato prontamente, e pubblicamente, fatto lamento [2].

Ma insomma, per quanto riguarda le scuole elementari, non è come per gli asili infantili pei quali v'è tutto da fare, ossia non c'è da lamentarsi di una assoluta mancanza di disposizioni legislative; ci sono, e provvedono con criteri generali assai buoni, all'avviamento alla matematica; sennonchè nella scuola elementare italiana, anche dopo la riforma del 1904 e i programmi del 1905, vi sono troppe cose che

[1] Op. cit.

[2] Cfr. Frattini, Articolo critico sui nuovi programmi per le scuole elementari (Pubblicato nel giornale « La Scuola Educatrice » del 1905). Cfr. A. Conti, *Aritmetica razionale* (3ª ediz. Bologna, Casa ed. Zanichelli, 1906).

distraggono gli insegnanti e gli alunni da quello che v'è di più fondamentale per l'iniziazione di questi allo studio della lingua nazionale e della matematica.

È bensì vero che nella parte generale delle Istruzioni citate si legge: (1) « I « programmi non debbono esser mai interpretati estensivamente... La divisione for« malmente necessaria dei programmi e delle relative istruzioni per materia e per « argomento non devesi intendere come una dissociazione dei varî rami di studio: « questi debbono invece esser trattati in continua connessione fra loro con metodo « sintetico ed intuitivo... ». Con questi e con altri ottimi precetti il legislatore ha voluto prevenire un pericolo da esso stesso presentito, che cioè dinanzi a un programma ove compaiono distintamente tanti diversi titoli: lingua italiana, aritmetica e geometria, calligrafia, disegno, nozioni varie, racconti storici, nozioni di geografia ecc. il maestro credesse di dover frazionare l'orario quotidiano in quarti d'ora e mezz'ore dedicate alla storia, alla geografia, al disegno, alle nozioni varie...

Ma nonostante questi buoni precetti è generalmente accaduto proprio quello di cui il legislatore aveva mostrato di preoccuparsi, vuoi perchè di solito non si leggono nemmeno o, leggendole, non si meditano abbastanza le istruzioni allegate ai programmi ufficiali, quasi per timore di averne diminuita la propria individualità, vuoi, sopratutto, perchè di molti Comuni, anche importanti e notoriamente solleciti di cure per l'istruzione, i programmi e le istruzioni governative vengono a poco a poco interamente travisati in programmi e istruzioni particolareggiate, che davvero attentano all'individualità dell'insegnante, inceppandone ogni personale iniziativa con disposizioni che di bimestre in bimestre, di settimana in settimana, di giorno in giorno, d'ora in ora vengono sbocconcellando l'insegnamento e togliendogli tutto quel carattere sintetico ed intuitivo raccomandato dal legislatore.

Ecco perchè, anche per l'insegnamento delle prime nozioni di matematica nelle scuole elementari, i maestri *non possono*, generalmente, attenersi ai criterî, buoni in massima, suggeriti dalle istruzioni governative. *Non possono*; ma quanti fra essi, anche potendo, *saprebbero* interpretare realmente il pensiero del legislatore?

Con quale preparazione matematica si presentano essi all'esercizio del loro magistero? La loro iniziazione si è compiuta nel modo assai imperfetto, su cui già ci siamo intrattenuti; la loro istruzione è proseguita nella scuola tecnica o nella scuola complementare, e poi nei tre corsi che costituiscono, in Italia, la scuola normale propriamente detta, tre corsi ove, per dar posto a un numero considerevolissimo d'insegnamenti, tutti addensati in questi tre anni, si è riserbato alla matematica un orario insufficientissimo; di *due* ore settimanali, con un programma d'aritmetica razionale, di geometria piana e solida, di algebra, di metodologia, di computisteria ed economia domestica... e con l'obbligo di una prova scritta d'esame, la cui istituzione, di data recente (2), fu accolta, sì, con piacere dagli insegnanti, i quali però avrebbero desiderato che, contemporaneamente, fosse stato accresciuto l'orario del loro insegnamento, per avere il tempo necessario per un'adeguata preparazione alla prova predetta.

I programmi per l'insegnamento della matematica nelle scuole complementari e

(1) Boll. Uff. del Min. della P. I. del 2 marzo 1905.

(2) Introdotta col Regolamento sugli esami del 1904.

nelle scuole normali sono ancora quelli pei quali, fino da sette anni fa, un Congresso promosso dall'Associazione Mathesis [1] espresse il voto che i programmi stessi fossero riformati, in modo da toglierne certe notevoli sproporzioni esistenti nelle classi complementari e certe assurdità, specialmente per le classi normali, ove, tanto per dare qualche esempio tipico, si raccomanda, nelle annesse istruzioni, di insegnare, nella prima classe, la geometria *col metodo deduttivo,* e pertanto si pone nella classe prima l'argomento della misura della circonferenza e del cerchio, e nella classe seconda la teoria della proporzionalità, e quella della similitudine dei poligoni!... e così si pone nella prima classe la teoria della misura delle figure piane e nella seconda classe i concetti di numero, di rapporto e di proporzione!

L'angustia dell'orario assegnato alle lezioni di matematica nelle scuole normali non permette di intrattenere gli allievi e le allieve così come occorrerebbe, sui mezzi più idonei a rendere efficace l'insegnamento dell'aritmetica e geometria nelle scuole primarie: v'è appena il tempo di sfiorare qualche cosa, quando se ne presenti l'occasione nell'esposizione delle varie teorie, e il meglio che rimane a farsi è di rinviare gli allievi e le allieve alla lettura e alla meditazione di alcuni buoni libri di metodo, di cui, fortunatamente, non v'è difetto in Italia dacchè il Bustelli, il Ciamberlini, il Frizzo, in eccellenti pubblicazioni [2] raccolsero il frutto dei loro pazienti studi e della loro esperienza per agevolare ai maestri il modo di far penetrare nella mente del fanciullo dei sani concetti matematici, senza sforzo del bimbo anzi con suo diletto e interessamento.

Il maestro « nelle scuole elementari *istilla*, mentre nelle scuole medie *espone* « e nelle scuole superiori *discute*; l'idea che dall'insegnante, coll'attrazione della « persuadente parola penetra nel cervello del fanciullo, che frequenta la scuola « primaria, vi resta come nel granito scolpita. Se questa idea non è esatta per quanto « altri tenti successivamente di sradicarla o rettificarla, essa, molto probabilmente, « sotto forma meno rigida ed assoluta, riapparirà, e sarà d'uopo che i nuovi istitu- « tori adoperino una cura costante, affettuosa ed intelligente, perchè l'erroneo con- « cetto venga interamente eliminato dalla mente del fanciullo » [3].

Di ciò giustamente preoccupandosi, gli insegnanti di matematica delle scuole normali curano, in modo speciale, l'esattezza del loro linguaggio, e non tralasciano occasione per dare, ai loro alunni e alle loro alunne, dei consigli, sia d'indole generale, sia su particolari argomenti, affinchè essi sappiano *quante e quali idee matematiche* possano *istillarsi* nelle tenere menti infantili senza perciò torturare i fanciulli, anzi divertendoli... Ma quel poco a cui essi arrivano, nelle angustie dell'orario tra cui devono dibattersi è generalmente, e quasi per intero, neutralizzato

[1] Cfr. A. Conti, Relazione sull'insegnamento della matematica nelle scuole normali. Atti del II Congresso dei professori di matematica delle scuole medie italiane promosso dall'associazione Mathesis. Livorno 1901, tip. R. Giusti.

[2] A. Maria Bustelli, *L'insegnamento dell'aritmetica e della geometria nelle scuole primarie,* (tip. Lapi, Città di Castello 1889). C. Ciamberlini, *Sull'insegnamento dell'aritmetica pratica e della geometria nelle scuole primarie,* 2ª ed., Bologna, tip. Zanichelli, 1902. G. Frizzo, *L'insegnamento della matematica nelle scuole primarie* (Padova, Fratelli Drucker), 1898.

[3] G. Frizzo, op. cit.

dalla assoluta mancanza di coordinazione fra i varî indirizzi a cui sono improntati gli insegnamenti impartiti agli allievi-maestri, e in special modo fra l'indirizzo metodologico particolare a ciascun insegnante per la propria disciplina e quello che per tutte le discipline è improntato alle vedute dell'insegnante di pedagogia, del direttore della scuola normale e dei maestri delle classi elementari di tirocinio annesse alle scuole normali.

Con l'attuale ordinamento delle scuole normali e con le vigenti disposizioni relative al tirocinio accade non di rado che l'allievo-maestro si trovi dinanzi *almeno* a tre indirizzi diversi: a quale egli deve attenersi?

Si tratta, ad esempio, d'una lezione per la quarta elementare sulle figure piane e sulle regole per misurare la superficie dei principali poligoni (i temi delle lezioni sono assegnati ai tirocinanti dall'insegnante di pedagogia, d'accordo coi maestri delle classi di tirocinio). L'insegnante di matematica, domandato di qualche consiglio, oppure in altra occasione, mostra agli allievi che v'è modo di portare i fanciulli a conoscenza delle più importanti proprietà della equivalenza dei poligoni fino anche a quella di Pitagora senza perciò affaticar troppo i ragazzi, anzi divertendoli a disegnare, a tagliare, a incollare, a colorire, a osservare... Ma l'insegnante di pedagogia o il direttore della scuola o il maestro o la maestra della classe di tirocinio osserveranno, sovente, all'allievo-maestro che sta tutto bene quello che ha insegnato il professore di matematica, ma che per questi giuochi e trastulli ci vuol del tempo, a scapito di tutto il *programma* da svolgersi (di lingua, di storia, di geografia, di nozioni varie, di disegno, di calligrafia...) mentre che è così comodo dire al fanciullo che la superficie del rettangolo si misura moltiplicando la base per l'altezza e analogamente pel triangolo, per il trapezio... Il bambino, osserveranno ancora all'allievo-maestro, impara subito (*a memoria*) queste regolette ed è in grado di fare degli esercizi numerici, acquistando sempre maggiore abilità di calcolo e assimilando ugualmente (?) queste nuove nozioni geometriche...

Altra volta si tratterà d'una lezione sui cambiamenti d'unità di misura, sul sistema metrico decimale insomma: l'insegnante di matematica avrà spiegato tutta *l'inesattezza delle uguaglianze del genere delle seguenti*:

$$\text{km } 5 = \text{km } 5 \times 1000 = \text{m. } 5000 \quad ; \quad \text{hg } 250 = \text{hg } 250 : 10 = \text{kg } 25 \text{ ecc.}$$

Pertanto l'allievo-maestro troverà, non di rado, che gli alunni della scuola elementare sono abituati appunto a dire che si trasformano chilometri in metri moltiplicando per 1000 e così kg in grammi, e a scrivere delle uguaglianze del genere suaccennato; se si proverà a correggere, a modificare tale abitudini, non sarà improbabile che gli si dica che queste sono *pedanterie*... non si osa dire però altrettanto per gli errori di grammatica e di sintassi, anche quando questi possano considerarsi come semplici errori di forma e non di concetto!

Che cosa dovrà fare perciò l'insegnante di matematica? Egli persevererà nell'opera sua con tenacia e con fede, in attesa di tempi migliori e d'ulteriori e più felici e più precise disposizioni legislative, che conducano a un effettivo miglioramento della preparazione matematica dei maestri elementari e quindi, con una più razionale iniziazione allo studio della matematica, contribuiscano a render sempre migliori l'istruzione e l'educazione scientifica delle future generazioni!

Z. G. DE GALDEANO

QUELQUES MOTS SUR L'ENSEIGNEMENT MATHÉMATIQUE EN ESPAGNE

Je vous prie de me pardonner si je vous importune quelques minutes; parce que n'ayant pu hier assister au Congrès, je n'ai pu rien dire concernant l'enseignement en Espagne. Je vais m'exprimer télégraphiquement.

Malgré quelques tentatives individuels, les luttes de la politique ont dominé en Espagne, au point qu'aucune école de mathématiques ne put jamais y prendre racine; et depuis un demi siècle aucun législateur n'a donné un plan complet d'enseignement, qui est resté cristallisée.

Cependant il y a presqu'un mois, les premières intelligences d'Espagne, unies dans une seule pensée, se sont groupées pour constituer l'*Asociacion española para el progreso de las ciencias*, et ont décidé que le premier Congrès scientifique aura lieu à Saragosse au mois d'octobre, comme premier acte public de la dite association, et d'une rennaissance des sciences, notamment positives.

En Mathématiques, les plus récentes théories commencent à prendre une place dans l'enseignement, presqu'aux embranchements de la Physique mathématique qui expliquent M. ECHEGARAY et TERRADAS à Madrid et à Barcelona. Les noms de THOMSON, MAXWELL, GIBBS, LORENTZ, etc., et ceux de M. CANTOR, DARBOUX, KLEIN, POINCARÉ, PICARD, etc., sont déjà connus par leurs ouvrages.

Moyennant la publication de la *Nueva enciclopedia matematica* et d'autres ouvrages philosophiques et pedagogiques, j'ai intenté réunir ces modernes vues de la Mathématique. Parce que, contre la difficulté du progrès indéfini de la science, il faut employer les méthodes pédagogiques, en vue d'établir l'équilibre entre celui-là et la potentialité intellectuelle.

En résumé, le schematisme, par des images embrassant les systèmes, le cycle qu'imite la Nature dans la croissance par *intus-suceptionem* et l'élémentalisation, qui place chaque nouvelle idée ou théorie dans le lieu qui lui corresponde, dans l'état d'équilibre du système, sont les trois moyens qui donnent les conditions pour l'égalité de l'effort intellectuel et la resistance toujours croissante qui offre la variété à présént très considérable dans le domaine de la science.

E. BEKE

UEBER DEN JETZIGEN STAND DES MATHEMATISCHEN UNTERRICHTES UND DIE REFORMBESTREBUNGEN IN UNGARN

In kurzen Worten will ich über den mathematischen Unterricht in Ungarn berichten um dann die Bestrebungen zu bezeichnen, die bei uns in Bezug auf die Umgestaltung und Ergänzung dieses Unterrichtes im Gange sind.

Die ungarischen Mittelschulen sind zweierlei: Gymnasien und Realschulen, beide 8 klassig. Wir könnten aber auch mit einer kleinen Uebertreibung behaupten, dass vier verschiedene Lehrgänge bestehen; denn im Gymnasium hat der Schüler die Wahl zwischen Latein mit Griechisch und Latein ohne Griechisch, während er in der Realschule facultativ Latein lernen kann.

Der Lehrstoff des Mathematischen Unterrichts ist in beiden Schulen beinahe derselbe: in den unteren 3 Klassen Rechenunterricht, in den folgenden 5 Klassen Algebra welche mit den quadratischen Gleichungen und den Elementen der Combinatorik, abschliesst, der Geometrische Unterricht ist in den unteren 4 Klassen ein propedeutischer um die geometrische Anschauung zu entwickeln, und mit Cirkel und Lineal einfache Constructionen ausführen zu können, in den oberen 4 Klassen wird Geometrie, Trigonometrie, auch einiges aus der sphaerischen Trigonometrie gelehrt, in den Realschulen auch analytische Geometrie, in den oberen 3 Klassen dieser Schule auch Darstellende Geometrie resp. Orthogonale Projection. In den Gymnasien fehlt die Darstellende Geometrie gänzlich, hingegen wird der Koordinatenbegriff im Anschluss an die Behandlung der Functionen erster und zweiter Ordnung in die Algebra eingeführt.

Der Lehrstoff selbst macht wohl noch nicht den Unterricht aus. Das allerwichtigste ist die Methode, die Behandlung des Stoffes. Und da kann ich Ihnen sagen, dass bei uns in Ungarn die Mathematik wohl schon lange her, einzelne Ausnahmen ausgenommen, in völlig rationeller, modern paedagogischer Weise behandelt wird; der Rechenunterricht ist praktisch angelegt, ist in steter Verbindung mit dem alltäglichen Leben und dient dazu, um in den Schülern ein Interesse für die zahlenmässige Behandlung aller, in ihren Gesichtskreis gehörenden Dinge zu erwecken, und damit auch die wirtschaftliche Erziehung vorzubereiten. Das Rechnen bewegt sich an vielen Schulen in sogenannten Sachkreisen und wird der Wirklichkeit entnommenen und auch sachlich zusammenhängenden Aufgaben geführt. Der officielle Lehrplan bezeichnet sogar die sachlichen Kreise, aus denen die Rechenaufgaben zu nehmen seien, um dadurch auch die Sachkenntniss der Schüler zu vertiefen. Der praktische Sinn, der stete Zusammenhang mit der Wirklichkeit, und womöglich eine sachliche Grundlage charakterisirt den ungarischen math. Unterricht: die volkswirtschaftlichen Momente in dem algebraischen Unterricht überhaupt im Zusammenhang mit der Zinseszinsenrechung und auch in Anwendug auf die allereinfachsten Grundbegriffe der Wahrscheinlichkeitsrechnung, die Feldmessung in der Geometrie, physikalische und andere sachliche Verhältnisse werden stets in dem mathematischen Unterricht herangezogen. Dass der Unterricht zumeist heuristisch ist, was Herrn Marotte in deutschen Schulen so sehr gefiel, ist so selbstverständlich, dass wir in Ungarn daran garnicht denken können, dass im mathematischen Unterrichte auch ein anderer Vorgang, als die fortwährende Beschäftigung der ganzen Klasse, und das intensive Zusammenarbeiten des Lehrers und der Schüler zum Ziele führen könne.

Nun will ich Ihnen über unsere Reformbestrebungen einiges sagen. Im Grossen und Ganzen stehen wir alle unter dem Einfluss der Bewegung welche von Herrn Prof. Klein inaugurirt und von der deutschen Comission weiter gefördert wurde. Die Reformbewegung gerieth bei uns eigentlich vor 2 Jahren in Fluss, als ich auf der Jahresversammlung des ung. Professorenvereins die Ziele und die Aufgaben der ungarischen Bewegung bezeichnete. Der Landesverein der Professoren constituirte dann unter meinem Vorsitz eine Comission, bestehend aus den bedeutendsten Mittelschullehrern, und ausser mir noch aus zwei Hochschullehrern. Seither beschäftigte sich diese Commission eingehend mit den Fragen des mathematischen Unterrichts, jedes Mitglied der Comission eine wichtige Frage behandelnd.

Die Bestrebungen kann ich im Anschlusse an die bekannten auswärtigen Bestrebungen in kurzen Worten bezeichnen. Perry betont das *Practische* in dem math. Unterricht; Klein charakterisirt die ganze Bestrebung in dem kurzen, ein ganzes Programm bedeutenden Ausdrucke des *functionalen Denkens*. Unsere Comission ging ebenfalls in dieser Richtung; das konnten wir um so eher thun, als wir in beiden Beziehungen in unserem Lehrplan gehörige Vorbereitung hatten; mehr als z. B. in Deutschland. Was das praktische in dem Unterricht anbelangt, darauf wies ich schon hin, und das functionale Denken lag auch nicht weit von unseren früheren Bestrebungen, da dank des Einflusses, den schon in den 70er Jahren Professor J. König und unser aufgeklärte Pädagoge M. von Kármán in Bezug des Lehrplanes ausübten, die Behandlung der Functionen erster und zweiter Ordnung, sogar die Behandlung der extremen Werthe dieser Function in unseren Lehrplan aufgenommen wurde. Den erwähnten Gesichtspunkten fügte unsere Comission noch das *wirtschaftliche Interesse* hinzu, da nach unserer Auffassung eine der Hauptaufgaben des mathematischen Unterrichtes die Entwickelung des allgemeinen volkswirtschaftlichen Sinnes sei.

Unser Programm besteht also im Folgenden: eine bedeutende *Reduction* des Lehrstoffes, aus welchem alles überflüssige, zufällige, aus alten Lehrplänen übernommene auszuscheiden sei, eine *ökonomische Behandlung* des Stoffes z. B. in dem Sinne, dass die Geometrie jeher rechnerisch vorgehen und damit die verschiedenen Umwege beseitigen könne, die Einführung der *graphischen Behandlung* von den allerersten Schritten an, um dadurch den ganzen Lehrstoff anschaulicher zu gestalten, die *Einführung der Elemente der Differential und Integralrechnung* um dadurch einerseits die stereometrischen Berechnungen zu vereinfachen, den physikalischen Unterricht aufrichtiger und intensiver zu gestalten und die allgemeine mathematische Bildung der kommenden Generationen zu heben; die tiefere mathematische Erziehung durch Entwickelung des *functionalen Denkens* von den allerersten Anfängen an, eine naturgemässe *Verschmelzung des stereometrischen* und planimetrischen Unterrichtes mit *Heranziehung der Elemente der darstellenden* Geometrie, und in jeder Beziehung die *engste Anschliessung* der Mathematik an die Wirklichkeit.

Unsere Comission ist mit ihrer Arbeit beinahe fertig; eines unserer Mitglieder, Herr GOLDZIHER stellte die ganze Biographie der Reformbestrebungen zusammen, und in unserem Musee paedagogique werden alle, sich auf die Reformbestrebungen beziehenden Veröffentlichungen gesammelt; derselbe referirte auch darüber wie diese Bestrebungen sich in den verschiedensten Ländern gestalten; es wurden die sämmtlichen mathematischen Lehrpläne behandelt, die verschiedenen möglichen Reductionen, die durchgehende functionale Behandlung des ganzen Lehrstoffes ins einzelne, die Einschaltung der darstellenden Geometrie, der Zusammenhang mit dem physikalischen Unterricht, die heranzuziehenden Elemente der Differential und Integralrechnung besprochen, in welcher Beziehung eine in der University Extension gehaltene aus 6 Vorlesungen bestehende Differential und Integralrechnung gute Dienste leistete. Die Verhandlungen der Comission, welche sich auf die erwähnten Momente und auf mehrere andere Fragen beziehen, werden in nicht langer Zeit publicirt, um sämmtliche Lehrer mit den Bestrebungen der Comission zu befreunden.

Ich weiss, dass die wichtigste Frage, die Sie an mich stellen würden, die ist, wie das Alles ins Praktische übertragen wird. Da kann ich Ihnen nur sagen, dass wir alle in dieser Beziehung die Franzosen beneiden. Sie sprachen nicht viel, sie verhandelten nicht zu lange, sondern dem kaum ausgesprochenen Wort folgte die That: Die Werke TANNERY's und BOREL's sind die am deutlichsten sprechende Thaten. Wir in Ungarn hoffen auch, dass wir nicht den beschwerlichen, langen Weg des Experimentirens, gehen werden müssen, denn im Wetteifern der Schulen werden die Erfolge sehr oft fälschlich gedeutet und dadurch auch der Fortschritt gefährdet. Wir hoffen nämlich dass der gründliche, bis ins Einzelne ausgearbeitete Vorschlag der Comission einerseits die Behörde, andererseits die Lehrer von der Nothwendigkeit und Zweckmässigkeit des Fortschrittes überzeugen wird.

Der wirkliche Erfolg hängt aber von den Lehrern ab. Die Organisation und der Lehrplan und Alles, was daran hängt bildet nur den Rahmen; Leben und Geist in die Schüler bringt nur der Lehrer. Und das ist eben eine der wichtigsten Fragen, mit welcher sich unsere Comission befasst. Die Ausbildung der Lehrer muss praktischer werden, die Universität muss sich in dieser Beziehung den Ausprüchen der Mittelschule besser anpassen. Die angewandte Mathematik muss auch bei uns, wenn auch nicht in solchem, vielleicht zu weit gehenden Masse, wie in Deutschland zu ihren Rechten kommen. Nach unserer Auffassung muss ein jeder aus der Fülle schöpfen; um gut das gewöhnliche Rechnen unterrichten zu können, muss sich der Lehrer mit kaufmännischem Rechnen, mit politischer Arithmetik, oder wie M. CANTOR sagt mit dem Rechnen des täglichen Lebens genau bekannt machen und um in den Schülern ein volkwirtschaftliches Interesse zu entwickeln, muss er selbst, wenigstens encyclopaedisch Nationaloekonomie und auch Statistik studieren; um Trigonometrie gut und sachlich unterrichten zu können, muss er wenigstens in den Grundzügen die Geodesie und Astronomie studieren nicht um etwa diese Wissenszweige in die Mittelschule zu tragen, sondern um dem, in der Schule Vorzutragendem eine sichere, breitere Unterlage verschaffen, um auch das Kleinste aus dem Grossen nehmen zu können. Das ist unserer Ansicht nach die allererste Aufgabe, mit welcher wir uns zu befassen haben, und sie ist auch die schwierigste Aufgabe; denn in Ungarn haben wir leider nur 2 Universitäten, wir sind also nicht in der glücklichen Lage, wie z. B. Italien, wo so viele sich auch ex offo mit der höheren Wissenschaft befassen. Bei uns müssen auch mehrere Mittelschullehrer Arbeiter der Wissenschaft sein und dazu ist es nöthig, dass sie eine genügend breite wissenschaftliche Ausbildug bekommen; wie dann diese theoretische Ausbildung auch praktisch vertieft, in Bezug auf die Mittelschule wertvoller, philosophisch tiefer, allgemeiner zu machen wäre, damit müssen wir uns — ich glaube aber auch in allen anderen Ländern, Sie alle — beschäftigen. Das ist, vie ich erwähnte das schwierigste Problem der Reformbestrebungen.

Wir sind also, wie Sie sehen, auch am Wege, den mathematischen Unterricht in gehörigem Sinne umzugestalten. Viel Erfolg können wir in dieser Richtung noch nicht aufweisen, aber doch ist das Eis schon gebrochen; in einzelnen Schulen wird schon jetzt Differential- ünd Integralrechnung vorgetragen; sogar in einem Mädchengymnasium; sogar die Maturitäts-Aufgabe war ein Maximumproblem, welches eine tüchtige Differentiation erforderte. Nach meiner Erfahrung befasst sich die Jugend sehr gerne damit; in zwei meiner Volkshochschulklassen nahmen sehr viele Schüler aus den Mittelschulen teil und arbeiteten tüchtig; in einer, für Mittelschüler verfassten Zeitschrift, welche einer unserer Comissionsmitglieder L. Rátz, redigirt, finden die, aus der Infinitesimalrechung genommenen Aufgaben die meisten Auflösungen.

Der Erfolg ist im Anwachsen, aber, wie es scheint, werden wir auch mit Gegnern zu kämpfen haben. Ich spreche nicht von denjenigen, die überhaupt einer jeden Änderung gegenüber sich feindselig verhalten; ich meine diejenigen, welche es vom wissenschaftlichem Standpunkte aus nicht für möglich halten die Infinitesimalrechung erfolgreich in den Mittelschulen zu behandeln und es als einen wissenschaftlichen Rückgang betrachten, wenn diese Fragen wieder ohne wissenschaftliche Strenge behandelt werden; andere hingegen — und damit ist man auch schon öffentlich hervogetreten — fürchten eine neue Ueberbürdung. Den ersteren gegenüber sind wir bewaffnet mit Picard's Auffassung, dass wenn bei der ersten Behandlung der Dinge gleich die wissenschaftliche Strenge hervortreten würde, die grössten Entdeckungen überhaupt ausbleiben möchten. Die guten alten Zeiten, wo wir als Kinder aus Navier und Lübsen unsere ersten Kenntnisse zogen, waren nicht so schlecht, wie man es glaubt. Den anderen antwortete schon unsere Comission damit, dass sie in dem Verein der Schulärzte, wo die Frage der Ueberbürdung aufgeworfen wurde, die Herrn Ärzte überzeugen konnten, dass wir auf eine Reduction und durch die bessere, ökonomische Behandlung des Lehrstoffes, trotz der neu hinzutretenden Elemente auf eine Erleichterung des mathematischen Unterrichtes hinzielen. Natürlich vorausgesetzt, was in Schulangelgenheiten das Alfa und Omega ist: dass wir gute, wissenschaftlich und practisch ausgebildete, philosophisch und paedagogisch geschulte, human denkende und fühlende und vor Allem, den Lehrstoff völlig beherschende Lehrer besitzen. Damit schliesse ich in der Hoffnung, dass Sie uns Ungarn als Ihre fleissige, strebsame Mitarbeiter betrachten, die mit Ihnen gemeinschaftlich auf eine Evolution des math. Unterrichtes hinarbeiten.

G. GALLUCCI

LA QUISTIONE LOGICA E LA QUISTIONE GNOSEOLOGICA NEI PRINCIPII DELLA MATEMATICA

Gli studî critici sui principî delle matematiche hanno ultimamente assunto tale sviluppo da costituire da sè soli un nuovo ramo della scienza. Se si volessero raccogliere tutte le monografie e discussioni sull'importante argomento, dai poderosi lavori pubblicati dalla scuola di WUNDT nei *Philosophische Studien*, ai notevoli articoli della *Revue de Métaphisique* e della *Rivista di matematica*, si verrebbero a formare parecchi grossi volumi; senza contare gli sviluppi di metodologia scientifica, che si trovano nei già classici trattati di logica da STUART-MILL a WUNDT e SIGWART. E già molte questioni sono mature per una trattazione sistematica come lo dimostra la comparsa di volumi recentissimi, che hanno arricchita la letteratura scientifica, opere dovute a matematici del più alto valore: POINCARÉ, ENRIQUES, HILBERT. Tutto questo movimento del pensiero scientifico contemporaneo s' inquadra meravigliosamente nello sviluppo che ha avuto la filosofia dopo la grande rivoluzione kantiana.

Chi, da semplice spettatore, assiste allo svolgersi delle varie discussioni, le quali talvolta prendono forma di vivace polemica, è preso da un certo sbalordimento. Anche a prescindere dalla naturale difficoltà delle questioni, la multiplicità dei punti di vista sotto cui sono guardate da filosofi e matematici di varie scuole è un serio ostacolo per l'esatta comprensione dello stato attuale dei varî problemi. Spesso ci si trova davanti a scienziati che non s'intendono perchè parlano linguaggi diversi; ed anche quando si ha la fortuna di incontrarne due che vanno d'accordo, si deve purtroppo notare qualche discrepanza in quistioni di non secondario interesse.

Per acquistare una visione sintetica possibilmente chiara dello stato attuale di questi studî è necessario tener sempre presente davanti alla mente una distinzione fondamentale: fra la quistione logica e la quistione gnoseologica. Solo così riuscirà forse possibile trovare il terreno sul quale potrebbero andare d'accordo quelli che militano in campi opposti.

PAOLO DU BOIS-REYMOND nella sua opera profonda sui principî dell'analisi credette aver trovata la risoluzione dell'antinomia fondamentale in cui ci s'imbatte nella critica dei concetti di irrazionale e di limite. Egli disse che « le difficoltà inerenti a questi concetti non sono di natura puramente matematica, altrimenti sarebbero state già da lungo tempo appianate » (veduta giustissima!) ed aggiunse che « la soluzione dell'enigma è che esso è e sarà sempre un enigma; solo questo enigma è ridotto alla sua più semplice espressione psicologica: vi sono per lo spirito due modi completamente diversi di comprendere la realtà e che hanno egual diritto ad essere prese come intuizioni fondamentali delle scienze esatte, perchè nessuna di esse conduce a risultati assurdi ». Queste due intuizioni diverse furono da lui impersonate nei dui tipi dell'empirista e dell'idealista. L'empirista si rifiuta di accettare qualsiasi concetto cui non corrisponda una rappresentazione sensibile, per conseguenza egli contesta all'idealista il dritto di parlare del segmento rettilineo *perfetto*, della *misura perfetta*, ecc. Il segmento ideale del geometra non è che « il termine *arbitrariamente* ammesso di una serie di rappresentazioni sempre più precise, per la quale l'esistenza del termine non può dimostrarsi. L'idealista invece crede fermamente alla *realtà obbiettiva* delle costruzioni ideali, quantunque queste non siano sensibilmente rappresentabili.

L'idealista e l'empirista non vanno d'accordo perchè hanno una concezione diversa della *realtà matematica*; per il secondo la realtà è solo il dato sensibile, per il primo invece il campo della realtà è più vasto, perchè comprende anche le costruzioni che il matematico fonda sui dati dell'esperienza servendosi della libera attività del suo spirito. Entrambi non escono dal campo gnoseologico.

Ebbene, oggi la distinzione di Du Bois-Reymond non è più sufficiente; un terzo interlocutore è intervenuto nel dibattito: il logico matematico, che alla quistione gnoseologica sostituisce *sic et simpliciter* la quistione logica. Egli ha una concezione della realtà matematica, che si contrappone a quella dell'idealista e dell'empirista. Reale è per lui tutto ciò che lo spirito costruisce senza contraddizione.

Dal punto di vista puramente logico si bada solo al rigore formale. Una teoria matematica è perfetta quando i concetti fondamentali di essa sono costruiti mediante un sistema di definizioni e postulati indipendenti fra loro e compatibili, e che costituiscono gli elementi necessari e sufficienti per lo sviluppo deduttivo. La genesi storica o psicologica di essi concetti non impone alcun legame al matematico-logico, che afferma recisamente il suo dritto di creare *ex nihilo*, per così dire, gli enti che vuole studiare senza tener conto del loro grado di realtà concreta e badando solo alle condizioni logiche cui deve soddisfare il sistema di definizioni e postulati. Due conseguenze si ricavano: 1° la possibilità di costruire teorie di enti, che non hanno alcun legame con la realtà concreta, cioè di enti che trascendono le nostre facoltà conoscitive, ad es. la 4ª dimensione ed il segmento infinitesimo attuale geometricamente intesi; 2° la possibilità di costruire in varî modi una stessa teoria, mutando il sistema di definizioni e postulati; la scelta fra questi modi va fatta col solo criterio della semplicità e della comodità (criterio prammatistico, o più precisamente teleologico). Insomma il motto del logico matematico è « *das Wesen der Mathematik liegt in ihrer Freiheit* » (Cantor). E qui Kant potrebbe osservare: « la colomba leggera, che nel suo libero volo fende l'aria, ha sentita la resistenza di questa ed ha pensato che volerebbe ancora meglio nel vuoto ».

Chi si pone dal punto di vista gnoseologico muove una obbiezione fondamentale. Il vostro concetto della realtà, dice al logico puro, non solo si contrappone alla coscienza comune, ma è monco e non riesce ad evitare la quistione gnoseologica. Difatti un concetto può essere contradditorio non solo formalmente, ma anche intrinsecamente. Quando un concetto viene trasportato arbitrariamente da un campo A ad un campo B essenzialmente distinto dal primo, diventa intrinsecamente contradditorio. Ad esempio il concetto dello spazio a 4 dimensioni inteso analiticamente non è contradditorio, ma se si vuol intendere *fisicamente* diventa ipso facto un ircocervo.

È dunque necessario distinguere i varî campi della conoscenza, cioè le varie forme dell'intuizione; e la quistione gnoseologica scacciata dalla porta rientra per la finestra.

Un'altra obbiezione e di non poco momento fa il filosofo al logico puro. Si può impunemente trascurare il *contenuto* dei concetti nella elaborazione logica? Un episodio notevole della cronaca scientifica contemporanea dimostra di no. Si è voluto costruire il concetto delle varie classi di numeri transfiniti senza aver prima elaborato convenientemente il contenuto, cioè facendo astrazione dal *λόγος τῆς οὐσίας*. Ebbene, dopo una lunghissima discussione non si è riusciti ancora a risolvere in modo soddisfacente le contraddizioni che si sono affacciate nello sviluppo della teoria; le dichiarazioni che un illustre analista, il Borel, ha fatte in proposito, sono molto impressionanti. E ciò non pertanto la teoria degl'insiemi resterà nella scienza, come uno dei più grandi acquisti, per quella parte che non dipende dai numeri transfiniti e che ha prodotto tanti notevoli progressi nella teorica delle funzioni. E già si può prevedere che, anche quei teoremi del Cantor nella cui dimostrazione si fa uso del transfinito, saranno stabiliti indipendentemente da questo. Un bellissimo esempio l'ha dato il Lindelöf dimostrando il teorema di Cantor-Bendixon con delle semplici considerezioni sui punti di condensazione degl'insiemi (Acta Mat., vol. 29, 1905).

Si aggiunga che l'irrigidimento della veduta formalistica dei principî della matematica può condurre a queste conseguenze: 1° l'identificazione della logica con la matematica, che anche in questo congresso è stata combattuta dall'autorevole parola di Itelson; 2° uno spirito di sottigliezza esagerata, una certa, direi quasi, ossessione del dubbio pervade la critica di concetti per se stessi chiarissimi. Gli è che si vuol dare l'ostracismo all'intuizione lì dove essa regna sovrana. E si è avuta la reazione: noi abbiamo intesa la voce possente di Poincaré, che si è ribellato alle esagerazioni della logica matematica; 3° un certo *radical scepticism* che penetra precisamente in quella rocca formidabile, che sino ad ora è stata considerata come l'asilo della verità indiscutibile: « i matematici non conoscono ciò di cui trattano e non sanno se ciò che dimostrano è vero ». Così il Russell, e Benedetto Croce, lo prende in parola e nega in conseguenza il *valore teorico* delle matematiche, nega anzi l'esistenza della matematica come scienza. Il Croce non aveva il diritto di prendere alla lettera la frase paradossale di Russell, ma bisogna pur confessare che l'autore dei *Principles of Mathematics* è stato molto imprudente.

Conclusione.

I due punti di vista logico e gnoseologico s'integrano e si correggono a vicenda. La critica dei principî della matematica appartiene nello stesso tempo alla matematica ed alla filosofia, quindi è necessario trovare un terreno comune sul quale sia possibile l'accordo fra matematici e filosofi. E questo accordo si potrà avere solo in base a reciproche concessioni.

Il filosofo deve discendere dal suo seggio olimpico dal quale contempla l'assoluto spirito, l'assoluto vero; nella trattazione dei principî della scienza egli deve prima di tutto interrogare quelli che della scienza intensamente vivono e deve informarsi dell'evoluzione, che le idee direttrici hanno subìto per effetto dei recenti sviluppi. Non deve far giustizia sommaria di tutto ciò che in questi sembra contraddire alla gnoseologia kantiana od hegeliana, ma deve vagliare tutto e scegliere quegli elementi vitali che sono necessari per una più esatta determinazione del campo della conoscenza umana. E sopratutto nessun preconcetto deve guidarlo nel giudizio su alcune conclusioni che a prima vista sembrano paradossali; altrimenti non potrà comprendere la vera portata di certi recenti studi sulla natura della definizione e sull'indipendenza dei postulati.

D'altra parte il matematico deve abbandonare la sua diffidenza per le alte speculazioni filosofiche con la scusa che queste sono sempre in evoluzione. È proprio delle dottrine filosofiche l'essere perennemente in evoluzione. Ed infatti la filosofia, la vera filosofia, prende alimento dalla scienza; se questa si evolve e si elabora continuamente, lo stesso deve avvenire della filosofia. Il matematico non può e non deve disconoscere l'importanza fondamentale del problema della conoscenza, quale fu posto per la prima volta da Kant, cioè: determinare in qual modo lo spirito umano esplica la sua attività nella costruzione dell'esperienza. Il problema non si può trattare prescindendo dall'osservazione e studio della scienza viva, della scienza nel suo continuo divenire; e questo studio può condurre ad una *gnoseologia positiva* che dev'essere la base della costruzione filosofica. Questo, si può dire, è il *leit-motiv* del magnifico libro dell'Enriques: *I problemi della scienza.* L'Enriques però non assurge ad una vera costruzione filosofica; ma questa non sarà difficile se matematici e filosofi riuniranno i loro sforzi per la rielaborazione di una critica della ragione, nella quale la dottrina della conoscenza non avrà l'immobilità e rigidità dello schema kantiano; l'*intuizione*, le *categorie*, l'*a priori* saranno intesi in senso più lato cioè come partecipanti in certo modo della mobilità dello spirito vivente ed attivo.

A. EMCH

DER RECHENKÜNSTLER WINKLER UND SEINE METHODEN

Eine der interessantesten Gestalten auf dem Gebiete der Rechenkunst ist der grosse Kopfrechner JOHANN JAKOB WINKLER. Während über eine Reihe von Vertretern derselben Geistesrichtung in verschiedenen Abhandlungen eingehend berichtet wird, findet man über WINKLER fast nichts vor und es ist der Zweck dieser Mitteilung, einige genauere Angaben über diesen merkwürdigen Mann zu machen.

Er wurde am 23. Februar 1831 in Wermatswil als Sohn des ULRICH WINKLER und der ELISABETH, geb. ENDERLIG, geboren. WINKLER war mit einer AMALIE KAROLINE FORSTINGER von Karlsruhe verheiratet, hat aber keine Nachkommen. Ueber ihren Aufenthalt ist in der Heimatgemeinde nichts bekannt, obschon sie laut Familienregister noch am Leben ist und im 81. Lebensjahre stünde. WINKLER war der zweite von 10 Kindern und sein Grossvater stammte aus Zell im Tösstale und wurde im Jahre 1829 als Bürger von Uster aufgenommen.

WINKLER hatte ein phänomales Zahlengedächtnis und eine riesige Rechnungsfertigkeit, die er nach seinen eigenen Angaben jeden Tag übte und üben musste. Er war sehr kurzsichtig und liess sich daher die Aufgaben und Zahlen vorlesen, gewöhnlich zweimal, so dass er während der grössten Rechnung weder die Aufgabe, noch irgend welche Zwischenresultate notiert sehen konnte, auf diesen Umstand war er stolz und hob wiederholt hervor, diese durch nichts unterstützte Gedächtniskunst hätte noch niemand fertig gebracht. Häufig war er mit einer Aufgabe fertig bevor sie zum zweitenmal gelesen war. WINKLER löste so ziemlich jede Aufgabe, welche in Rechnungsform gebracht werden konnte und bediente sich dabei, wie der berühmte französische Rechner JACQUES INAUDI einer Annäherungsmethode, indem er Näherungswerte bestimmte und dann den wahren Wert durch Interpolation erhielt. Irgend welche Logarithmen berechnete er auf sieben Dezimalen und auch Nummern zu gegebenen Logarithmen bestimmte er mit gleicher Leichtigkeit. Von andern Rechnungskünstlern unterschied er sich dadurch, dass er auch Aufgaben aus der Physik in seinen Bereich zog.

Dass ein Kern Wahrheit in der Tatsache liegt, dass WINKLER gelegentlich flunkerte, geht daraus hervor, dass es nach den Untersuchungen BINET's über den Rechenkünstler INAUDI fast ausgeschlossen ist, in so kurzer Zeit 120 Ziffern auswendig zu lernen. Wenn also WINKLER behauptete, das ohne Mnemotechnik tun zu können, so ist die Tatsache noch keineswegs festgestellt. Sehr deutlich geht dies aus dem Artikel des Herrn Dr. H. LAURENT über « Calcul Mental » in der *Grande Encyclopédie* hervor, in welchem er schreibt: « Ich habe einen jungen Engländer WINKLER gekannt und unglücklicherweise seine Spur verloren, welcher wunderbare Rechnungen ausführte. Hatte man ihm zweimal 5000 Zahlen vorgesagt, so konnte er nach 14 Tagen dieselben in gleicher Ordnung hersagen. Es ist jedoch klar, dass eine solche Leistung nur durch Mnemotechnik erklärlich ist. In einer Sitzung, welcher auch der Arithmologe LEBESGUE und der Abbé MOIGNO beiwohnten, gab ich WINKLER die Aufgabe, eine fünfstellige Zahl in die Summe von vier Quadraten zu zerlegen und nach drei Minuten gab er verschiedene Lösungen des Problems. LEBESGUE behauptete, dass es ihn 14 Tage nehmen würde, um die Aufgabe zu lösen ».

WINKLER gab vor eine Methode zu besitzen und sagte: Wenn ihr sie kennen würdet, so würdet ihr gerade so schnell rechnen, wie ich, ich habe kein Gedächtnis und habe Mühe, eine Fabel auswendig zu lernen.

Nach einer brieflichen Mitteilung hat Herr Dr. LAURENT in Paris WINKLER gut gekannt. In der *Grande Encyclopédie* ist er irrtümlicherweise als Engländer angeführt. Offenbar ging WINKLER von England nach Paris und es ist ja wohl möglich, dass er an letzterem Orte den Glauben erweckte, er sei Engländer. Er soll auch in Oxford an der Universität eine Vorstellung gegeben haben. Nach einer Mitteilung von Herrn Professor ELLIOT ist jedoch in Oxford, sowie im übrigen England nichts über WINKLER bekannt.

Herr LAURENT teilt ferner mit, dass WINKLER im Gegensatz zu INAUDI, MONDEUX, etc. ein gebildeter Mann und guter Mathematiker war. Er beschäftigte sich mit höherer Analysis und interessierte sich für Literatur und Philosophie. Er gab vor, dass seine Kunst auf einer Methode beruhe, die er für 100000 Fr. verkaufen würde. Das war Ende der 60 er Jahre, als WINKLER etwa 38 Jahre alt sein mochte.

Er war auch in Solothurn und andern Schweizerstädten bekannt, wo er zu wiederholtenmalen Vorstellungen gab.

Was nun WINKLER's Methode anbelangt, so glaube ich nicht, dass dahinter ein grosses Geheimnis steckte. Ein gewisser G. von TOBEL gab in Zürich im Verlage von MEYER und ZELLER eine Brochüre mit dem Titel: Sammlung sehr wertvoller Rechnungsformeln, Aufgaben und Tabellen, leichtverständlich für jedermann, von J. J. WINKLER, speziell für Kopfrechner, heraus. Dieselbe enthält nichts als eine zum Schnellrechnen zugestutzte Anwendung der Logarithmen und algebraischen Formeln, wie sie aus folgender Darstellung hervorgeht:

Um zum Beispiel den Logarithmus einer Zahl., z. B. 9368754 zu berechnen, zerlegt er die Zahl in $9000000 + 368754$ und nennt 9000000 die Grundzahl A. Davon ist 368754 circa 4 %, also $9368754 = A + \frac{4 . A}{100} + 875$ oder $= A . 1{,}04 + 8754$. Die Zahl $A . 1{,}04 = 9360000$ nennt er die zweite Grundzahl B. Davon ist 8754 circa 9 Zehntausenstel oder 8424. Also $9368754 = A . 1{,}04 + A . 1{,}04 \frac{9}{10000} + 330 =$ $A . 1.04 . 1{,}0009 + 330$. Die Zahl $A . 1{,}04 . 1{,}0009 = 9368424$ wird 3. Grundzahl C genannt. Davon ist 330 circa 3 pro Hunderttausend, oder 281. Also $9368754 =$

A.1,04.1,0009.1,00003 + 49. Die 4. Grundzahl lautet D = 9368705, wovon 49 cirka 5 Millionstel, oder 47 ist. Folglich 9368754 = A.1,04.1,0009.1,00003. 1,000005 + 2 und als fünfte Grundzahl E = 9368752. Der Rest 2 ist beinahe 2 Zenmillionstel von E, also schliesslich

$$9368754 = 9000000 \,.\, 1{,}04 \,.\, 1{,}0009 \,.\, 1{,}00003 \,.\, 1{,}000005 \,.\, 1{,}0000002$$

und

$$\log 9368754 = \left\{\begin{array}{ll} \log 9000000 & = 6{,}954\ 2425 \\ \log 1{,}04 & = 0{,}017\ 0333 \\ \log 1{,}0009 & = 0{,}000\ 3907 \\ \log 1{,}00003 & = 0{,}000\ 0130 \\ \log 1{,}000005 & = 0{,}000\ 0022 \\ \log 1{,}0000002 & = 0{,}000\ 0002 \\ \hline & = 6{,}971\ 6819 \end{array}\right.$$

Nun wusste WINKLER alle Logarithmen von 1 bis 100, sowie die meisten von 100 bis 1000 und diejenigen von der Form $100p$, $1000p$, etc. auswendig, so, dass er mit Hülfe seines riesigen Zahlengedächtnisses imstande, war nach dem vorhergehenden Schema Logarithmen zu berechnen.

Der WINKLER'sche Ansatz läuft darauf hinaus, eine Zahl n als Produkt von der Form

$$n = a.\left(1 + \frac{p_1}{q_1}\right)\left(1 + \frac{p_2}{q_2}\right)\left(1 + \frac{p_3}{q_3}\right)\ldots$$

darzustellen. Man sieht, dass schon eine solche Darstellung kopfrechnerisch grosse Anforderungen stellt, welche in Verbindung mit der Aufstellung und Addition der Teillogarithmen jedenfalls blos einem Kopfrechner ersten Ranges gelingen dürfte. In ähnlicher Weise fand er den Numerus zu einem gegebenen Logarithmus. WINKLER bediente sich bei grössern Potenz-Wurzel-Zinseszins-und Rentenrechnungen hauptsächlich der Logarithmen und auswendiggelernter Zinstabellen. Auch waren ihm alle Schnellrechnungsregeln, welche sich aus der Algebra ergeben geläufig. Z. B. löste er mit Hülfe der bekannten Formeln fast blitzschnell alle Aufgaben über arithmetische Reihen verschiedener Ordnung.

Eine Multiplikation, wie 696.604 machte er natürlich nach der Formel

$$(600 - 4)\ (600 + 4) = 360000 - 16 = 359984,$$

und so noch unzähliges mehr aus dem Bereiche der Rechentechnik.

Fasst man die Leistungen WINKLER's zusammen, so muss gesagt werden, dass er ohne Zweifel der grösste aller Rechenkünstler war. Seine wunderbaren Leistungen beruhten auf einer ausserordentlichen Rechnungsfertigkeit, einem phänomalen durch Mnemotechnik unterstützten Gedächtnis, sowie auf seiner nicht ungewöhnlichen mathematischen Bildung.

WINKLER starb am 25. August 1893 an Hirnschlag im Kantonsspital von Stans, arm und verlassen und ohne jeglichem Mittel.

GINO LORIA

SUR LES MOYENS POUR FACILITER ET DIRIGER LES ÉTUDES SUR L'HISTOIRE DES MATHÉMATIQUES

I.

Dans un article qu'il a récemment publié (¹), M. Eneström a dit que, le nombre des personnes qui s'occupent de l'histoire des mathématiques étant désormais considérable, l'instant était arrivé pour fixer le plan suivant lequel les recherches futures doivent être menées. Quoiqu'il semble qu'en général les savants d'une spécialité quelconque forment plutôt une troupe de volontaires sans discipline, qu'une armée régulière connaissant et respectant des lois et des règlements, la question mise à l'ordre du jour par le savant dirécteur de la *Bibliotheca Mathematica* est sans doute importante puisqu'on sait que la plus grande diversité d'opinions règne aujourd'hui sur la route qu'on doit suivre dans cette sorte de recherches, car les uns s'occupent exclusivement des oeuvres sans donner la moindre attention aux auteurs, tandis que d'autres n'ont des yeux et des oreilles que pour les détails biographiques et un trop grand nombre trouvent bon de séparer les découvertes mathématiques de tout ce qui a trait à l'histoire générale de la pensée et à l'histoire politique, montrant le mathématicien comme un être isolé, qui n'a aucun rapport avec le monde ou il vit et qui se soustrait à toute influence extérieure.

Mais il y a une autre question analogue à celle soulevée par M. Eneström et qui me parait digne de tout notre interêt.

Il est vrai que le nombre des culteurs de l'histoire des mathématiques est aujourd'hui assez grand; mais il est également vrai qu'il y a des personnes qui voudraient bien se vouer à cet ordre de recherches et qui ne le peuvent pas faute de moyens d'instruction, semblables à ceux qui se trouvent sous la main de tous ceux qui veulent se vouer aux autres branches de l'érudition. Des instituts ou l'on montre comment on fait des recherches sur l'histoire des mathématiques, j'en connais seulement un, le « Seminar » fondé à Munich et dirigé par le regretté A. von Braunmühl.

(¹) *Ueber planmässige Arbeit auf dem mathematisch-historischen Forschungsgebiete* (Bibl. mathem., 3. Folge, Bd. VIII, p. 1 e suiv.).

Si cet exemple donné par notre illustre collègue était suivi dans un nombre considérable d'écoles supérieures, la question dont je m'occupe serait d'emblée résolue; mais on ne peut avoir de grandes espérances dans la fondation de beaucoup de chaires officielles de l'espèce indiquée, ni mêmes dans de cours libres, car les personnes qui pourraient les tenir sont pour la plus part absorbées par d'autres occupation officielles.

Or, je me rappelle qu'un Saint [1] a dit qu'il y a trois manières pour apprendre une chose: la manière *meilleure* est de la professer, l'*execellente* est de l'écouter de la voix d'un maître, la *bonne* de l'apprendre par un livre. Eh ! bien, si nous ne pouvons pas transformer ceux qui aspirent à devenir des historiens des mathématiques en des professeurs ou en des étudiants, mettons entre leurs mains un bon livre qui leur épargne les douloureuses incertitudes, les faux pas, la perte de temps que subirent tous ceux qui durent chercher tous seuls leur route! C'est la célèbre loi de Mach sur l'*économie de la pensée* qui conseille d'adopter ce moyen; c'est une assemblée comme celle devant j'ai l'honneur de parler qui est appelée à décider de cette entreprise, à en fixer le plan et à repartir le travail entre les personnes qui sont à même de la mener à bout.

Pour préparer l'échange d'idées qui doit aboutir à ce resultat, je vous demande la permission d'exposer quelques observations personnelles et de faire quelques propositions sur les sujets qui, suivant mes idées, devraient être traitées dans le *Manuel pour l'aspirant-historien des mathématiques*, dont je crois la compilation urgente.

II.

L'histoire des mathématiques, comme toute branche de l'histoire, est une reconstruction du passé à l'aide des sources existantes; par conséquent les procédés qu'on y emploie ne sont pas différents, dans le fond, de ceux dont on fait usage, par exemple. dans l'histoire de la littérature. Or c'est mon opinion que cette analogie a été trop généralement méconnue ou oubliée et que, de l'isolement qui en résulta, l'histoire des mathématiques a souffert un arrêt ou des déviations dans son développement. C'est pour cela que je voudrais que le *Manuel* dont nous nous occupons commençât par un aperçu sur les recherches qui aboutirent à la création de la *Mhéthode historique*, qui est une des gloires du siècle passé; je crois cela d'autant plus nécessaire car beucoup de personnes ont la fausse idée que pour écrire un chapitre d'histoire des mathématiques il est toujours suffisant de recueillir et d'exposer un certain nombre de faits analogues, sans s'apercevoir que de cette manière on ne s'élève pas au dessus du modeste niveau du simple annaliste faisant une énumeration des princes qui ont régnés dans une certaine époque, des batailles qui furent livrées, des traités signés et des modifications qui s'ensuivirent dans la constitution des états; or il faut répandre la convinction que la *euristique*, ou doctrine des sources, représente, non la *dernière*, mais la *première* phase de toute histoire.

Ces généralités épuisées (et pour les écrire je ne saurais conseiller des guides meilleurs des célèbres traités de M. Bernheim), il faudrait dire quelque chose sur les

[1] S. François de Sales.

procédés qu'on emploie aujourd'hui pour étudier « scientifiquement » l'histoire de la littérature, procédés que, si je ne me trompe, l'historien des mathématiques pourra très-utilement employer dans plusieurs circonstances; il sera bon même de remarquer que l'histoire des sciences est en réalité si étroitement liée à celle des ouvrages littéraires qu'il existe d'excellentes histoires de la littérature embrassant aussi l'analyse des productions scientifiques; un exemple célèbre de ce système est offert par la grande *Storia della letteratura italiana* de Tiraboschi.

À ces remarques générales il est nécessaire de faire suivre un aperçu sur le meilleurs ouvrages généraux de consultation, aides indispensables qui font épargner un temps immense; j'ajoute que parmi ces sources d'informations il est nécessaire de comprendre les traité de chronologie et de métrologie, tels que ceux de Ideler et Hultsch, et les bonnes histoires des instituts d'instruction et de sociétés savantes, car elles donnent de précieux renseignements sur l'état général de la culture, sur la tendence des esprits dans une certaine époque et enfin sur le côté didactique de l'activité de savants illustres.

III.

Après cela on peut bien se tourner aux sujets particulier au *Manuel* dont il s'agit, en exposant avant tout les différentes idées qu'ont manifesté Cantor, Eneström, Paul Tannery, etc. sur le but, la méthode, la direction, les bornes que doivent avoir les recherches sur l'histoire des mathématiques, en les comparant à celles appliquées par ceux qui écrivirent des histoires d'autres sciences positives et en discutant la possibilité d'une *histoire générale des sciences.* Un point délicat est celui des erreurs scientifiques. Notre science n'élève pas ses constructions sur les ruines d'édifices plus anciens; les propositions qu'on a dû rejeter sont ou le produit de paralogismes ou l'effet de changements de la significations de certains mots téchniques. De la première espèce sont les essais sur la quadrature du cercle et la trisection de l'angle, et sur eux l'historien pourra en général suivre exemple donné par l'Institut de France en « passant à l'ordre du jour ». De l'autre espèce sont les propositions d'analyse (comme celle de l'existence de la dérivée d'une fonction continue) qui ne subsistent plus à cause de la métarmophose subie de nos temps par la notion de fonction; or les phénomènes de cette espèce méritent, suivant mon sentiment, toute l'attention de l'historien, car il sont de ceux qui justifient l'ancienne opinion que l'histoire est la maîtresse de la vie.

Tout cela formera un préambule extrèmement utile à l'analyse des histoires des mathématiques existantes qu'on devra faire avec tout le soin et l'étendue désirables, car c'est seulement l'étude approfondie des maîtres qui donne la force et le pouvoir de les suivre dans leurs chemin glorieux et la constatation des fautes qu'on a commises permet bien souvent d'éviter d'y retomber. Le nombre des *histores générales*, des mathématiques n'est pas grand; au contraire les travaux ayant pour but l'histoire de notre science dans une époque détérminée ou dans un pays particulier, ou bien l'histoire d'une théorie, d'une question ou même d'un seul problème, sont extrèmement nombreux; ces travaux rarement ont été l'objet de pubblication séparée, pour la plus grande partie il se trouvent épars un peu partout: dans les recueils des académies scientifiques ou littéraires, dans les journaux de science, d'art ou d'érudition et il y en aussi un bon nombre qui parurent comme thèses de doctorat ou en appendice de programmes scolaires. Pour que le bilan de ces contributions, bien souvent importantes, réusisse complet il faut faire appel aux savants de tous les pays; c'est seulement par leurs efforts combinés qu'il sera possible de rendre assez complète cette « bibliographie des monographies historiques » base indispensable pour l'« histoire des histoires des mathématiques » dont on commence à sentir le besoin. Je suppose qu'un travail de ce genre soit compris dans le programme du dernier volume de l'*Encyklopädie der mathematischen Wissenschaften;* mais sans doute il ne pourra atteindre dans cet ouvrage l'extension qu'il faudra lui donner dans le *Manuel*, car il faut que celui fasse connaitre exactement quelles sont les recherches q'uon a déjà faites et qu'il mette en évidence celles qui possèdent un caractère d'urgence. Qu'il me soit permis de remarquer que pour ce qui a rapport à l'Antiquité classique, on pourrait pour cela se servir très-utilement des magnifiques Rapports périodiques publiés dans ce dernier quart de siècle par M. Heiberg; de graves difficultés au contraire se recontreront par rapport à l'Orient, car, si je suis bien informé, aucun journal ne donne de comptes-rendus réguliers des recherches des orientalistes relatives aux sciences exactes; je remarque cela parce que c'est un des points le plus délicats et importants qui sont offert par la préparation due *Manuel.*

Dans la hiérarchie des productions de la pensée la biographie occupe un rang plus bas que l'histoire; mais les biographies des savants illustres fournissent des matériaux d'une valeur inéstimable à tout historien. Par conséquent il est de toute nécéssité de recueillir avec soin et de classer avec jugement tous les donnés fournis par les nécrologies des personnages le plus éminents, en particulier par celles écrit par les contemporains. Le nombre vraiment énorme de pubblications de cette espèce peut se mésurer « ad oculum » en feuilletant les dernières pages de l'excellent *Handwörterbuch* de Poggendorff, ou il y a la liste des sources utilisées, et en remarquant qu'aujourd'hui cette collection ne peut plus se considérer comme complète. Et même sans avoir recours à cet ouvrage superbe, il est aisé de former une idée de la quantité énorme des renseignements que l'on peut tirer des recueils biographiques, si on remarque qu'il n'y a pas d'académie ou d'université, si modeste qu'elle soit, qu'il n'y a pas même de compagnie religieuse, pas même de region, qui n'ait pas payé une dette de reconnaissance envers ceux qui enrichirent le patrimoine intellectuel de l'humanité. Or pour éviter que ces travaux soient oubliés et stériles au fond de nos bibliothèques, le *Manuel* contiendra une liste le moins incomplète que possible des biographies des mathématiciens; évidemment sa compilations ne peut être que le produit d'un travail collectif international; et pour qu'elle acquière son plus haut degré d'utilité j'exprime le désir qu'elle donne, pour chaque savant, des notices sur sa correspondance, si elle existe, car la collection des lettres portant la signature ou l'adresse de Guido Grandi (1), Franchini (2), Flauti (3), Lorgna (4),

(1) La corréspondence de Grandi est conservée dans la Bibliothèque de l'Université de Pise.

(2) Bibliothèque de Lucque.

(3) La corréspondence de Flauti se trouve chez sa famille.

(4) Comp. Bullettino Boncompagni, t. VI, p. 101.

Riccardi (1), Santini (2), Genocchi (3) etc., est sans doute un document scientifique d'une valeur hors ligne, pour éclaircir, dans tous ses recoins, la vie scientifique du temps auquel il se rapporte.

IV.

Ce que je viens d'exquisser forme la partie générale du *Manuel*.

On devrait ensuite s'occuper de l'exposition des moyens à employer pour mener à bout des recherches sur l'histoire des mathématiques. Il sera bon de séparer ce qui touche à l'Antiquité et au Moyen-Age de ce qui se rapport aux temps postérieurs à l'invention de l'imprimerie; la nécessité de cette séparation n'a pas besoin de démonstration pour quiconque connait la portée immense de la révolution apportée par Gutenberg dans les moyens de transmission de la parole écrite.

Pour faire des recherches sur la pensée des mathématiciens dans les temps les plus reculés, il est en général nécessaire de disposer d'une science philologique et paléographique très-considérable, tandis qu'il suffit de connaitre seulement les premiers éléments de la science du nombre et de l'étendue. En conséquence le principe de la division du travail conseillerait que nous laissions aux savants ayant l'habitude de lire et d'interpréter les anciens manuscrits les recherches se rapportant à la géométrie et à l'arithmétique des Grecs et des Romains, tout en nous déclarant prêts à suivre l'exemple donné par M. Zeuthen, toujours disposé à commenter les résultats des fouilles de son savant collègue M. Heiberg. Si cette proposition trouvait un accueil favorable, il serait bon de prier le professeurs de philologie grecque et latine de conseiller leurs élèves de ne pas écarter de leurs discussions les manuscrits mathématiques, en faisant valoir que ceux-ci pourront fournir le sujet d'investigations bien plus utiles que celles ayant comme point de départ les ouvrages, justement oubliés, de certains philosophes ou littérateurs de dernier rang. Toutefois pour rendre possible que quelque mathématicien occupe la place malheureusement laissée vide par Paul Tannery, il est nécessaire que le *Manuel* donne un ample résumé des procédés suivis dans la classification et l'étude des différents manuscrits d'un même ouvrage, de manière que l'« apparatus criticus » cesse d'être un de ces instruments mistérieux que les seuls docteurs-ès-lettres sont autorisés à employer. Cela n'est pas encore suffisant: pour rendre possibles de nouvelles recherches pour éviter qu'elles se dirigent vers des champs si explorés qu'on ne peut espérer que d'y faire quelque maigre glainure, il est indispensable de pouvoir mettre sous les yeux de l'élève des listes de manuscrits mathématiques; par conséquent le *Manuel* devrait contenir de larges extraits des Catalogues des manuscrits existants, avec des renseignements suffisants pour répondre à ces questions: où se trouvent des manuscrits d'un certaine ouvrage? cet ouvrage est-il encore inédit?

Les remarques que je viens de faire rapport au monde grec et au monde latin peuvent se répéter rapport à la littérature orientale; il est à désirer que des spécia-

(1) Comp. Bullettino Boncompagni, t. VIII, p. 13.

(2) Comp. Bullettino Boncompagni, t. XI, p. 10.

(3) Tous les papiers laissés par Genocchi se trouvent à la Bibliotèque de Plaisance.

listes suivent l'exemple de MM. Carra de Vaux et Nallino, qui emploient leur profond savoir philologique au service des mathématiques; mais il est à souhaiter aussi que M. Suter ne reste pas le seul mathématicien qui s'occupe de la science des Arabes; c'est pour cela que le *Manuel* contiendra un chapitre qui serve de guide aux culteurs des mathématiques désireux de faire progresser nos connaissances sur des peuples vers lesquels se tournent les regards de tous ceux qui répètent encore l'ancien mot « ex Oriente lux ».

J'ajoute enfin que, ce que nous savons aujourd'hui rapport aux mathématiques du Moyen-Age étant encore bien insuffisant, si quelq'un, soit-il littérateur ou savant, voudra poursuivre les recherches restées incomplètes depuis la regrettable mort de Maximilien Curtze, il peut d'avance compter sur l'approbation générale; le *Manuel* devra rendre possible et relativement facile la tâche de cet investigateur par des renseignements sur les manuscrits pas encore explorés et sur les difficultés qu'offre leur déchiffrement: il est nécessaire d'avertir que, la philologie du Moyen-Age étant encore toute à faire, les aides que les gens de lettres peuvent nous offrir, sont encore, malheureusement, très bornés.

V.

L'invention de l'imprimerie a mis des barrières infranchissables à la science paléographique; par conséquent ceux qui se vouent à l'histoire des sciences dans l'Age moderne sont dispensés de s'emparer d'une science, désormais exacte, dont le maniement exige une habilité considérable. Mais comme les recherches mathématiques accomplies dans ces derniers siècles visent à des buts bien plus elevés que ceux que se proposaient les anciens, l'historien doit disposer de connaissances mathématiques très-étendues, je dirais même plus étendues, si non plus profondes, que celles dont ont besoin les specialistes d'une branches déterminée des sciences exactes.

Pour épargner la peine et l'ennui de longues recherches bibliographiques, il serait bon de mettre sous les yeux de tout historien des mathématiques modernes une liste axacte des « Oeuvres complètes » qu'on a dejà faitdes mathématiciens les plus illustres: la compilation de cette liste est un travail ni long ni difficile et qui sera utile pour une autre raison: dès qu'il sera fini, il rendra évidents des phénomènes qu'on pourrait bien dire des injustices; p. ex. n'est-il pas étrange que l'on n'ait pas encore songé à réunir les travaux de géomètres tels que Chasles, Kummer, Genocchi, tandis que d'autres personnes, dont l'influence a été bien moindre, ont obtenu ce suprème des honneurs posthumes auxquels un savant peut aspirer?...

Non moins nécessaire, mais bien plus difficile à rédiger est une liste complète des pubblications périodiques renfermant des travaux mathématiques. Des essais dans ce sens ont été déjà faits. M. S. H. Scudder a compilé en 1879 une bonne liste des pubblications périodiques en général (1) et en 1897 M. H. Carrington Bolton a fait un catalogue des journaux scientifiques et téchniques (2); le *Manuel* devra contenir

(1) Catalogue of scientific serials published by the Harward University, 1879.

(2) *A catalogue of scientific and technical periodicals 1665-1895*, II ed. (Smithsonian miscellanous collections, vol. XL, 1897).

un résumé de ces travaux rélatif exclusivement aux sciences exactes. Mais il ne faut pas oublier que M. FELIX MÜLLER, que tout le monde connait comme une autorité bibliographique, a récemment ([1]) compilé une liste de l'espèce indiquée, qui, après quelques additions, arrivera au degré de perfection auquel peut aspirer toute oeuvre humaine. A ce sujet je veux faire une remarque: tout le mond sait que, la spécialisation étant un produit de la science moderne, jusqu'en 1850 et même après un bon nombre de travaux mathématiques se trouvent répandus un peu partout; de manière qu'il y a de recueuils, quelquefois très-étendus, ne renfermant qu'un très-petit nombre de mémoires mathématiques; comme ces recueuils sont en général les plus rares, je me permets de recommender aux jeunes-gens repandus dans tout le monde de suivre l'exemple que j'ai donné il y a quelque temps, en pubbliant un dépouillement raisonné d'une ancienne pubblication périodique italienne ([2]). Tout travail fait en cette diréction serait sans doute utilisé ou au moins cité dans le *Manuel* dont je m'occupe.

Des aides extrèmement précieux pour l'historien des mathématiques modernes sont représentés par les bibliographies mathématiques; la plus ancienne que je connaisse est la « Bibliotheca mathematica » de MURHARD (Leipsic 1798), à laquelle suivirent dix ans après un grand repertoire de J. D. REUSS ([3]) et de nos jours le *Mathematischer Bücherschatz* de M. WÖLFFING. Peut-être qu'il y aura plusieurs autres bibliographies plus anciennes et plus modernes; celles que je connais le mieux pour m'en être servi bien souvent sont le « Catalogue of scientific papers » publié par la Société Royale de Londres et le « Répertoire bibliographique des sciences mathématiques », qui est publié à Paris par une Commission internationale. J'ajoute que M. VALENTIN depuis longtemps prépare avec le soin le plus scrupuleux une grande bibliographie mathématique, qui comprendra, différemment de celles que je viens de citer, les années antérieures à 1800.

Tous ces recueuils bibliographiques devront être analysés dans le *Manuel* pour en faire ressortir les qualités et les défauts ([4]); ce qui donnera l'occasion pour parler des différentes manières employées pour faire les citations, depuis l'origine de l'imprimerie jusqu'à BALTHASAR BONCOMPAGNI, pour faire remarquer tous les dangers qu'offrent les « citations de seconde main » et pour énumerer les cas ou l'on pourra l'adopter faute de mieux.

Enfin le *Manuel* devra contenir des indications sur les journaux historiques et sur ceux renfermant des comptes-rendus des travaux mathématiques; jusq'à peu près 1850 il faut pour cela avoir recours aux revues générales de la littérature; mais pour les productions contemporaines le Jahrbuch fondé par ORTHMANN, le Bulletin de M. DARBOUX, la Revue sémestrielle des pubblications mathématiques etc., permettent à tout

([1]) *Abgekürzte Titel von Zeitschriften mathematischen Inhalts* (Jahresber. der Deutschen Mathem.-Vereinig., Bd. XII, 1903, p. 427 et suiv.).

([2]) *Il « Giornale de' Letterati d'Italia » di Venezia e la « Raccolta Calogerà » come fonti per la storia delle matematiche nel secolo XVIII* (Abhandlungen zur Gesch. der Mathem., Bd. IX, 1899, p. 241 et suiv).

([3]) *Repertorium commentationum a soc. litt. secundum disc. ordinem* (t. VII, Gottingae, 1908).

([4]) Comp. E. WÖLFFING, *Ueber die bibliographischen Hilfsmittel der Mathematik* (Jahresber. der Deutschen Math.-Ver., Bd. XII, 1903, p. 408).

le monde de connaître ce que contient et comment est jugé tout ce qui parait sur l'horizon mathématique.

VI.

Les sujets que je viens d'énumérer sont ceux qui, suivant ma faible expérience, me semblent former le bagage indispensable pour tout historien des mathématiques; en conséquence j'ai rédigé une table des matières du *Manuel* dont je propose la compilation et qui pourra servir de base pour la discussion qui va suivre. Permettez-moi que, pour finir, j'en donne lecture à la Section:

MANUEL POUR LES RECHERCHES SUR L'HISTOIRE DES MATHÉMATIQUES.

I. Généralités sur la nature, le but et les méthodes de la recherche historique. La « méthode historique ».

II. Méthodes employées pour l'étude « scientifique » de la littérature; bornes de leurs applicabilité aux recherches sur l'évolution d'autre manifestations de la pensée. Les ouvrages de consultations en général (dictionnaires, encyclopédies, histoires des universités, des sociétés savantes, etc.). Chronologie et métrologie.

III. Des différentes diréction que l'on peut suivre dans les études sur l'histoire des sciences en général et des mathématiques en particulier. Analyse des principales histoires générales des mathématiques. Matériaux pour une « histoire des histoires des mathématiques ». Les biographies et la correspondence de savants illustres.

IV. Nécessité de considérer separément ce qui se rapporte aux temps antérieurs à l'invention de l'imprimerie de ce qui a trait aux temps postérieurs. Recherches sur l'histoire des mathématiques dans l'Antiquité et le Moyen-Age. Généralités sur l'étude des manuscrits; catalogues des manuscrits; etc.

   a) Les mathématiques des Grecs.
   b) Les mathématiques des Romains.
   c) Les mathématiques des peuples de l'Orient.
   d) Les mathématiques au Moyen-Age.

V. Le livre imprimé et son histoire. Liste des « Oeuvres complètes » des grands mathématiciens modernes. Les recueils académiques et les journaux scientifiques. La bibliographie moderne et ses procédés; aides et secours qu'elle offre à l'historiens des mathématiques.

F. AMODEO

APPUNTI SU BIAGIO PELICANI DA PARMA

Il pensiero di fare questa comunicazione mi è venuto poco tempo fa, quando ebbi la fortuna di avere nelle mani quella rarissima collezione di trattati di matematica stampata a Venezia nel 1505 a cura e spese di OTTAVIO SCOTI, cittadino di Monza, che però vien ricordata sotto il nome del primo trattato che essa contiene: *Questio de modalibus* BASSANI POLITI.

Io ricordava che il CANTOR, a pag. 166 del vol. II delle sue *Vorlesungen* (2ª ediz.), parlando di BIAGIO PELICANI, aveva detto: « Egli si occupò fra l'altro di « Statica e di Prospettiva e scrisse oltre a ciò dei commenti alla *latitudines formarum* « di Oresme. Quest'ultimo commento è apparso stampato nel 1482 (1), ma oggi ap- « partiene alle rarità appena ritrovabili, e le notizie su di esso sarebbero ancora de- « sideratissime tanto per la nota importanza dell'opera commentata, quanto per « assodare fino a quanto egli sia meritevole della celebrità acquistata nei suoi « tempi » (2).

Ed appunto in questa collezione doveva essere contenuto il commento citato e ciò era ricordato tanto dal BONCOMPAGNI nel vol. IV del suo Bullettino (p. 497, 1871) quanto dal RICCARDI nella *Biblioteca matematica italiana.* Ed anzi il RICCARDI aggiunge, dopo aver citato il suddetto commento nelle due edizioni da lui conosciute (3), che gli è ignoto « se si sia stampato il trattato *de ponderibus*, diversi codici del quale sono indicati dal BONCOMPAGNI nelle notizie delle versioni fatte da

(1) Bisogna correggere 1486.

(2) « Er beschäftigte sich unter anderem mit Statik und Perspective und schrieb überdies Erläuterungen zu den Latidudines formarum des Oresme. Letztgenannter Commentar ist 1482 in Padua im Drucke erschienen, gehört aber heute zu den kaum auffindbaren Seltenheiten, und doch wären Nachrichten über ihn sehr erwünscht, sowohl wegen der uns bekannten Bedeutsamkeit des erläuterten Werkes, als auch um ein Urtheil zu gewinnen, wie weit die Berühmtheit des Verfassers eine verdiente war ».

(3) Per la prima edizione cita: *Incipit perutilis tractatus de latitudinibus formarum secundum Reverendum doctorem magistrum Nicolaum Horen* (di 20 carte nell'ultima delle quali è detto che fu finita di stampare il 18 febbraio 1486) e dice che nel recto della 12ª carta sta scritto: *Incipiunt questiones super tractatu de latitudinibus formarum per venerandum doctorem magistrum Blasium de Parma de pelicanis* (e finisce colla data, mese ed anno suddetto).

Platone Tiburtino » (p. 54 e seg. della Nuova Acc. Lincei). Sicchè unica opera stampata che finora si ricordi del PELICANI è il suddetto commento.

Ma quale non fu la mia meraviglia quando nello spogliare quel prezioso volume trovai che, non uno, ma due trattati vi erano del PELICANI e che il secondo trattato è addirittura ignoto? Eppure tanto il BONCOMPAGNI che il RICCARDI, due finissimi ricercatori di opere rare, hanno descritto la *collezione matematica di* OTTAVIO SCOTI minutamente, ne hanno contate le carte in numero di 74 in tutto, hanno riportato l'ultimo periodo dell'ultima carta, ed hanno dato l'elenco dei trattati in esso contenuti nel numero di *sette*. Invece in essa vi sono due altri trattati sconosciuti finora e sono:

Questio subtilis doctoris Johannis de Casali de velocitate motus alteriotiones (carte 58 a 71 verso);

Questio Blasii de Parma de tactu corporum durorum (carta 71 verso 2ª col., 74 recto).

Quindi è assodato che vi è un'opera di GIOVANNI DE CASALI da esaminare, e che le opere stampate di BIAGIO da Parma finora venute a luce sono due: Il commento sul trattato *de Latitudinibus formarum* di ORESME, e le *Questioni sull'urto o contatto dei corpi duri* [1].

Come abbia potuto avvenire questa distrazione nei due citati valorosi storiografi, e in tutti quelli che hanno avuto per le mani il libro suddetto, spiegherò in poche parole. L'editore cominciò a far stampare quest'opera in folio di cm. 20 per 28,5 a due colonne per pagina in quaderni variabili di 10, di 8, di 6, o di 4 carte l'uno, e nel primo quaderno incluse il frontespizio, ove mise, con ortografia che lascia anche a desiderare, l'elenco dei titoli dei *sette* trattati. Sono questi i sette trattati notati da BONCOMPAGNI e da RICCARDI. Però quando l'editore giunse alla fine del quaderno ottavo, pensò d'inserire nella collezione gli altri due trattati e, non volendo rifare il frontespizio, sul dorso dell'ultima pagina del 10° quaderno (cioè nel *verso* di quella carta che nel *recto* porta l'ultimo periodo citato) stampò a caratteri grossi i due titoli dei due ultimi trattati. L'elenco della collezione corretto nella ortografia è perciò il seguente:

Questio de modalibus Bassani Politi (carte 2 a 4 recto, numerate);

Tractatus proportionum introductorius ad calculationes Suiset [2] (carte 4 verso a 8, numerate);

Tractatus proportionum Thome Bradwardini (carte 9-16, numerate);

Tractatus proportionum Nicholai Horen (carte 17-26, non numerate);

Tractatus de latitudinibus formarum ejusdem Nicholai (carte 27-29, non numerate);

Tractatus de latitudinibus formarum Blasii de Parma (carte 30 a 32 recto, non numerate);

Tractatus de [3] *sex incovenientibus* (carte 33-58 recto 1ª col., non numerate);

[1] Il PELICANI stesso nella 32ª carta afferma di aver scritto delle *Questioni sul trattato delle proporzioni*, ma non risulta che siano state stampate.

[2] Ejusdem magistri BASSANI POLITI artium Doctoris.

[3] Il testo dice per isbaglio *Auctor sex inconvenientibus*.

Questio subtilis doctoris Johannis de Casali de velocitate motus alterationes (carte 58 recto 1ª col. - 71 verso, non numerate);

Questio Blasii de Parma de tactu corporum durorum (carte 71 verso 2ª col. - 74 recto, non numerate).

Termina il volume col seguente periodo:

Venetiis mandato et sumptibus heredum quondam nobilis Viri D. Octaviani Scoti Civis Modoetientis per Bonetum Locatellu Bergomensem presbyterum Kalendis Septembris 1505.

Cui segue il registro dei 10 quaderni e l'emblema di Ottavio Scoti.

* * *

Dalla lettura dei due trattati di Biagio da Parma risulta che il cognome suo invece che Pelacani si deve scrivere Pelicani e che la questione sull'urto contatto dei corpi duri è stata oggetto di una disputa da lui tenuta a Bologna.

Il primo (1) occupa in tutto 10 colonne di stampa. Comincia così:

Incipiunt questiones super tractatu de latitudinibus formarum determinate per venerandum doctorem magistrum Blasium de Parma de Pelicanis; e termina con queste parole: *Espliciunt questiones super tractatu de latitudinibus formarum magistri Johannis* (2) *Horen determinate per venerandum doctorem artium magistrum Blasium de Parma de Pelicanis.*

L'altro trattato occupa 4 colonne di stampa, e comincia così:

Blasii de Parma de tactu corporum durorum questio; e finisce: *Esplicit questio Bononie disputata per Reverendissimum doctorem magistrum Blasium de Parma omnium. septem artium professorem. Parisius doctoratum, etc.*

Nel primo dei due trattati suddetti, quello ritenuto commento all'opera di Oresme intorno alla legge con cui variano le ordinate delle curve piane o, come egli dice, le latitudini delle forme, si discutono, col solito metodo della scolastica, tre questioni:

1ª questione: Se la latitudine di qualsivoglia forma sia sempre uniforme o difforme;

2ª questione: Se vi sia qualche forma uniformemente difforme che cominci a *non grado;*

3ª questione: Se a qualsivoglia latitudine uniformemente difforme corrisponda il suo grado medio.

Sulla prima questione si risponde che no; e per venire a questa conclusione egli non segue l'Oresme col parlare solo di forme geometriche piane, ma eleva il concetto di forma al suo più ampio significato. E comincia a parlare di forme *sostanziali* e di forme *accidentali;* le sostanziali le suddivide in *estese* e *non estese* e ciascuna di queste in altre specie; le *accidentali* le suddivide in *graduali* e *non graduali*, e ciascuna di queste in altre e così seguitando; ed è notevole che fa entrare

(1) Questo primo trattato sarà ristampato per esteso negli Annali del R. Istituto tecnico di Napoli del 1909, vol. 25.

(2) Per errore invece di *Nicholai.*

anche il tempo come termine di paragone per le suddivisioni successive. Poi le stesse forme accidentali le suddivide in *divisibili* e *non divisibili*. Né egli si limita, quando parla di forme geometriche, alla concezione delle forme a due dimensioni, *estensione* e *intensione* (o *longitudine* e *latitudine*), ma considera anche quelle a tre dimensioni *longitudine, latitudine* e *profondità*, ed insiste inoltre che la uniformità della forma è relativa al soggetto ed al tempo, quindi fa entrare anche una quarta dimensione nelle sue considerazioni.

Fatto ciò egli definisce che cosa sia una latitudine uniforme rispetto al soggetto e rispetto al tempo, e che cosa sia una latitudine difforme rispetto al soggetto, rispetto al tempo e rispetto ad entrambi gli elementi.

E finisce con 9 conclusioni, per mettere in chiaro che il problema posto in questo modo non ammette che le latitudini delle forme possano essere sempre uniformi o difformi.

È notevole la prima conclusione che dice: ogni parte del fuoco è tanto calda quanto tutto il fuoco; e la terza ove porta il corpo umano come esempio di forma sostanziale che non può essere uniforme o difforme perché è indivisibile.

Sulla seconda questione, egli comincia dal voler mettere in chiaro la definizione della latitudine uniformemente difforme; poiché, egli dice che molti sbagliano nel definirla.

E dopo aver affermato che se a è una latitudine uniformemente difforme essa è difforme (si noti questa indicazione di una cosa con la lettera a), egli comincia dal citare la definizione dell'autore, Oresme, e dice che non è buona.

La definizione di Oresme era questa:

Latitudo uniformiter difformis est illa: cujus est aequalis excessus graduum inter se equaliter distantium.

Pare che egli interpreti che se 8 è la distanza fra' due gradi, 8 debba essere l'eccesso del grado, se sei, sei, se quattro, quattro (cioè con nostro linguaggio che la linea retta che debba rappresentare questa forma sia inclinata a 45 gradi con la linea delle longitudini) il che non appare ad una interpretazione liberale della riportata definizione. Ne critica altre due (delle quali non dice gli autori) e poi conchiude che la definizione più chiara è la seguente:

Latitudo uniformiter difformis est latitudo difformis: cujus quarumlibet trium partium extensive equalium ab invicem eque distantium situantur ut prime ad secundam sicut 2 ad tertiam equales intensive sunt excessus talis est prime ad secundam sicut 2 ad tertiam loquendo de partibus totalibus quantitatis intensive.

Dopo passa a discutere che cosa si debba intendere per *grado* e *non grado*, quale è cioè la qualità del grado, e fa lunghe disquisizioni per conchiudere che come il punto indivisibile è infinitesima parte della linea ed è termine della linea, così qualunque parte infinitesima è termine, e che quindi terminare a *non grado* vuol dire passare da un dato grado a un grado infinitamente piccolo.

In base a questa disquisizione egli (dopo aver fatte diverse conchiusioni sul cominciare e terminare delle latitudini estensive ed uniformi) cita che Oresme aveva detto che nessuna latitudine uniformente difforme può cominciare a *non grado* e terminare a *non grado*, e con un esempio di forma in cui entrano pietre e mattoni fa vedere come si debba correggere questa sua conchiusione.

Sulla terza questione si ferma un po' più a lungo. Prima fa delle premesse, che sono in relazione con le diverse classi di latitudini che egli ha formulate innanzi e nelle quali non crediamo utile seguirlo. Poi si sofferma a fare delle considerazioni geometriche semplicissime e a dimostrarle: che cioè, la congiungente i due punti medî di due lati di un triangolo è metà del terzo lato; che il parallelogrammo limitato da questa congiungente e dal terzo lato è equivalente al triangolo; e che il triangolo staccato dalla detta congiungente nel dato triangolo è quarta parte del triangolo intero.

Dopo fa 8 conclusioni sul quesito, fra le quali citeremo la 3ª, che dice che in ogni latitudine uniformemente difforme, che o comincia a *non grado* o termina a *non grado*, il grado medio è metà del massimo suo grado; e la 5ª ove dice che nelle latitudini uniformemente difformi vi sono infinite loro parti che hanno lo stesso grado medio. Egli tende in sostanza a far vedere che non sempre esiste nella forma il grado medio.

Infine in un quarto articolo presenta delle eccezioni a quanto egli ha detto, eccezioni che sono dipendenti dalle qualità di latitudini che egli considera, e che egli ricava da un corpo a forma di colonna, dal calore, dalle latitudini dipendenti insieme dal tempo e dal calore, e così via.

***

Dall'esame di questo trattato resta assodato che la concezione di Nicola Oresme fu allargata, ingigantita e complicata da Biagio Pelicani deviandola dalla dritta via che avrebbe dovuto percorrere per arrivare più presto alla concezione della Geometria analitica di Descartes. E gli altri trattati della *Collezione matematica di Ottavio Scoti* stanno lì a provare, anche con una sola rapida scorsa, qual'è quella che nella fretta del momento ho potato darci, che questa amplificazione della questione fatta dal Pelicani colpì nel genio del tempo; poiché fu subito accettata e seguìta da altri, mentre le idee semplici e piane di Oresme furono messe addirittura da banda.

Ciò naturalmente non sarebbe successo, se il Pelicani non avesse acquistato con la sua dottrina un grande ascendente sui suoi contemporanei; perciò questo trattato non fa scapitare la sua fama; ma nemmeno la conferma nel senso che sarebbe desiderato dalla storia del progresso della teoria della rappresentazione analitica delle curve. Resta quindi ad esaminare quanto egli abbia contribuito alla scienza con la disputa che tenne a Bologna sull'urto o contatto dei corpi duri, questione che fu ancora dopo di lui per circa due secoli nell'infanzia. Ma il tempo non mi è bastato per superare le difficoltà che la lettura del trattato presenta, e su di esso io mi riserbo di riferire in altra occasione ed in altro luogo.

G. PITTARELLI

DUE LETTERE INEDITE DI LAGRANGE ALL'ABATE DI CALUSO ESISTENTI NELL'ARCHIVIO STORICO MUNICIPALE DI ASTI

È ben noto come Luigi Lagrange, nato il gennaio del 1736 a Torino, il 21 agosto 1766 per suggerimento di D'Alembert fu chiamato da Federico II a Berlino, come capo della Sezione matematica di quell'Accademia; e fu così successore di Euler. Morto Federico II, egli fu invitato da Vittorio Emanuele I a tornare a Torino, e da Luigi XVI ad andare a Parigi. Preferì Parigi e vi si stabilì nel 1787.

Permettetemi di ricordare come il marchese Caracciolo, rappresentante del Re di Napoli presso quello di Sardegna e legato con Lagrange da grandissima amicizia, avesse fatto a questo delle proposte per andare a Napoli. Ciò prova ancora una volta quello che il collega Loria affermò nella sua conferenza di mercoledì, che, cioè, anche all'epoca del nostro servaggio politico, uomini illuminati non mancarono che amassero i buoni studî e le nostre discipline matematiche, e ne onorassero i cultori, secondo le proprie forze e le circostanze!

Tornando a Lagrange, ho l'onore di presentare a voi a nome del Municipio di Asti le fotografie, in doppia copia, di due lettere ch'Egli scrisse all'abate Tommaso Valperga di Caluso, e che ora si conservano nell'archivio storico municipale della suddetta città, dove io le ritrovai nel luglio del 1904. Esse datano l'una da Berlino (3 luglio 1784), l'altra da Parigi (28 aprile 1788): non sono di argomento scientifico; ma possono servire benissimo alla biografia dell'Uomo.

Nella prima lettera Lagrange parla dello Scheele del chimico di Stokolma che fu eletto socio straniero di quella che allora divenne Accademia delle Scienze di Torino, il 21 marzo 1784, e ne parla nei termini che si potranno leggere nella lettera stessa.

All'Abate, che gli aveva fatto l'invito d'inviargli qualche Memoria per l'Accademia, promette di soddisfarlo, scegliendo tra quelle delle quali poteva disporre; ma ci fa anche sapere ch'egli diviene di giorno in giorno di più difficile contentatura per le sue Memorie, e invece di aumentare il numero di quelle stampate, desidera piuttosto di poterne sopprimere una parte, o almeno ridurle a poche pagine.

Nell'altra lettera avvisa l'Abate d'inviargli due esemplari della « Meccanica analitica », allora pubblicata, l'uno per l'Accademia, come tributo di riconoscenza e di rispetto, e l'altro per l'Abate medesimo, al quale soggiunge: « *io vorrei* (traduco) *avere qualche cosa di meglio ad offrirvi per convincervi di tutta la mia stima e per meritare la vostra* ».

Si vede poi che l'Abate gli aveva richiesto qualche scritto per l'inserzione nel volume IV degli Atti. Egli scrive in proposito: « temo forte (traduco anche quì) « di non poter rispondere alla richiesta come io desidererei. Lasciando Berlino ho preso « quasi congedo dalla geometria, e il cerchio di distrazioni in mezzo alle quali vivo « qui è poco proprio a rianimare la mia antica passione per questa scienza ».

Si sente da queste due lettere, scritte a un antico amico e confratello, tutta la mitezza, e anzi la timidezza, dell'animo di LAGRANGE, ma anche la stima grande e sincera ch'egli aveva di colui al quale scriveva, e dello SCHEELE, e del CONTE DI SALUZZO, ufficiale del genio, fondatore, col medico CIGNA e con LAGRANGE, di quella Società privata che divenne poi l'Accademia delle Scienze di Torino, e del chimico marchese di BREZÉ (Argentero di Bersezio, marchese Gioacchino), membro dopo il 1770 di quella.

E ben era degno della stima di un tanto uomo l'abate di CALUSO, al quale Egli si rivolgeva per ricordarsi agli altri amici. Il segretario generale dell'Accademia e poi direttore della classe fisica nei primi del secolo scorso, era una di quelle figure dagli aspetti svariati, che nella storia della coltura meritano sempre un posto segnalato. Era amicissimo, oltre che di LAGRANGE, anche di V. ALFIERI, i due maggiori spiriti che avesse prodotto allora il Piemonte, tanto che l'autobiografia dell'ALFIERI è piena del nome dell'Abate, come di *amico incomparabile*, di *ottimo degli uomini* ecc. E tra una memoria e un'altra di matematica e di fisica ch'egli veniva pubblicando nei volumi accademici di Torino, insegnava all'ALFIERI, come questi afferma, *a gustare e sentire e discernere la bella e immensa varietà de' versi di Virgilio* (1), e gli dava per iscritto *fratellevoli e luminosi avvisi su le traduzioni dal greco!*

Io consegno dunque queste due lettere di L. LAGRANGE a un tanto amico, nelle mani dei due Presidenti odierni della nostra Sezione IV, signori prof. PICARD e SIMON, l'uno della Francia, l'altro della Germania. È un caso fortuito, ma bello, che questi due egregi scienziati ricevano pel nostro Congresso questo dono della città di V. ALFIERI, che ricorda l'Uomo sommo, il quale, divenuto già celebre nella patria Torino, illustrò poi col suo nome e con le sue opere immortali prima Berlino e poi Parigi.

Dopo ciò ecco le due lettere di LAGRANGE, delle quali mantengo l'ortografia.

A' Monsieur
Monsieur l'Abbé de Caluso
de l'Academie des Sciences
à Turin.

Monsieur,

Je ne connois M. Schèele que par ses ouvrages et ses decouvertes, j'ignore meme sa demeure, mais je tacherai de lui faire passer votre lettre par la voie du Ministre de Suede. Je ne doute pas

(1) *Vita di V. Alfieri scritta da esso*, Torino, Paravia e C., 1903, cap. VII, p. 165.

qu'il ne soit très flatté de cette distinction, et l'Academie doit l'etre de son coté d'avoir été une des premieres à lui rendre les honneurs dus a son merite. Je suis très sensible à l'invitation dont vous m' honorez, et je voudrais pouvoir y repondre d'une maniere proportionnée au cas que j'en fais; mais quoique j'aie pleusieurs memoires dont je puis disposer, je ne saurais me resoudre a vous en envoyer quelques uns, que dans le cas où ils seroient necessaires pour completer le volume, qu' il conviendroit d'ailleurs, à l'exemple des principales Academies, de destiner presqu'uniquement aux travaux des membres ordinaires. Je deviens de jour en jour plus difficile sur les miens, et au lieu d'augmenter le nombre de mes memoires imprimés, je desirerois fort de pouvoir en supprimer une partie, ou du moins la reduire a peu de pages. Je suis enchanté d'avoir une occasion de vous renouveller les temoignages des sentimens que vous m'avez inspirés depuis longtems et aux quels notre nouvelle confraternité a ajouté encore.

Ayez la bonté de m' acquitter envers M. le Comte de Saluces pour toutes les choses obligeantes qu'ils a daigné m'ecrire, et d'agréer les assurances de la haute estime et de la respectueuse consideration avec laquelle j'ai l'honneur d'être

Monsieur

à Berlin le 3 Juillet
1784

Votre tres humble et tres
obeissant serviteur
DE LA GRANGE

Paris, le 28 avril 1788.

Monsieur,

Quoique je n'aie pas encore reçu le paquet que vous avez la bonté de m'ennoncer, je suis trop sensible à l'honneur que vous me faites par le present que vous m'avez destiné pour que je ne m'empresse pas a vous en remercier. Permettez moi de vous prier en meme temps d'accepter comme un faible retour de ma part un exemplaire da ma mecanique analitique qui vient de paraitre. Je voudrais avoir quelque chose de mieux a vous offrir pour vous convaincre de toute mon estime et pour meriter la votre. Je prends la liberté de vous en envoyer aussi un pour l'Academie, et je vous serai infiniment obligé de me faire l'honneur de la presenter de ma part a cette Compagnie comme un tribut de reconnaissance et de respect que je lui dois. Quant au desir que vous voulez bien me temoigner d'avoir quelque chose de moi pour l'inserer dans le quatrieme volume, je crains fort de n'y pouvoir repondre comme je le desirerais. J'ai presque pris congé de la geometrie en quittant Berlin, et le cercle de distractions au milieu duquel je vis ici est peu propre a ranimer mon ancienne passion pour cette science. Ayez la bonté de dire a M. le Marquis de Brezé combien je suis sensible à son souvenir; j'espere qu'il ne doutera jamais de mon devouement comme je ne doute pas de ses bontés. Oserois-je vous prier encore de faire agréer à M. le Comte de Saluces mes hommages et mes sinceres excuses de ce que j'ai manqué de repondre dans le temps a la lettre dont il m'a honoré par M. de Landriani? Je tacherai de reparer cette faute par mon zele à le servir si je puis lui etre bon a quelque chose dans ce pais. J'ai l'honneur d'être aver la consideration la plus distinguée,

Monsieur

Votre tres humble et tres
obeissant serviteur
DE LA GRANGE

N. B. - La Sezione approvò la proposta che una delle copie fosse data alla Biblioteca della Facoltà di Scienze dell'Università di Roma, l'altra a quella dell'Accademia dei Lincei.

F. AMODEO

SULLA NECESSITÀ DI FORMARE UN ARCHIVIO DELLE SCIENZE MATEMATICHE

Chiunque imprenda a trattare una scienza storica si deve non una volta sola arrestare innanzi a questa difficoltà: Sono io sicuro che quest'idea che ora io trovo estrinsecata, non sia stata da altri manifestata precedentemente?

E purtroppo ora in tantissime occasioni manca la possibilità di rispondere a questa dimanda, e molte volte soltanto il caso guida uno storico a risolvere una di queste difficoltà, quando egli meno se lo aspetti e nel momento che egli si accingeva a tutt'altra ricerca. E ciò è non solo vero in riguardo al passato, ma anche in riguardo alle teorie che si vanno concretando al presente, per la qual cosa niente di più insicuro dei nomi che attualmente si affibbiano ai teoremi delle diverse branche matematiche, che battezzati in fretta dal primo ammiratore di uno scienziato, sono poi riconosciuti a breve intervallo di tempo di una più remota priorità. E questo inconveniente apporta un falso giudizio in danno egualmente dei più umili cultori che dei grandi innovatori della Scienza; perchè se spesso accade che il nome di un grande pare sicura malleveria, che altri di più modesta apparenza non avesse potuto ideare quello stesso teorema, e perciò si sottrae a questi il merito che gli spetta, altre volte avviene, che l'idea di un cultore modesto può aver apparenza di novità, mentre già qualche grande ingegno l'aveva con noncuranza fatta palese, come per incidente, in mezzo ad altre verità da lui ritenute più interessanti, e l'aureola di questi viene in parte diminuita. Più grave è la conseguenza per la Storia, che da queste sviste viene falsata, e si dà allo sviluppo delle idee un andamento tutt'affatto diverso da quello che in realtà avrà avuto.

La necessità quindi di sopprimere queste difficoltà per i tempi già passati e di preparare tutte le facilitazioni affinchè, per i tempi che corrono, non si ricada fra non molto nello stesso inconveniente, vale a dire di mettere la Storia delle Matematiche su di una via che non abbia più bisogno di essere rifatta, è così evidente che io non mi dilungo a dire altro, nella certezza che essa già è condivisa dalle vostre menti.

Mi accingo invece a indagare come si possa ottenere di raggiungere nel modo migliore lo scopo che vi ho delineato. E per facilitare a me stesso la ricerca del metodo che bisogna seguire basterà accennare un poco allo svolgimento della storia dei tempi antichi e alla formazione della storia nei nostri ultimi secoli.

Per quanto riguarda la formazione della storia dei nostri ultimi secoli, prenderò come tipo il MONTUCLA. Egli, appassionato lettore delle opere matematiche e instancabile ricercatore, mise su, in un tempo non lungo, due grandiosi volumi che apparvero e sono meravigliosi ad ogni lettore per il lavoro che quelli gli dovettero costare. Se non che alla lettura attenta di questi volumi, per parte di ciascun matematico, di ogni regione, o centro scientifico europeo, risaltarono subito le dimenticanze, i difetti di quella storia. Ogni lettore conosceva nella sua branca e nella sua regione non un nome solo, non un libro solo che a MONTUCLA era sfuggito; e come poteva essere diversamente? Ma che forse queste esplosioni hanno potuto diminuire il merito del grandioso lavoro di MONTUCLA? Niente affatto. Si conchiuse che bisognava leggere le opere dimenticate, rintracciarne altre che indubbiamente dovevano esserci e riordinare le date degli avvenimenti delle teorie e delle scoperte.

E qui, come era avvenuto nella stessa mente di MONTUCLA, si sviluppano due tendenze storiche: gli storici per regione, gli storici per branche, che io personifico in LIBRI e in CHASLES. Ciascuno portò le sue rivendicazioni, questi per la branca geometrica, l'altro per la vita matematica italiana. Ma l'uno e l'altro furono incompleti; perchè CHASLES non ebbe il tempo di leggere tutte le opere geometriche e tutte analizzarle attentamente, e nè potette averle tutte a sua disposizione; e LIBRI non potette tutta far risaltare la coltura italiana, perchè tutte le biblioteche d'Italia non potettero essere da lui rovistate. Intanto l'uno e l'altro trovarono imitatori e continuatori, e sempre edificando gli uni sugli altri e correggendo e proporzionando meglio in base a nuove scoperte, siamo giunti fino all'opera di MORITZ CANTOR, la più magistrale, la più grandiosa che ormai si possogga.

Ma con questa è fatta la Storia universale delle matematiche?

Bisogna, invece di rispondere, chiedere al venerato Maestro: Avete potuto Voi leggere tutte le opere che sono state dimenticate dagli altri; avete potuto rileggere in modo completo quelle che già erano esaminate, per assicurarvi se il giudizio dato era esatto e se la lettura precedente è stata esauriente? Io risponderò per lui con le sue parole indirizzate a me in una lettera che io conservo come prezioso suo ricordo, e che egli mi spedì il 5 marzo 1902, in seguito alla pubblicazione della mia *Vita matematica napoletana*; egli scrisse: « *È chiaro che i libri, che per la loro rarità, soltanto nelle biblioteche della patria dei loro autori si trovano, altrove siano sconosciuti. Perciò le ricerche speciali come le sue devono aiutare a riempire gli involontarii vuoti delle cognizioni storiche* » (1).

Ed ecco dunque che fra mezzo secolo gli storici si troveranno per rispetto al nostro Maestro nelle stesse condizioni in cui si trovava egli rispetto al MONTUCLA, allo CHASLES, al LIBRI. E la storia cambierà sempre, e financo nelle linee principali

(1) « Es ist ja begreiflich, dass Bücher, welche selbst in der Heimat ihres Verfasses zu den Seltenheiten der Bibliotheken gehören, anderwärts ganz umbekannt sind. Da müssen Einzeluntersuchungen wie die Ihrige helfen, umbeabsichtigte Lücken in der Geschichtskenntiss auszufüllen ». (Da una lettera del 5 marzo 1902).

essa potrà subire fluttuazioni; non dico nulla di quello che avverrà nelle parti secondarie.

A far risaltare il mio pensiero prendo ad esempio le qualità della storia delle matematiche del LIBRI. Chi legge quest'opera è tutto compreso di meraviglia per lo stile che la informa, per l'entusiasmo che in ogni pagina risalta, per la passione che l'autore poneva nelle sue ricerche, e ognuno si augurerebbe di sapere scrivere la Storia con eguale attraente stile. Ma se poi si riguarda il contenuto, e si chiede la sintesi di ciò che si legge, non si può negare che il lettore resta sconfortato, poichè una sintesi storica non si può ricavarla dall'opera sua, se non si conosce la storia. Molto spesso l'autore mentre parla di un periodo storico, e di una certa epoca, trascinato dalla sua stessa fluidità di pensiero, e di stile, trascorre e parla di uomini e di opere che a quella non appartengono, senza avvisarne il lettore, oppure esce in considerazioni estranee alle matematiche, perchè egli si entusiasma di altre ricerche che la sua mente accarezza, e delle quali a lui non sarebbe mancato il materiale per farle. Eppure la sua Storia è rimasta ed è consultata avidamente, perchè il suo gran valore sta nelle note, che costituiscono la più gran parte dell'opera; là egli ci presenta o brani di opere fin allora sconosciute, o rarissime a trovarsi, o riassunti del contenuto di altre opere rare o di lettura difficile; è per esse che la Storia del LIBRI sarà sempre utilmente sfogliata.

Questo mio giudizio, che io non credo non si possa sottoscrivere anche da altri fra voi, mi richiama all'altro punto storico di cui voleva parlarvi, a quello della creazione della Storia antica.

Qual'è l'opera che ha dato il maggiore impulso alla formazione della storia dell'antichità per quei periodi per i quali le opere corrispondenti non sono arrivate fino ai nostri tempi? Non le storie, che non sono pervenute a noi che soltanto in brani insignificanti, che hanno potuto a mala pena segnare le colonne migliarie del progresso scientifico dell'evo antico; non i giudizî in essi contenuti, che si son dovuti rivedere e financo mutare; ma in gran parte lo strato fondamentale, la base granitica di tutto l'attuale edifizio storico dell'epoca antica è stata la *Collezione matematica* di PAPPO, e non già nella parte dove egli ha data la sua contribuzione originale di matematico, ma in quella dove egli è stato più fedele espositore del contenuto delle opere altrui. Pochi cenni su qualche opera ora perduta son bastati a far cercare la *divinazione* di quell'opera. Che cosa non si sarebbe fatto se egli avesse dato qualche maggiore dettaglio sul numero e sugli enunciati delle proposizioni, e se non avesse taciuto il nome suo o di altri per riguardo alla scoperta di tanti teoremi da lui citati? Quanto non sarebbe ancora più innanzi lo studio e non sarebbero più sicure le conclusioni della storia di quel periodo?

Un'opera matematica della quale sian note le definizioni fondamentali, la lista ordinata delle proposizioni che contiene in ogni sua parte, è un'opera nota, e se anche si perdesse, l'opera si riprodurrebbe.

E se EUCLIDE, DIOFANTO e TOLOMEO, invece di darci soltanto un corpo compiuto della scienza da essi trattata, avessero voluto dirci pure da quali autori hanno essi tratte le teorie diverse, o i più rilevanti teoremi, quante altre facilitazioni non ne avrebbe avuto la storia, e quanti problemi ora insoluti o insolvibili non sarebbero decifrati?

Da questa indagine risulta evidente che affinchè la Storia delle Matematiche possa avviarsi alla sua sistemazione definitiva, occorre innanzi tutto che sia ordinato il materiale storico, poi occorre che lo storico se ne serva secondo il suo genio gli detta. Questa seconda parte è tutta eventuale e la lasciamo risolvere al caso che crei lo Storico. Quello che possiamo fare è la preparazione completa del materiale storico, ed urge che si faccia, e per esso occorre non l'opera di un solo, nè di dieci, nè di cento persone, ma l'opera di tutti i matematici del mondo, dai modesti ai grandi, in un periodo di tempo non limitato dalla fretta, ma dalla coscienza dei collaboratori, e dal bisogno della Scienza.

Occorre che si crei l'*Archivio delle Matematiche.*

Che cosa è quest'Archivio delle Matematiche?

È la raccolta dei fascicoli che con un unico formato e con un unico tipo di carattere ed in una lingua possibilmente unica contengano in breve ciascuno il riassunto completo di tutte le idee e di tutti i teoremi di ciascuna delle opere matematiche di tutti i tempi e di tutto il mondo.

Questi fascicoli si potrebbero stampare in qualunque parte del mondo, da qualunque gruppo di matematici, o da' matematici isolati.

Ed io assumerei come tipo di formato e di carattere quello dell'attuale « Enciclopedia delle Matematiche ».

Ognuno dei suddetti fascicoli rappresenterebbe per l'Archivio ciò che è la scheda di un'opera nello schedario di una biblioteca; una opportuna notazione decimale dovrebbe segnare il posto del fascicolo nella raccolta ordinata per soggetto; il nome dell'autore basterebbe a segnarne il posto in una seconda raccolta ordinata alfabeticamente: la data della pubblicazione dell'opera riassunta ne fisserebbe il posto in una terza raccolta ordinata cronologicamente.

Tutti questi fascicoli dovrebbero essere acquistati da tutte le biblioteche più importanti del mondo e riuniti, man mano che si vanno stampando, in appositi casellarî o in volumi che non si dichiareranno mai completi.

La critica storica, nella formazione di questi riassunti, dovrebbe essere bandita, oppure limitata alla constatazione delle ripetizioni di cose già note: basterà che il riassunto sia fatto fedelissimamente, che le idee oscure sian fatte chiare, oppure che si dichiari che sono incomprensibili. Poche pagine debbono bastare per opere voluminose. Per esempio, il trattato delle sezioni coniche di Apollonio potrebbe essere riassunto in tante pagine quanti sono i libri che lo compongono, ed in egual modo si potrebbe riassumere l'opera degli *Elementi* di Euclide; ma non sempre il numero delle pagine potrà essere proporzionale al volume dell'opera. Vi saranno delle piccole opere che sono esse stesse il riassunto di idee numerose e feconde e queste avranno forse bisogno di dilucidazioni più larghe dell'opera. La nomenclatura di ogni teoria dovrebbe essere resa più possibilmente uniforme, ma in parentesi dovrebbesi sempre in carattere diverso riportare il nome prescelto dall'autore che si riassume. Non un teorema o un'avvertenza che non fosse stata già fatta precedentemente dovrebbe essere trascurata, nè si dovrebbe cambiar l'ordine adottato dall'autore che si riassume. Poco o nessun peso si dovrebbe dare alle dimostrazioni, salvo quando le dimostrazioni sono esse stesse una novità sul passato o formano un'indimenticabile modello, o costituiscono un originale metodo; ma in ogni caso dovrebbero essere sempre rapidamente accennate.

*
* *

In ogni nazione dovrebbe esserci un comitato centrale che raccoglie e coordina le pubblicazioni dei riassunti delle opere di quella nazione e dovrebbe corrispondere con qualunque collaboratore della nazione per informarlo se il riassunto di una determinata opera esiste e all'occorrenza dare notizia di qualche proposizione in essa contenuta. Un comitato centralissimo di tutte le nazioni dovrebbe coordinare tutta l'opera ed essere al caso di poter informare i comitati nazionali se esiste un riassunto di una qualunque opera, di una qualunque nazione. Con ciò nessun lavoro sarebbe duplicato o sprecato.

I vantaggi di un siffatto archivio sono tanti, che diviene ozioso di stare a dimostrarli; ne citerò qualcuno solamente. Cesserebbe in gran parte la preoccupazione della perdita delle opere; sarebbe ridotto a minimi termini l'inconveniente per le biblioteche e per i centri di studî di non possedere un esemplare di un'opera rara; ogni studioso avrebbe alla sua portata di mano un primo *accessit* a tutta la scienza pubblicata nei più remoti angoli della terra, e potrebbe limitare il bisogno di studiare le opere originali a quelle che effettivamente gli risulterebbero necessarie pel suo particolare scopo; sarebbe effettivamente possibile di fare la vera enciclopedia matematica sul tipo del Formulario di PEANO; poichè ora il tentativo che si sta facendo è molto lontano dal darci tutto ciò che il pensiero umano ha escogitato, e più che *enciclopedia* si può dire raccolta di monografie e riassunti, non di tutte, ma delle principali e più note teorie di una determinata branca della matematica, caratterizzati dalla tendenza speciale dell'autore della monografia.

Resta a considerare l'entità del lavoro e della spesa. Il lavoro è immenso, la spesa è enorme. Ma questo lavoro, suddiviso fra le centinaia di coscienziosi lavoratori e cultori speciali delle singole teorie, e conoscitori della bibliografia del proprio paese verrà ridotto a dosi che non spaventa più nessuno. La spesa viene coperta dall'obbligo che avrebbero le biblioteche, che si rispettano, di acquistare ciascuna tre copie almeno di ogni riassunto per formare la collezione per soggetto, l'alfabetica e la cronologica; e non mi pare che sia esagerato sperare da questa contribuzione anche un compenso per chi si pone con lena a un tal lavoro.

Un abbozzo dell'archivio da me propugnato è embrionale nella pubblicazione fatta dal benemerito prof. LAMPE, al quale io mando un affettuoso saluto e mi faccio interprete della riconoscenza di tutti i matematici del mondo pel lavoro a cui ha saputo così sapientemente sobbarcarsi e continuare per tanti anni con una costanza così meravigliosa. Così come è fatta quella pubblicazione è sempre la prima a cui il ricercatore ricorre quando gli occorrono indicazioni bibliografiche. Ma da questa pubblicazione all'Archivio ci corre ancora molto. Solo l'Archivio potrà rendere allo scienziato ricercatore di nuove verità, e allo scienziato indagatore della storia delle scoverte matematiche quel benefizio che tutti desideriamo. È però innegabile che per gli anni della durata della pubblicazione dello *Jahrbuch über die Fortschritte der Mathematik*, il lavoro per lo Archivio sarà di molto facilitato, come sarà facilitato dal *Formulario matematico* di PEANO, per quanto riguarda le opere già da lui sfogliate.

Veggo che è tempo di concludere, e perciò io presento il seguente ordine del giorno:

« Il Congresso internazionale dei Matematici, udita la proposta del prof. AMODEO, sulla formazione di un Archivio delle Matematiche, fa voti:

« 1° Che in ogni centro scientifico si costituiscano i matematici della regione in comitato per lo spoglio e riassunto di tutte le opere, a preferenza dei matematici di quella regione, e s'incarichi della pubblicazione di ciascun riassunto in opuscolo separato, di formato identico a quello adottato dalla « Enciclopedia matematica » che ora si sta pubblicando, in una delle quattro lingue ammesse nei Congressi, ed in numero di esemplari sufficienti perchè se ne possano provvedere tre a ciascuna delle biblioteche dei centri scientifici del mondo.

2° Che in ogni Nazione si formi un comitato centrale che raccolga le notizie degli opuscoli stampati e in corso di studio per informarne chiunque aspiri a collaborare, onde non avvenga spreco di energie.

« 3° Che un Comitato centrale si assuma il compito di Comitato centralissimo di tutte le Nazioni,

« 4° Che le biblioteche di tutti i centri scientifici del modo assumano l'impegno di acquistare a prezzo determinato i riassunti pubblicati per costituire ciascuna il proprio Archivio delle Matematiche » [1].

[1] Il Congresso approvò la proposta contenuta in quest'ordine del giorno, emendata nel senso di affermare in massima la convenienza di creare un Archivio delle scienze matematiche senza entrare affatto nei particolari (cfr. vol. I, pag. 50).

E. DE AMICIS

L'EQUIVALENZA IN PLANIMETRIA
INDIPENDENTEMENTE DALLE PROPORZIONI E DAL CIRCOLO

Per completare, nelle nostre Scuole Medie, la esposizione della teoria dell'equivalenza dei poligoni, occorre, come è noto, stabilire ad un certo punto il teorema:

ε) « *Se un triangolo ha gli angoli uguali a quelli di un secondo triangolo,* « *il rettangolo di un lato dell'uno e un lato dell'altro è equivalente al rettangolo* « *dei lati corrispondenti a quei due* ».

Quanto più presto la proposizione *ε* verrà stabilita, tanto maggiore vantaggio didattico potrà ricavarsene; e tanto maggior vantaggio scientifico verrà pure a conseguirsi, quanto meno, per stabilirla, si sarà fatto ricorso ad elementi estranei alla natura della questione.

Nella maggior parte dei nostri testi scolastici tale proposizione viene dedotta, come negli *Elementi di Euclide*, dalla teoria delle proporzioni. Nella *Geometria piana* di F. Giudice (Palermo, 1890) viene invece stabilita indipendentemente dalle proporzioni, ma con l'aiuto di proposizioni relative al circolo, quali l'inversa di quella sulla uguaglianza degli angoli iscritti in un medesimo arco e quella sull'equivalenza dei rettangoli delle parti di due corde che si tagliano, dedotta quest'ultima col noto procedimento di Euclide e cioè col sussidio pure del teorema di Pitagora. Tale via, che era stata tenuta fin dal 1881 dal prof. G. Biasi (in un suo corso di lezioni litografato) e fu poi seguìta dal prof G. Testi (Livorno, 1896) e ultimamente dal prof. G. Riboni (Bologna, 1907), non ci pare però consigliabile, appunto perchè veniamo per tal guisa a precluderci l'applicabilità della proposizione *ε* alla dimostrazione dei preaccennati teoremi, di Pitagora cioè e delle trasversali nel circolo.

E, pure evitando la teoria delle proporzioni propriamente detta, ma sempre ricorrendo a proprietà del circolo, tale proposizione può essere stabilita con procedimenti varî, fra i quali sono particolarmente da ricordare quelli del prof. L. Rajola-Pescarini (Napoli, 1876), del prof. Hilbert (Leipzig, 1899), del prof. G. Vailati (Comunicazione al II Congresso di Mathesis, Livorno, 1901; e Bollettino di Matematica, Bologna, 1902) e del prof. B. Levi (Livorno, 1903).

Indipendente invece tanto dalle proporzioni come dal circolo è la dimostrazione data dal De Paolis (Torino, 1884), basata però sul teorema di Desargues pel caso dei triangoli omotetici « *Se due triangoli prospettivi hanno due coppie di lati* « *corrispondenti fra loro rispettivamente paralleli, avranno anche la terza coppia* « *di lati paralleli* » dimostrato col sussidio della Stereometria. Nè può dirsi « *af-*

fatto indipendente dalla teoria delle proporzioni » la dimostrazione che di quest'ultimo teorema ha dato il prof. A. Faifofer (Venezia, 1898), riesposta poi dal prof. F. Palatini (Livorno, 1899) ([1]), basata com'è, con un processo di « esaustione », non solamente sulla esistenza di una parte aliquota di un segmento dato la quale risulti minore di un altro segmento dato per quanto piccolo, sul teorema « Dato un un fascio di parallele e due trasversali, *a due o più segmenti eguali* della prima trasversale *corrispondono altrettanti segmenti eguali* fra loro della seconda trasversale, e *alla somma* di due o più segmenti della prima trasversale *corrisponde la somma* dei corrispondenti segmenti della seconda trasversale » e sull'altro « Se due segmenti sono divisi in uno stesso numero di parti eguali e fra le rette che congiungono ogni coppia di punti di divisione, corrispondenti, ve ne sono *due* parallele, tali congiungenti saranno *tutte* parallele fra loro », ma eziandio sul confronto fra due segmenti dal punto di vista della esistenza, o meno, di una loro *sottomolteplice comune*, sulla distinzione cioè fra grandezze commensurabili e grandezze *incommensurabili* (A. Faifofer, *Elementi di Geometria*, Ed. 13ª, p. 153, ultima riga).

Il procedimento che ora passo ad esporre, e che adopero da un triennio nelle mie lezioni all'Istituto Tecnico, evita invece indiscutibilmente le proporzioni, nè fa uso delle proprietà del circolo, e, *basato sostanzialmente soltanto sulla equivalenza dei parallelogrammi che hanno rispettivamente uguali le basi e le altezze*, serve a stabilire nel modo più diretto la proposizione ε, e senza uscire dal campo della *Planimetria* (intesa nel tradizionale significato scolastico, piuttosto che nel senso ristrettivamente scientifico di *Geometria del piano*) conduce anche al predetto teorema sui triangoli omotetici e perciò pure a quello, più generale, di Desargues sui triangoli omologici complani.

*
* *

Stabilita (sulla base della definizione di equivalenza suggerita dal Duhamel e con l'aiuto della proposizione archimedea) la equivalenza dei parallelogrammi equibasici ed equialti e dedottane l'equivalenza dei *parallelogrammi laterali di un gnomone* ([2]), nonchè la corrispondente proposizione inversa ([3]), e l'equivalenza dei

([1]) Della dimostrazione ideata dal prof. Faifofer è pur fatto uso negli *Elementi di Geometria* del prof. M. Gremigni (Firenze, 1908; *Planimetria*, Libro III, p. 17).

([2]) Il teorema (fig. A) « *Sono equivalenti i parallelogrammi laterali di un gnomone* »

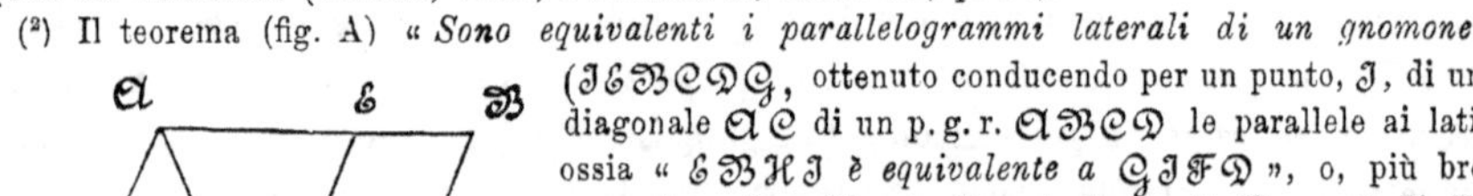

(𝔍𝔈𝔅ℭ𝔇𝔊, ottenuto conducendo per un punto, 𝔍, di una diagonale 𝔄ℭ di un p. g. r. 𝔄𝔅ℭ𝔇 le parallele ai lati), ossia « 𝔈𝔅ℌ𝔍 *è equivalente a* 𝔊𝔍𝔉𝔇 », o, più brevemente, « I ⊔ II » è dimostrato negli *Elementi di Euclide* (vedine p. es. la versione del Tartaglia, Venezia 1569, p. 33 *eversa* e cfr., per la denominazione di *gnomone*, a p. 40) facendo ricorso alla *equivalenza per sottrazione*, che può però facilmente essere evitata, basandosi sulla già stabilita equivalenza dei parallelogrammi equibasici ed equialti, mediante opportuno tracciamento di parallele alla diagonale considerata (F. Giudice, *Geom. Piana*, Brescia 1897, p. 87; M. Gremigni, *El. di Geom.*, Firenze 1904; *Planim.* Libro II, p. 135).

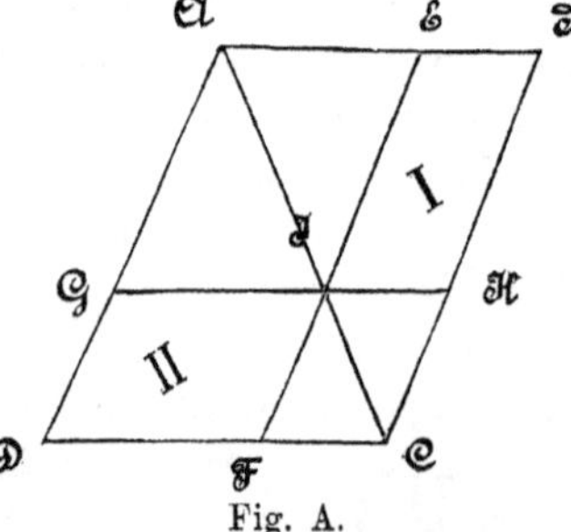

Fig. A.

([3]) Tale proposizione inversa è enunciata nel seguente modo: β) « *Si parallelogrammum di-*

parallelogrammi cantonali di un gnomone doppio ([1]), già considerata da PROCLO ([2]), ciò basta per dimostrare senz'altro la proposizione:

δ) *Se due rettangoli sono equivalenti e altri due, ad essi rispettivamente*

« *visum fuerit in quatuor parallelogramma, ita ut ex illis duo adversa sint aequalia: consistent* « *reliqua duo circa diametrum* » dal CLAVIO, il quale (*Opera Mathematica*, Moguntiae 1612, T. I), dopo di aver dimostrato il *teorema del gnomone*, *α*) « *In omni parallelogrammo complementa* « *eorum, quae circa diamétrum sunt, parallelogrammorum, inter se sunt aequalia* », aggiunge (l. c., p. 72): « *Conversum quoque hujus theorematis cum* PELETARIO *demonstrabimus hoc modo...* ». E, basandosi sul già stabilito teorema diretto, cioè su *α*, prova, valendosi della fig. B, che « *Se*

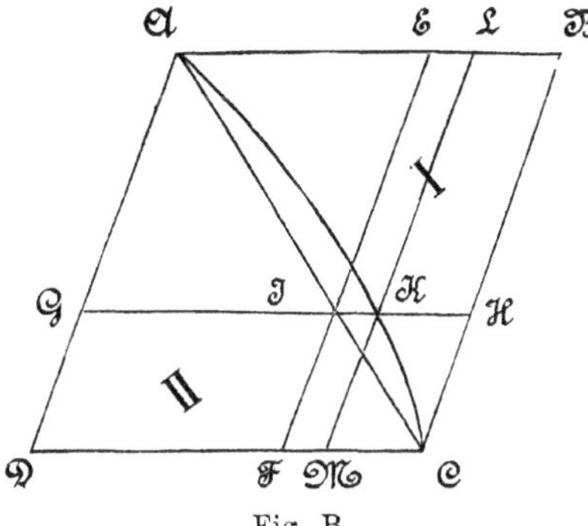

Fig. B.

I $\sqcup$ II, *cioè se il p.g.r. 𝔈𝔅ℌ𝔍 è equivalente al p.g.r. 𝔊𝔍𝔉𝔇 e gli angoli ℌ𝔍𝔈 e 𝔊𝔍𝔉 sono opposti al vertice, e le rette 𝔅𝔈 e 𝔇𝔊 s'incontrano in 𝔄 e 𝔅ℌ e 𝔇𝔉 in ℭ, il punto 𝔍 dovrà trovarsi sulla diagonale 𝔄ℭ del così ottenuto p.g.r. 𝔄𝔅ℭ𝔇* », cioè la proposizione *β*, con semplicissima dimostrazione per assurdo, la quale termina così: « ... *erit etiam 𝔅ℌ𝔎𝔏 maius quam 𝔅𝔈𝔍ℌ*, PARS QUAM TOTUM », usufruendo pertanto implicitamente di ciò che oggidì è chiamato il *postulato della equivalenza*.

([1]) Conducendo (fig. C) per 𝔑 e 𝔖 le parallele ad 𝔄ℭ fino rispettivamente ad incontrare

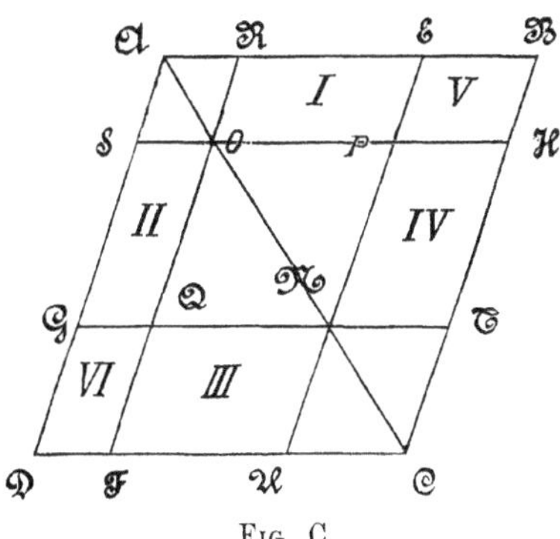

FIG. C.

𝔅ℭ e 𝔇ℭ e basandosi poi sulla equivalenza dei parallelogrammi equibasici ed equialti e sulla transitività della relazione di equivalenza, provasi (senza ricorrere a sottrazioni di poligoni) che « V $\sqcup$ VI », vale a dire: *γ*) « *Sono equivalenti i parallelogrammi cantonali di un gnomone doppio* » (𝔒𝔉𝔈𝔅ℭ𝔇𝔊𝔔, ottenuto conducendo per due punti, 𝔒, 𝔐, di una diagonale 𝔄ℭ di un p. g. r. 𝔄𝔅ℭ𝔇 le parallele ai lati).

([2]) *Eodem modo hoc theorema demonstratur a* PROCLO *etiamsi duo parallelogramma circa diametrum non conjungantur in puncto 𝔍, sed vel unum ab altero sit semotum, vel ambo se*

« *equibasici, sono pure equivalenti, il rettangolo della prima e ultima altezza è* « *equivalente a quello delle altre due* ». Più concisamente: Se b', b'', a', a'', a''', a'''' sono segmenti,

$$\begin{matrix} b'a' \sqcup b''a'' \\ b'a'''' \sqcup b''a''' \end{matrix} \supset a'a'''' \sqcup a''a'''.$$

E riferendoci alla fig. F:

$$\begin{matrix} \text{I} \sqcup \text{II} \\ \text{III} \sqcup \text{IV} \end{matrix} \supset \text{V} \sqcup \text{VI}.$$

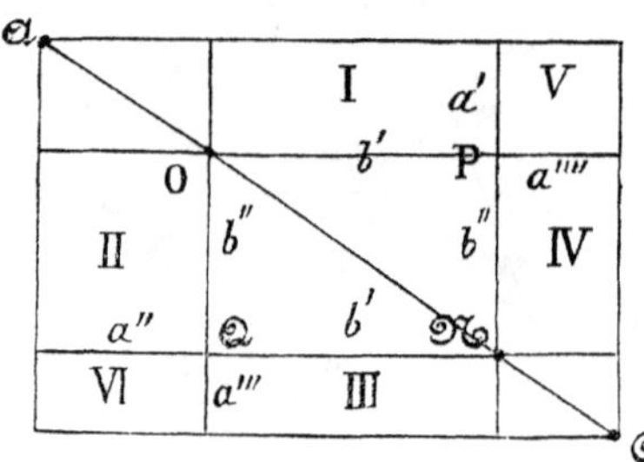

Fig. F.

Infatti, costruito il rettangolo $b'b''$, ossia O P M Q, e fiancheggiatolo coi rettangoli I, II, III, IV, per la β (terz'ultima nota), perchè I ⊔ II, sarà O sulla diago-

mutuo intersecent ». Così il Clavio (o. c., p. 72), in uno *scolio* alla proposizione α (43ª del I Libro d'Euclide), riferendosi alla fig. A ed accompagnandola con la fig. D e la fig. E, che si trovano in Proclo e sono riportate anche nell'*Euclide* del Commandino (Urbino 1575, p. 28). — Nelle osservazioni del Proclo alla precitata proposizione α (pp. 416-18 dei suoi *Commentarii in primum Euclidis elementorum librum*, Ed. Friedlein, Leipzig, Teubner 1873) è notato che i casi (figg. A, D, E)

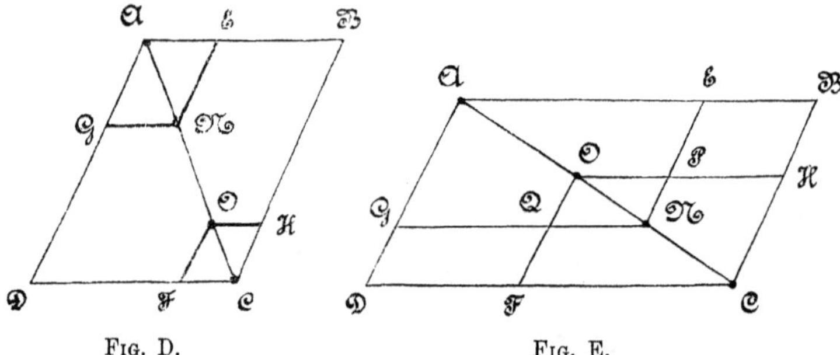

Fig. D. Fig. E.

sono tre, « *nè più nè meno* » (οὔτε πλείους οὔτε ἐλάσσους), e che nel 2° *le figure che sopravanzano* (παραπληρώματα, *complementa* come dice il Clavio, *supplementi* come dicono altri) sono pentagoni, anzi *quinquelateri* « πεντάπλευρα ». Nel 3°, invece dei pentagoni intrecciati, si considerano appunto quei due altri *parallelogrammi*, P E B H e Q F D G, che abbiamo detto *cantonali*, e si dimostra la loro equivalenza, per sottrazione, provando prima quella dei trapezî situati dalle due parti della diagonale. Spiegasi infine perchè la parola παραπλήρωμα non venga definita da Euclide nella lista delle definizioni poste in principio al libro e qual sia inoltre il senso della locuzione « *parallelogrammi costruiti intorno alla diagonale* » (περὶ διάμετρον).

nale $\mathcal{A}\mathcal{N}$, e, perchè III ⊔ IV, sarà $\mathcal{N}$, sulla diagonale $\mathcal{O}\mathcal{C}$; dunque, per la γ (penultima nota), V ⊔ VI, come volevamo dimostrare (¹).

* * *

Ecco, ciò posto, come (con procedimento perfettamente omogeneo alla natura della questione e del tutto analogo a quello che ho esposto fin qui) pervengo a dimostrare la proposizione ε.

Se i triangoli Δ e Δ', ai quali essa si riferisce, sono rettangoli, si potrà collocarli con le ipotenuse adiacenti e da una medesima banda rispetto alla retta delle ipotenuse, e coi cateti corrispondenti rispettivamente paralleli, cioè nel modo indicato dalla fig. G, nella quale mediante le linee punteggiate si è completata *la figura*

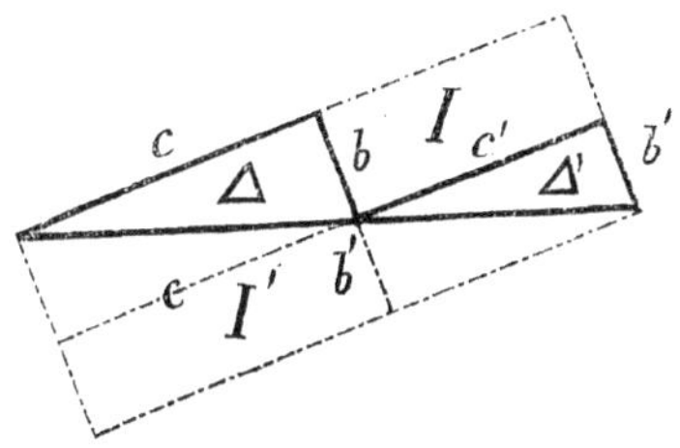

Fig. G.

del teorema del gnomone, di cui I e I' sono parallelogrammi laterali, e perciò I ⊔ I', cioè bc' ⊔ $b'c$; vale a dire: la proposizione ε è intanto provata pel caso in cui i lati dei due triangoli che si considerano sono un cateto dell'uno ed un cateto dell'altro e i loro corrispondenti.

Potremo poi collocare gli stessi triangoli Δ e Δ', cioè $\mathcal{A}\mathcal{B}\mathcal{C}$ e $\mathcal{A}'\mathcal{B}'\mathcal{C}'$, rettangoli in $\mathcal{A}$ e $\mathcal{A}'$, con un cateto $\mathcal{B}'\mathcal{A}'$ di Δ' adiacente alla ipotenusa a, ossia $\mathcal{B}\mathcal{C}$,

(¹) Di questa semplice dimostrazione (alla quale sono giunto variando in alcuni punti, e ricollegando direttamente alle già note proposizioni sull'equivalenza dei parallelogrammi, un procedimento indicatomi dal chiaro collega prof. G. Biasi, in una lettera sua del 26 novembre 1901) può dirsi che è pienamente connaturata alla proposizione da dimostrarsi; alla quale pertanto si perviene, con questo metodo, *senza deviazioni*. Altrettanto non può ripetersi di altre dimostrazioni allo stesso riguardo, le quali invece dipendono dai teoremi sulle trasversali nel circolo o sugli angoli iscritti, o dalla teoria delle proporzioni, o dalla solita proposizione relativa ai triangoli omotetici, o da quella di Pappo sopra uno speciale esagono, che è un caso particolare dell'*esagono di Pascal* e che nelle *Collectiones* è chiamato βωμίσκον « *quod parvi altaris imaginem referat* » (Pappi Alexandrini *Mathematicae Collectiones a Commandino in latinum conversae, Pisauri 1588, fo. 245 verso*), della quale il prof. Hilbert (*Grundlagen der Geometrie*) espone ben tre dimostrazioni, di cui l'ultima (o. c., Ed. 2ª) è precisamente quella stessa che leggesi in Pappo. — Con ragionamento analogo a quello tenuto per la δ, e riferendosi alla fig. C anzichè alla fig. F, dimostrasi pure la seguente proposizione, di cui la δ è caso particolare: « *Se quattro p. g. r. sono* « *fra loro equiangoli, e il I° è equivalente al II°, e il III°, che ha un lato uguale ad un lato* « *del primo, é equivalente al IV°, che ha un lato uguale ad un lato del secondo, allora anche i due p. g. r. equiangoli ai precedenti ed aventi per lati, l'uno gli altri due lati del I° e IV°, e l'altro i rimanenti due lati del II° e III°, saranno equivalenti* ».

di Δ, e l'altro cateto b' perpendicolare alla retta di quel cateto e di quella ipotenusa, e pure da una medesima banda di tal retta, nel modo indicato dalla fig. H, ove mediante linee punteggiate si è completata *la figura del teorema di* PAPPO (*Collectiones*, Liber IV, prop. I) *relativo all'equivalenza di parallelogrammi costruiti sui lati di un triangolo.* Si ottiene così il rettangolo ba', ossia $\mathfrak{A}\mathfrak{C}\mathfrak{C}'\mathfrak{D}$, il quale risulta equivalente al p. g. r. $\mathfrak{B}\mathfrak{C}\mathfrak{C}'\mathfrak{E}$, che alla sua volta è equivalente al rettangolo $\mathfrak{A}'\mathfrak{C}'\mathfrak{E}\mathfrak{F}$, ossia $b'a$; e perciò $ba' \sqcup b'a$; vale a dire la proposizione ε resta provata anche pel caso in cui i lati dei triangoli che si considerano siano un cateto dell'uno e l'ipotenusa dell'altro e i loro corrispondenti.

La proposizione ε rimane così stabilita pei triangoli rettangoli. Essa può poi subito essere estesa ai triangoli obliquangoli. Siano infatti gli angoli del triangolo $\mathfrak{A}\mathfrak{B}\mathfrak{C}$ uguali ai corrispondenti angoli del triangolo $\mathfrak{A}'\mathfrak{B}'\mathfrak{C}'$ e vogliasi dimostrare che $bc' \sqcup b'c$. Condotte le altezze $\mathfrak{A}\mathfrak{D}$ e $\mathfrak{A}'\mathfrak{D}'$, ossia h e h', si avranno (fig. K)

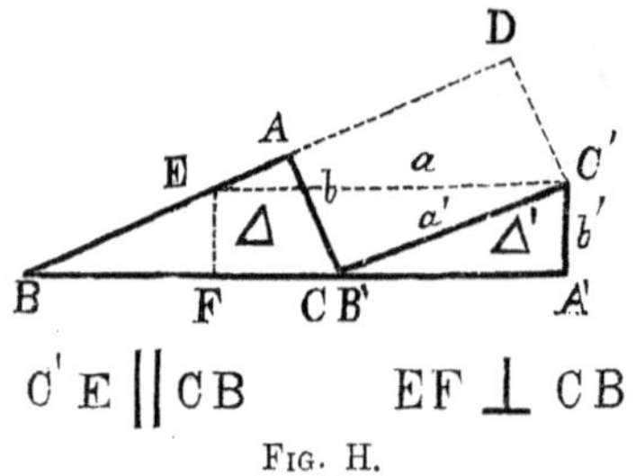

FIG. H.

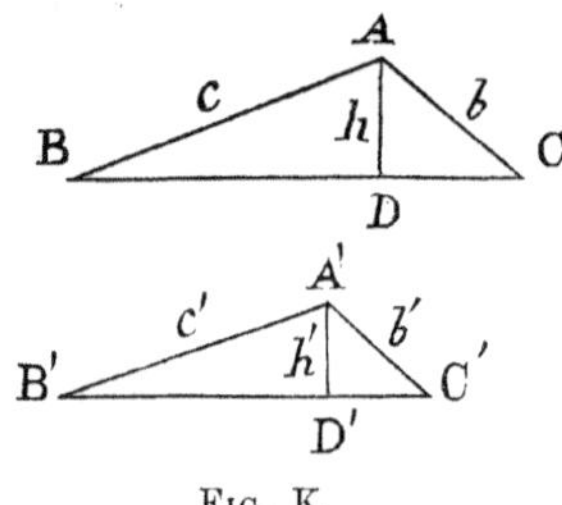

FIG. K.

le due coppie di triangoli, rispettivamente equiangoli, $\mathfrak{A}'\mathfrak{C}'\mathfrak{D}'$ e $\mathfrak{A}\mathfrak{C}\mathfrak{D}$, $\mathfrak{B}'\mathfrak{A}'\mathfrak{D}'$ e $\mathfrak{B}\mathfrak{A}\mathfrak{D}$, rettangoli in $\mathfrak{D}$ e $\mathfrak{D}'$, e perciò:

$$h'b \sqcup hb'$$

$$h'c \sqcup hc',$$

donde, per la δ,

$$bc' \sqcup b'c,$$

come volevasi dimostrare ([1]).

Osservazione. — Stabilita così la ε, se ne deduce tosto col sussidio della δ il sovraricordato TEOREMA DI DESARGUES PEI TRIANGOLI OMOTETICI, che pertanto rimane dimostrato *planimetricamente*; e si deduce pure facilmente l'importante TEOREMA SULL'EQUIVALENZA DEI PARALLELOGRAMMI EQUIANGOLI ED EQUILATERI « *Se una coppia di p. g. r., fra loro equiangoli, sono equivalenti, ogni altra coppia di p. g. r. fra loro equiangoli, e rispettivamente equilateri con quelli, saranno equivalenti* », che può anche stabilirsi direttamente, per farne poi la base di molteplici deduzioni, come ho esposto in una Comunicazione al III Congresso della Associazione « Mathesis » (Napoli, 1903).

([1]) Non è superfluo notare che questa dimostrazione non esclude che i triangoli $\mathfrak{A}\mathfrak{B}\mathfrak{C}$ e $\mathfrak{A}'\mathfrak{B}'\mathfrak{C}'$ possano essere rettangoli in $\mathfrak{A}$ e $\mathfrak{A}'$. In altri termini, potevamo anche esimerci dal dare pei triangoli rettangoli una dimostrazione apposita pel caso relativo ai soli cateti (fig. G); ma l'abbiamo data perchè molto più semplice di altre, note, per il medesimo caso.

L. E. J. BROUWER

DIE MOEGLICHEN MAECHTIGKEITEN

Wenn man untersucht, wie die mathematischen Systeme zustande kommen, findet man, dass sie aufgebaut sind aus der Ur-Intuition der Zweieinigkeit. Die Intuitionen des continuierlichen und des discreten finden sich hier zusammen, weil eben ein Zweites gedacht wird nicht für sich, sondern unter Festhaltung der Erinnerung des Ersten. Das Erste und das Zweite werden also *zusammengehalten*, und in dieser Zusammenhaltung besteht die Intuition des continuierlichen (continere = zusammenhalten). Diese mathematische Ur-Intuition ist nichts anderes als die inhaltslose Abstraction der Zeitempfindung, d. h. der Empfindung von « fest » und « schwindend » zusammen, oder von « bleibend » und « wechselnd » zusammen.

Die Ur-Intuition hat in sich die Möglichkeit zu den beiden folgenden Entwickelungen:

1) Die Construction des Ordnungstypus ω; wenn man nämlich die ganze Ur-Intuition als ein neues Erstes denkt, kann man ein neues Zweites hinzudenken, das man « drei » nennt, u. s. w.

2) Die Construction des Ordnungstypus η; wenn man die Ur-Intuition empfindet als den Uebergang zwischen dem « Ersten für sich » und dem « Zweiten für sich », ist die « Zwischenfügung » zustande gekommen.

Natürlich kann man stets ein ganzes schon mittelst der Ur-Intuition aufgebautes mathematisches System als neue Einheit nehmen, und hieraus erklärt sich die unendliche Fülle der in der Mathematik möglichen Systeme, die indes alle auf die beiden genannten Ordnungstypen zurückzuführen sind.

In dieser Weise betrachtet, würde es nur eine unendliche Mächtigkeit geben, nämlich die abzählbare, und andere als abzählbare fertige discrete Systeme sind in der Tat nicht aufzubauen. In zwei Weisen hat aber eine höhere Mächtigkeit in der Mathematik Sinn:

1) Man kann eine Methode zur Bildung eines mathematischen Systems angeben, die aus jeder gegebenen zum Systeme gehörigen abzählbaren Menge ein neues gleichfalls zum Systeme gehöriges Element erzeugt. Mit einer solchen Methode sind aber wie überall in der Mathematik nur abzählbare Mengen zu construieren, das ganze System ist niemals zu construieren, weil es eben nicht abzählbar sein kann. Es ist

unrichtig, dieses ganze System eine mathematische Menge zu nennen, denn es ist nicht möglich, es aus der mathematischen Ur-Intuition fertig aufzubauen. Beispiele sind: das Ganze der Zahlen der zweiten Zahlenklasse, das Ganze der definierbaren Punkte auf dem Continuum, das Ganze der mathematischen Systeme.

2) Man kann das mit dem discreten gleichberechtigten Continuum als Matrix von Punkten oder Einheiten betrachten, und annehmen, dass zwei Punkte dann und nur dann als verschieden zu betrachten sind, wenn sie sich in ihrer Lage auf einer gewissen Skala von Ordnungstypus η unterscheiden lassen. (Man könnte hinsichtlich der Unterscheidung der Punkte andere Annahmen machen, wie die nicht-Archimedischen Continua zeigen, aber diese Annahmen sind immer auf die erste zurückzuführen). Man bemerkt dann, dass das in dieser Weise definierte Continuum sich niemals als Matrix von Punkten erschöpfen lässt, und hat der Methode zum Aufbau mathematischer Systeme hinzugefügt die Möglichkeit, über eine Skala vom Ordnungstypus η ein Continuum (im jetzt beschränkten Sinne) hinzulegen.

Sei nun eine beliebige Menge M Teilmenge einer Menge von der Mächtigkeit des Continuums, so kann man dieses Continuum auf ein lineares Continuum zwischen 0 und 1 abbilden, und erscheint somit die Teilmenge auf diesem Continuum linear geordnet. In der Menge M existiert nun eine abzählbare Teilmenge M_1, mit Hülfe deren sie zu definieren ist. Diese Menge M_1 kann in folgender Weise in Beziehung gesetzt werden zur Skala der Zahlen $\frac{a}{2^n}$ zwischen 0 und 1.

Die Gesamtheit der Punkte von M_1 approximieren wir durch Dualbrüche. Jede Ziffer ist entweder durch die ihr vorangehende bestimmt, oder lässt noch die Wahl zwischen 0 und 1 offen; wir construieren nun eine Verzweigungskette, in der jeder Zweig sich einfach fortsetzt, falls die Wahl nicht frei ist, und sich in zwei Zweige spaltet, falls sie frei ist, und vernichten sodann jeden Zweig, der sich an keiner weiteren Stelle mehr spaltet. Ist dies, von der ersten Dualstelle anfangend, an allen Stellen vollführt, so wird am gebliebenen Residu noch einmal diese Vernichtungsoperation vorgenommen. Schliesslich ist dann übriggeblieben entweder nichts, oder eine unendliche Verzweigung, in der jeder Zweig sich weiterhin wieder spaltet. Im zweiten Falle enthält die Menge M_1 Teilmengen vom Ordnungstypus η; im ersten Falle nicht.

Es kann nun sein, dass ausser der abzählbaren Menge M_1 von der angegeben ist, dass sie zu M gehört, die Definition von M noch Angabe einer zweiten abzählbaren Menge M_2 erfordert, die zu M sicher nicht gehören darf (¹), aber nach Aufstellung dieser beiden Mengen kann die Bestimmung von M nur noch in einer Weise vervollständigt werden, nämlich, im Falle dass M_1 Teilmengen vom Typus η besitzt, durch die Vollführung der Operation des Continuierlichmachens in einer oder mehreren dieser Mengen, natürlich unter Tilgung der durch M_2 ausgeschlossenen Punkte.

(¹) Falls man in der Menge der ausgeschlossenen Punkte auch die Operation des Continuierlichmachens hätte ausgeführt, so kommt dies schliesslich auf dasselbe hinaus, als ob man nur eine abzählbare Reihe von Punkten hätte angegeben für M_1 und M_2, während das weitere nur auf eine Vorgreifung in die spätere Wahl zwischen Vollführen oder Unterlassen des Continuierlichmachens für die verschiedenen Teilmengen von M_1 vom Typus η hinauskommt.

Wird die Operation wenigstens einmal vollführt, so ist die Mächtigkeit von M jene des Continuums; wird sie nicht vollführt, so ist M abzählbar.

Es existiert also nur eine Mächtigkeit für mathematische unendliche Mengen, nämlich die abzählbare. Man kann aber hinzufügen:

1) *die abzählbar-unfertige*, aber dann wird eine *Methode*, keine Menge gemeint;

2) *die continuierliche*, dann wird freillch etwas Fertiges gemeint, aber nur als *Matrix*, nicht als Menge.

Von anderen unendlichen Mächtigkeiten, als die abzählbare, die abzählbar-unfertige, und die continuierliche, kann gar keine Rede sein.

G. DELITALA

LA TETRAGONOMETRIA PIANA

NELLE SCUOLE SECONDARIE

Oggetto della presente comunicazione è di coordinare e completare alcuni risultati, che già videro la luce in sedi opportune, diretti a fornire dei materiali utili per migliorare i metodi d'insegnamento della *Trigonometria* nelle scuole secondarie e riparare così a quei difetti lamentati da qualche oratore di questa Sezione nella seduta di giovedì.

Sarà pure un modesto contributo alla *Geometria receute* o del *triangolo*, intorno alla quale molti illustri autori continuano a dedicare con lena incessante le loro ricerche, per giungere qualche volta per vie diverse e con mezzi diversi ai medesimi risultati.

La *Tetragonometria piana*, secondo l'etimologia della parola, suona quella parte delle Matematiche elementari che si propone la risoluzione del tetragono completo e ne studia le sue proprietà giovandosi delle funzioni circolari o goniometriche.

Nella *Trigonometria* dati 3 elementi del triangolo, fra i quali sia compreso almeno un lato, si determinano i restanti elementi. Nella *Tetragonometria* dati 5 dei suoi elementi si possono trovare i rimanenti; si potrà estendere la risoluzione al pentagono completo noti essendo 7 dei suoi elementi; ed in generale si può con metodo sistematico dedurre la risoluzione dell'n-gono completo conoscendo $(2n - 3)$ dei suoi elementi, fra i quali sia compreso almeno un lato (nn. 3-9-11 dell'Elenco di pubblicazioni qui unito).

Mentre colla *Trigonometria ordinaria* si ritrovano e si dimostrano le proprietà metriche già note della Geometria, colla *Tetragonometria* non solo si riscontrano e si dimostrano le medesime proprietà, ma se ne deducono delle nuove, e la *Trigonometria* stessa si può riguardare come caso particolare della *Tetragonometria*, quando uno dei vertici coincide con uno degli altri tre o cade sopra un lato del triangolo e sul prolungamento.

Altro vantaggio della *Tetragonometria* si ha nel fatto che mentre le formule della *Trigonometria ordinaria* si basano sul postulato d'EUCLIDE, ossia sui principî della *Geometria euclidea*, la quale corrisponde precisamente al caso della *Geometria non-euclidea*, quando in questa i lati del triangolo sono infinitamente piccoli, le formule della *Tetragonometria piana* godono il carattere di appartenere ai principî fondamentali della *Geometria non-euclidea* più generale della prima. Infatti, è risaputo essere una conseguenza di quest'ultima *Geometria* che le relazioni metriche delle figure piane dipendono da una lunghezza k che non può essere determinato *a priori*; ma se questo parametro deve restare indeterminato dal punto di vista logico od astratto, non è più tale quando si scende ai casi pratici o concreti, ed allora bisogna fissarlo, e perciò non vi è altro modo di determinarlo che ricorrendo all'osservazione.

Il celebre LOBACEFSKI, fondatore della *Geometria non-euclidea*, i due BOLYAI, RIEMANN, HELMOLTZ, BATTAGLINI, BELTRAMI, KLEIN, TAURINUS, DE-TILLY, GENOCCHI ecc. nelle loro classiche Memorie hanno dimostrato questo concetto fondamentale. Essi, partendo dalle funzioni iperboliche relative alla base k, hanno dimostrato che la *Geometria euclidea* non è altro che la *Geometria pratica* (in senso lato) che corrisponde al particolare valore di $k = \infty$ e sono giunti alla indiscutibile conclusione che il V postulato d'EUCLIDE è indimostrabile e bisogna ammetterlo come una verità sperimentale.

Fin dall'anno 1898 nello studio di un problema di *Geodesia elementare* conosciuto comunemente col nome di *POTHÉNOT*, ho trovato un nuovo metodo per la risoluzione dell'importante problema mediante l'uso di un *segmento fisso* (n. 9), del quale ho indicato la costruzione geometrica e l'espressione analitica.

Le formule alle quali sono pervenuto sono le seguenti:

$$(1) \qquad \begin{cases} x = \dfrac{bc}{q} \operatorname{sen}(\alpha - A) \\ y = \dfrac{ca}{q} \operatorname{sen}(\beta - B) \\ z = \dfrac{ab}{q} \operatorname{sen}(\gamma - C) \end{cases}$$

$$(2) \qquad q^2 = b^2 \operatorname{sen}^2 \gamma + c^2 \operatorname{sen}^2 \beta + 2bc \operatorname{sen} \beta \operatorname{sen} \gamma \cos(\alpha - A)$$

o le altre due analoghe che da quest'ultima si possono ottenere colla rotazione ciclica delle lettere. Le a, b, c ; A, B, C sono gli elementi del triangolo di riferimento ABC; α, β, γ sono le *coordinate angolari* del quarto vertice D del tetragono completo che per la convenzione stabilita debbono soddisfare alla relazione di condizione:

$$(3) \qquad \alpha + \beta + \gamma = \pm 2\pi$$

secondochè sono descritte nel senso dell'ordine ciclico dei vertici del triangolo o nel senso inverso; x, y, z sono le *coordinate ceviane* dello stesso vertice D rispetto al triangolo di riferimento. Siccome uno dei lati del triangolo prolungato indefinitamente divide il piano in due regioni, si adotta la convenzione di assumere positive le *coordinate ceviane* del quarto vertice che si trova nella regione del triangolo, negative quando giace nell'altra regione.

In altro studio (n. 4) ho introdotto un secondo parametro Δ, la *costante angolare* del vertice D rispetto al triangolo di riferimento, col quale le formule di risoluzione diventano:

$$(4)\quad \begin{cases} x = \dfrac{b \operatorname{sen} C \operatorname{sen}(\alpha - A)}{\Delta} = \dfrac{c \operatorname{sen} B \operatorname{sen}(\alpha - A)}{\Delta} \\ y = \dfrac{c \operatorname{sen} A \operatorname{sen}(\beta - B)}{\Delta} = \dfrac{a \operatorname{sen} C \operatorname{sen}(\beta - B)}{\Delta} \\ z = \dfrac{a \operatorname{sen} B \operatorname{sen}(\gamma - C)}{\Delta} = \dfrac{b \operatorname{sen} A \operatorname{sen}(\gamma - C)}{\Delta} \end{cases}$$

$$(5)\quad \Delta^2 = \operatorname{sen}^2\alpha \operatorname{sen}^2(\beta - B) + \operatorname{sen}^2\beta \operatorname{sen}^2(\alpha - A) + \\ + 2 \operatorname{sen}\alpha \operatorname{sen}\beta \operatorname{sen}(\alpha - A) \operatorname{sen}(\beta - B) \cos C$$

o le altre due analoghe a quest' ultima.

È notevole che il nuovo parametro Δ è indipendente dai lati del triangolo, ed i due parametri sono legati fra di loro dalla relazione:

$$(6)\quad \frac{q}{\Delta} = \frac{a}{\operatorname{sen} A} = \frac{b}{\operatorname{sen} B} = \frac{c}{\operatorname{sen} C} = 2R$$

che include il noto *teorema dei seni* della Trigonometria ordinaria.

In un successivo studio (n. 7) si è trovato un terzo parametro lineare h, *valore dell'altezza equivalente* del vertice D rispetto al triangolo di riferimento, esso è rappresentato dall'altezza d'un triangolo equivalente a quello di riferimento avente per base il segmento fisso q. Esiste cioè la relazione:

$$(7)\quad \frac{bc \operatorname{sen} A}{q} = \frac{ca \operatorname{sen} B}{q} = \frac{ab \operatorname{sen} C}{q} = \frac{2\Omega}{q} = h.$$

E le formule di risoluzione diventano:

$$(8)\quad \begin{cases} x = h \dfrac{\operatorname{sen}(\alpha - A)}{\operatorname{sen} A} \\ y = h \dfrac{\operatorname{sen}(\beta - B)}{\operatorname{sen} B} \\ z = h \dfrac{\operatorname{sen}(\gamma - C)}{\operatorname{sen} C}. \end{cases}$$

Le citate combinazioni di formule risolvono il problema fondamentale della Tetragonometria piana: « Dati 5 dei 12 elementi principali del tetragono completo, fra i quali sia compreso almeno un lato, trovare i 7 restanti elementi ».

In altro successivo studio (n. 11) oltre i 12 elementi principali del tetragono completo si sono considerati i 6 angoli secondarî A_1, A_3 ; B_1, B_2 ; C_1, C_2 misurati nel senzo dell'ordine ciclico dei vertici del triangolo di riferimento, e si sono stabilite altre due terne di relazioni fra questi nuovi elementi, cioè:

$$(9) \qquad \begin{cases} A = A_2 - A_1 + 2\pi \\ B = B_2 - B_1 + 2\pi \\ C = C_2 - C_1 + 2\pi \, . \end{cases}$$

Si osserva che tutte le possibili disposizioni della figura, tetragono piano, si riducono alle tre seguenti: 1ª, il quarto vertice D cade nell'interno del triangolo di riferimento; 2ª, esso cade fuori del triangolo e in uno dei suoi angoli; 3ª cade fuori del triangolo e in uno degli angoli formati dai prolungamenti dei lati. Nel 1° caso le formule (9) si mantengono inalterate; nel 2° caso si mantiene il termine costante 2π solo nella relazione dell'angolo in cui cade il punto; nel 3° caso si sopprime in tutte il termine costante 2π.

La seconda terna di formule di risoluzione è:

$$(10) \qquad \begin{cases} \dfrac{b \operatorname{sen} \alpha}{a \operatorname{sen} \beta} = \dfrac{\operatorname{sen} B \operatorname{sen} \alpha}{\operatorname{sen} A \operatorname{sen} \beta} = \dfrac{\operatorname{sen}(-B_1)}{\operatorname{sen} A_2} \\[2ex] \dfrac{c \operatorname{sen} \beta}{b \operatorname{sen} \gamma} = \dfrac{\operatorname{sen} C \operatorname{sen} \beta}{\operatorname{sen} B \operatorname{sen} \gamma} = \dfrac{\operatorname{sen}(-C_1)}{\operatorname{sen} B_2} \\[2ex] \dfrac{a \operatorname{sen} \gamma}{c \operatorname{sen} \alpha} = \dfrac{\operatorname{sen} A \operatorname{sen} \gamma}{\operatorname{sen} C \operatorname{sen} \alpha} = \dfrac{\operatorname{sen}(-A_1)}{\operatorname{sen} C_2} \, . \end{cases}$$

Le relazioni (9) e (10) insieme alle sette precedenti forniscono un sistema di 13 equazioni fra altrettante incognite le quali premettono di risolvere il problema fondamentale della *Tetragonometria piana* sotto una forma più generale: « Di un tetragono completo dati 5 qualunque dei suoi 18 elementi di misura, fra i quali sia compreso almeno un lato, trovare i 13 restanti elementi ».

Ognuno vede come sotto questa forma più generale esso comprende moltissimi problemi della Geodesia elementare, fra i quali ricordo: il problema di Pothenot, quello di Hansen, quello di Nansen, quello della distanza inaccessibile ecc.

Proseguendo nelle ricerche, tenendo presente il suesposto principio di *Geometria non-euclidea*, in due successive Note (nn. 13-14) ho trovato la formula di risoluzione del *problema di* Snellius, *ampliato in generale*, che comprende come caso particolare pee $n = 1$, quello di Pothenot, sotto la forma seguente:

« Date le coordinate cartesiane dei tre vertici del triangolo di riferimento e « misurate le coppie di angoli α_i, β_i $(i = 1, 2, 3, \ldots, n)$ trovare l'azimut della « prima congiungente $(AP_1) = \theta_{a,1}$ ».

Si è trovato:

$$(11)\quad \begin{cases} \tan g\, \theta_{a,1} = \dfrac{(X_c - X_b)\cos\omega - (Y_c - Y_b)\,\mathrm{sen}\,\omega + (X_b - X_a)\,K}{(Y_c - Y_b)\cos\omega + (X_c - X_b)\,\mathrm{sen}\,\omega + (Y_b - Y_a)\,K} \\ \omega = \pm\left[\sum_1^n (\alpha_n + \beta_n) - n\pi\right] \\ K = \dfrac{\mathrm{sen}\,\beta_1\,\mathrm{sen}\,\beta_2\ldots\mathrm{sen}\,\beta_n}{\mathrm{sen}\,\alpha_1\,\mathrm{sen}\,\alpha_2\ldots\mathrm{sen}\,\alpha_n} \end{cases}$$

essendo ω l'angolo di deviazione dell'ultima congiungente $P_n C$ sulla prima congiungente $P_1 A$ (n. 19).

Le quali mi hanno condotto alle nuove formule di risoluzione, calcolabili direttamente per logaritmi, del problema di Pothénot e del conseguente problema della Tetragonometria piana:

$$(12)\quad \begin{cases} \dfrac{\mathrm{sen}\,B\,\mathrm{sen}\,\alpha}{\mathrm{sen}\,A\,\mathrm{sen}\,\beta} = \cot\varrho_1 \\ \mathrm{sen}\,\sigma_1 = \mathrm{sen}\,2\varrho_1 \cos(\gamma - C) \\ h = c\,\dfrac{\mathrm{sen}\,A\cos\varrho_1}{\sqrt{2}\,\mathrm{sen}\,\alpha\,\mathrm{sen}\left(\dfrac{\pi}{4} + \dfrac{\sigma_1}{2}\right)} \end{cases}$$

oppure le altre due terne analoghe che si ottengono colla rotazione ciclica delle lettere.

Le formule ottenute godono del carattere di generalità, così pure tutte quelle che dalle medesime si possono dedurre.

Del carattere di generalità si avvantaggia specialmente la Geometria se si considera che le proprietà di una figura si estendono pure al caso in cui uno dei suoi punti si allontani indefinitamente nel piano del triangolo di riferimento in direzione assegnata, il che può dar luogo al *tetragono* che dirò *immaginario*, per distinguerlo dal *tetragono reale* finora considerato, al quale si potranno estendere in virtù del principio di continuità le proprietà dimostrate pel tetragono reale.

Per la dimostrazione, richiamo due importanti proprietà che ho trovato in altro studio (n. 7) dell'*inversione isogonale*:

« 1°. Due punti *coniugati isogonali* hanno in valore assoluto gli stessi *parametri* q, Δ, h. 2°. Le *coordinate angolari* dell'uno sono date dalle funzioni circolari omonime delle *differenze angolari* dell'altro ».

Se si consideramo i punti del circolo circoscritto al triangolo di riferimento ed i corrispondenti punti isogonali si trovano p. es. per l'arco che chiude l'angolo A:

$$\begin{cases} P_a[\alpha_a = 2\pi - (B + C),\ \beta_a = B,\ \gamma_a = C],\ [q_a = 0,\ \Delta_a = 0,\ h_a = \infty], \\ \quad x_a = \dfrac{0}{0},\ y_a = \dfrac{0}{0},\ z_a = \dfrac{0}{0} \\ P'_a[\alpha'_a = -2\pi,\ \beta'_a = 0,\ \gamma'_a = 0],\ [q'_a = 0,\ \Delta'_a = 0,\ h'_a = \infty] \\ \quad x'_a = -\infty,\ y'_a = -\infty,\ z'_a = -\infty. \end{cases}$$

Altri due gruppi di formule analoghe esistono per gli altri due archi di cerchio circoscritto al triangolo.

Dunque il luogo degli inversi isogonali dei punti del cerchio circoscritto, che sono i vertici dei tetragoni immaginarî, hanno le coordinate trilineari (angolari e ceviane) tutte negative e si può affermare ch'esso è un cerchio di raggio infinito e concentrico a quello circoscritto.

Il che non è in contraddizione al concetto di cerchio-limite di LOBACEFSKI di cui è cenno nella celebre Memoria del BATTAGLINI quando scrive: « Nel sistema « di *Geometria non-euclidea* il piano è una superficie indefinita, essendo i suoi punti « all'infinito *tutti distinti* fra loro ed appartenenti ad una *circonferenza di circolo* « che ha per centro un punto *qualunque* del piano ed il raggio infinito ecc. » (1).

Pei tetragoni reali aventi il quarto vertice sulla circonferenza del cerchio circoscritto al triangolo di riferimento, le relazioni fra i tre parametri si presentano sotto forma indeterminata, e siccome si erano trovate le dette relazioni indipendenti dai due sistemi di coordinate trilineari, cioè:

$$\frac{q}{\Delta} = 2R\,,\ q \times h = 2\Omega \text{ e di conseguenza } h \times \Delta = \frac{\Omega}{R}$$

così queste proprietà del tetragono reale si estendono pure al tetragono immaginario.

Si deduce come conseguenza che se si immaginano i lati del triangolo di riferimento prolungati indefinitamente, essi divideranno il piano non già in 7 regioni come si ritiene comunemente nella *Geometria euclidea*, sibbene in 8 regioni, l'ottava delle quali è caratterizzata dall'avere le coordinate trilineari (angolari e ceviane) tutte negative.

Per le brevi considerazioni svolte credo poter concludere che le proposte formule della *Tetragonometria piana* si possono considerare appartenere alla *Geometria non-euclidea*, o meglio si potranno considerare come un capitolo della *Pangeometria* di LOBACEFSKI, scienza questa logica deduttiva fondata come è noto sulle 28 proposizioni di EUCLIDE e sulla negazione del V postulato, e che considera le rette parallele non equidistanti ma assintotiche.

Alla fine della sua opera così si esprime:

« ..... Un semplice colpo d'occhio sulle equazioni (19), che esprimono la di- « pendenza esistente fra i lati e gli angoli dei triangoli rettilinei, è sufficiente per « dimostrare che a partire di là la *Pangeometria diviene un metodo analitico che* « *rimpiazza e generalizza i metodi analitici della Geometria ordinaria*. Si po- « trebbe incominciare l'esposizione della Pangeometria delle equazioni (19), ed anche « cercare di sostituire a queste equazioni altre equazioni che *esprimerebbero le di-* « *pendenze fra i lati e gli angoli di ogni triangolo rettilineo ecc.* » (2).

(1) G. BATTAGLINI, *Sulla Geometria immaginaria di* LOBACEFSKI (Giornale di Matematica, Napoli, vol. V, pag. 230).

(2) *Pangeometria* per N. LOBACEFSKI. Versione dal francese (Giornale di Matematiche di G. Battaglini, vol. V, 1867, pag. 273).

Parole queste che io credo, con poco differente interpretazione, si possano applicare alle citate formule della *Tetragonometria piana* per le quali si può concludere: Esse sono semplici, simmetriche, generali, soddisfano alle esigenze della pratica e sono feconde di numerose applicazioni nel campo della *Geodesia elementare* (nn. 8, 12, 16, 15, 17, 18) e della *Geometria recente* (nn. 6, 10, 7), perciò le ho credute degne della vostra benevola attenzione.

È mia convinzione, sarebbe veramente utile e si renderebbe benemerito dell'insegnamento secondario chi cercasse d'introdurre nelle scuole con metodi elementari il concetto di Geometria non-euclidea sopra enunciato e che ebbi occasione di applicare nelle mie ricerche con buoni risultati. Esso potrà facilitare il raggiungimento di quell'ideale desiderato da tutti e proclamato dalle varie Sezioni di questo Congresso, cioè di contenere in poche leggi generali il maggior numero di cognizioni acquisite alla scienza. Infine per le formule proposte di *Tetragonometria piana* si potrebbero applicare le parole dette dall'illustre mio maestro, il prof. D'Ovidio, in una sua Conferenza tenuta a Napoli a proposito delle *coordinate triangolari*: « *esse hanno ormai il diritto di entrare nell'insegnamento* » (1) e non tardarono ad entrarvi.

Con questo augurio e con questa speranza termino questa qualunque comunicazione.

ELENCO DELLE PUBBLICAZIONI CITATE

1. *Contributo allo studio del problema di Pothènot.* — Accademia Reale delle Scienze di Torino. Anno 1897-98, vol. XXXIII, gennaio 1898.
2. *Le formule definitive di risoluzione del problema di Pothènot.* — L'Ingegneria Civile e Industriale. Torino, gennaio 2906, fasc. 1°.
3. *La risoluzione completa del tetragono piano.* — Periodico di Matematica. Livorno, 1901, t. XVI, gennaio-febbraio.
4. *Relazioni dipendenti da raggi uscenti da un punto ecc.* — Le Matematiche pure ed applicate. Città di Castello, 1901, Febby N. 1.
5. *Su di un sistema di coordinate trilineari.* — Le Mat. pure ed applicate. Città di Castello, 1902, t. II. Nn. 6-7.
6. *Un correlativo del teorema di Stewart.* — Periodico di Mat. Livorno, t. XVII, agosto 1901.
7. *Algunas propriedades de la inversion isogonal.* — Revista trimestral de Matematicas. Zaragoza, 1905, pp. 76-89.
8. *Nuova risoluzione di due problemi.* — L'Ing. Civ. Torino, 1901, vol. XXVII.
9. *La risoluzione del pentagono completo ecc.* — L'Ing. Civ. Torino, 1902, vol. XXVII.
10. *Nuove proprietà dei punti notevoli del triangolo.* — Periodico di Mat. Livorno, vol. XVIII, settembre-dicembre 1902.
11. *La risoluzione generale del tetragono completo e sue applicazioni ecc.* — Il Monitore tecnico. Milano, ottobre 1903, Nn. 28-29.

(1) E. D'Ovidio, *Nuova esposizione della teoria generale* ecc. (Giornale di Matematica di G. Battaglini. Napoli 1867, vol. VI, pag. 46).

12. *La risoluzione generale del problema di Hansen.* — L'Ing. Civ. Torino, 1903, vol. XXIX.
13. *Determinazione di una o più stazioni incognite ecc.* — L'Ing. Civ. Torino, 1902, vol. XXVII.
14. *Il segmento fisso nel problema di Snellius ampliato in generale.* — Il Monitore tecnico. 1902, vol. VIII, N. 21 e seg.
15. *Determinazione di un punto al vertice di piramide e relativa compensazione.* — Il Potitecnico. Milano, 1902.
16. *Per la misura indiretta delle distanze con una stazione unica.* — Il Politecnico. Milano, 1902.
17. *Il problema di Snellius ampliato in generale e relativa compensazione.* — L'Ing. Civ. Torino,
18. *Influenza degli errori angolari nel problema di Snellius ampliato ecc.* — L'Ing. Civ. Torino, 1902, vol. XXVIII.

INDICE DEL TERZO VOLUME

PARTE TERZA.

COMUNICAZIONI.

SEZIONE III-A.

Meccanica, Fisica matematica, Geodesia.

Sezione III-b.

Applicazioni varie della Matematica.

Sezione IV.

Questioni filosofiche, storiche, didattiche.

INDICE RIASSUNTIVO

PARTE PRIMA.

PARTE SECONDA.

PARTE TERZA.

COMUNICAZIONI.

INDICE DEGLI AUTORI

ERRATA-CORRIGE

VOLUME I.

Pag. 197; la riga 12 va corretta così: .... *astratte? E soddisfa essa pure alle condizioni alle quali deve esser assoggettato*

Pag. 199, riga 24; in luogo di « α », leggi « di α »

Pag. 204, righe 13-14; in luogo « della geometria non euclidea », leggi « delle geometrie non euclidee »

Pag. 207, riga 23; in luogo di « euclidee », leggi « non euclidee »

VOLUME II.

Pag. 57, righe 2, 3, 5, 7 e Pag. 59, riga 22; dopo il simbolo « $> k$ » si inseriscano le parole « together with certain of the points at wich it is $= k$ »

www.ingramcontent.com/pod-product-compliance
Lightning Source LLC
LaVergne TN
LVHW011248110826
845149LV00001B/72

* 9 7 8 1 4 1 8 1 8 5 7 1 8 *